VALENTINE

Volume One

THE ICE DEATH

Written by **Alex de Campi**

Art by **Christine Larsen**

Coloring by **Christine Larsen** *(chapters 1-4)*
and **Tim Durning** *(chapters 5-10)*

"Fanchon" art by **Cassandra James**

Cover painting by **Steven Belledin**

Book design by **Drew Gill**

IMAGE COMICS, INC.

Robert Kirkman - chief operating officer
Erik Larsen - chief financial officer
Todd McFarlane - president
Marc Silvestri - chief executive officer
Jim Valentino - vice-president

Eric Stephenson - publisher
Todd Martinez - sales & licensing coordinator
Jennifer de Guzman - pr & marketing director
Branwyn Bigglestone - accounts manager
Emily Miller - administrative assistant
Jamie Parreno - marketing assistant
Sarah deLaine - events coordinator
Kevin Yuen - digital rights coordinator
Tyler Shainline - production manager
Drew Gill - art director
Jonathan Chan - design director
Monica Garcia - production artist
Vincent Kukua - production artist
Jana Cook - production artist
www.imagecomics.com

VALENTINE, VOL. 1: THE ICE DEATH TP
First printing. September 2012.
ISBN: 978-1-60706-624-8

It really eats at me when I'm the dumbest person in the conversation. To her credit, Alex De Campi never, ever points out that this becomes the inevitable dynamic each and every time she and I sit down to talk. Instead, she simply comports herself with a grace and humility that most people with such extraordinary talent and ambition can't even begin to muster, and those who encounter her would do well to take notes. God knows I have.

Oh, not about being graceful and humble, not me. That ship has long ago sailed. What I take note of whenever I speak with Alex is how much she can teach me about the craft of storytelling. It became evident back in the fall of 2010, when she and I shared the stage at a pre-New York ComicCon discussion panel about the State Of Digital Comics or somesuch. I'd been invited to participate because I was an old-guard dude who'd recently been talking up quite loudly, with a volume inversely proportional to my actual strategy, the virtues of digital versus the pitfalls of print. Alex, by contrast, was softer-spoken but—as I discovered that day as she made her case and explained VALENTINE to a room full of journalists and retailers—was much deeper into the 21st century when it came to What Could Be Done than any of the rest of us.

Alex, as you're about to witness, had vision where the rest of us were still blundering around in the dark. With the brilliant webcomic VALENTINE, she and her collaborator, Christine Larsen, had not only pioneered some of the storytelling techniques that digital uses uniquely well and that print can't mimic—captions and art fading in and out, sudden juxtapositions left-turning the narrative, and more—but they did so while at the same time creating a work that would translate equally effectively in print. The fact that you're holding this volume in your hands right now is a testament to the fact that Alex and Christine are the first to do what no one else has yet done—blend the two media of pixel and ink into a narrative strong enough to achieve greatness in both.

This isn't logrolling on my part. I really am impressed. You can tell I'm impressed because, on the face of it, as a reader searching for something new, there is absolutely nothing in the list of the following keywords—"France," "Napoleon," "Russia," "cavalry," "historical novel"—that would ordinarily appeal to me on any level whatsoever. And yet, I love what you're about to read. I love it for its techniques, I love it for its craft and heart, I love it for its graphics, but most of all, I love it because it's a good story well told. Take a look for yourself, and welcome to the future.

Mark Waid
writer, editor, publisher, bon vivant
thrillbent.com

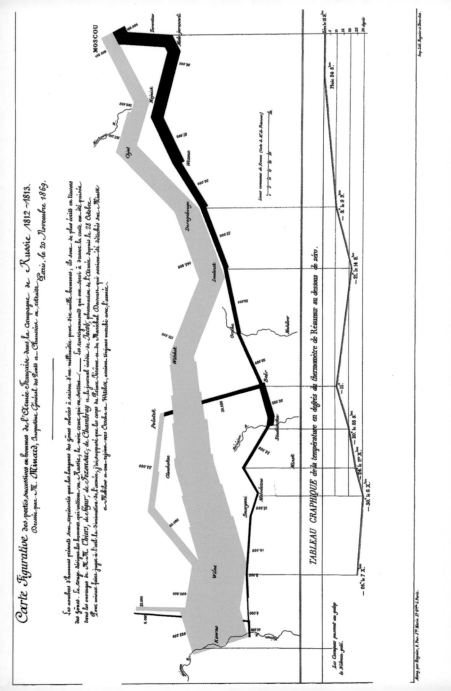

Carte Figurative des pertes successives en hommes de l'Armée Française dans la campagne de Russie 1812–1813.

Dressée par M. Minard, Inspecteur Général des Ponts et Chaussées en retraite.

Paris, le 20 Novembre 1869.

Les nombres d'hommes présents sont représentés par les largeurs des zones colorées à raison d'un millimètre pour dix mille hommes; ils sont de plus écrits en travers des zones. Le rouge désigne les hommes qui entrent en Russie, le noir ceux qui en sortent. —— Les renseignements qui ont servi à dresser la carte ont été puisés dans les ouvrages de MM. Thiers, de Ségur, de Fezensac, de Chambray et le journal inédit de Jacob, pharmacien de l'Armée depuis le 28 Octobre.
Pour mieux faire juger à l'œil la diminution de l'armée, j'ai supposé que les corps du Prince Jérôme et du Maréchal Davoust qui avaient été détachés sur Minsk et Mobilow et ont rejoint vers Orscha et Witebsk, avaient toujours marché avec l'armée.

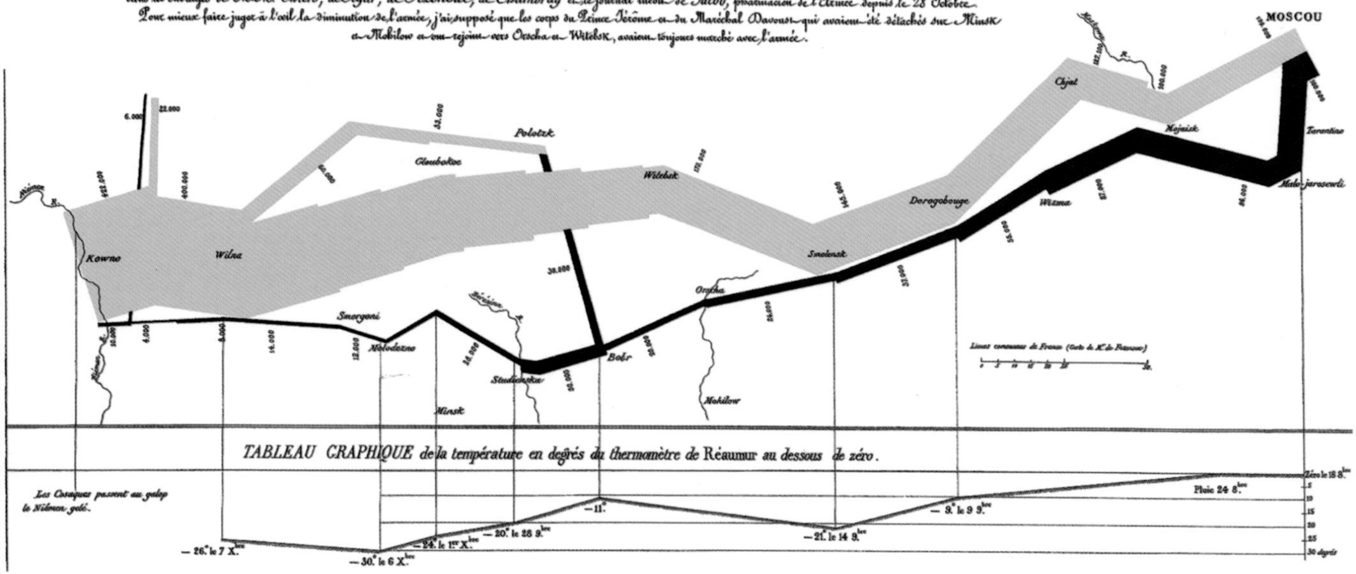

MOSCOU
Kowno
Wilna
Gloubokoe
Polotzk
Witebsk
Smolensk
Dorogobouge
Chjat
Mojaisk
Tarantino
Malo-jarosewli
Wizma
Orscha
Mohilow
Bobr
Studienska
Minsk
Molodezno
Smorgoni
422.000
400.000
22.000
6.000
60.000
33.000
175.000
145.000
127.100
100.000
96.000
87.000
55.000
37.000
24.000
20.000
50.000
30.000
28.000
12.000
14.000
8.000
4.000
10.000
TABLEAU GRAPHIQUE de la température en degrés du thermomètre de Réaumur au dessous de zéro.
Les Cosaques passent au galop le Niémen gelé.
Zéro le 18 8.bre
Pluie 24 8.bre
− 9° le 9 9.bre
− 21° le 14 9.bre
− 11°
− 20° le 28 9.bre
− 24° le 1.er X.bre
− 30° le 6 X.bre
− 26° le 7 X.bre
30 degrés

Autog. par Regnier, 8. Pas. S.te Marie S.t G.ain à Paris.

Imp. Lith. Regnier et Dourdet.

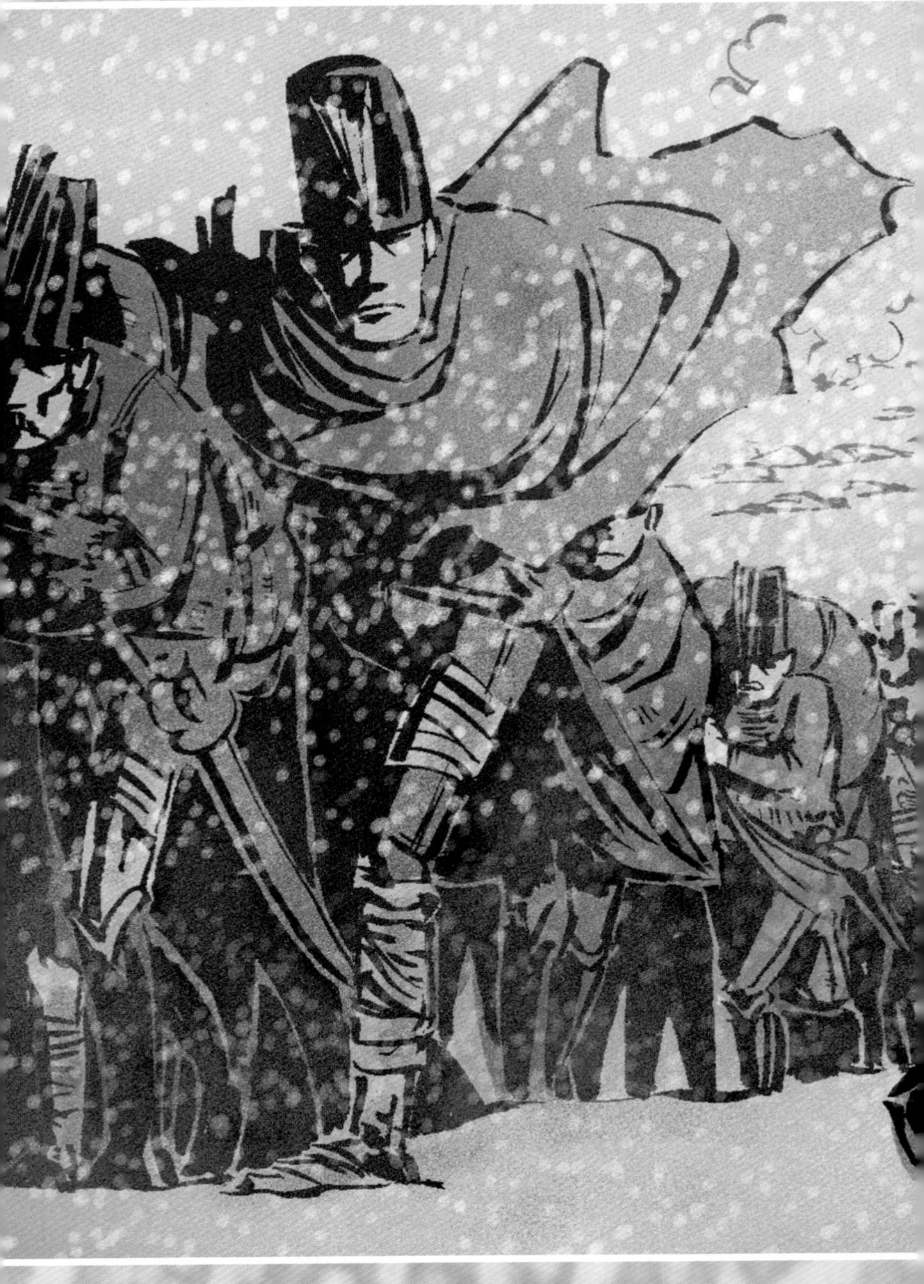

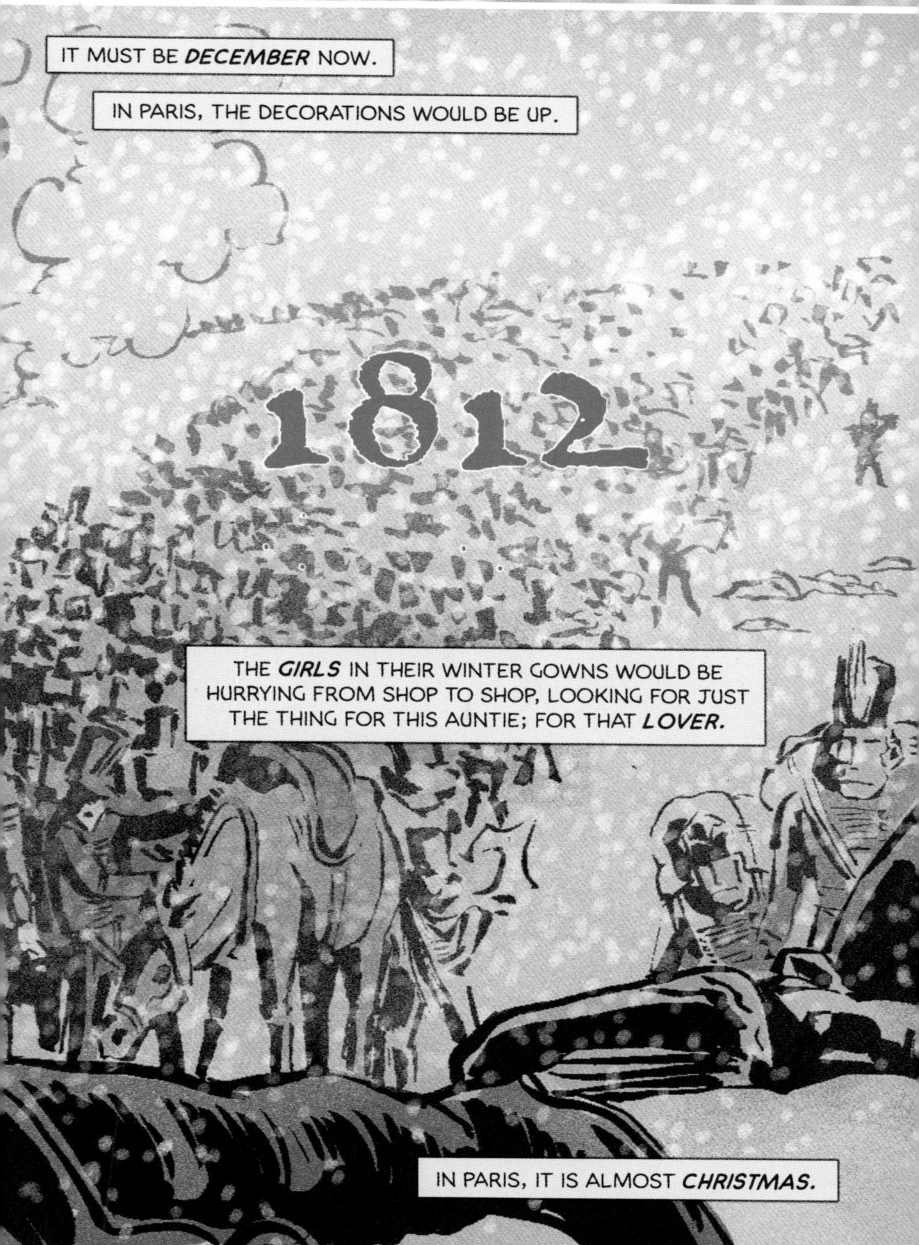
IT MUST BE *DECEMBER* NOW.
IN PARIS, THE DECORATIONS WOULD BE UP.
1812
THE *GIRLS* IN THEIR WINTER GOWNS WOULD BE HURRYING FROM SHOP TO SHOP, LOOKING FOR JUST THE THING FOR THIS AUNTIE; FOR THAT *LOVER.*
IN PARIS, IT IS ALMOST *CHRISTMAS.*

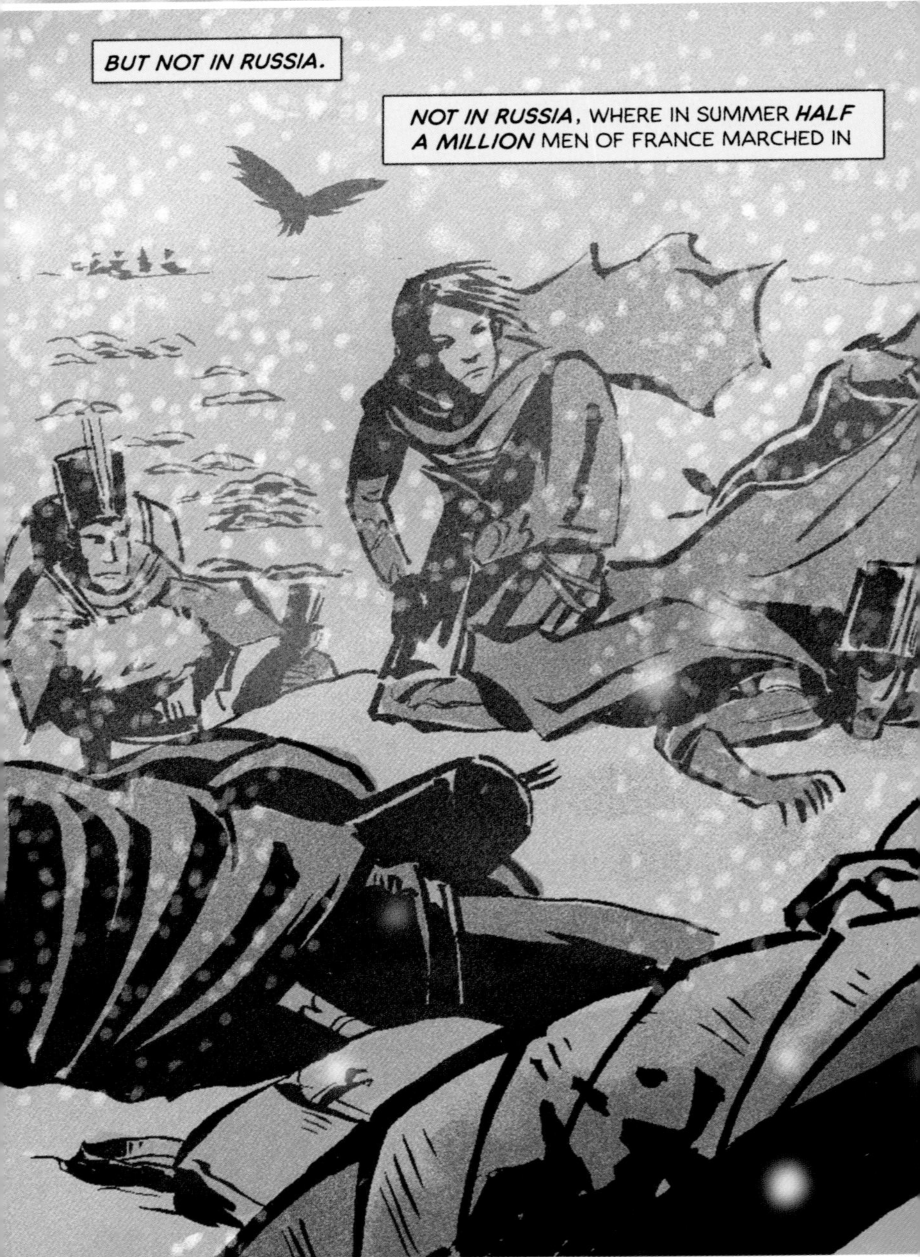
BUT NOT IN RUSSIA.
NOT IN RUSSIA, WHERE IN SUMMER HALF A MILLION MEN OF FRANCE MARCHED IN

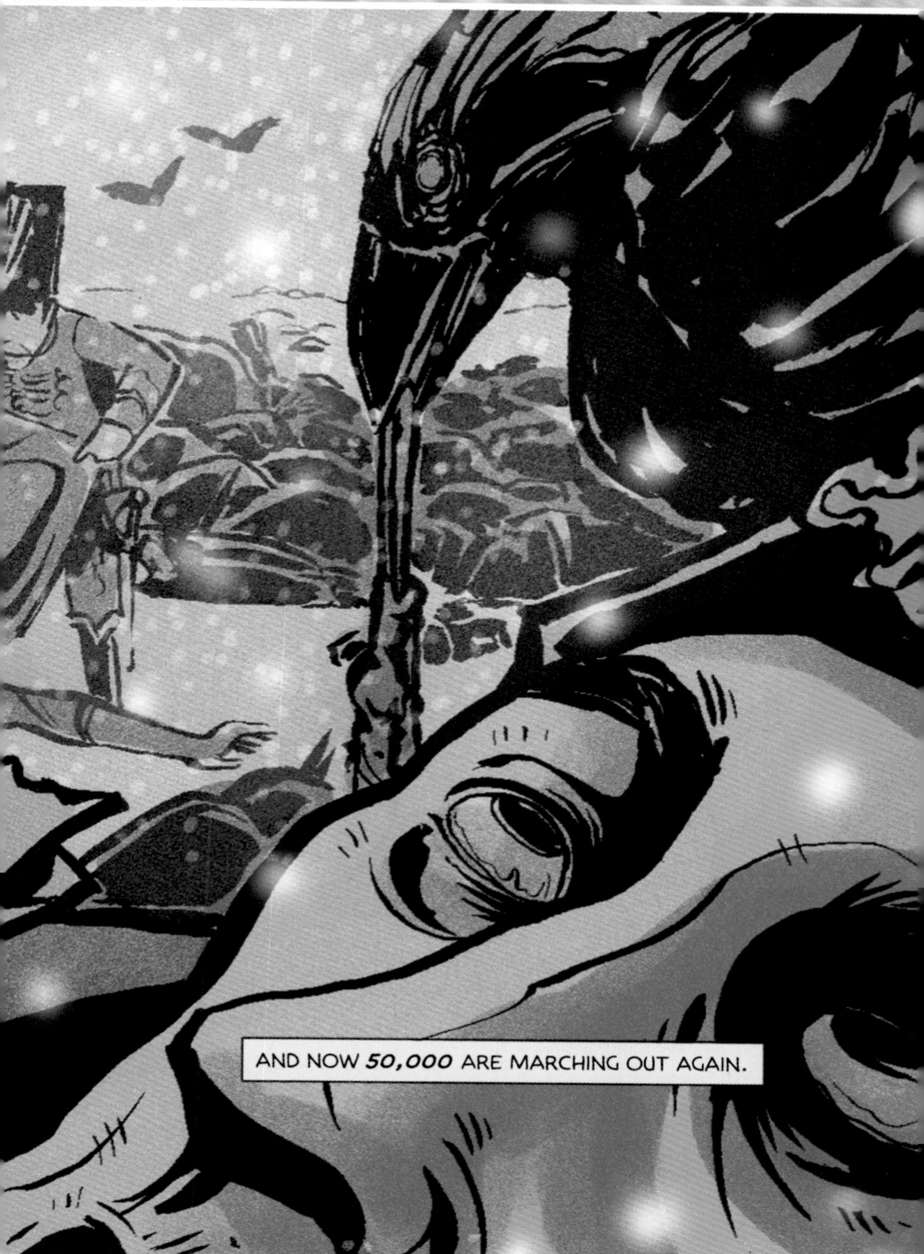
AND NOW 50,000 ARE MARCHING OUT AGAIN.

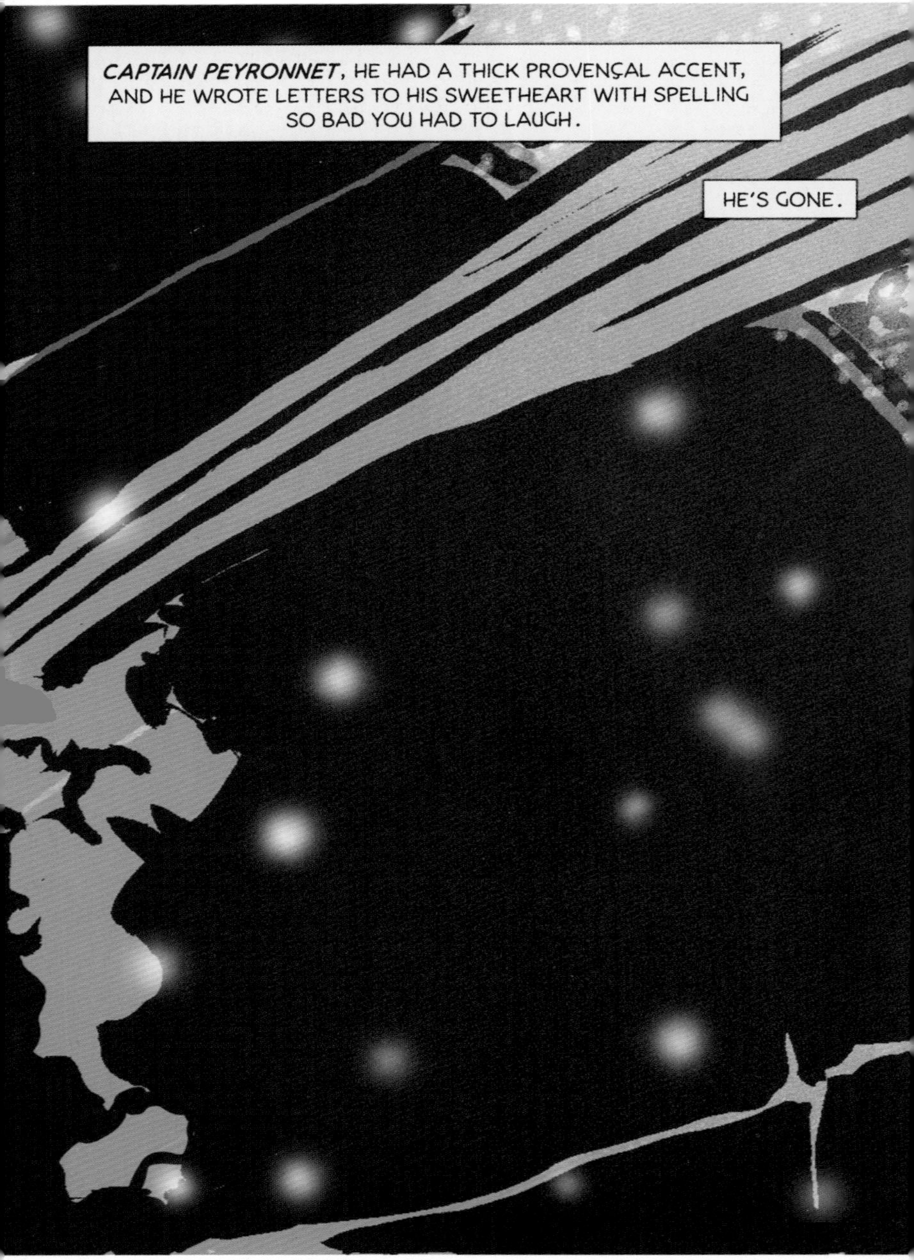
CAPTAIN PEYRONNET, HE HAD A THICK PROVENÇAL ACCENT, AND HE WROTE LETTERS TO HIS SWEETHEART WITH SPELLING SO BAD YOU HAD TO LAUGH.
HE'S GONE.

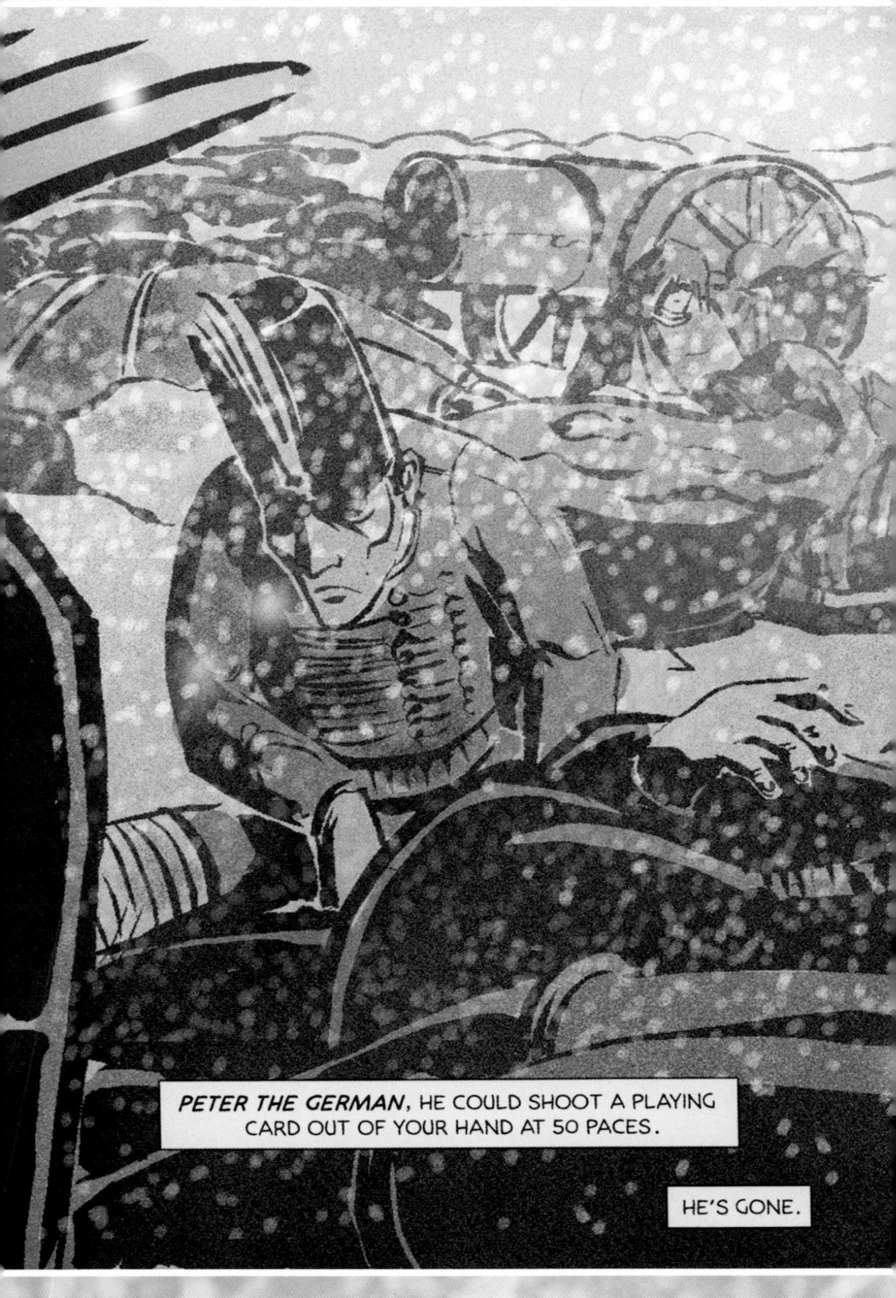
PETER THE GERMAN, HE COULD SHOOT A PLAYING CARD OUT OF YOUR HAND AT 50 PACES.
HE'S GONE.

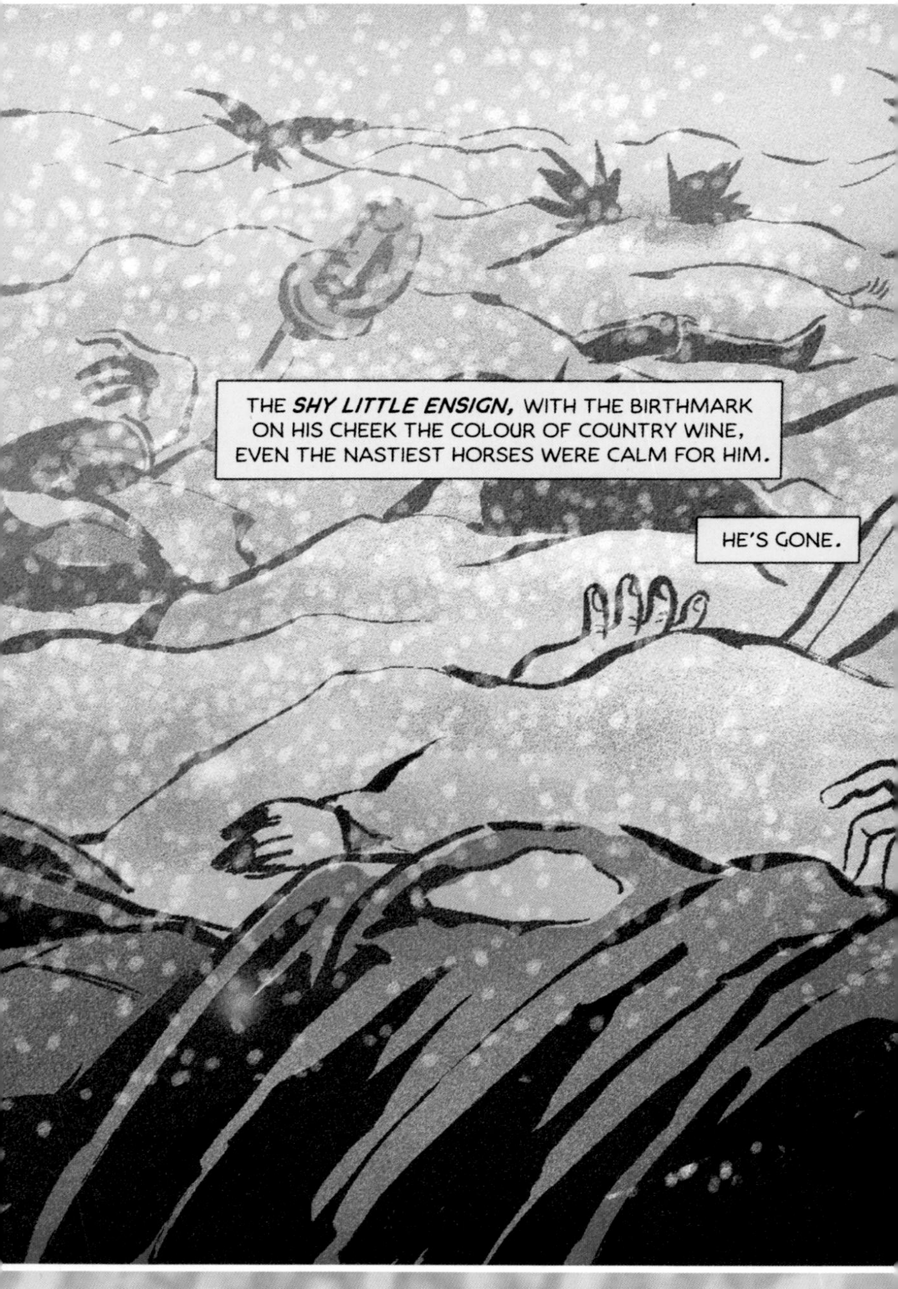
THE SHY LITTLE ENSIGN, WITH THE BIRTHMARK ON HIS CHEEK THE COLOUR OF COUNTRY WINE, EVEN THE NASTIEST HORSES WERE CALM FOR HIM.
HE'S GONE.

ROGER, HE'D SING DANCE-HALL SONGS AS HE MARCHED, AND HIS SKINNY FRIEND, WHAT WAS HIS NAME, THEY WERE GOING TO OPEN A RESTAURANT WHEN THEY GOT OUT.

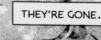
THEY'RE GONE.

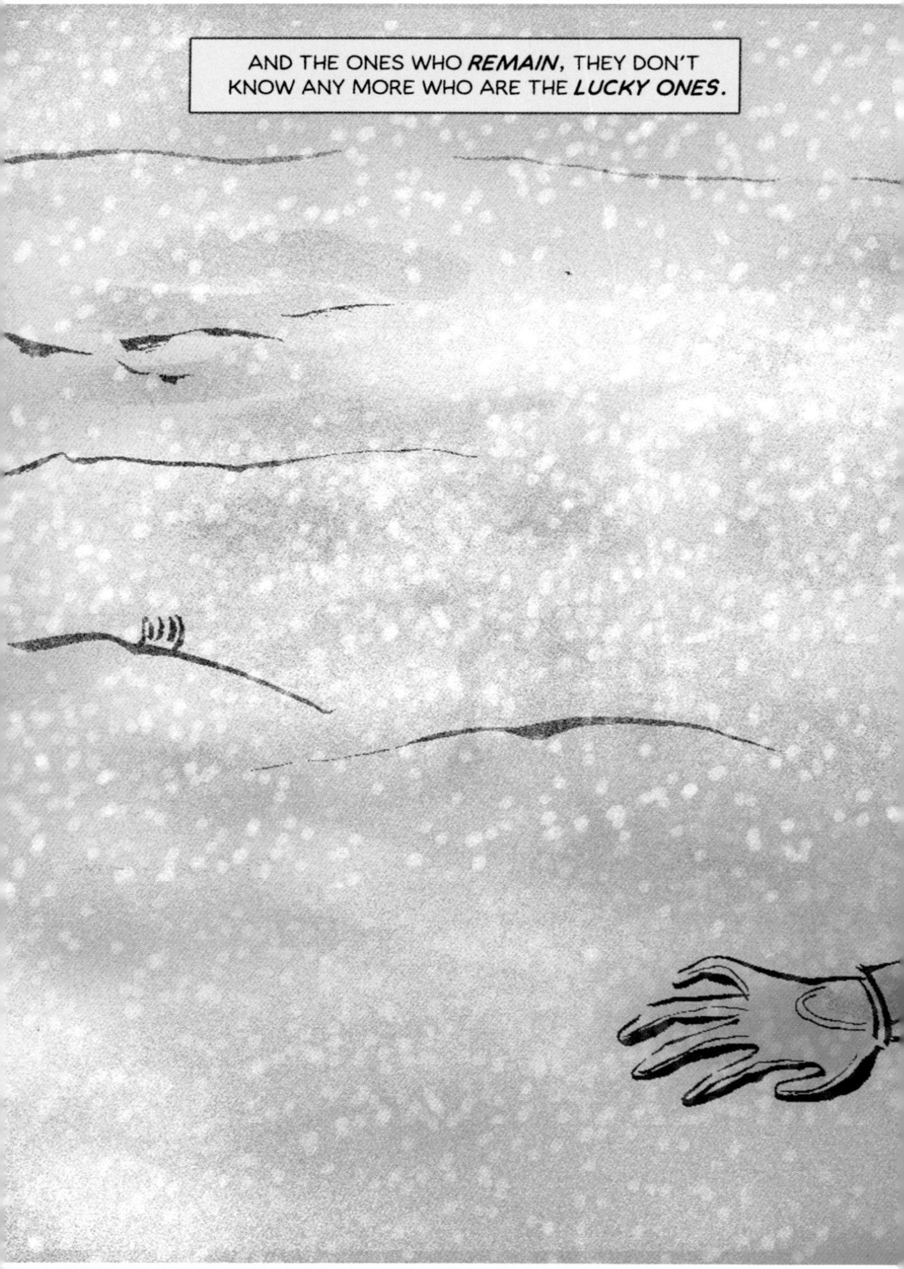
AND THE ONES WHO *REMAIN*, THEY DON'T KNOW ANY MORE WHO ARE THE *LUCKY ONES*.

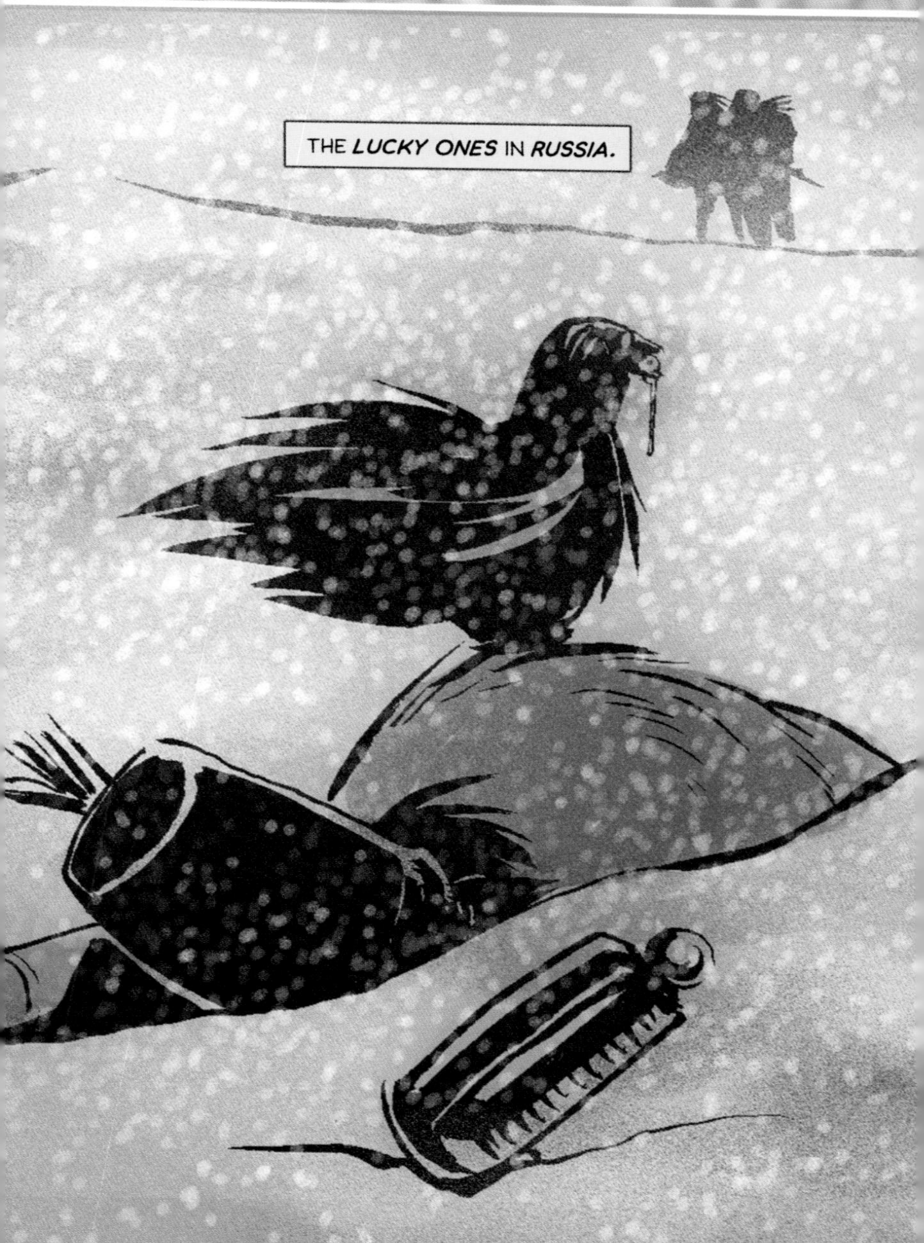
THE LUCKY ONES IN RUSSIA.

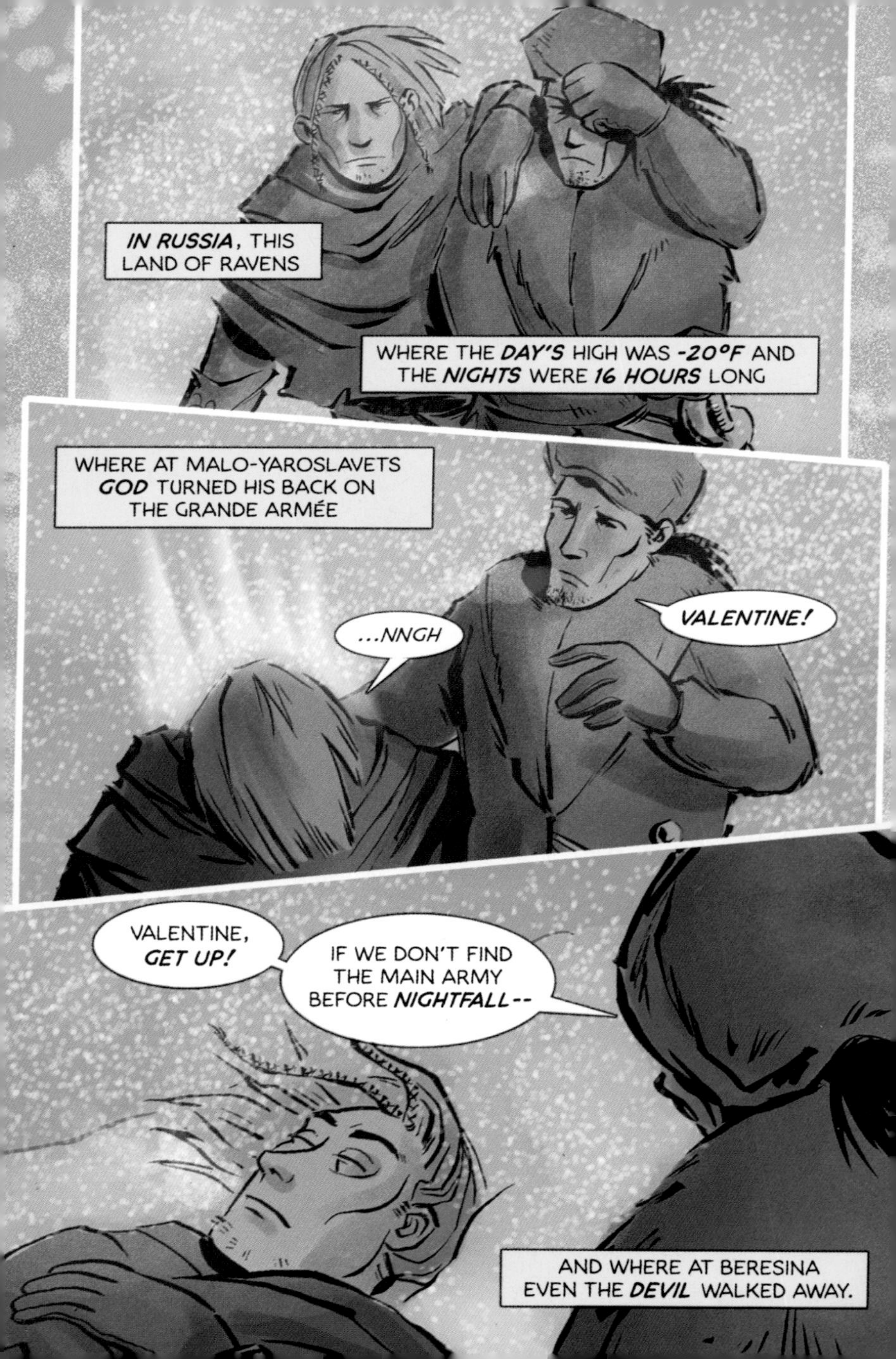
IN RUSSIA, THIS LAND OF RAVENS
WHERE THE DAY'S HIGH WAS -20°F AND THE NIGHTS WERE 16 HOURS LONG
WHERE AT MALO-YAROSLAVETS GOD TURNED HIS BACK ON THE GRANDE ARMÉE
...NNGH
VALENTINE!
VALENTINE, GET UP!
IF WE DON'T FIND THE MAIN ARMY BEFORE NIGHTFALL--
AND WHERE AT BERESINA EVEN THE DEVIL WALKED AWAY.

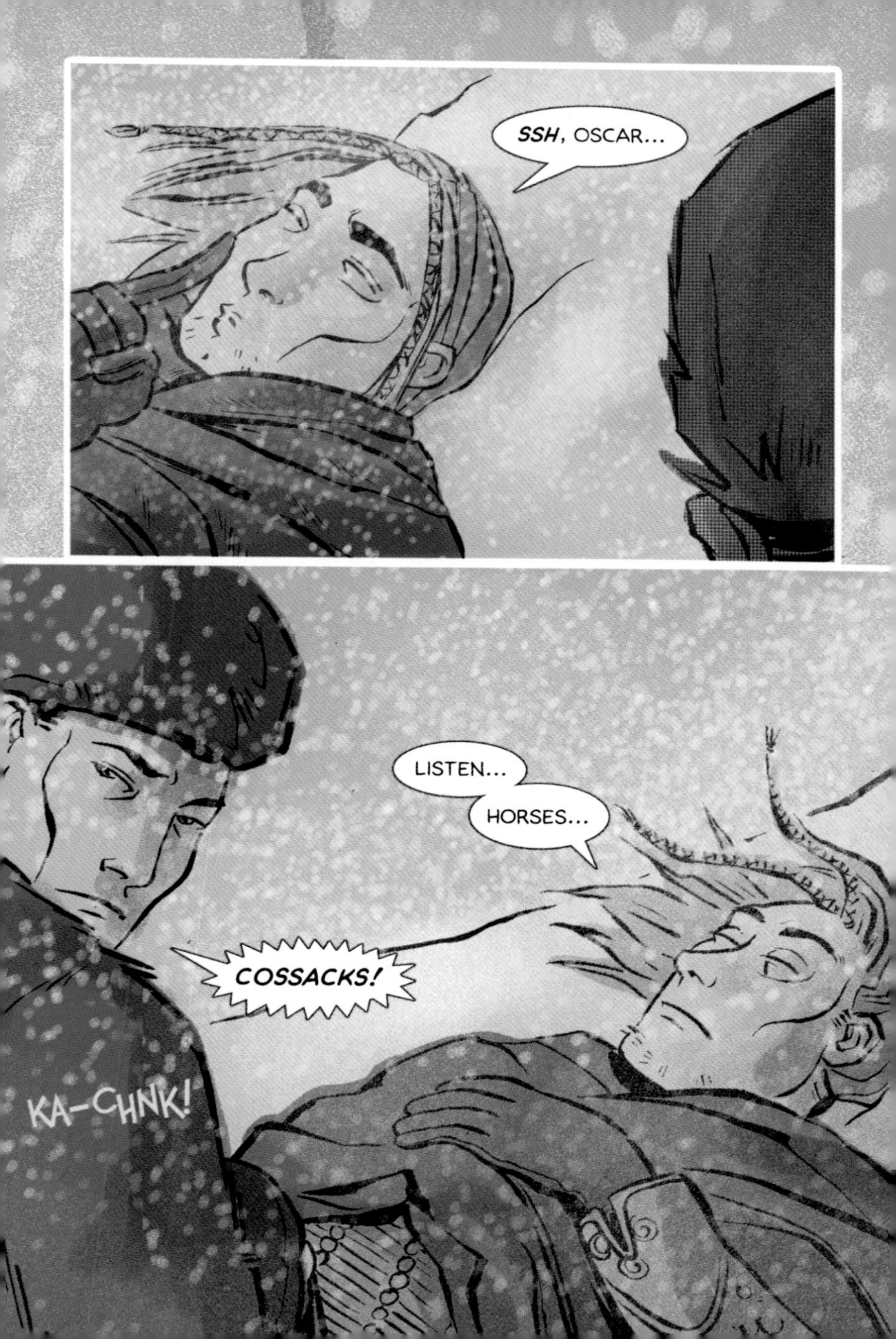
SSH, OSCAR...
LISTEN...
HORSES...
COSSACKS!
KA-CHNK!

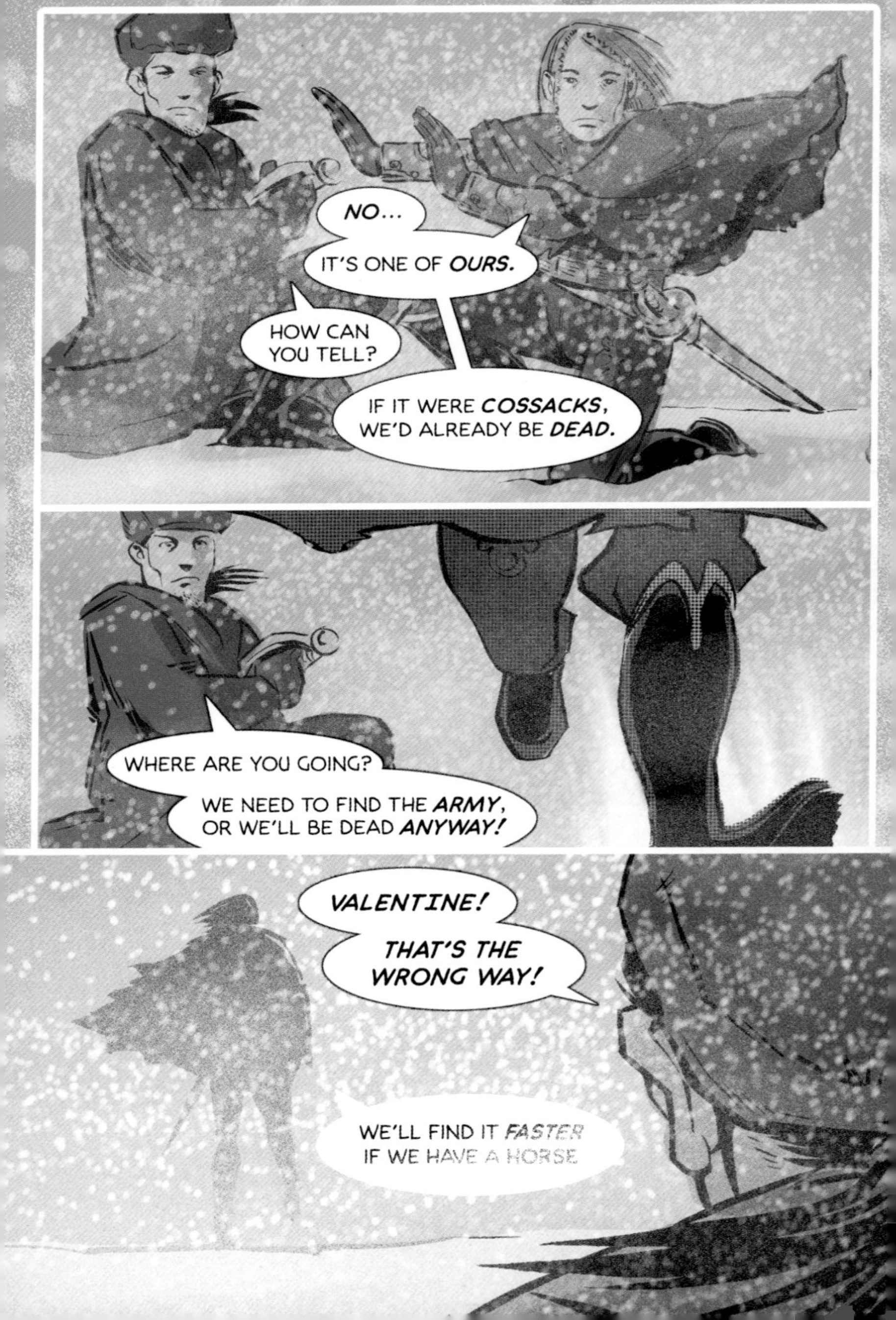
NO...
IT'S ONE OF OURS.
HOW CAN YOU TELL?
IF IT WERE COSSACKS, WE'D ALREADY BE DEAD.
WHERE ARE YOU GOING?
WE NEED TO FIND THE ARMY, OR WE'LL BE DEAD ANYWAY!
VALENTINE!
THAT'S THE WRONG WAY!
WE'LL FIND IT FASTER IF WE HAVE A HORSE

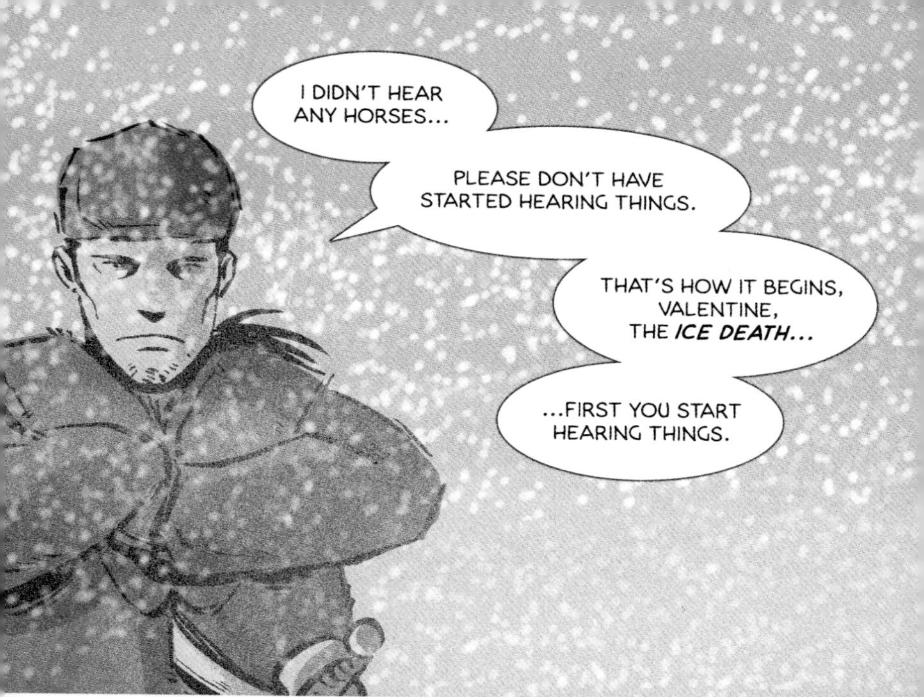
I DIDN'T HEAR ANY HORSES...
PLEASE DON'T HAVE STARTED HEARING THINGS.
THAT'S HOW IT BEGINS, VALENTINE, THE *ICE DEATH...*
...FIRST YOU START HEARING THINGS.

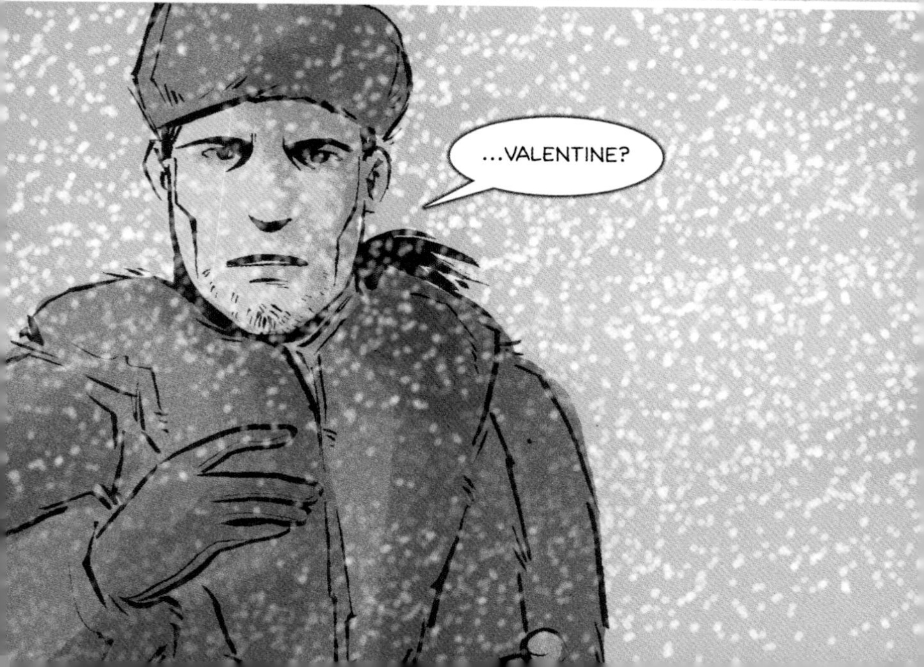
...VALENTINE?

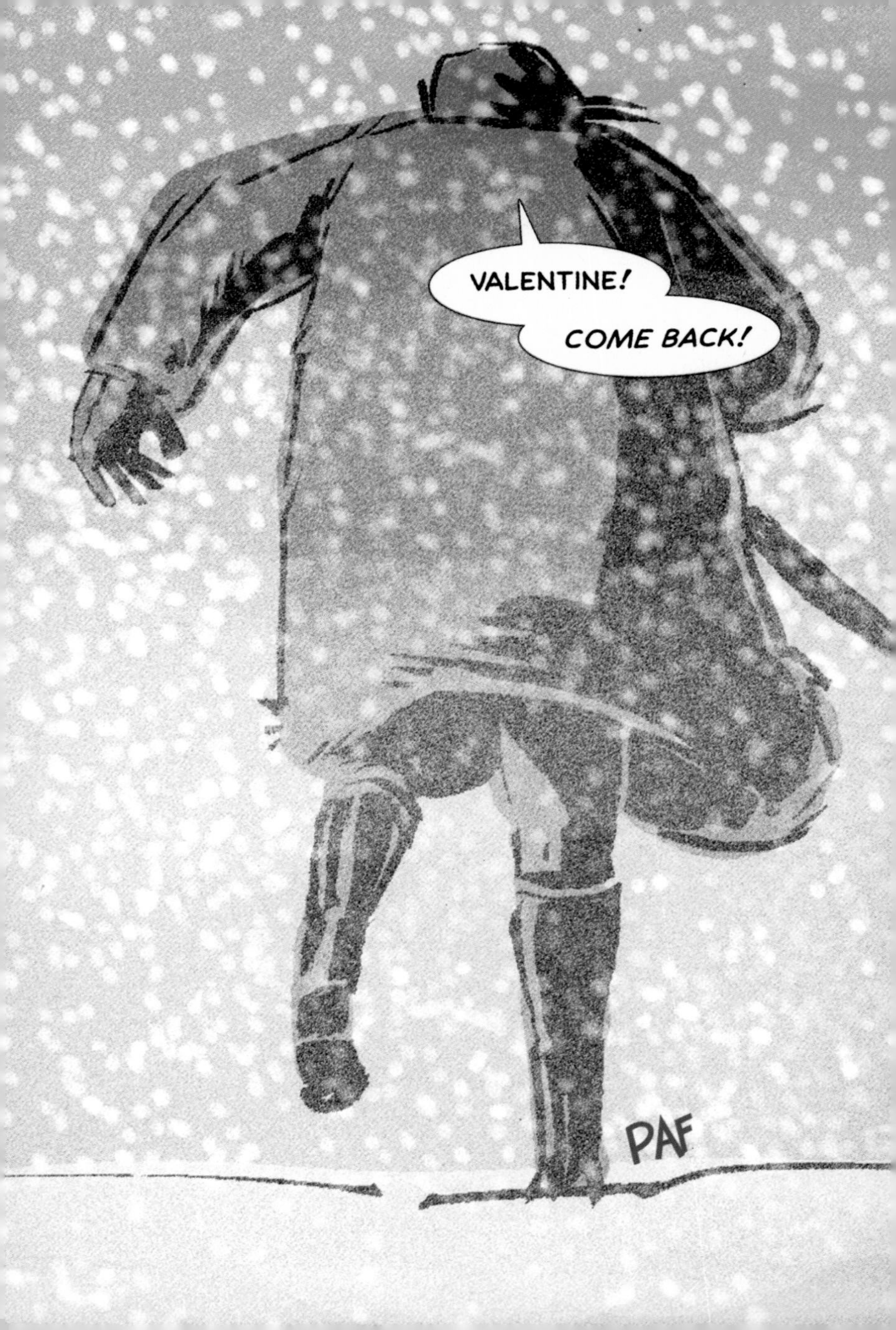
VALENTINE!
COME BACK!
PAF

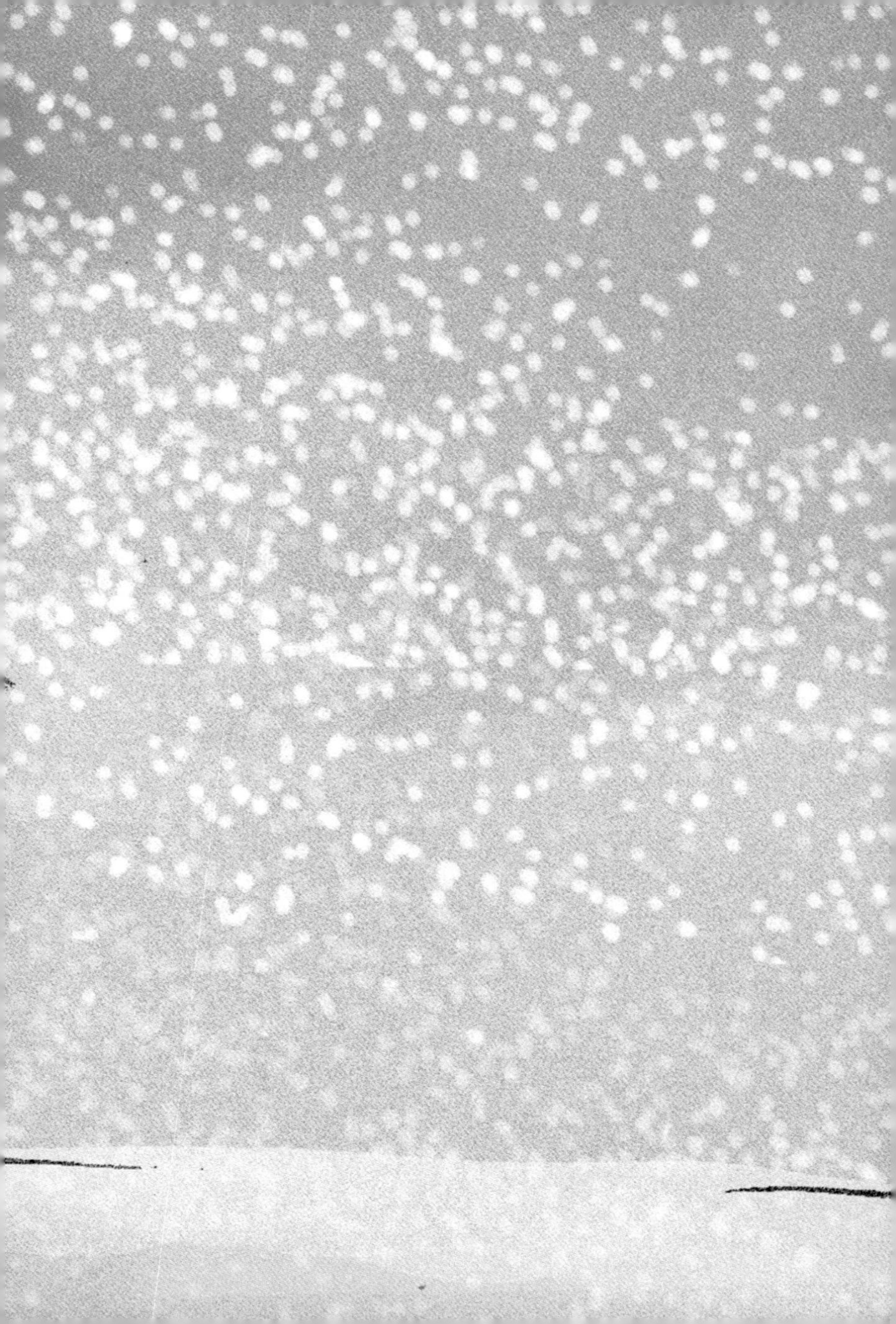

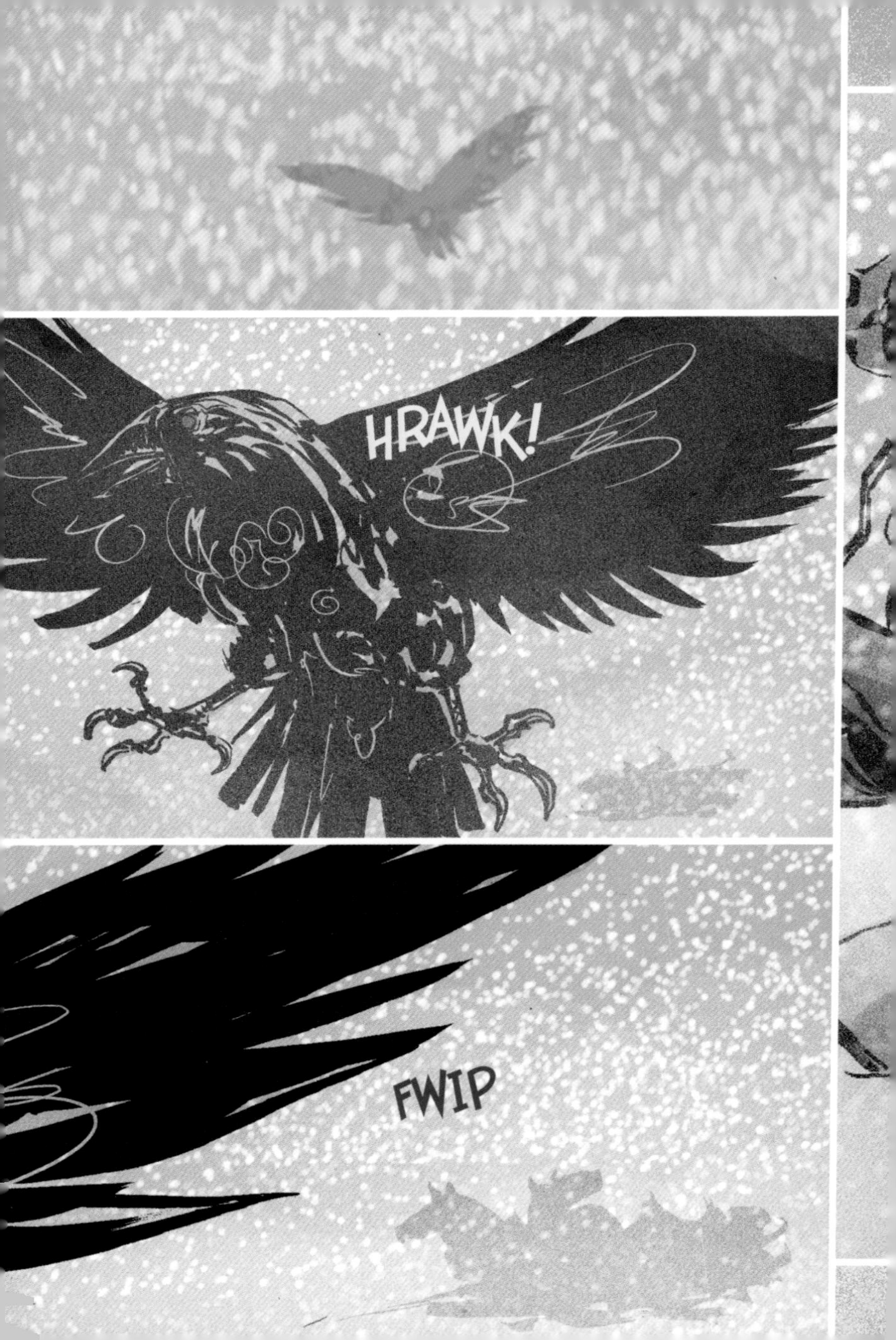
HRAWK!
FWIP

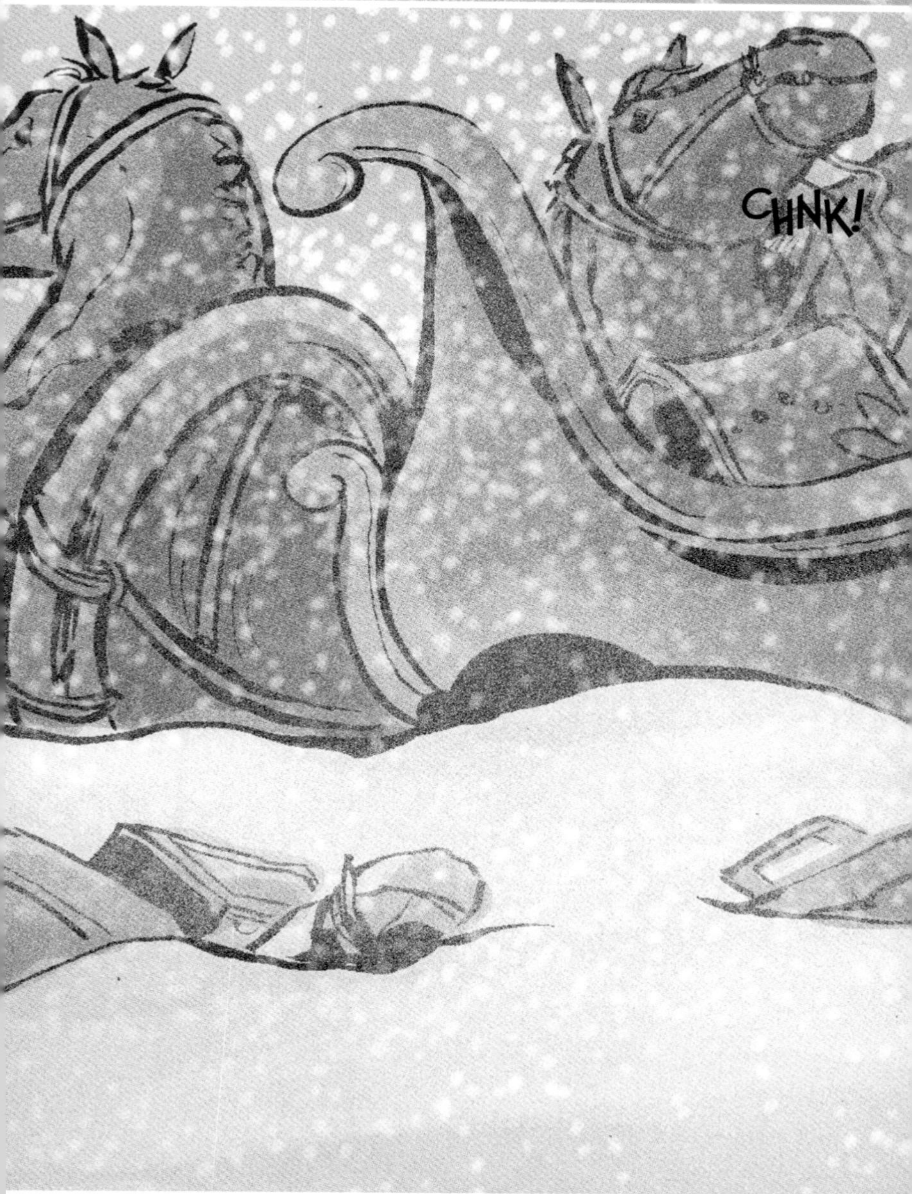
CHNK!

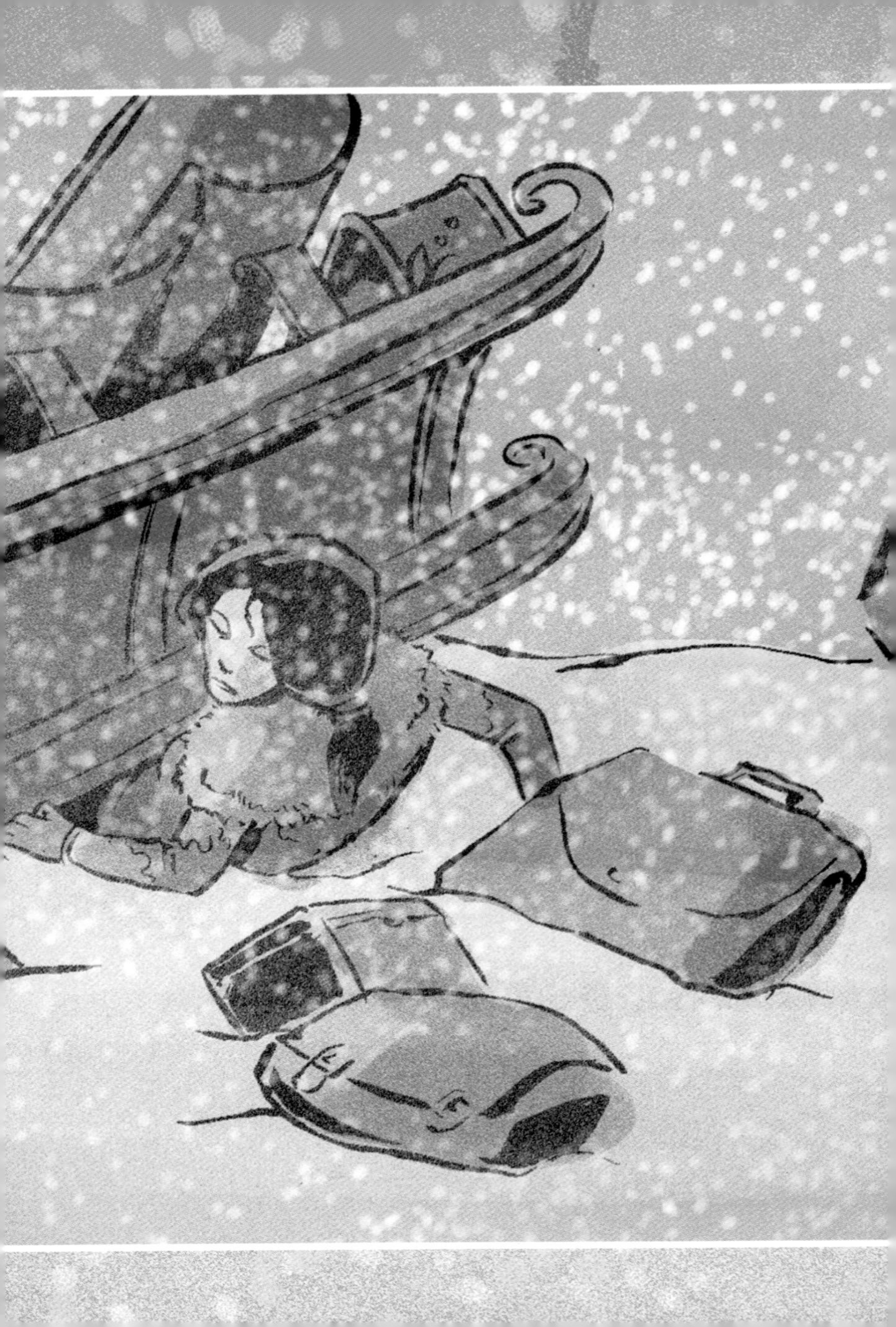

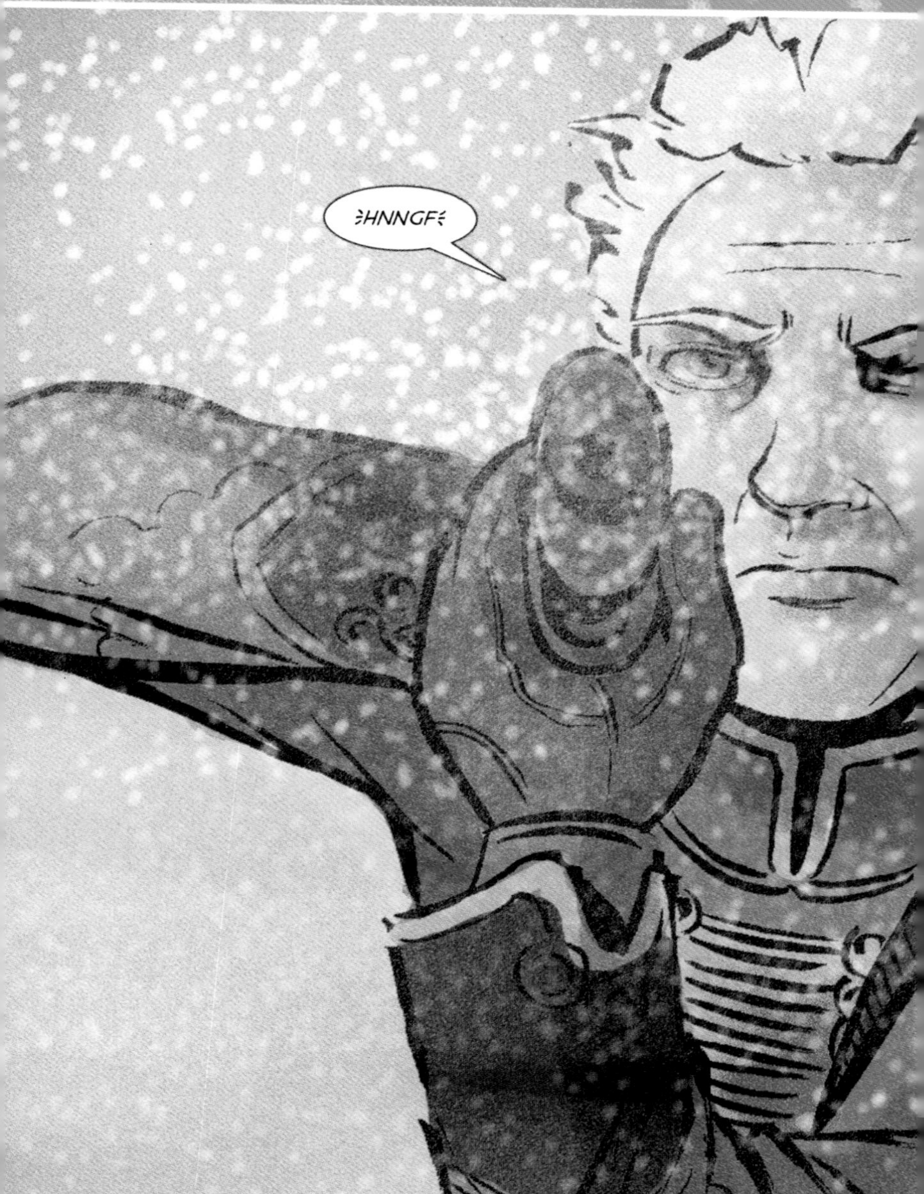
HNNGF

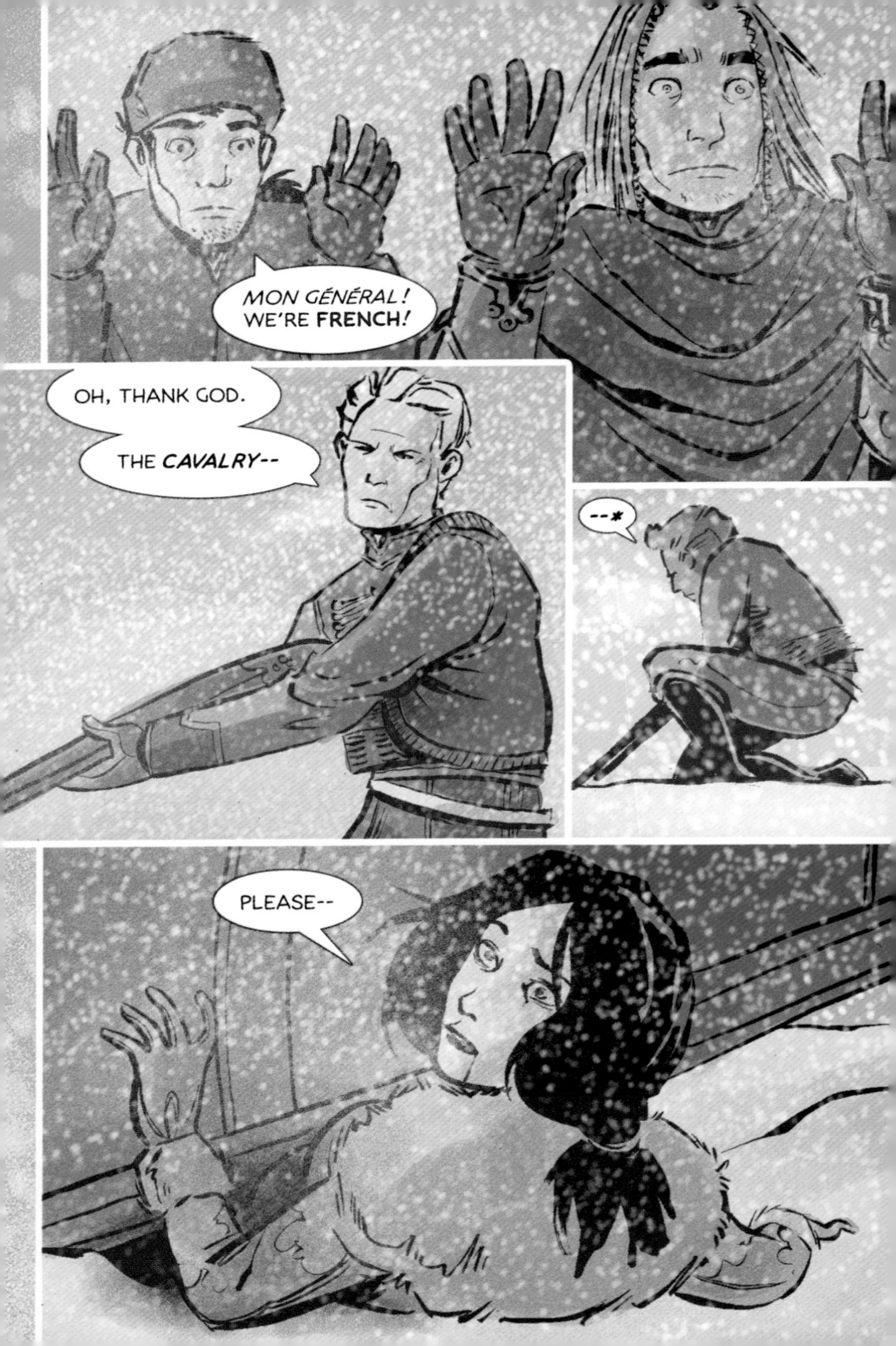
MON GÉNÉRAL!
WE'RE **FRENCH!**
OH, THANK GOD.
THE ***CAVALRY--***
--*
PLEASE--

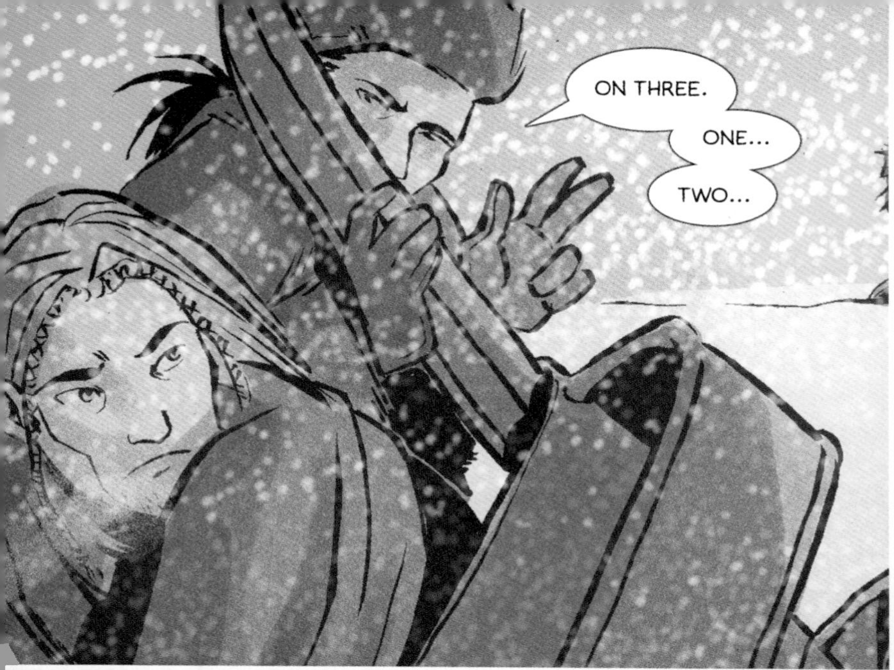
ON THREE.
ONE...
TWO...

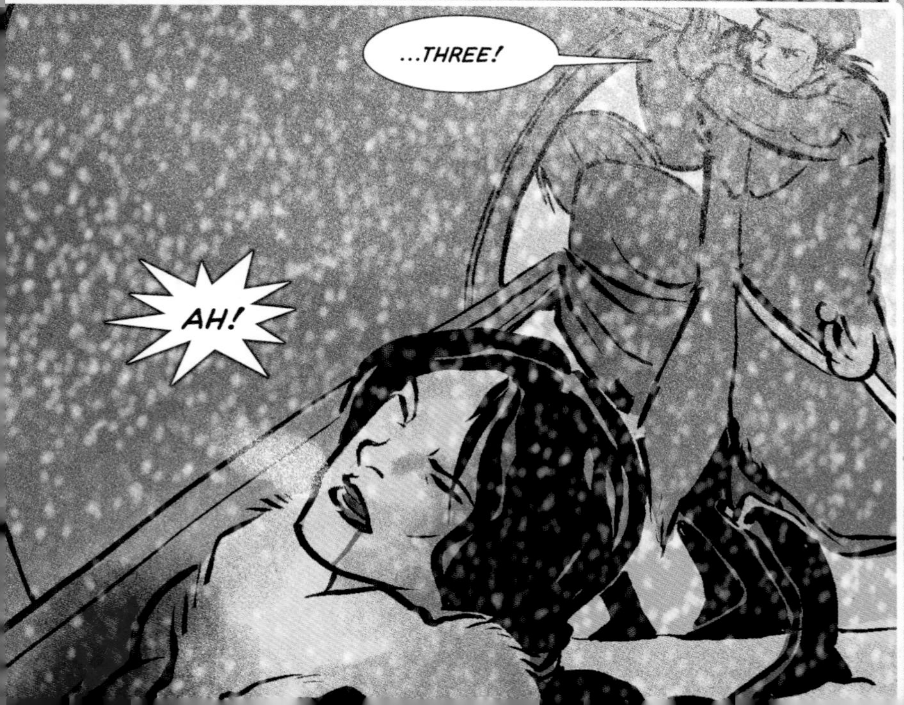
...THREE!
AH!

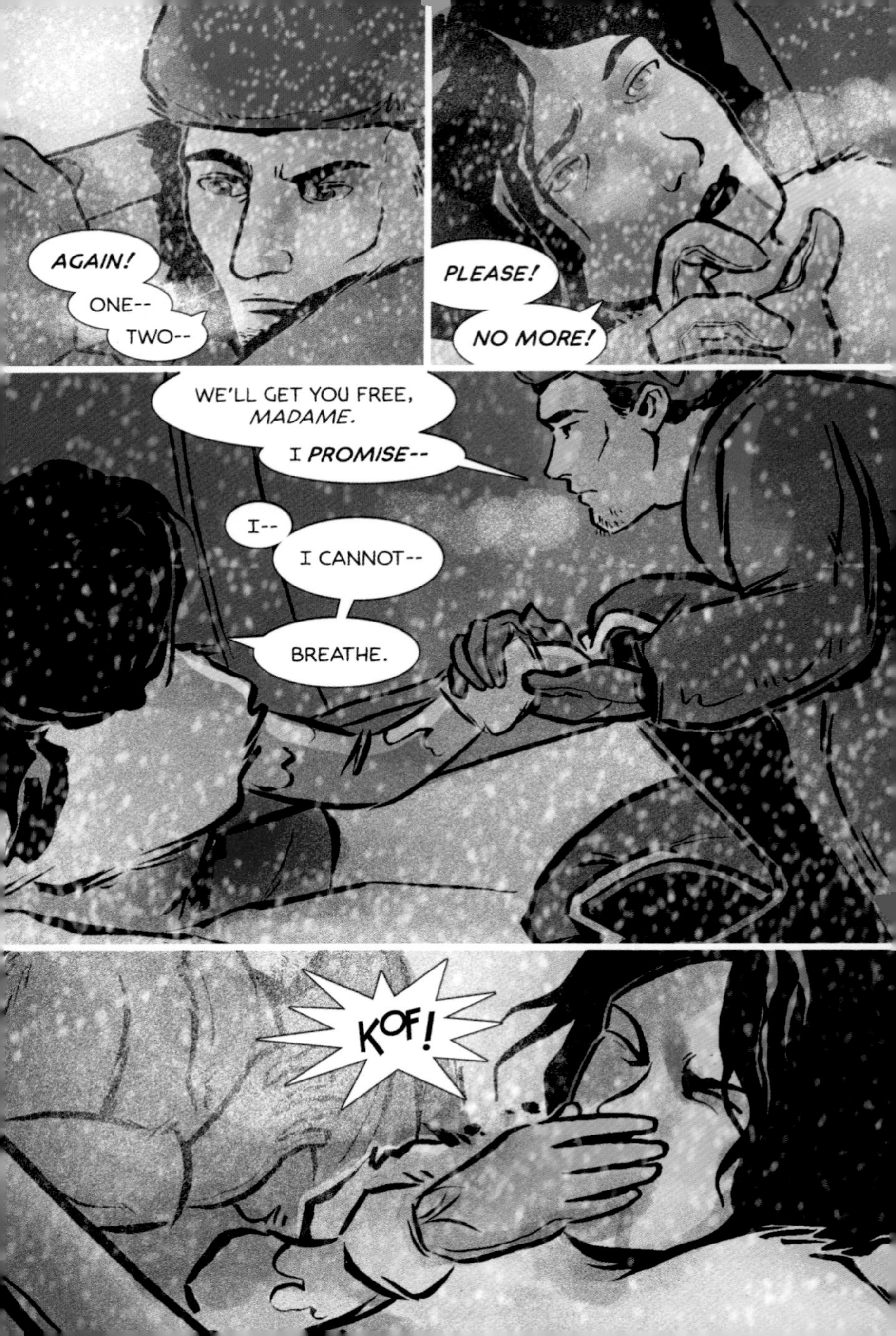
AGAIN!
ONE--
TWO--
PLEASE!
NO MORE!
WE'LL GET YOU FREE, MADAME.
I PROMISE--
I--
I CANNOT--
BREATHE.
KOF!

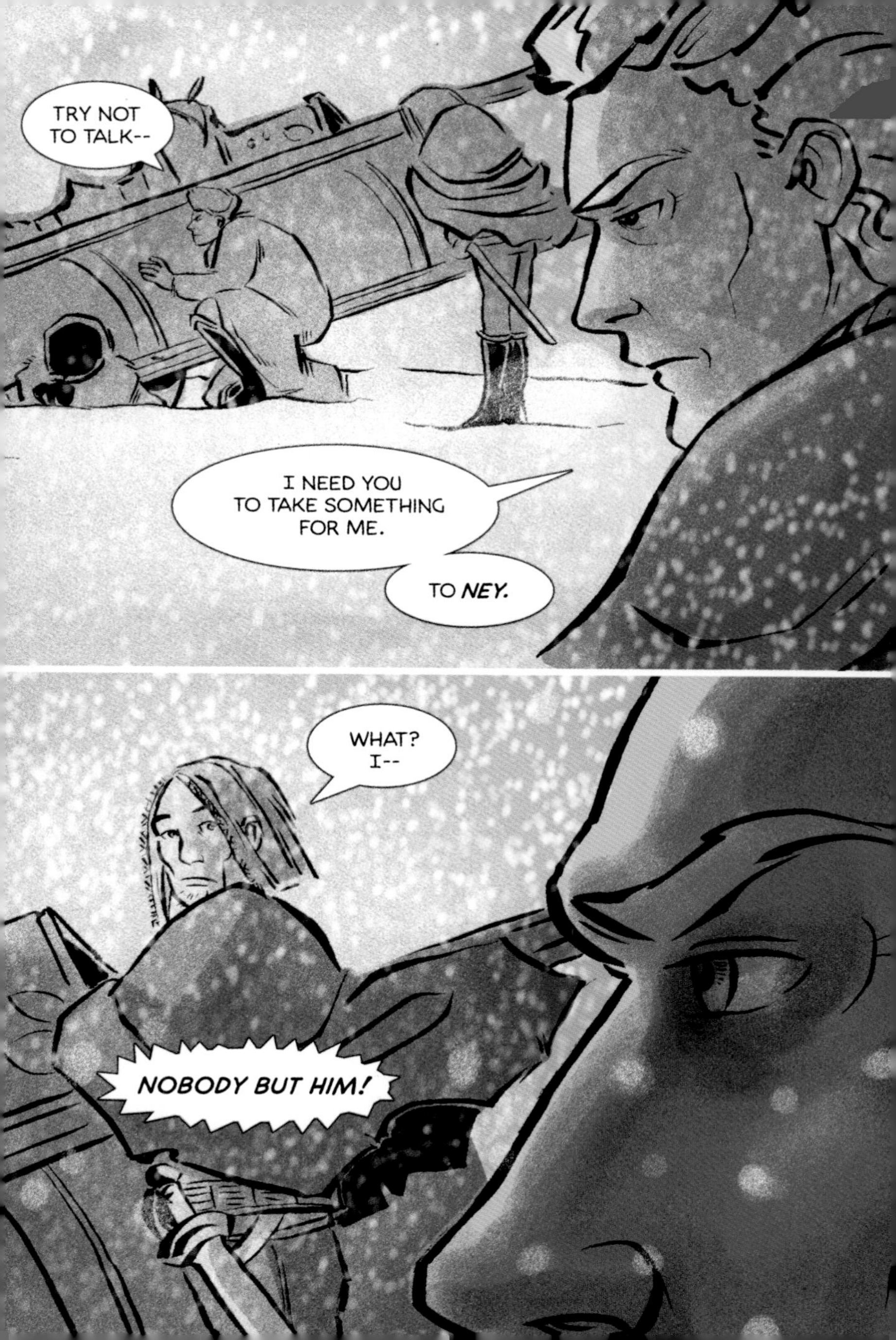
TRY NOT TO TALK--
I NEED YOU TO TAKE SOMETHING FOR ME.
TO NEY.
WHAT? I--
NOBODY BUT HIM!

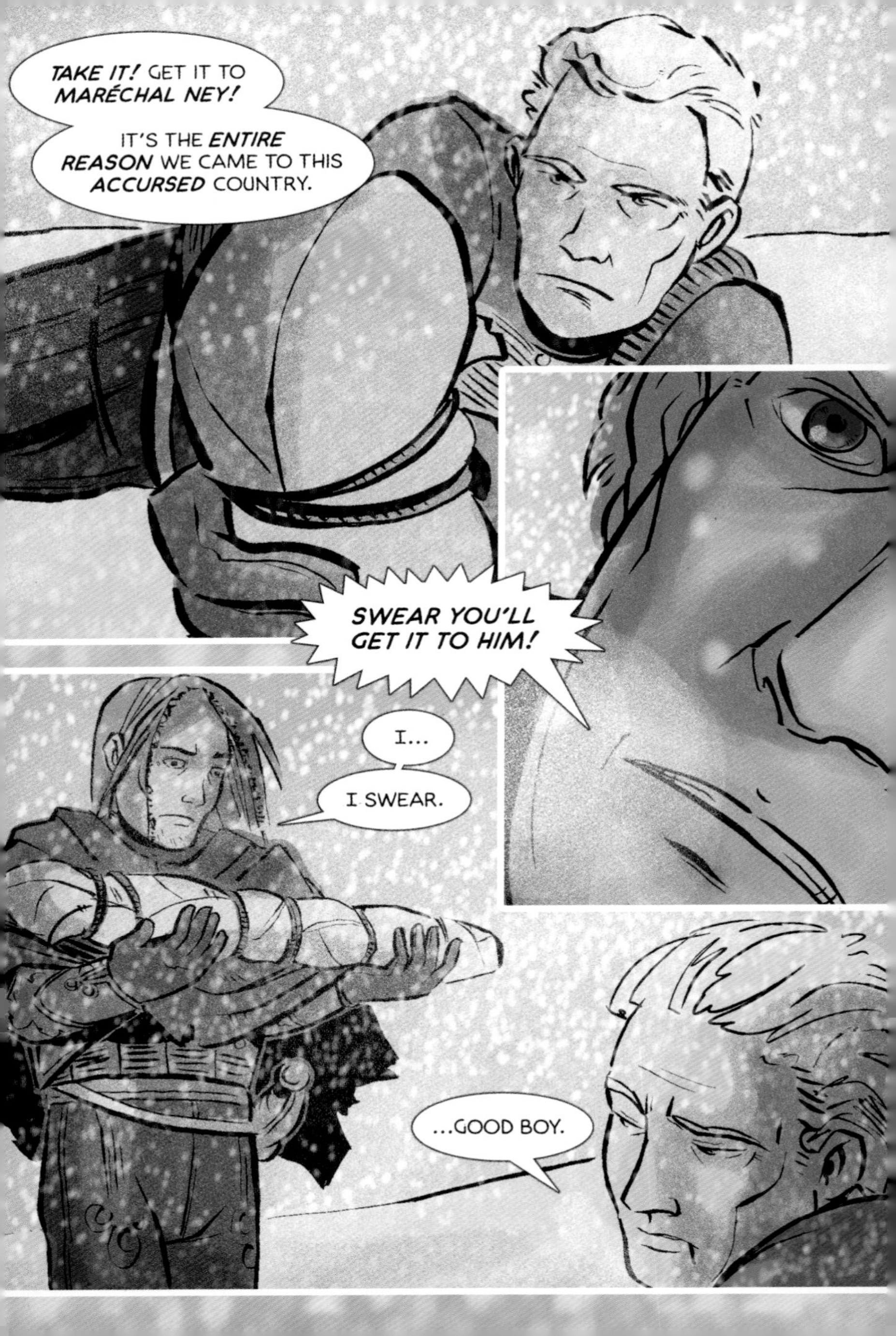
TAKE IT! GET IT TO MARÉCHAL NEY!
IT'S THE ENTIRE REASON WE CAME TO THIS ACCURSED COUNTRY.
SWEAR YOU'LL GET IT TO HIM!
I...
I SWEAR.
...GOOD BOY.

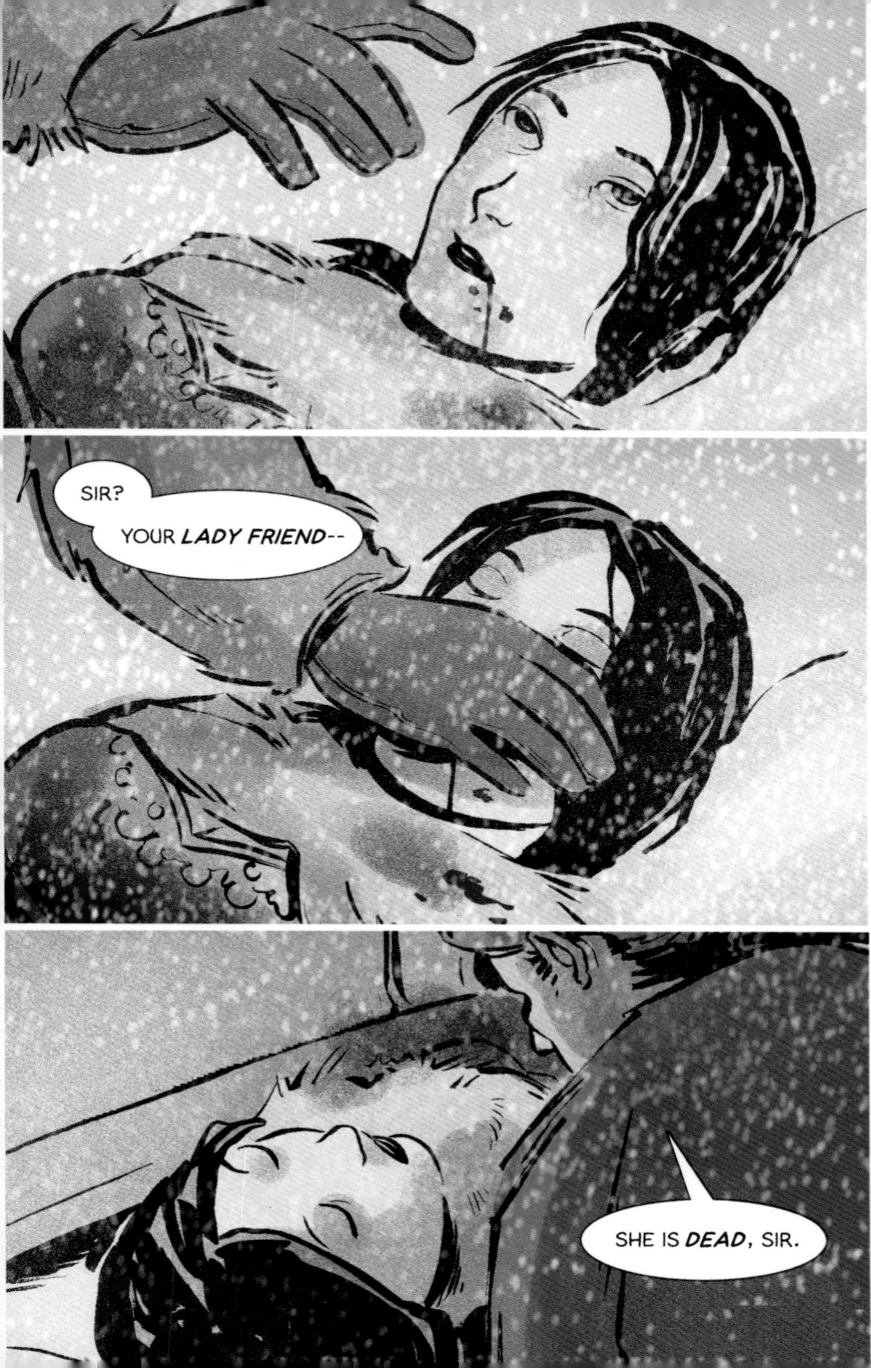
SIR?
YOUR *LADY FRIEND*--
SHE IS *DEAD*, SIR.

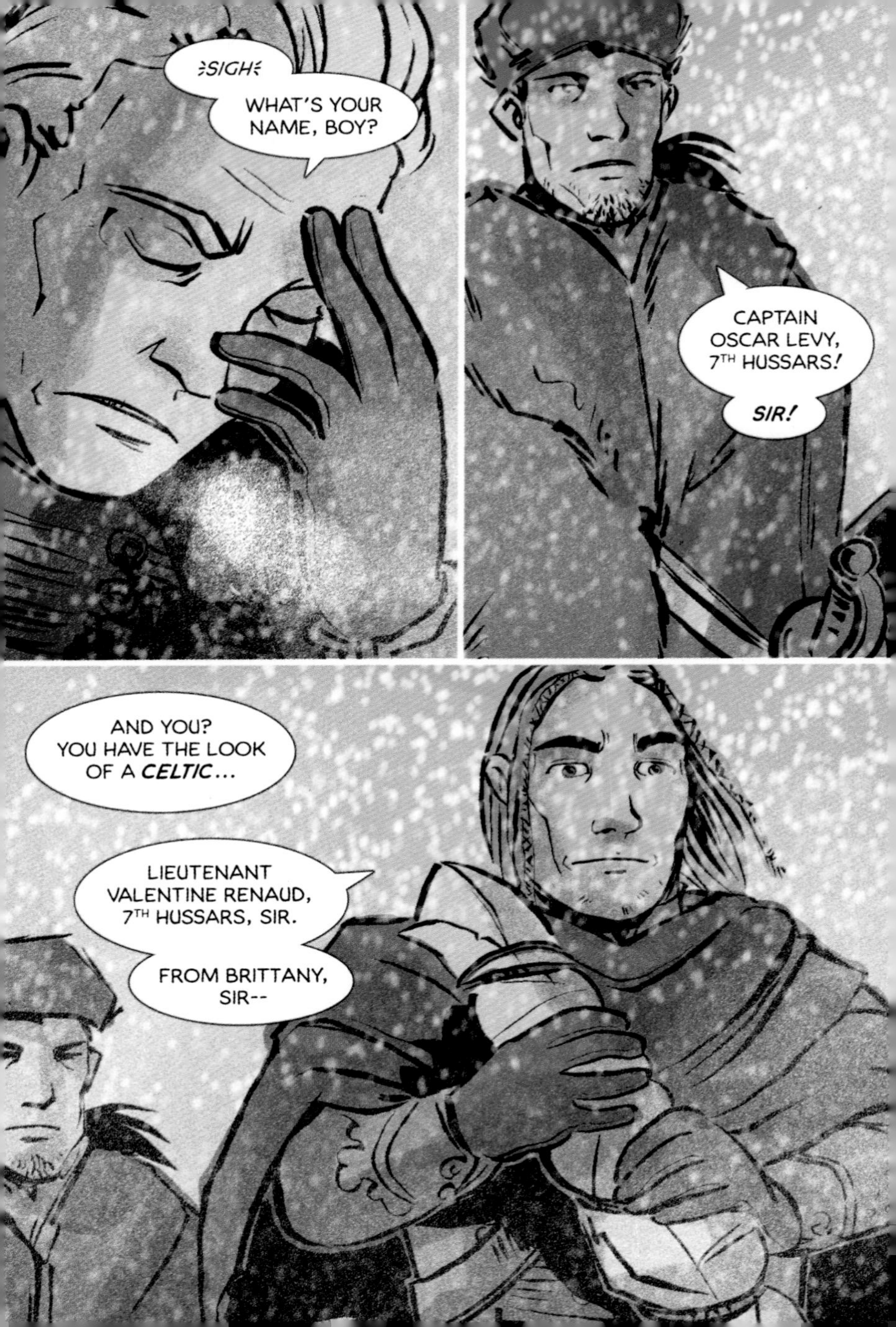

SIGH
WHAT'S YOUR NAME, BOY?
CAPTAIN OSCAR LEVY, 7TH HUSSARS!
SIR!
AND YOU? YOU HAVE THE LOOK OF A *CELTIC*...
LIEUTENANT VALENTINE RENAUD, 7TH HUSSARS, SIR.
FROM BRITTANY, SIR--

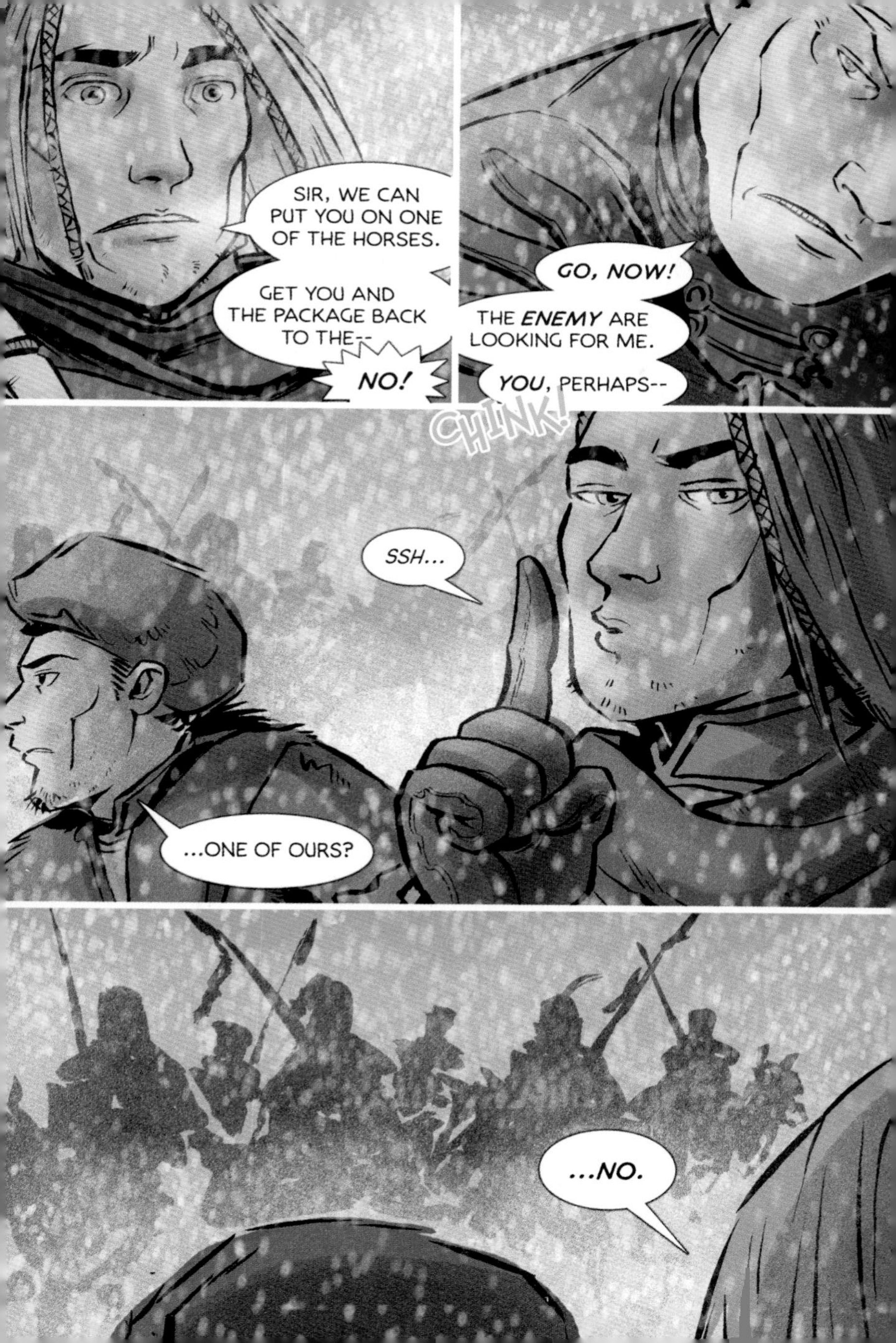
SIR, WE CAN PUT YOU ON ONE OF THE HORSES.
GET YOU AND THE PACKAGE BACK TO THE--
NO!
GO, NOW!
THE ENEMY ARE LOOKING FOR ME.
YOU, PERHAPS--
CHINK!
SSH...
...ONE OF OURS?
...NO.

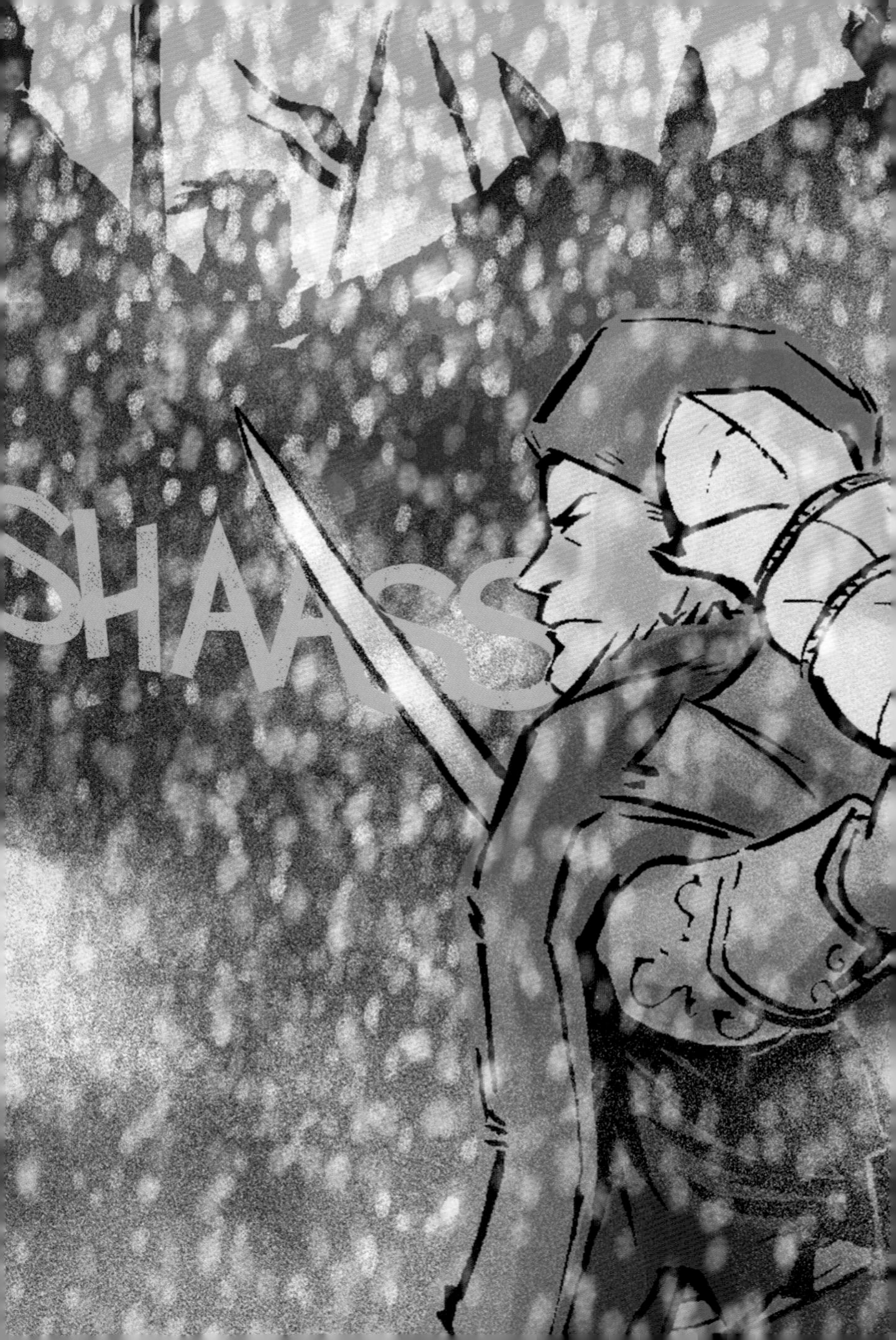
SHAASS

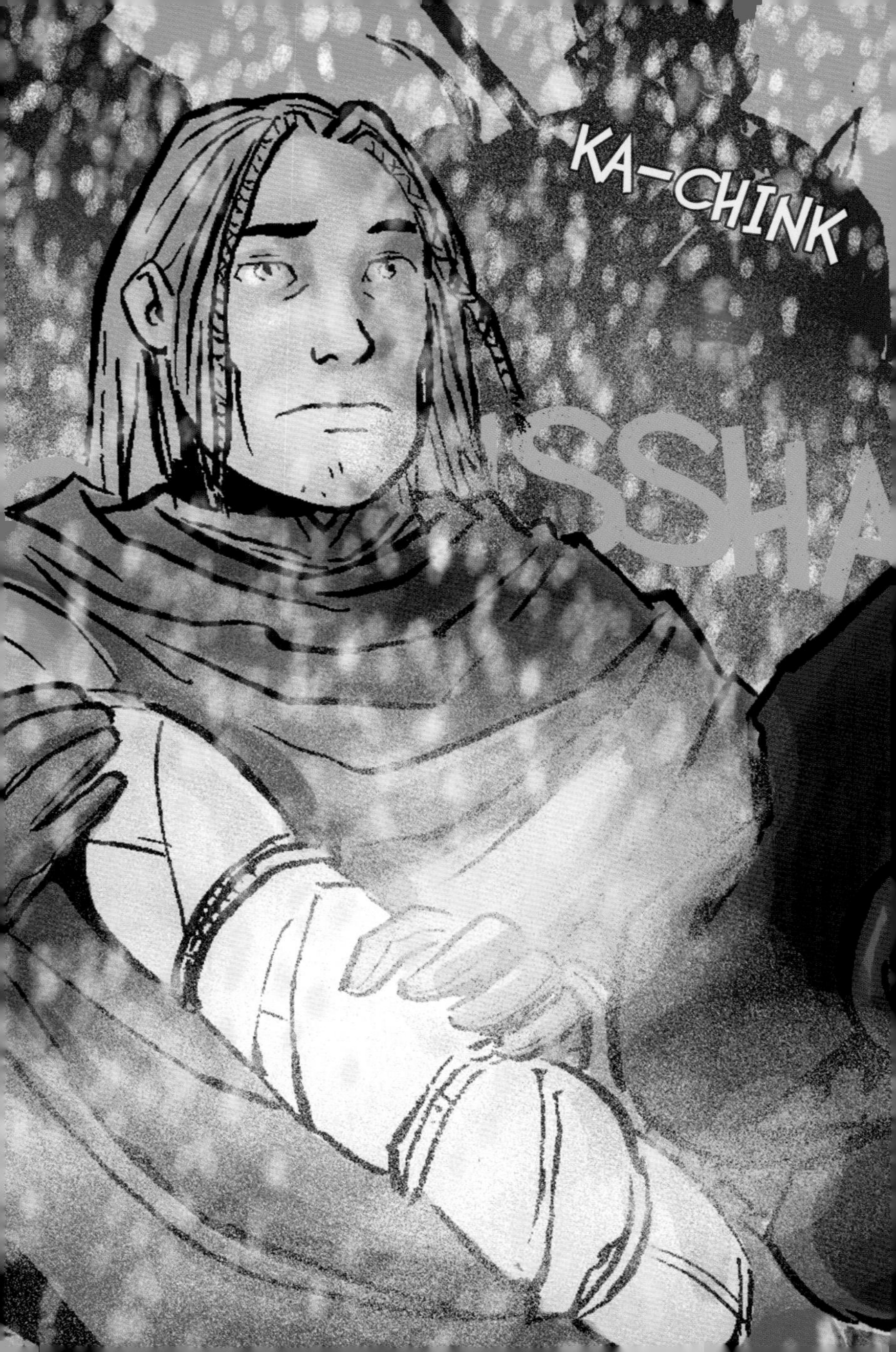
KA-CHINK
SSHA

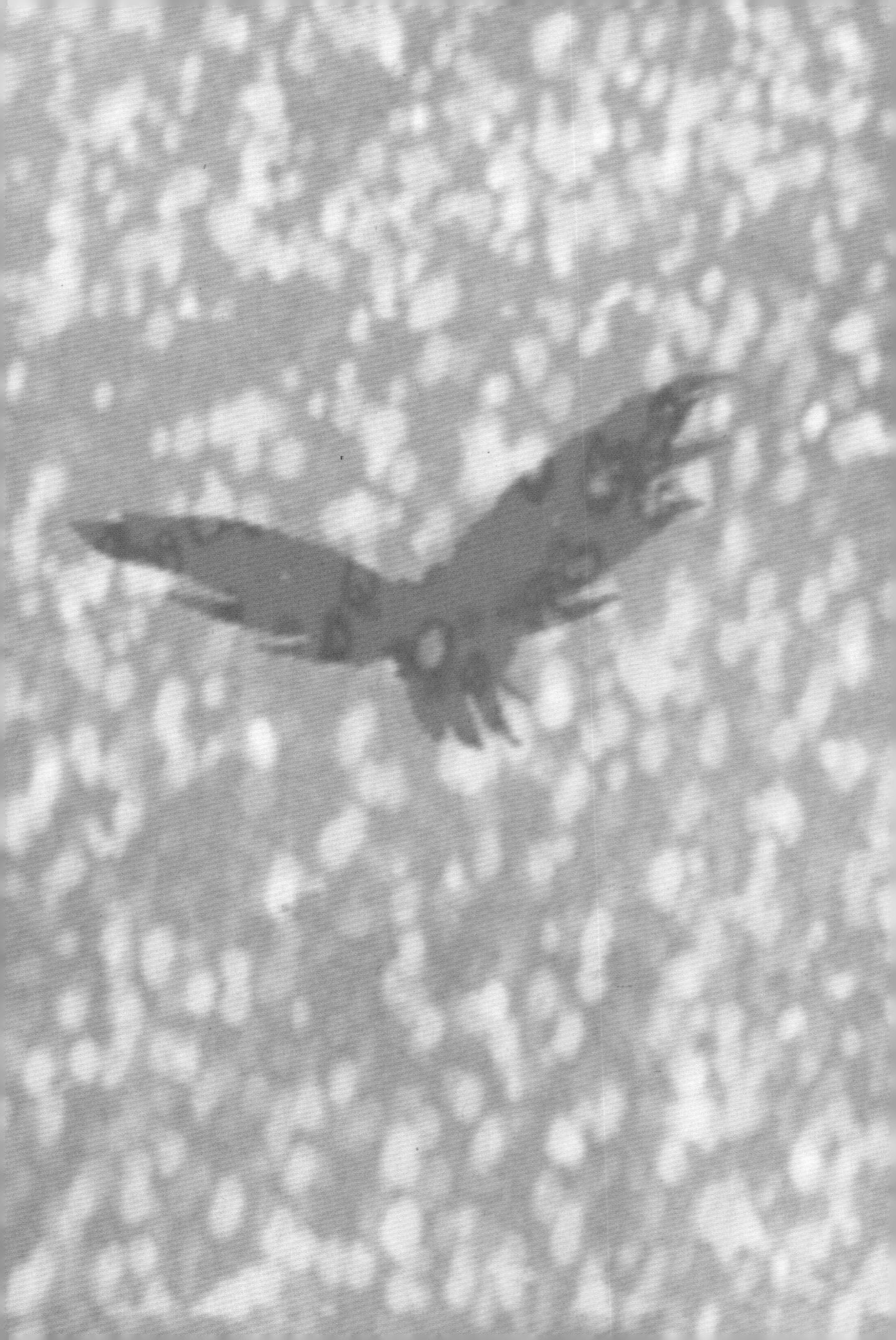

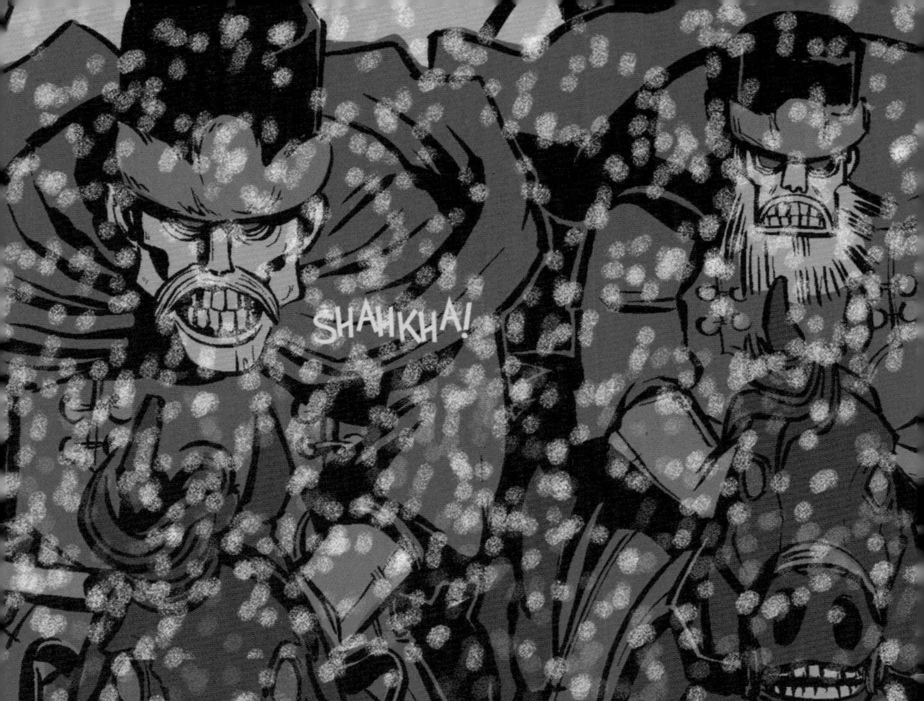
SHAHKHA!

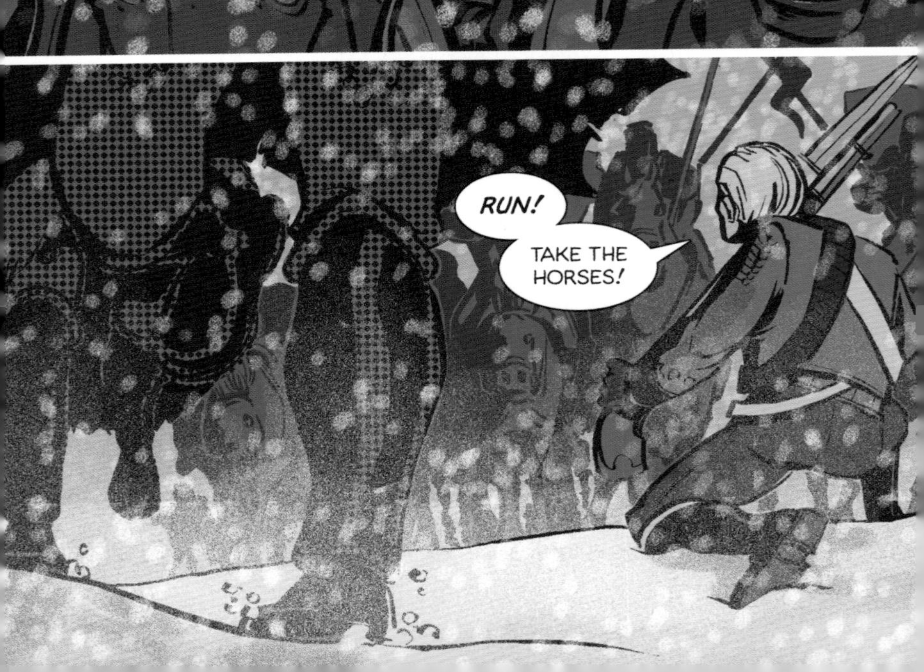
RUN!
TAKE THE HORSES!

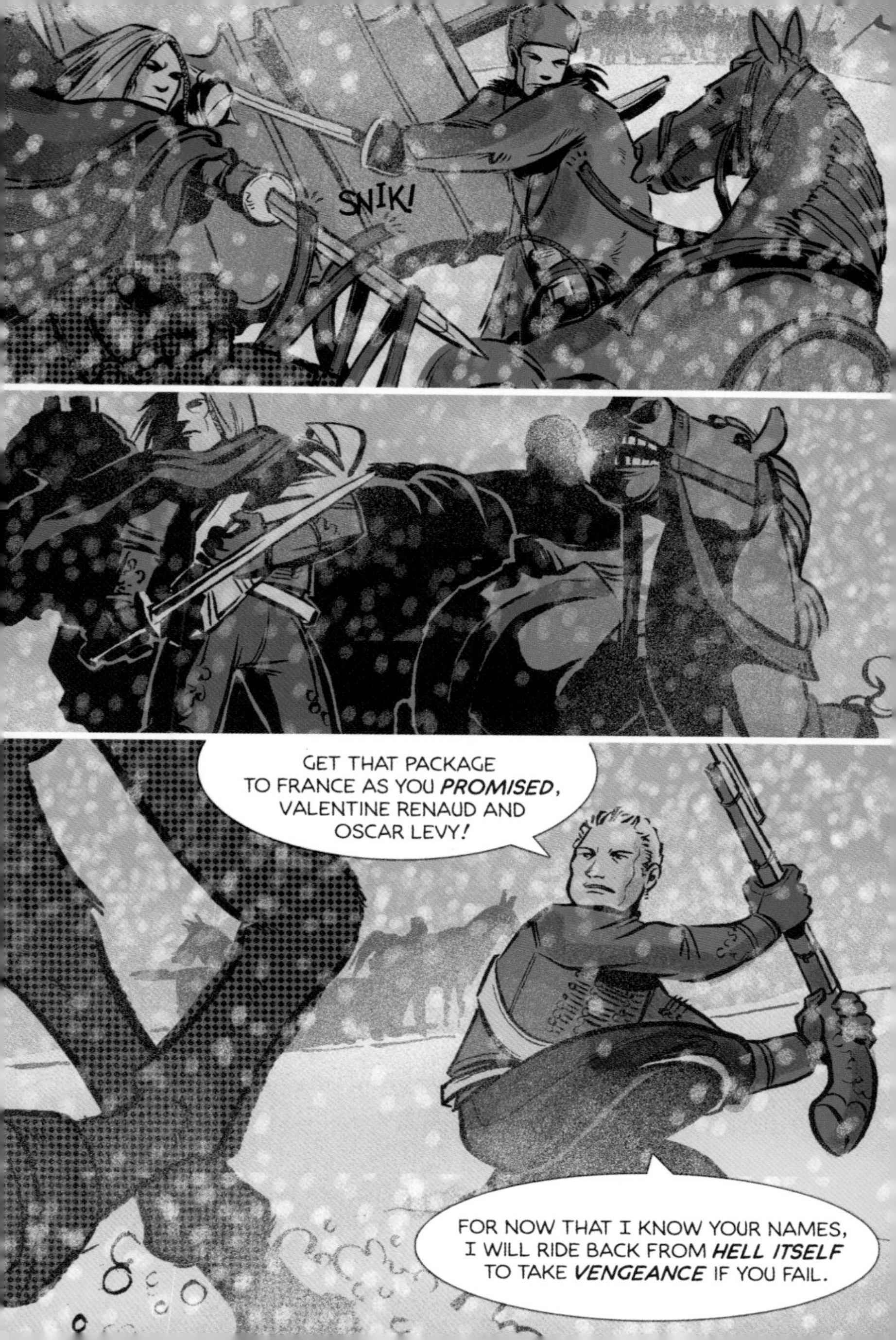
SNIK!
GET THAT PACKAGE TO FRANCE AS YOU *PROMISED*, VALENTINE RENAUD AND OSCAR LEVY!
FOR NOW THAT I KNOW YOUR NAMES, I WILL RIDE BACK FROM *HELL ITSELF* TO TAKE *VENGEANCE* IF YOU FAIL.

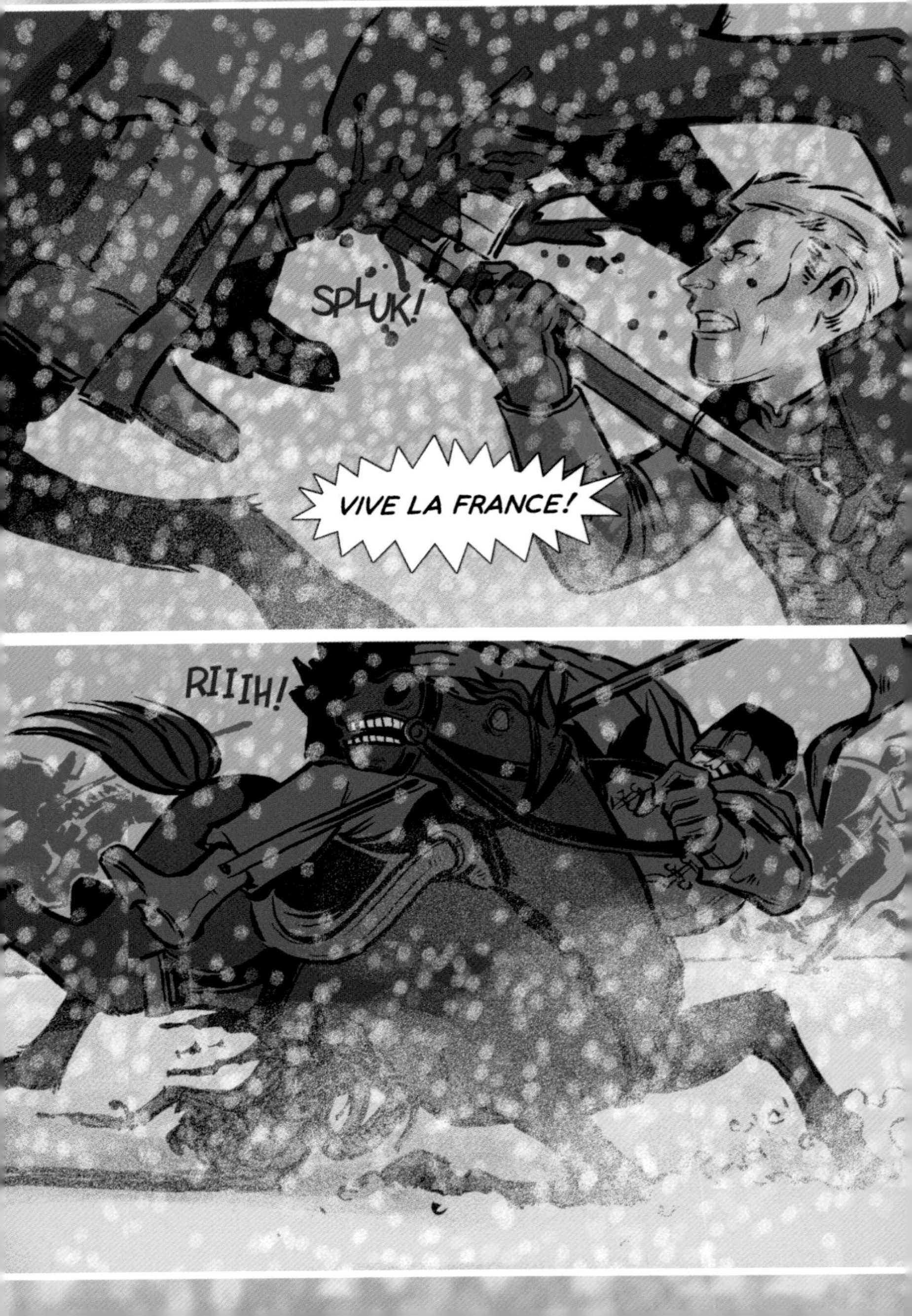
SPLUK!
VIVE LA FRANCE!
RIIIH!

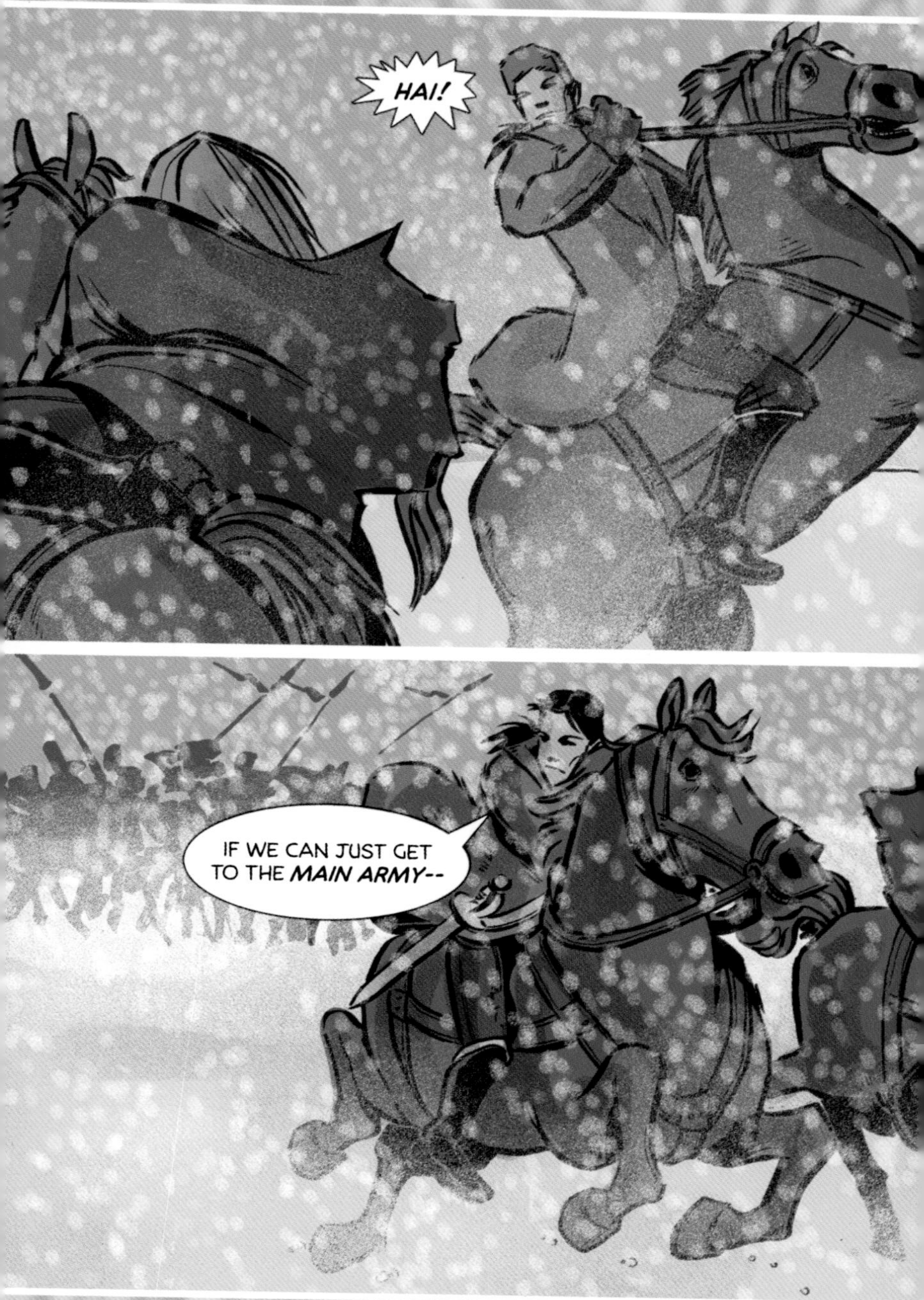
HAI!
IF WE CAN JUST GET TO THE *MAIN ARMY*--

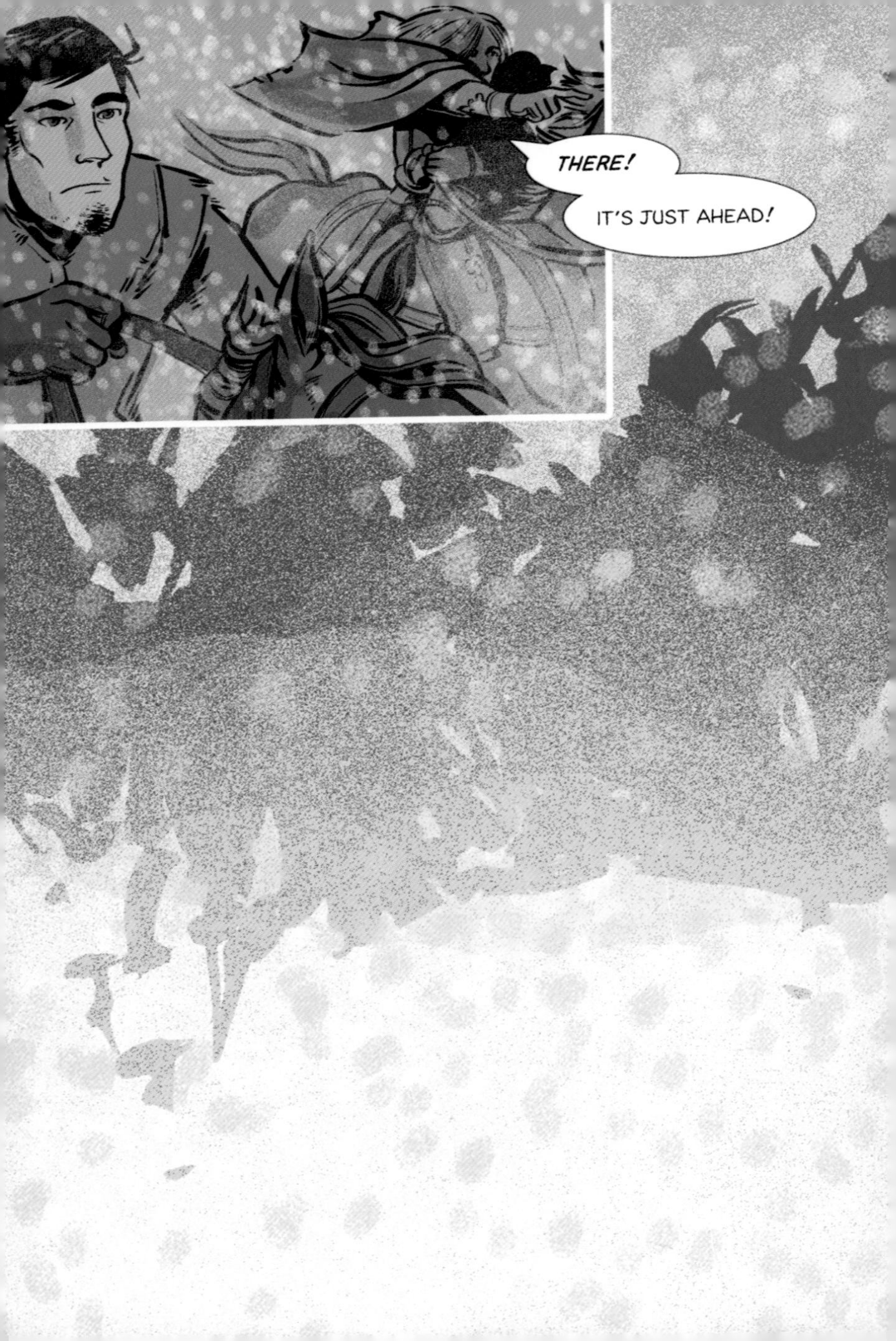
THERE!
IT'S JUST AHEAD!

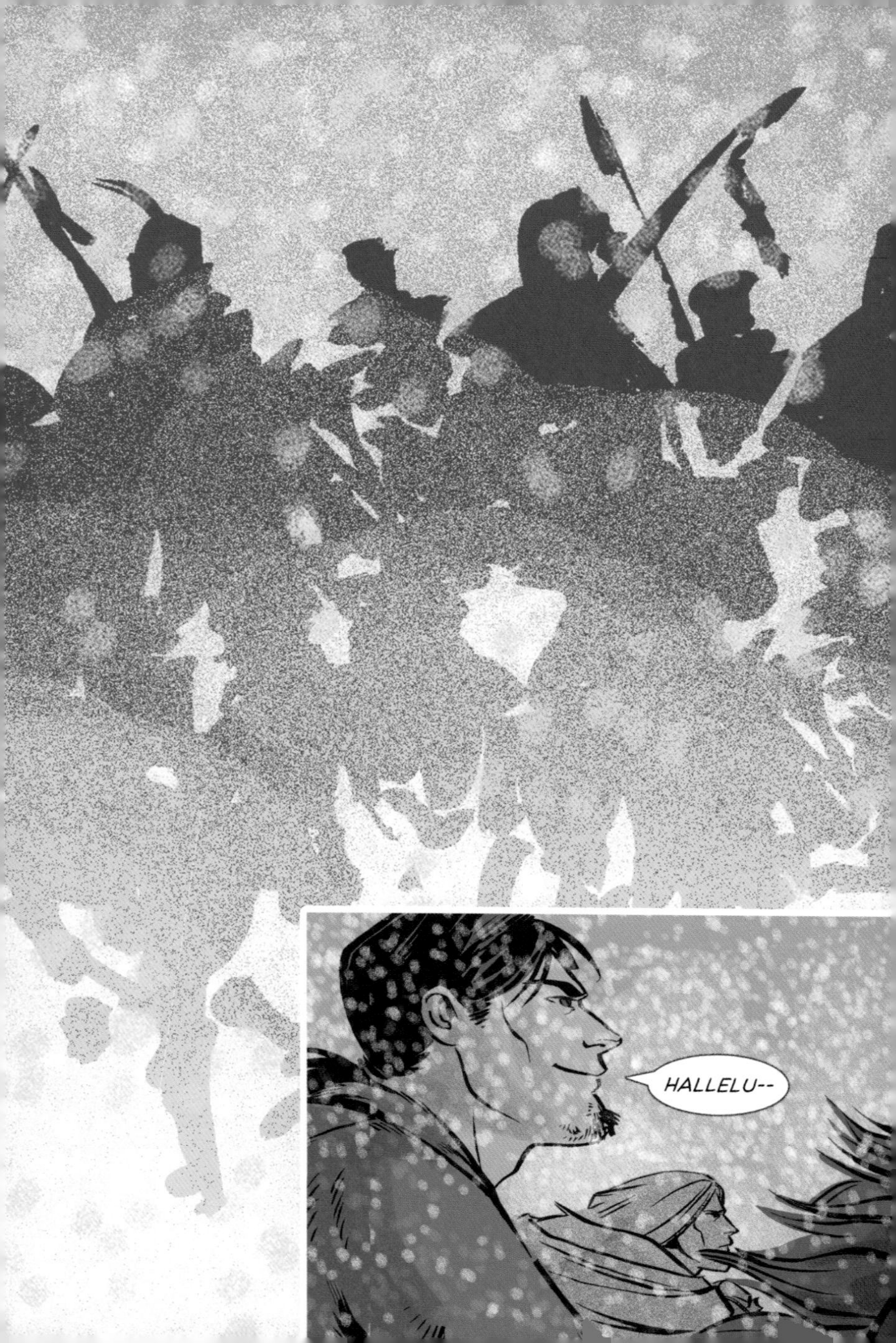
HALLELU--

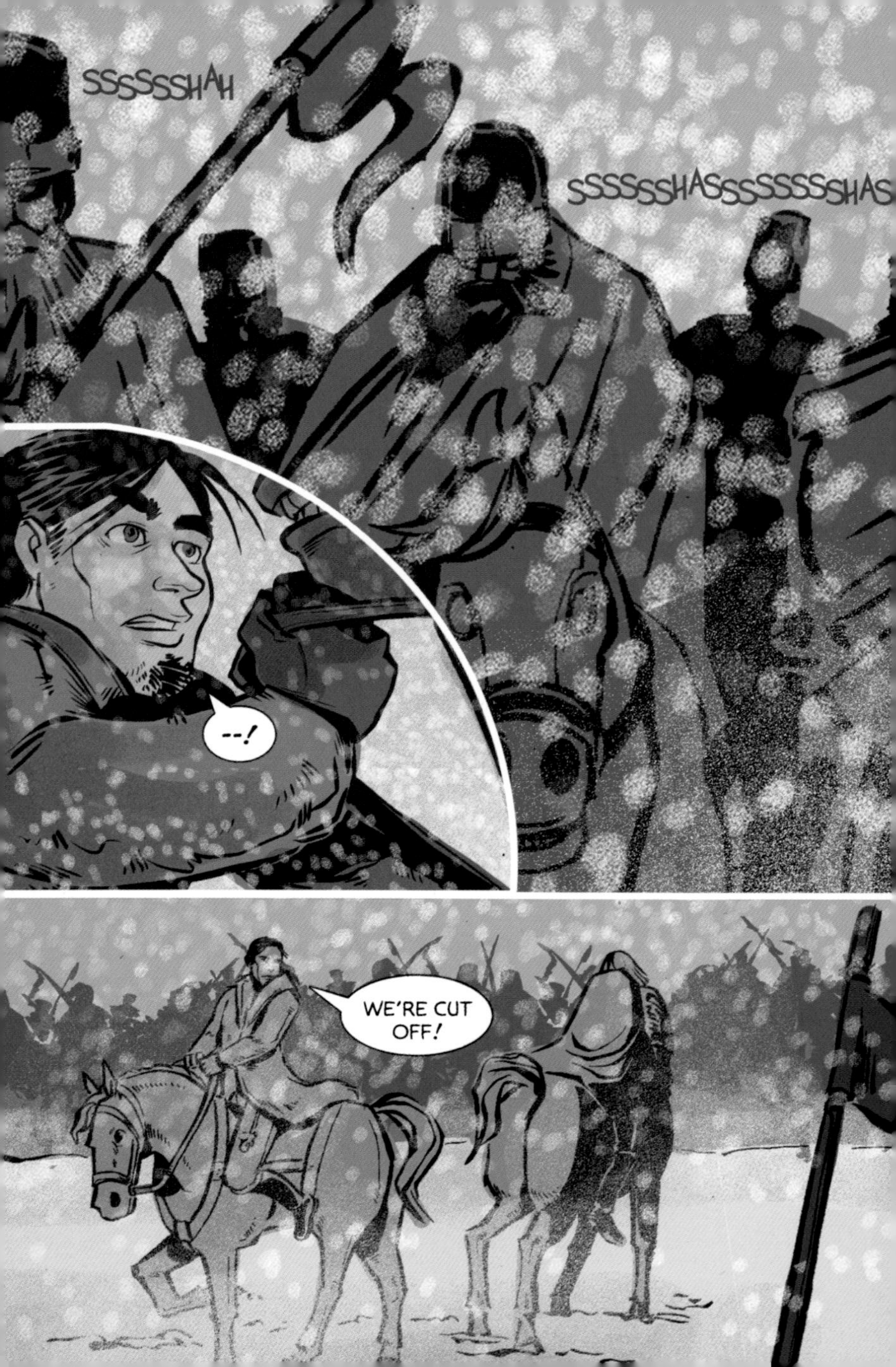
SSSSSSHAH
SSSSSSHASSSSSSSSSHAS
--!
WE'RE CUT OFF!

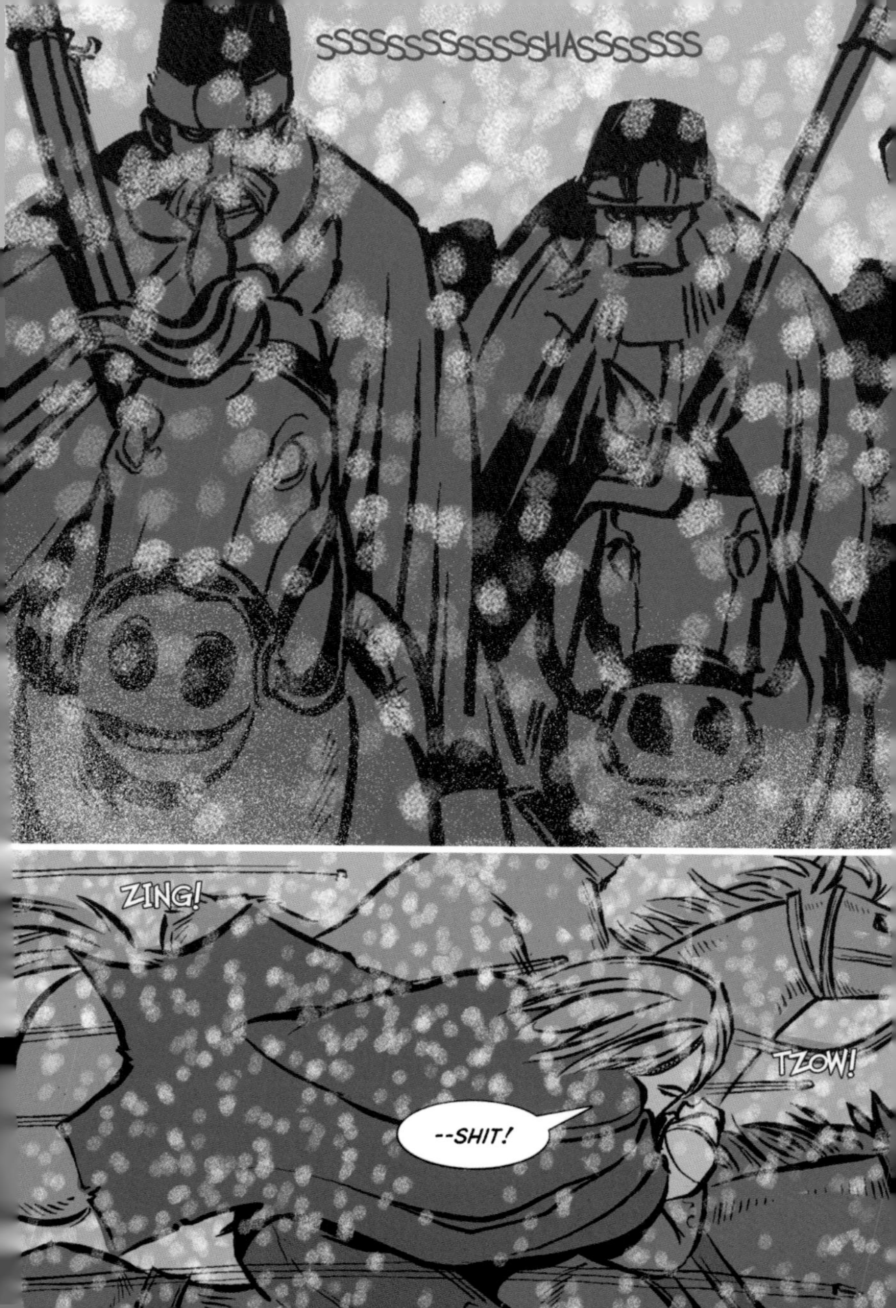
SSSSSSSSSSSSSHASSSSSSS
ZING!
TZOW!
--SHIT!

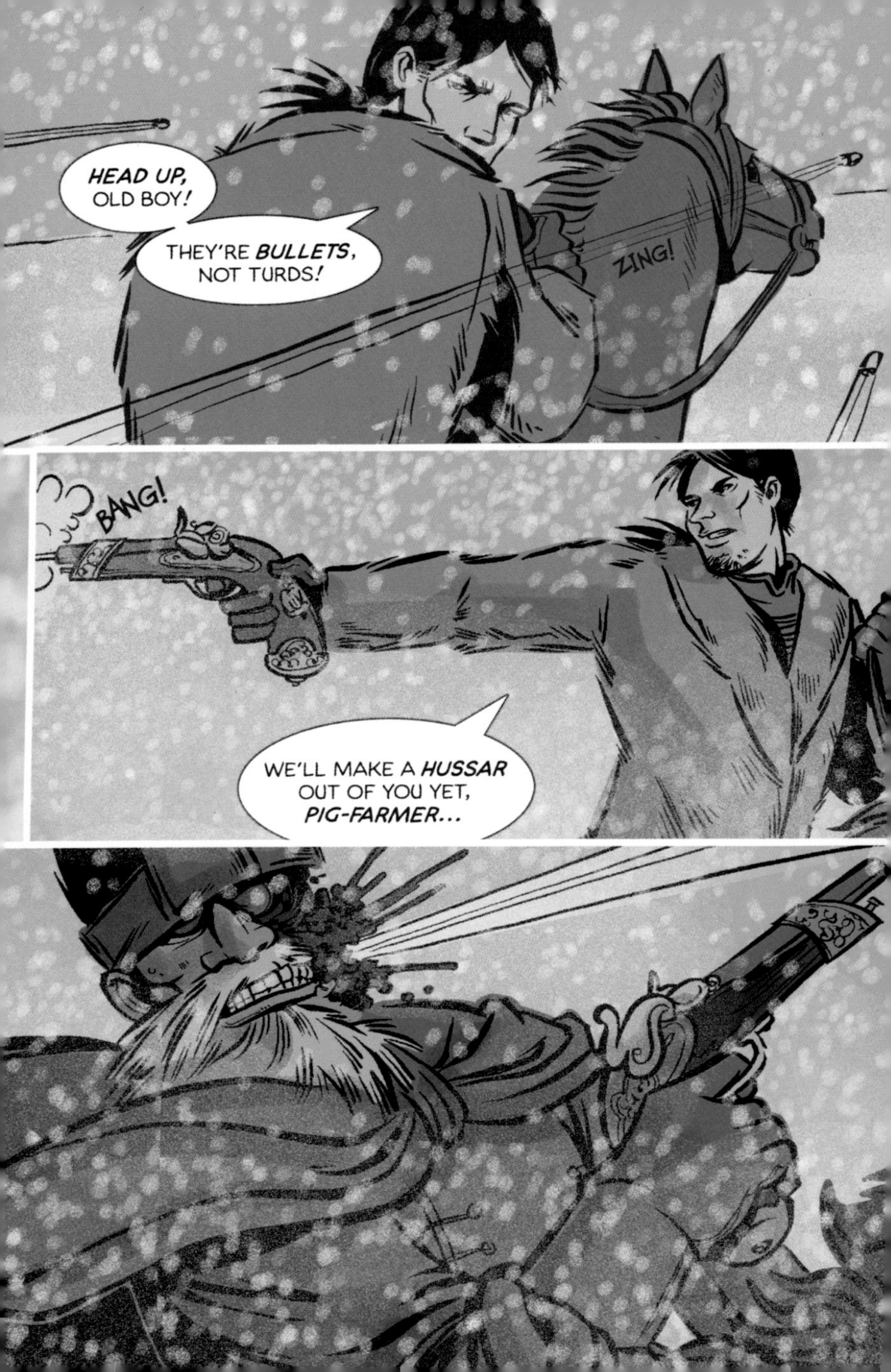
HEAD UP, OLD BOY!
THEY'RE BULLETS, NOT TURDS!
ZING!
BANG!
WE'LL MAKE A HUSSAR OUT OF YOU YET, PIG-FARMER...

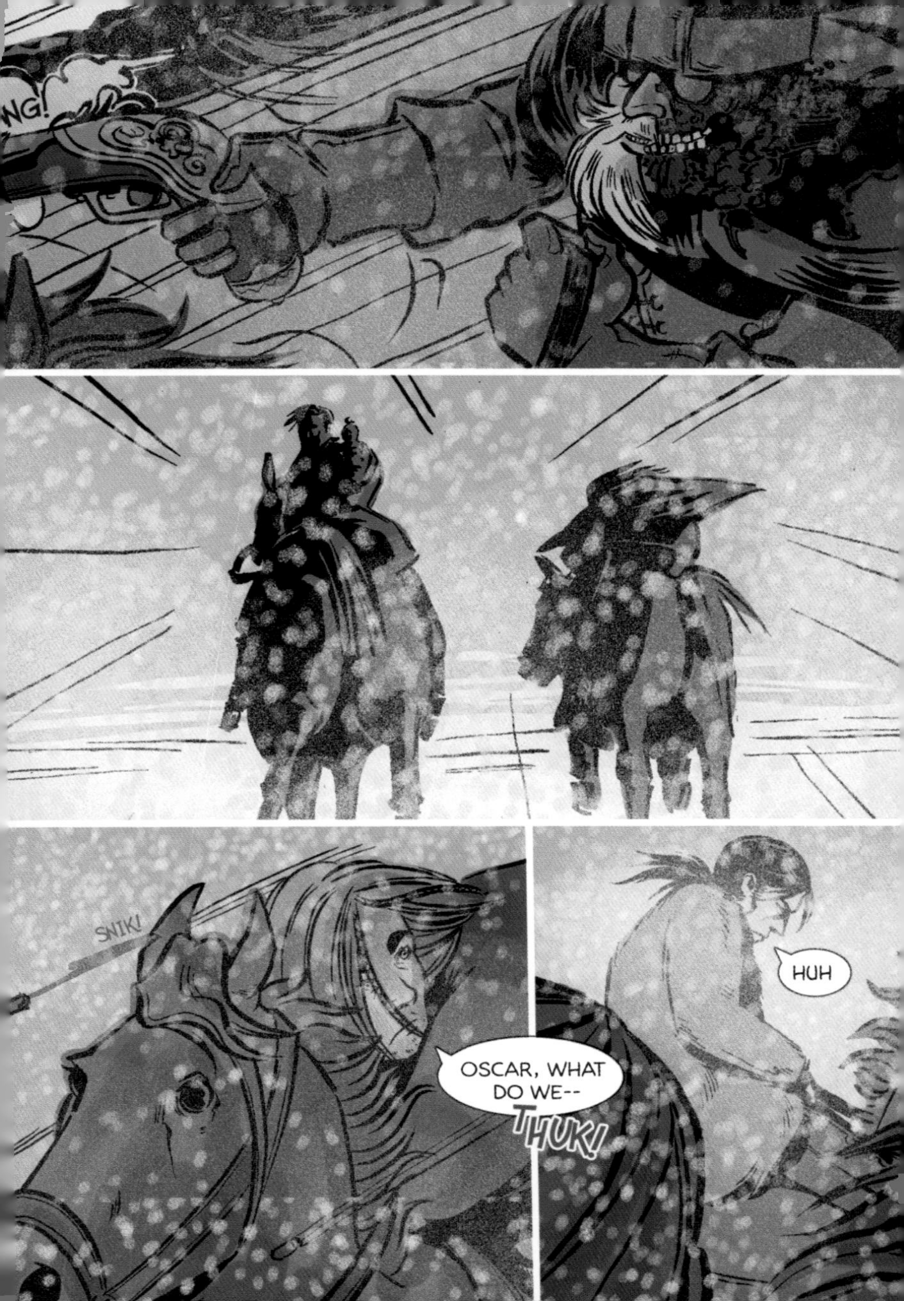
SNIK!
OSCAR, WHAT DO WE--
THUK!
HUH

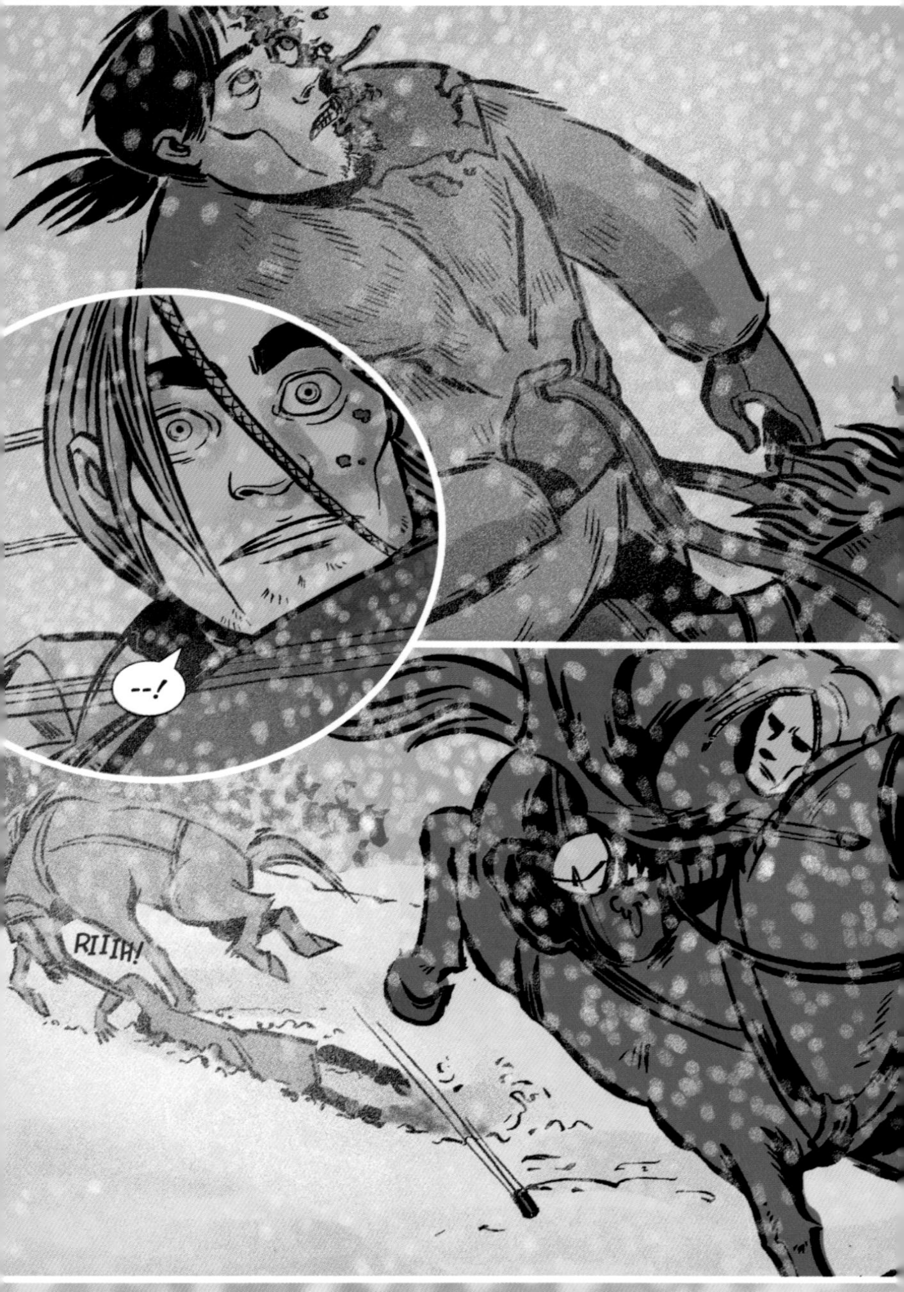
--!
RIIIA!

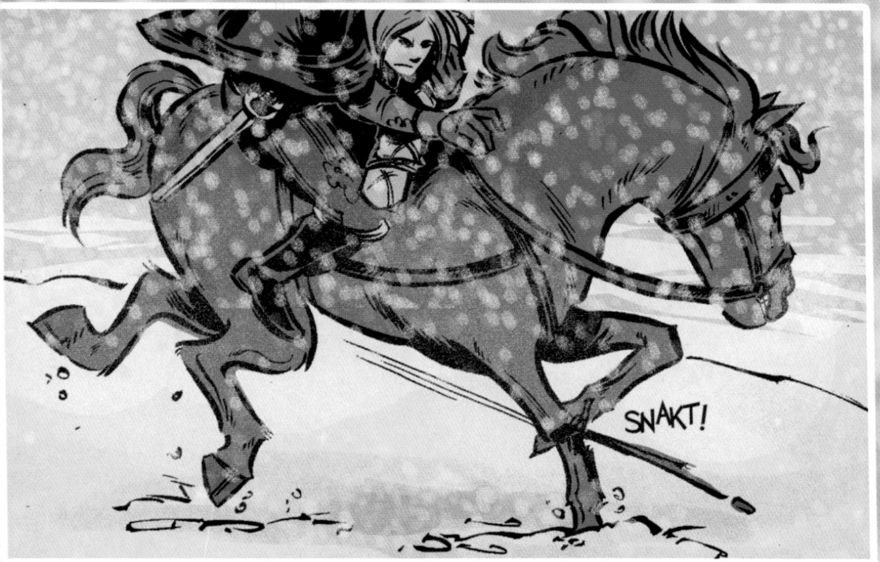
SNAKT!

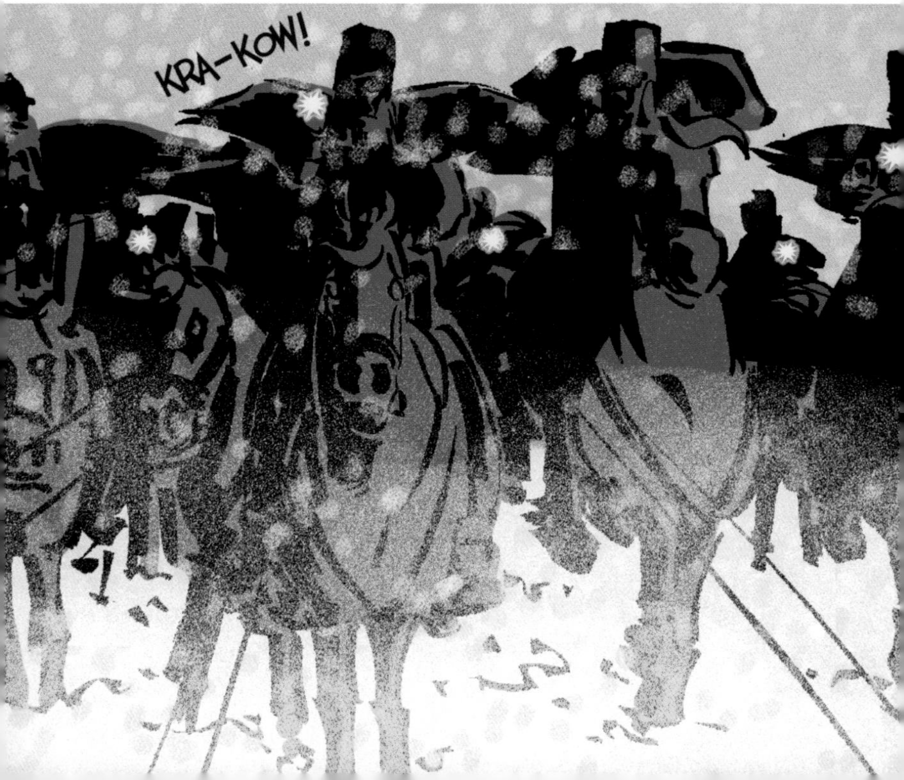
KRA-KOW!

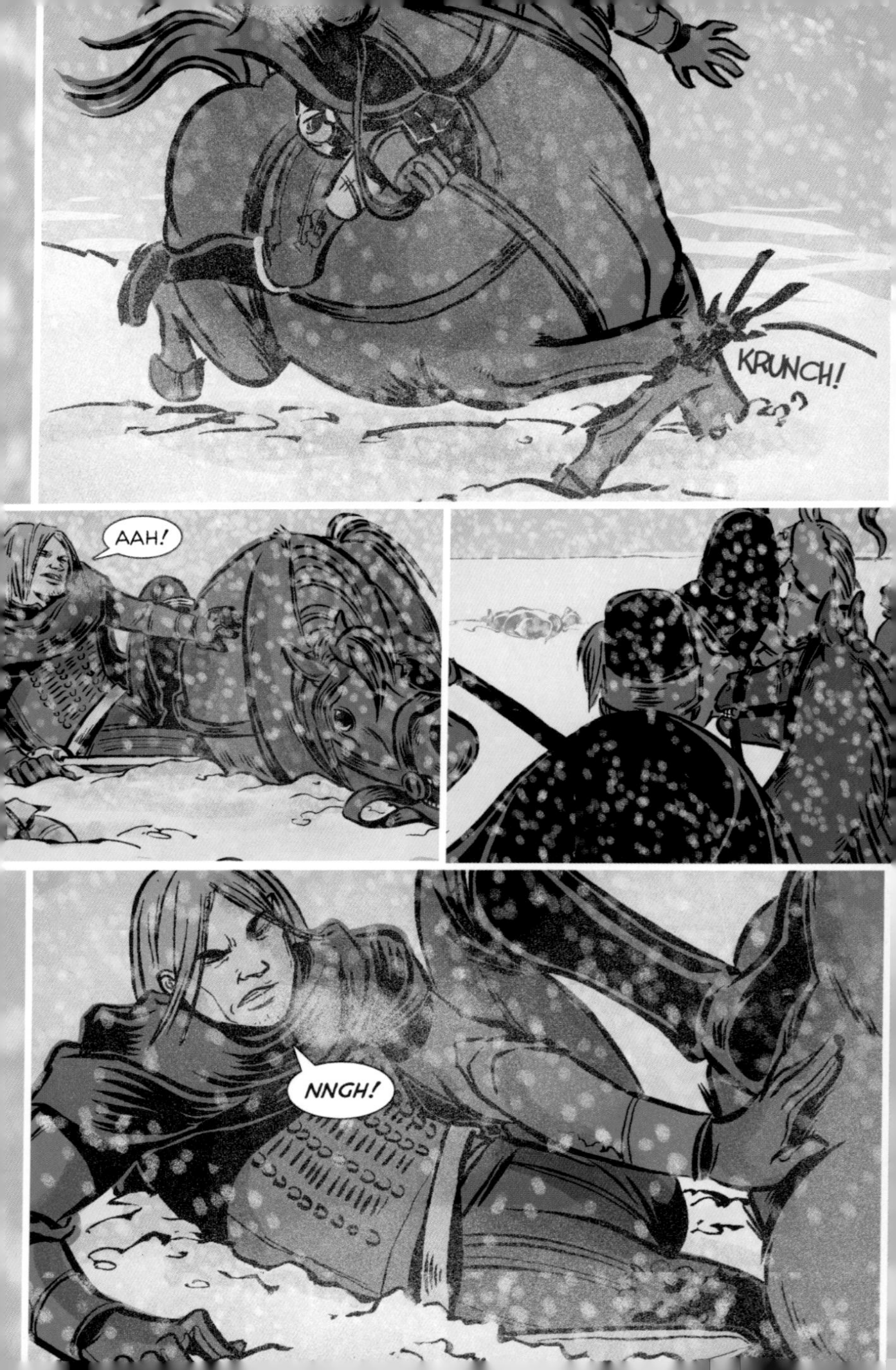
KRUNCH!
AAH!
NNGH!

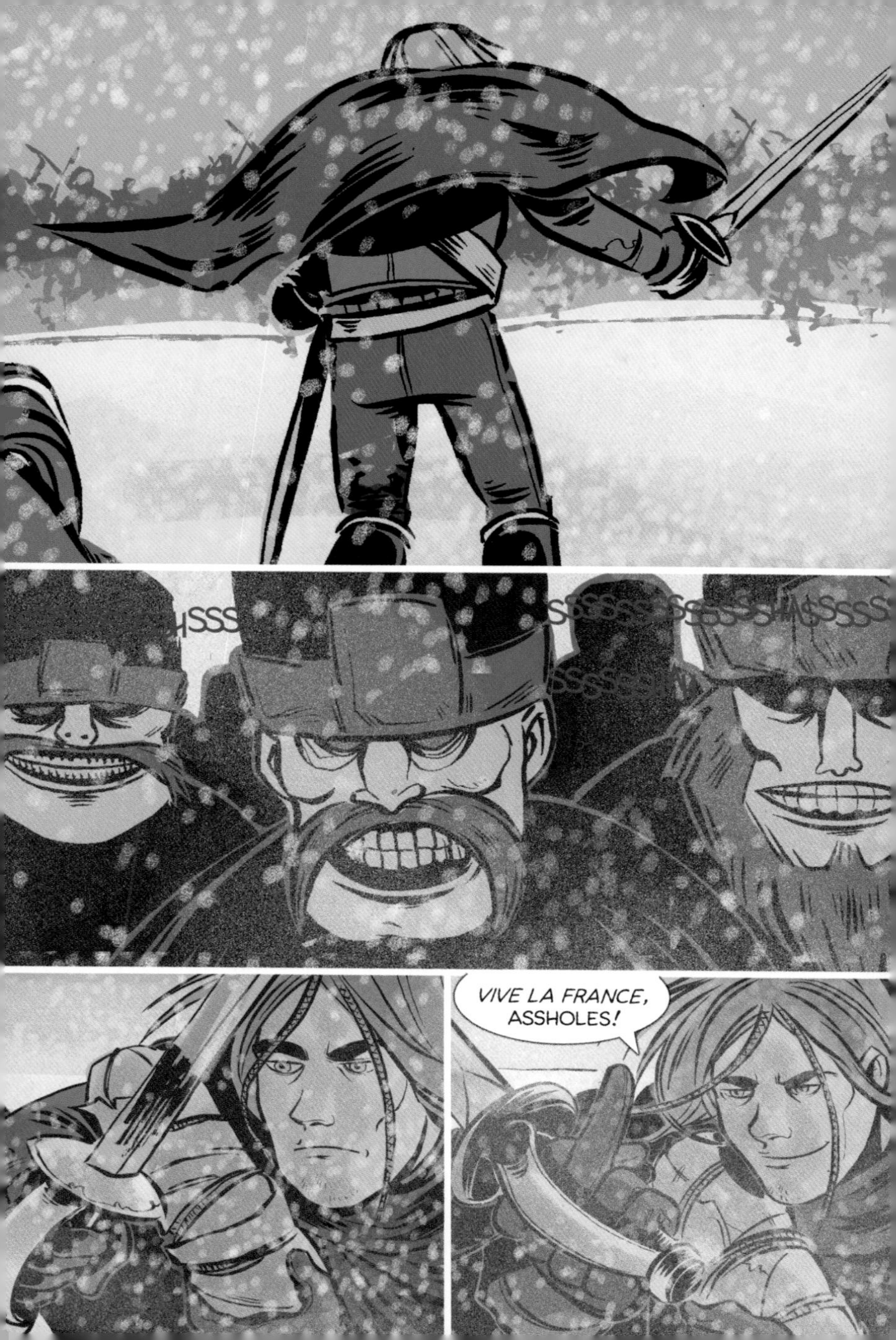
VIVE LA FRANCE, ASSHOLES!

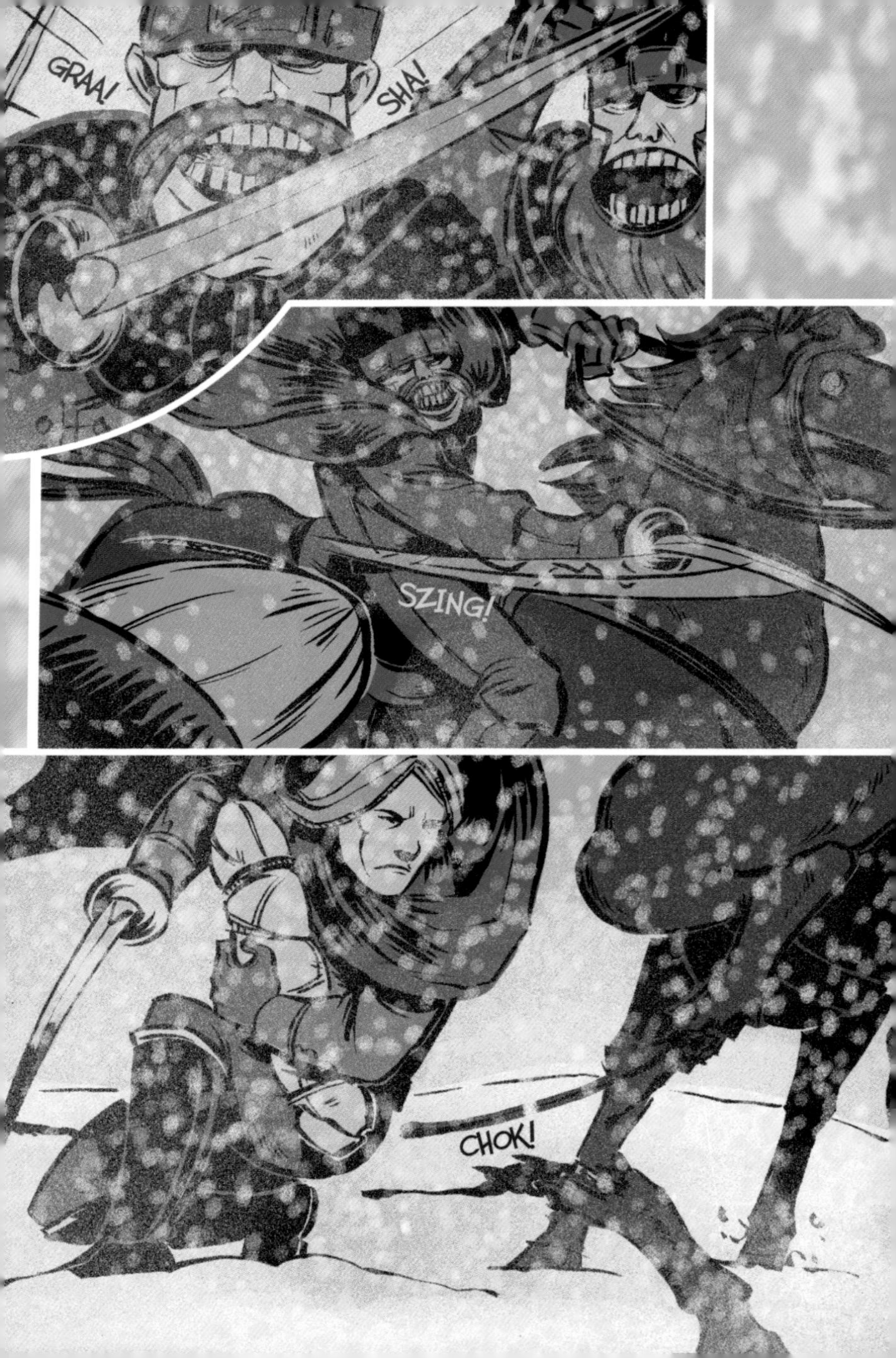
GRAA!
SHA!
SZING!
CHOK!

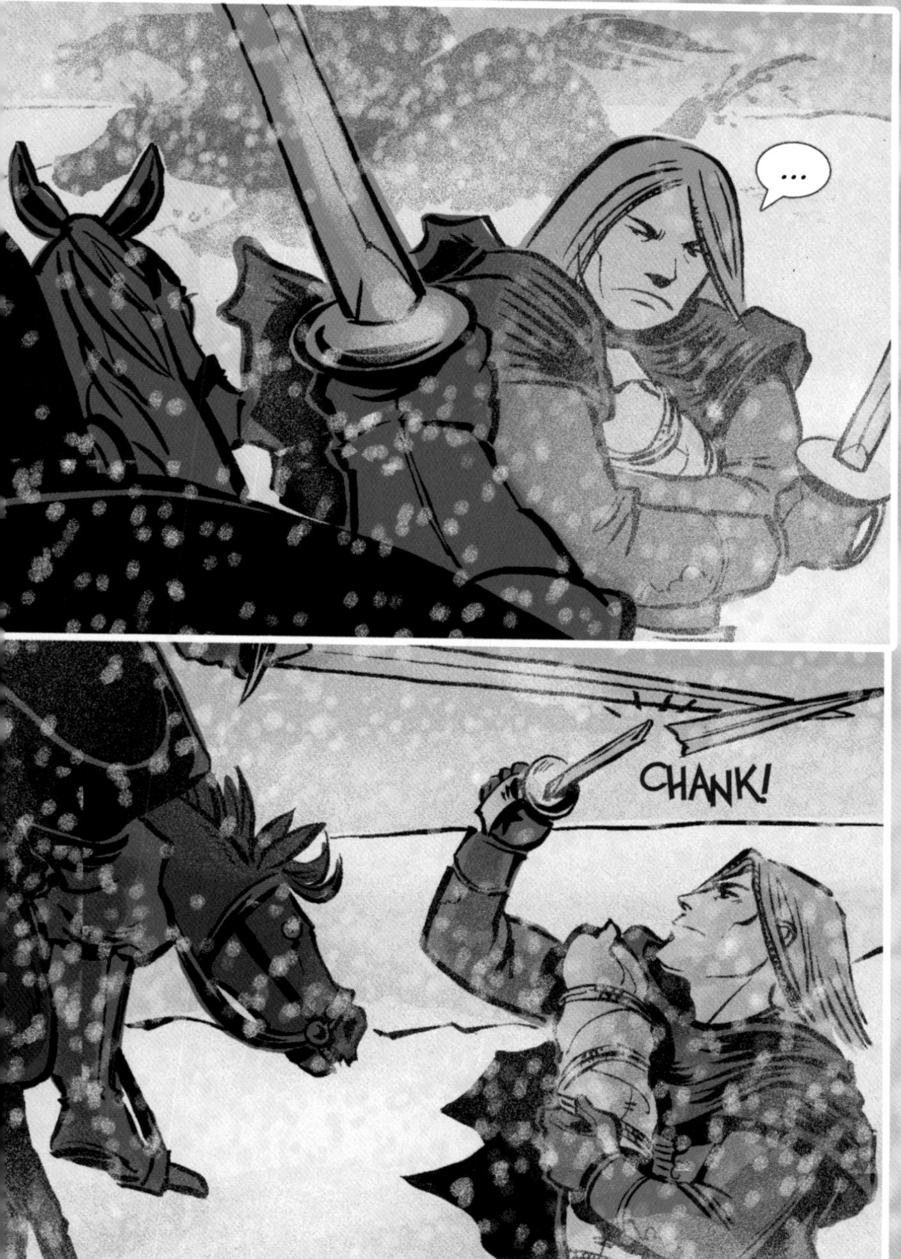
...
CHANK!

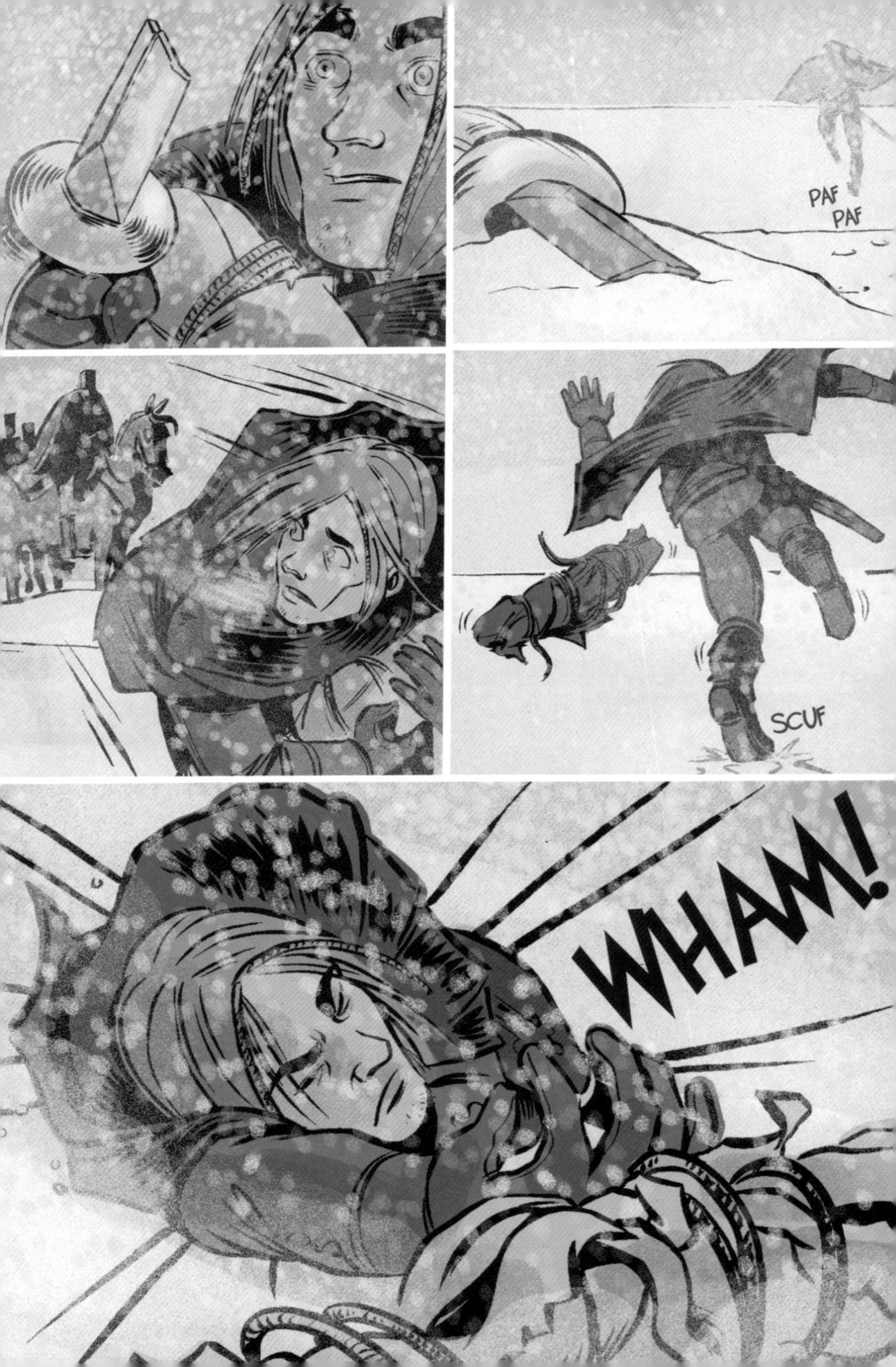
PAF
PAF
SCUF
WHAM!

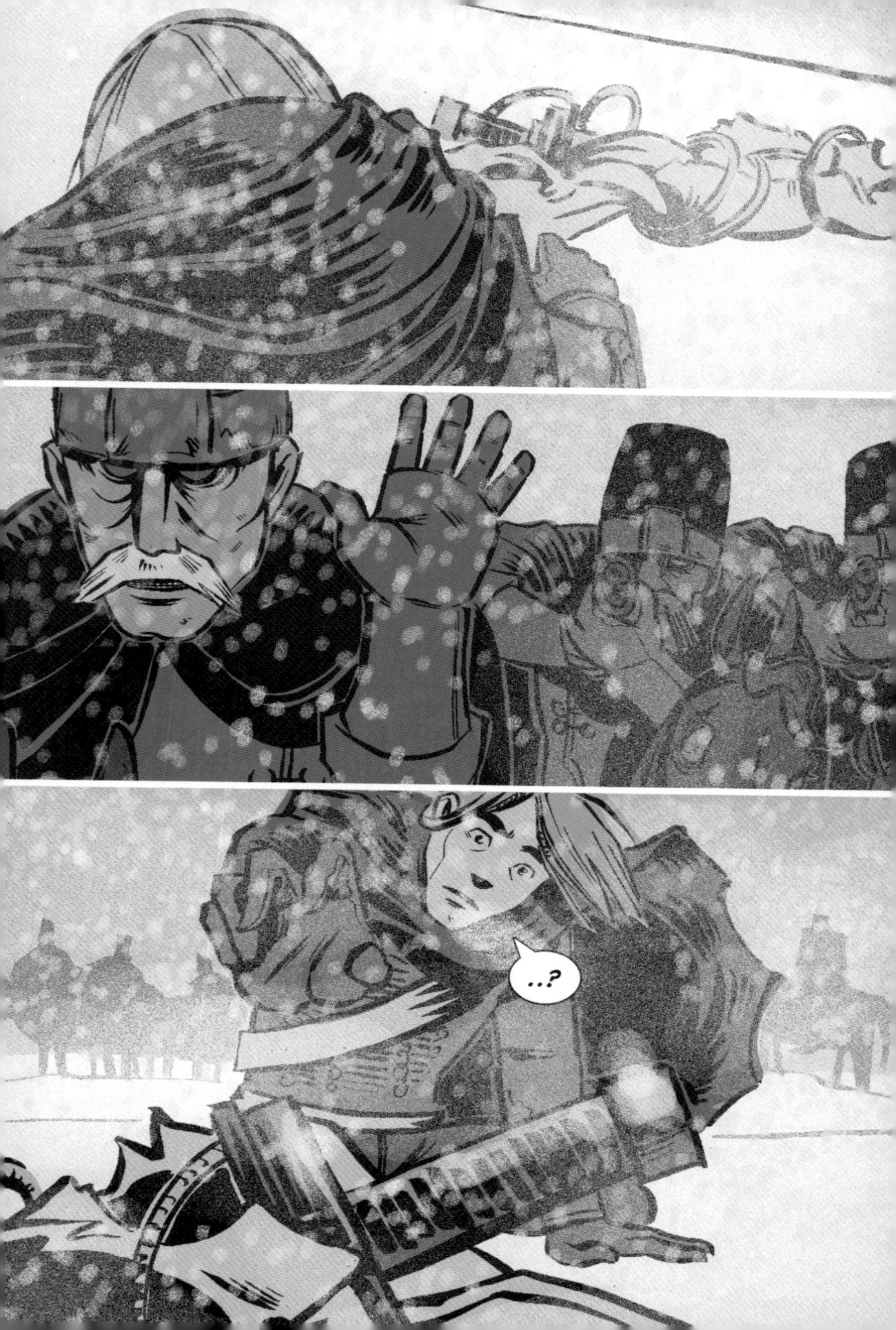
..?

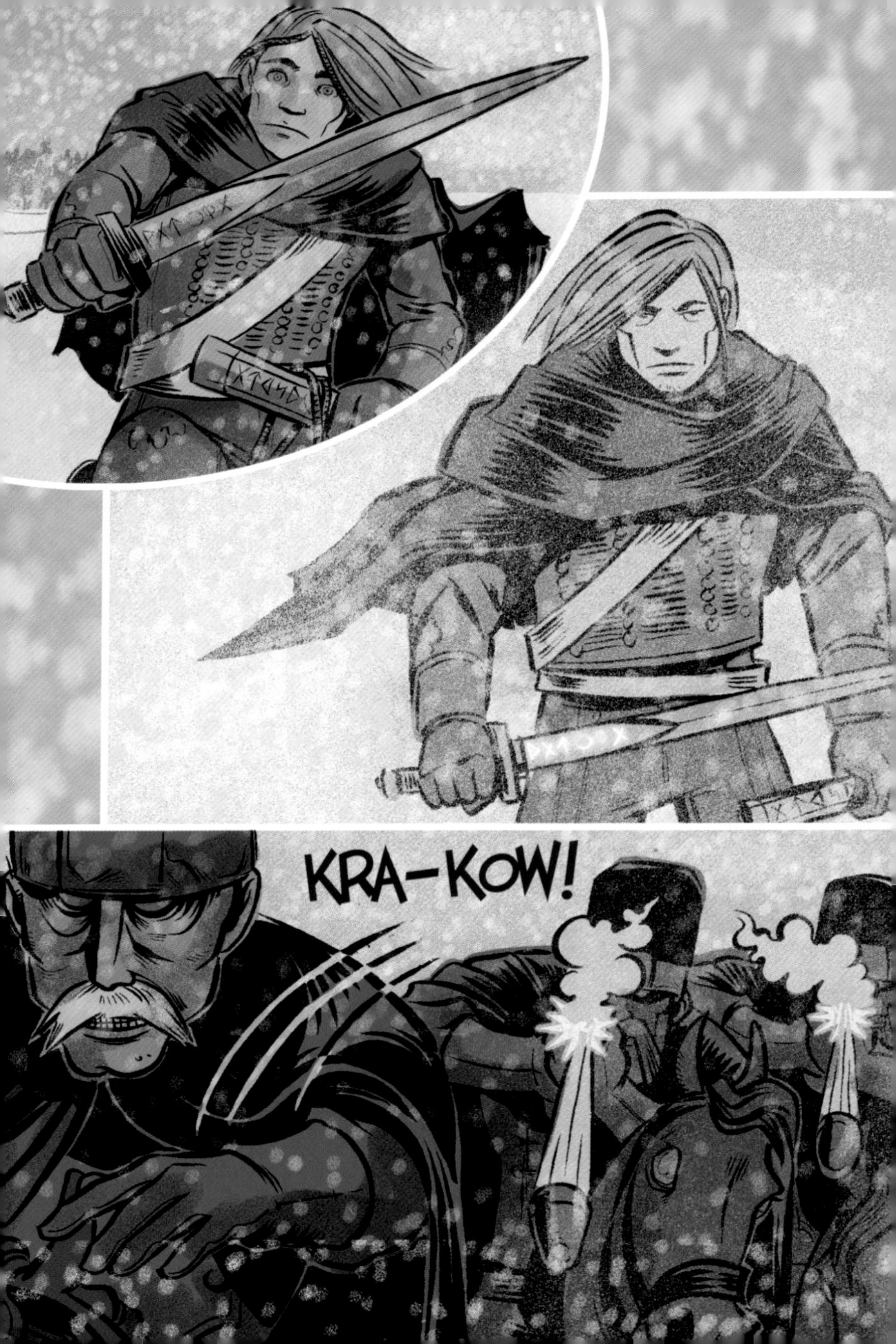
KRA-KOW!

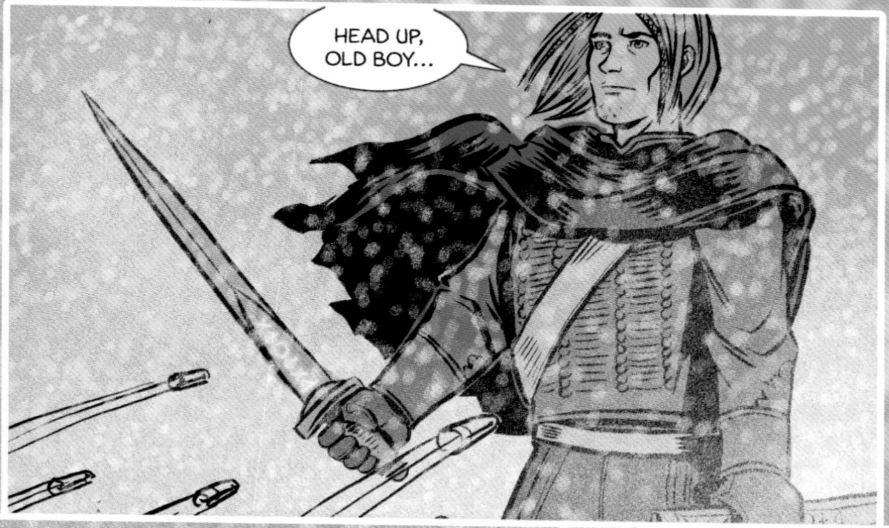
HEAD UP,
OLD BOY...

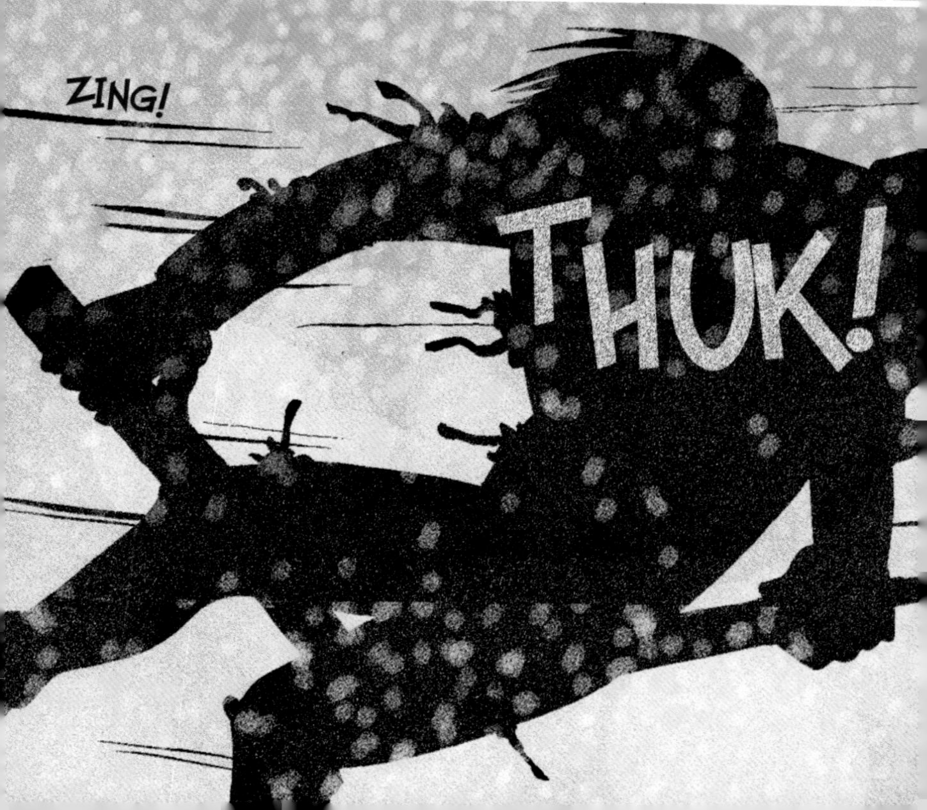
ZING!
THUK!

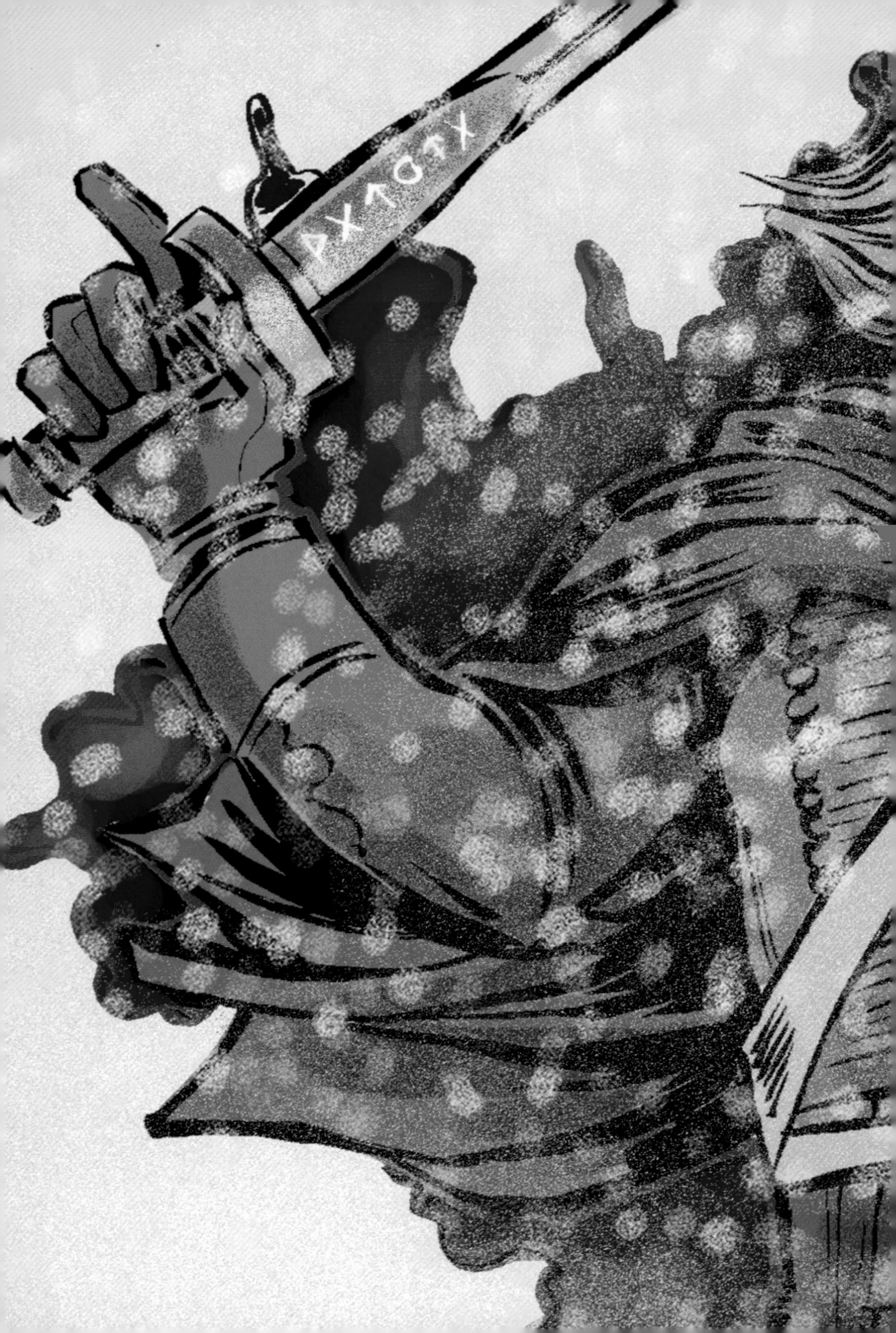

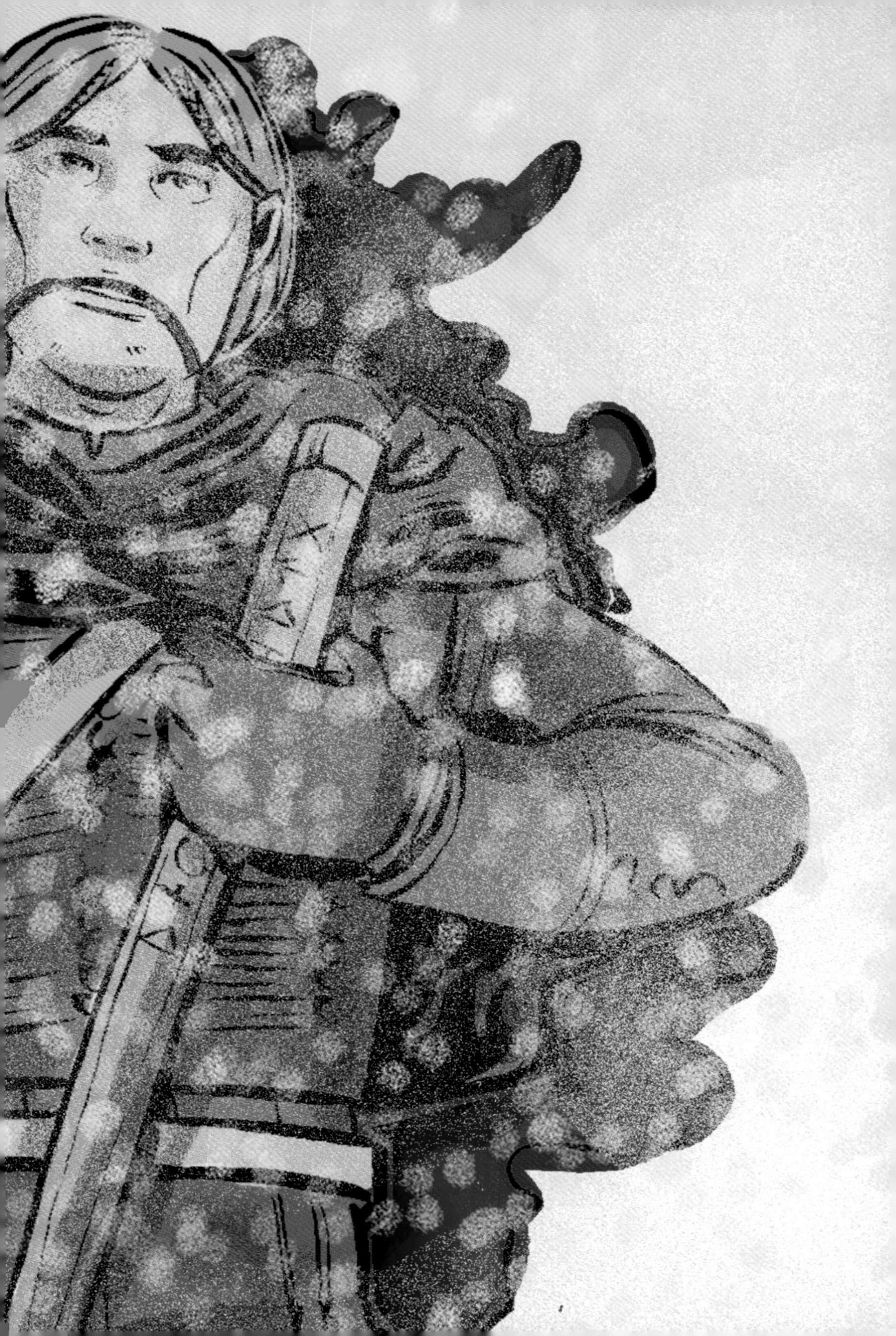

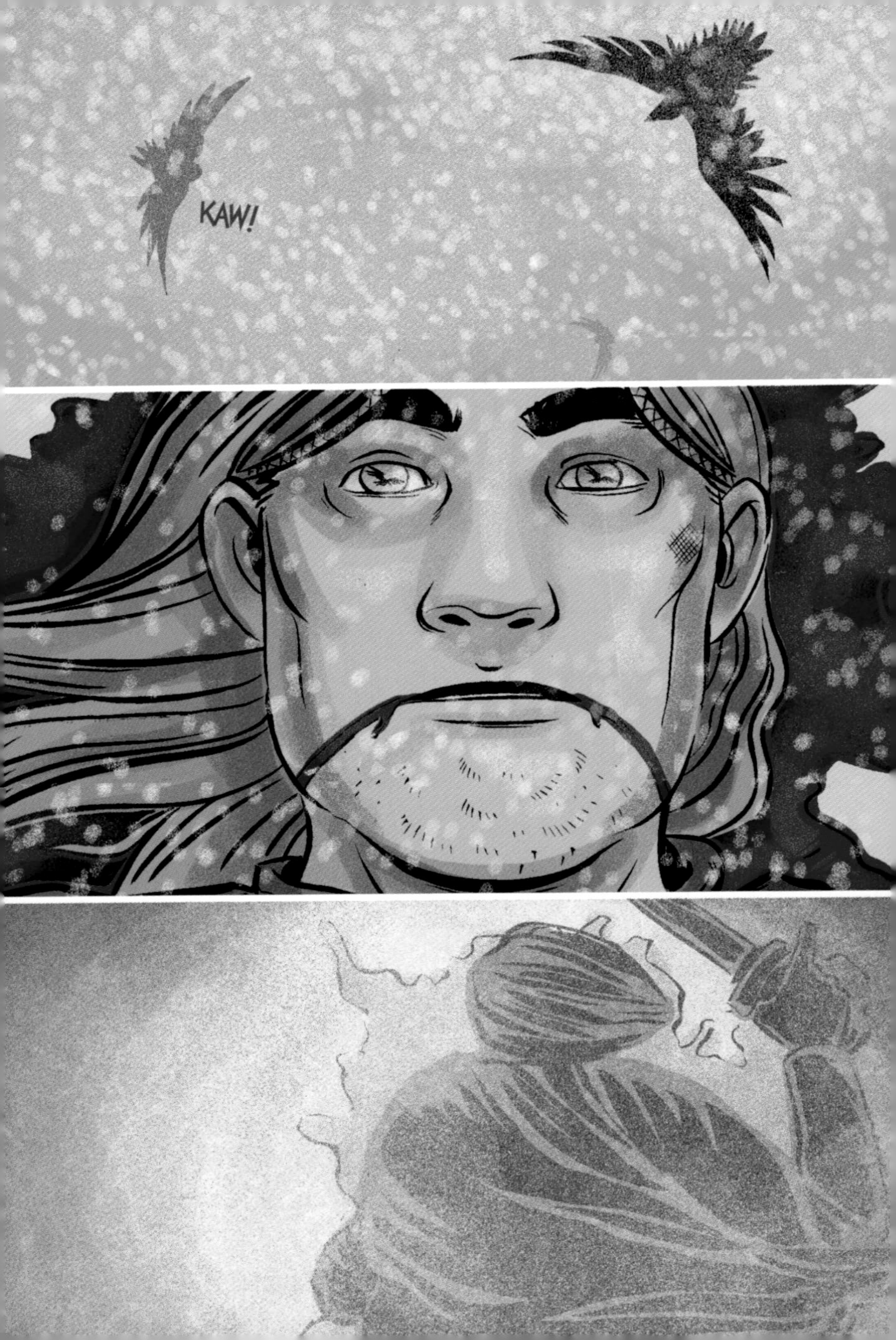
KAW!

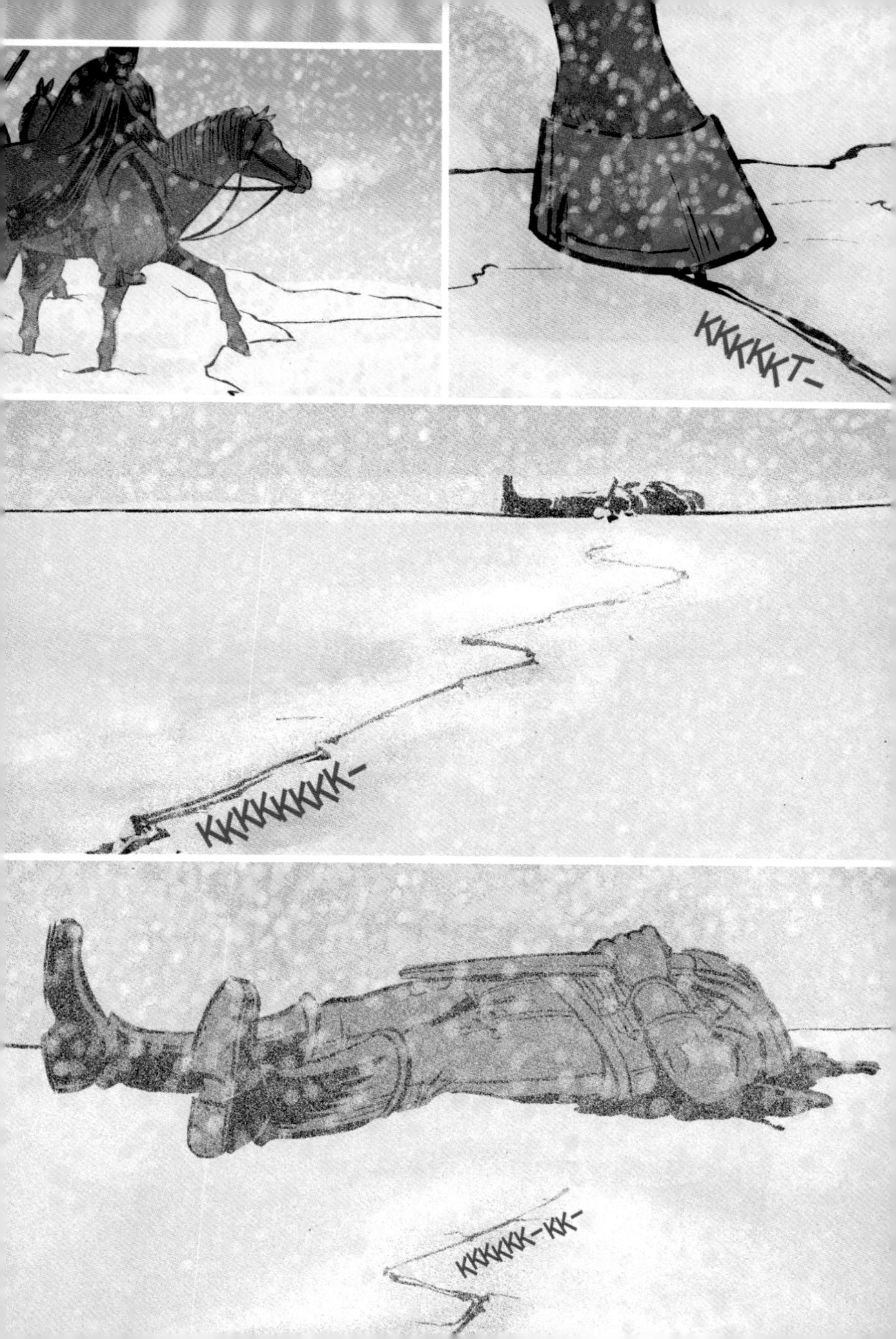
KKKKKT-
KKKKKKK-
KKKKK-KK-

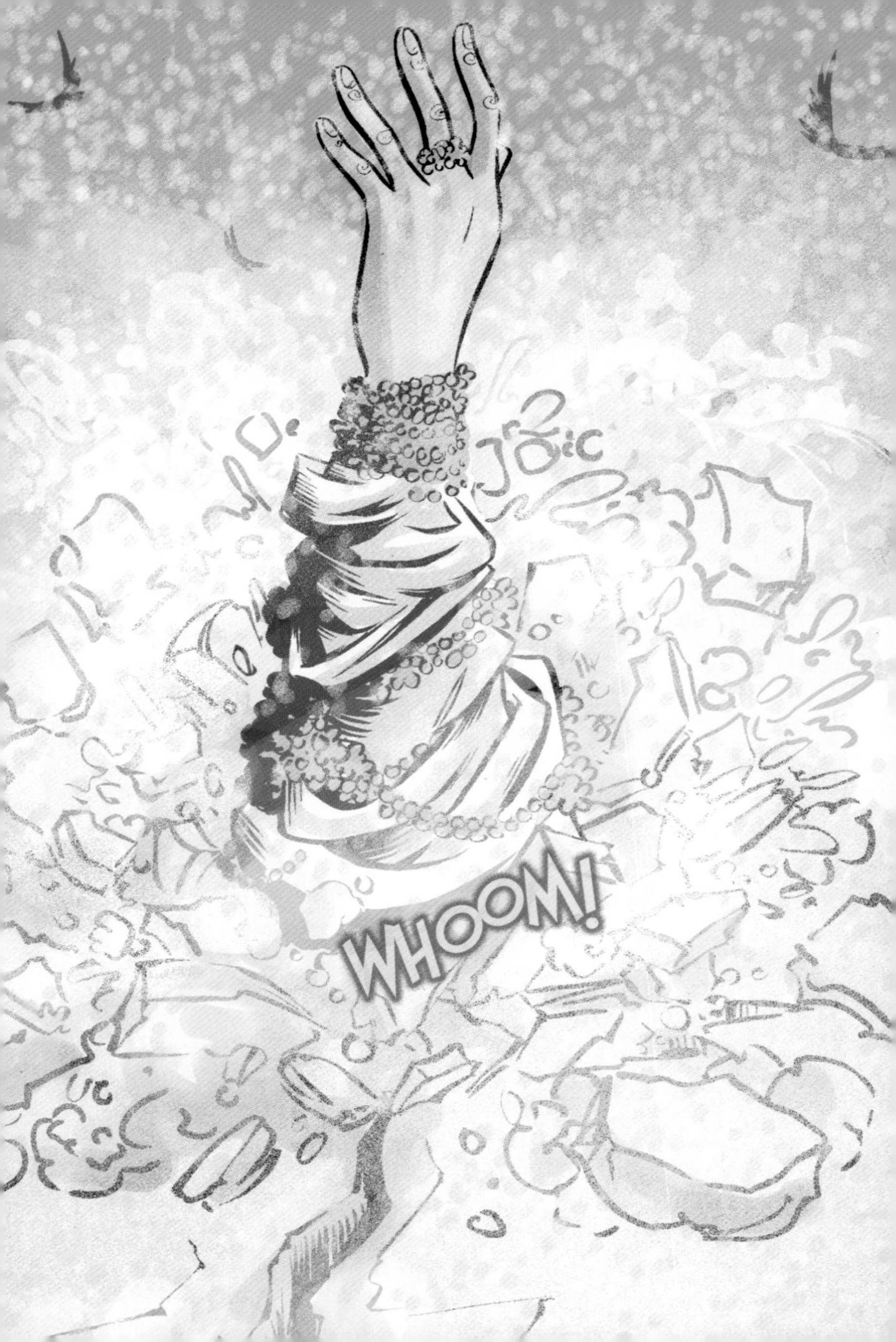
WHOOM!

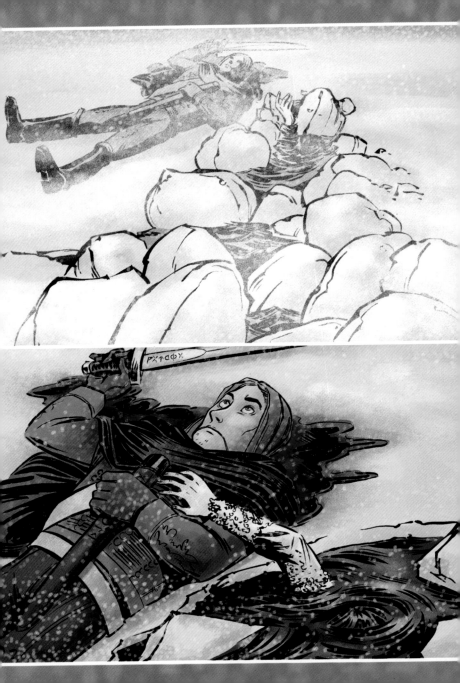

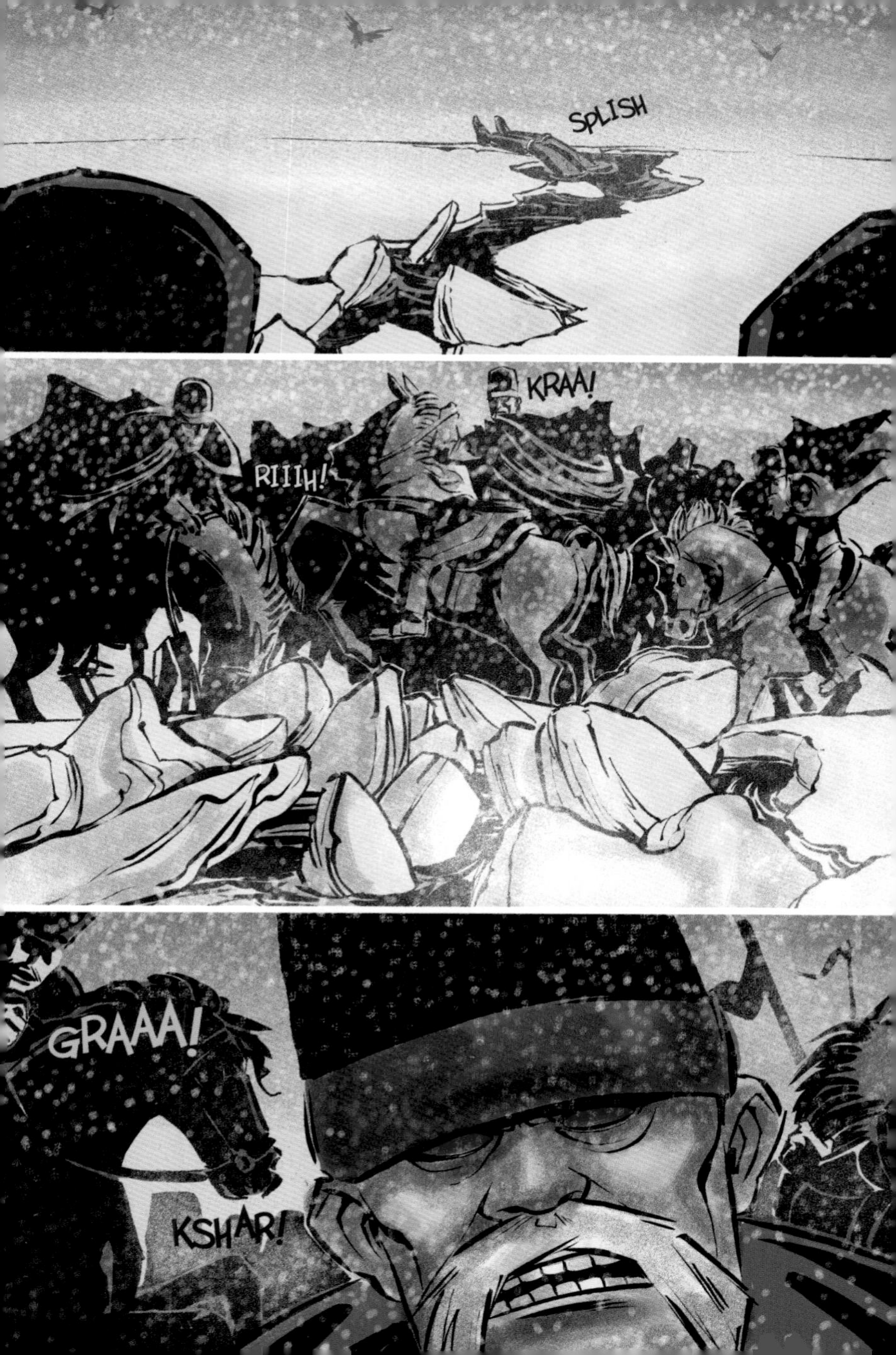
SPLISH
RIIIH!
KRAA!
GRAAA!
KSHAR!

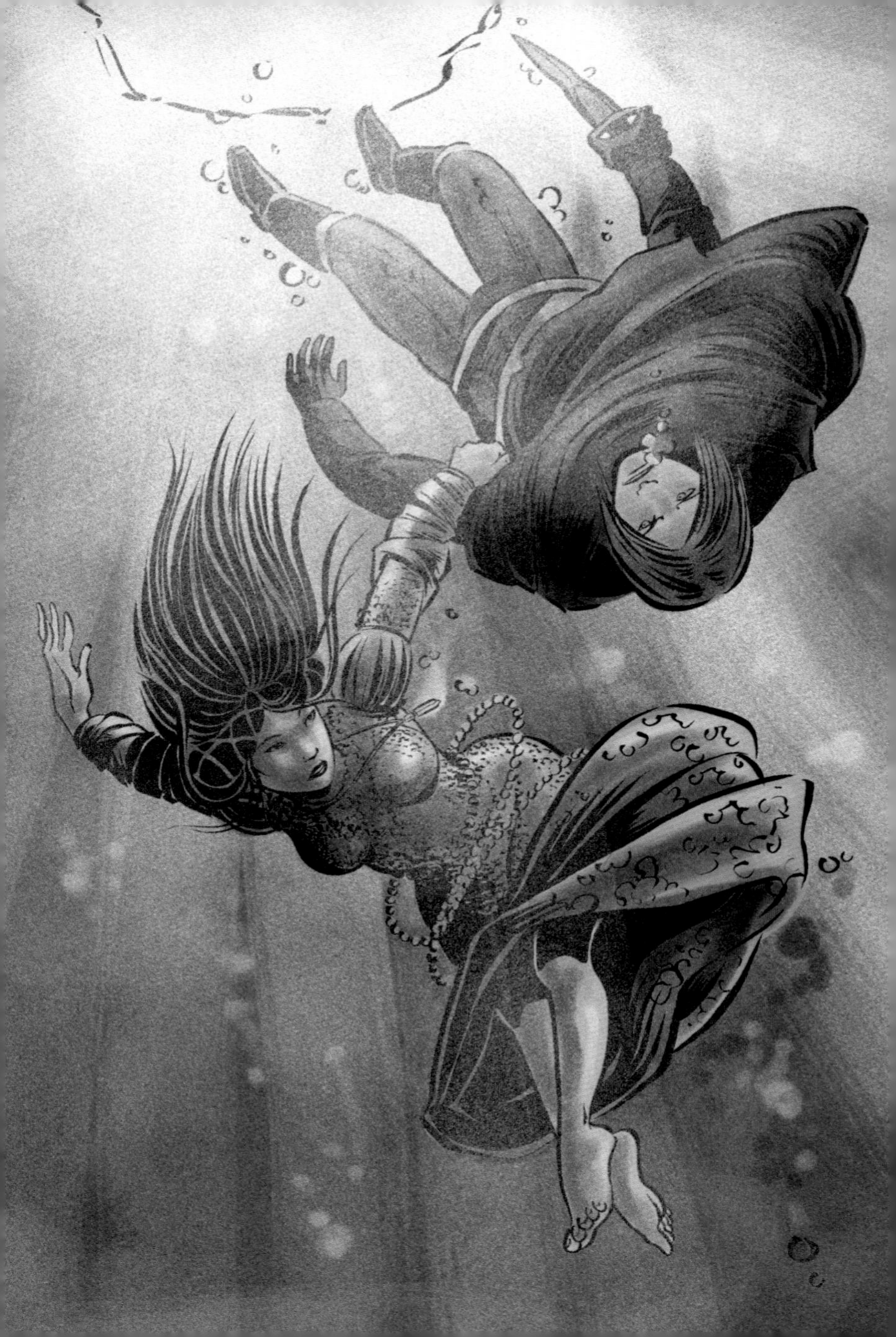

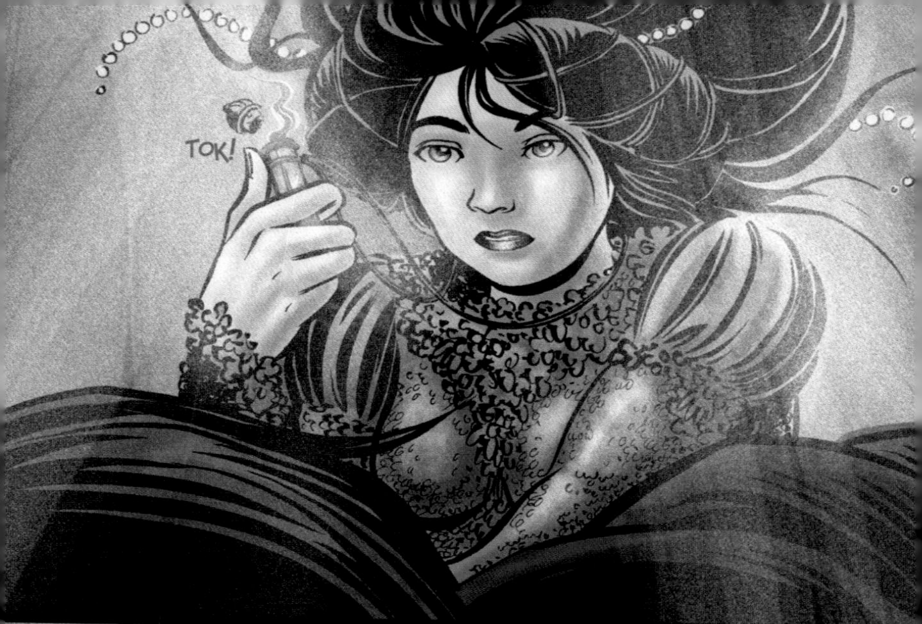
TOK!

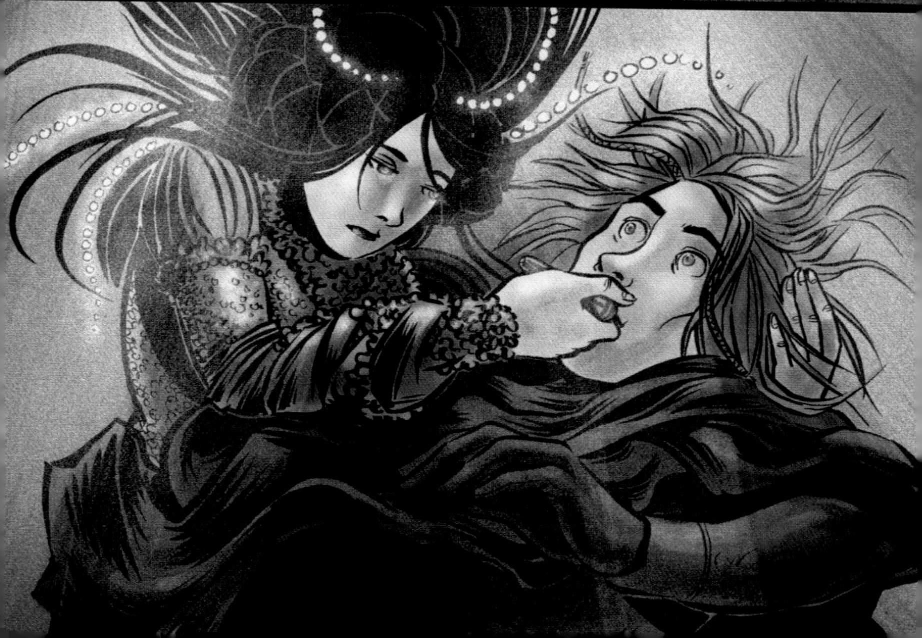

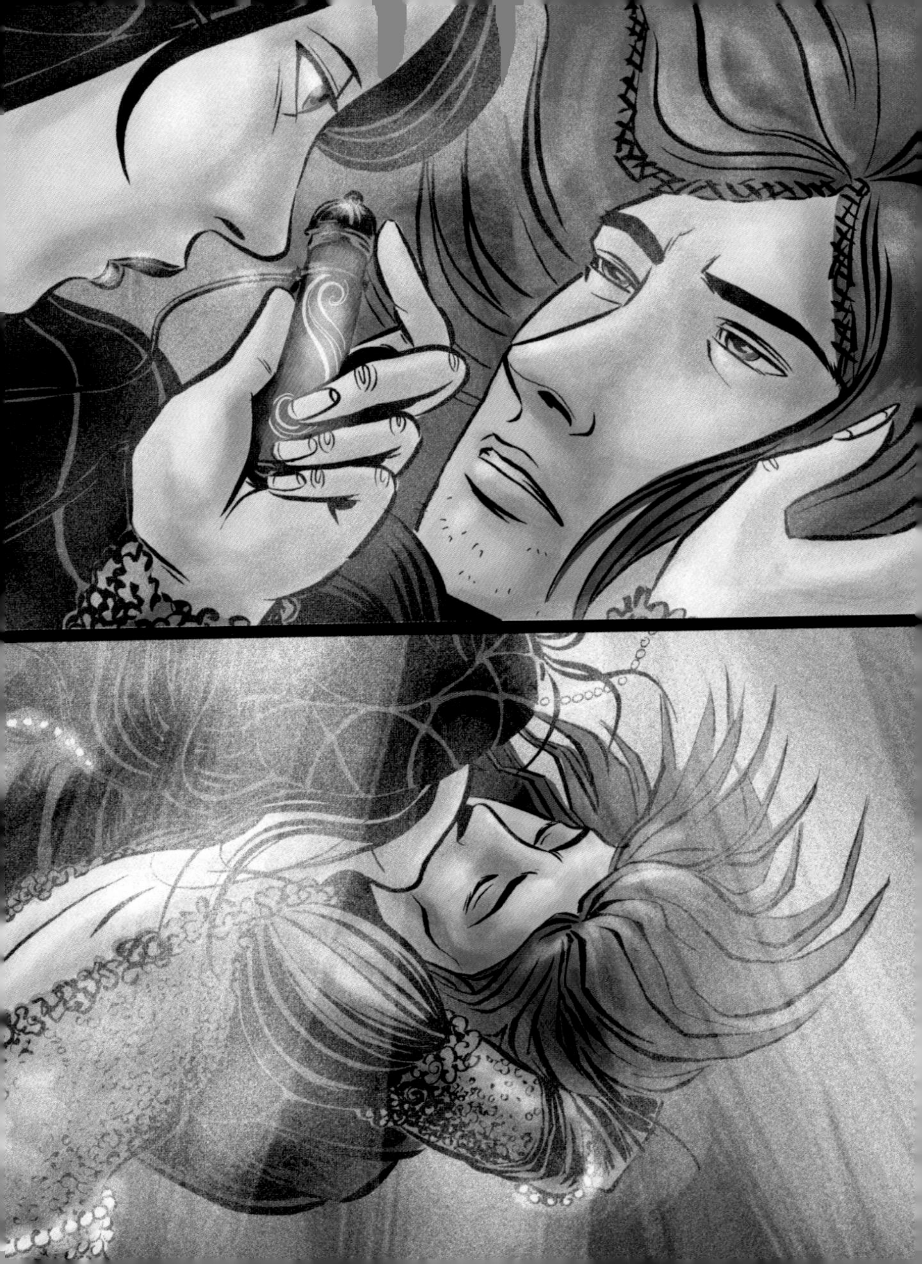

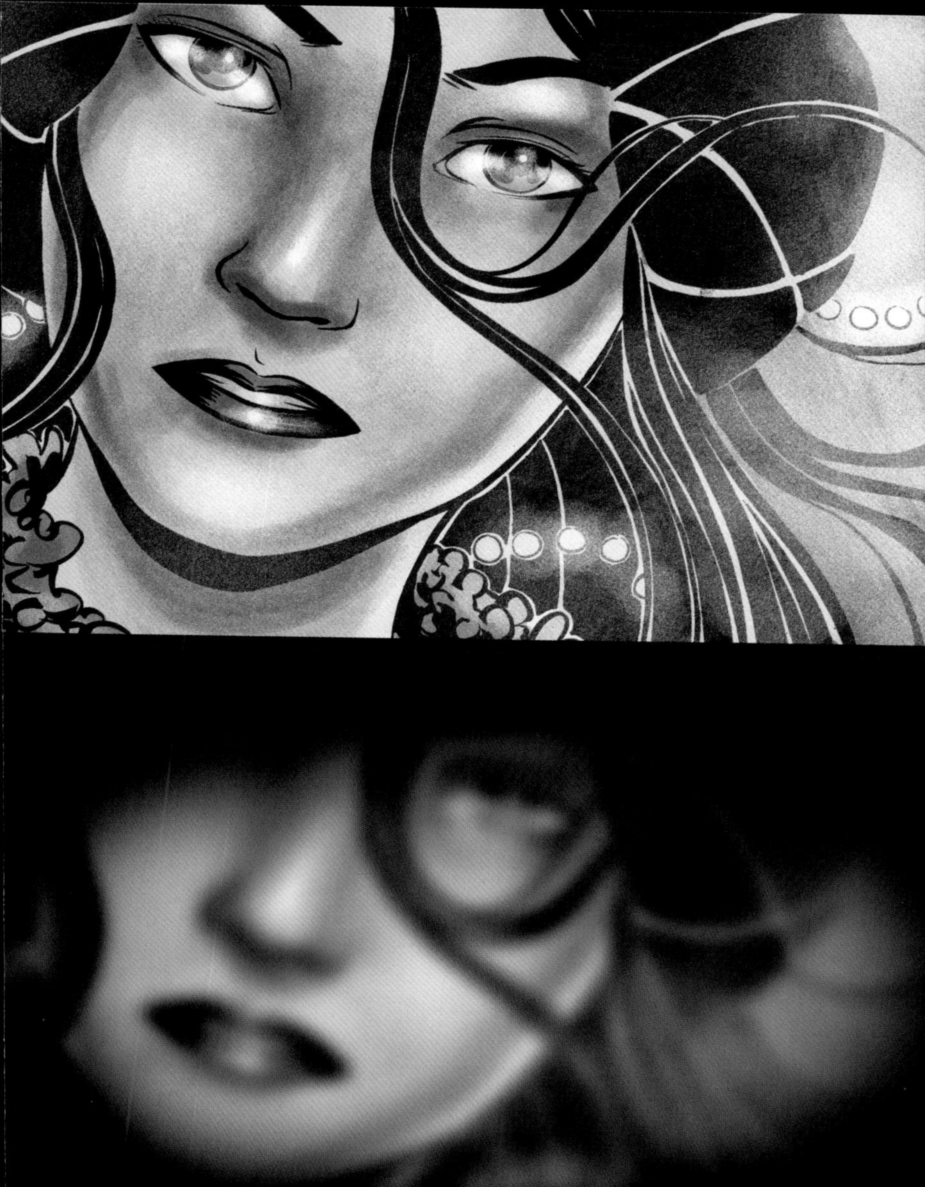

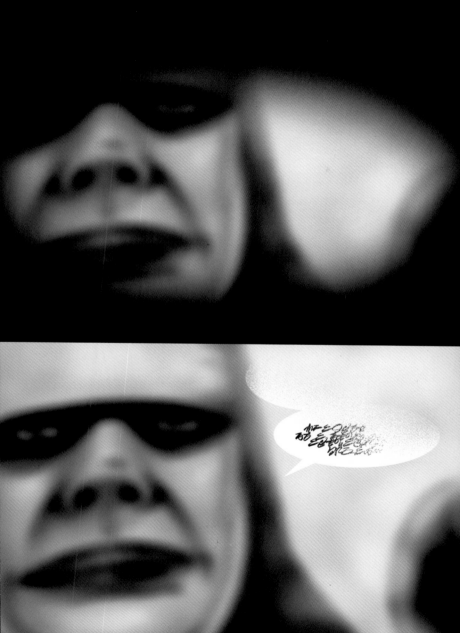

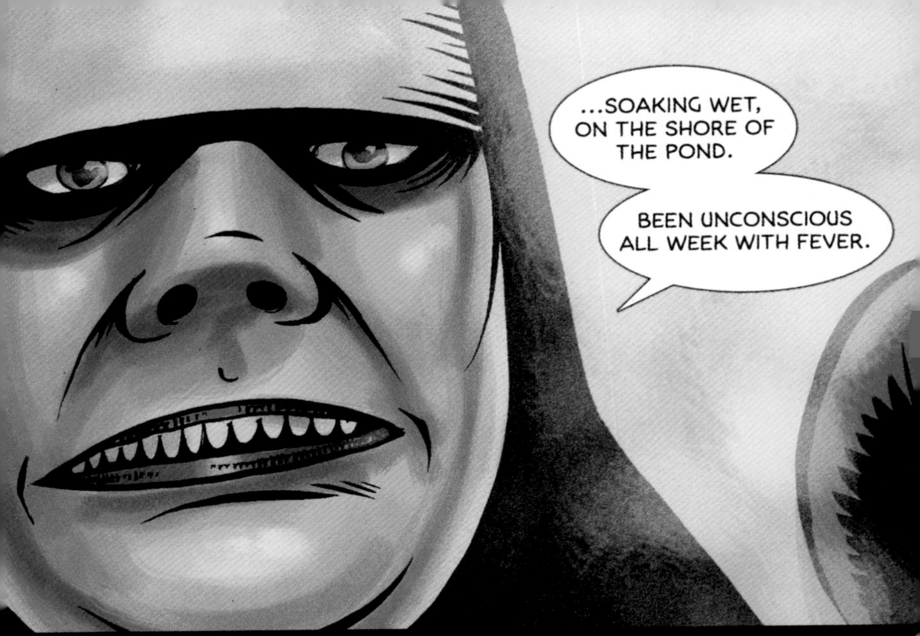
...SOAKING WET, ON THE SHORE OF THE POND.
BEEN UNCONSCIOUS ALL WEEK WITH FEVER.

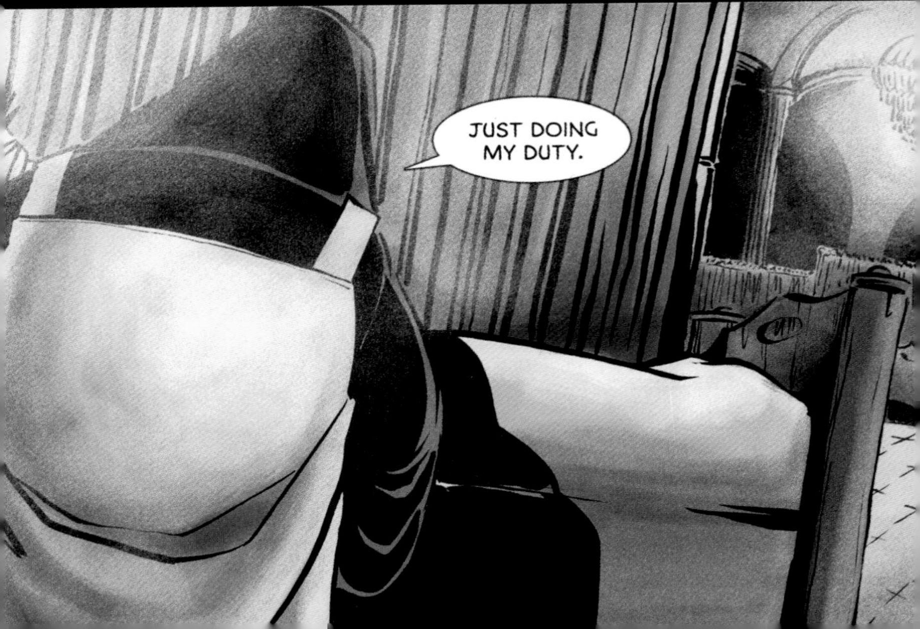
JUST DOING MY DUTY.

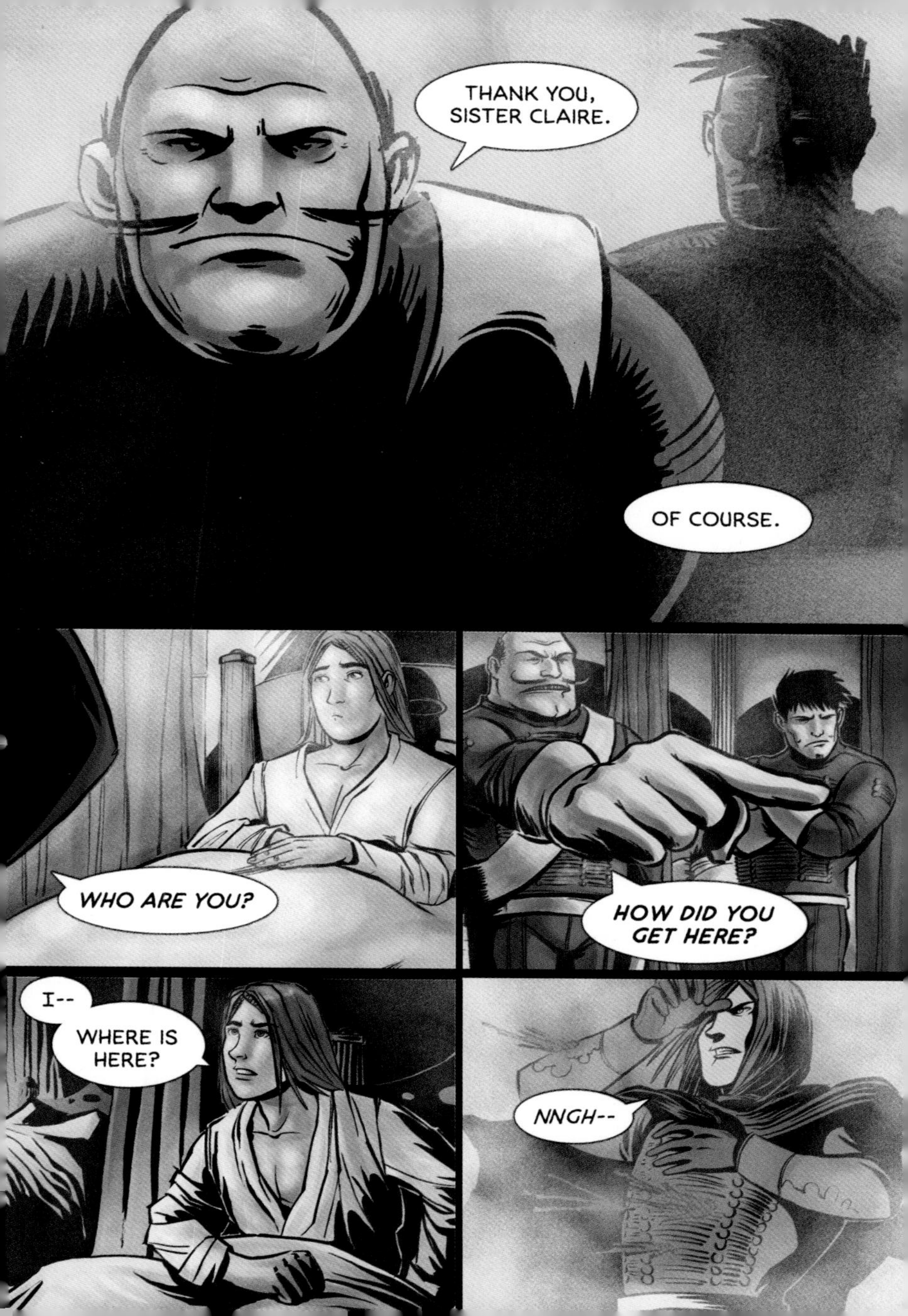
THANK YOU, SISTER CLAIRE.
OF COURSE.
WHO ARE YOU?
HOW DID YOU GET HERE?
I--
WHERE IS HERE?
NNGH--

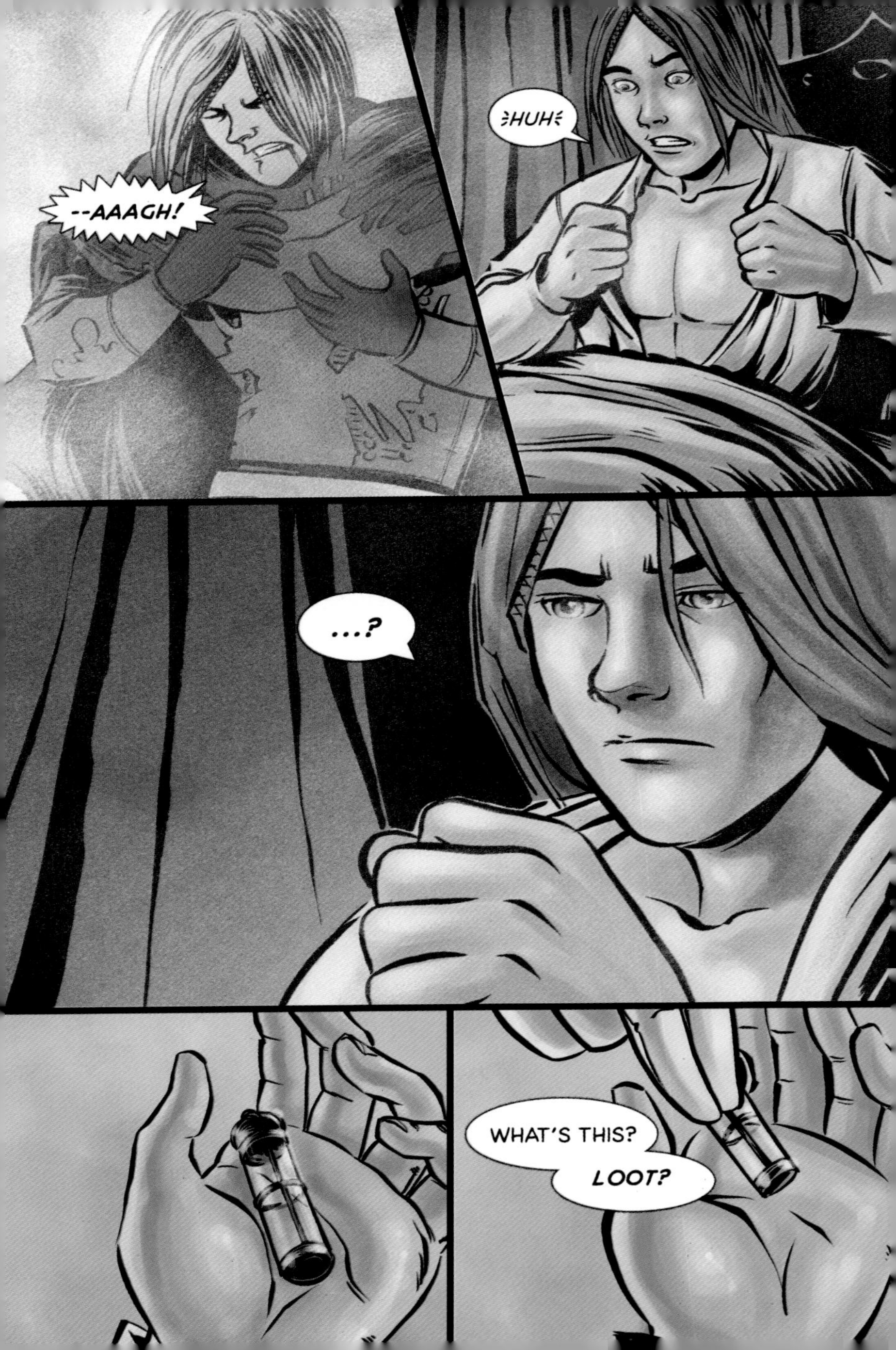
--AAAGH!
HUH
...?
WHAT'S THIS?
LOOT?

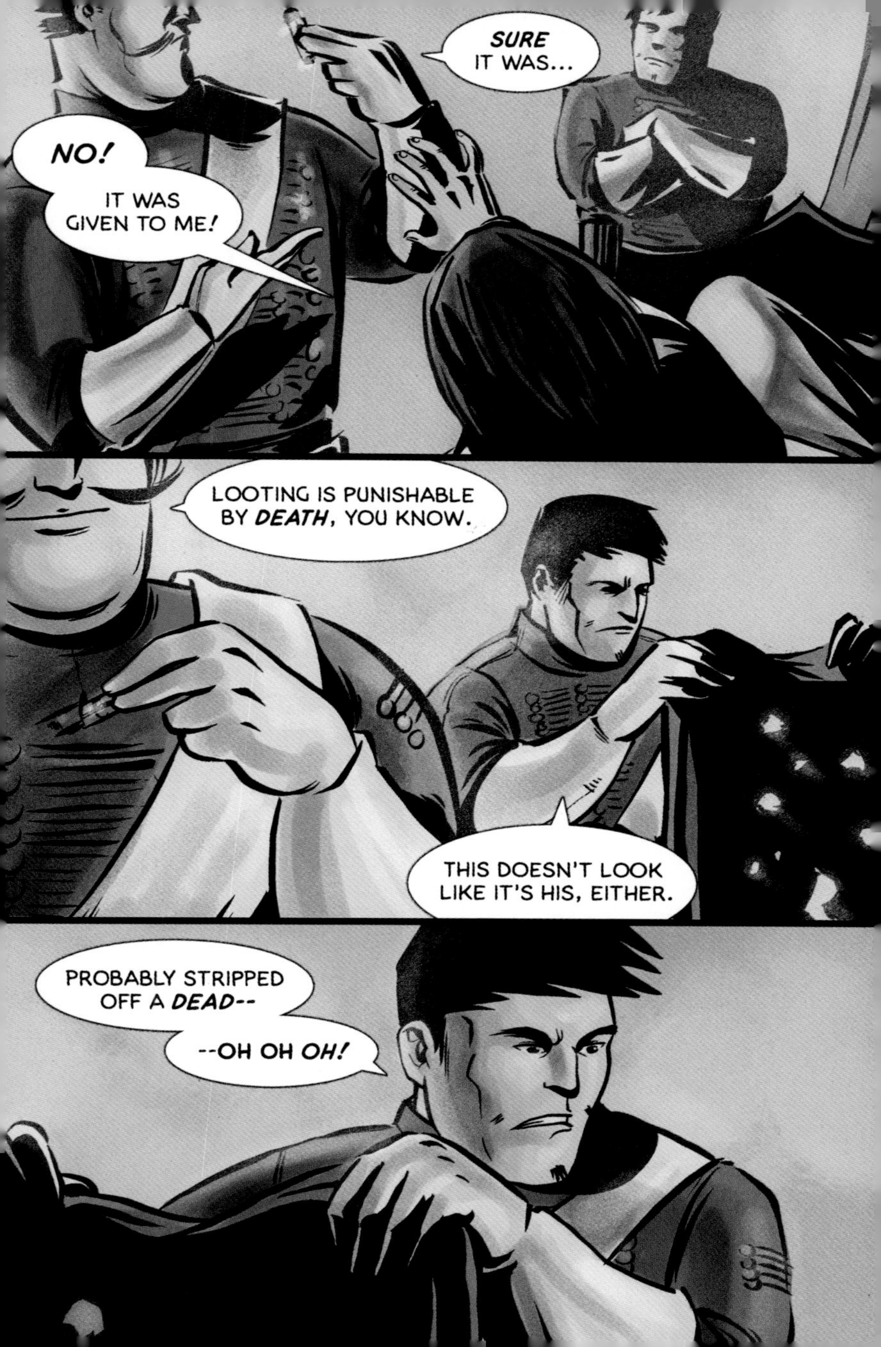
SURE IT WAS...
NO!
IT WAS GIVEN TO ME!
LOOTING IS PUNISHABLE BY DEATH, YOU KNOW.
THIS DOESN'T LOOK LIKE IT'S HIS, EITHER.
PROBABLY STRIPPED OFF A DEAD--
--OH OH OH!

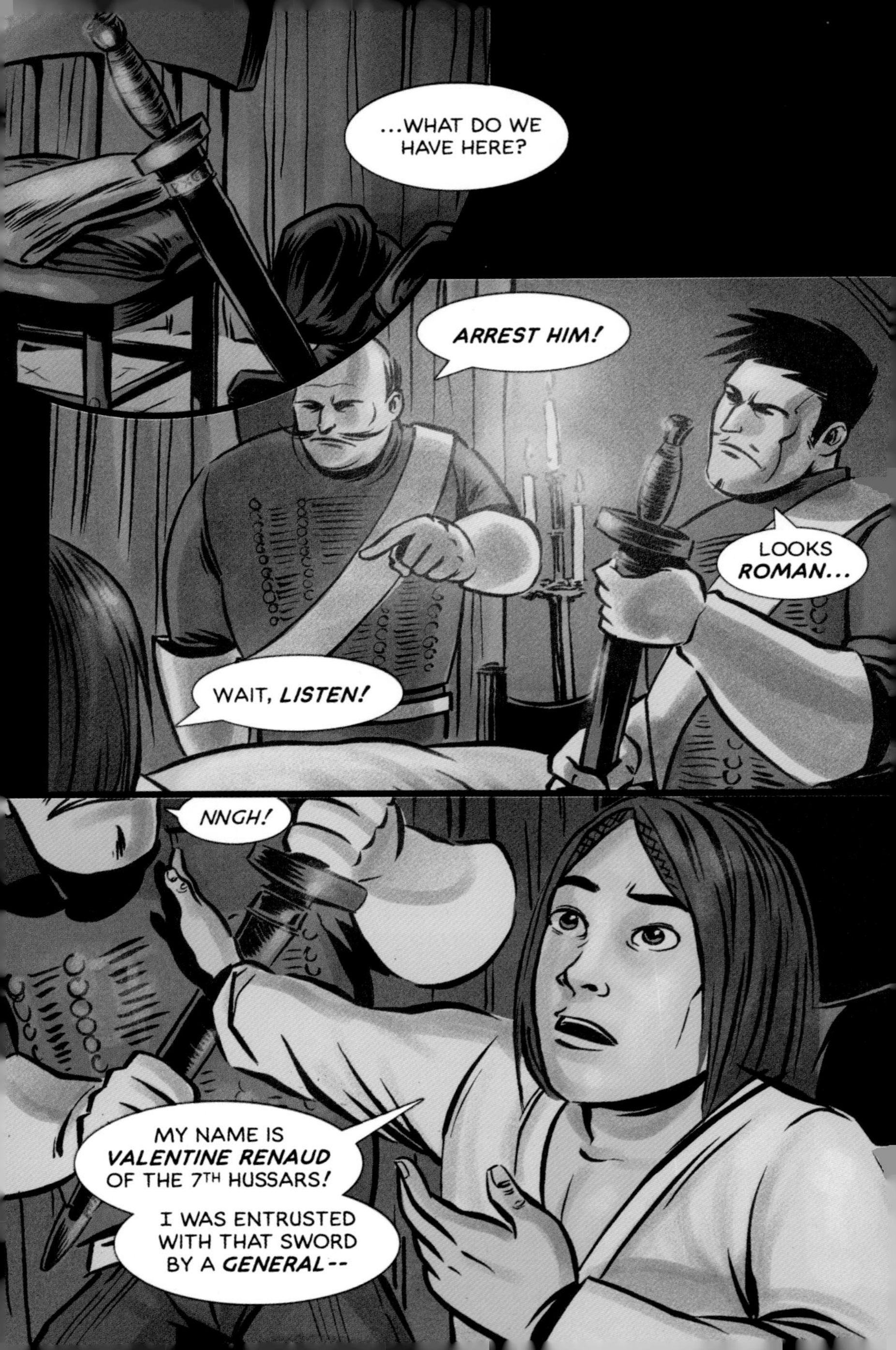
...WHAT DO WE HAVE HERE?
ARREST HIM!
LOOKS ROMAN...
WAIT, LISTEN!
NNGH!
MY NAME IS VALENTINE RENAUD OF THE 7TH HUSSARS!
I WAS ENTRUSTED WITH THAT SWORD BY A GENERAL--

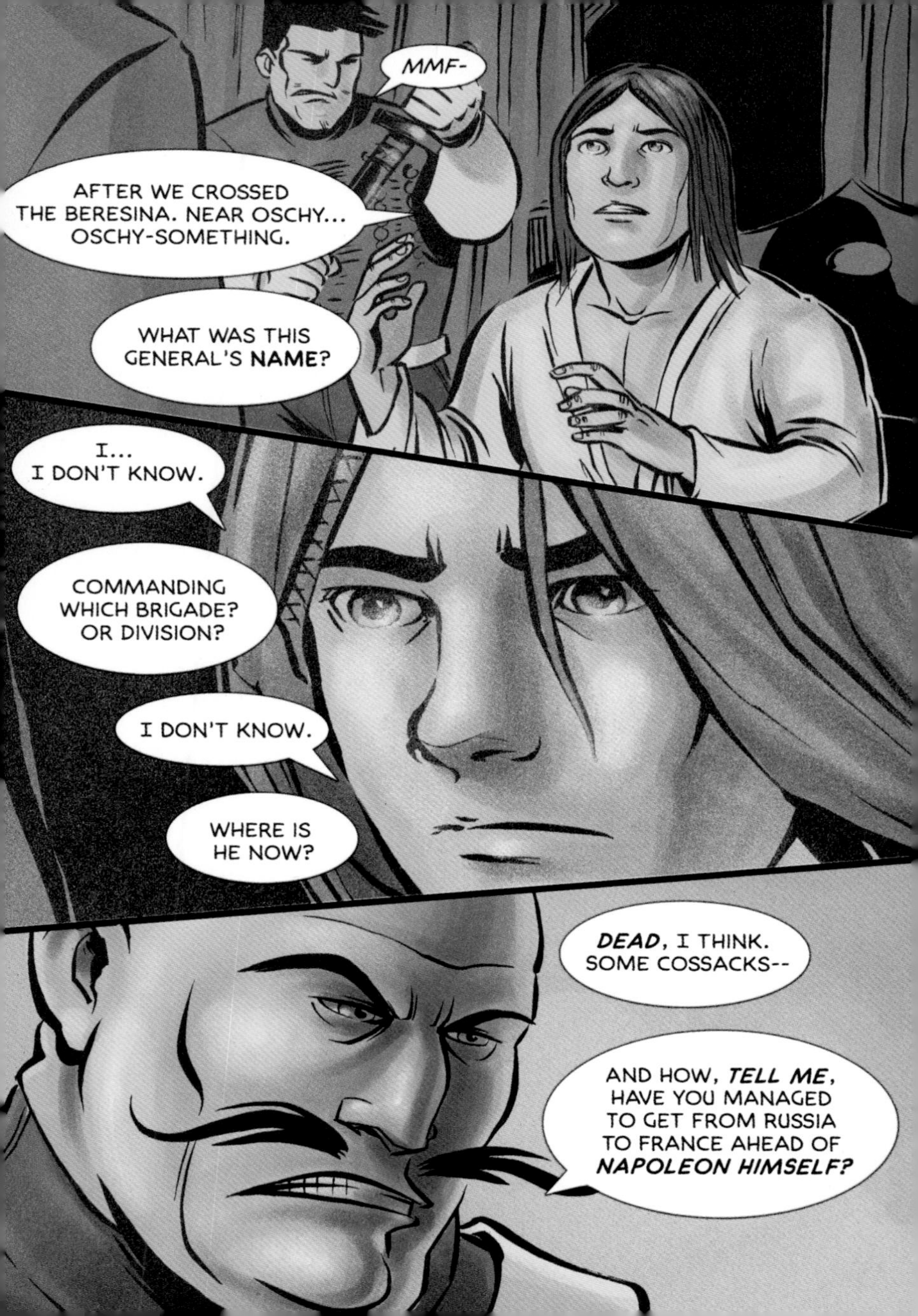
MMF-
AFTER WE CROSSED THE BERESINA. NEAR OSCHY... OSCHY-SOMETHING.
WHAT WAS THIS GENERAL'S **NAME**?
I... I DON'T KNOW.
COMMANDING WHICH BRIGADE? OR DIVISION?
I DON'T KNOW.
WHERE IS HE NOW?
DEAD, I THINK. SOME COSSACKS--
AND HOW, ***TELL ME***, HAVE YOU MANAGED TO GET FROM RUSSIA TO FRANCE AHEAD OF ***NAPOLEON HIMSELF?***

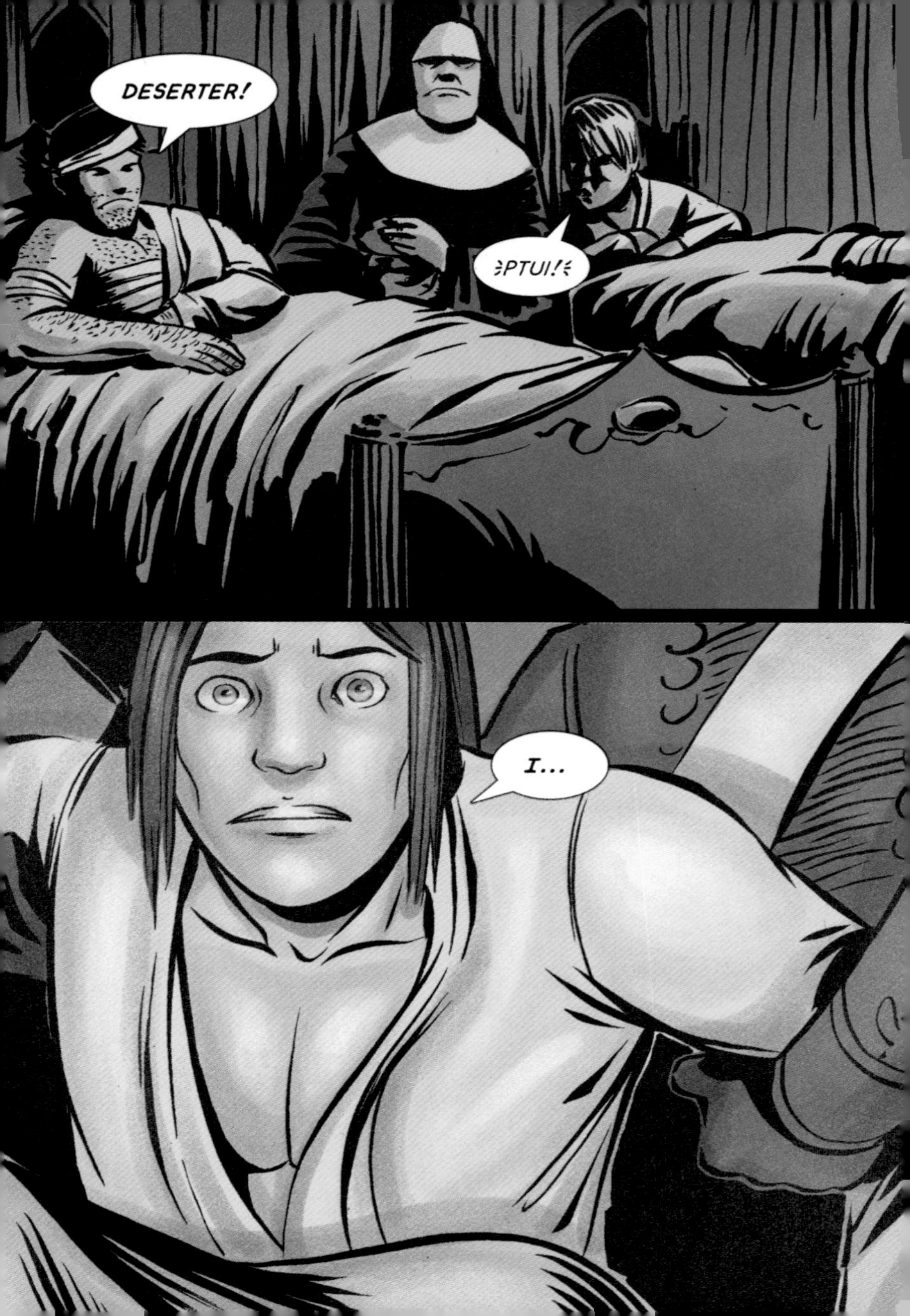
DESERTER!
PTUI!
I...

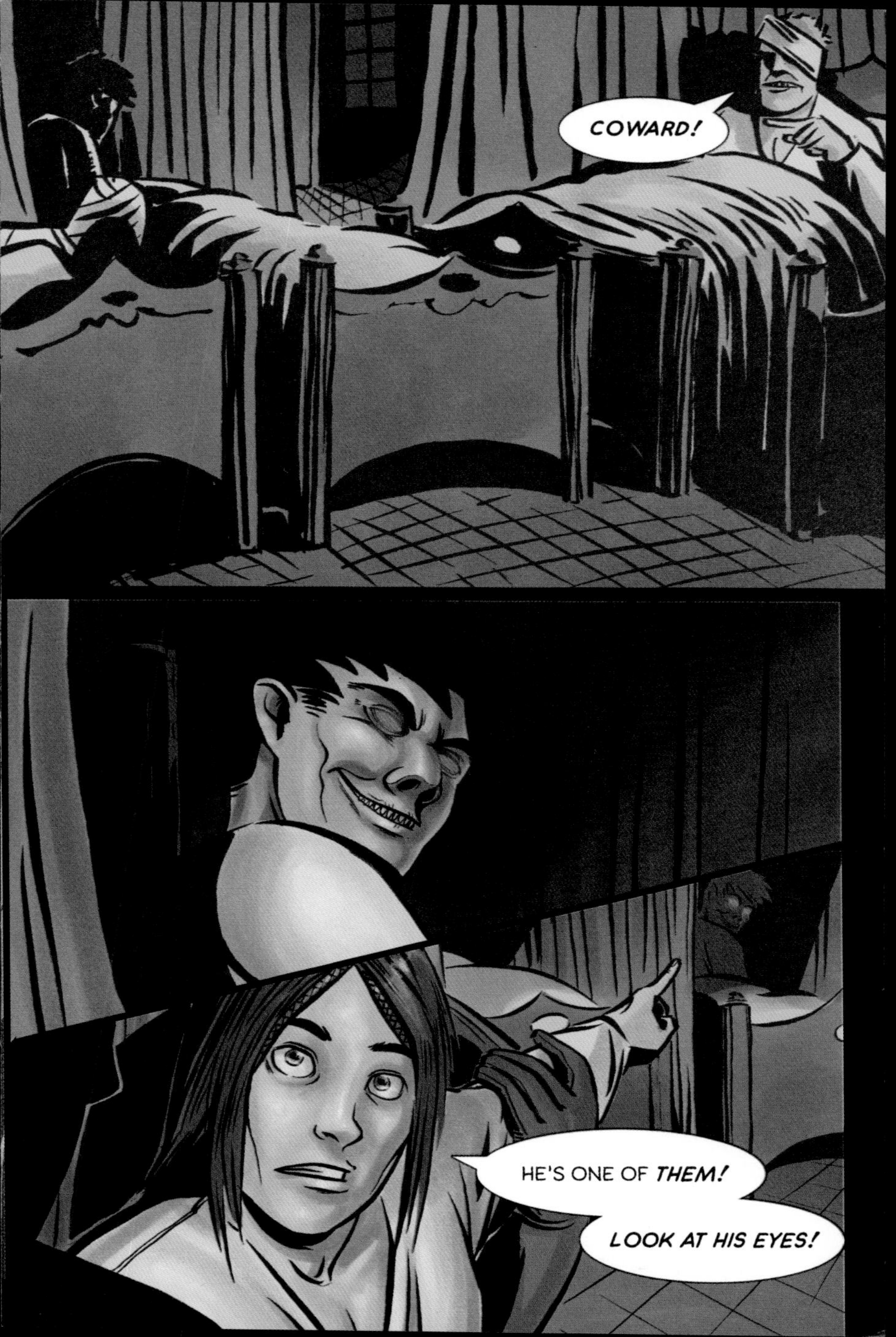
COWARD!
HE'S ONE OF THEM!
LOOK AT HIS EYES!

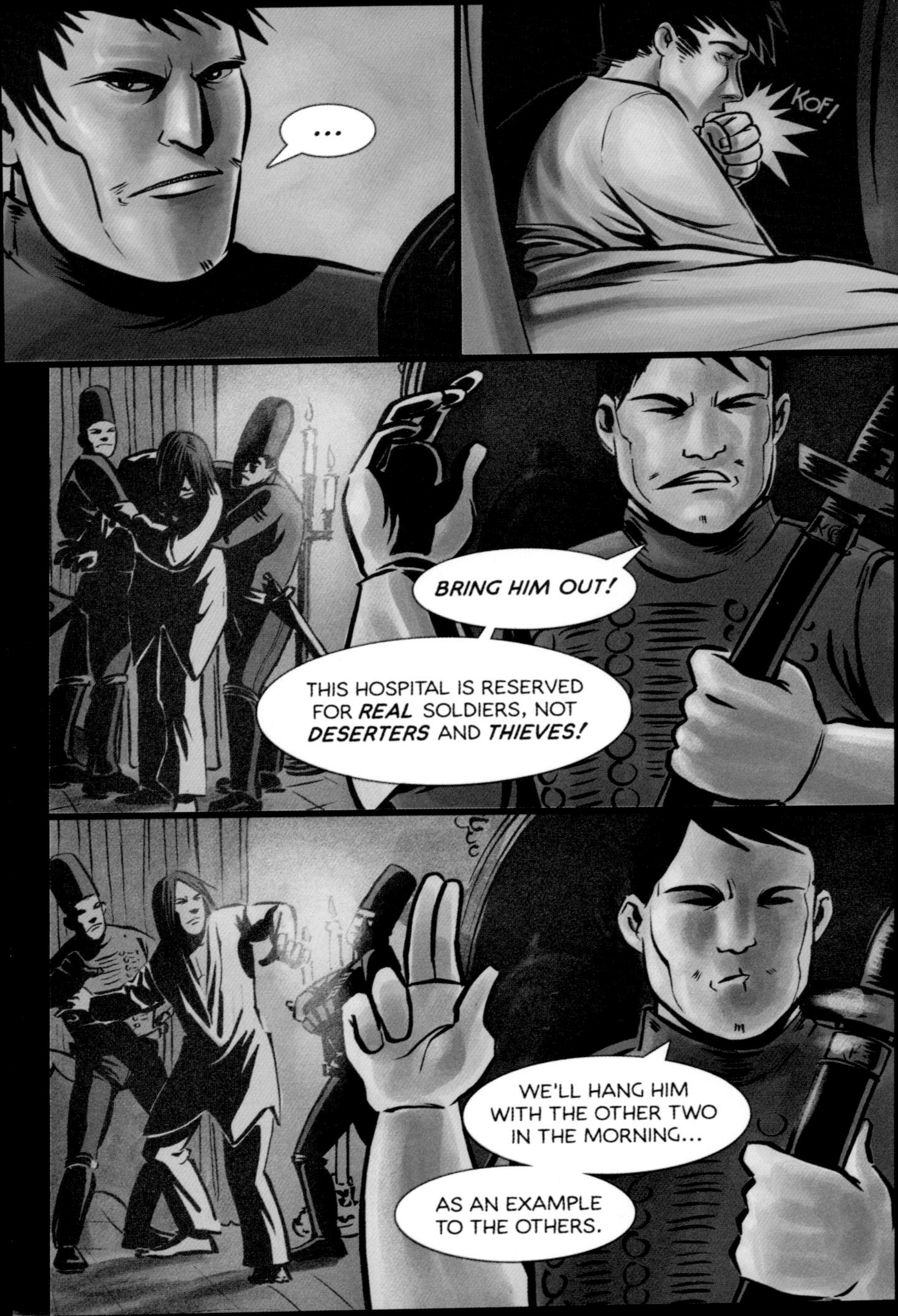
...
KOF!
BRING HIM OUT!
THIS HOSPITAL IS RESERVED FOR REAL SOLDIERS, NOT DESERTERS AND THIEVES!
WE'LL HANG HIM WITH THE OTHER TWO IN THE MORNING...
AS AN EXAMPLE TO THE OTHERS.

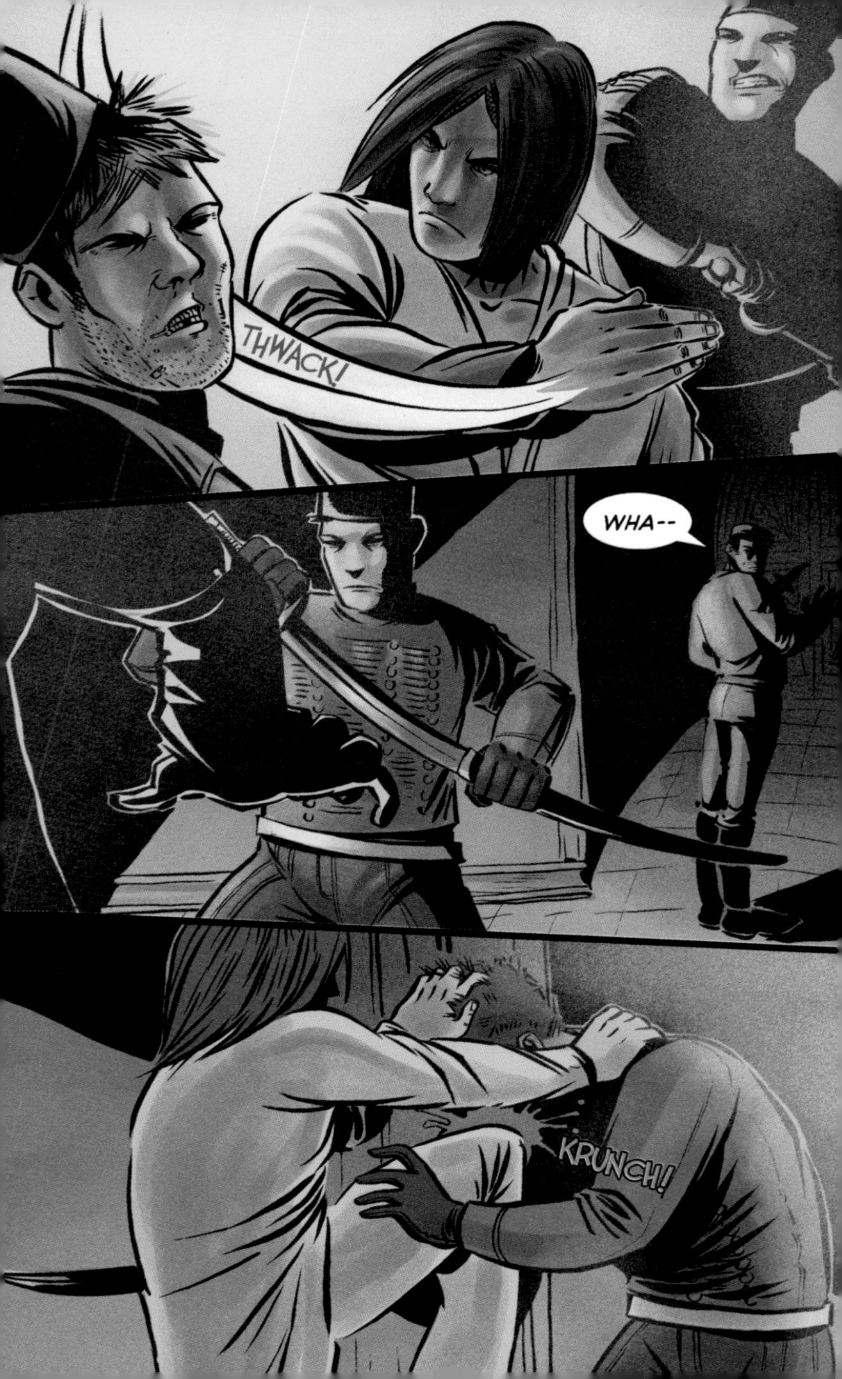
THWACK!
WHA--
KRUNCH!

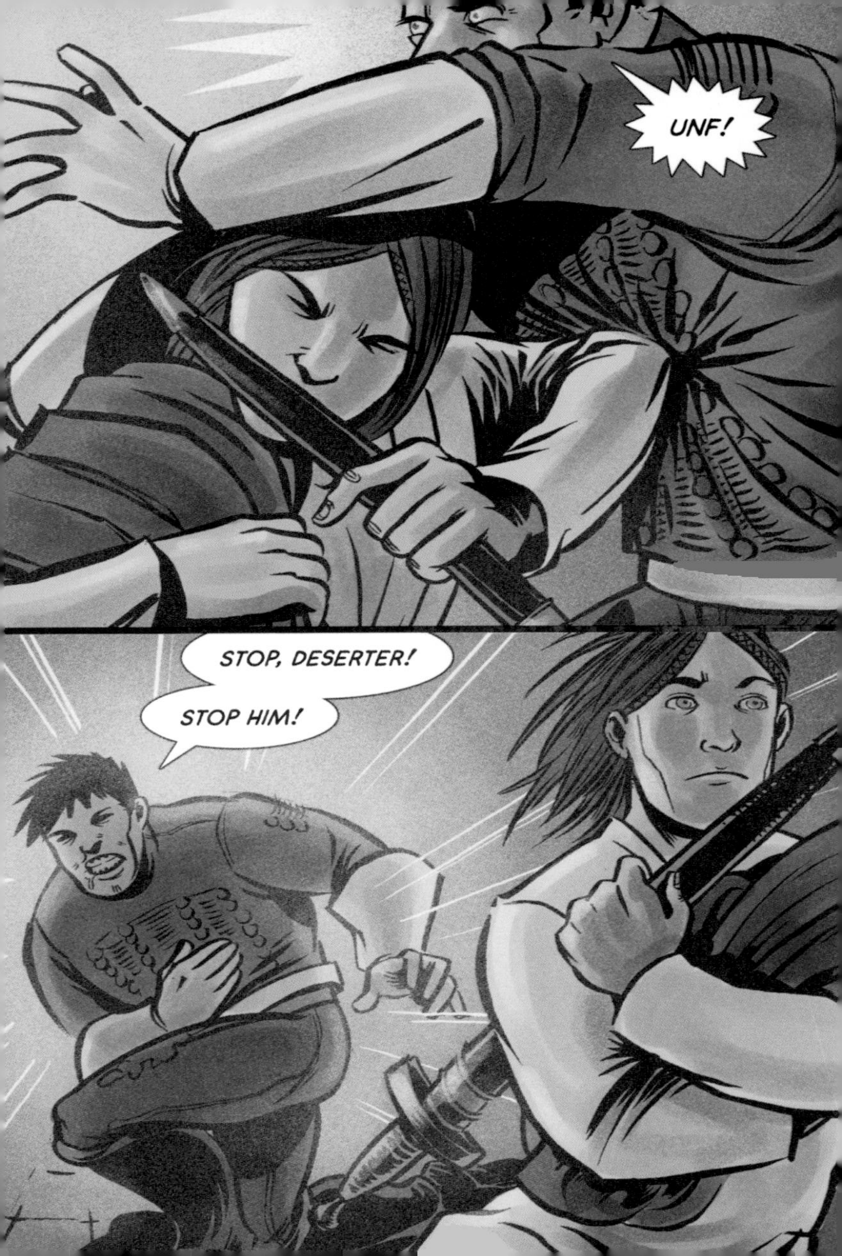
UNF!
STOP, DESERTER!
STOP HIM!

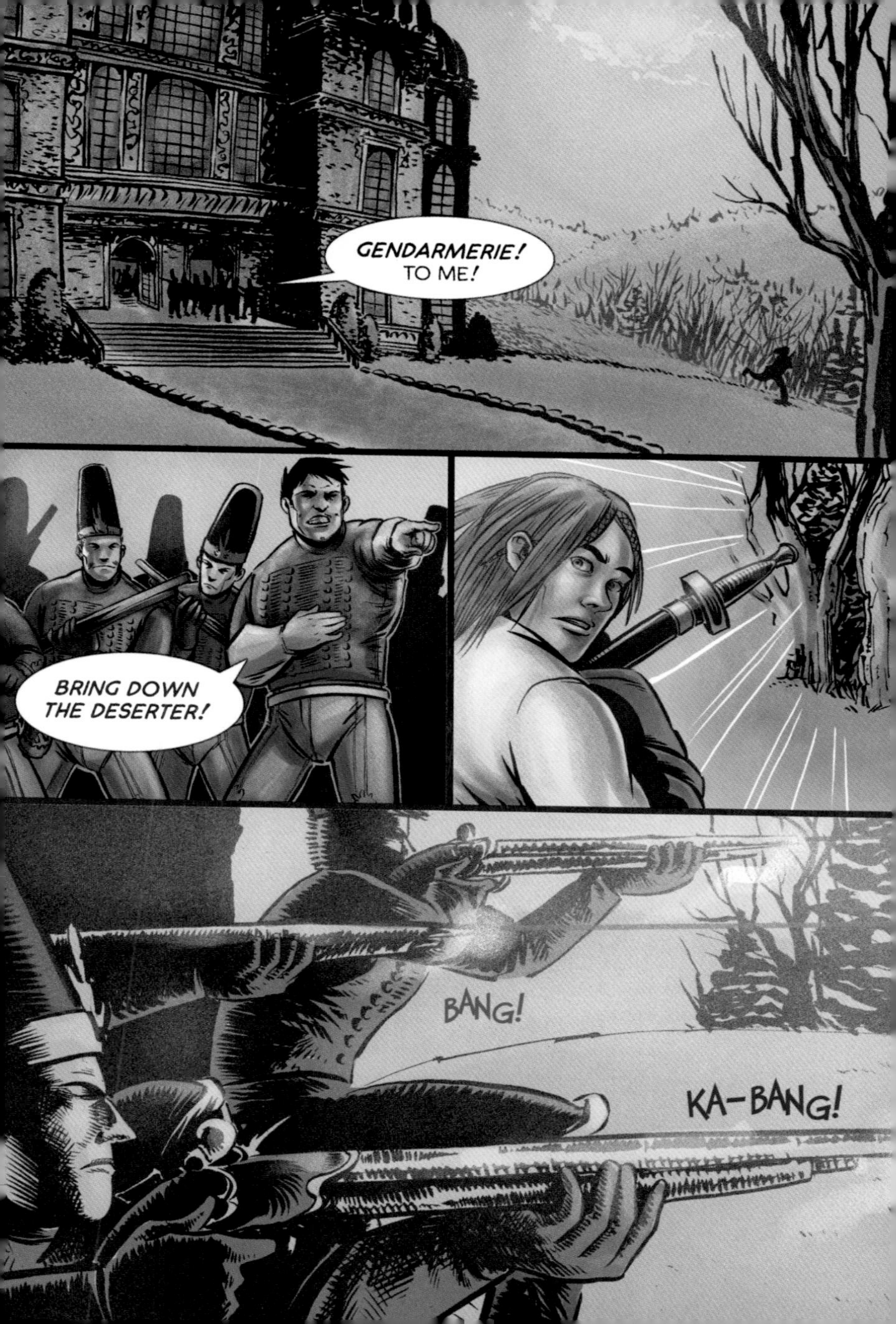
GENDARMERIE! TO ME!
BRING DOWN THE DESERTER!
BANG!
KA-BANG!

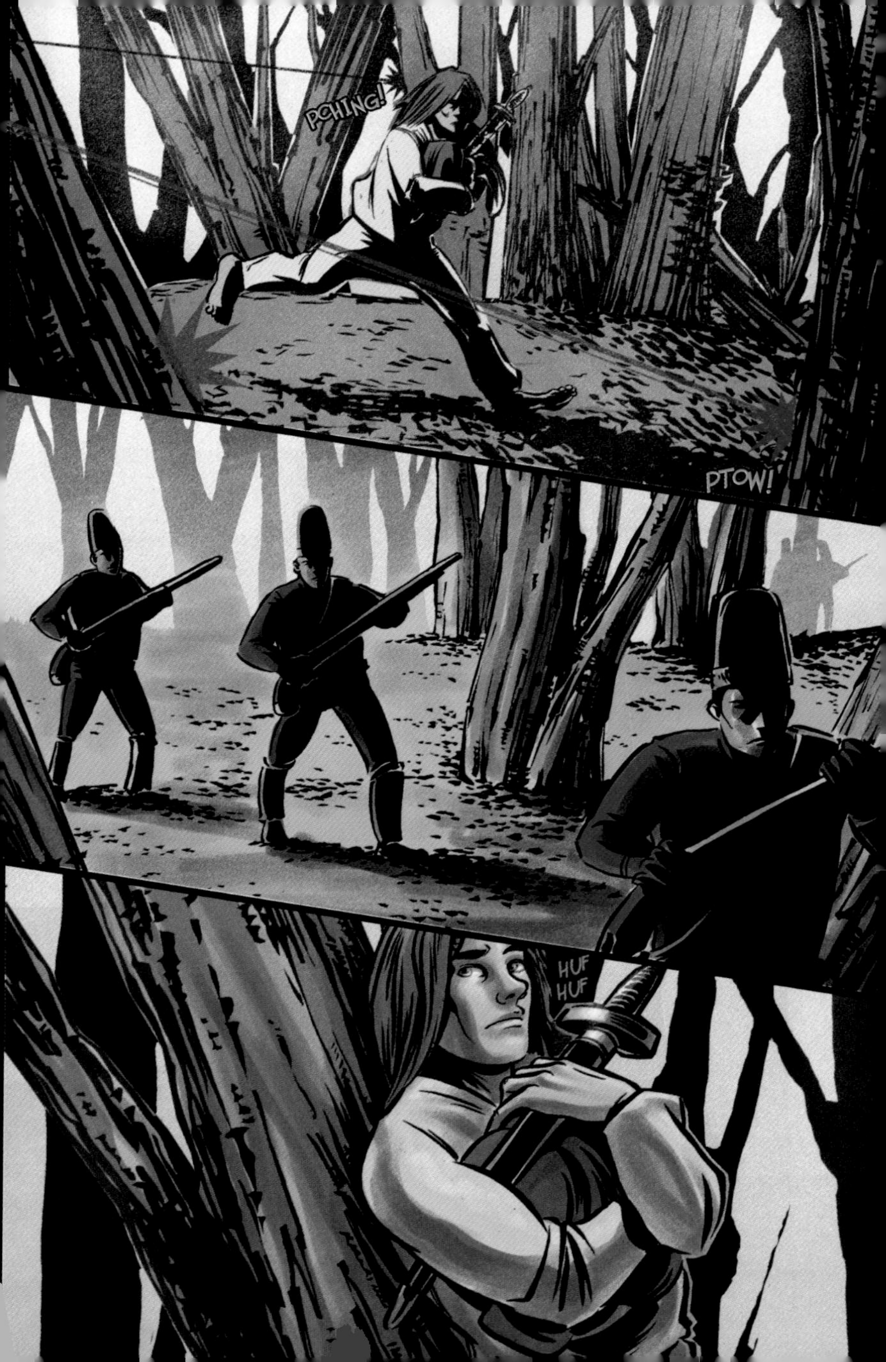
PCHING!
PTOW!
HUF
HUF

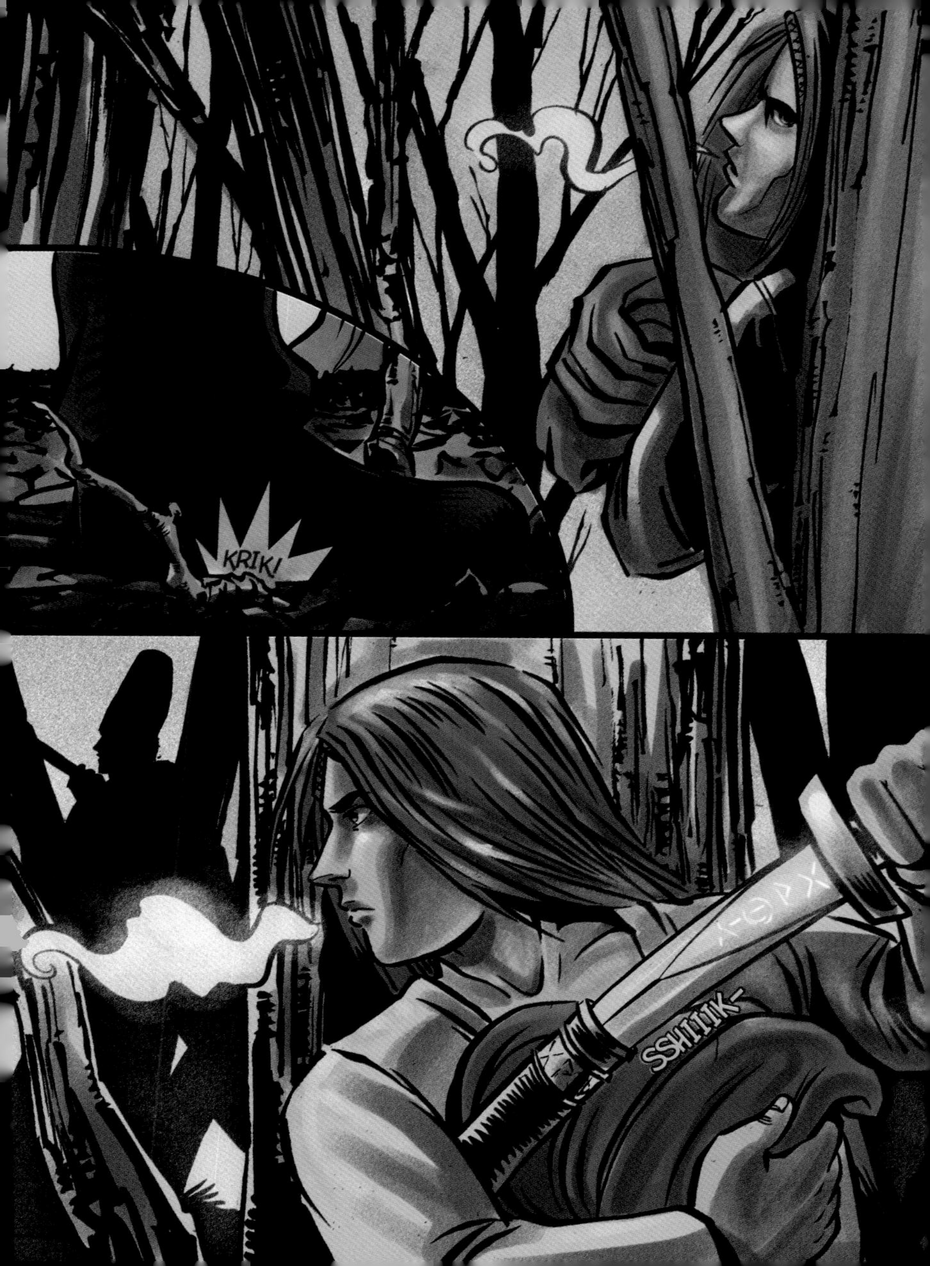
KRIK!
SSHIIIK-

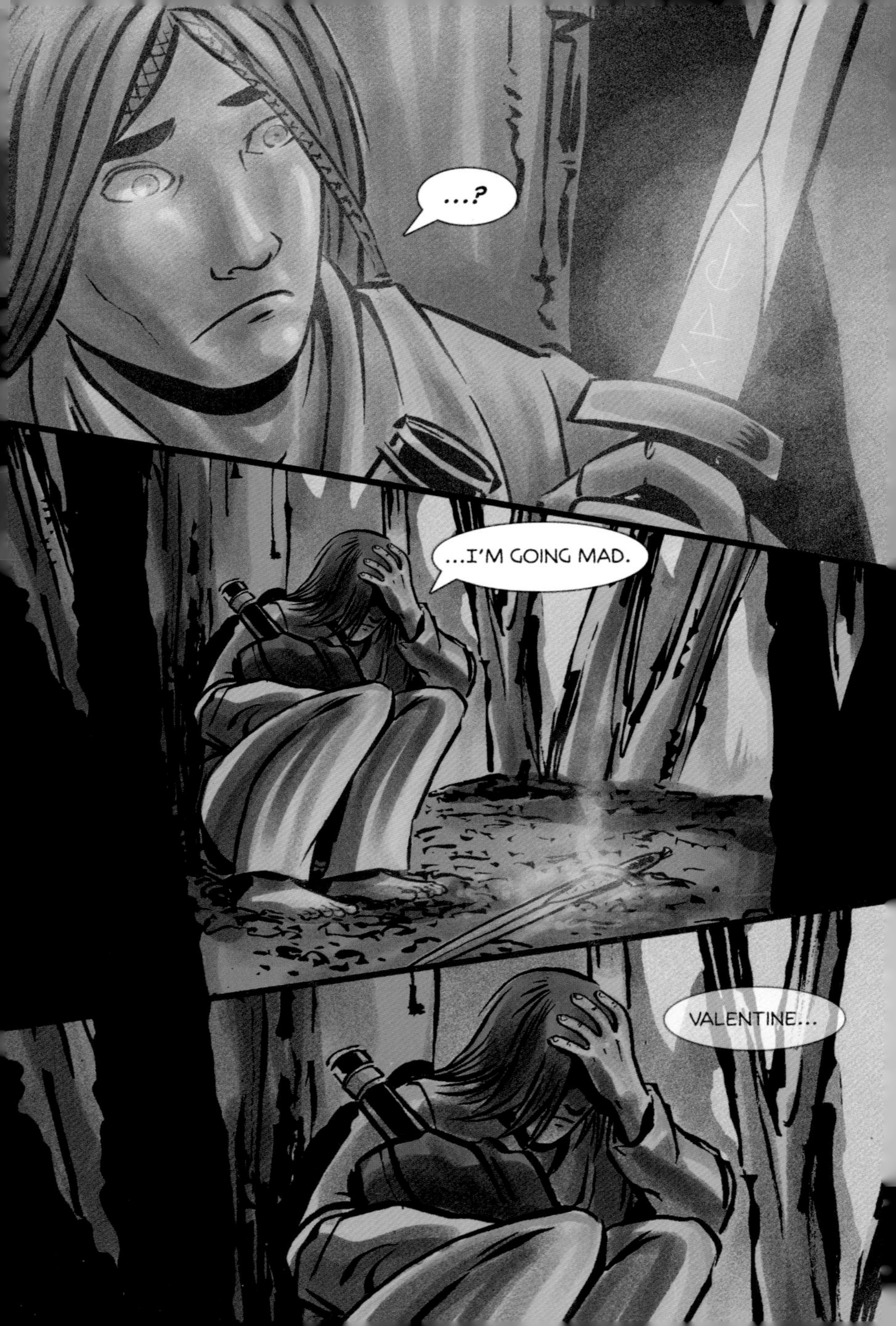
...?
...I'M GOING MAD.
VALENTINE...

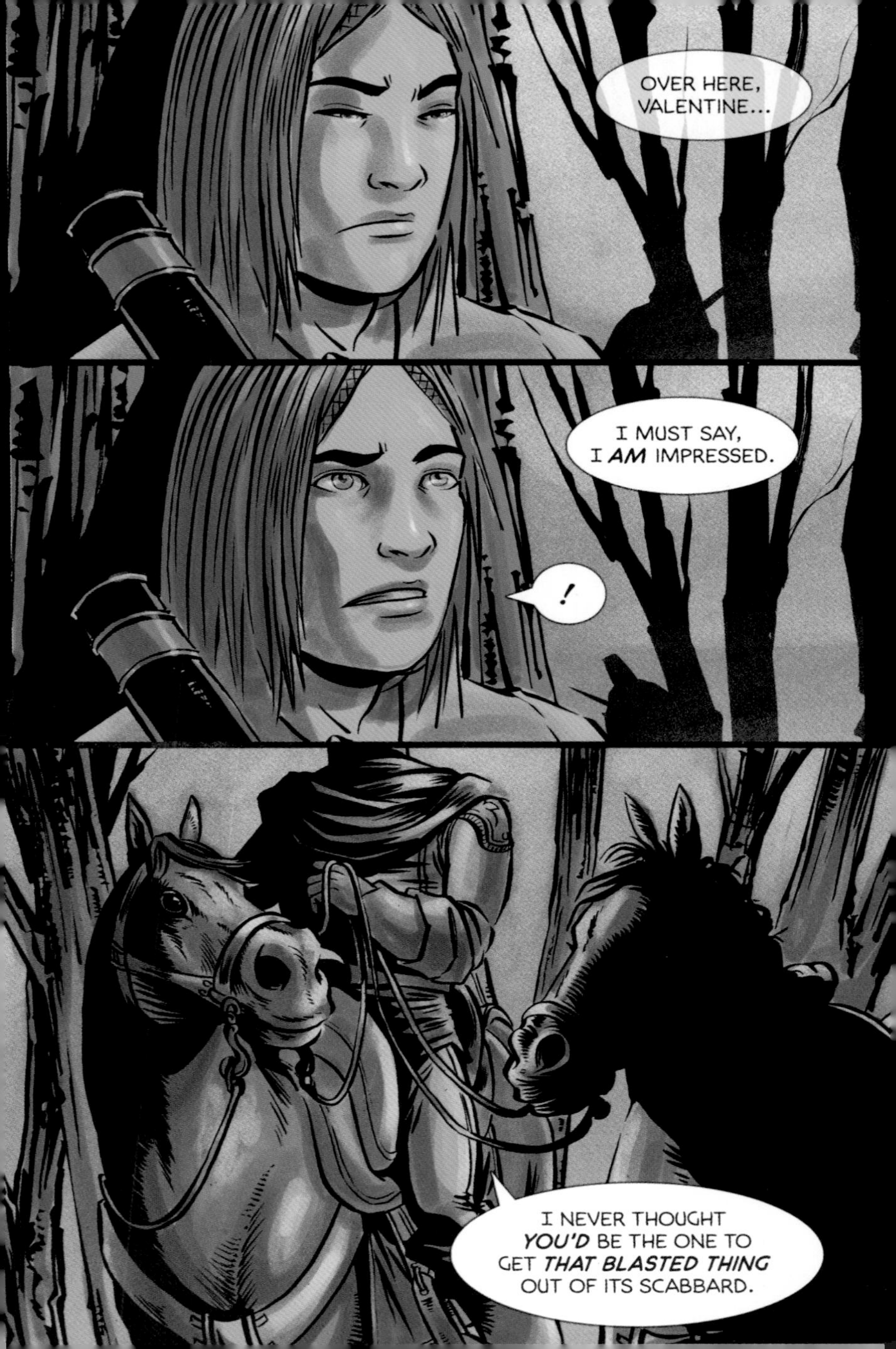
OVER HERE, VALENTINE...
I MUST SAY, I *AM* IMPRESSED.
!
I NEVER THOUGHT *YOU'D* BE THE ONE TO GET *THAT BLASTED THING* OUT OF ITS SCABBARD.

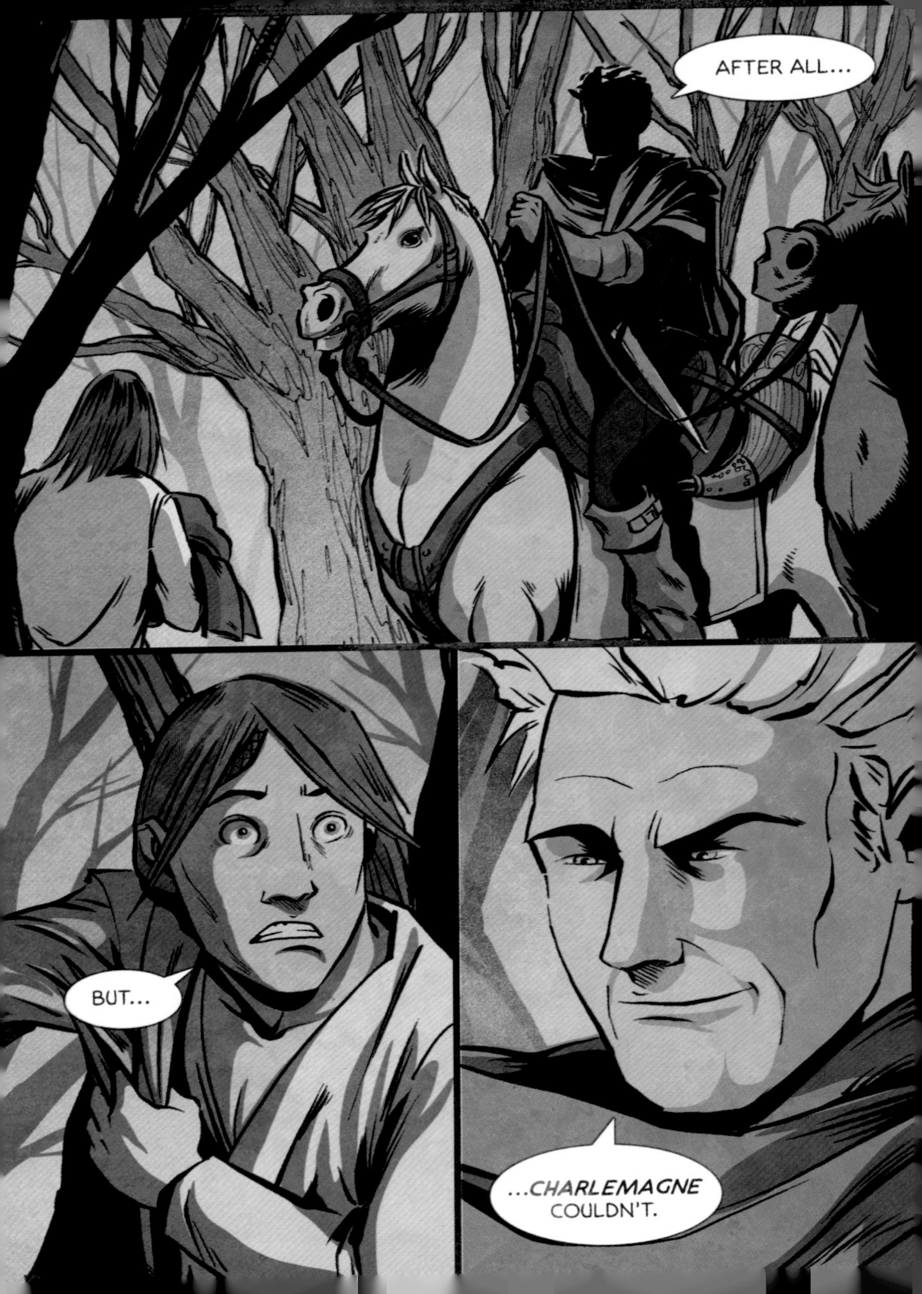
AFTER ALL...
BUT...
...CHARLEMAGNE COULDN'T.

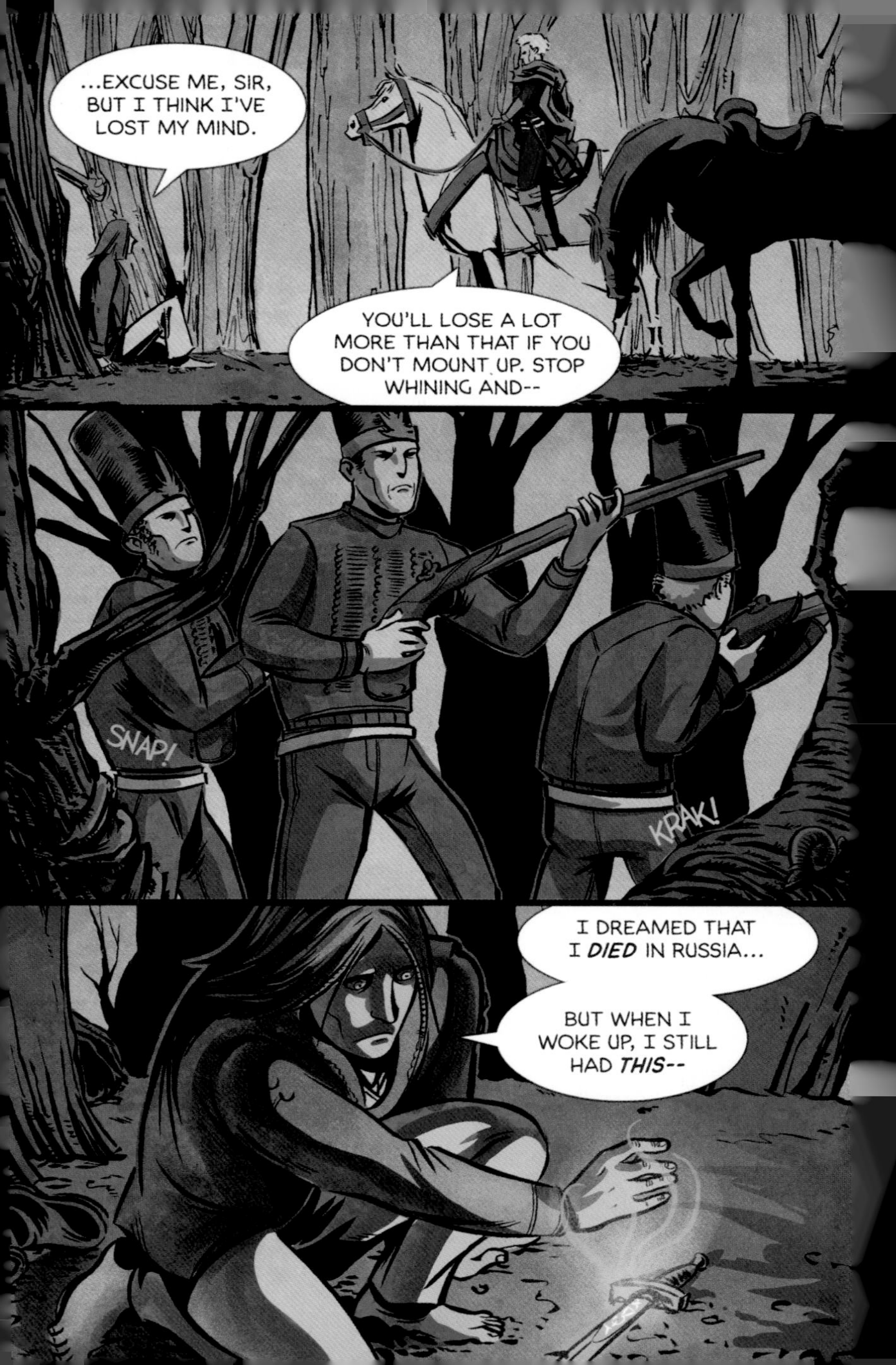
...EXCUSE ME, SIR, BUT I THINK I'VE LOST MY MIND.
YOU'LL LOSE A LOT MORE THAN THAT IF YOU DON'T MOUNT UP. STOP WHINING AND--
SNAP!
KRAK!
I DREAMED THAT I *DIED* IN RUSSIA...
BUT WHEN I WOKE UP, I STILL HAD *THIS*--

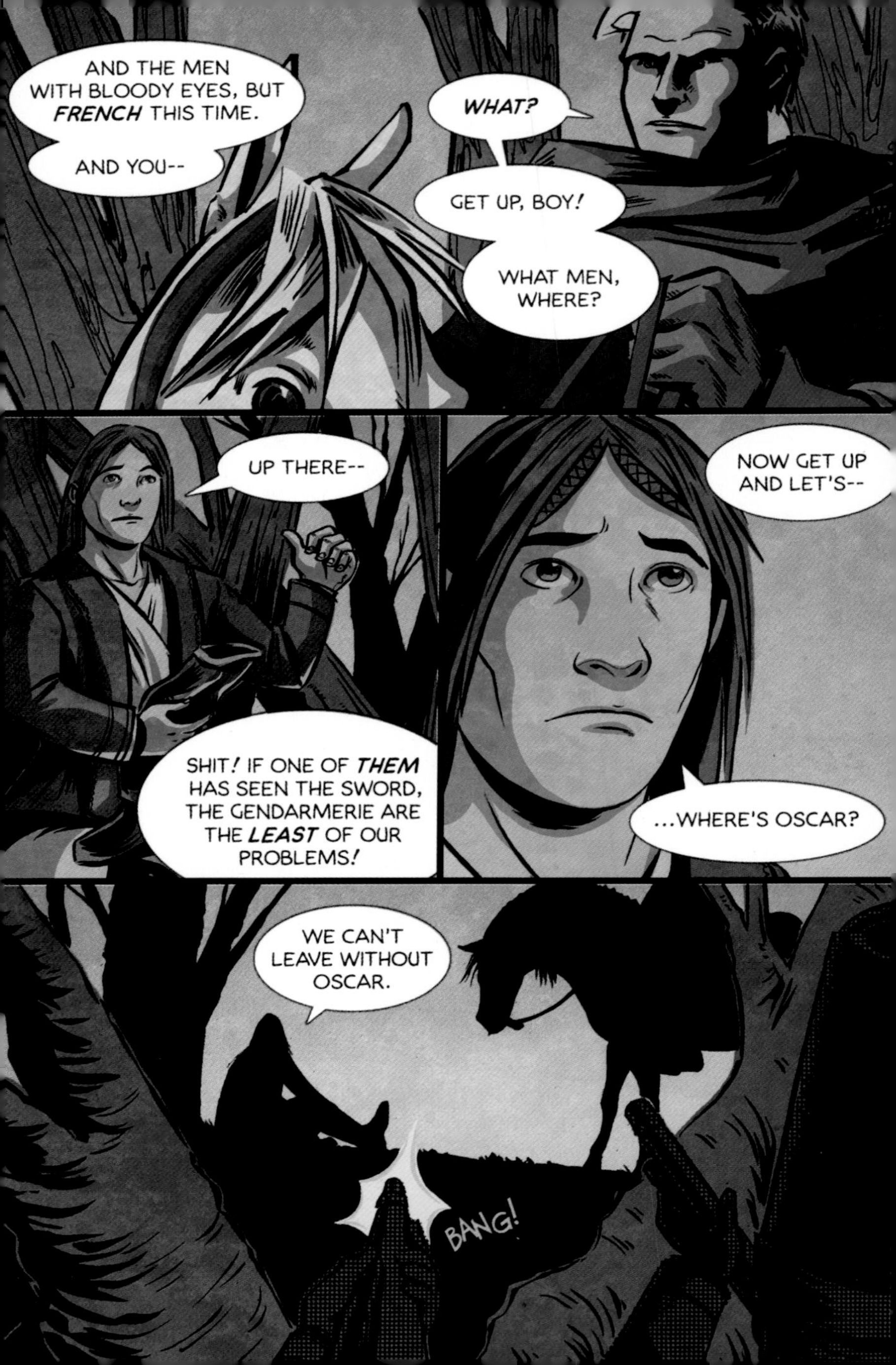
AND THE MEN WITH BLOODY EYES, BUT *FRENCH* THIS TIME.
AND YOU--
WHAT?
GET UP, BOY!
WHAT MEN, WHERE?
UP THERE--
NOW GET UP AND LET'S--
SHIT! IF ONE OF *THEM* HAS SEEN THE SWORD, THE GENDARMERIE ARE THE *LEAST* OF OUR PROBLEMS!
...WHERE'S OSCAR?
WE CAN'T LEAVE WITHOUT OSCAR.
BANG!

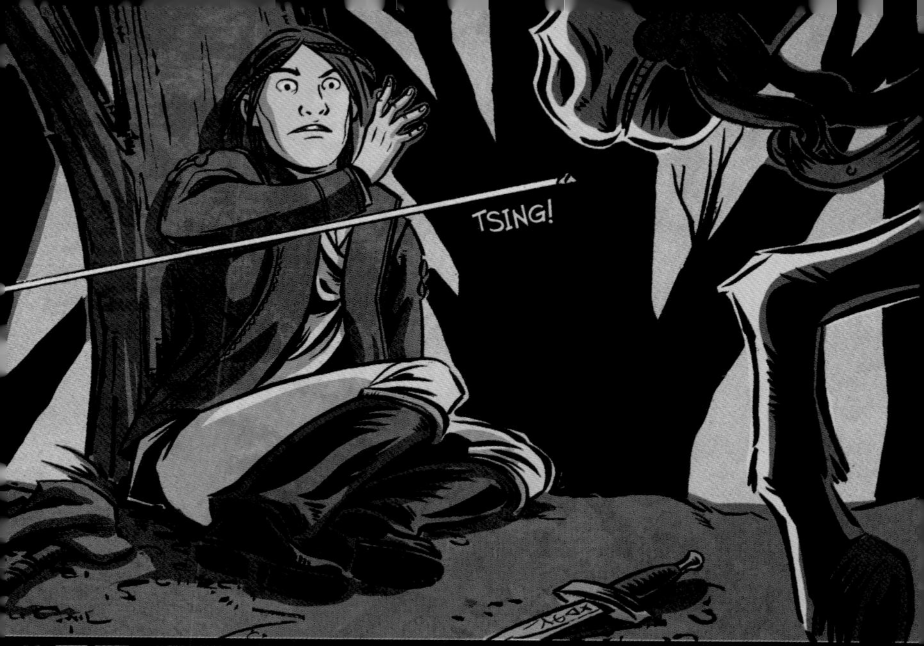
TSING!

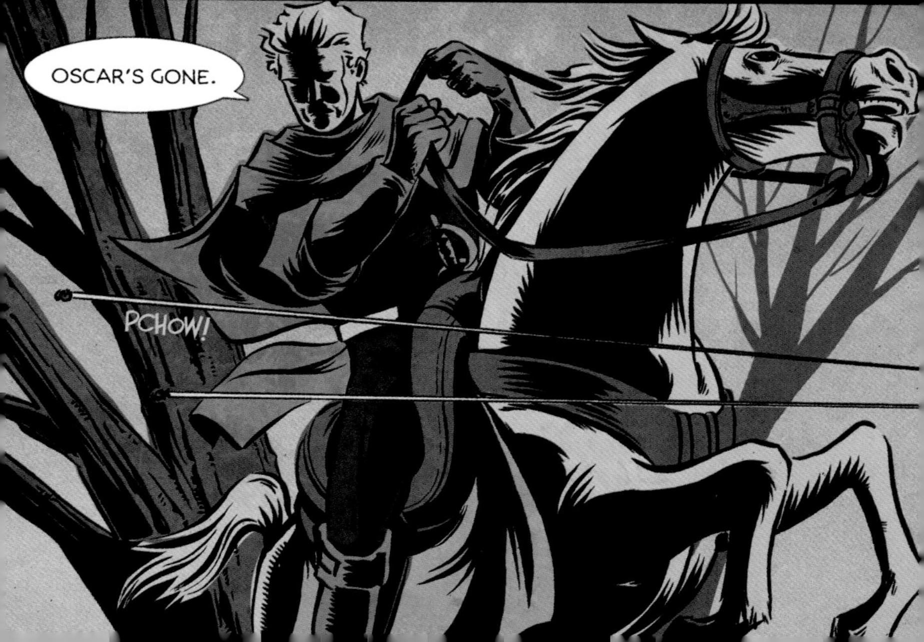
OSCAR'S GONE.
PCHOW!

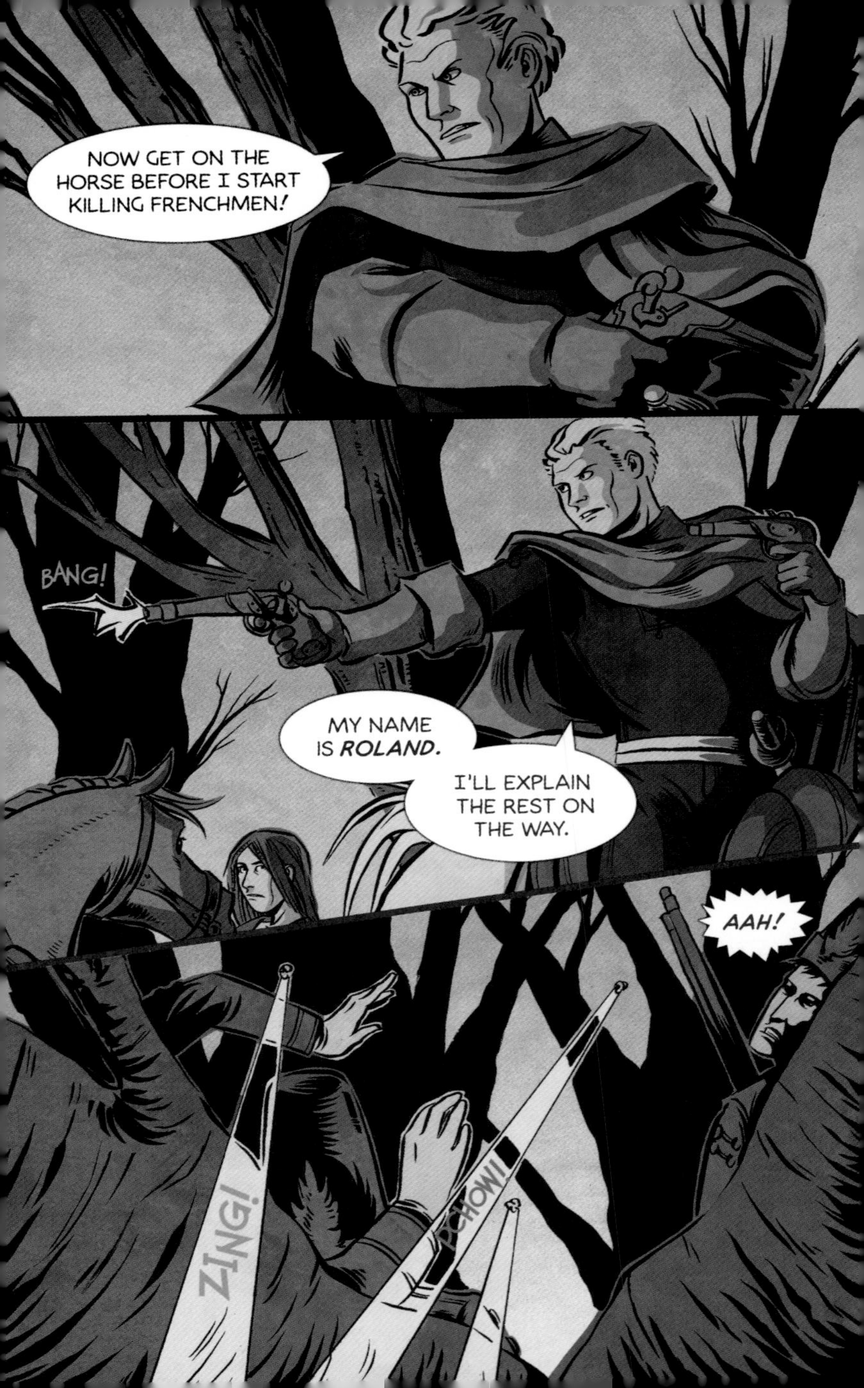
NOW GET ON THE HORSE BEFORE I START KILLING FRENCHMEN!
BANG!
MY NAME IS ROLAND.
I'LL EXPLAIN THE REST ON THE WAY.
AAH!
ZING!
PCHOW!

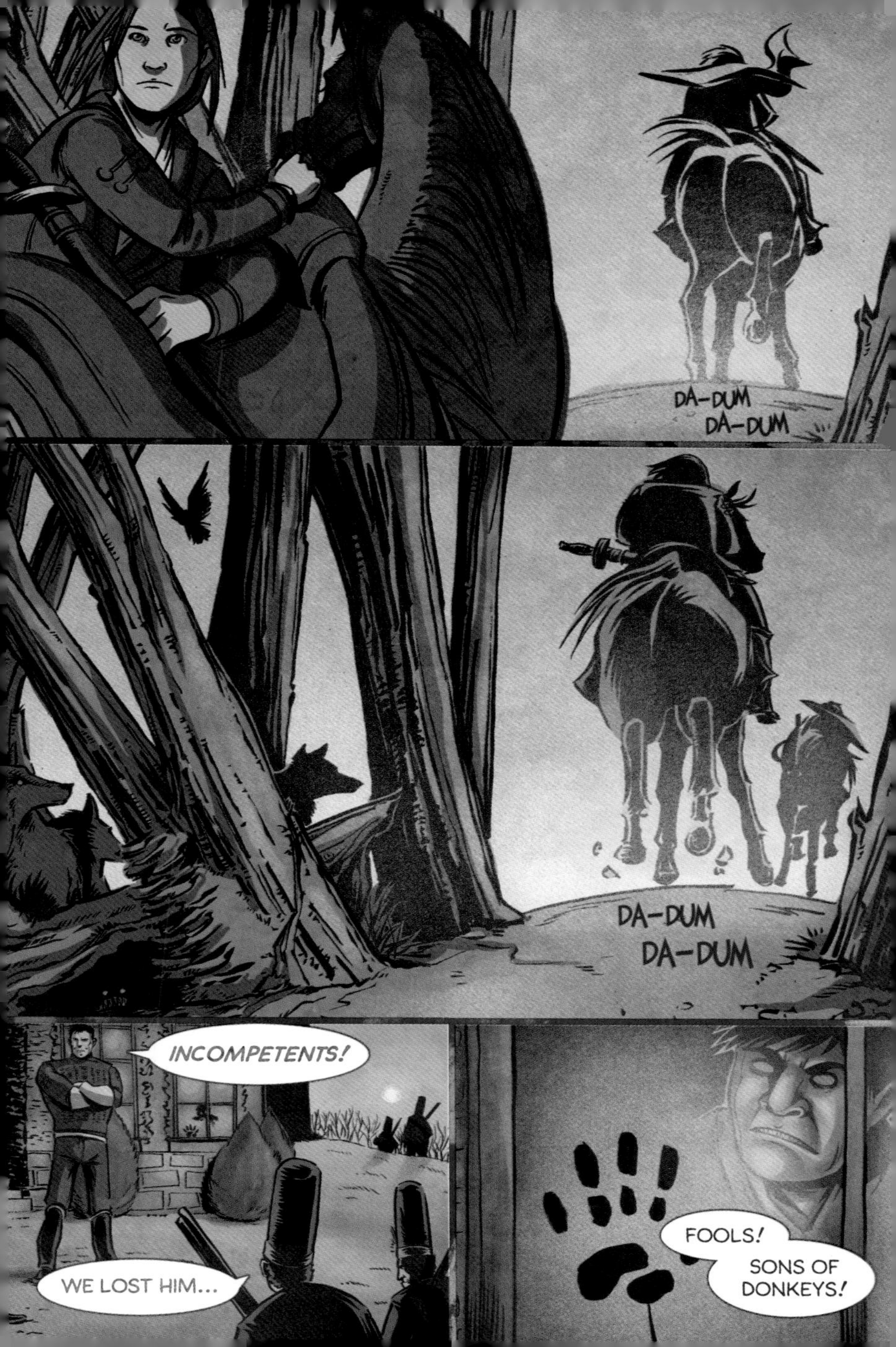
DA-DUM
DA-DUM
DA-DUM
DA-DUM
INCOMPETENTS!
WE LOST HIM...
FOOLS!
SONS OF DONKEYS!

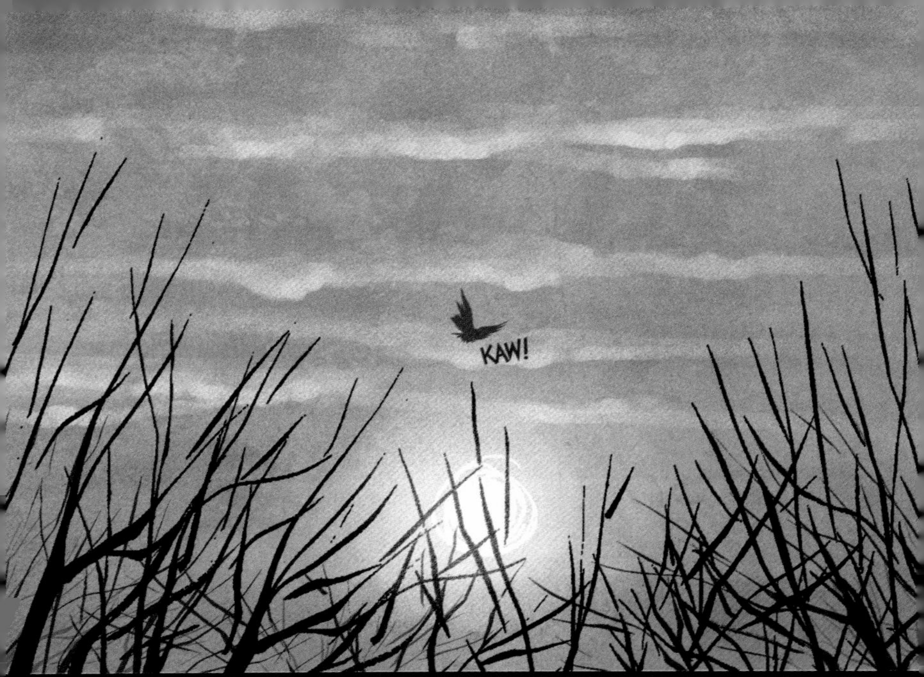
KAW!

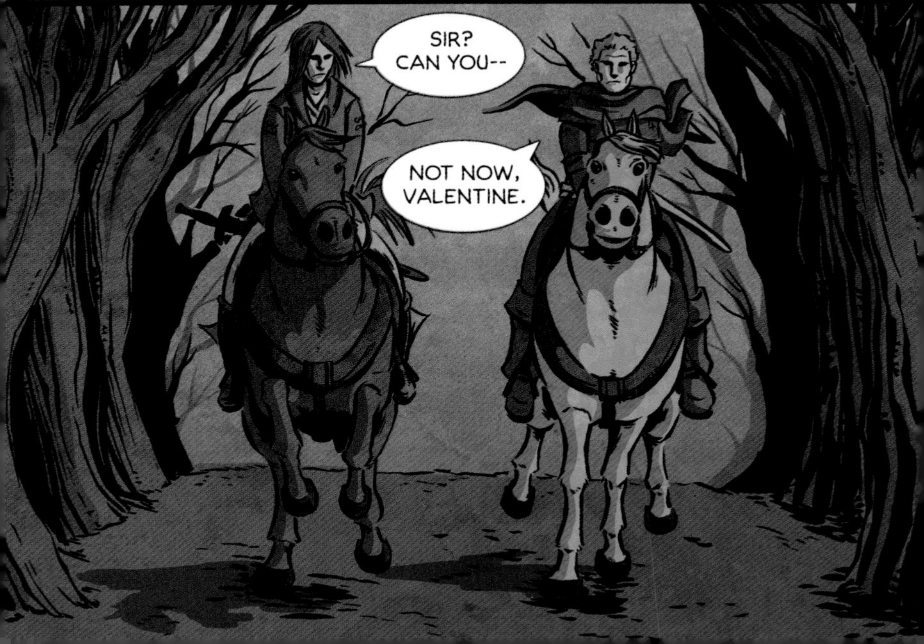
SIR?
CAN YOU--
NOT NOW,
VALENTINE.

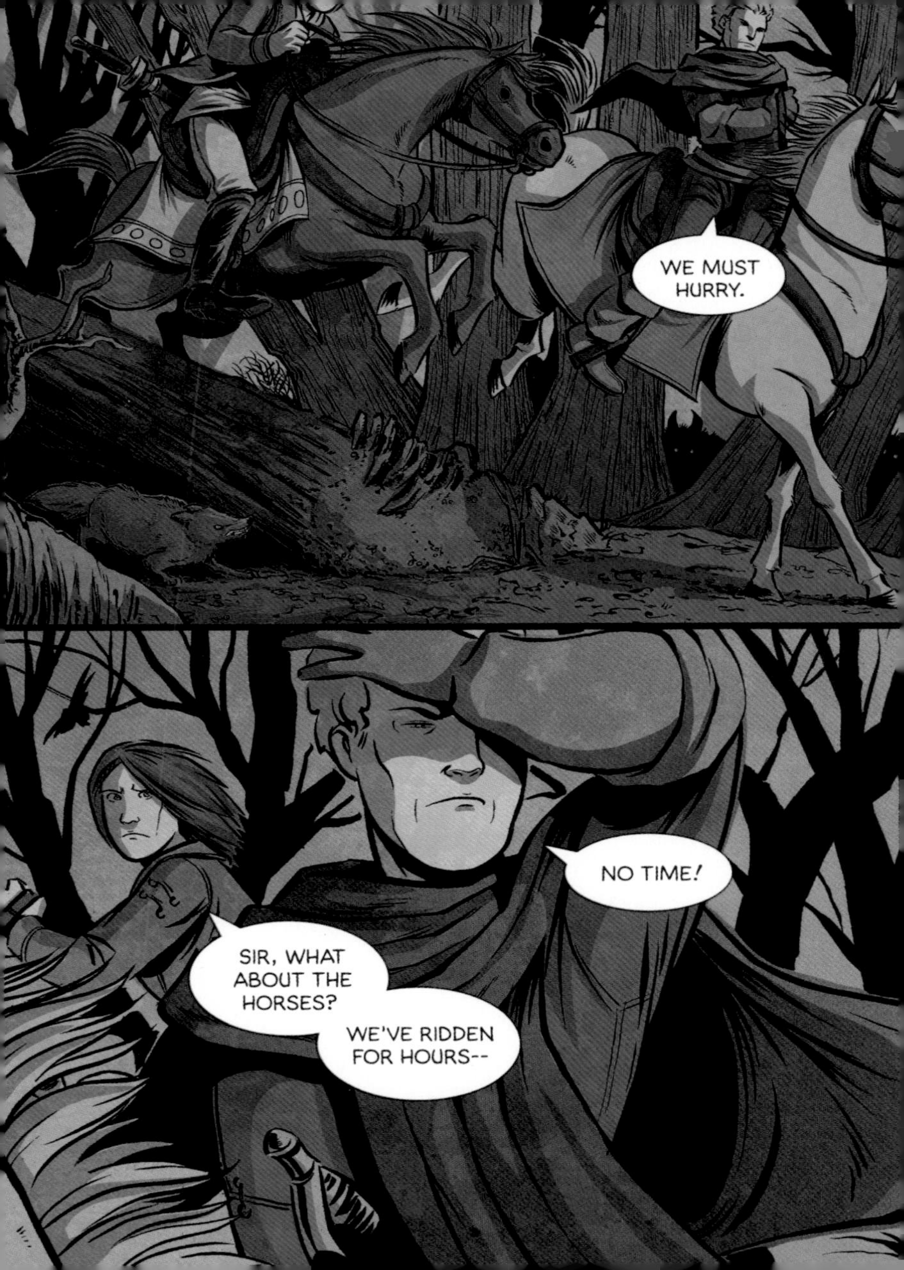
WE MUST HURRY.
SIR, WHAT ABOUT THE HORSES?
WE'VE RIDDEN FOR HOURS--
NO TIME!

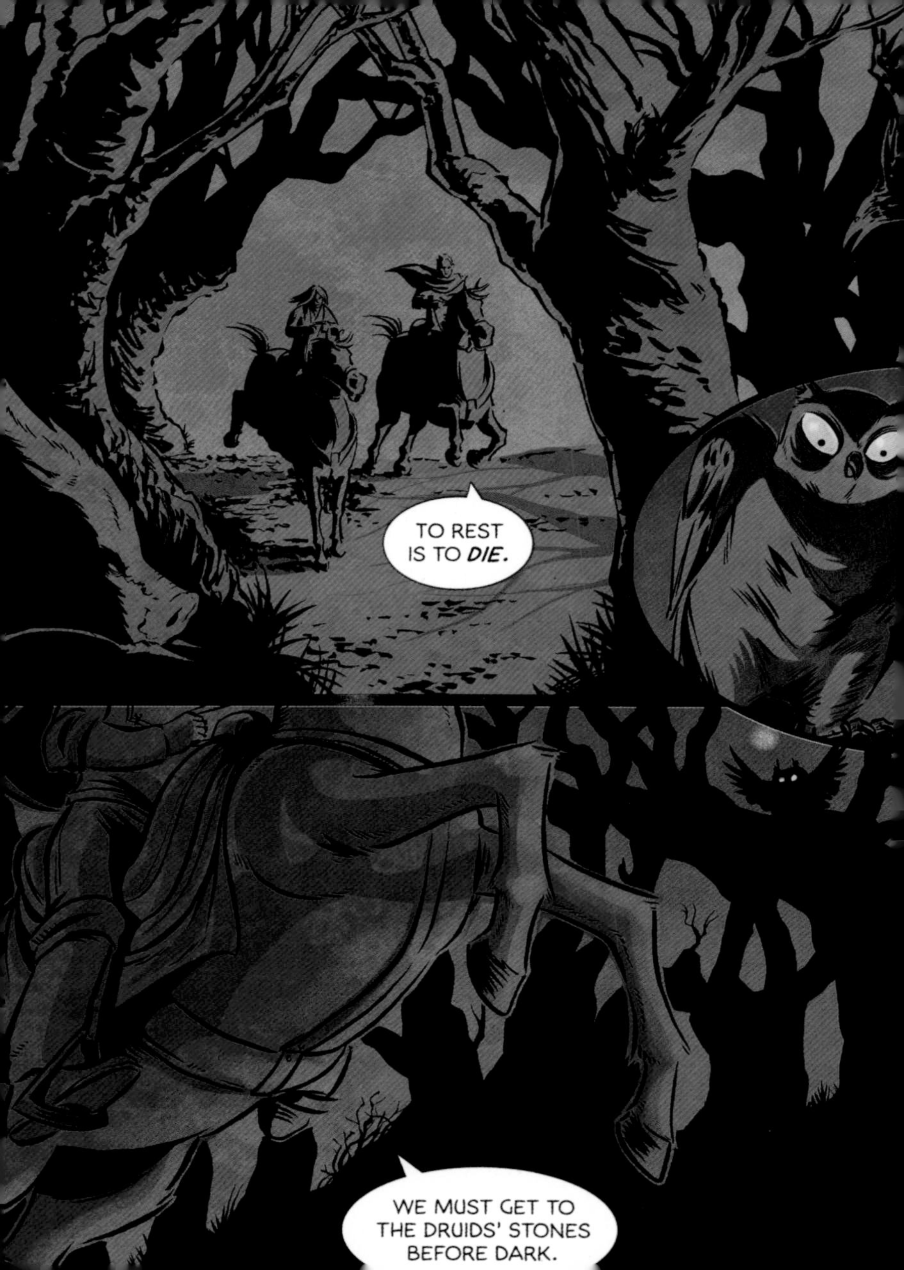
TO REST IS TO *DIE.*
WE MUST GET TO THE DRUIDS' STONES BEFORE DARK.

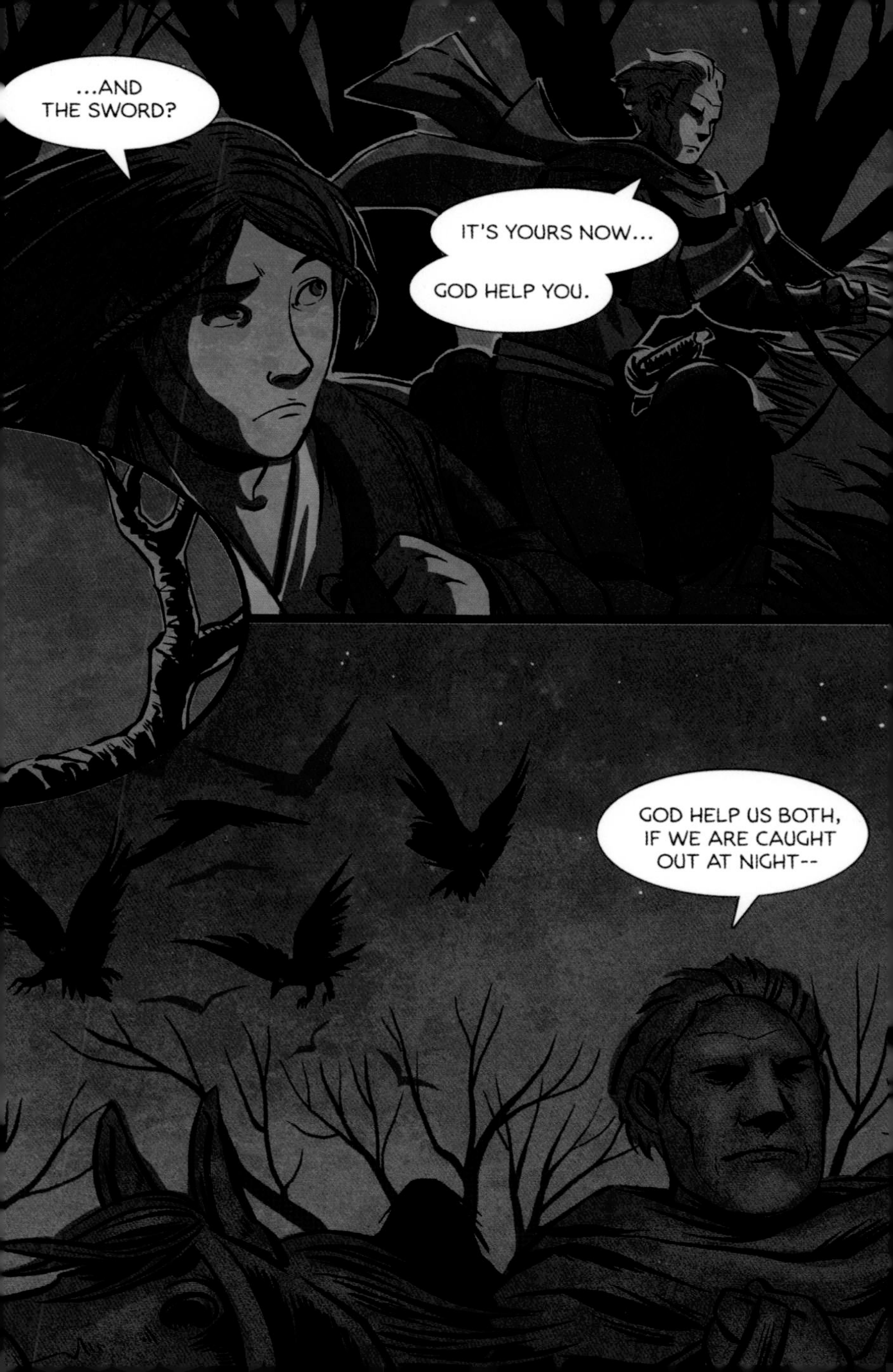
...AND THE SWORD?
IT'S YOURS NOW...
GOD HELP YOU.
GOD HELP US BOTH, IF WE ARE CAUGHT OUT AT NIGHT--

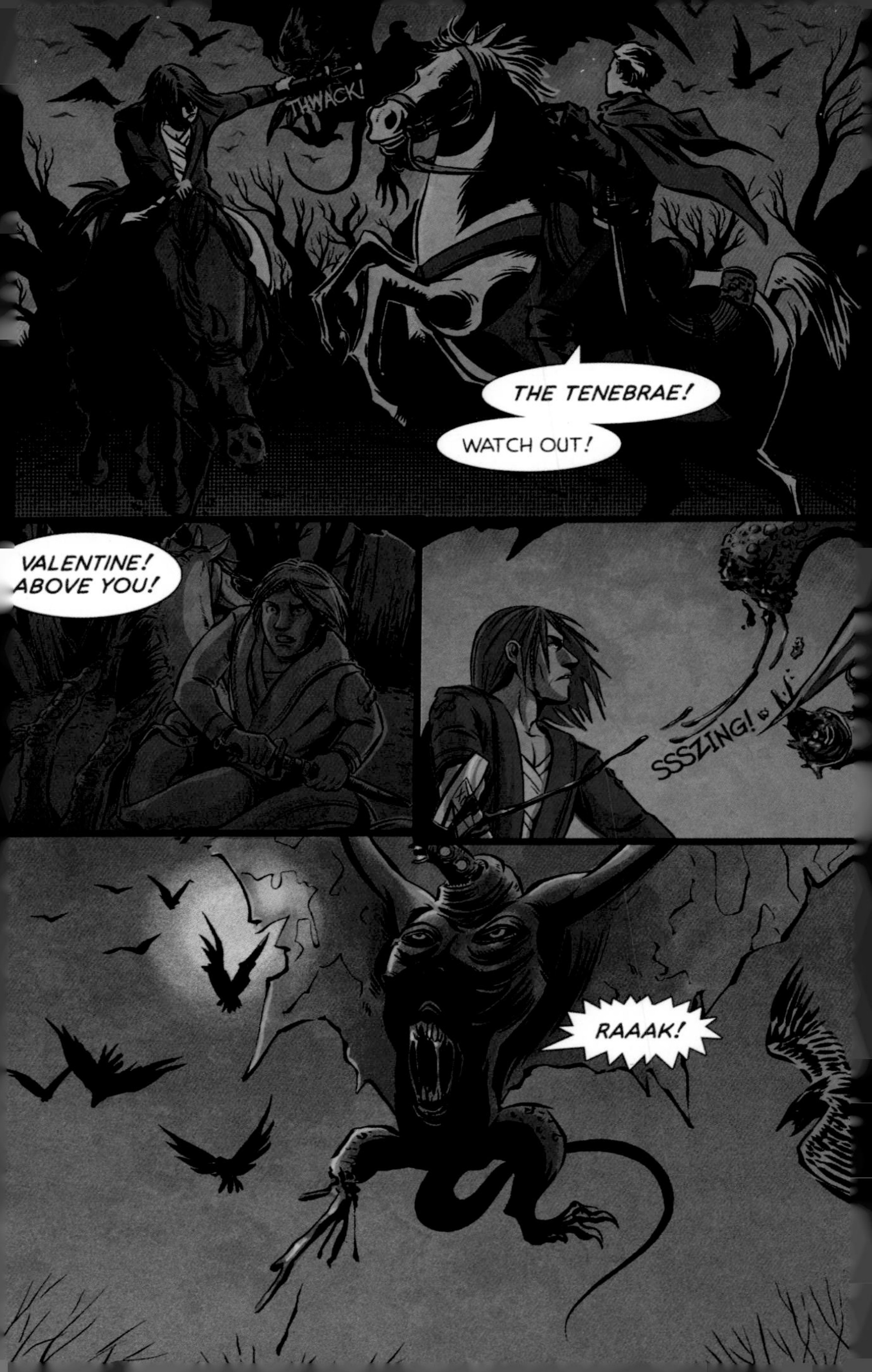
THWACK!
THE TENEBRAE!
WATCH OUT!
VALENTINE! ABOVE YOU!
SSSZING!
RAAAK!

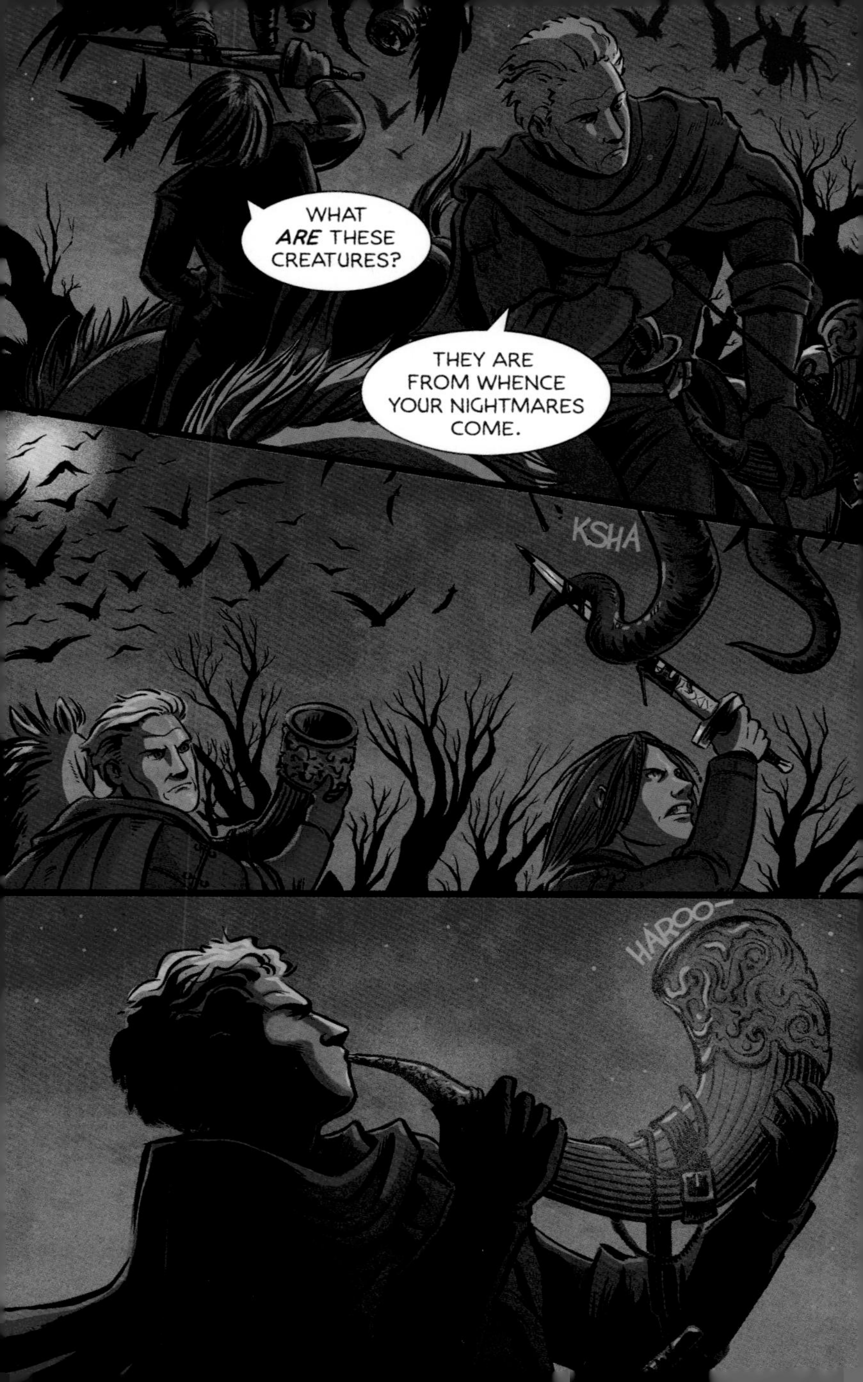
WHAT *ARE* THESE CREATURES?
THEY ARE FROM WHENCE YOUR NIGHTMARES COME.
KSHA
HAROO—

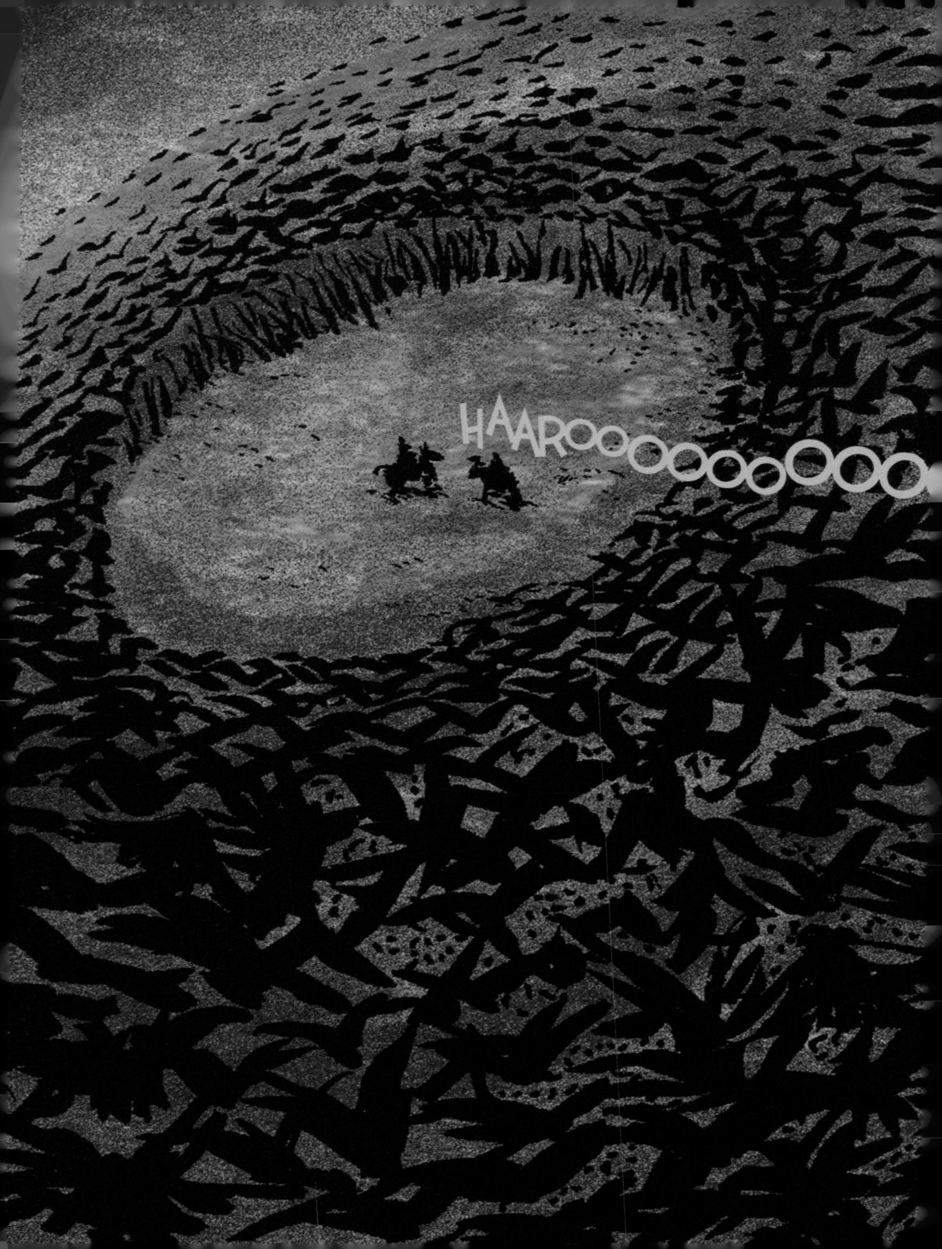
HAAROOOOOOOOOOOO

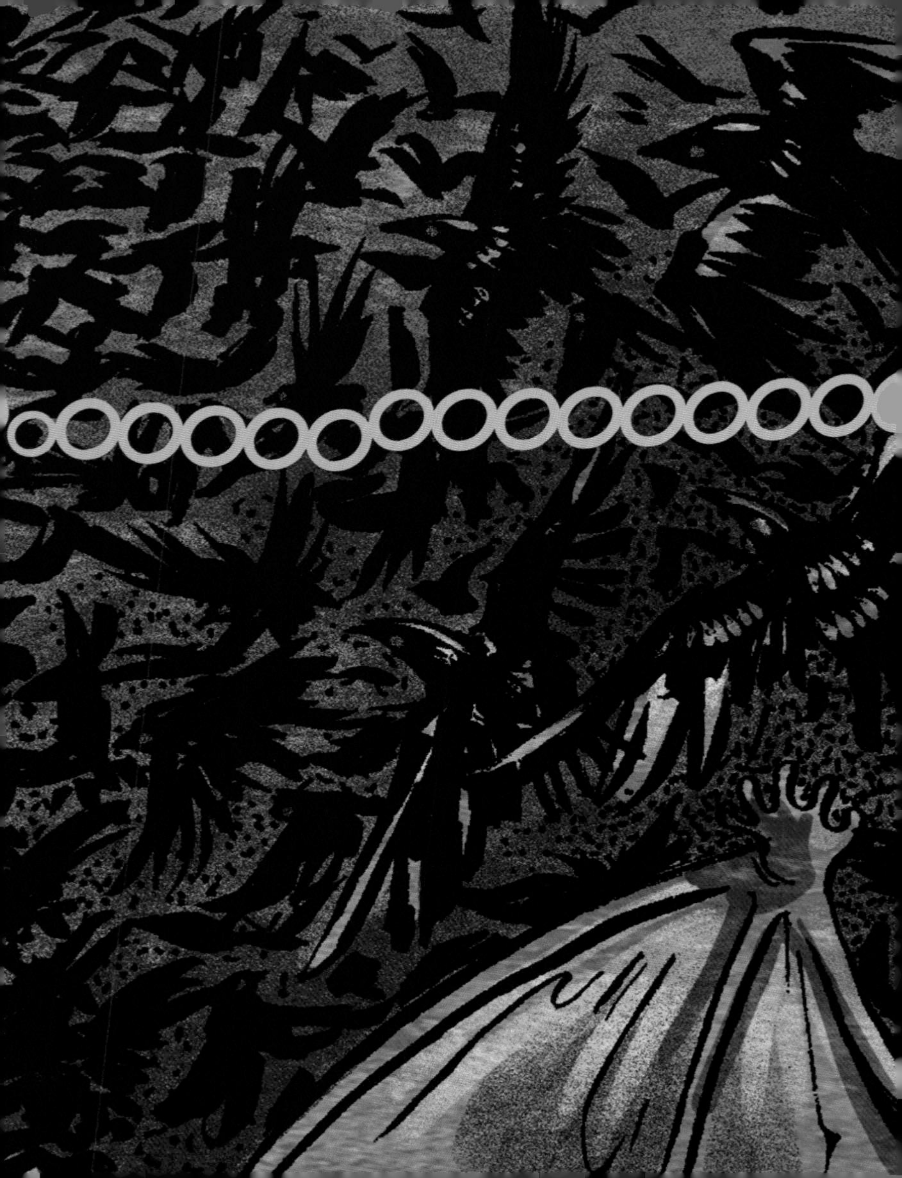

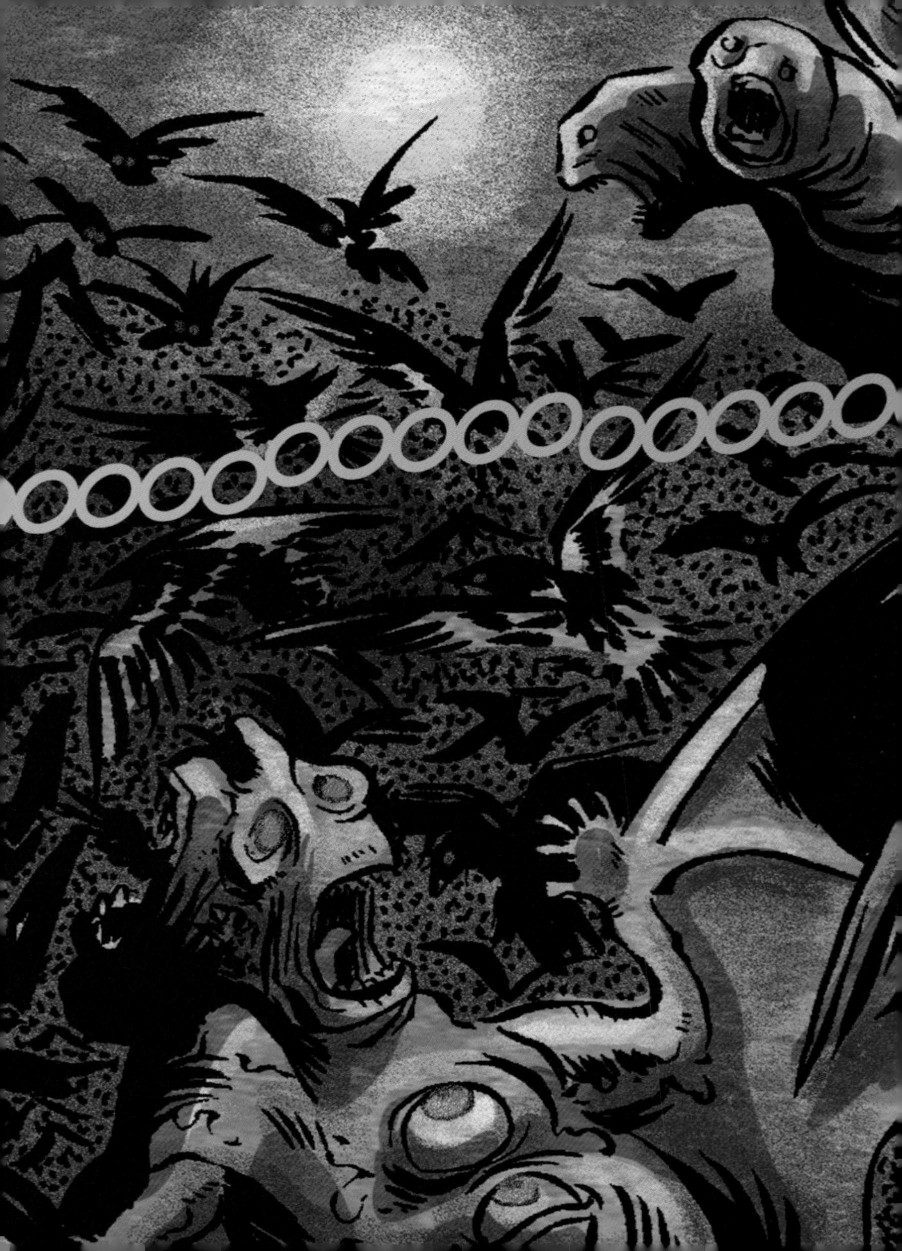

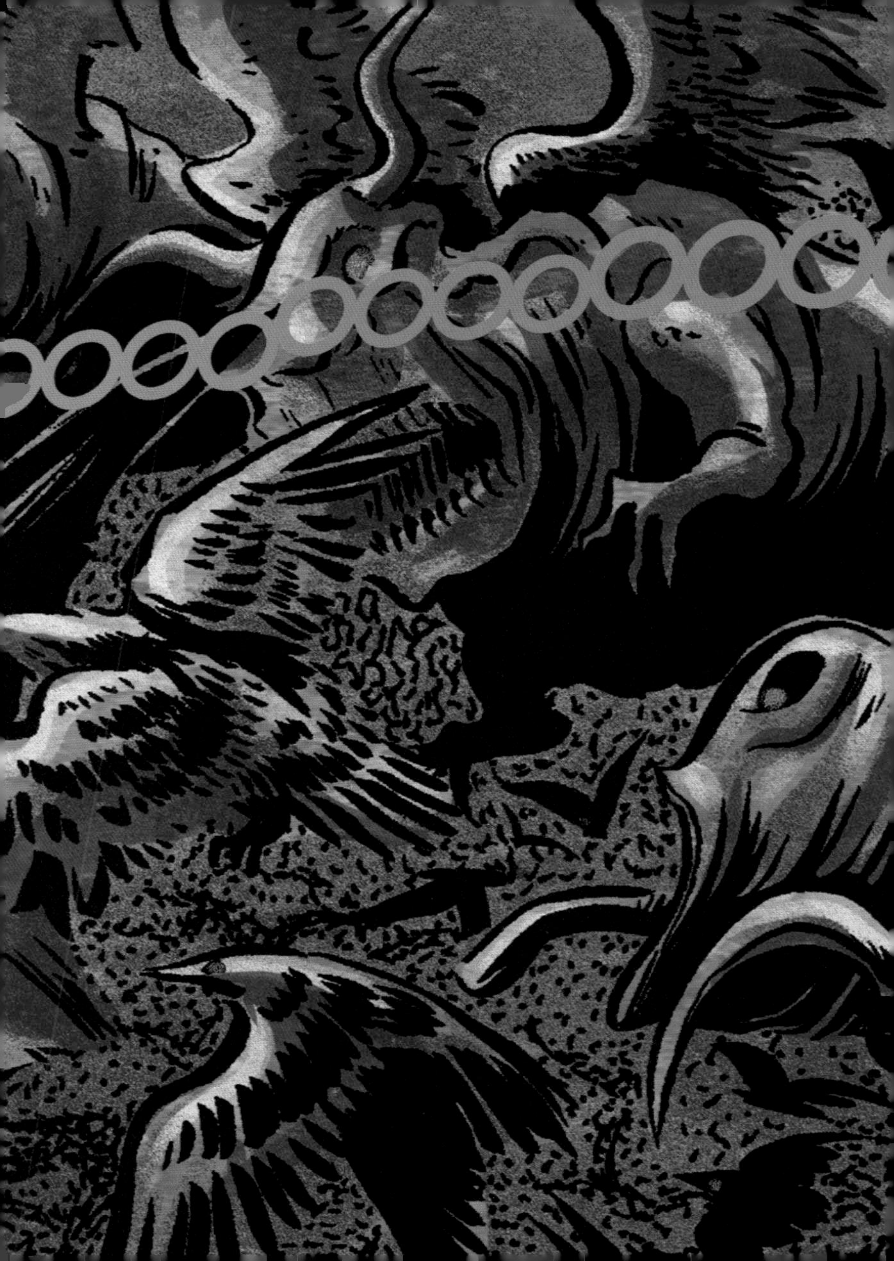

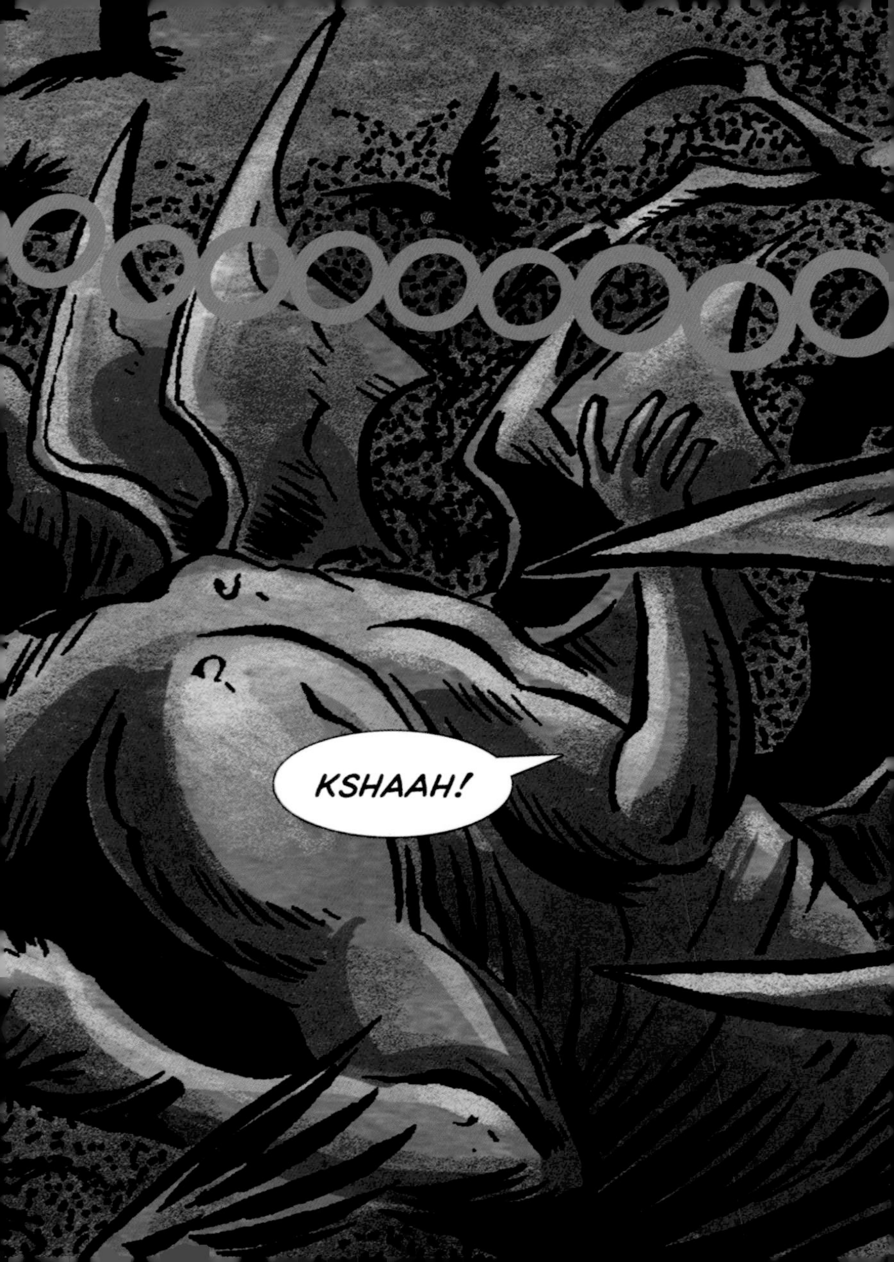
KSHAAH!

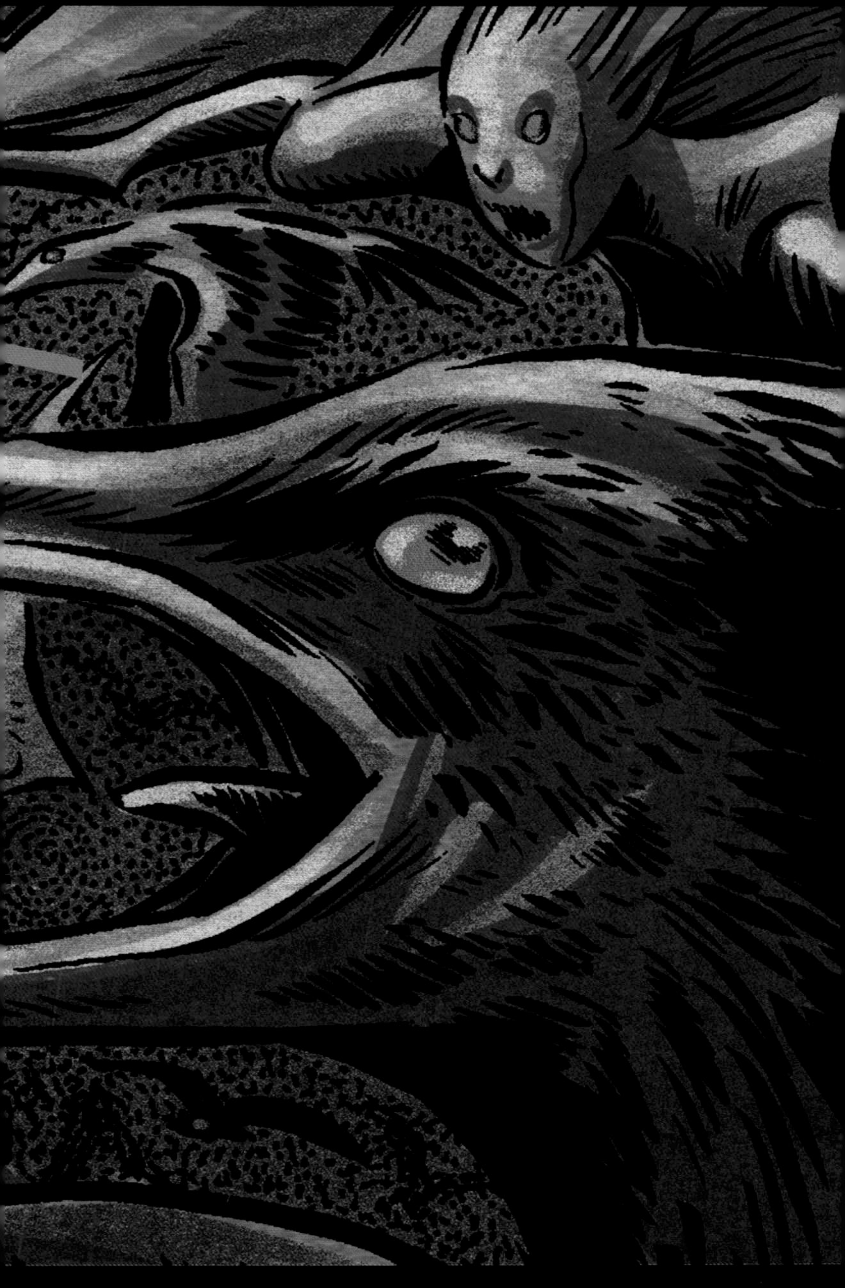

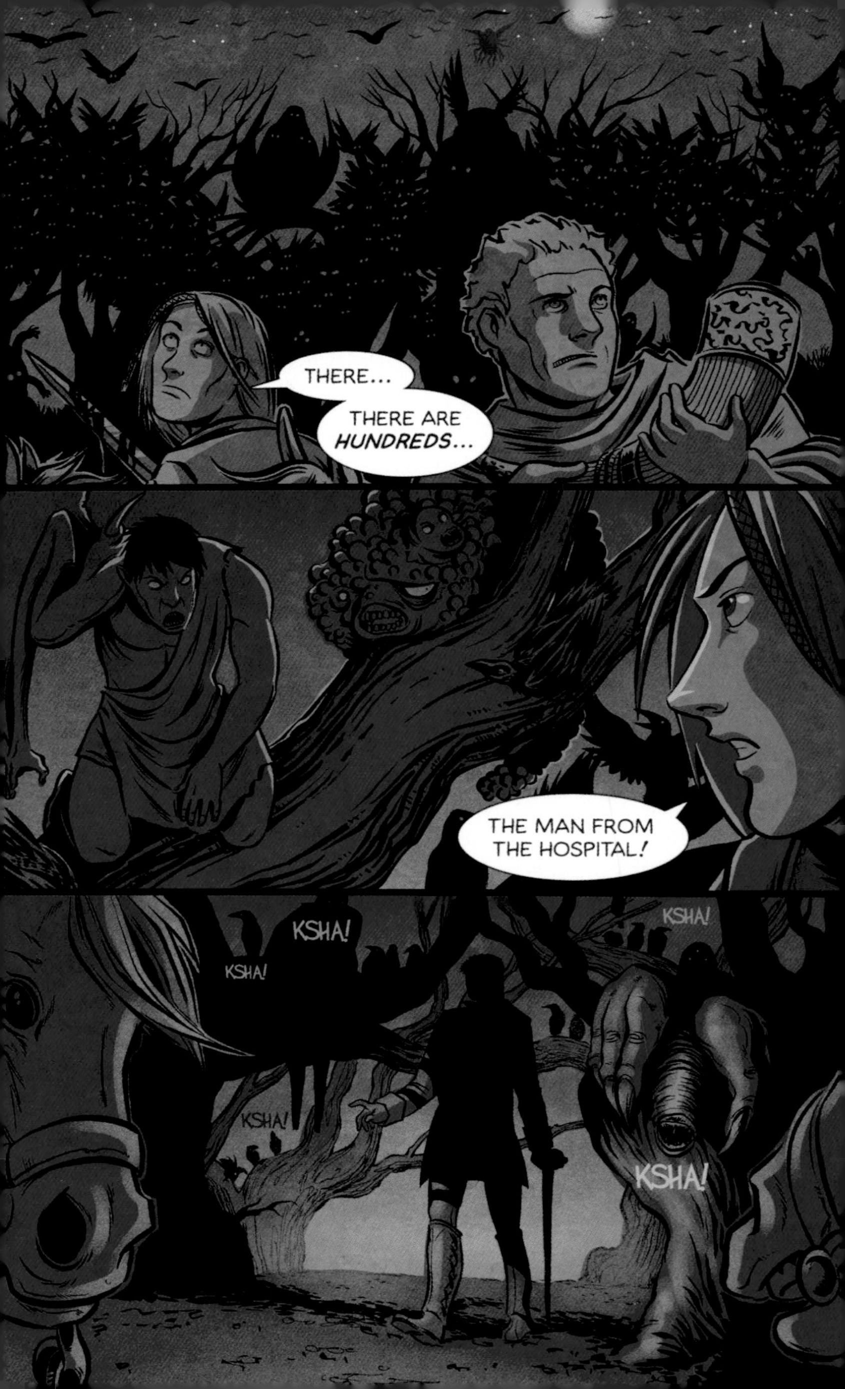
THERE...
THERE ARE *HUNDREDS*...
THE MAN FROM THE HOSPITAL!
KSHA!
KSHA!
KSHA!
KSHA!
KSHA!

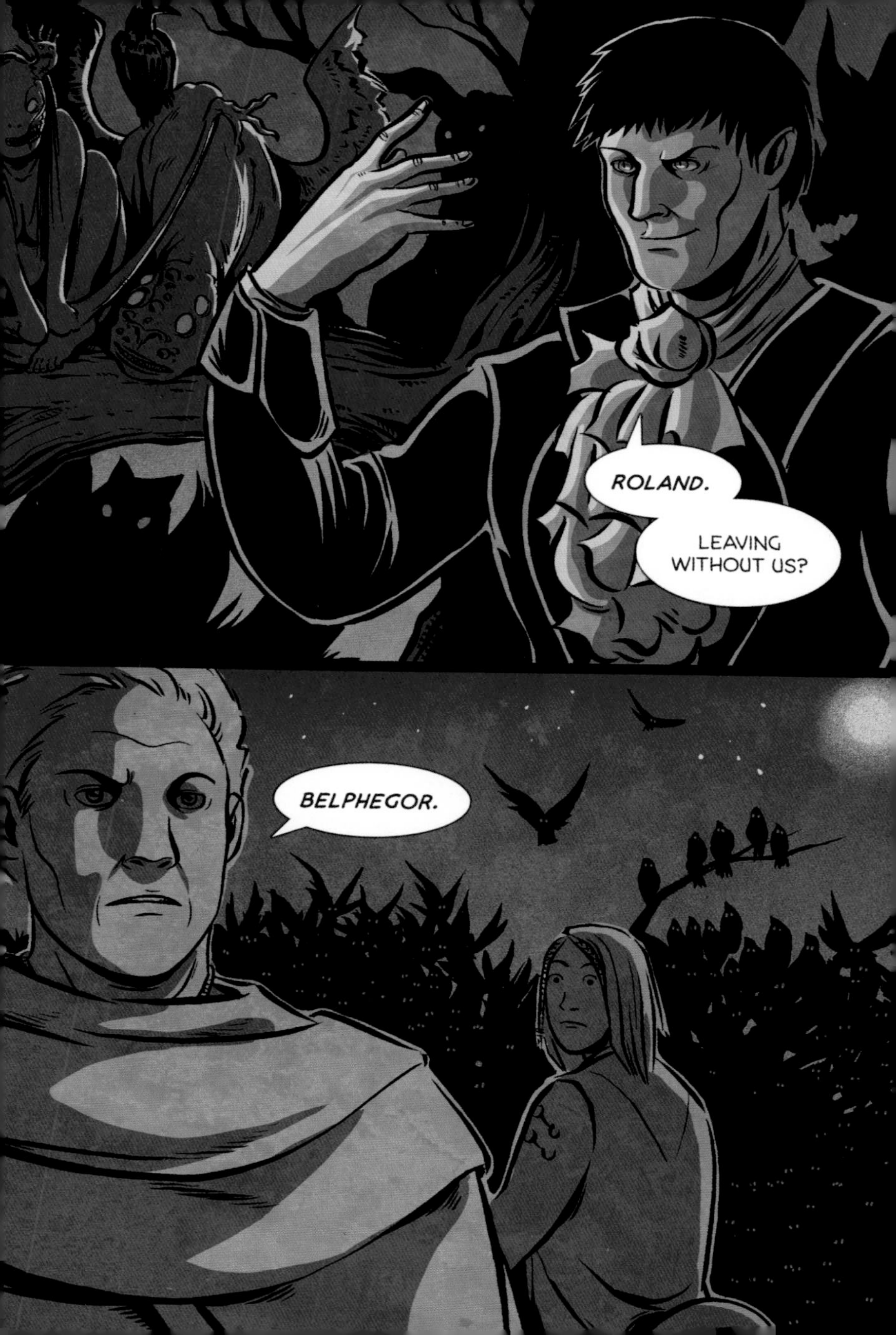
ROLAND.
LEAVING WITHOUT US?
BELPHEGOR.

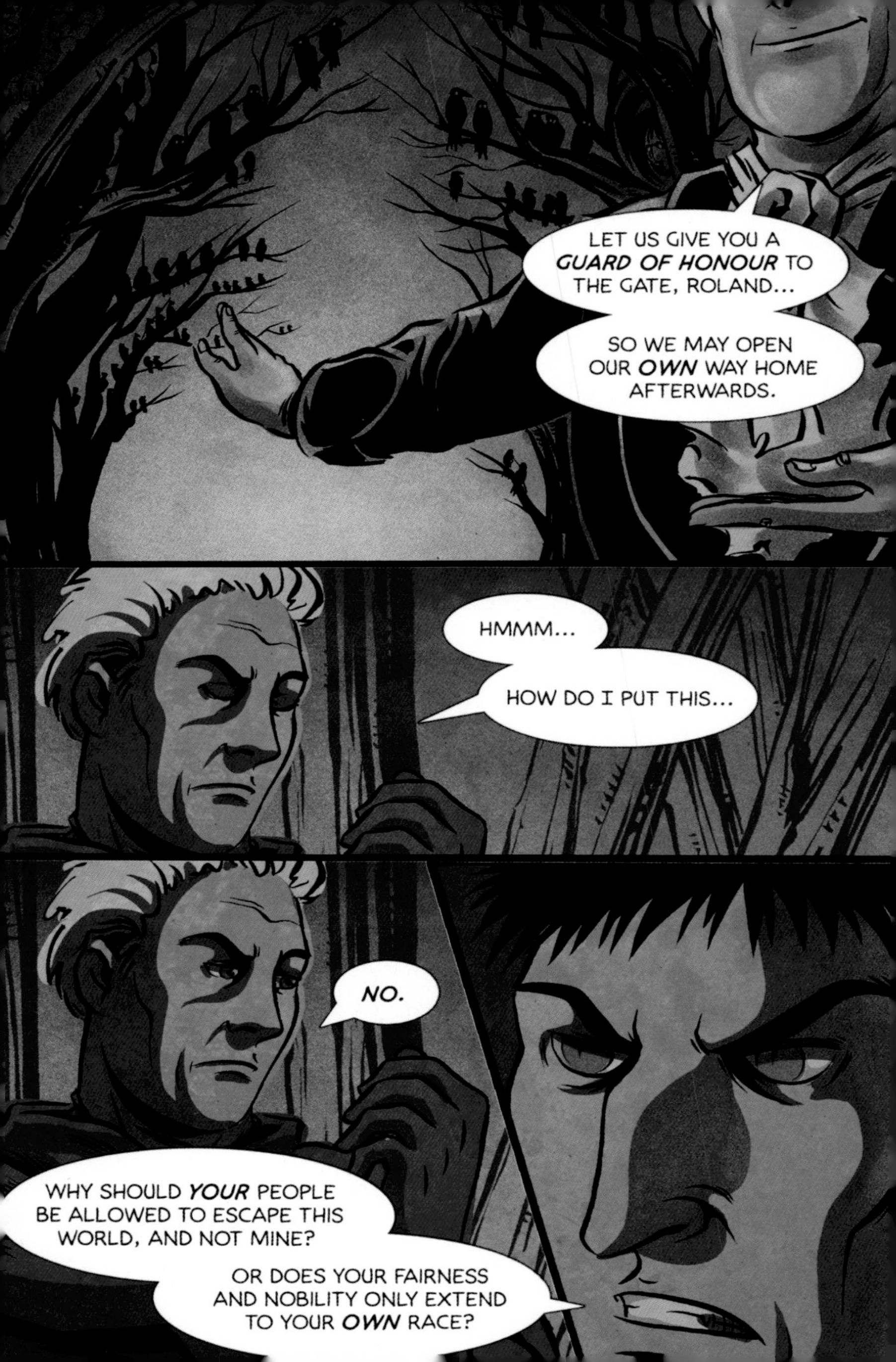
LET US GIVE YOU A *GUARD OF HONOUR* TO THE GATE, ROLAND...
SO WE MAY OPEN OUR *OWN* WAY HOME AFTERWARDS.
HMMM...
HOW DO I PUT THIS...
NO.
WHY SHOULD *YOUR* PEOPLE BE ALLOWED TO ESCAPE THIS WORLD, AND NOT MINE?
OR DOES YOUR FAIRNESS AND NOBILITY ONLY EXTEND TO YOUR *OWN* RACE?

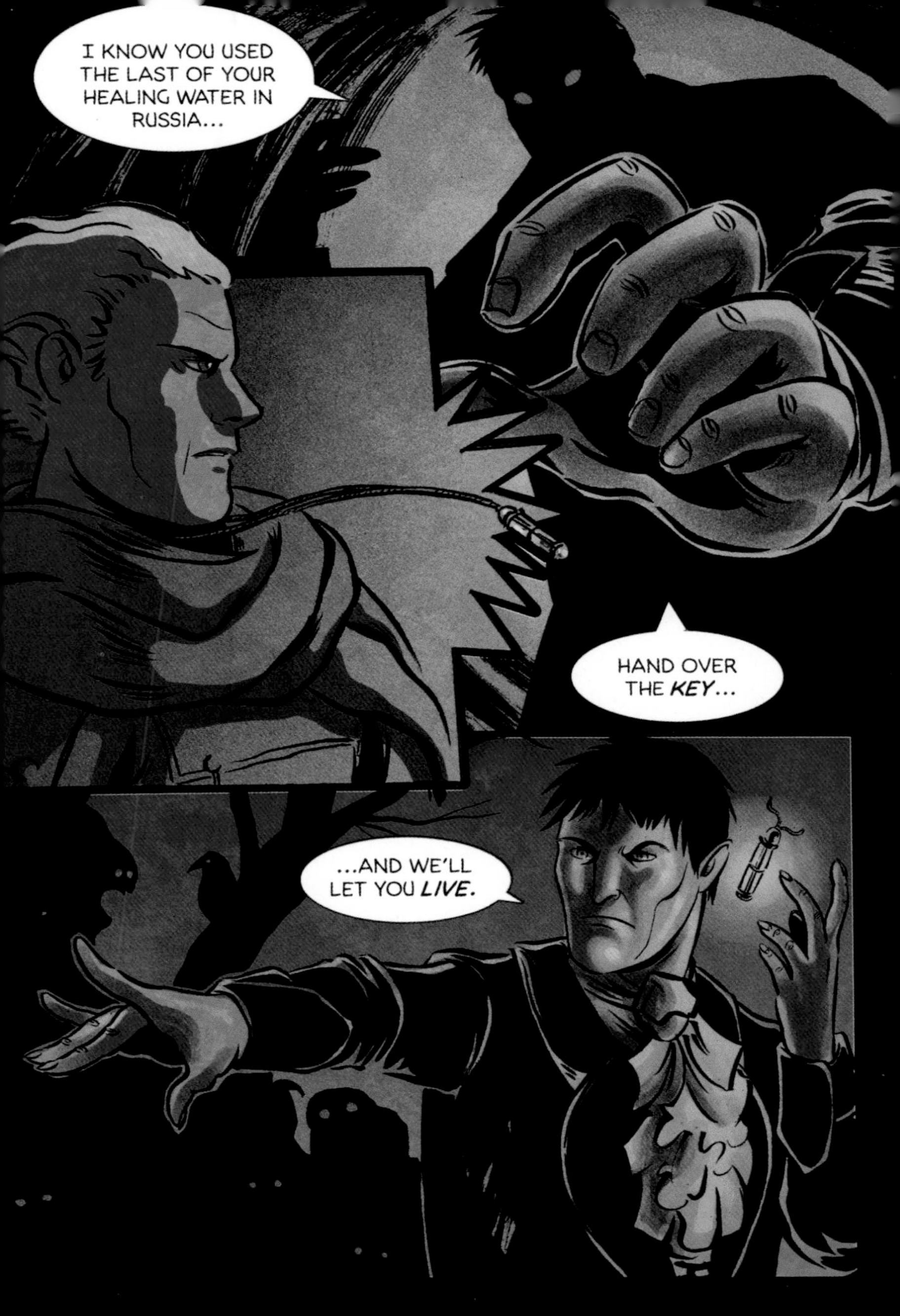
I KNOW YOU USED THE LAST OF YOUR HEALING WATER IN RUSSIA...
HAND OVER THE *KEY*...
...AND WE'LL LET YOU *LIVE.*

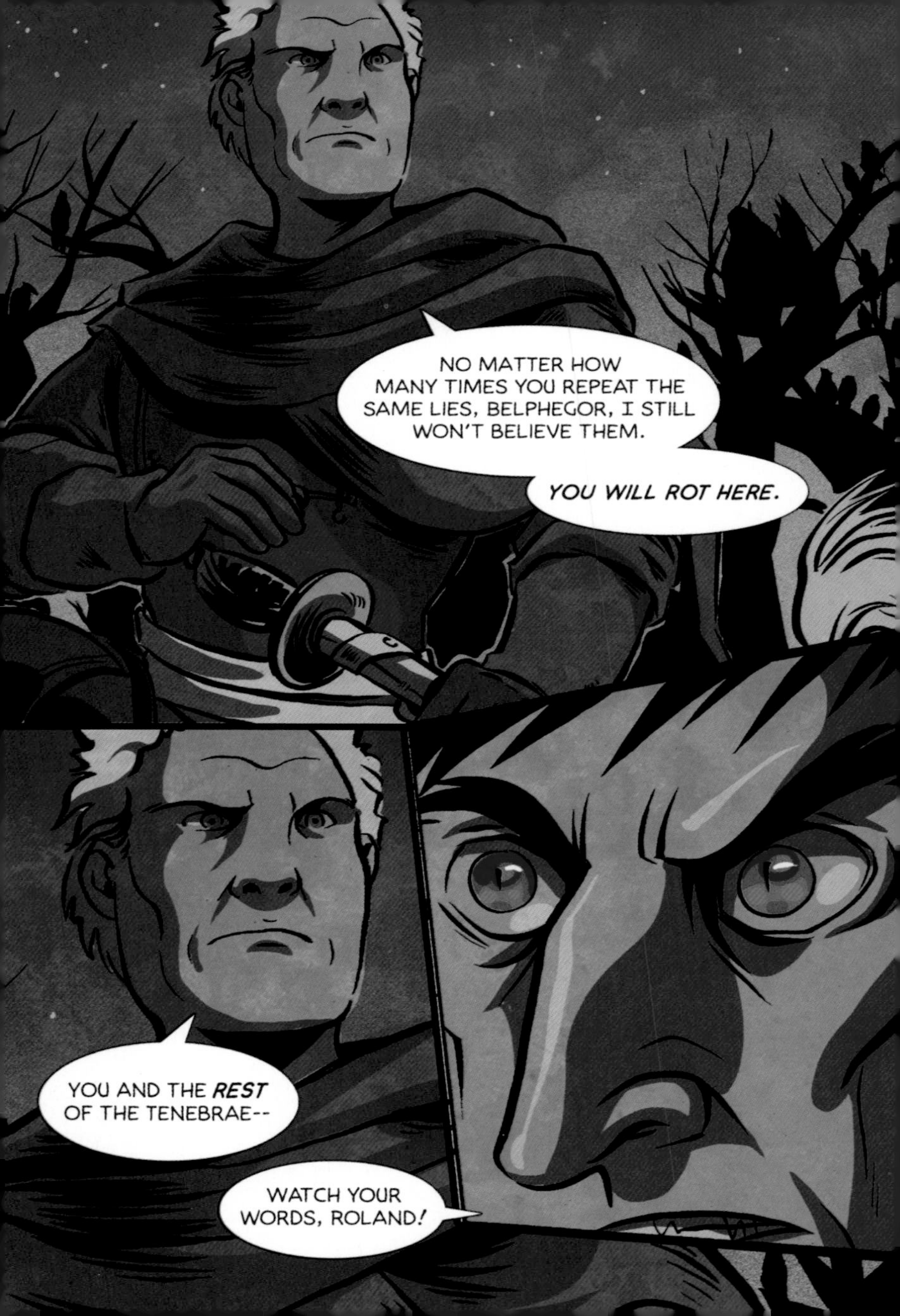
NO MATTER HOW MANY TIMES YOU REPEAT THE SAME LIES, BELPHEGOR, I STILL WON'T BELIEVE THEM.
YOU WILL ROT HERE.
YOU AND THE *REST* OF THE TENEBRAE--
WATCH YOUR WORDS, ROLAND*!*

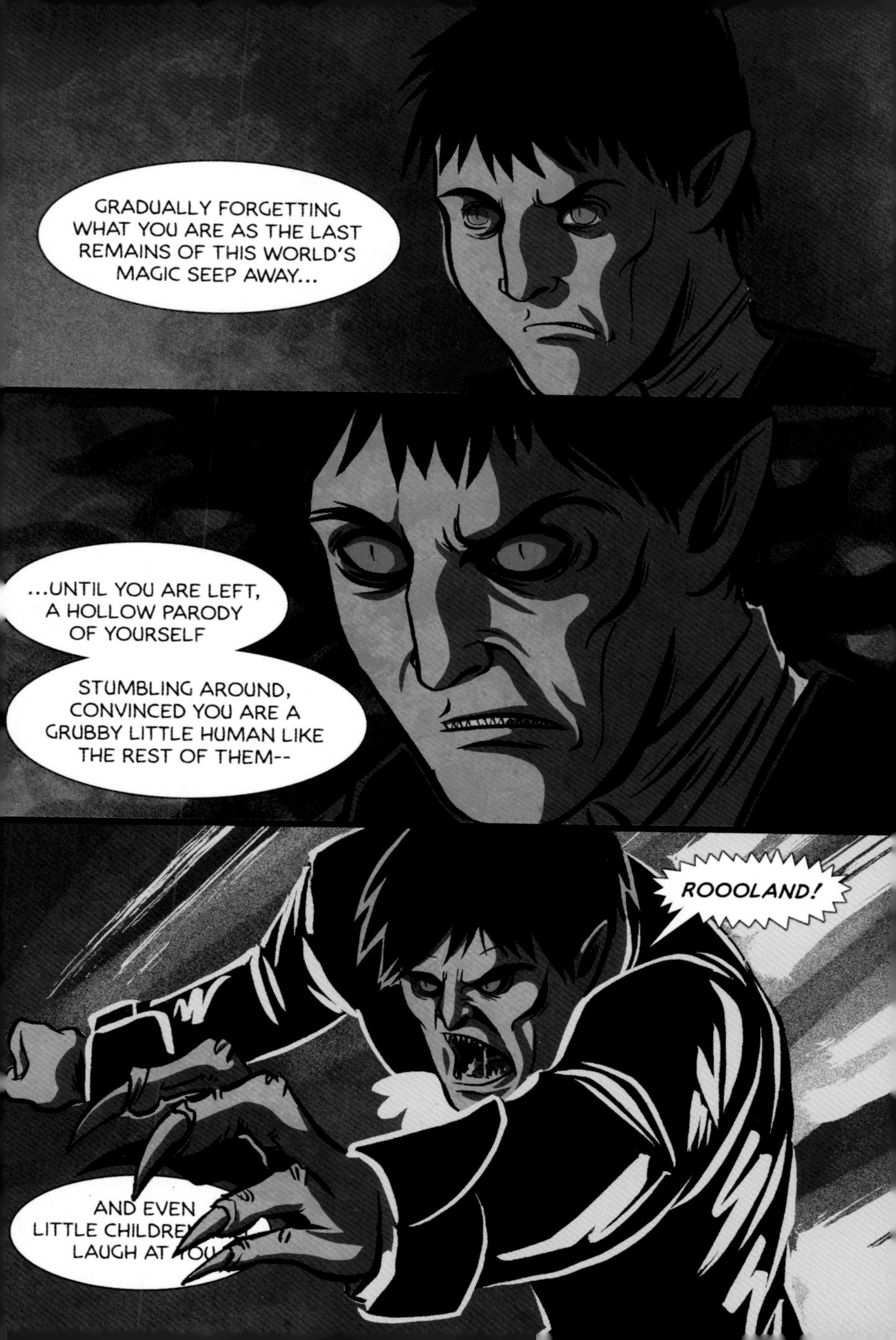
GRADUALLY FORGETTING WHAT YOU ARE AS THE LAST REMAINS OF THIS WORLD'S MAGIC SEEP AWAY...
...UNTIL YOU ARE LEFT, A HOLLOW PARODY OF YOURSELF
STUMBLING AROUND, CONVINCED YOU ARE A GRUBBY LITTLE HUMAN LIKE THE REST OF THEM--
ROOOLAND!
AND EVEN LITTLE CHILDRE
LAUGH AT

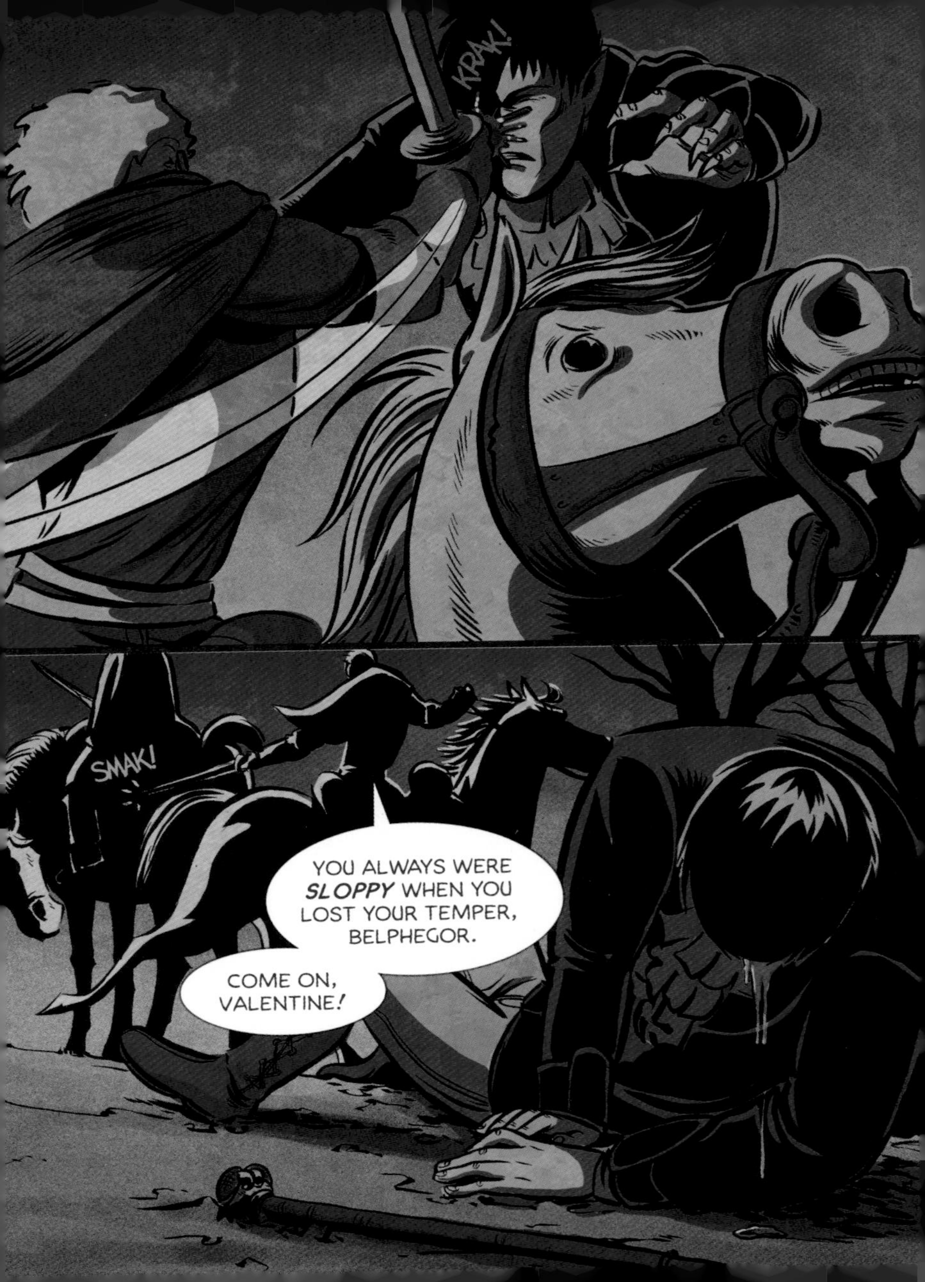
KRAK!
SMAK!
YOU ALWAYS WERE *SLOPPY* WHEN YOU LOST YOUR TEMPER, BELPHEGOR.
COME ON, VALENTINE!

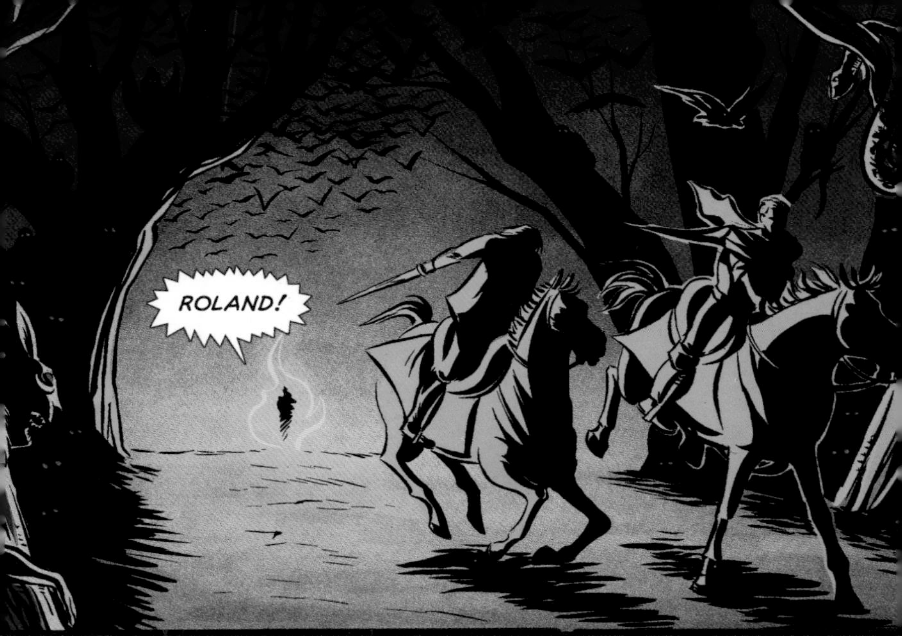
ROLAND!

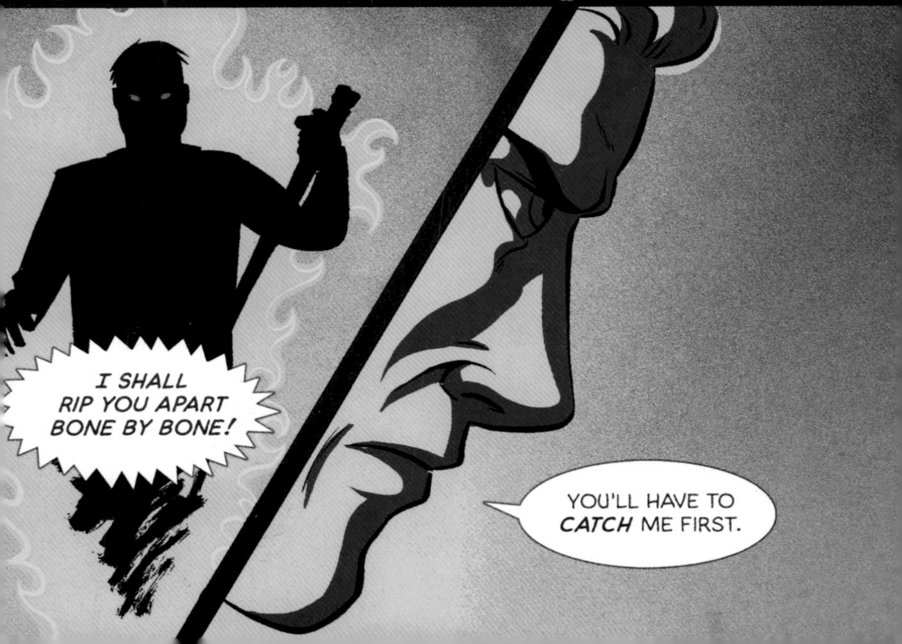
I SHALL RIP YOU APART BONE BY BONE!
YOU'LL HAVE TO *CATCH* ME FIRST.

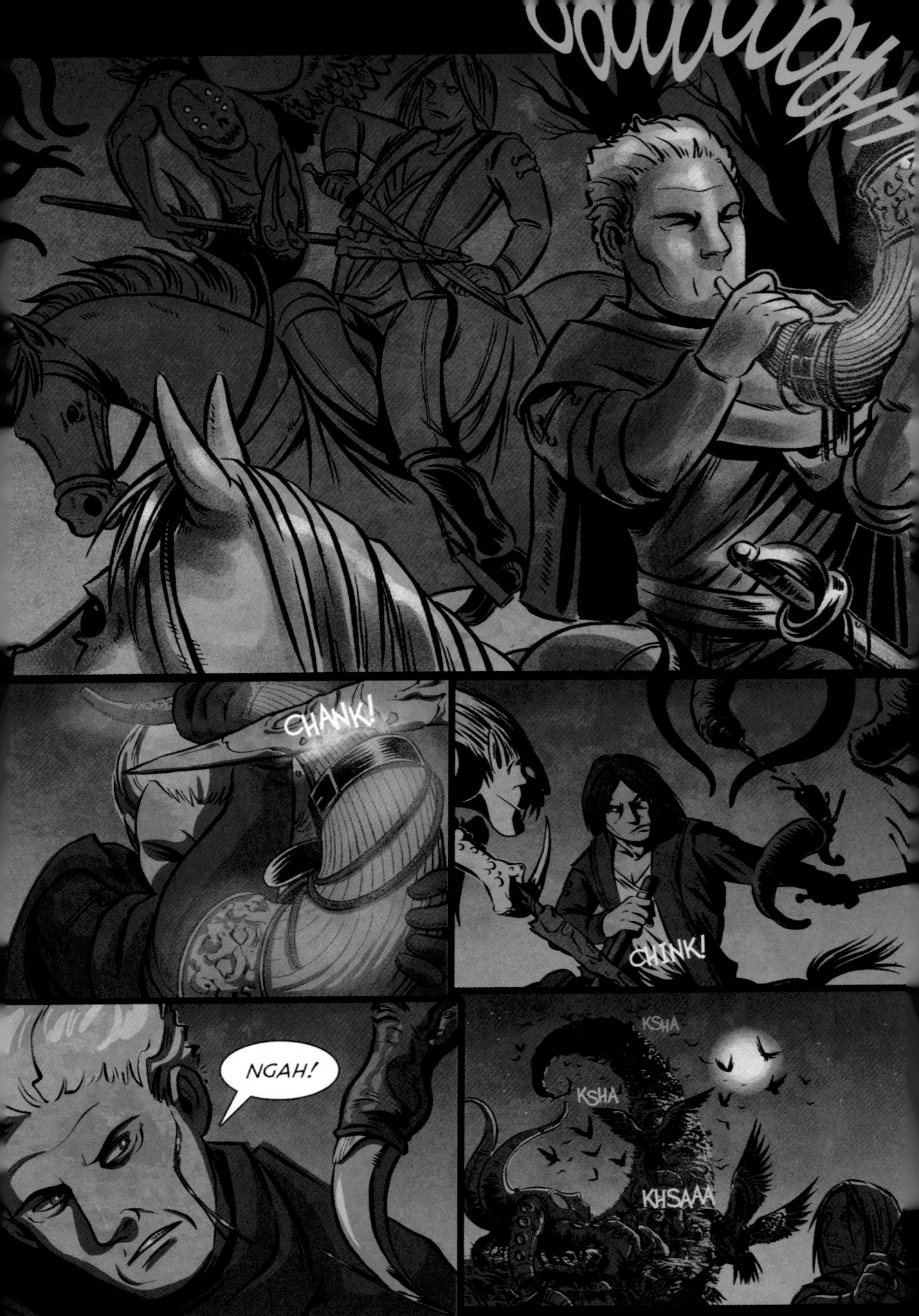
CHANK!
CHINK!
NGAH!
KSHA
KSHA
KHSAAA

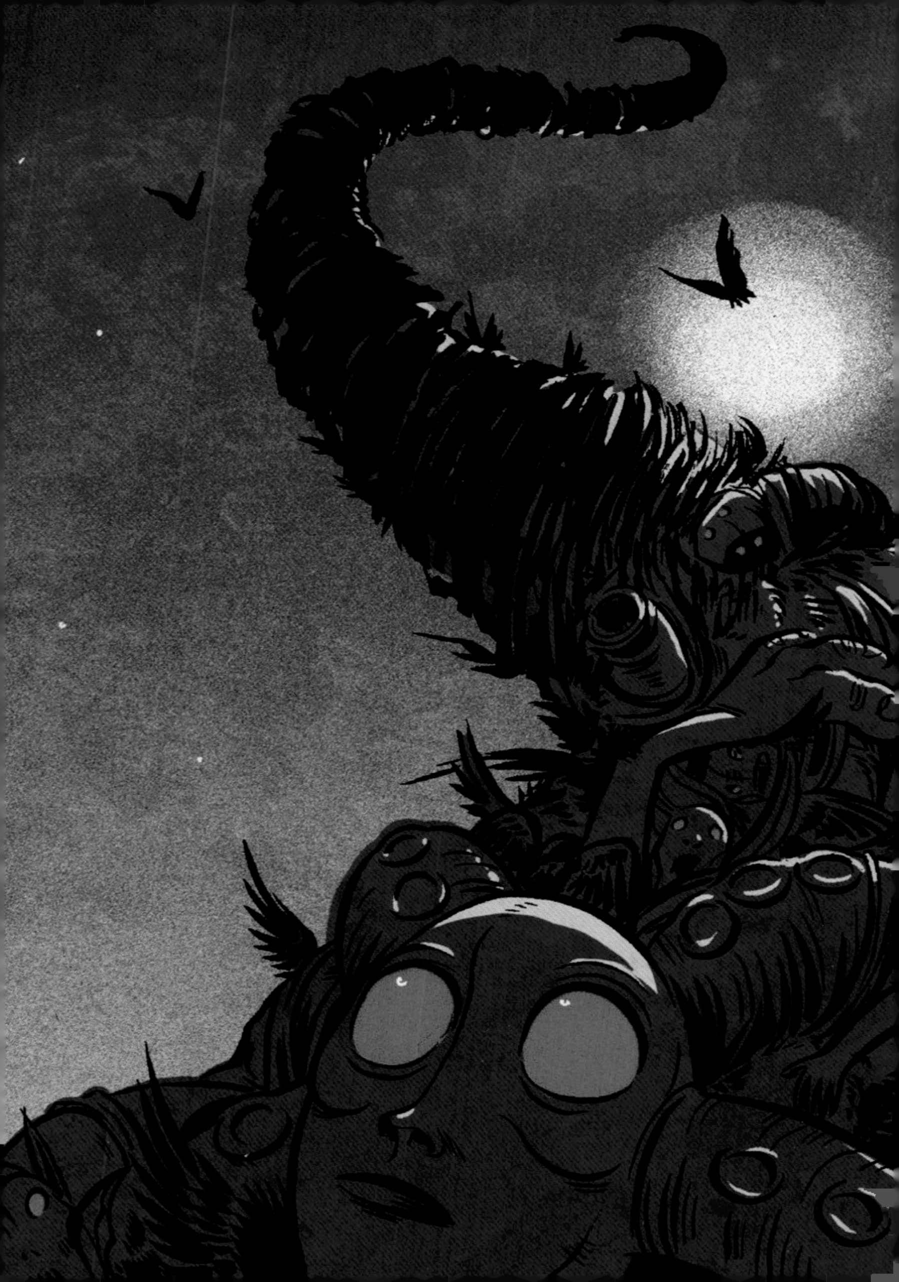

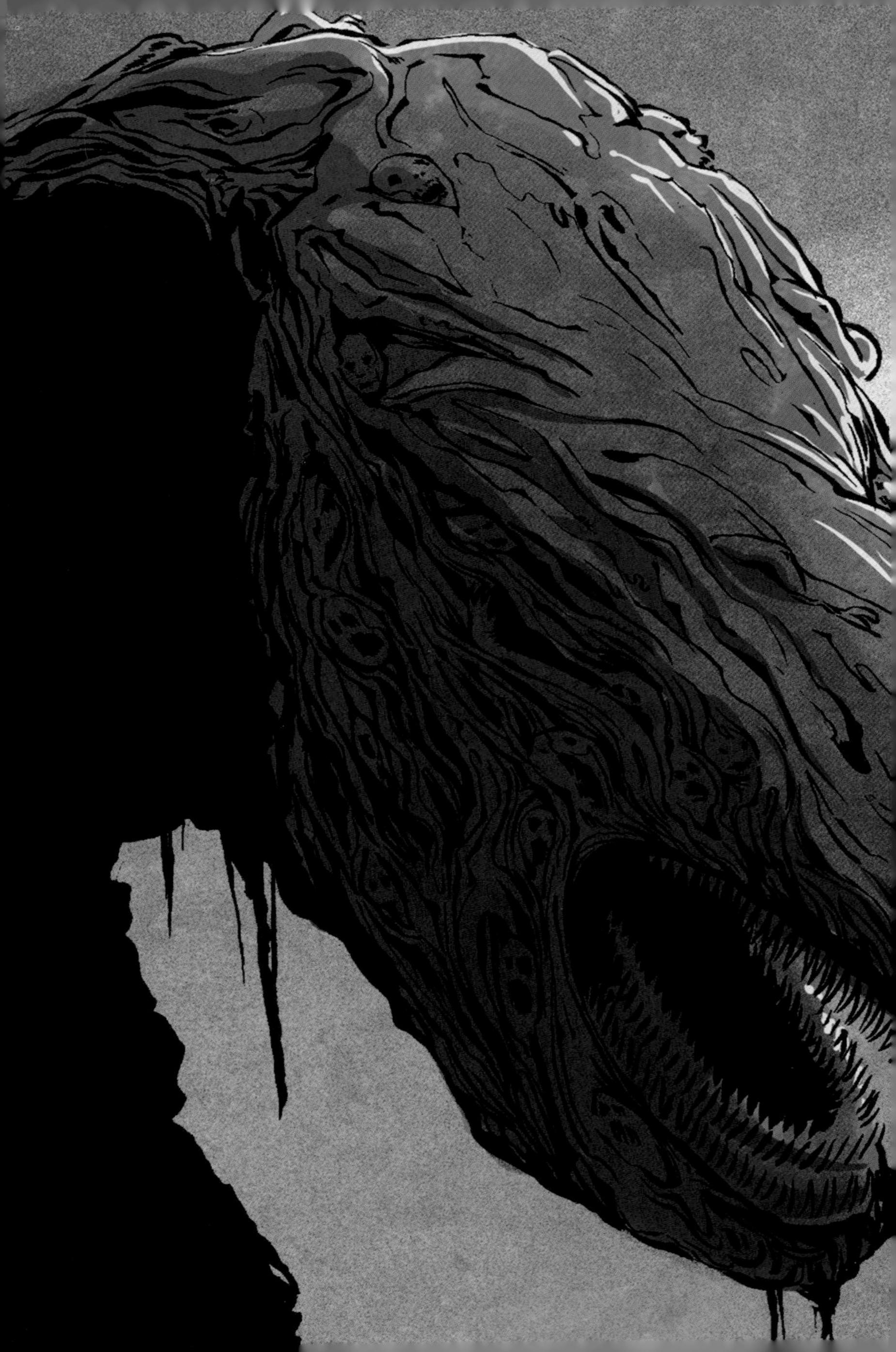

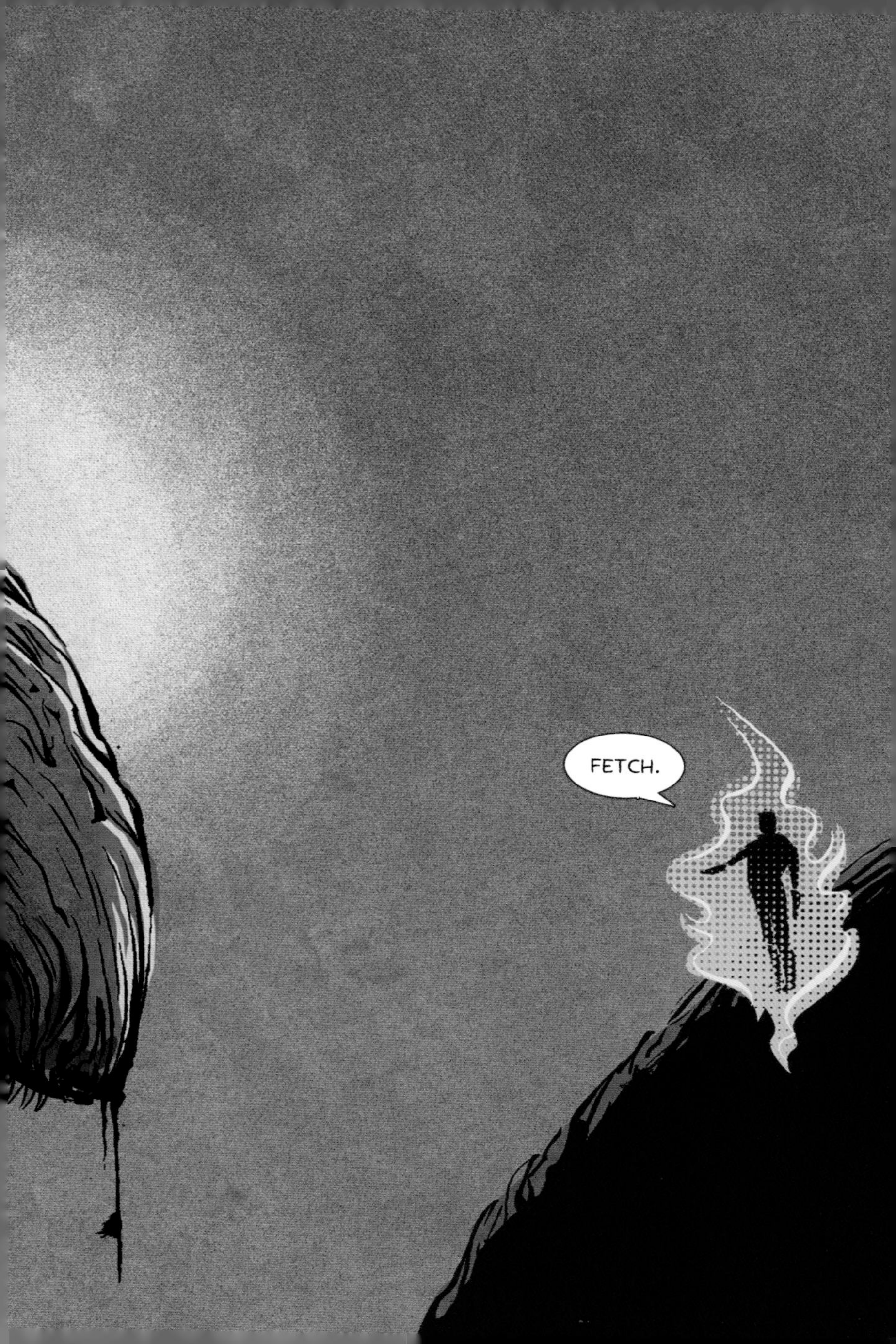
FETCH.

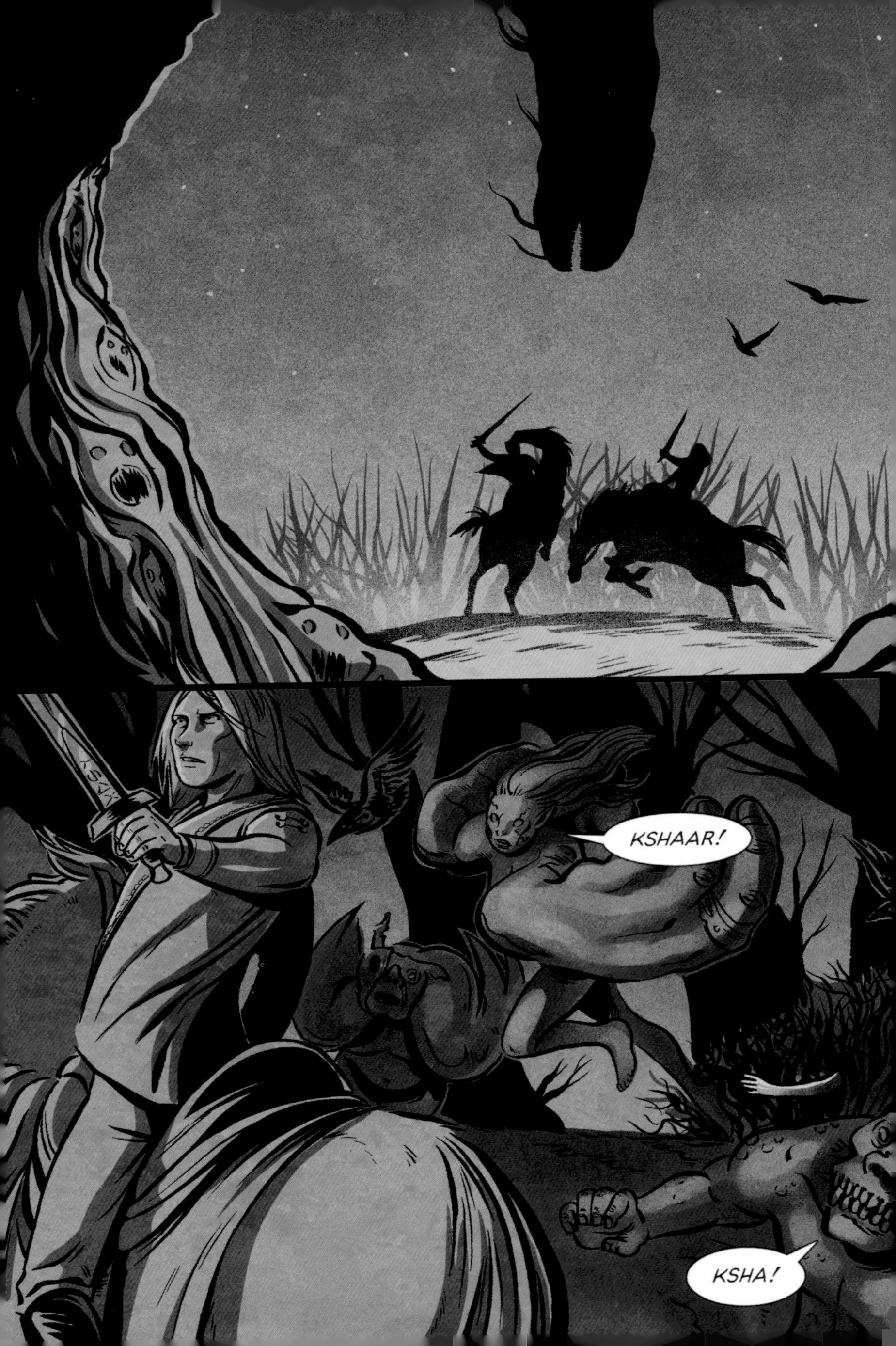
KSHAAR!
KSHA!

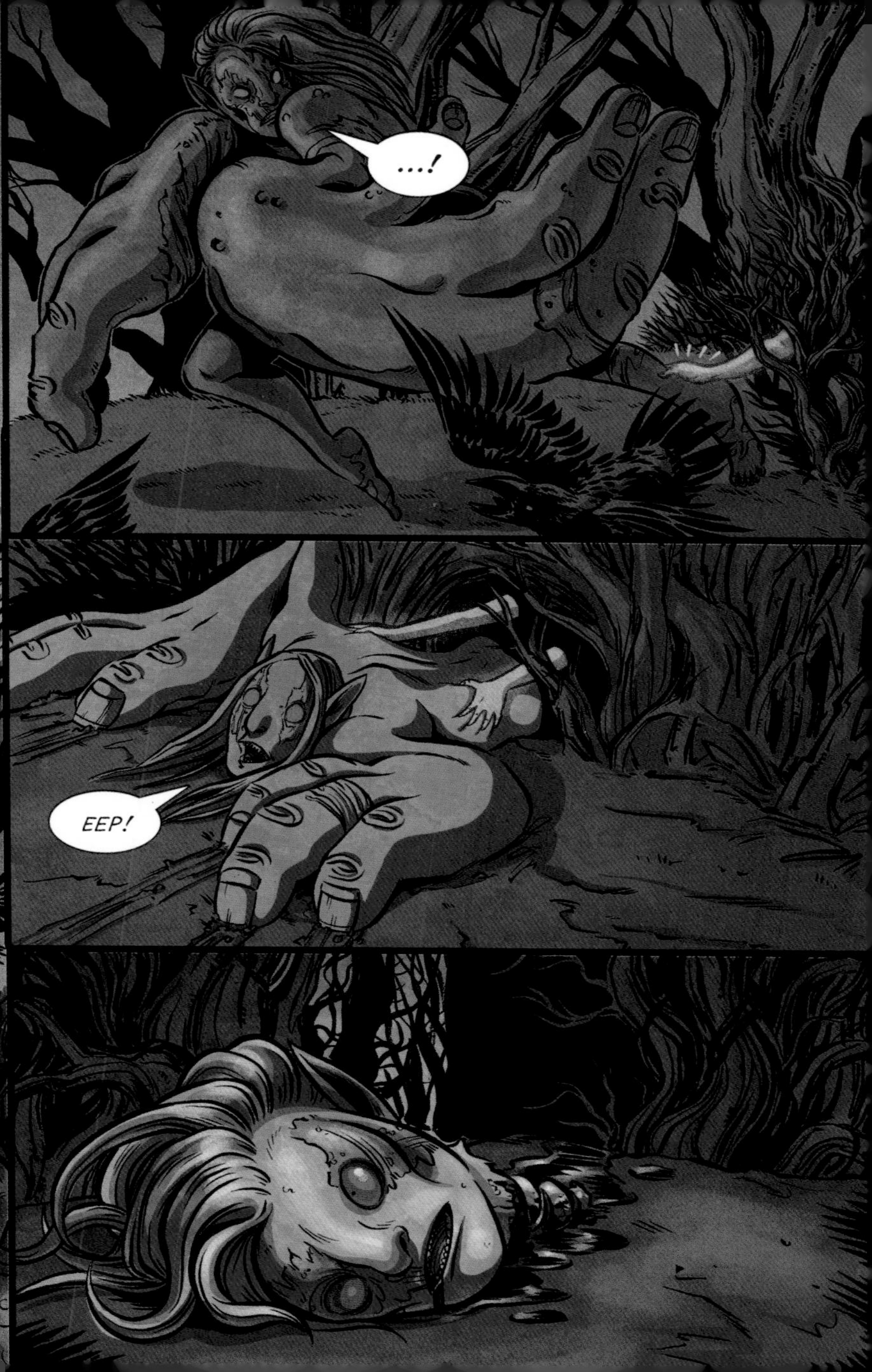

...!
EEP!

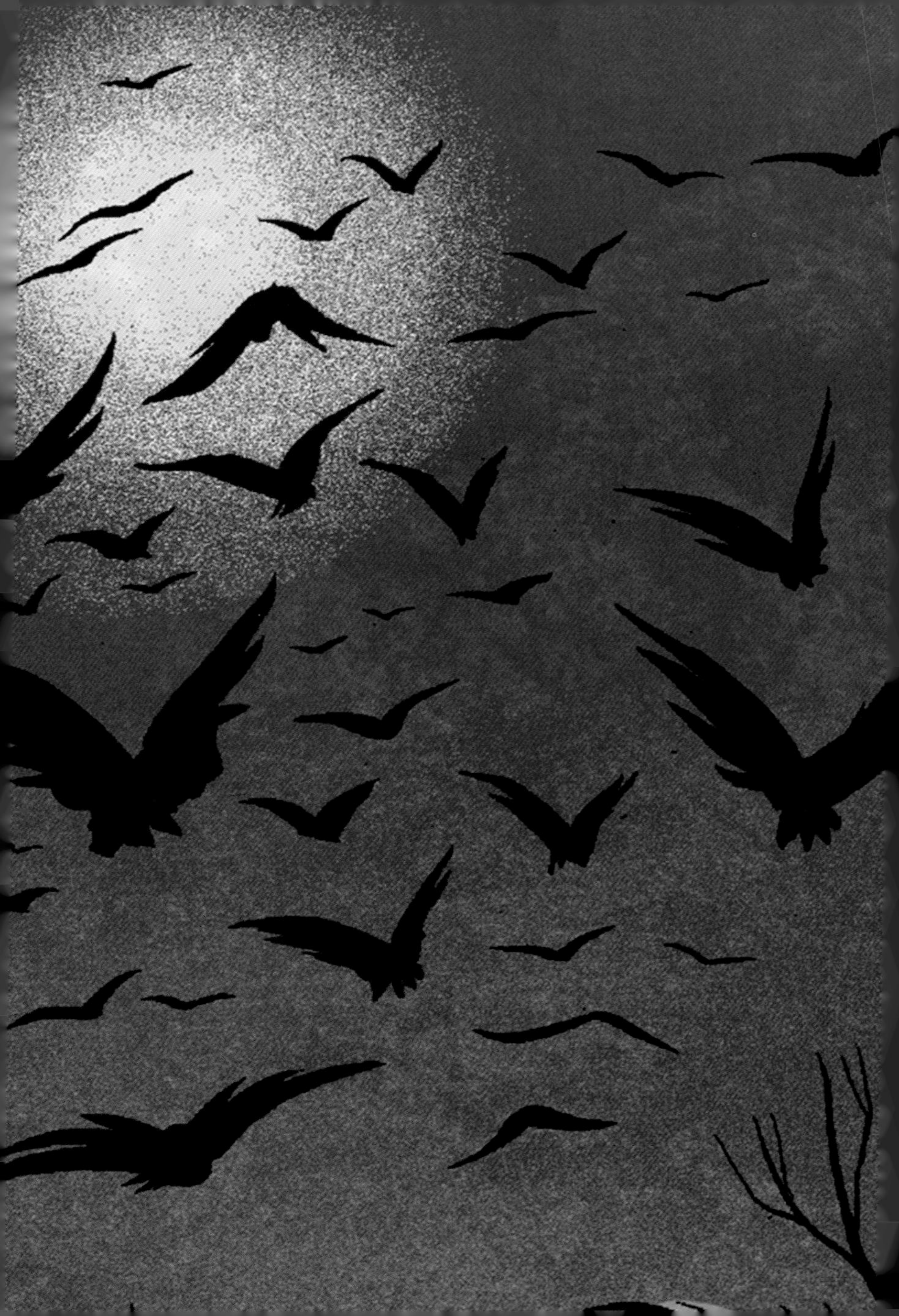

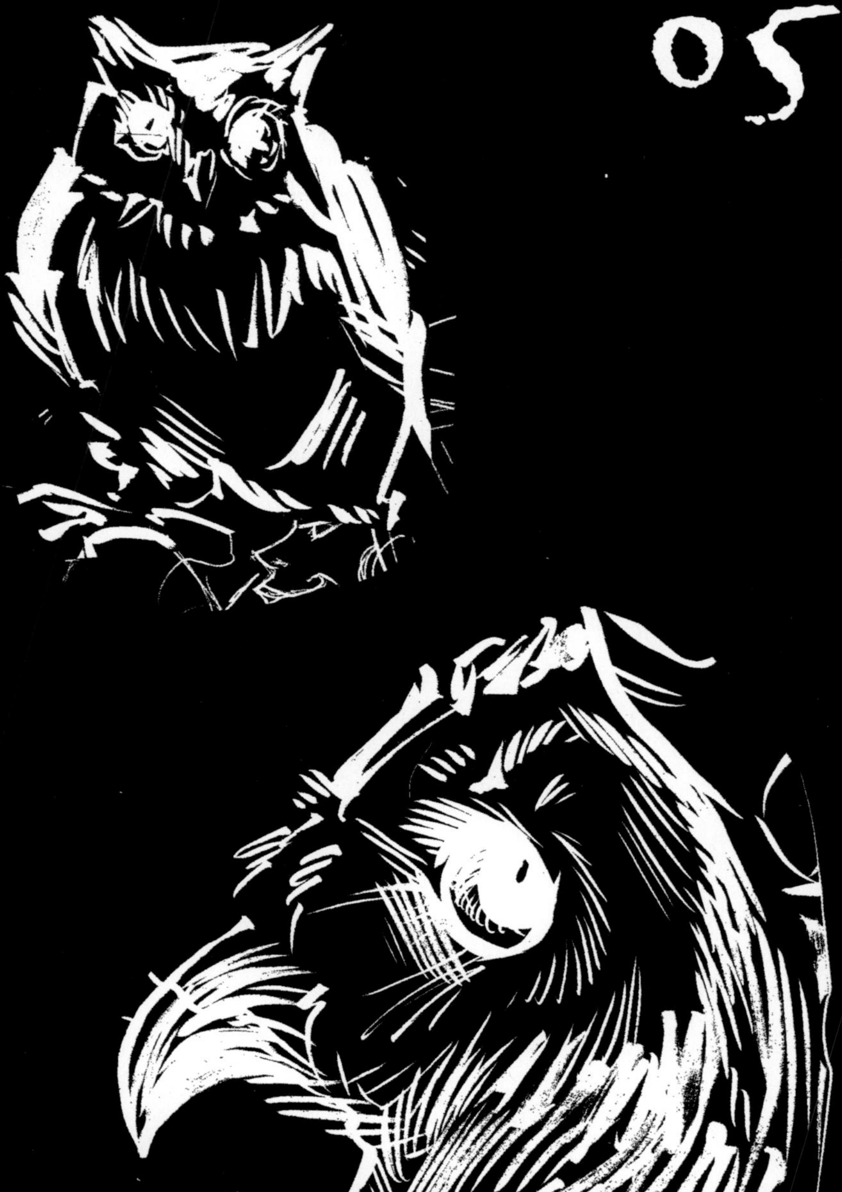
05

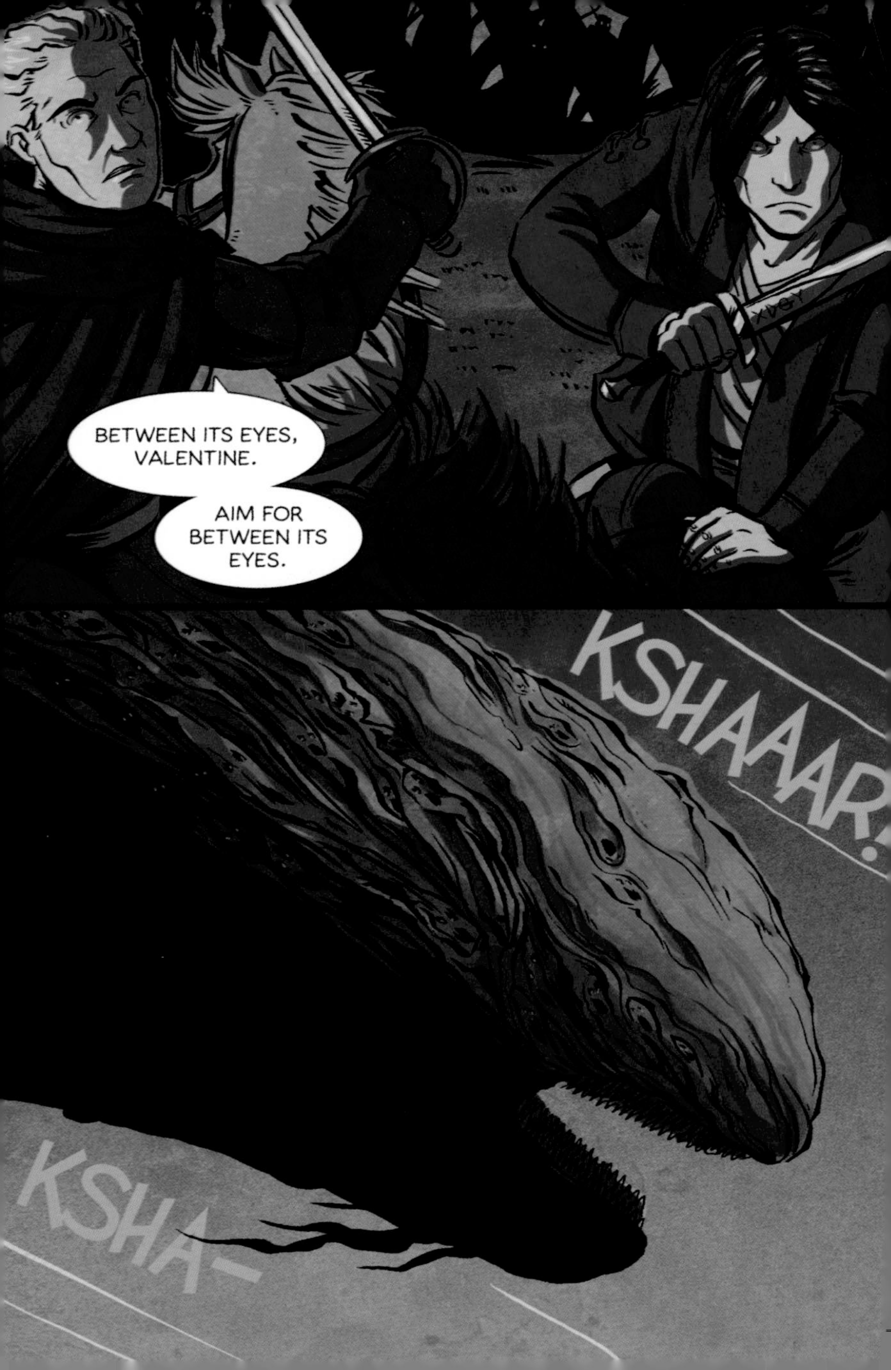
BETWEEN ITS EYES, VALENTINE.
AIM FOR BETWEEN ITS EYES.
KSHAAAR!
KSHA-

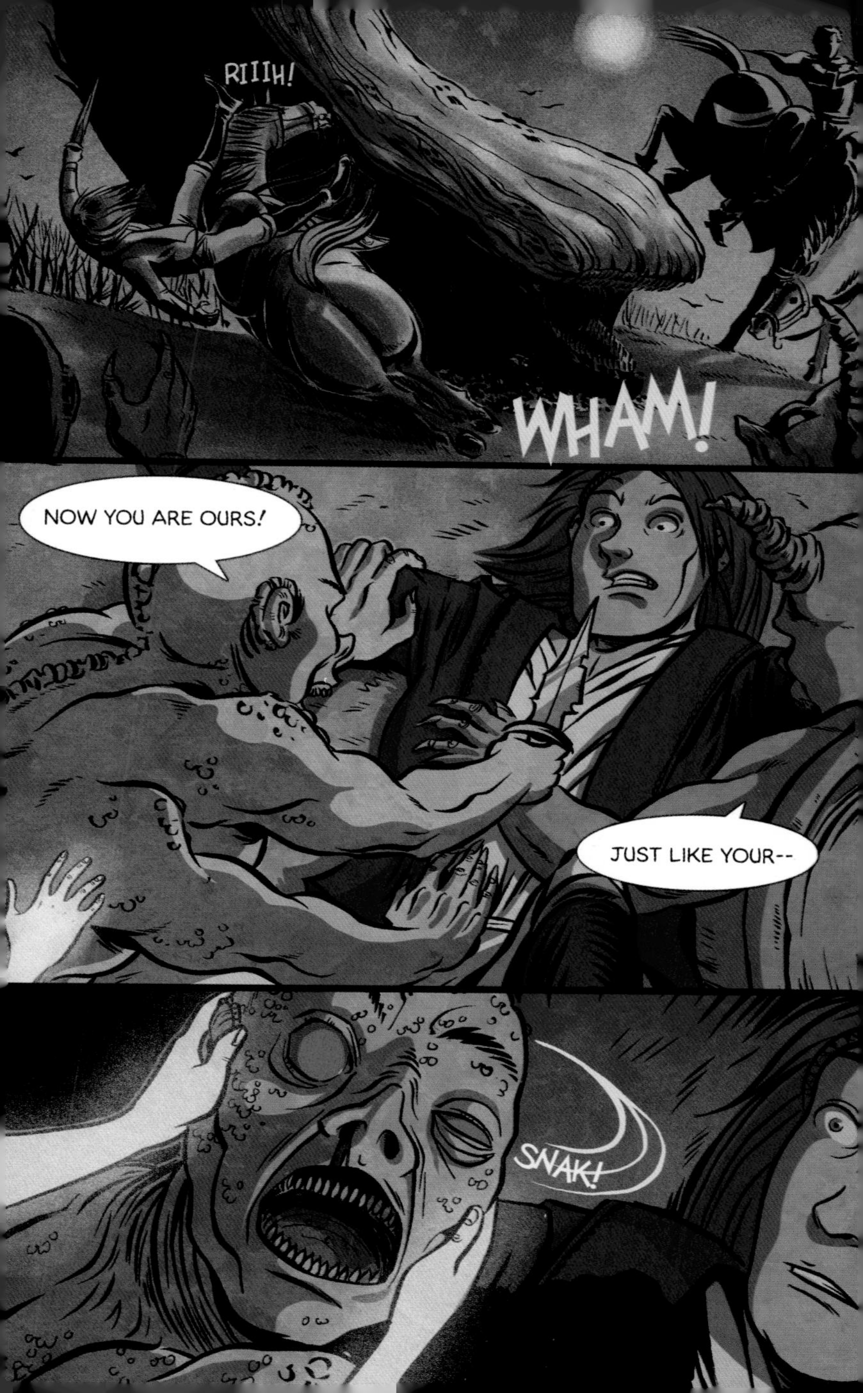
RIIIH!
WHAM!
NOW YOU ARE OURS!
JUST LIKE YOUR--
SNAK!

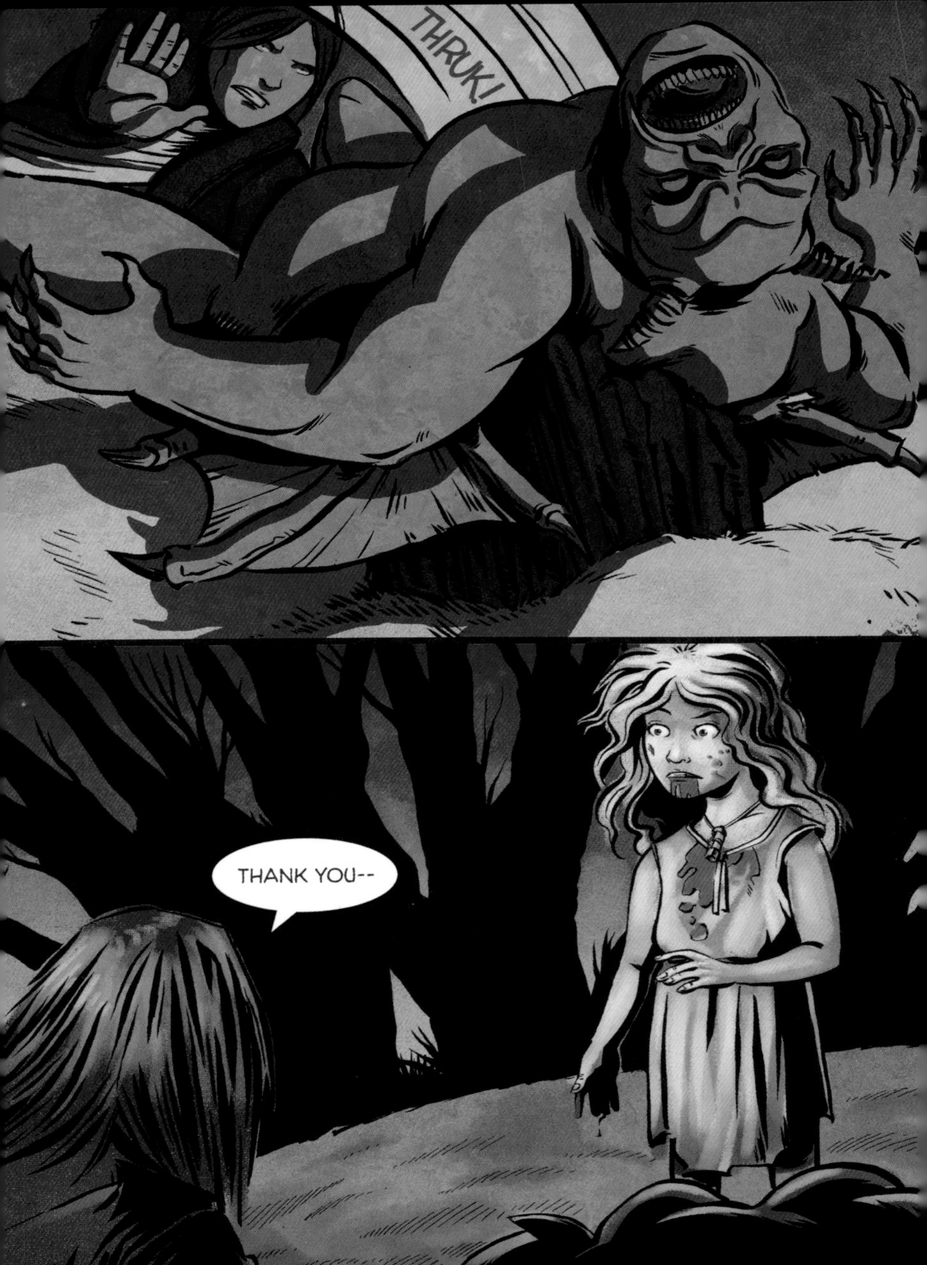
THRUK!
THANK YOU--

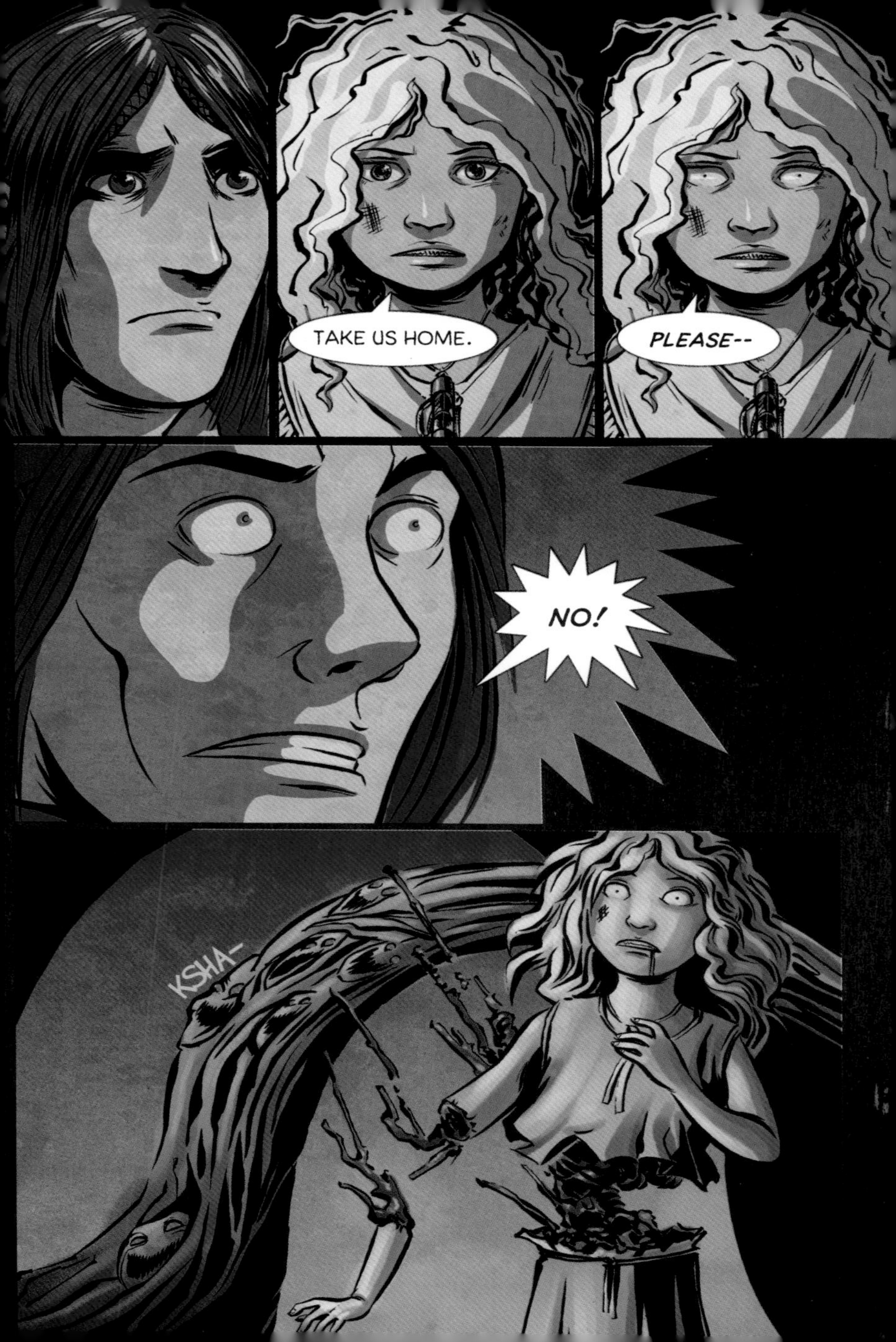
TAKE US HOME.
PLEASE--
NO!
KSHA-

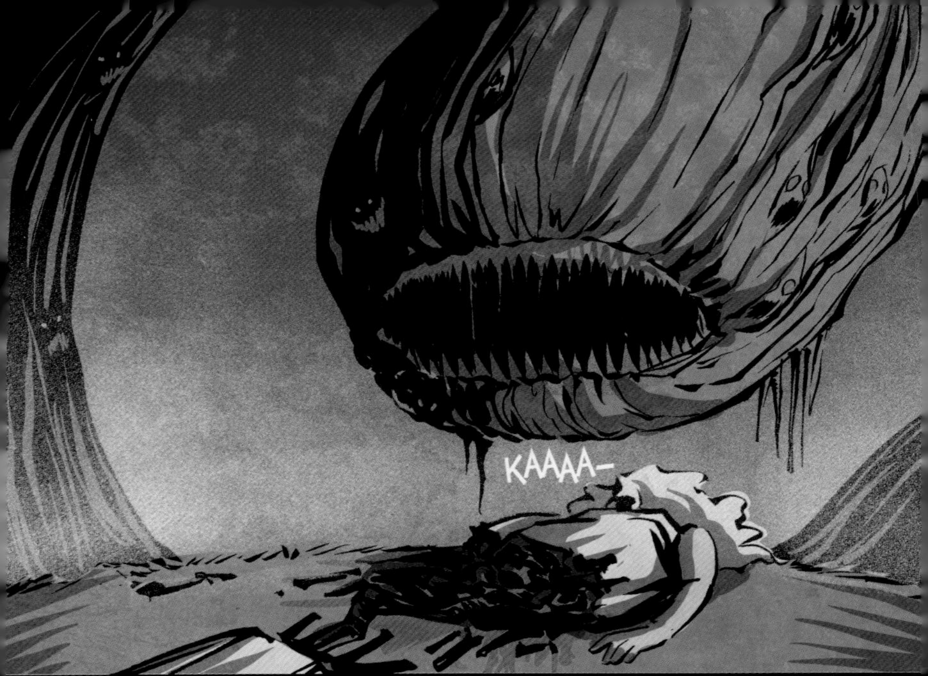
KAAAA-
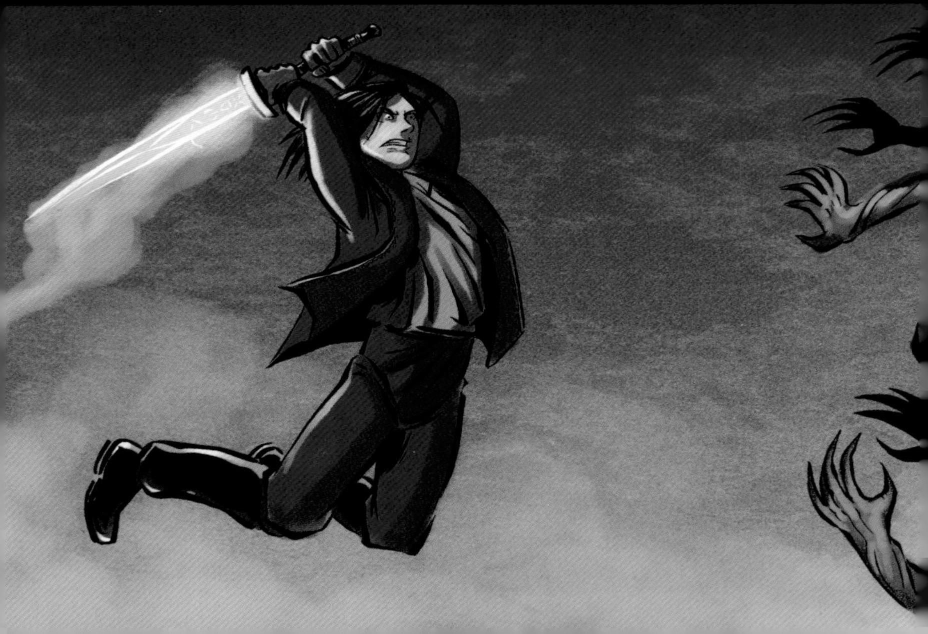

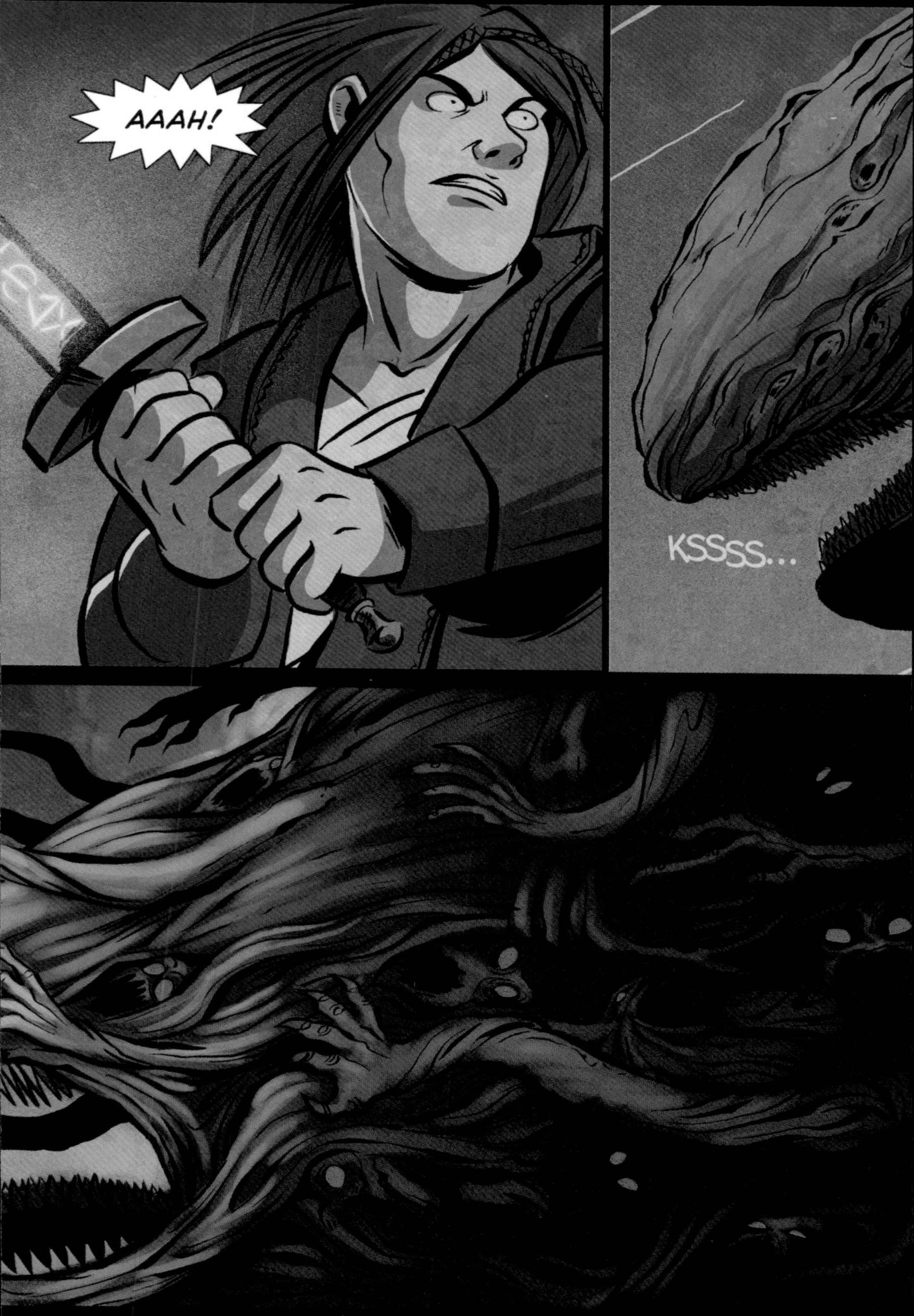
AAAH!
KSSSS...

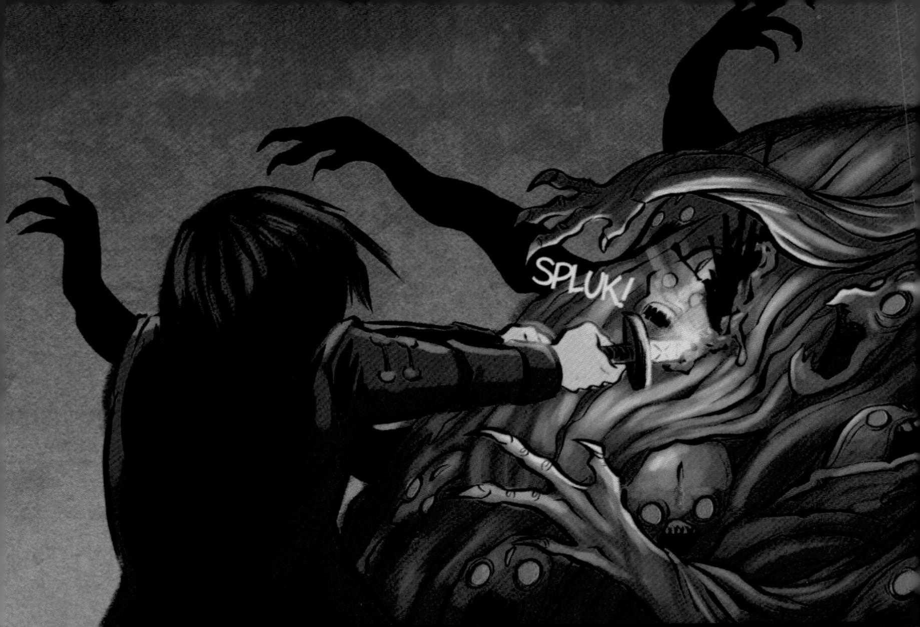
SPLUK!

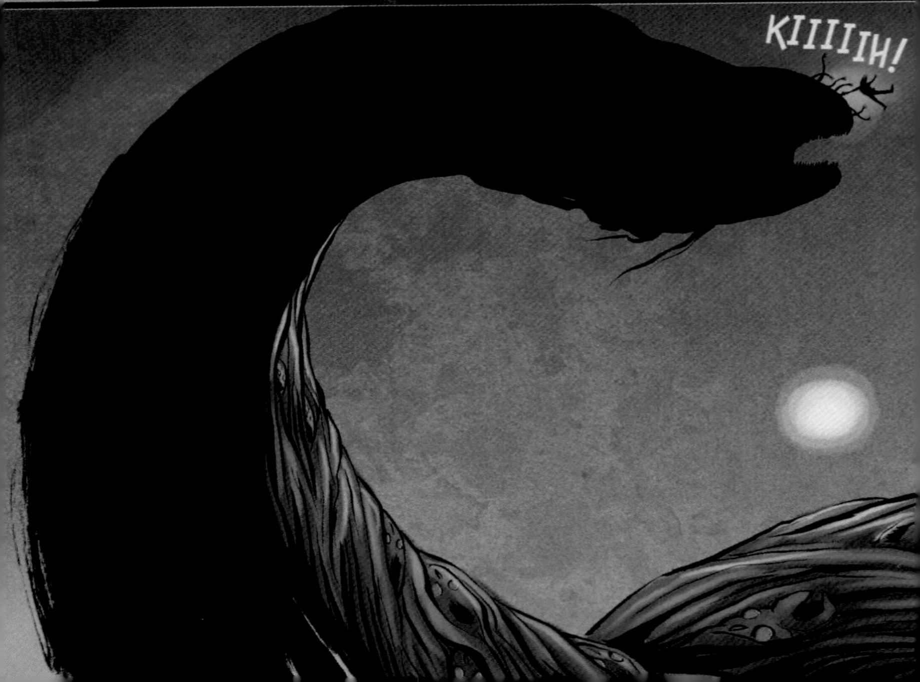
KIIIIIH!

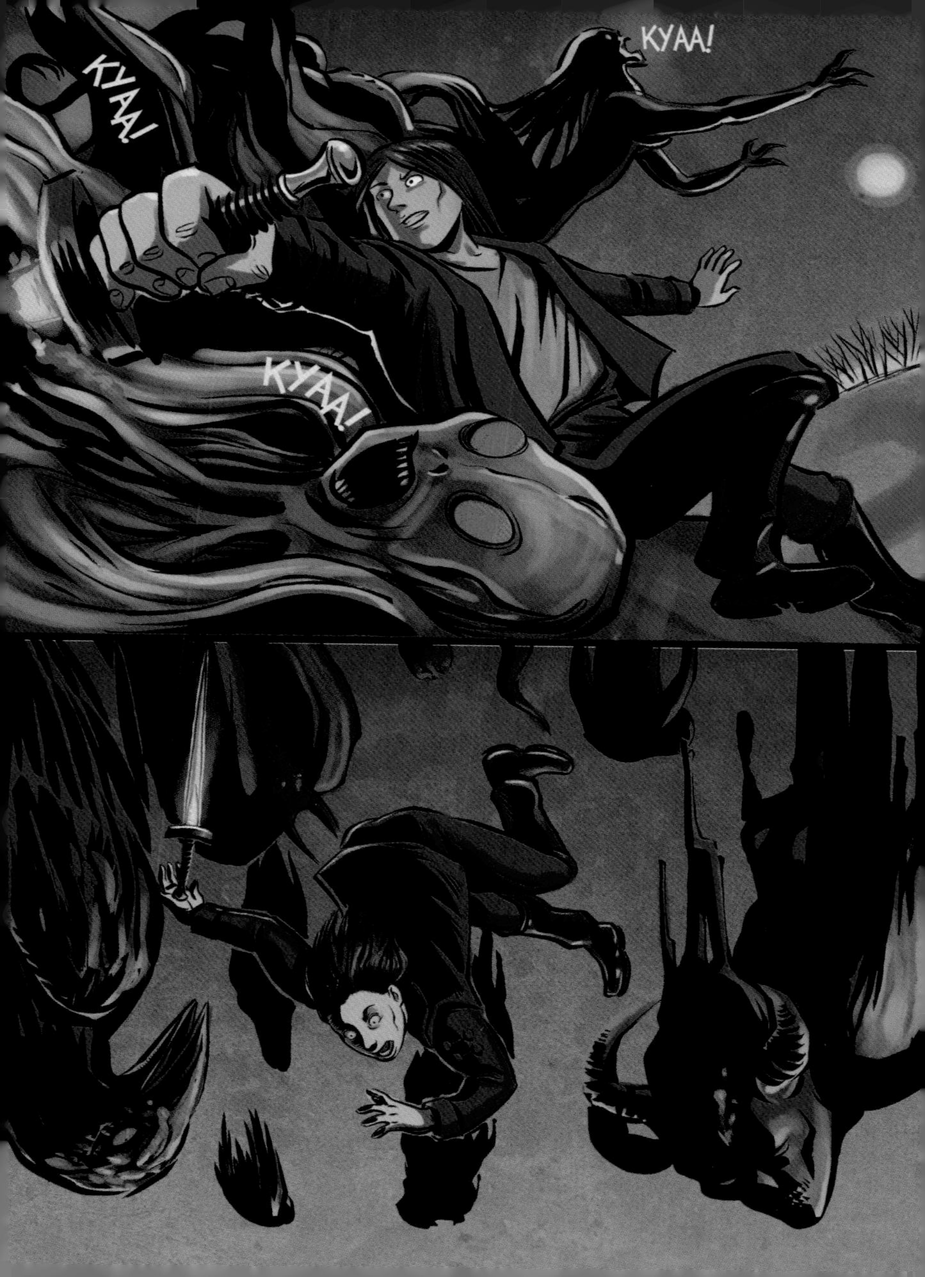
KYAA!
KYAA!
KYAA!

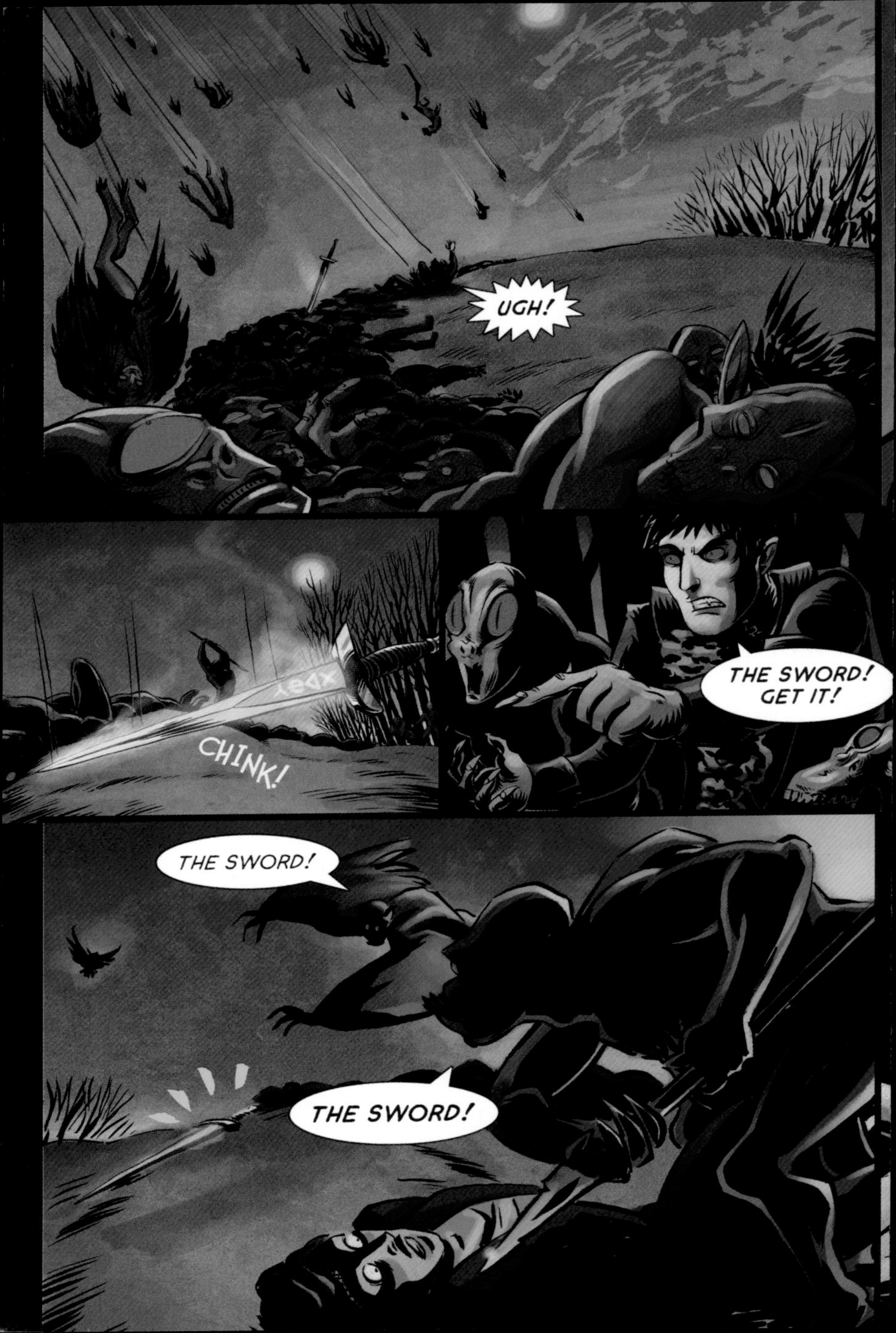
UGH!
CHINK!
THE SWORD! GET IT!
THE SWORD!
THE SWORD!

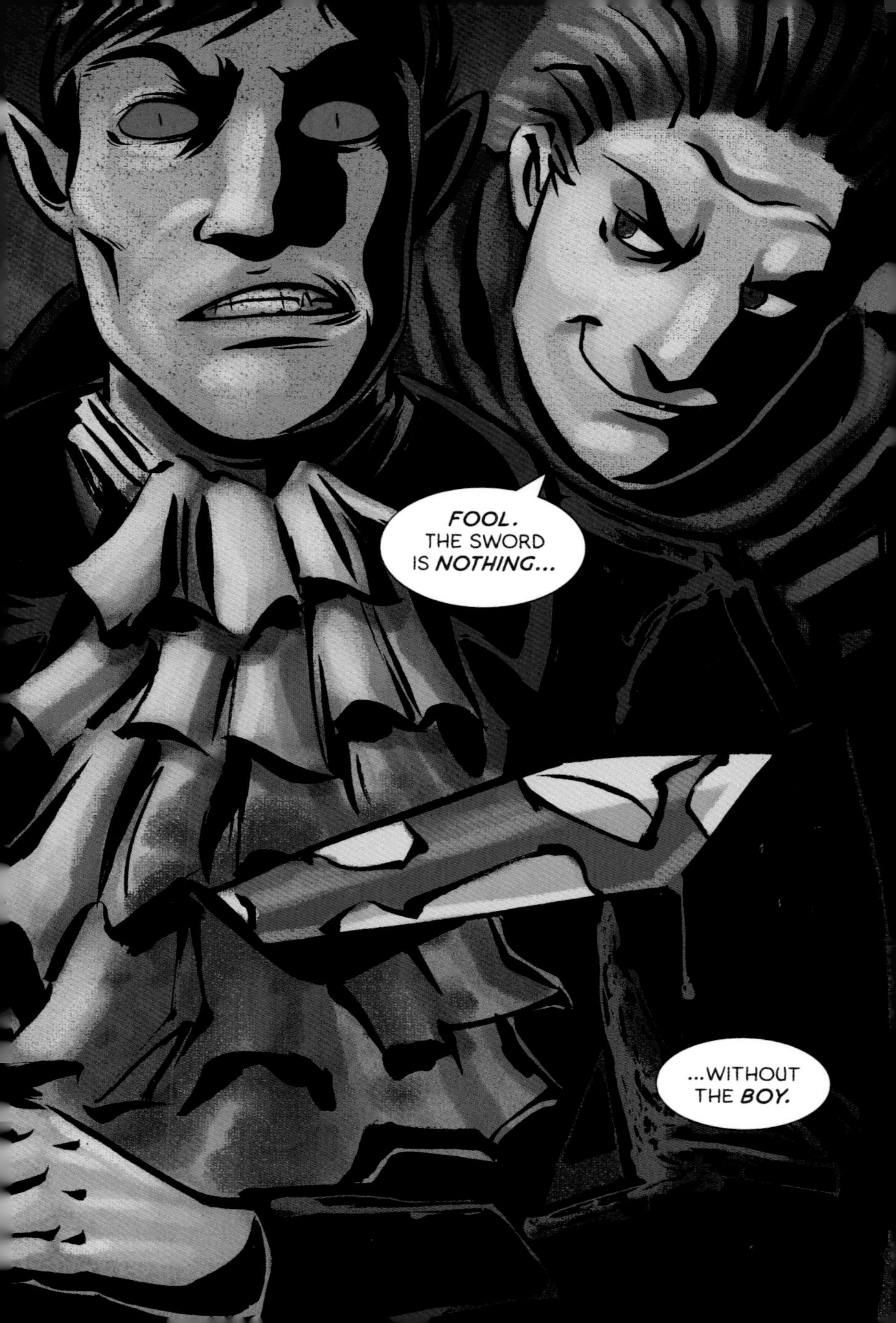
FOOL. THE SWORD IS *NOTHING...*
...WITHOUT THE *BOY.*

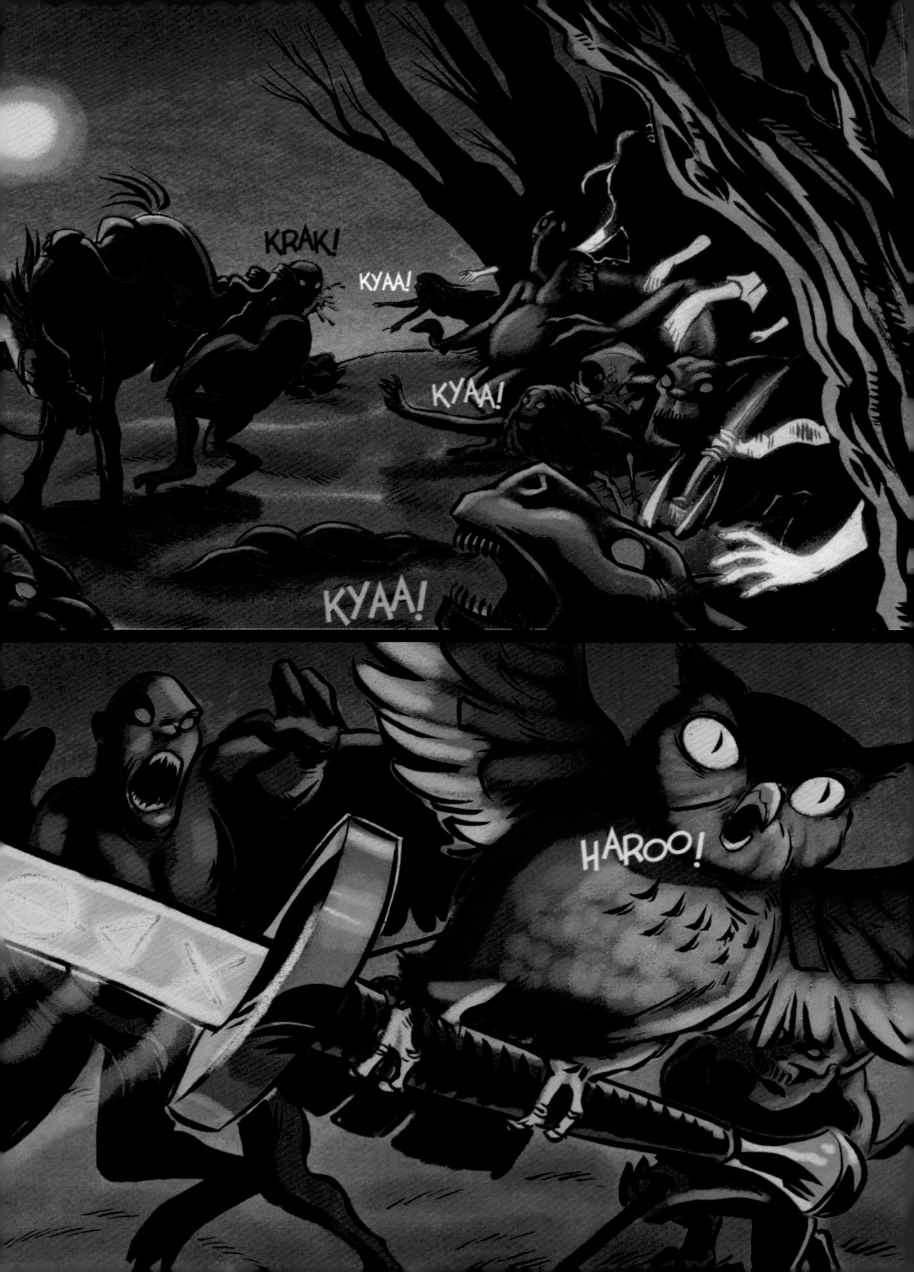
KRAK!
KYAA!
KYAA!
KYAA!
HAROO!

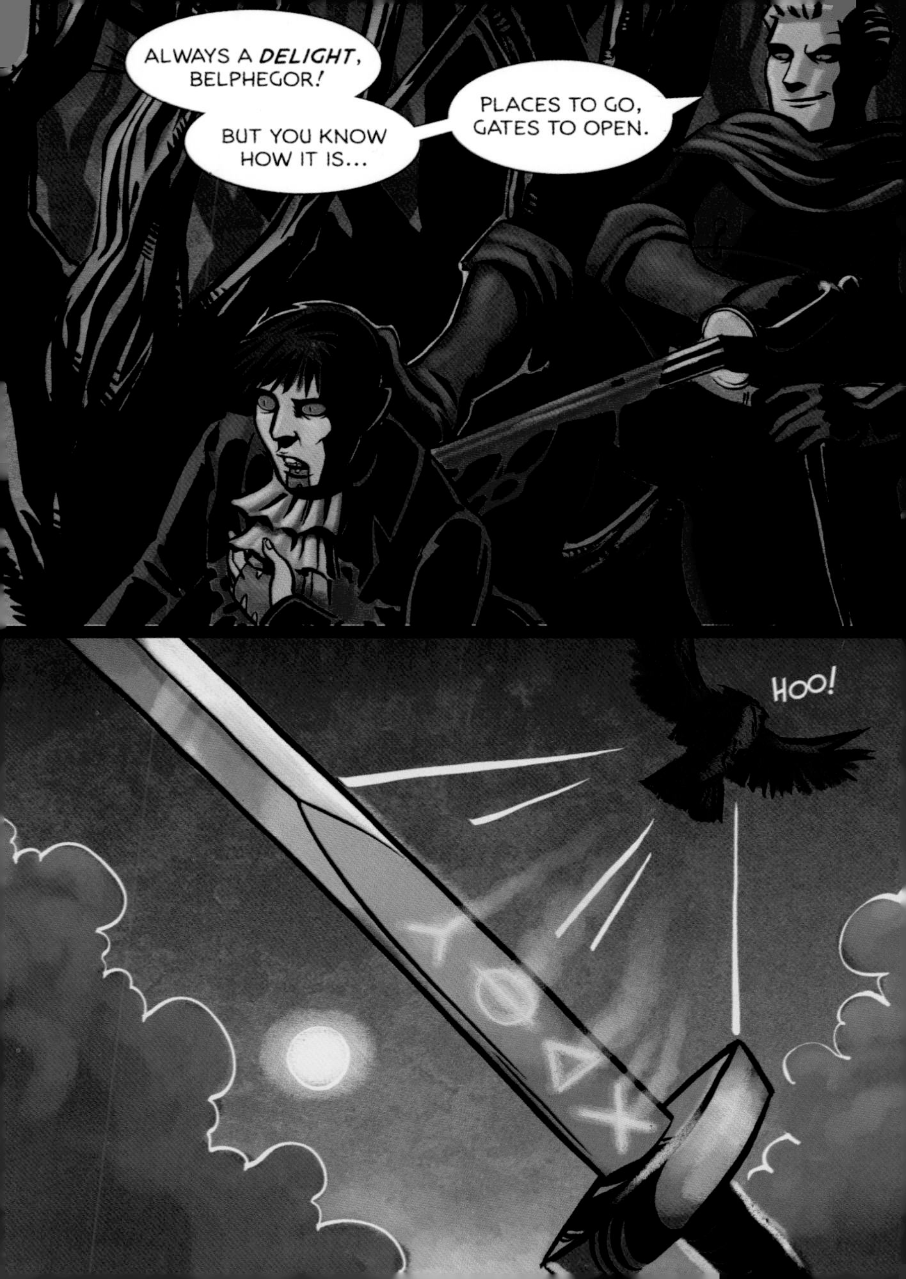
ALWAYS A DELIGHT, BELPHEGOR!
BUT YOU KNOW HOW IT IS...
PLACES TO GO, GATES TO OPEN.
HOO!

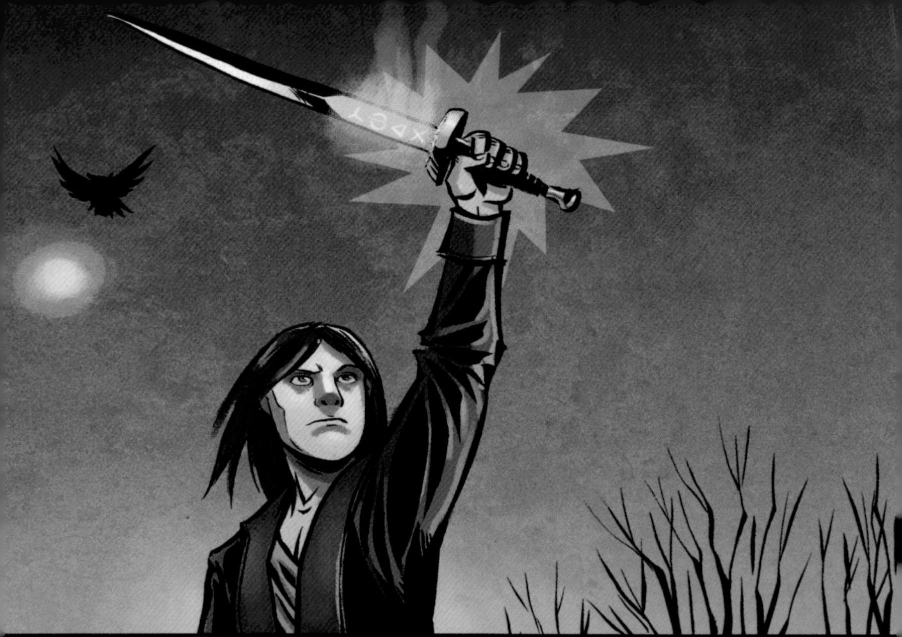

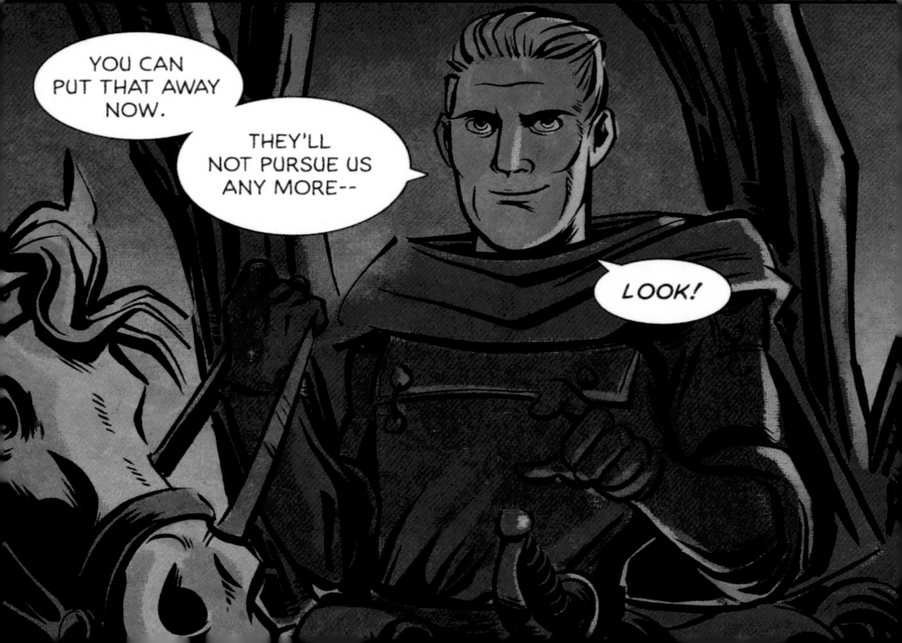
YOU CAN PUT THAT AWAY NOW.
THEY'LL NOT PURSUE US ANY MORE--
LOOK!

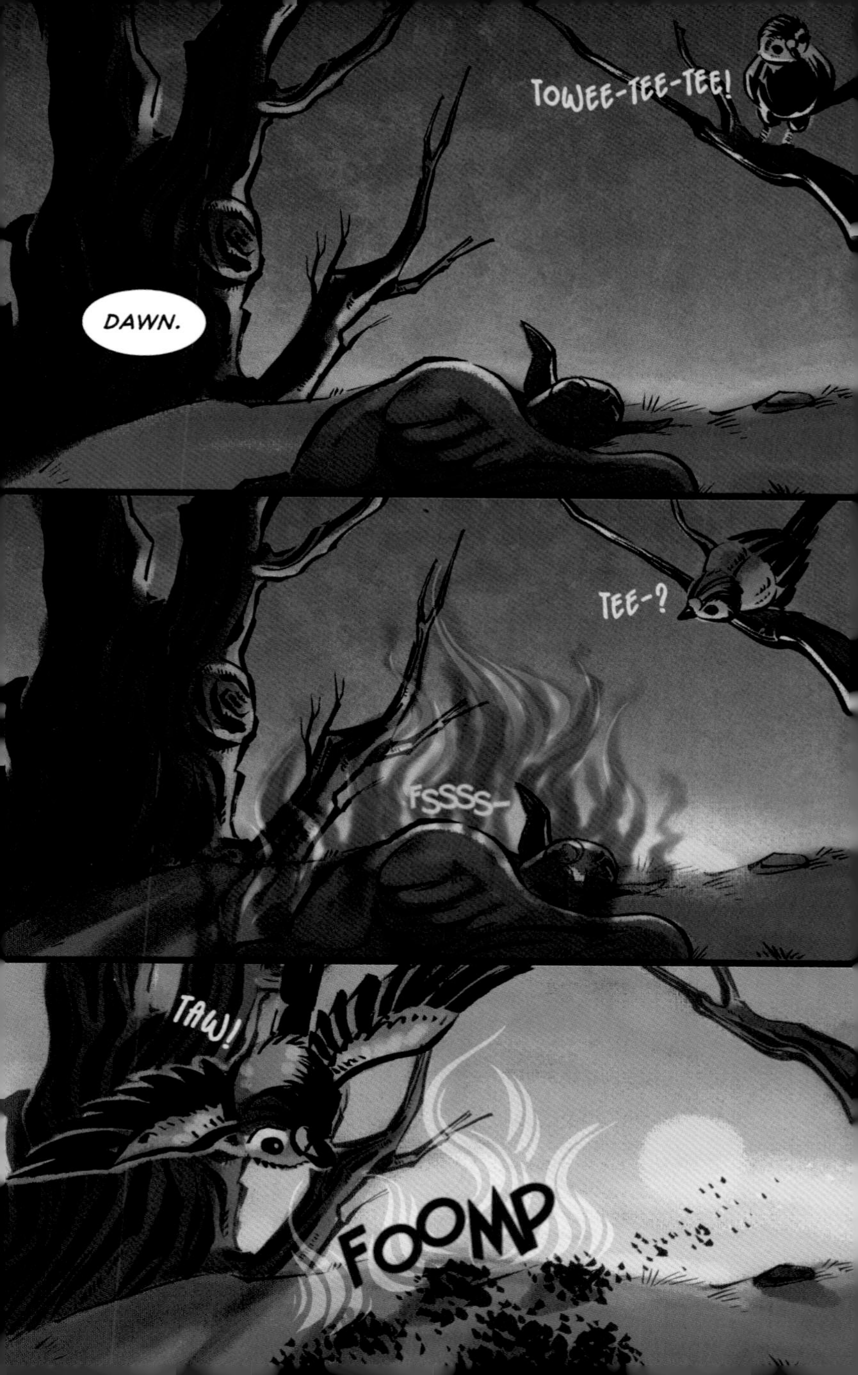
TOWEE-TEE-TEE!
DAWN.
TEE-?
FSSSS-
TAW!
FOOMP

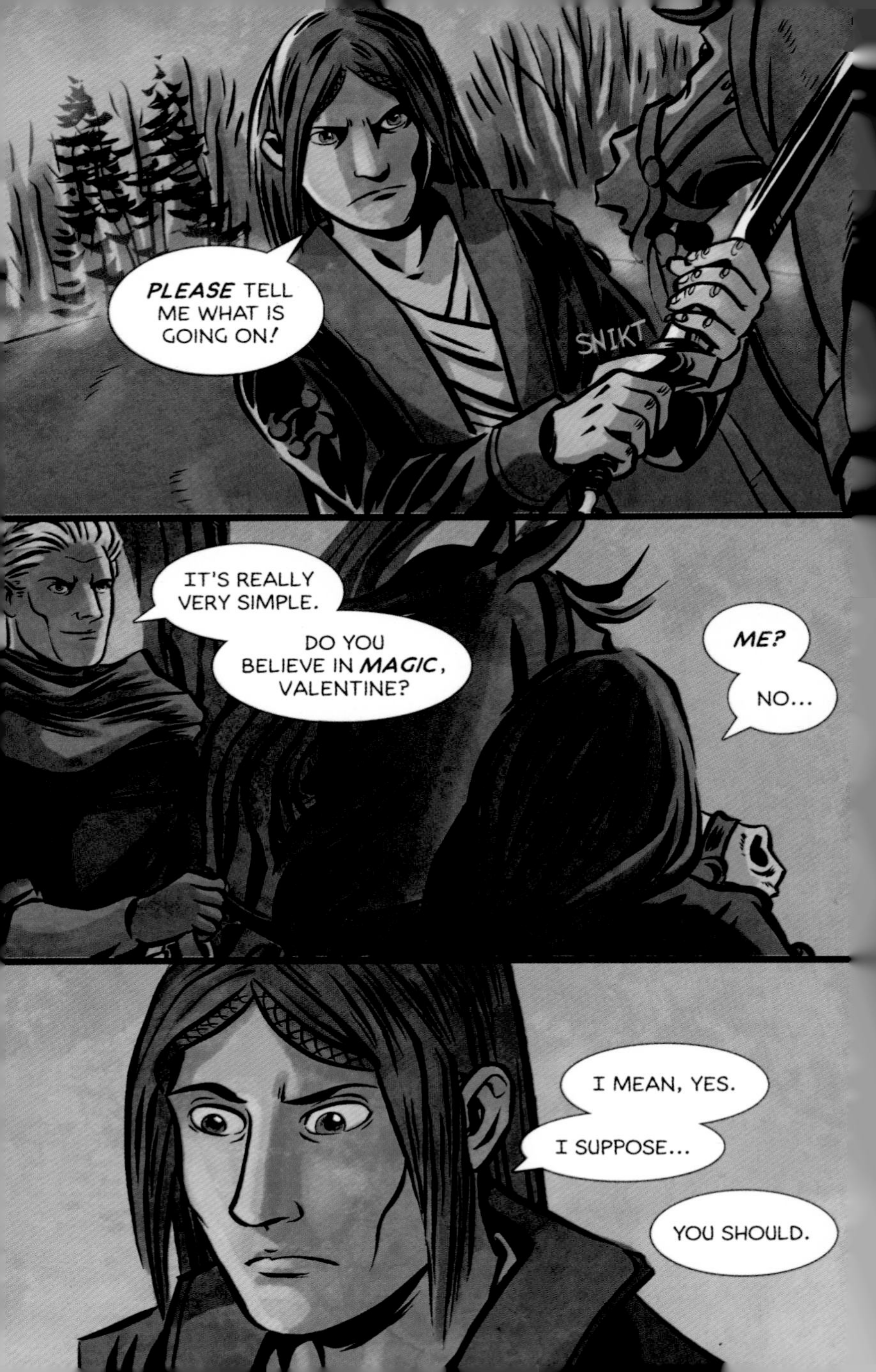
PLEASE TELL ME WHAT IS GOING ON!
SNIKT
IT'S REALLY VERY SIMPLE.
DO YOU BELIEVE IN MAGIC, VALENTINE?
ME?
NO...
I MEAN, YES.
I SUPPOSE...
YOU SHOULD.

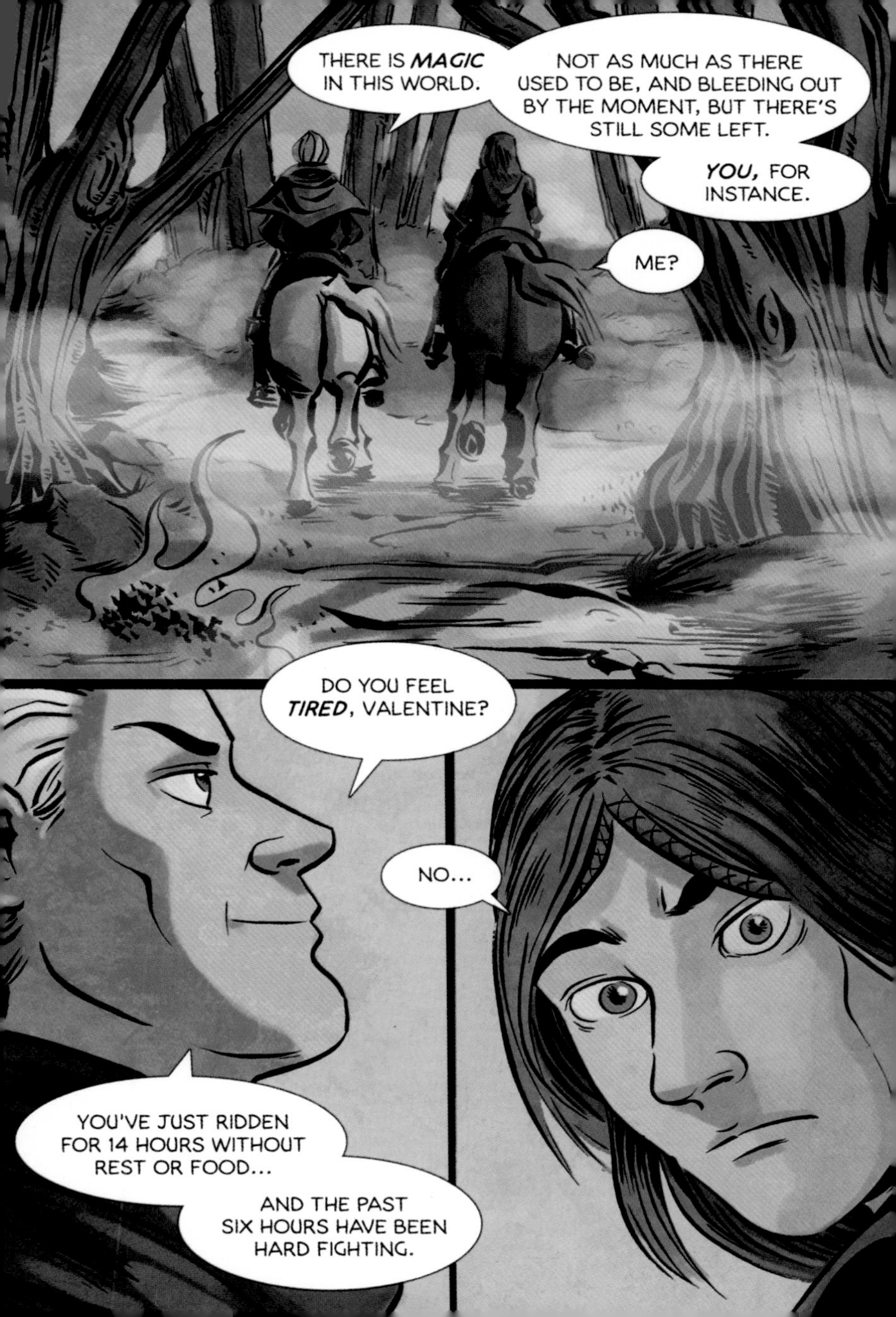
THERE IS *MAGIC* IN THIS WORLD.
NOT AS MUCH AS THERE USED TO BE, AND BLEEDING OUT BY THE MOMENT, BUT THERE'S STILL SOME LEFT.
YOU, FOR INSTANCE.
ME?
DO YOU FEEL *TIRED*, VALENTINE?
NO...
YOU'VE JUST RIDDEN FOR 14 HOURS WITHOUT REST OR FOOD...
AND THE PAST SIX HOURS HAVE BEEN HARD FIGHTING.

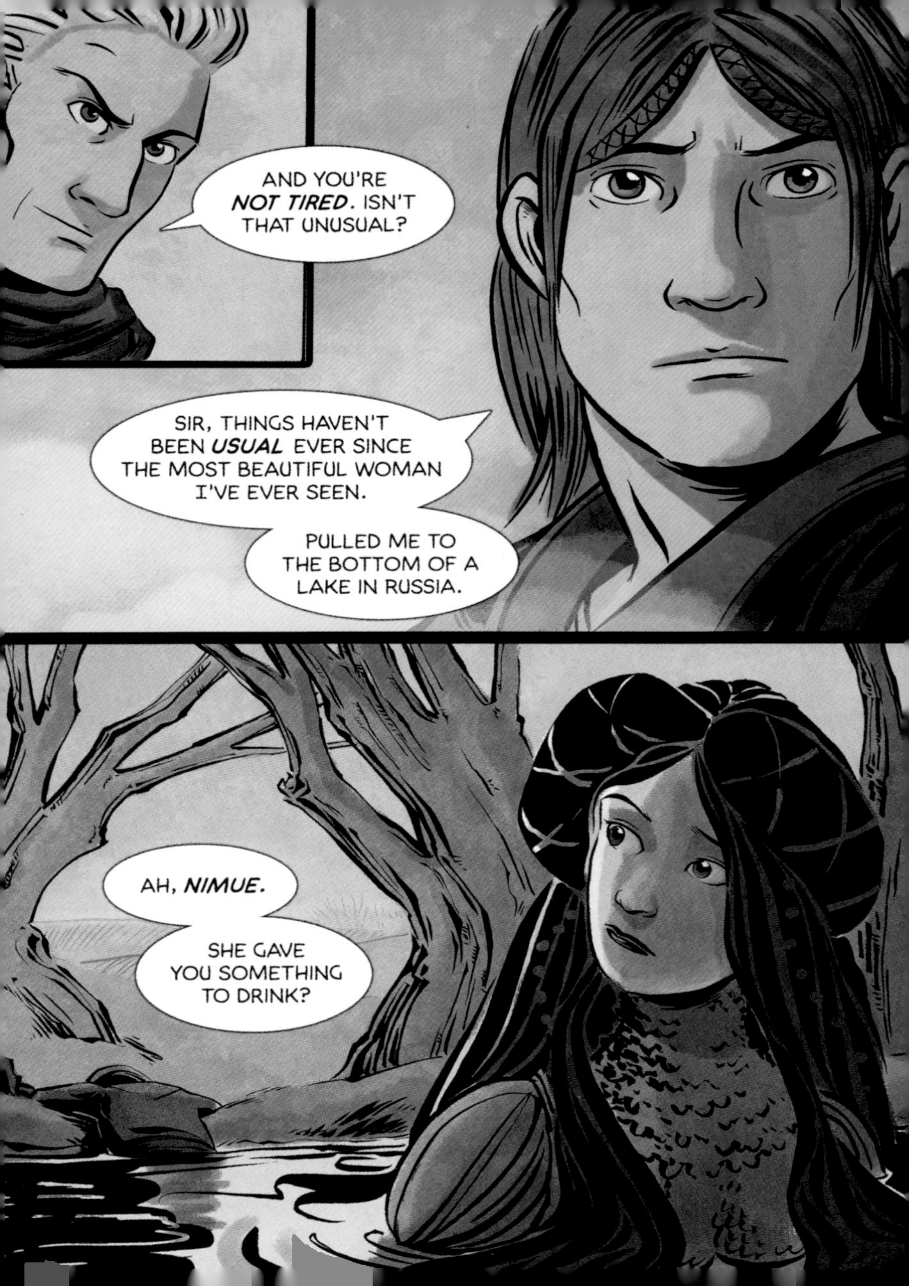
AND YOU'RE *NOT TIRED*. ISN'T THAT UNUSUAL?
SIR, THINGS HAVEN'T BEEN *USUAL* EVER SINCE THE MOST BEAUTIFUL WOMAN I'VE EVER SEEN.
PULLED ME TO THE BOTTOM OF A LAKE IN RUSSIA.
AH, *NIMUE.*
SHE GAVE YOU SOMETHING TO DRINK?

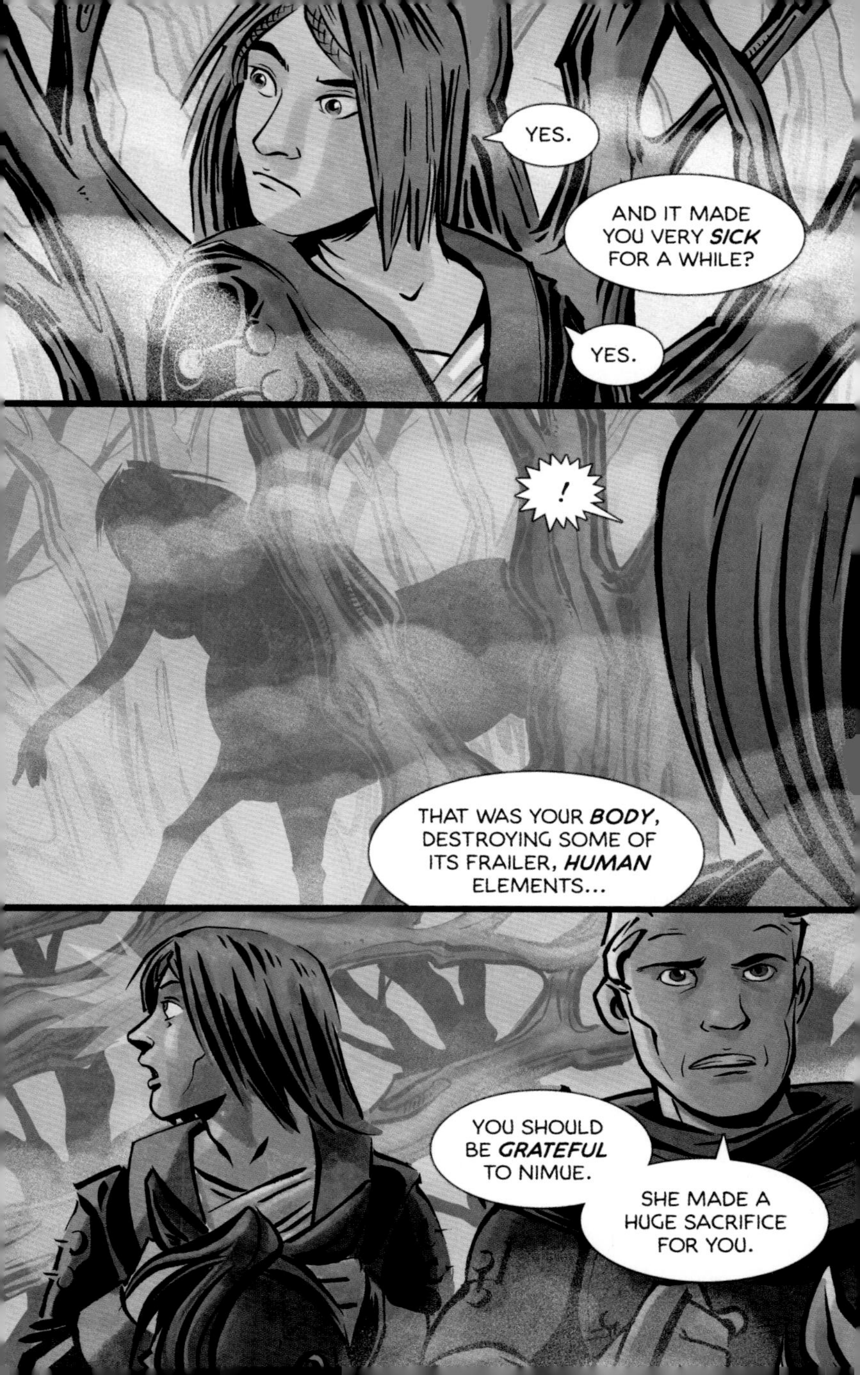
YES.
AND IT MADE YOU VERY *SICK* FOR A WHILE?
YES.
!
THAT WAS YOUR *BODY*, DESTROYING SOME OF ITS FRAILER, *HUMAN* ELEMENTS...
YOU SHOULD BE *GRATEFUL* TO NIMUE.
SHE MADE A HUGE SACRIFICE FOR YOU.

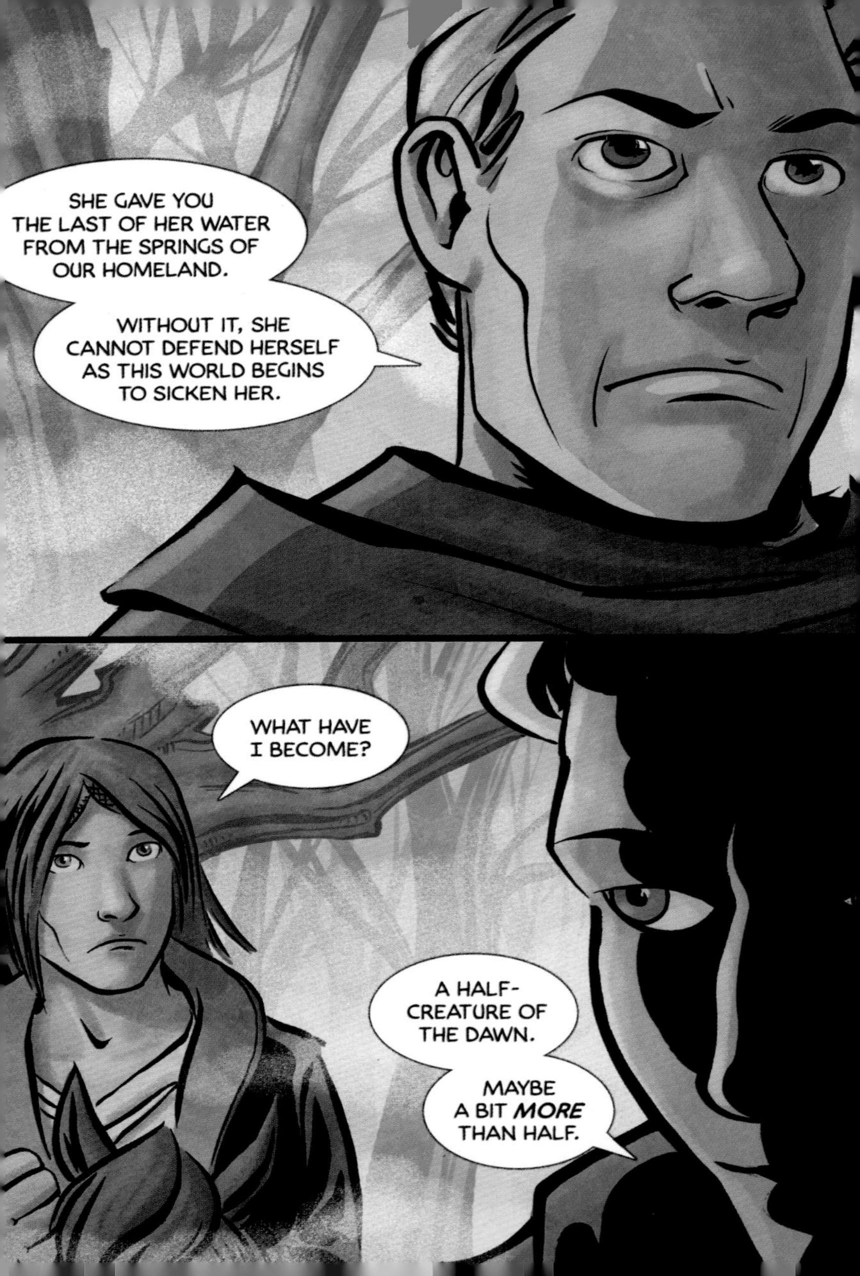
SHE GAVE YOU THE LAST OF HER WATER FROM THE SPRINGS OF OUR HOMELAND.
WITHOUT IT, SHE CANNOT DEFEND HERSELF AS THIS WORLD BEGINS TO SICKEN HER.
WHAT HAVE I BECOME?
A HALF-CREATURE OF THE DAWN.
MAYBE A BIT *MORE* THAN HALF.

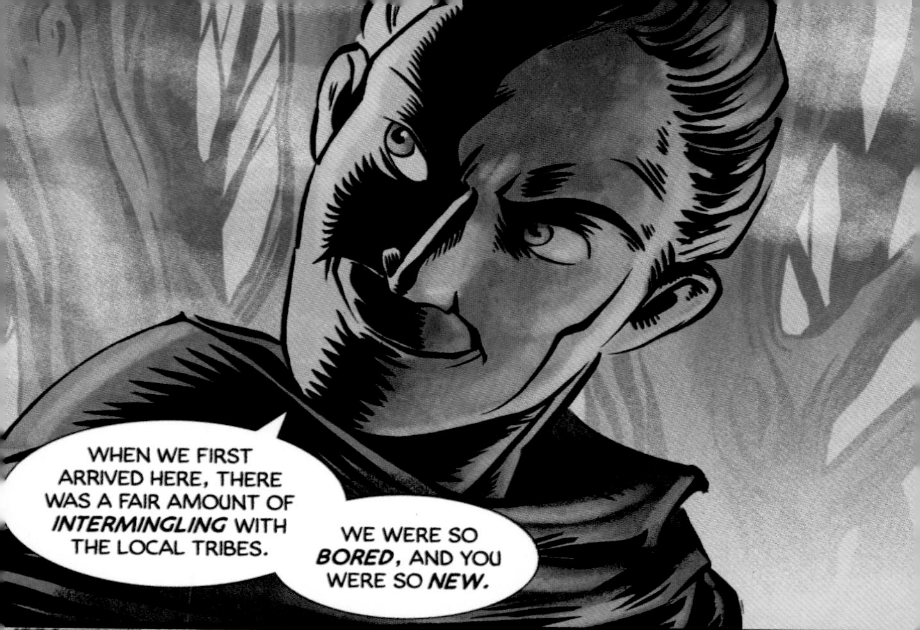
WHEN WE FIRST ARRIVED HERE, THERE WAS A FAIR AMOUNT OF *INTERMINGLING* WITH THE LOCAL TRIBES.
WE WERE SO *BORED*, AND YOU WERE SO *NEW.*

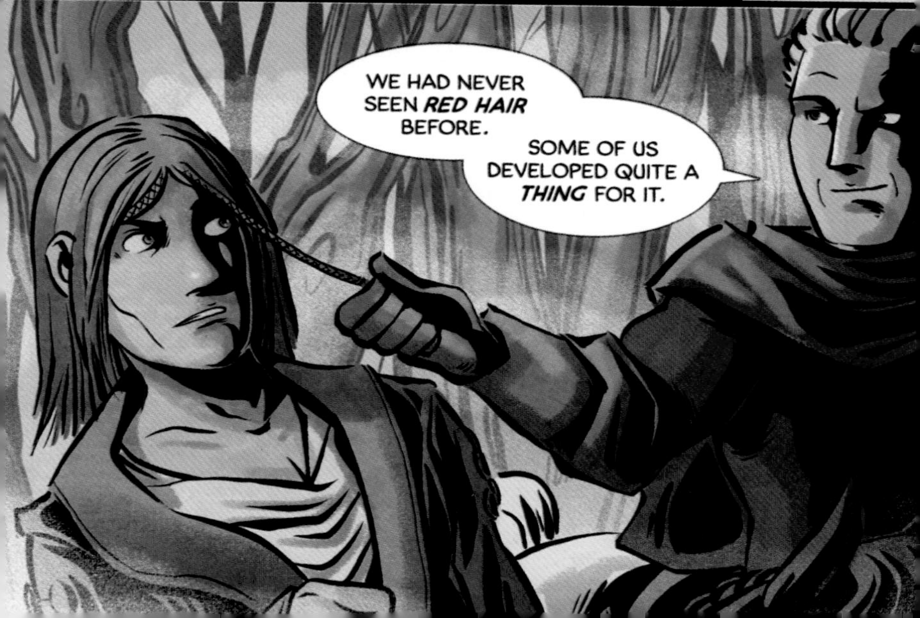
WE HAD NEVER SEEN *RED HAIR* BEFORE.
SOME OF US DEVELOPED QUITE A *THING* FOR IT.

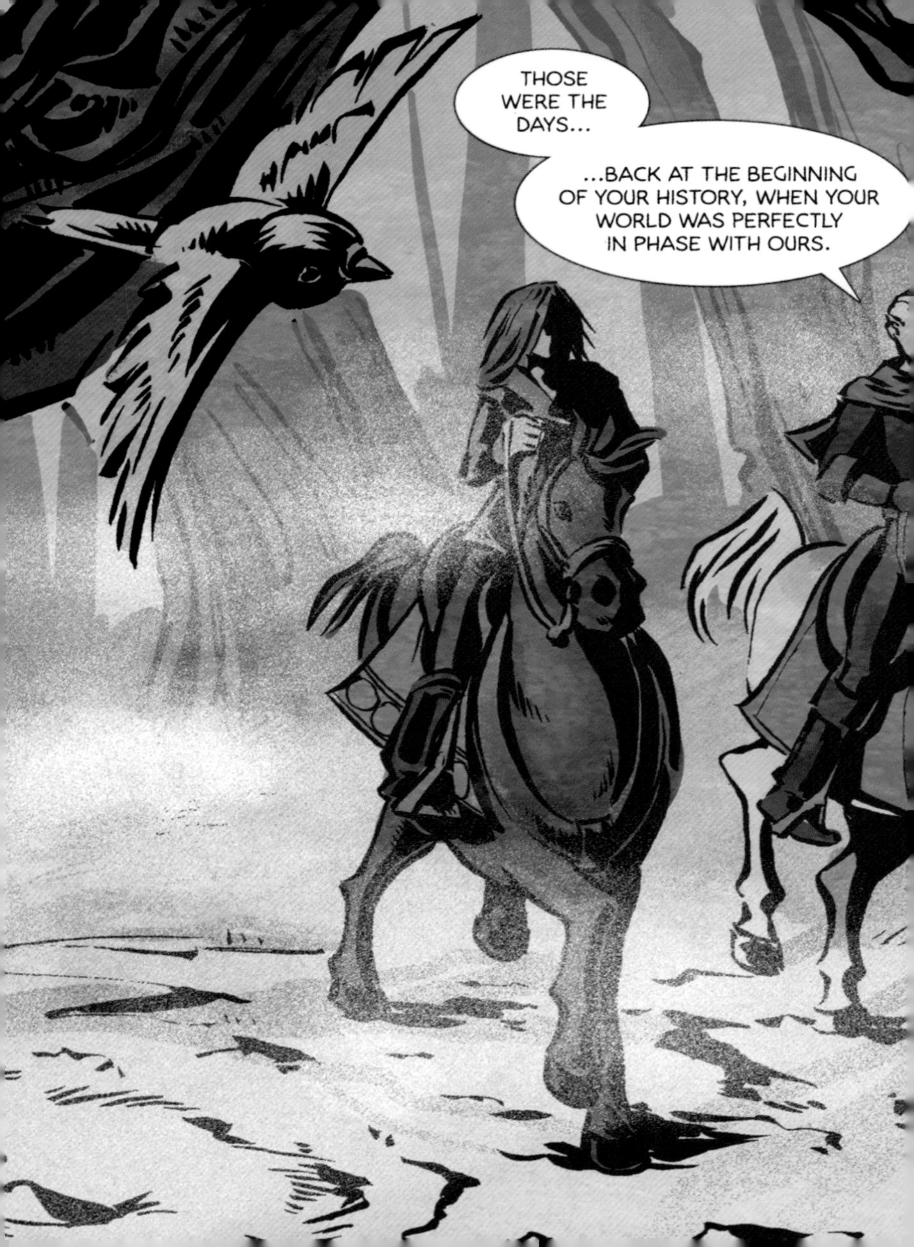
THOSE WERE THE DAYS...
...BACK AT THE BEGINNING OF YOUR HISTORY, WHEN YOUR WORLD WAS PERFECTLY IN PHASE WITH OURS.

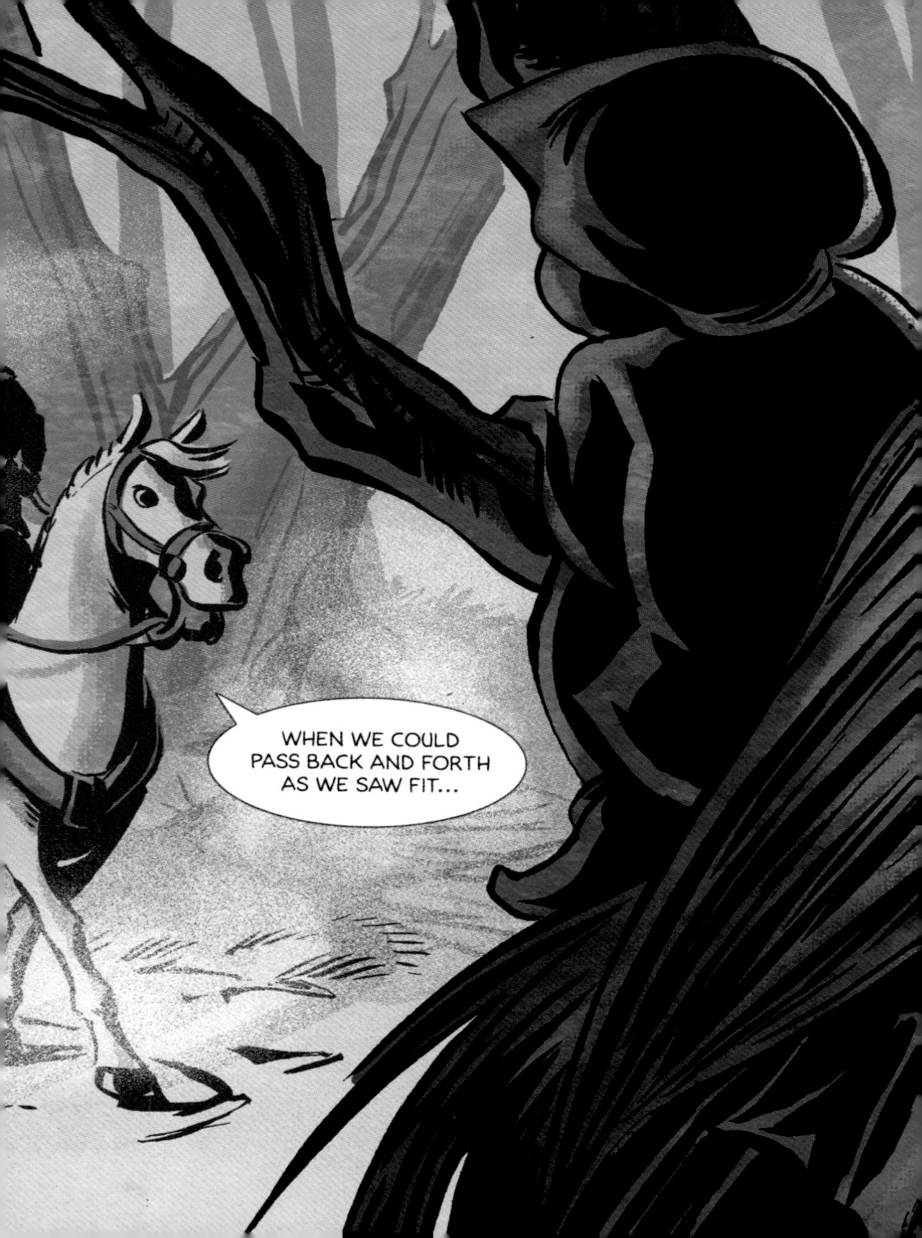
WHEN WE COULD PASS BACK AND FORTH AS WE SAW FIT...

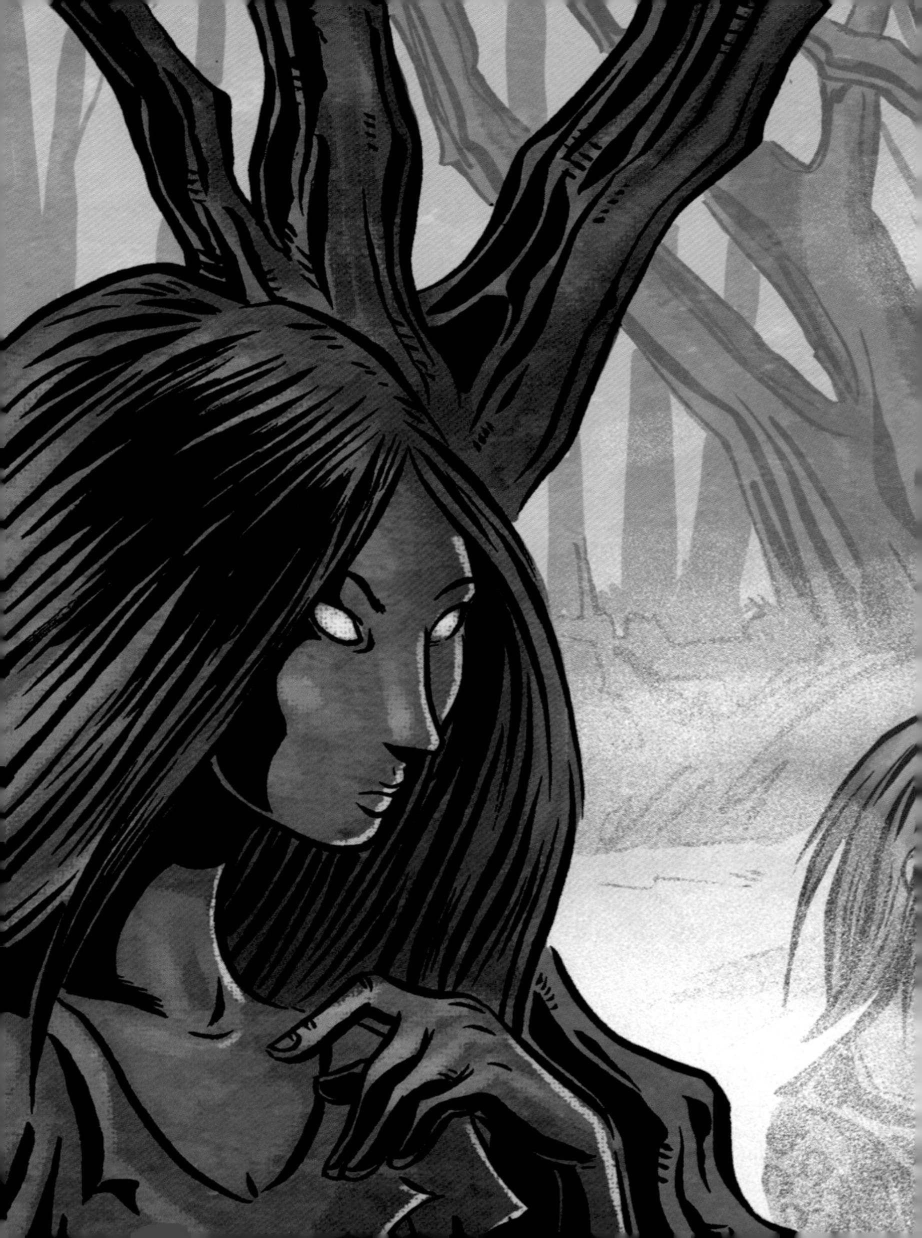

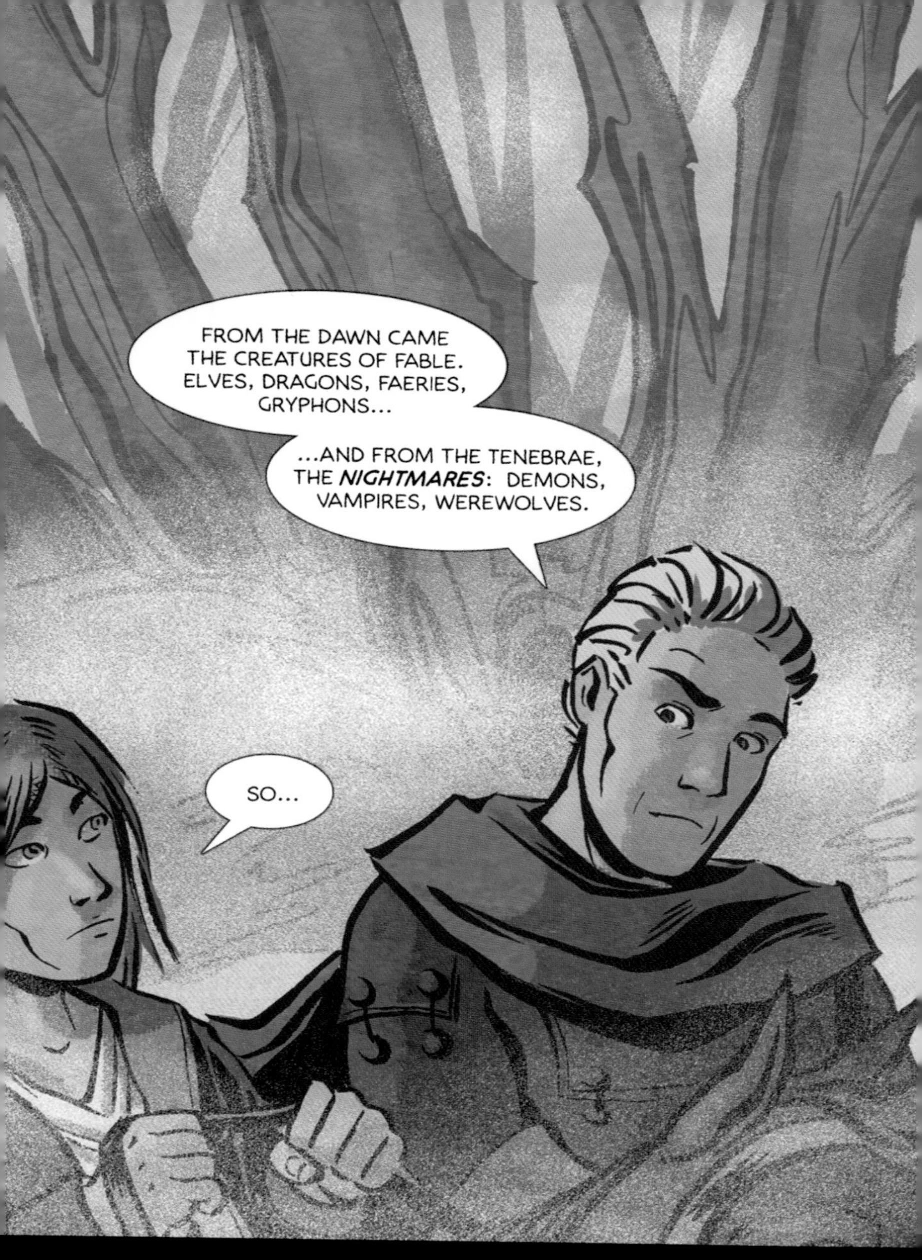
FROM THE DAWN CAME THE CREATURES OF FABLE. ELVES, DRAGONS, FAERIES, GRYPHONS...
...AND FROM THE TENEBRAE, THE ***NIGHTMARES***: DEMONS, VAMPIRES, WEREWOLVES.
SO...

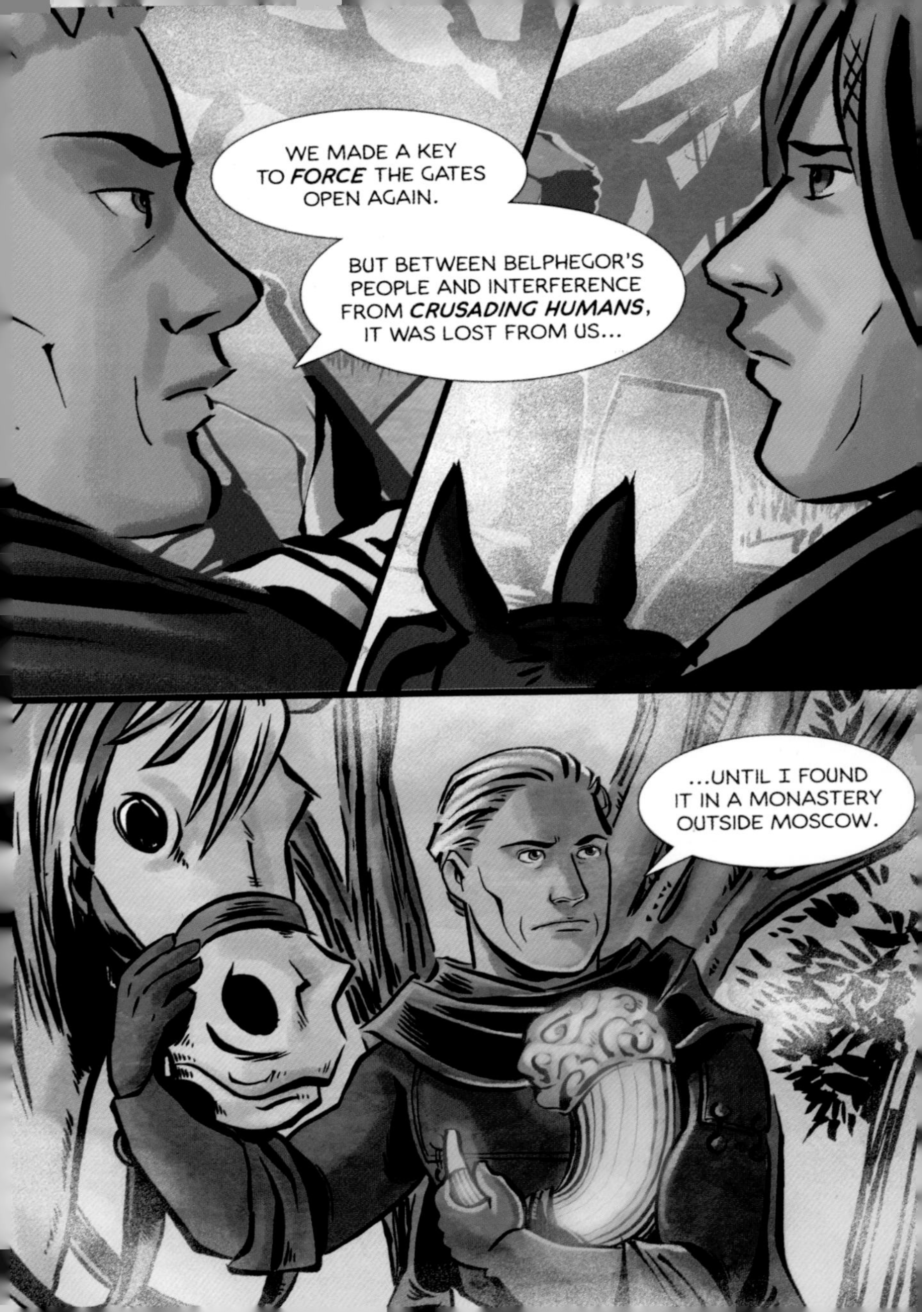
WE MADE A KEY TO *FORCE* THE GATES OPEN AGAIN.
BUT BETWEEN BELPHEGOR'S PEOPLE AND INTERFERENCE FROM *CRUSADING HUMANS*, IT WAS LOST FROM US...
...UNTIL I FOUND IT IN A MONASTERY OUTSIDE MOSCOW.

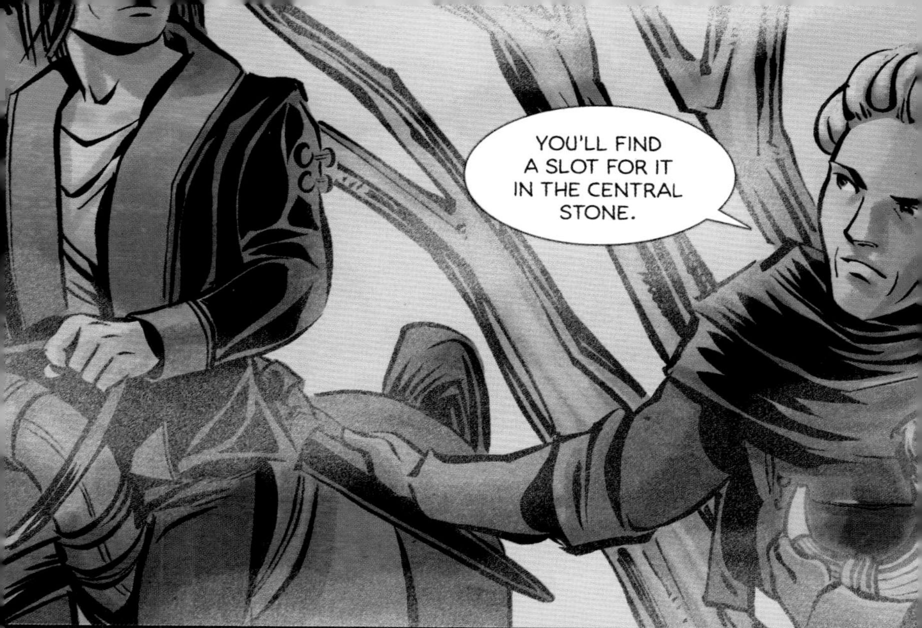
YOU'LL FIND A SLOT FOR IT IN THE CENTRAL STONE.
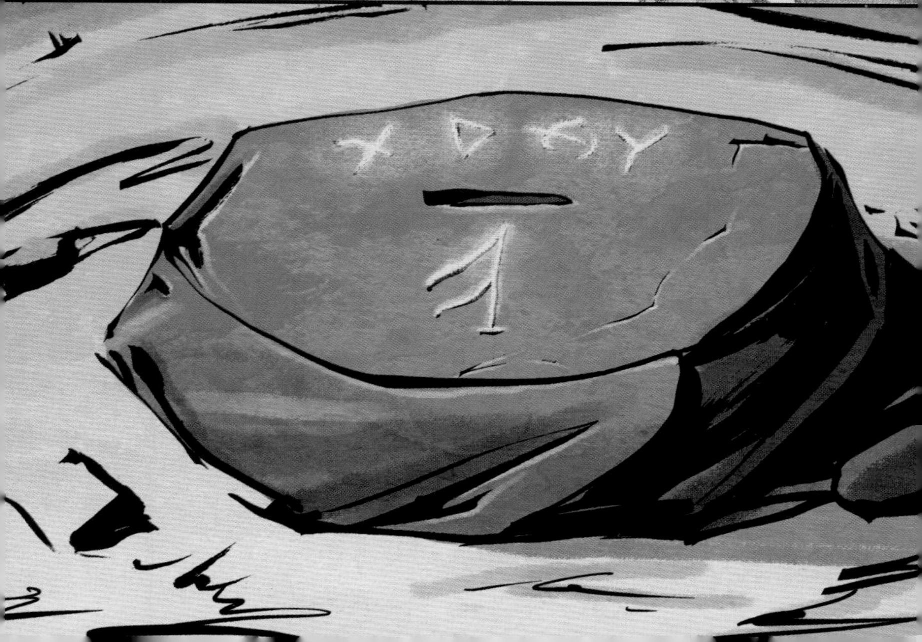

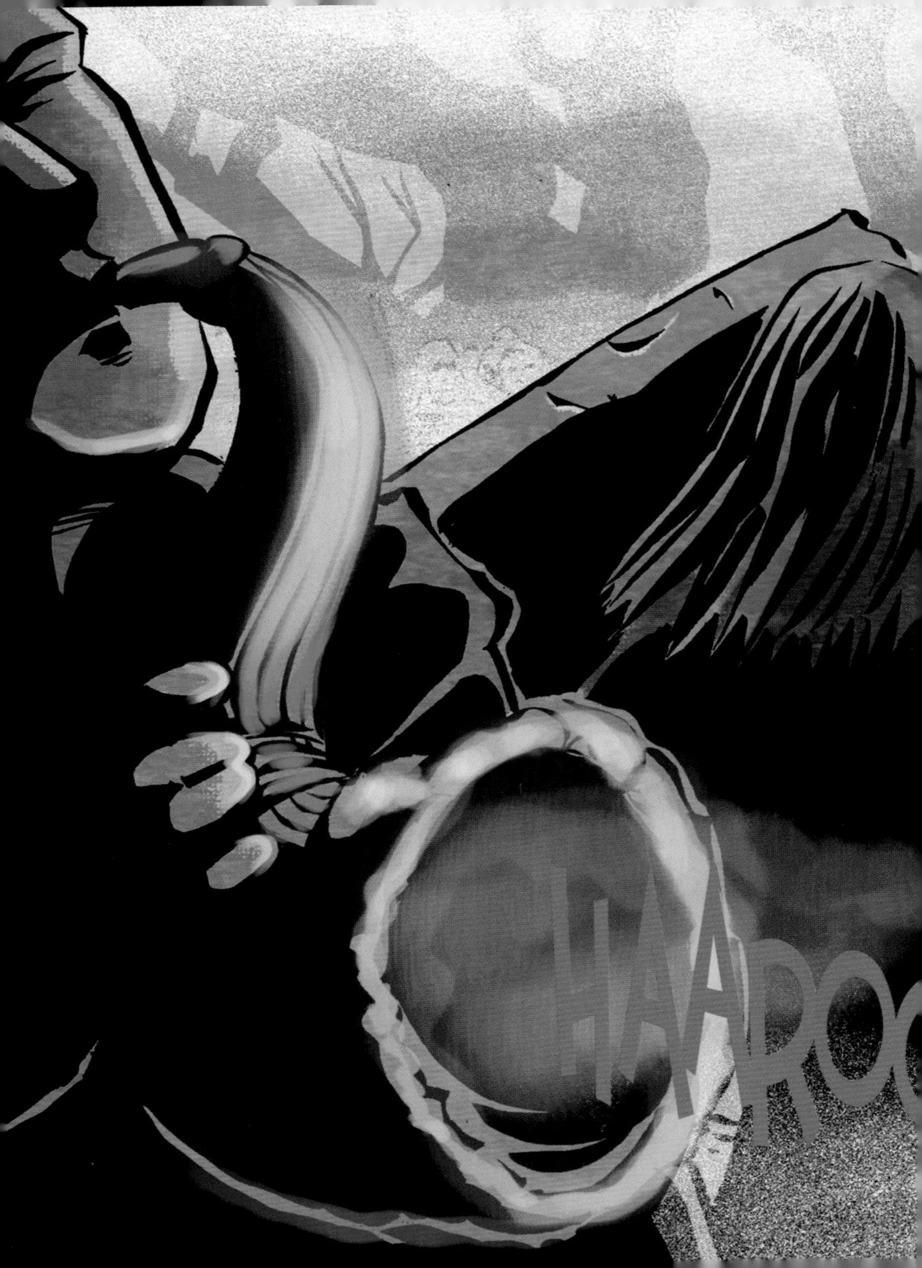
HAAROO

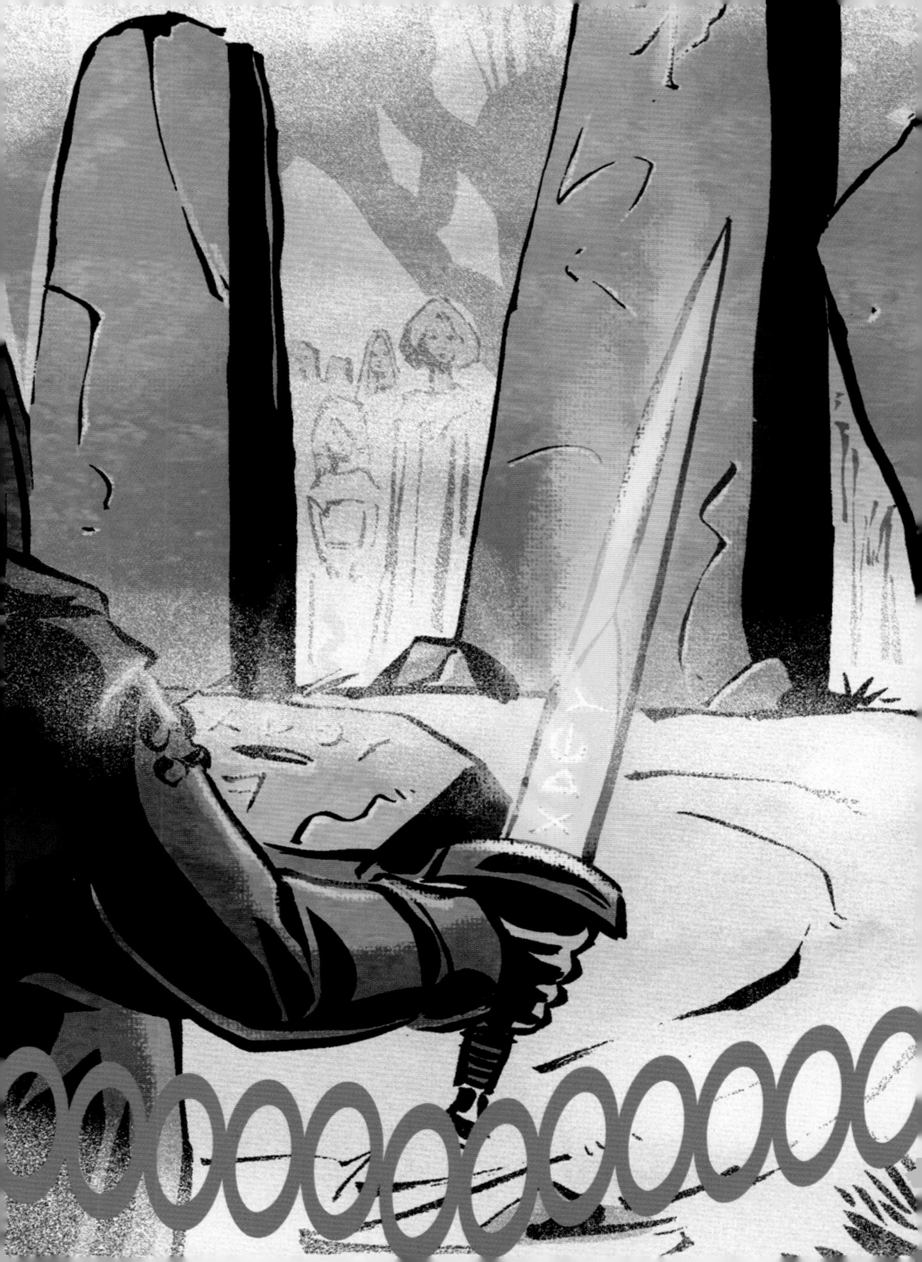
OOOOOOOOOOOO

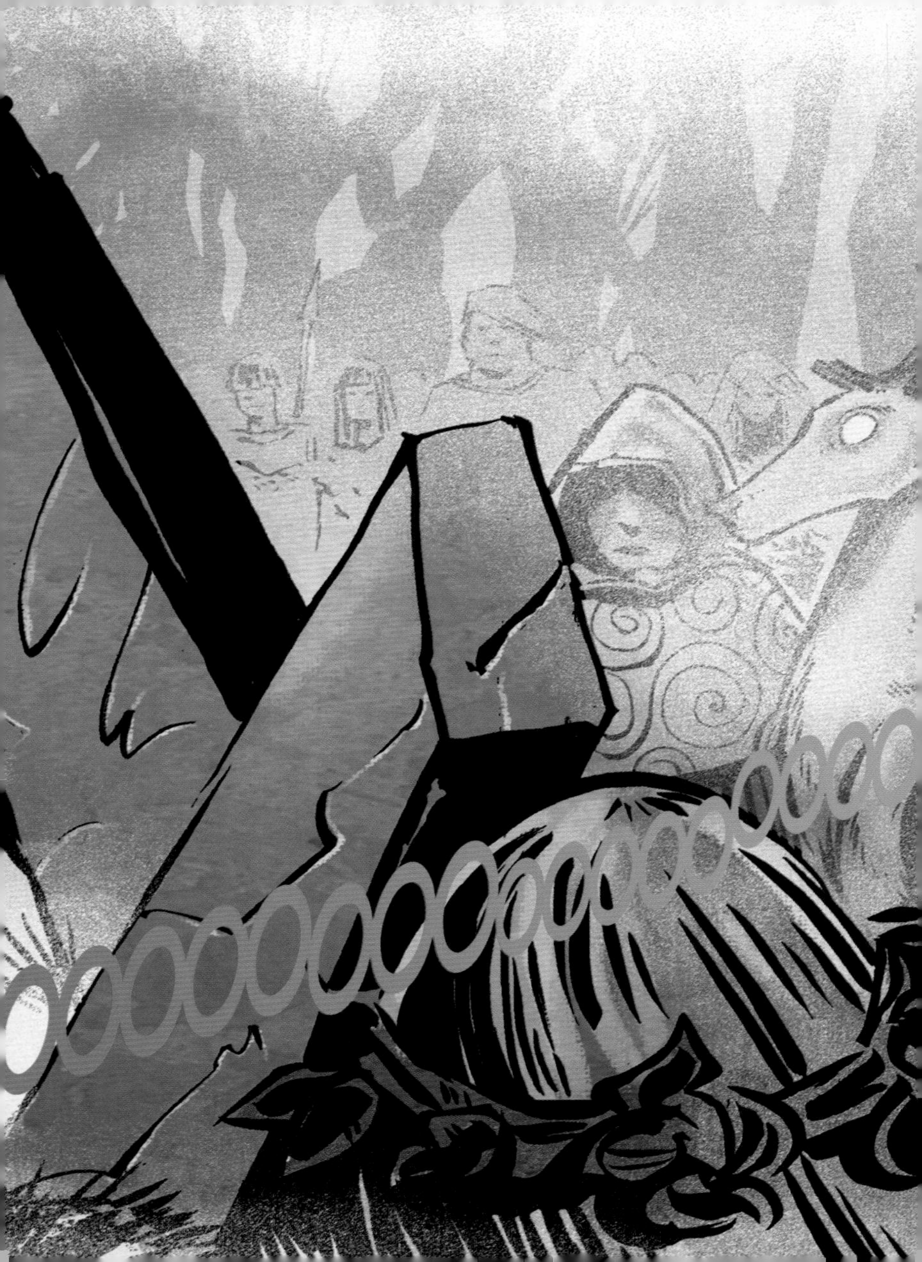
OOOOOOOOOOOOOOOOOOOOOOO

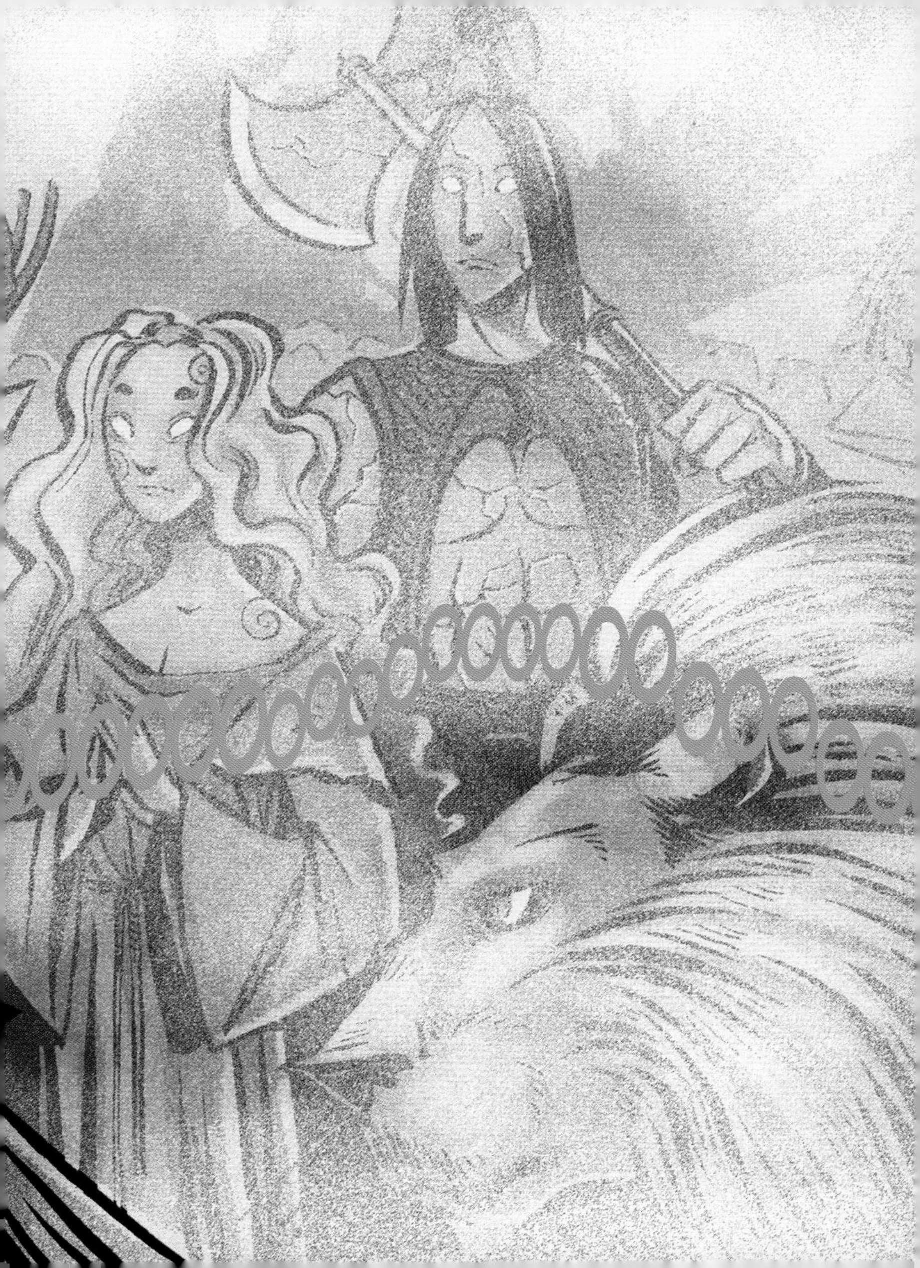

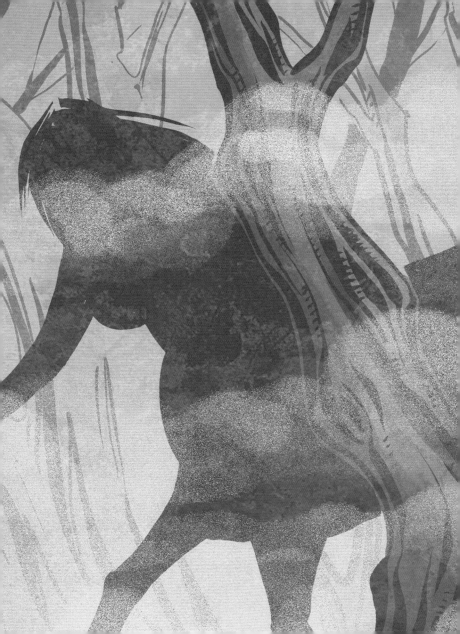

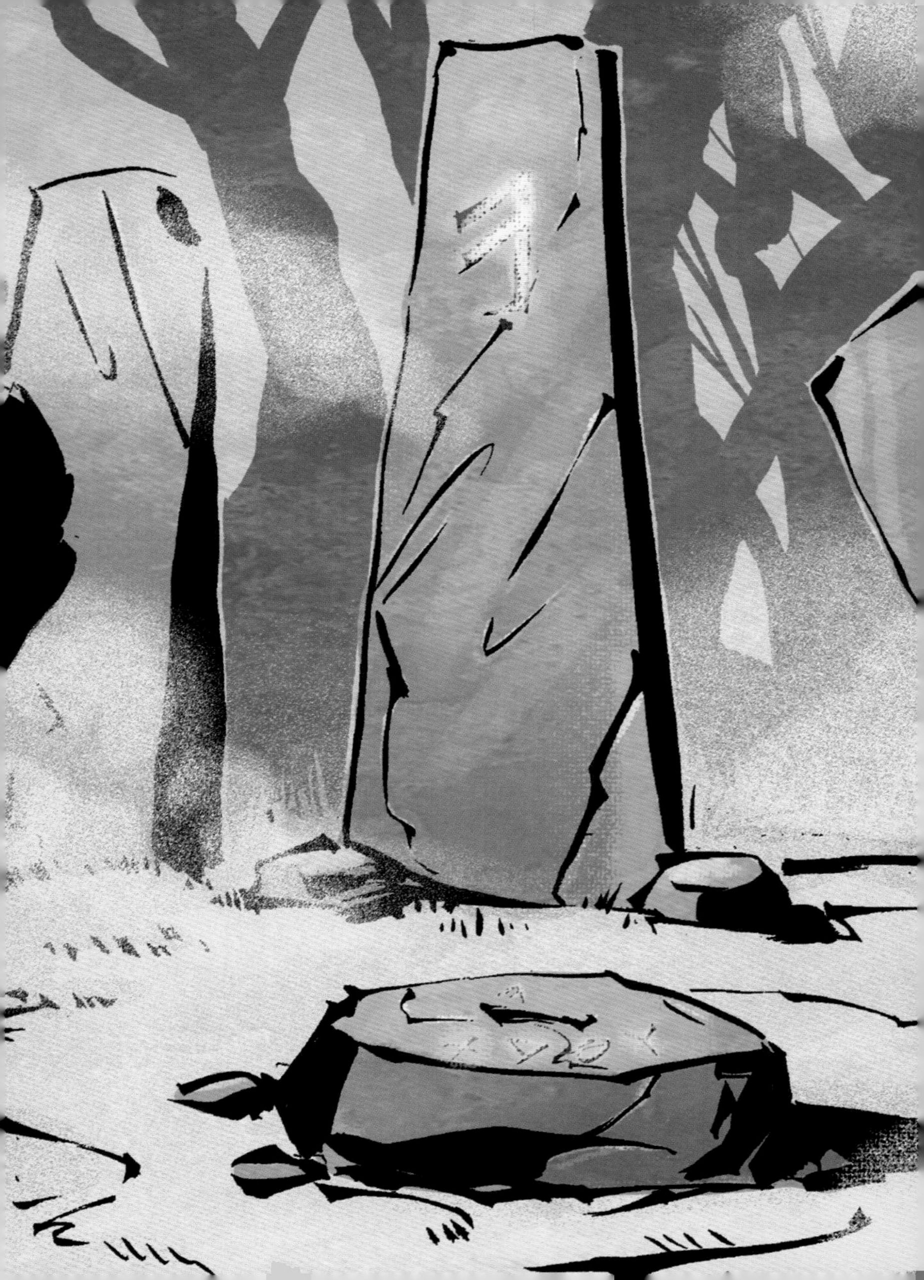

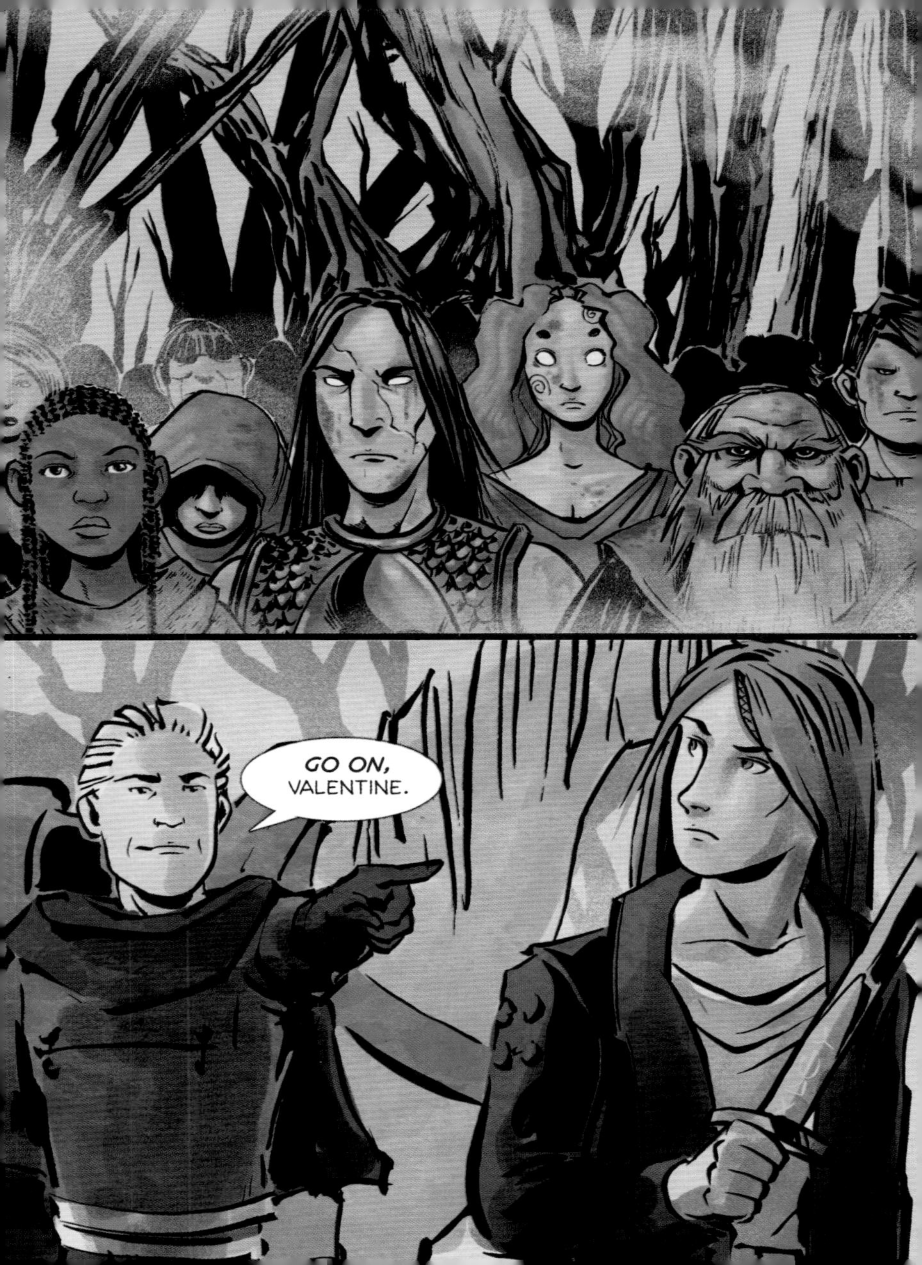
GO ON, VALENTINE.

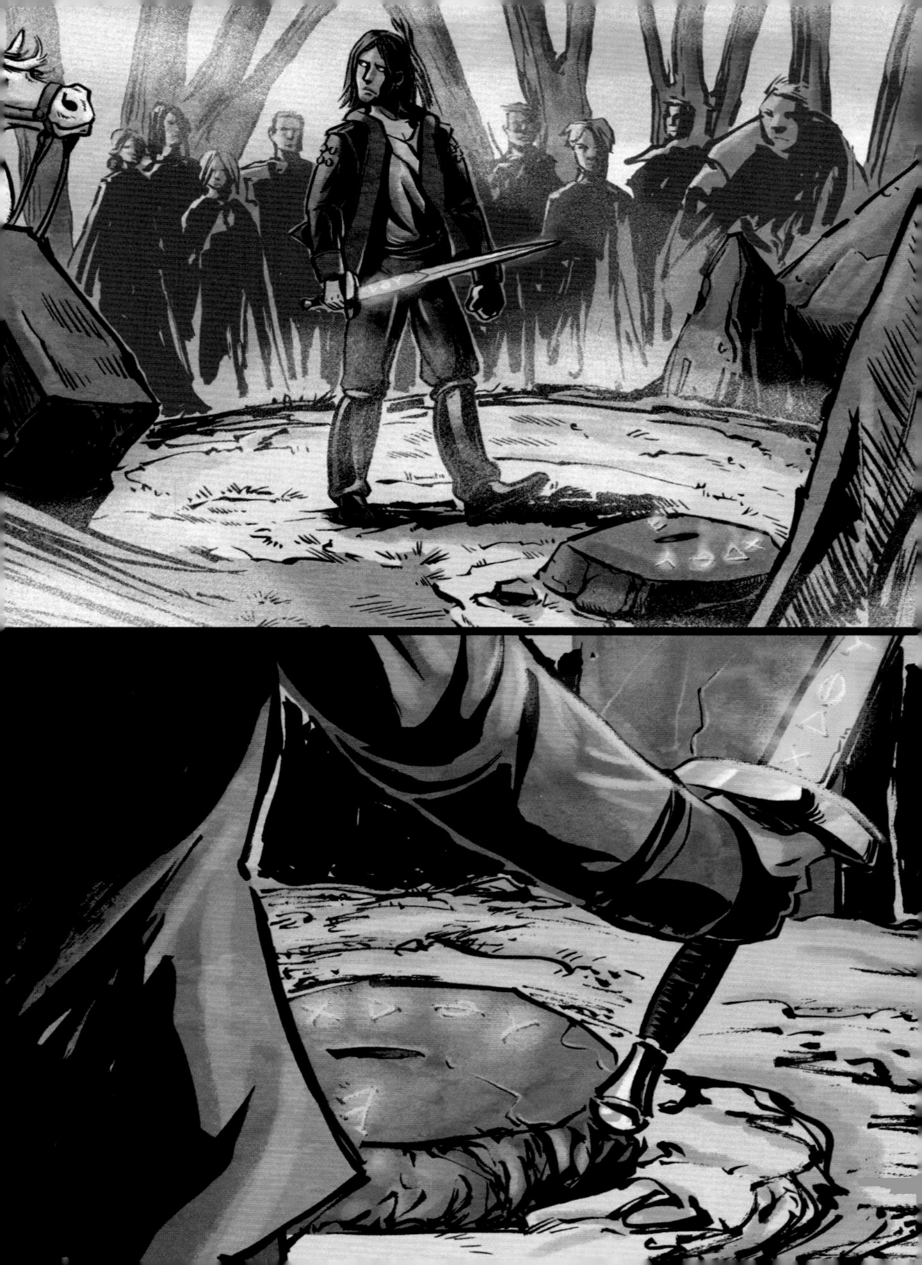

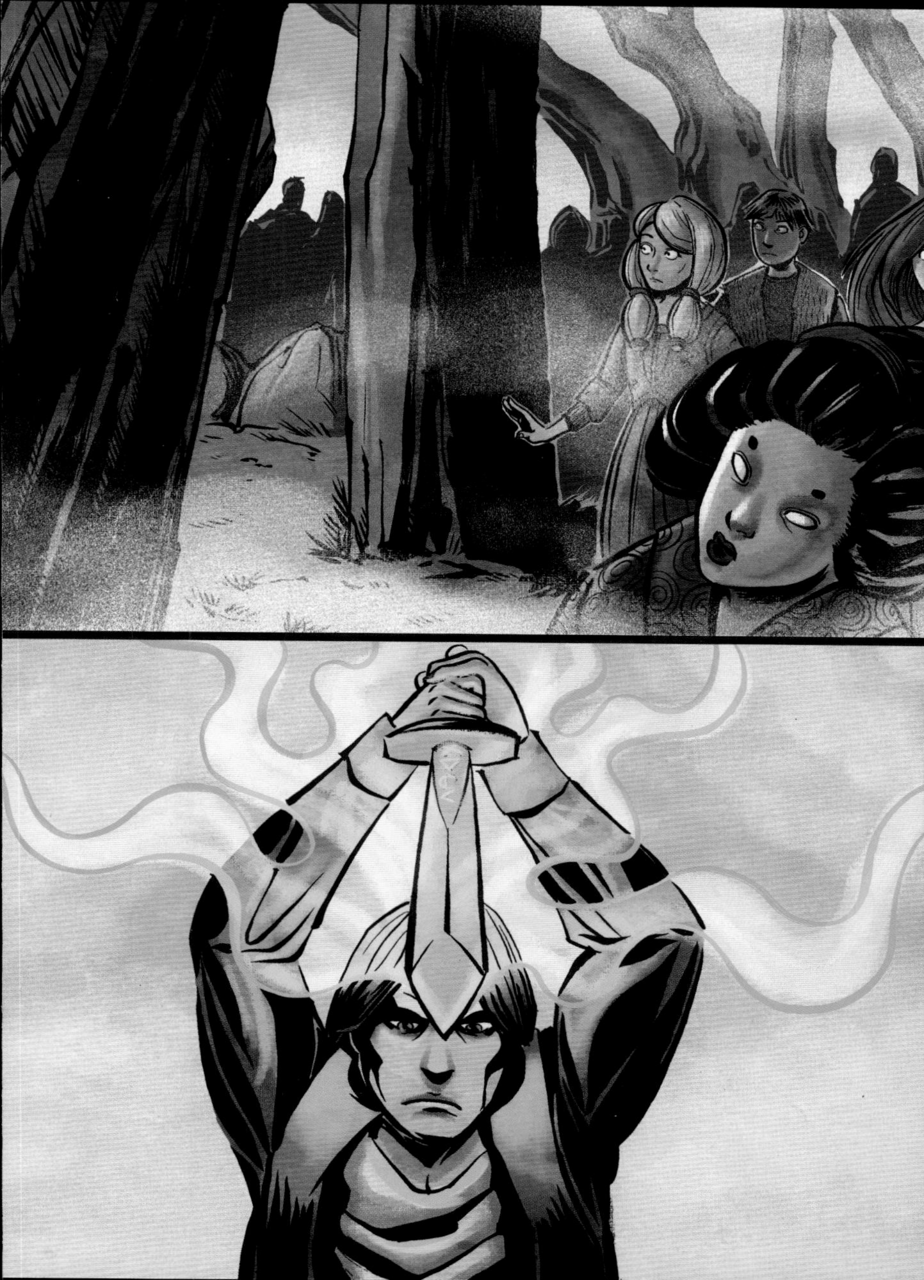

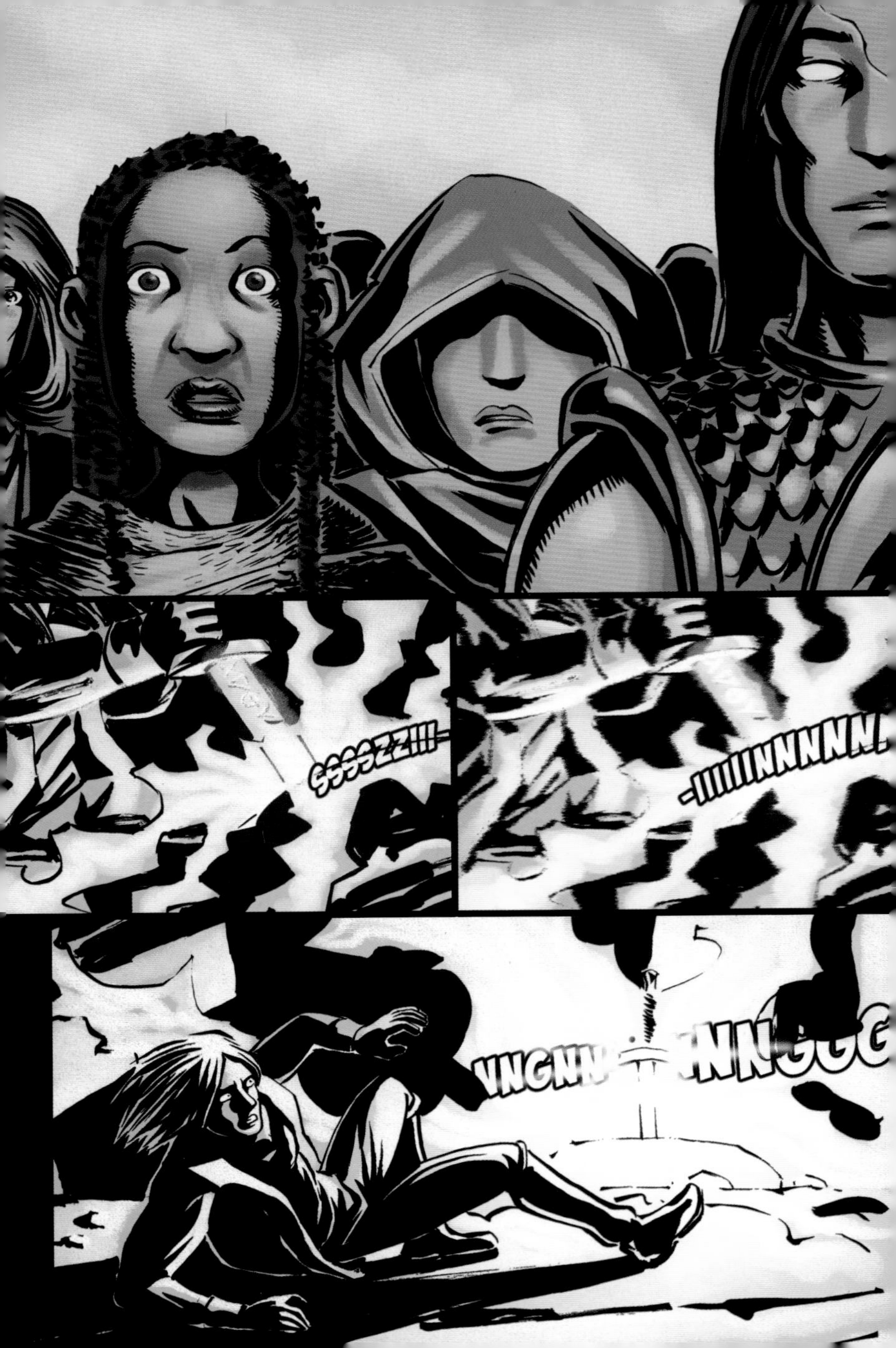
SSSSSZZIIII-
-IIIIIIINNNNNN!
VNGNN
NNGGG

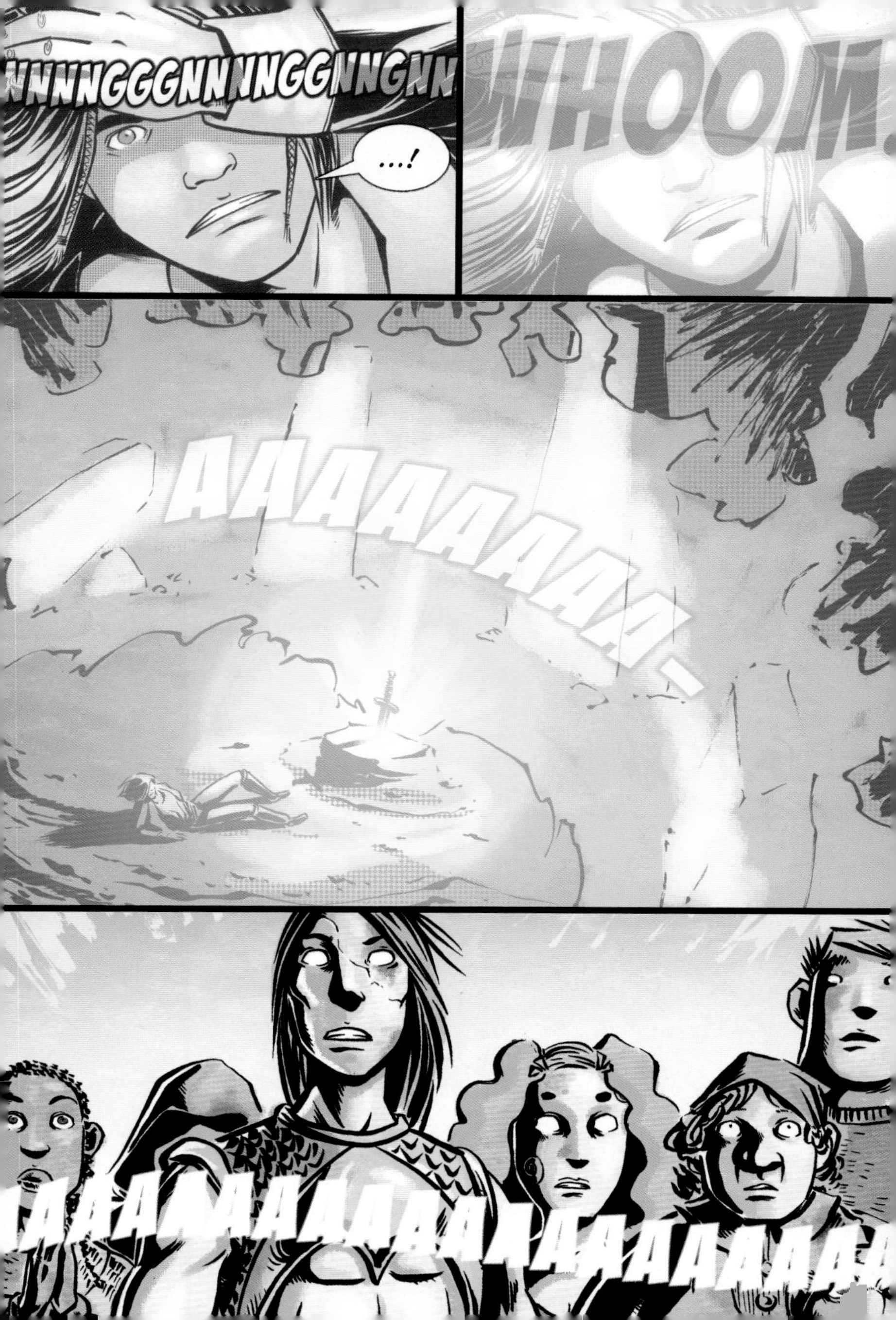
NNNNGGGNNNNGGNNGNN
...!
WHOOM!
AAAAAAAAA...
AAAAAAAAAAAAAAAAA

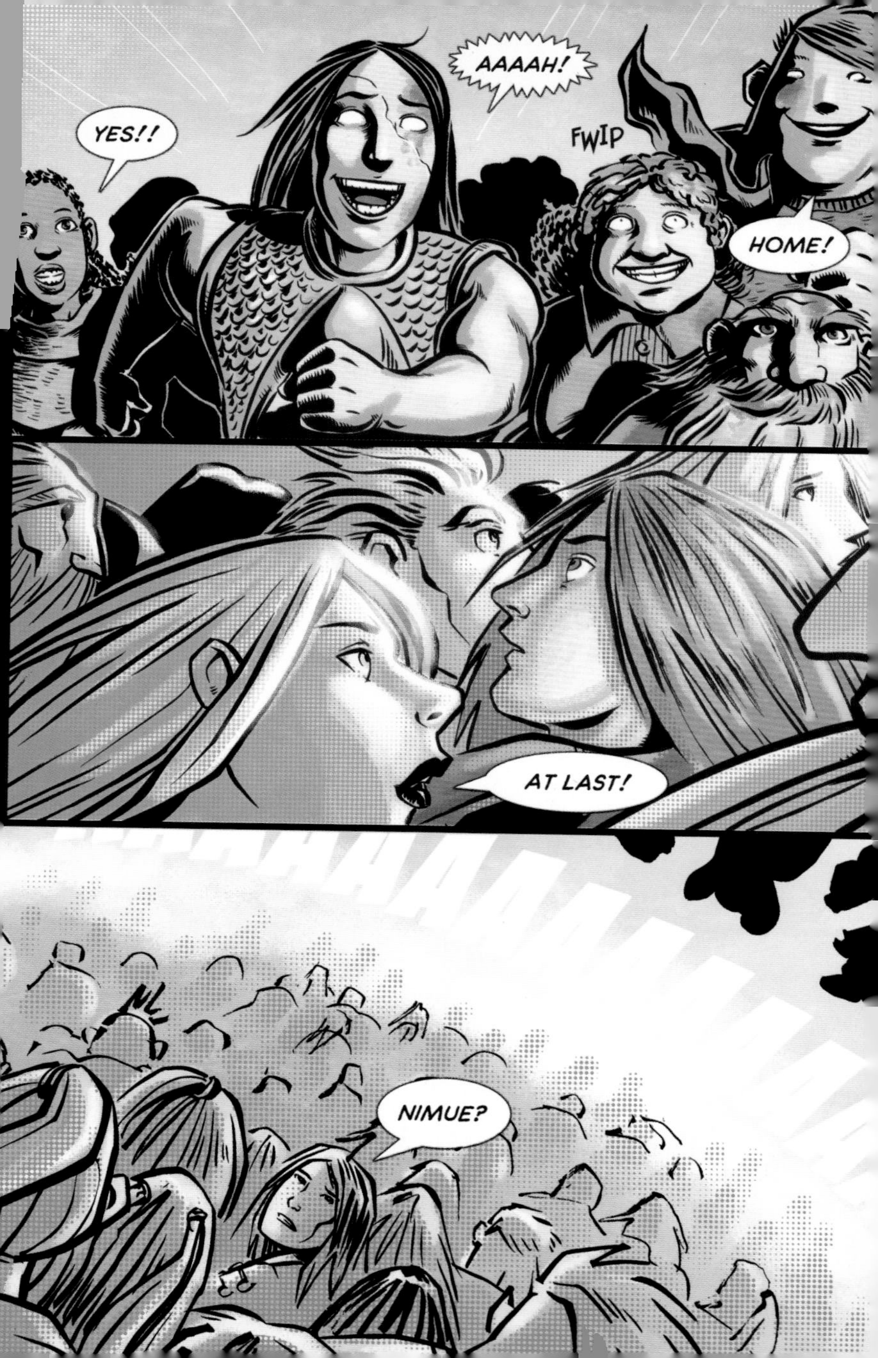
YES!!
AAAAH!
FWIP
HOME!
AT LAST!
NIMUE?

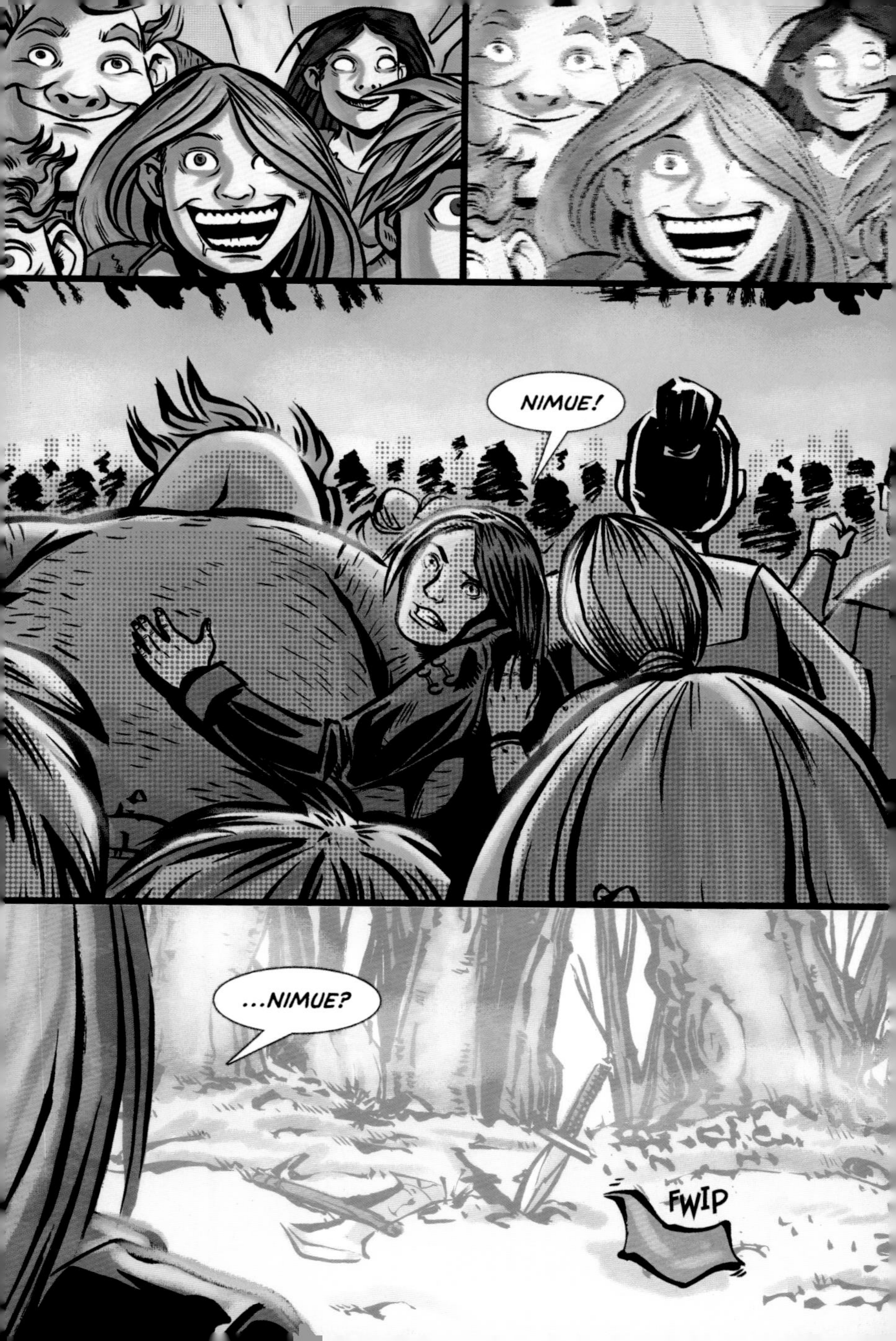
NIMUE!
...NIMUE?
FWIP

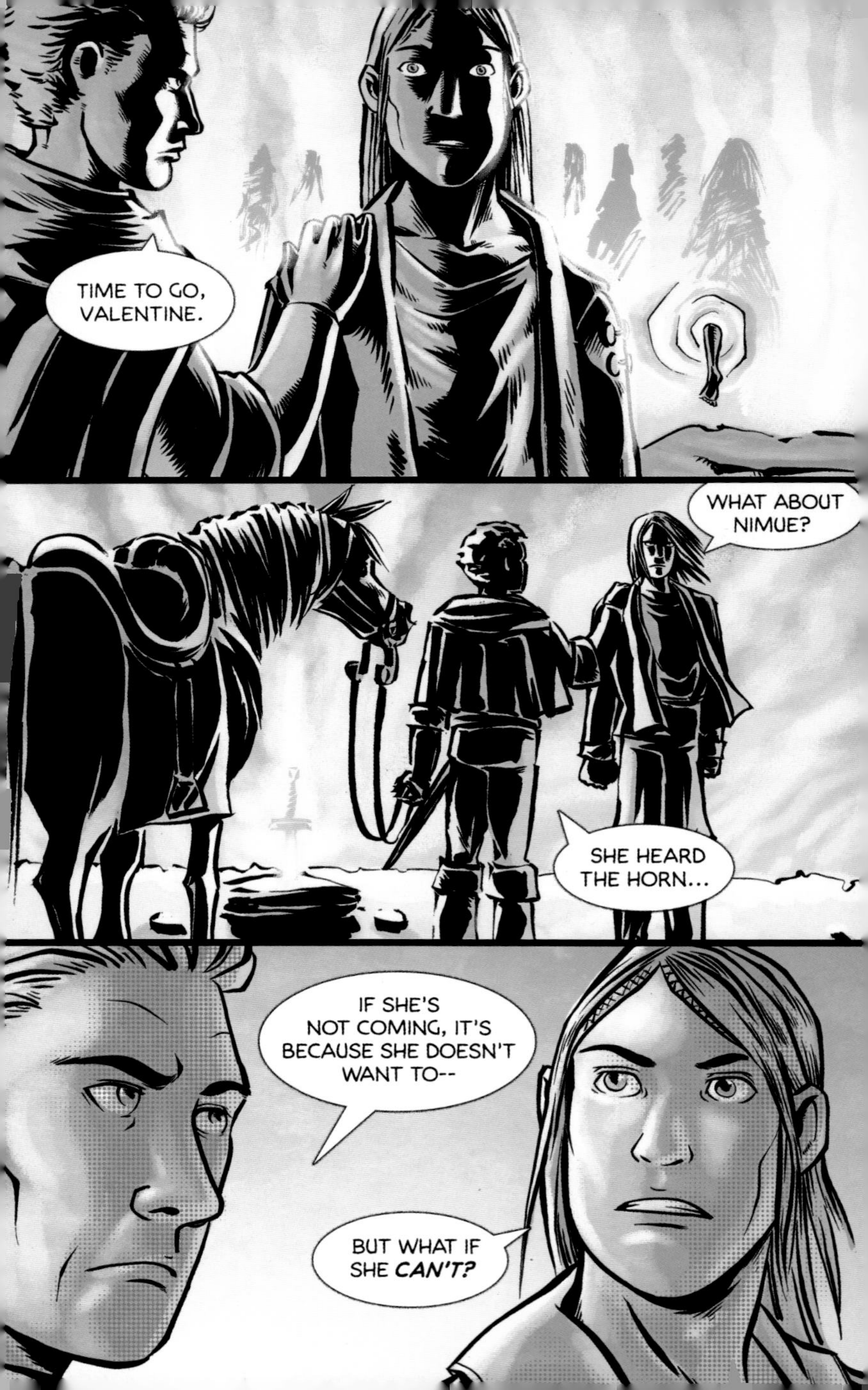
TIME TO GO, VALENTINE.
WHAT ABOUT NIMUE?
SHE HEARD THE HORN...
IF SHE'S NOT COMING, IT'S BECAUSE SHE DOESN'T WANT TO--
BUT WHAT IF SHE *CAN'T?*

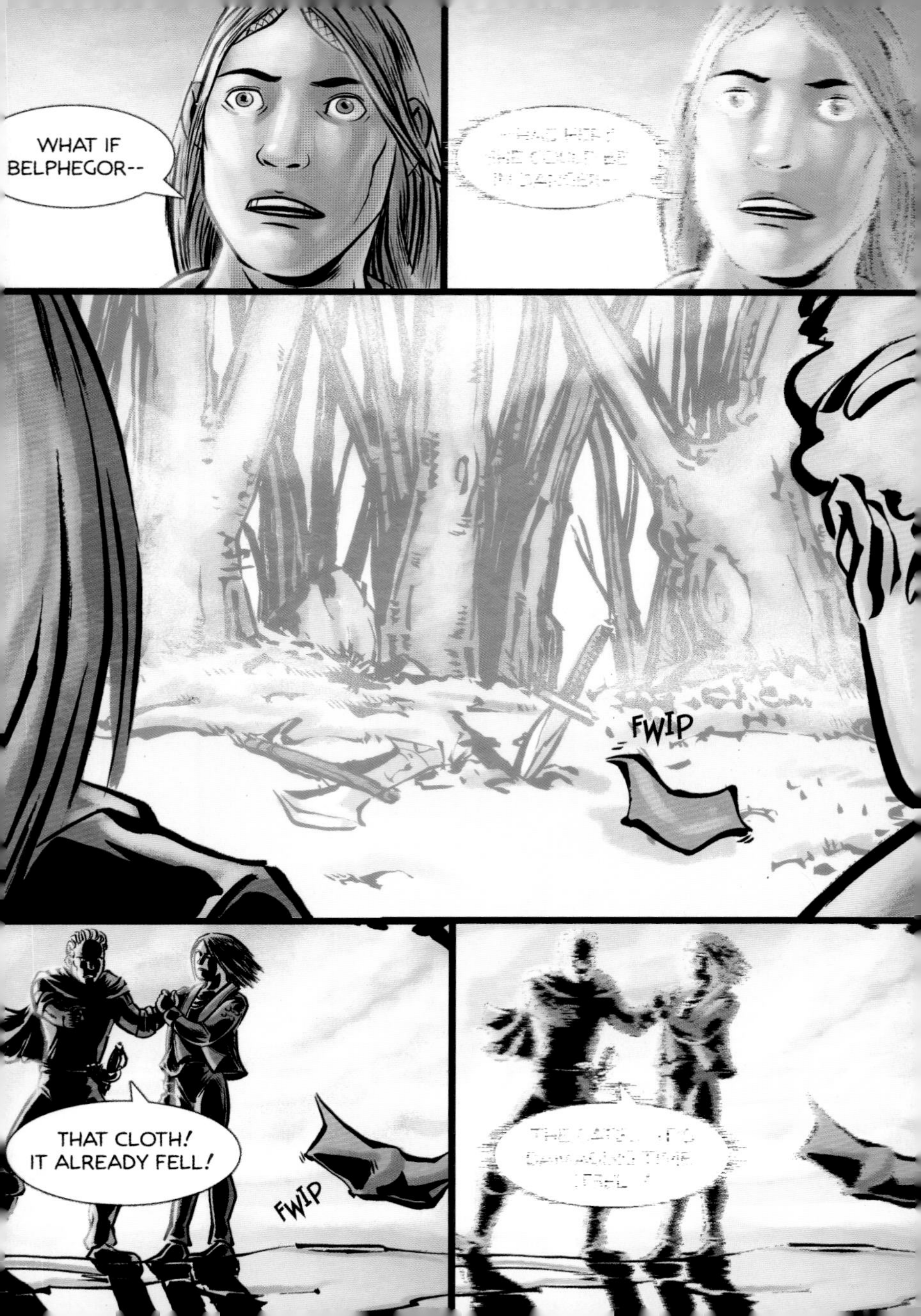
WHAT IF BELPHEGOR--
FWIP
THAT CLOTH! IT ALREADY FELL!
FWIP

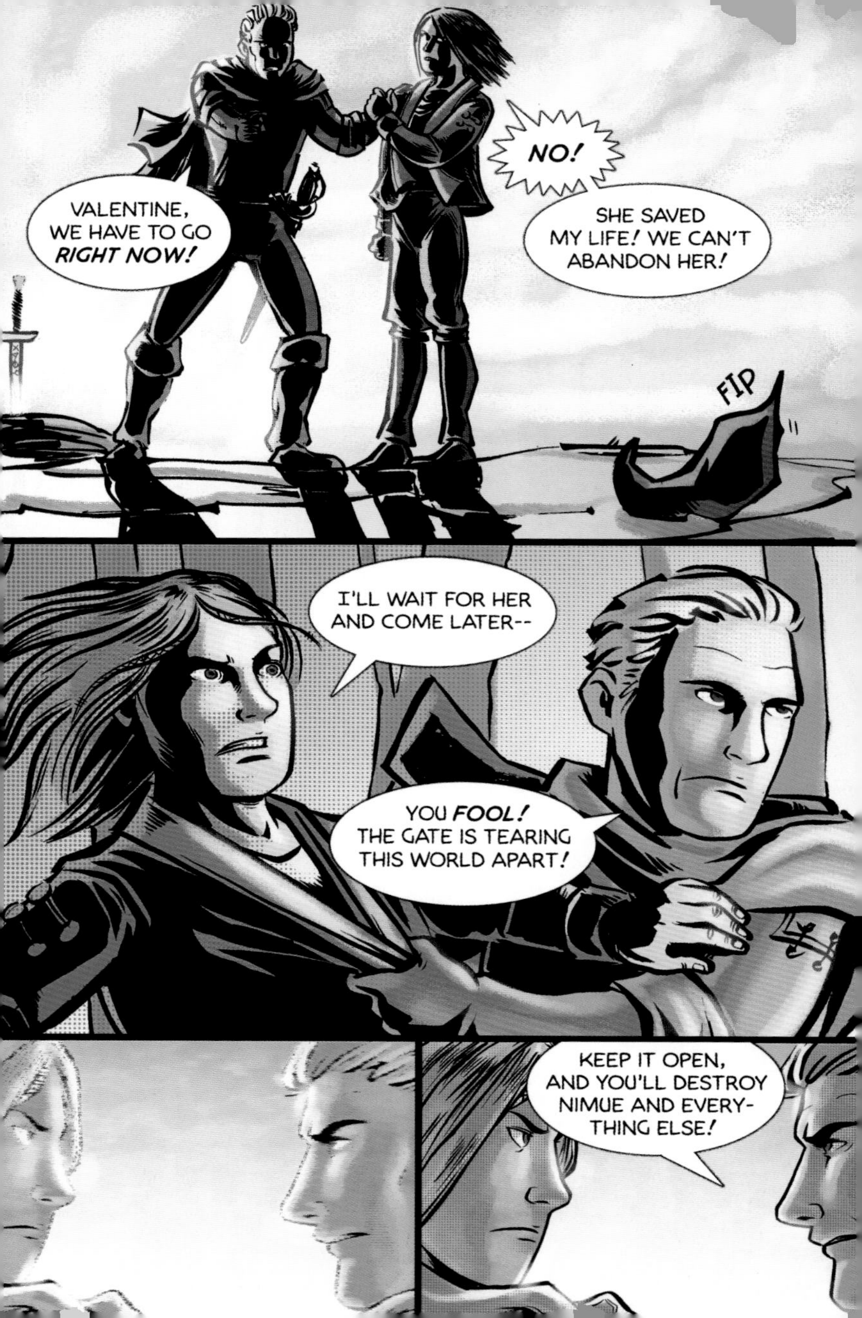
VALENTINE, WE HAVE TO GO *RIGHT NOW!*
NO!
SHE SAVED MY LIFE! WE CAN'T ABANDON HER!
FIP
I'LL WAIT FOR HER AND COME LATER--
YOU *FOOL!* THE GATE IS TEARING THIS WORLD APART!
KEEP IT OPEN, AND YOU'LL DESTROY NIMUE AND EVERY-THING ELSE!

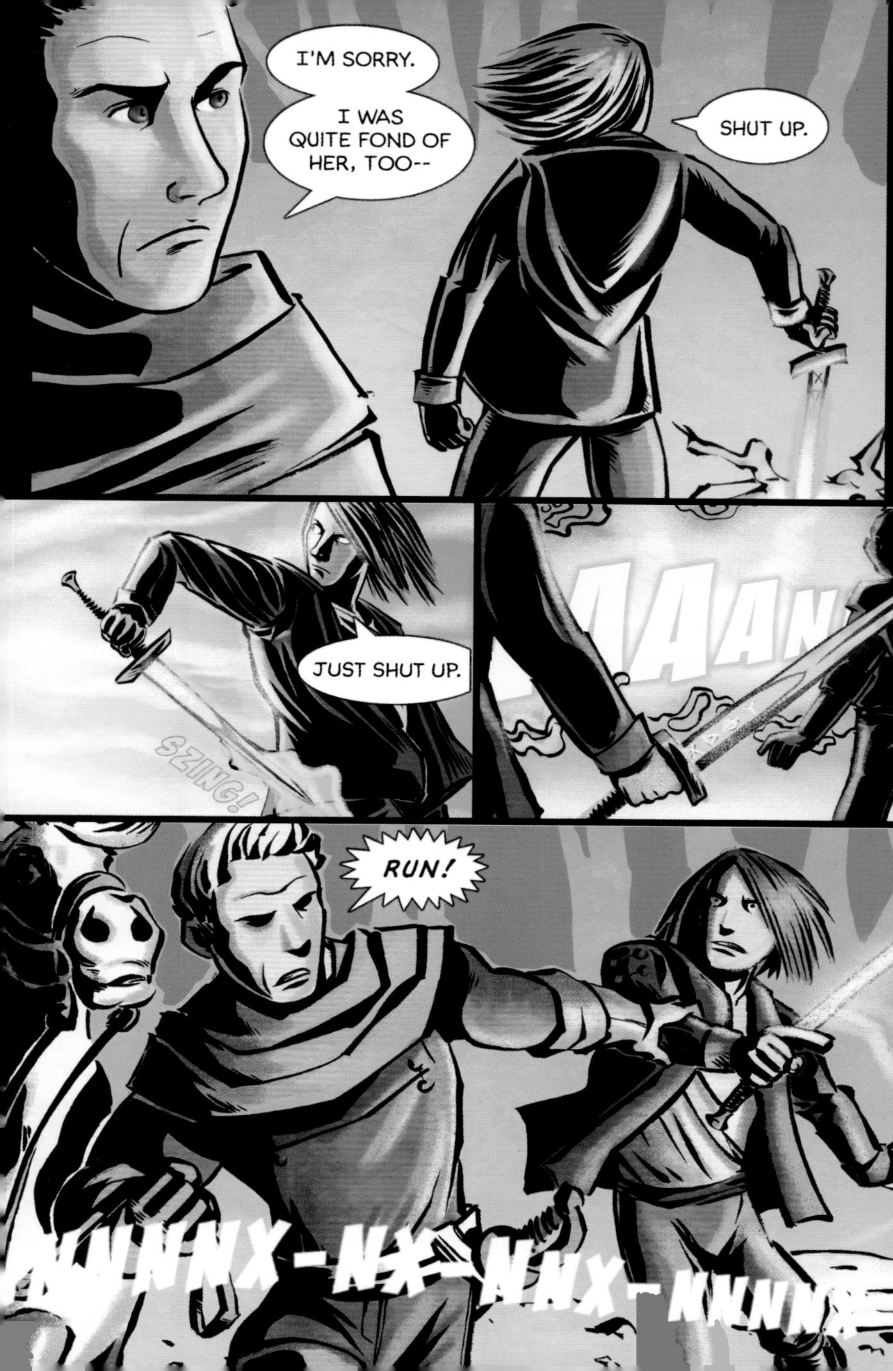
I'M SORRY.
I WAS QUITE FOND OF HER, TOO--
SHUT UP.
JUST SHUT UP.
SZING!
RUN!

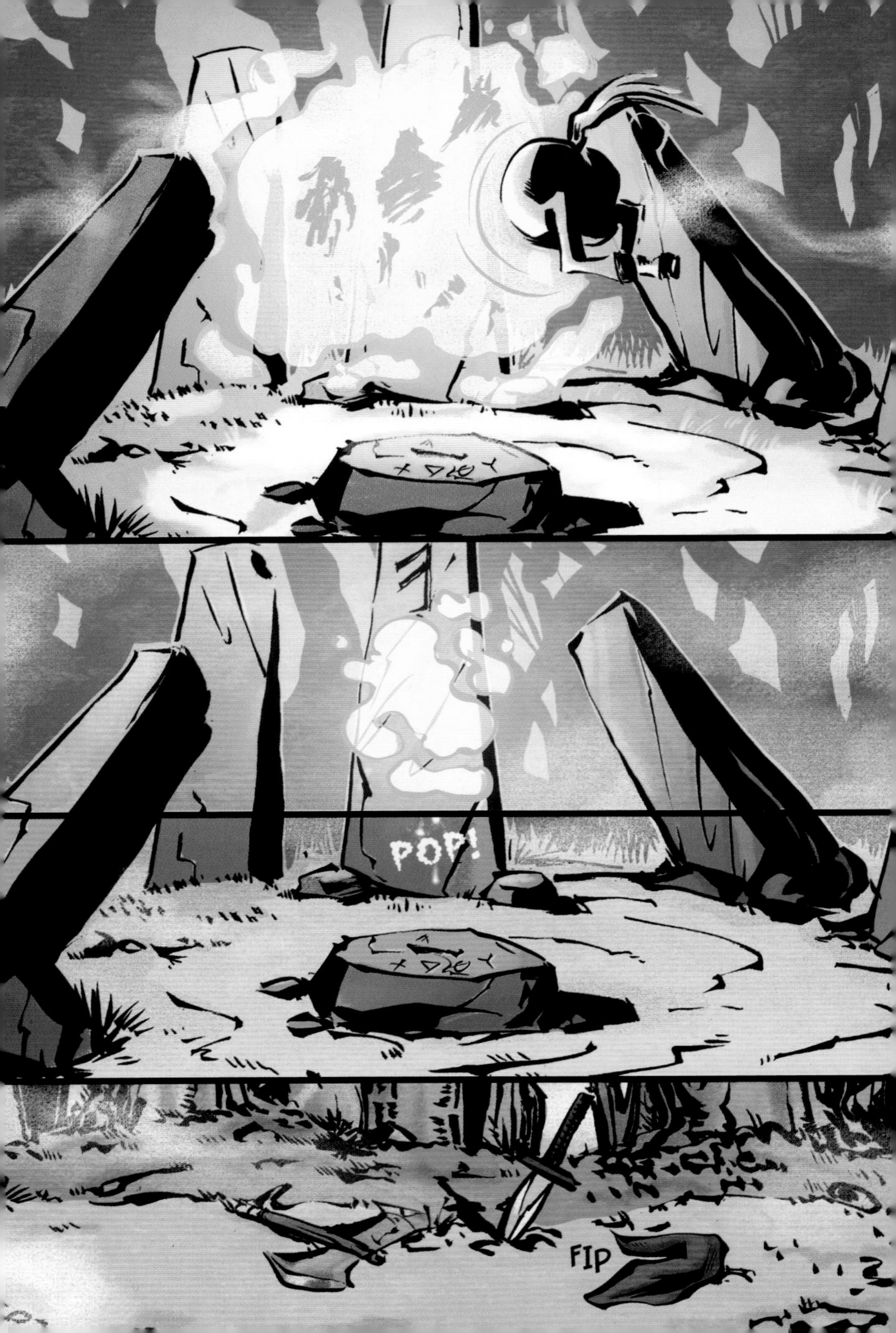
POP!
FIP

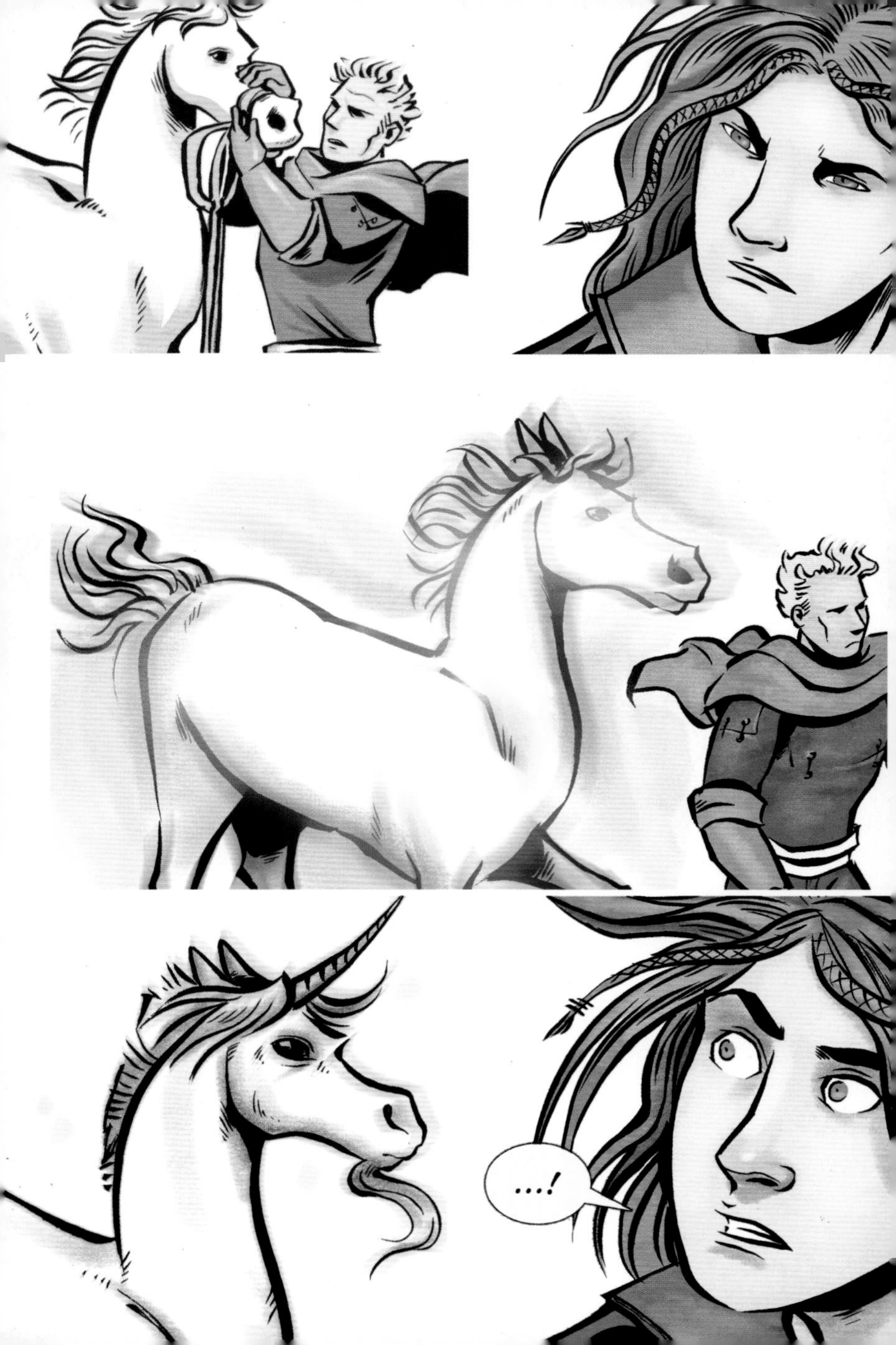
...!

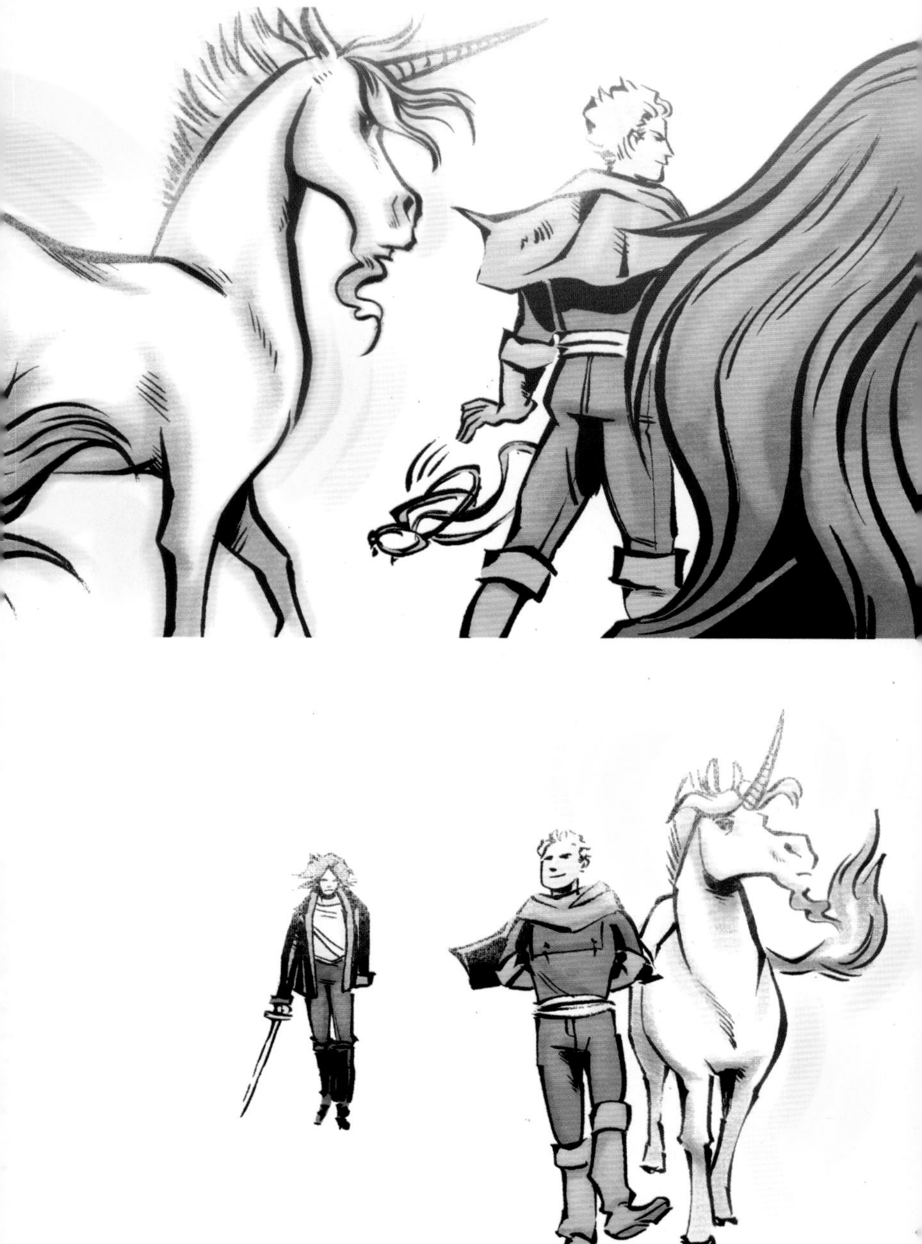

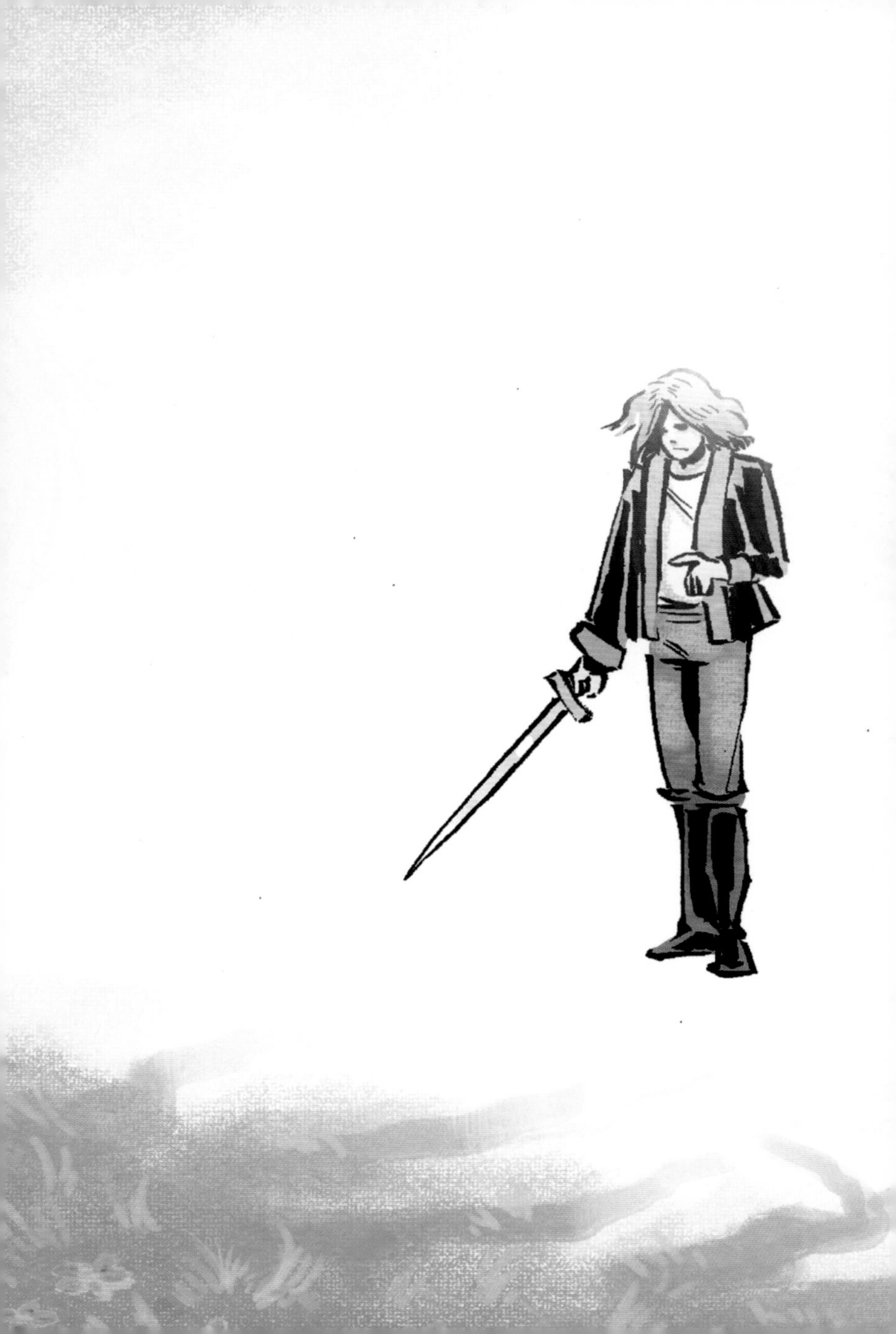

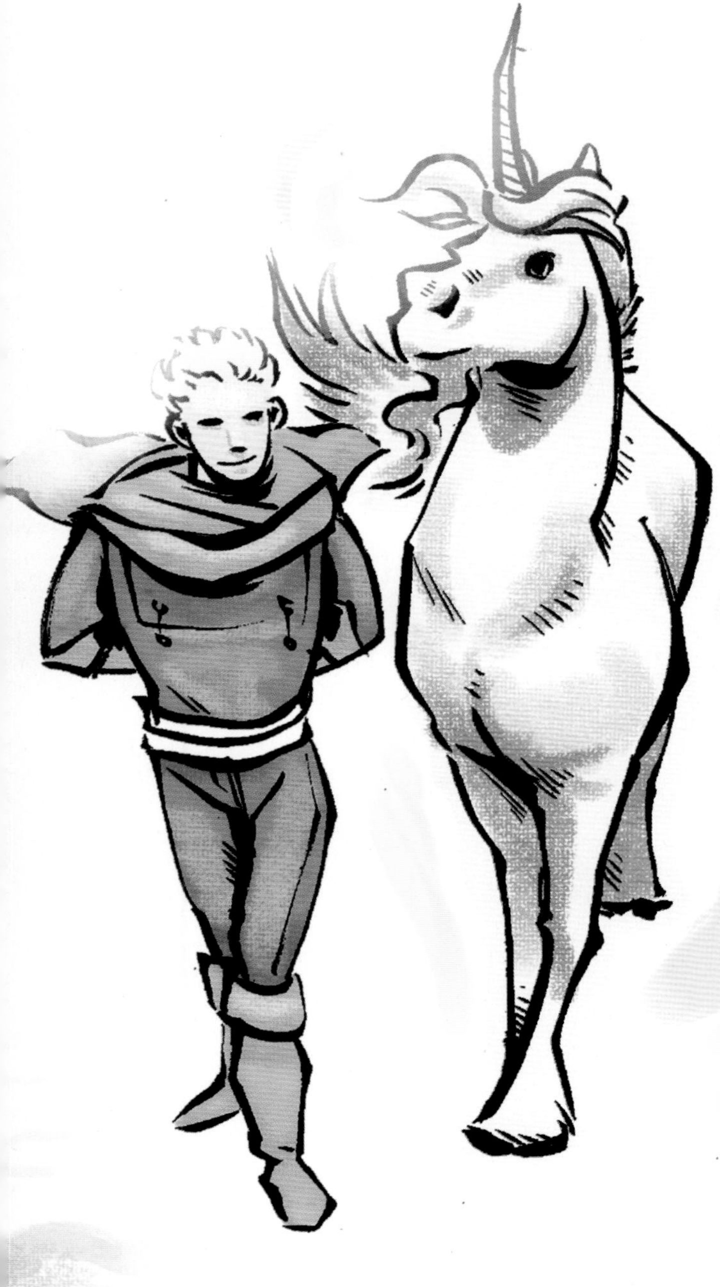

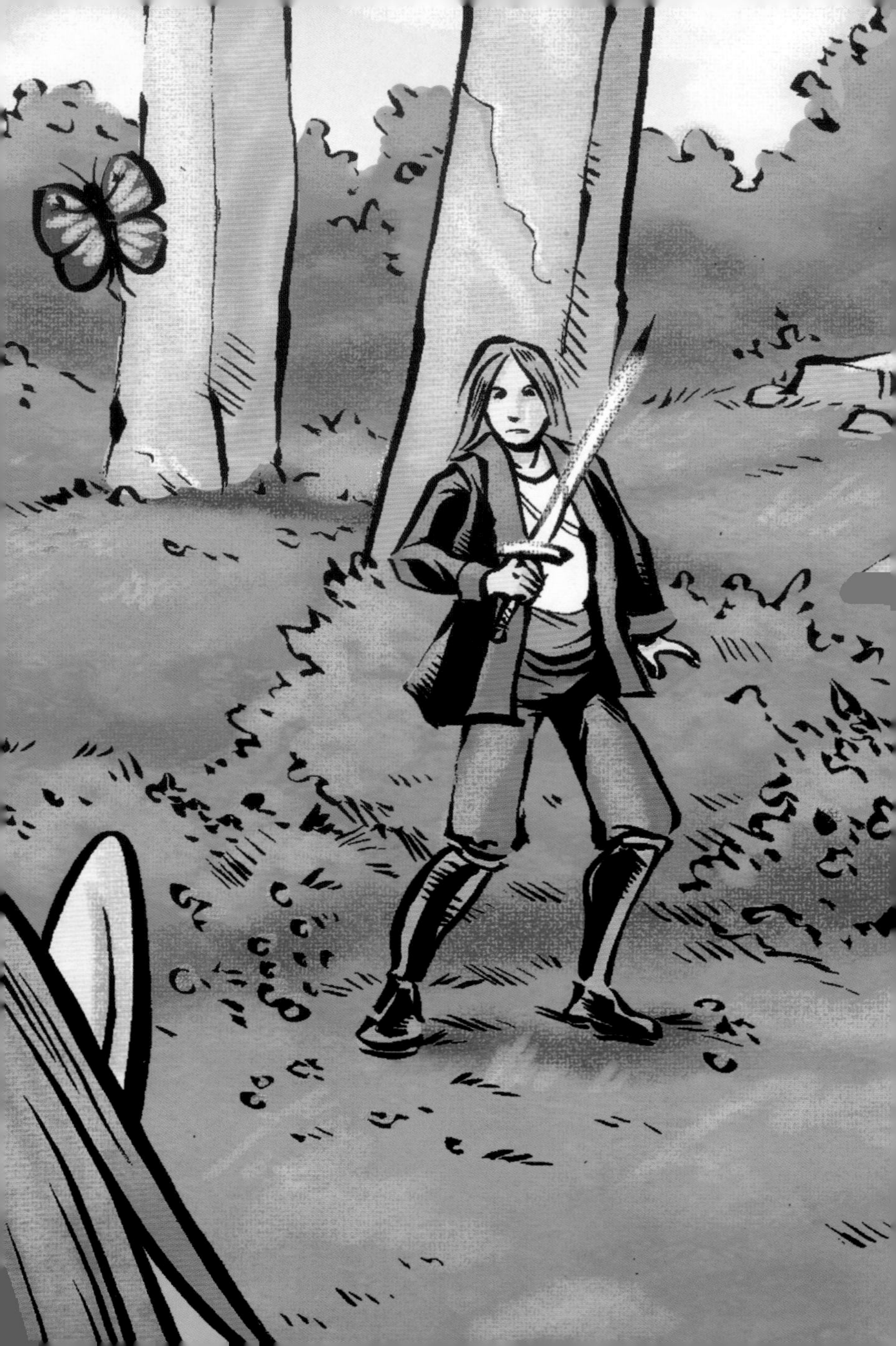

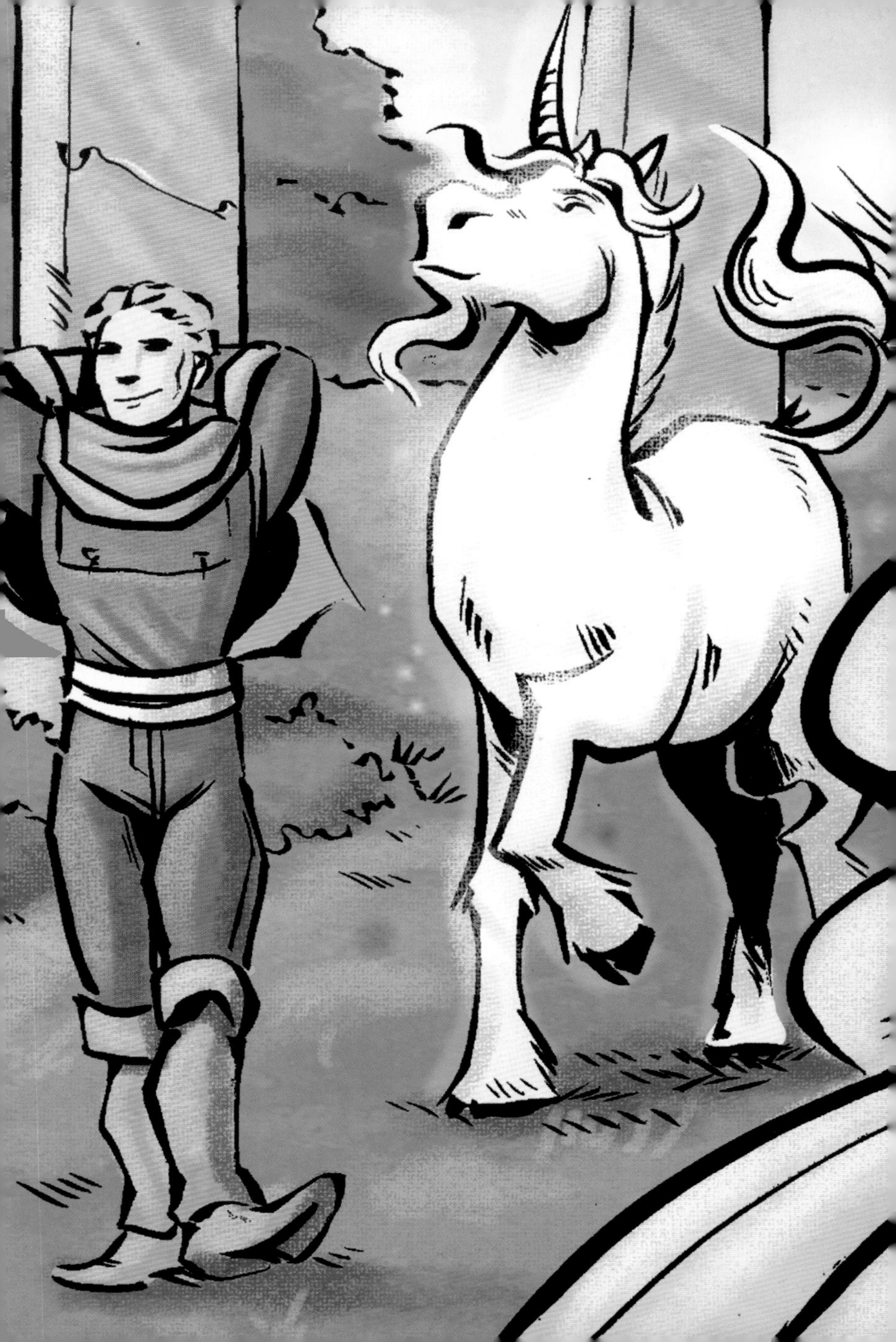

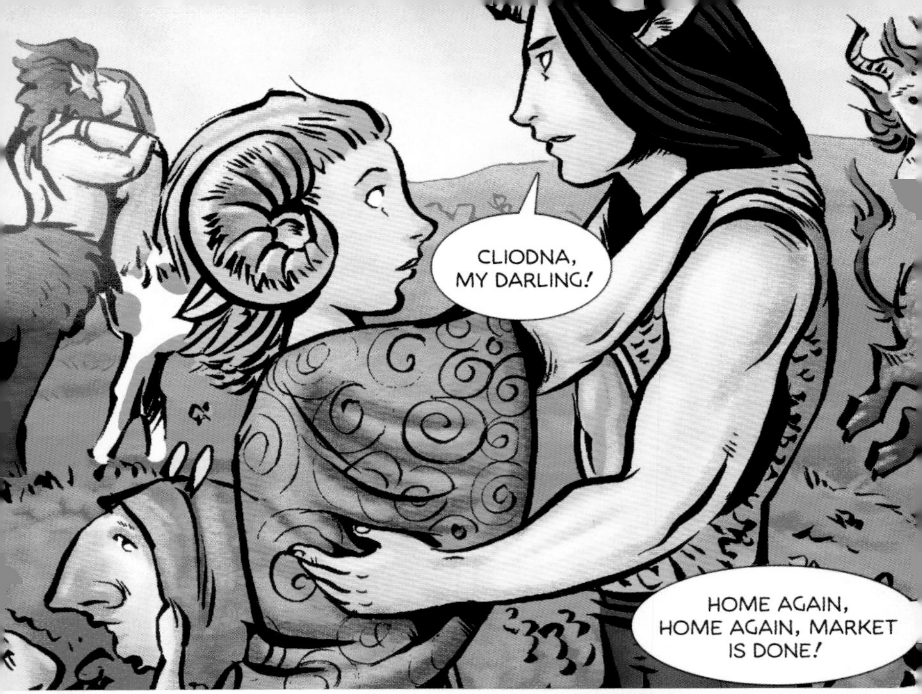
CLIODNA, MY DARLING!
HOME AGAIN, HOME AGAIN, MARKET IS DONE!

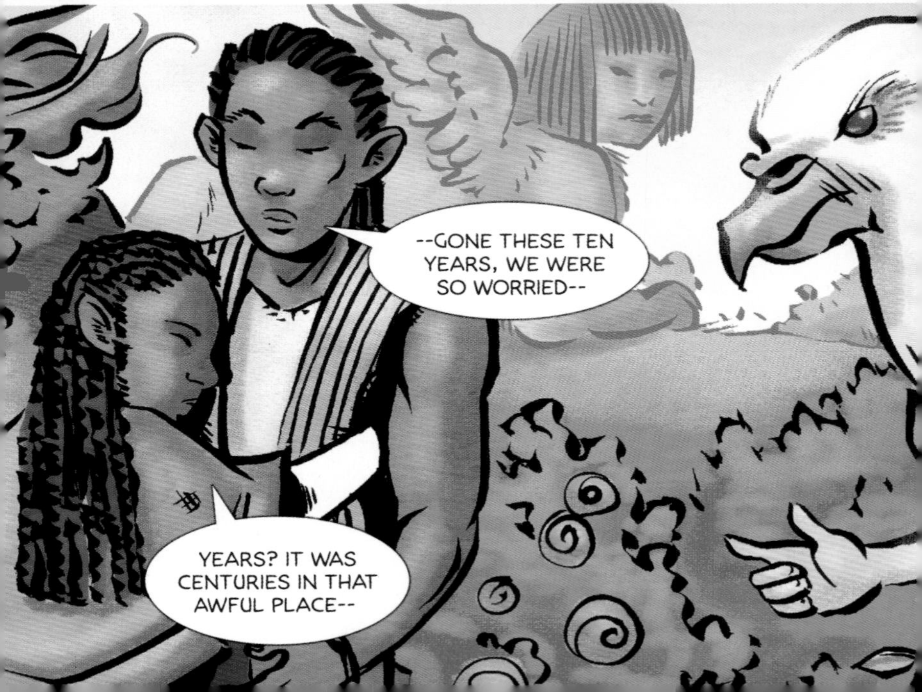
--GONE THESE TEN YEARS, WE WERE SO WORRIED--
YEARS? IT WAS CENTURIES IN THAT AWFUL PLACE--

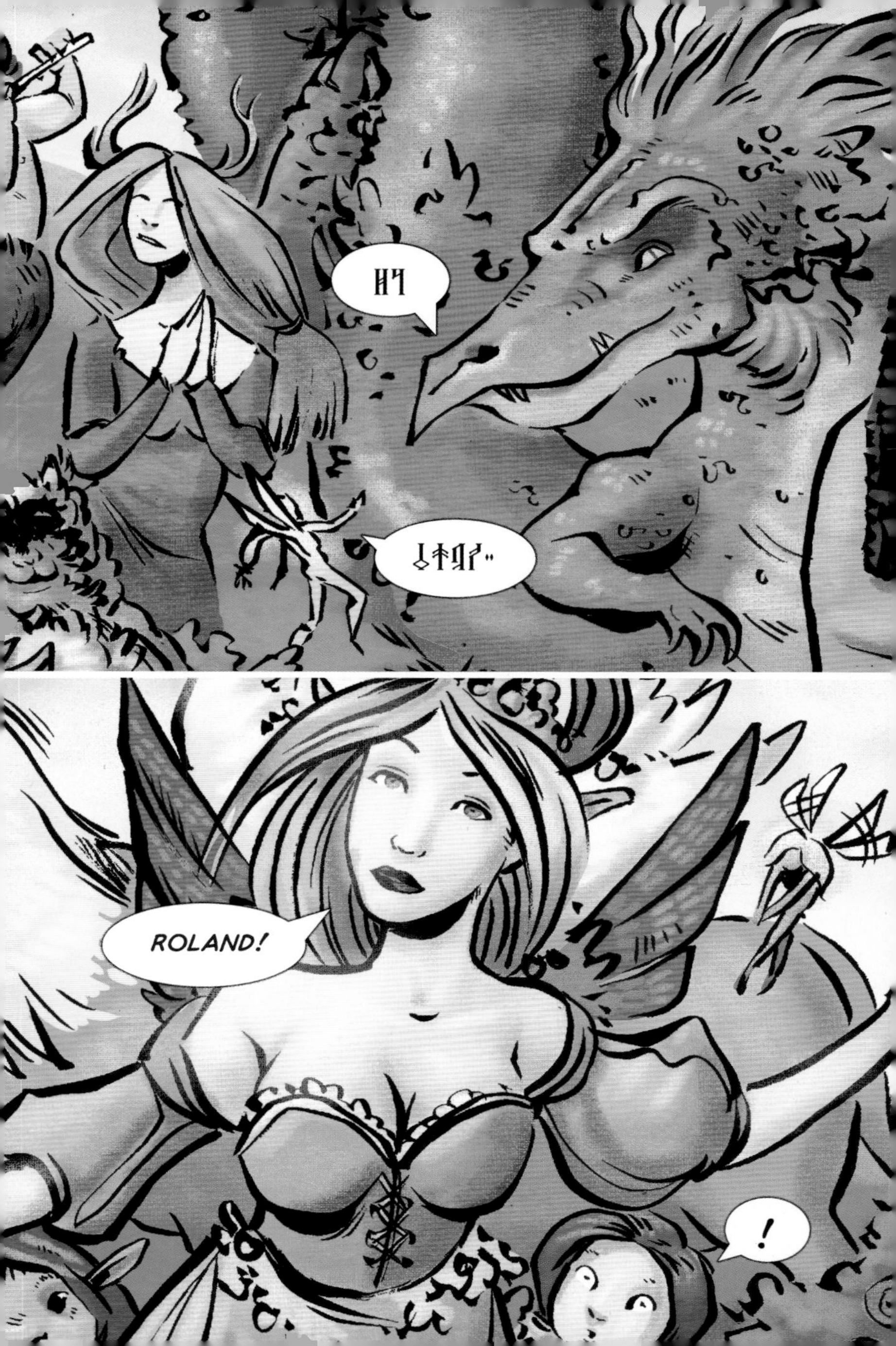
ROLAND!
!

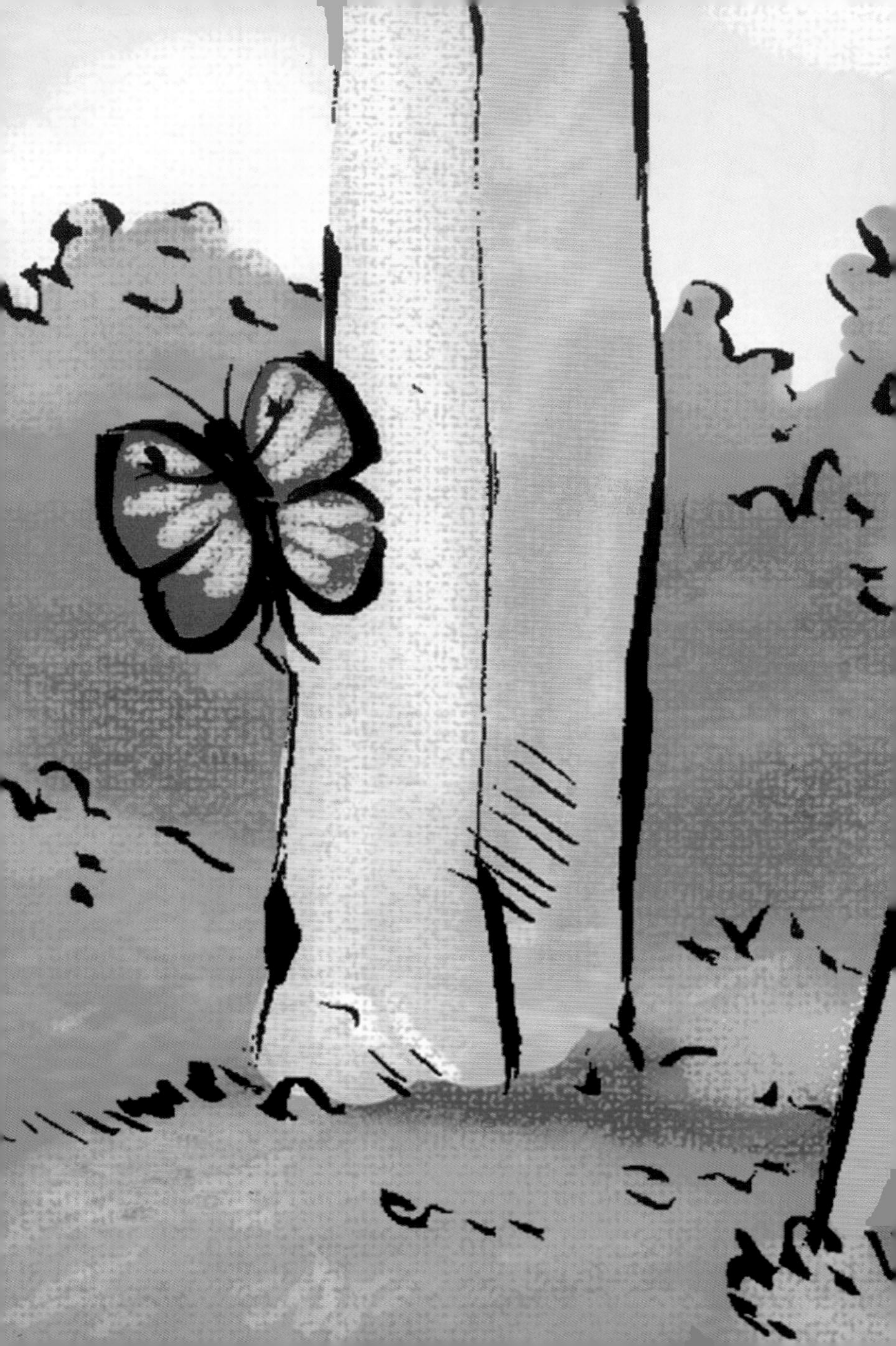

07

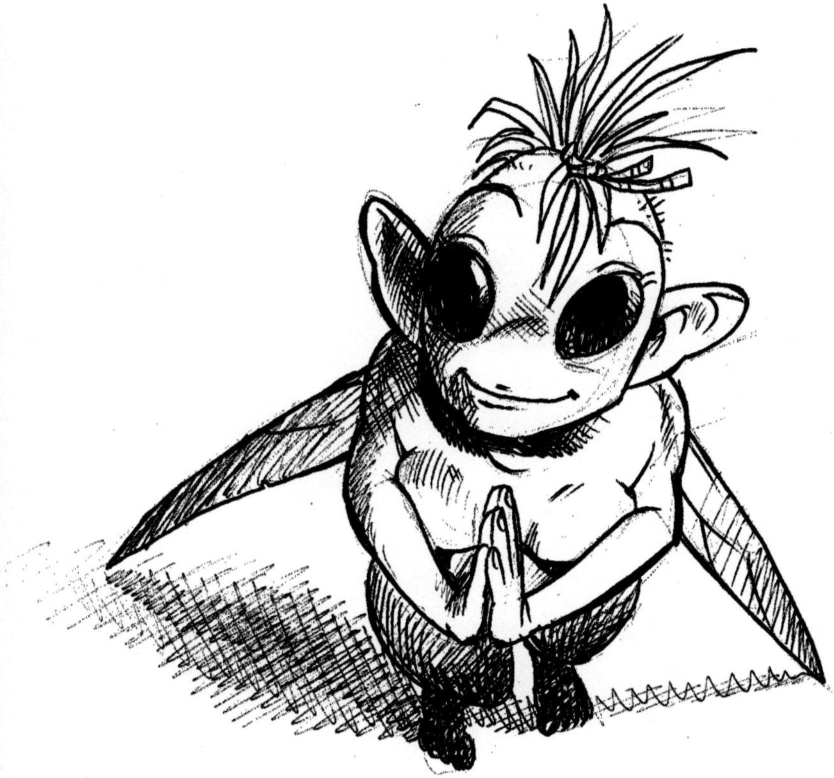

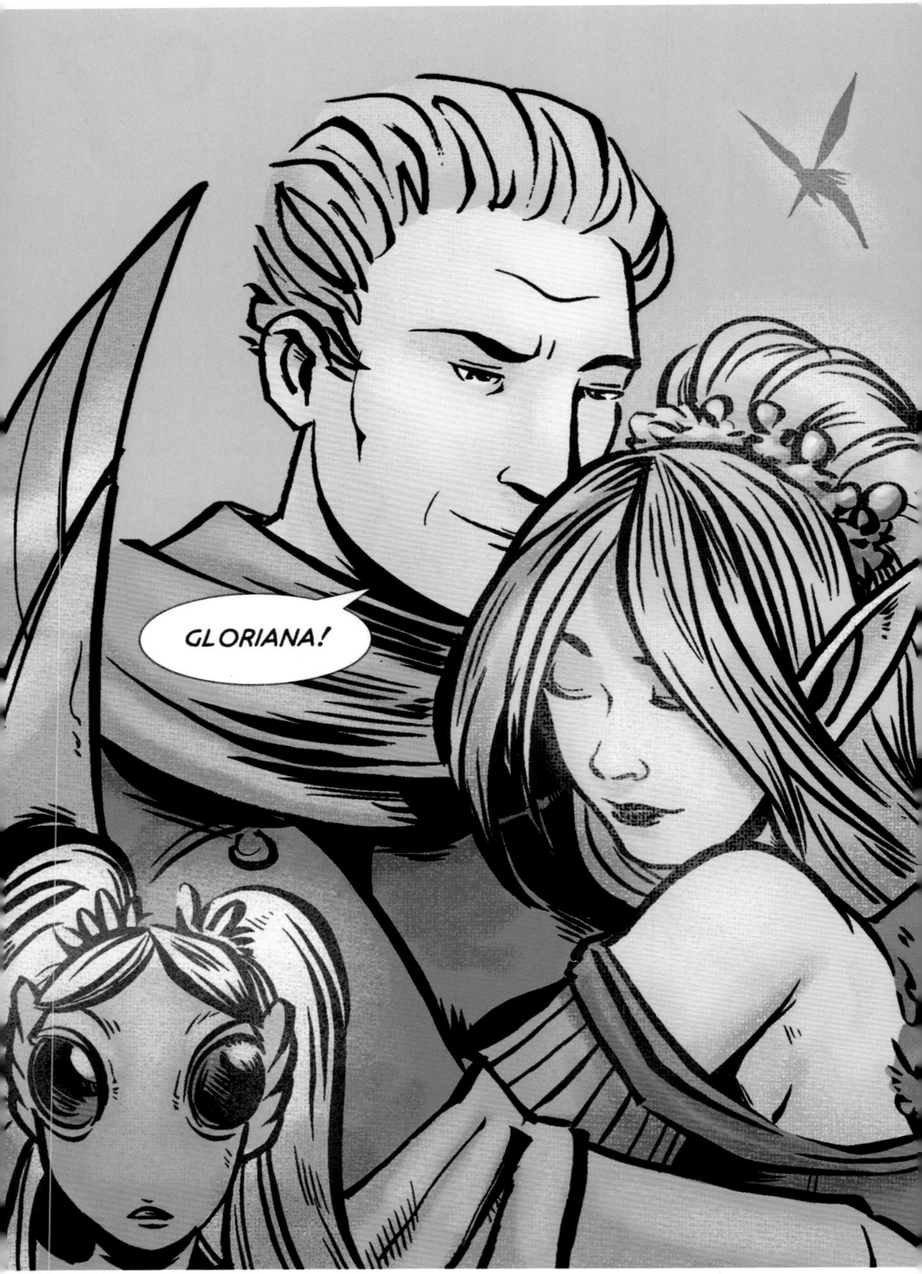
GLORIANA!

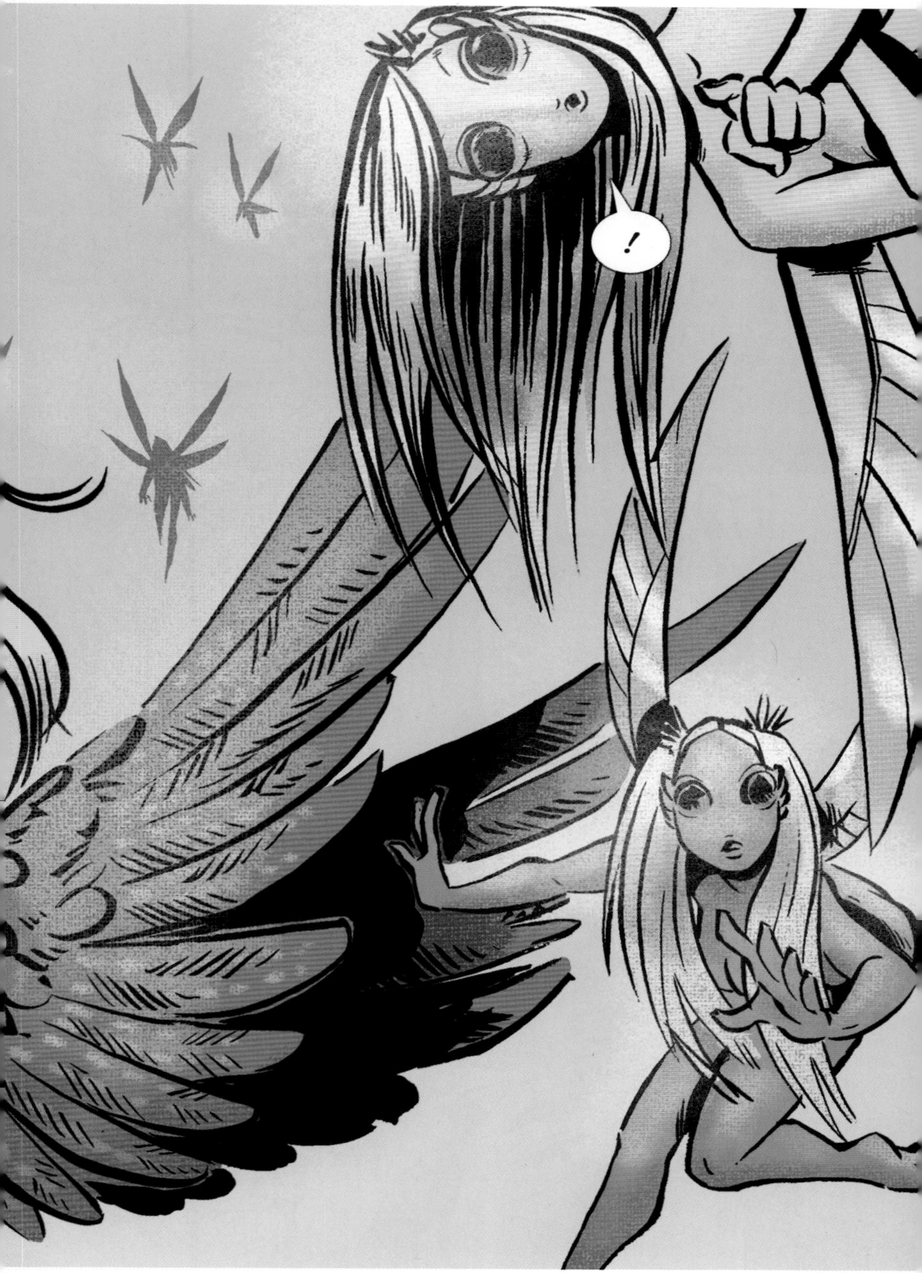
!

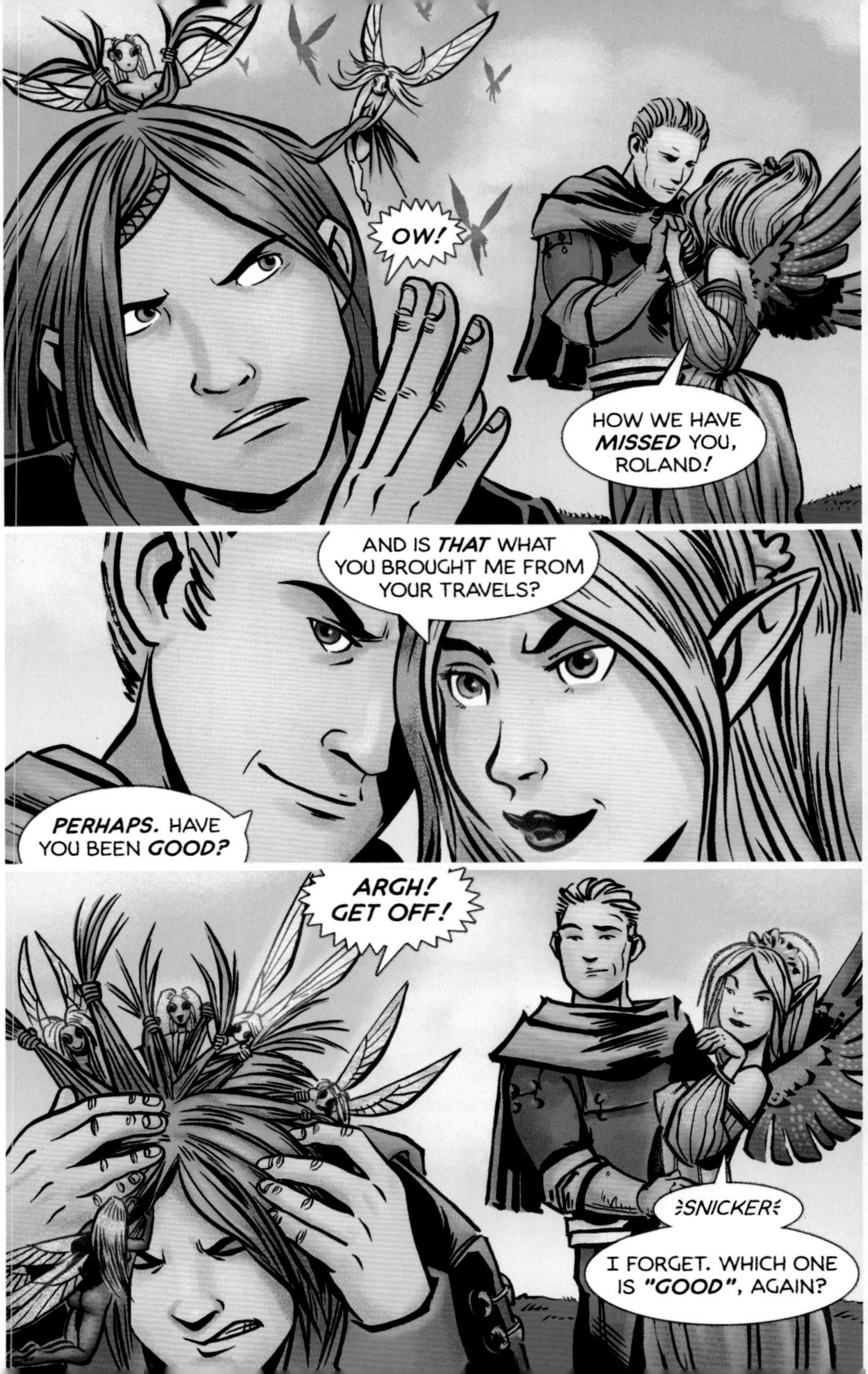
OW!
HOW WE HAVE MISSED YOU, ROLAND!
AND IS THAT WHAT YOU BROUGHT ME FROM YOUR TRAVELS?
PERHAPS. HAVE YOU BEEN GOOD?
ARGH! GET OFF!
SNICKER
I FORGET. WHICH ONE IS "GOOD", AGAIN?

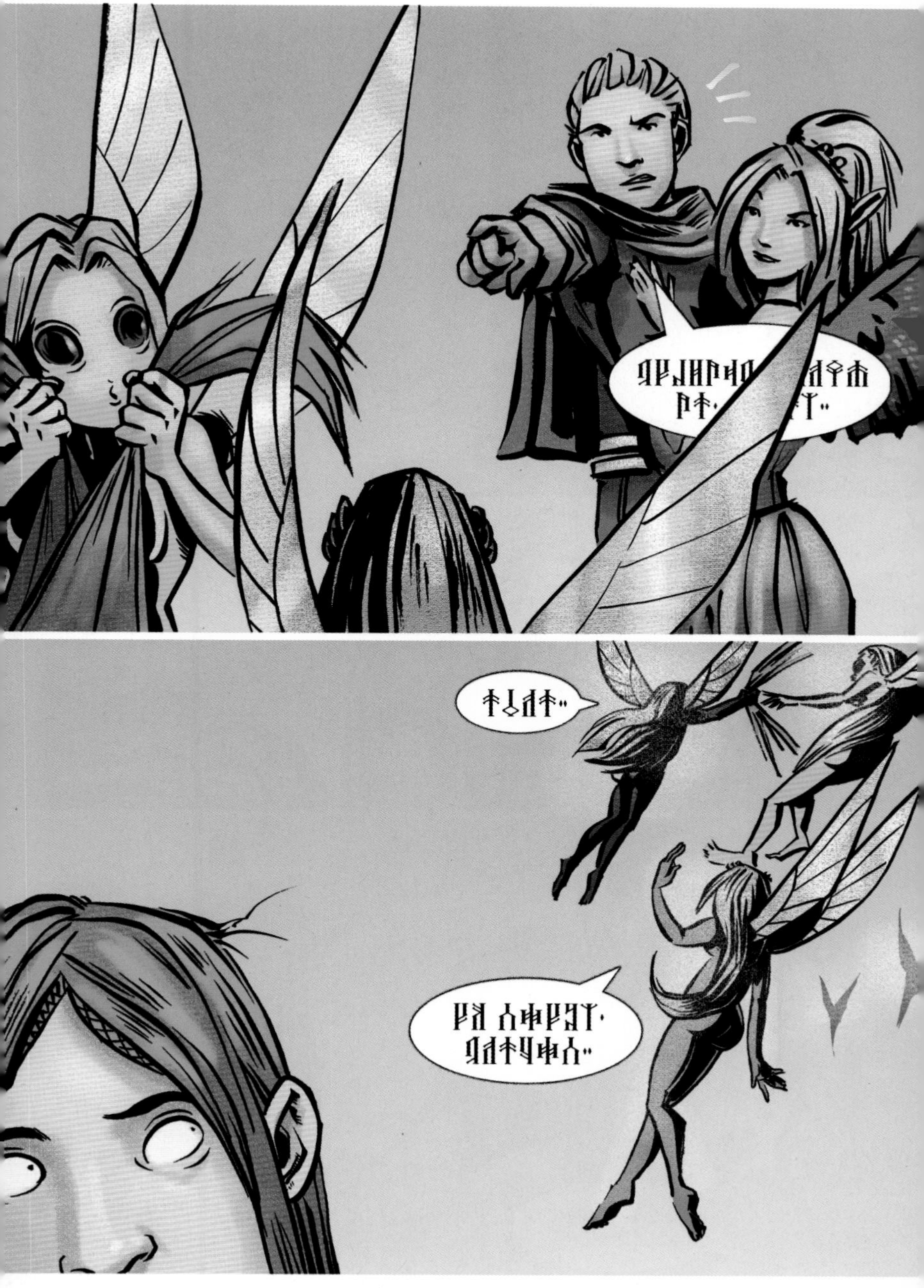

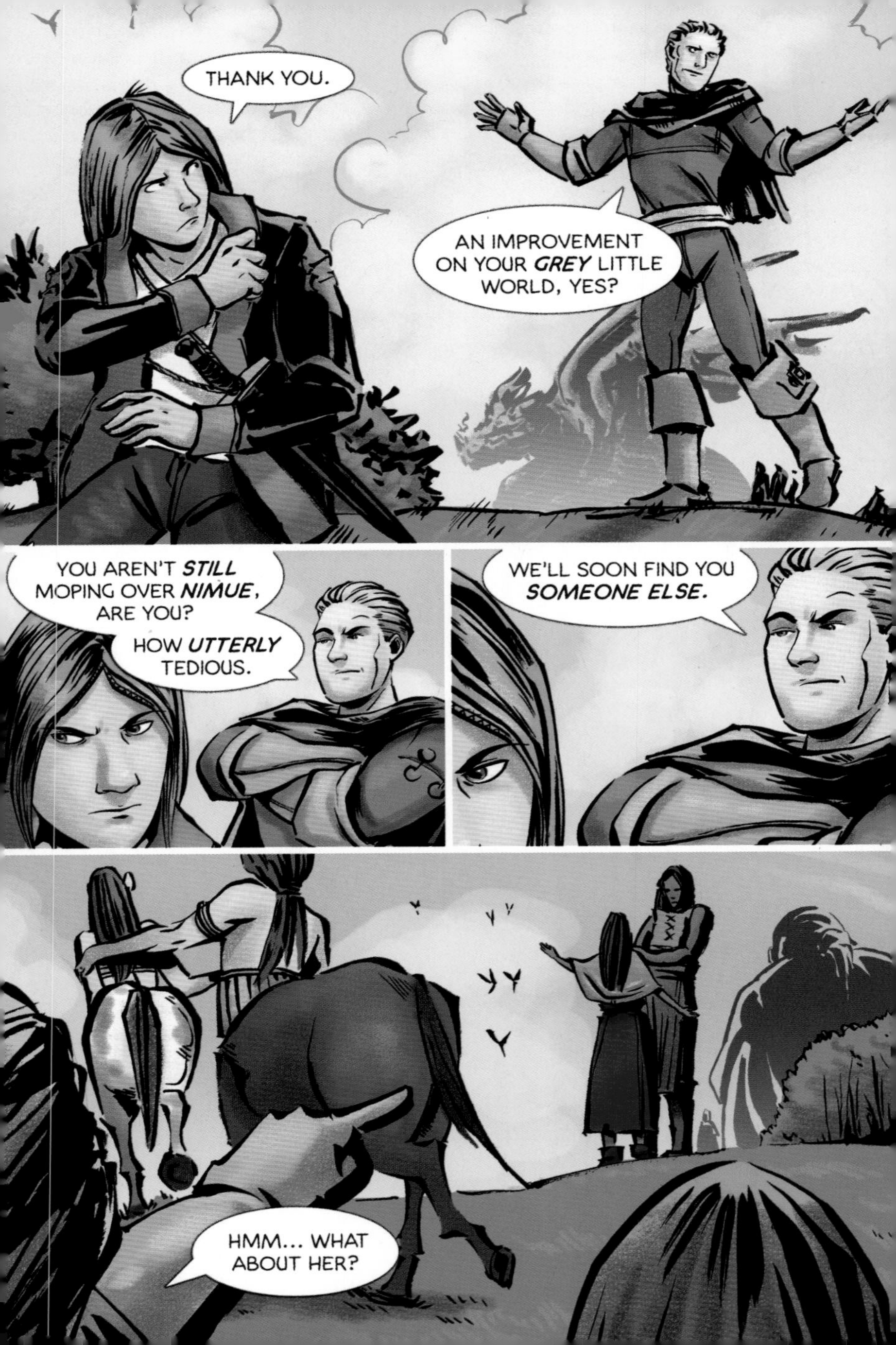
THANK YOU.
AN IMPROVEMENT ON YOUR *GREY* LITTLE WORLD, YES?
YOU AREN'T *STILL* MOPING OVER *NIMUE*, ARE YOU?
HOW *UTTERLY* TEDIOUS.
WE'LL SOON FIND YOU *SOMEONE ELSE.*
HMM... WHAT ABOUT HER?

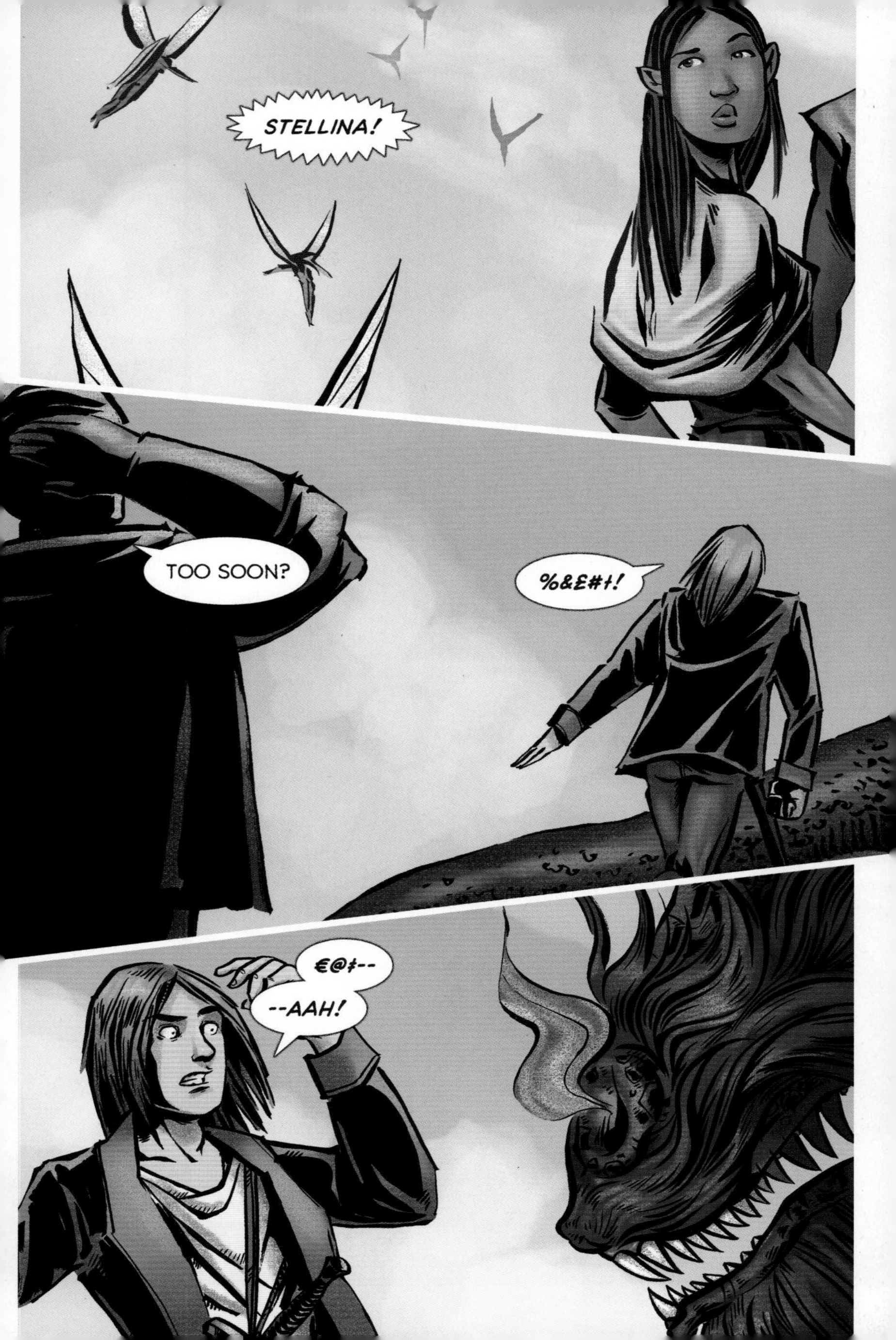
STELLINA!
TOO SOON?
%&£#†!
€@‡--
--AAH!

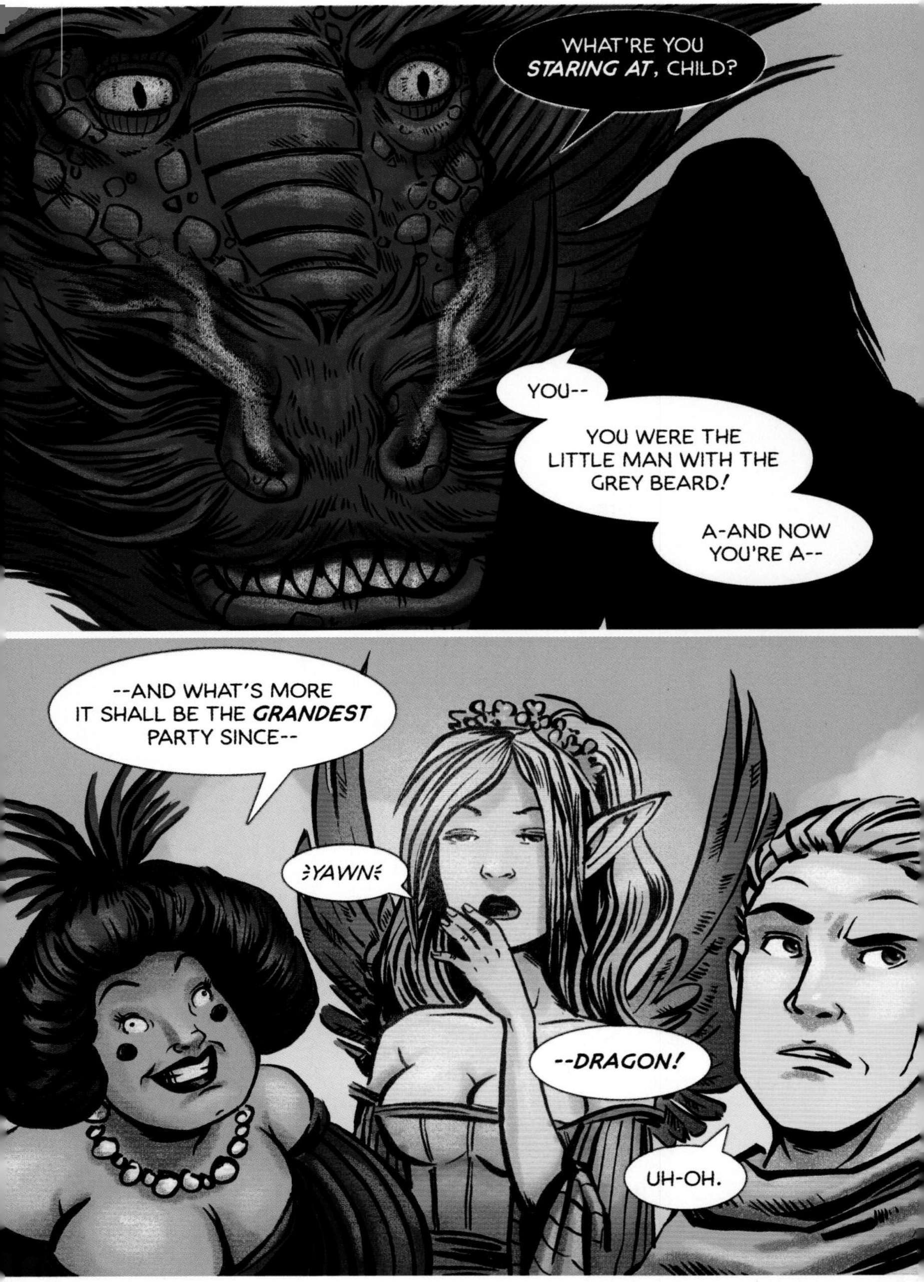
WHAT'RE YOU STARING AT, CHILD?
YOU--
YOU WERE THE LITTLE MAN WITH THE GREY BEARD!
A-AND NOW YOU'RE A--
--AND WHAT'S MORE IT SHALL BE THE GRANDEST PARTY SINCE--
YAWN
--DRAGON!
UH-OH.

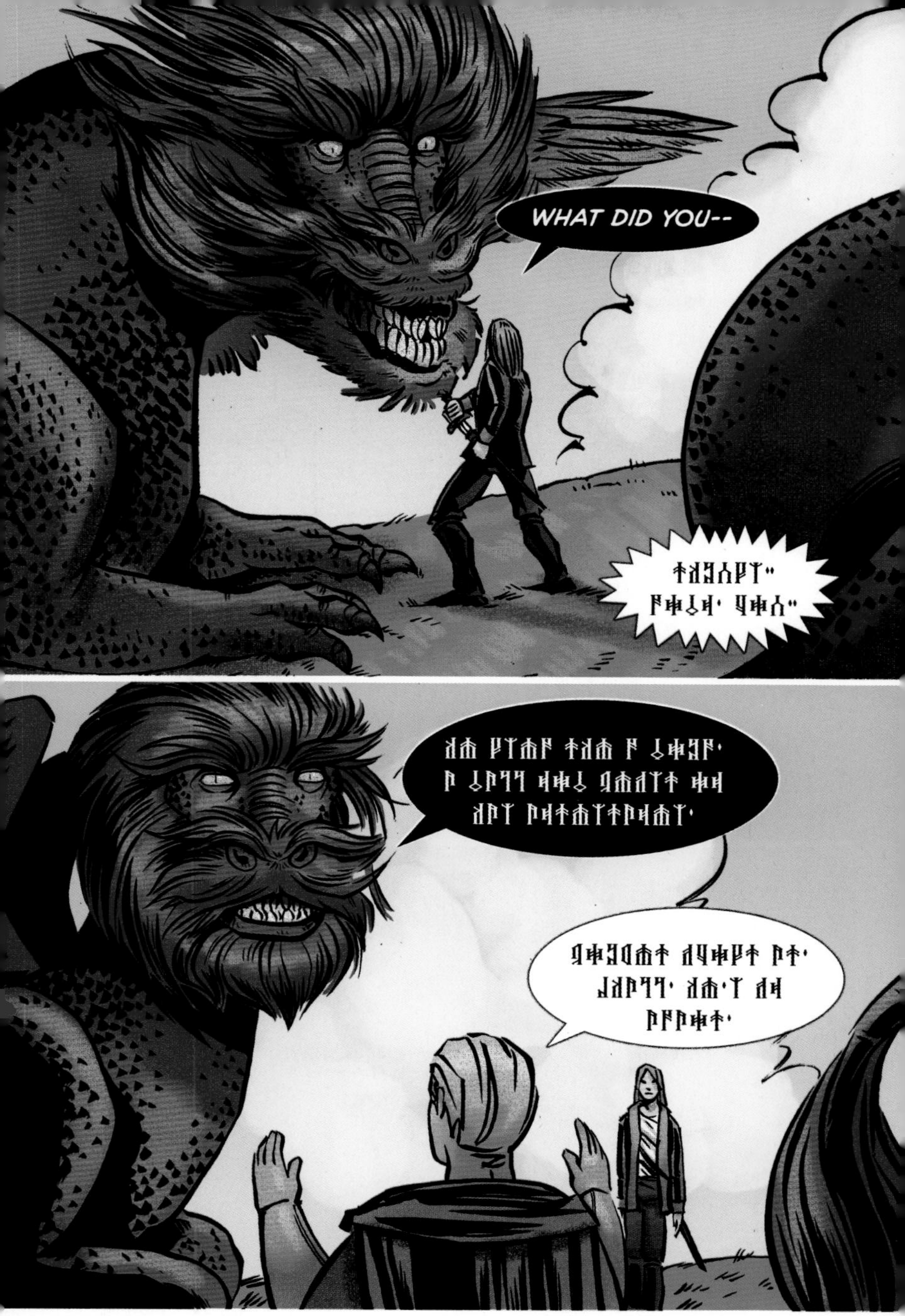
WHAT DID YOU--

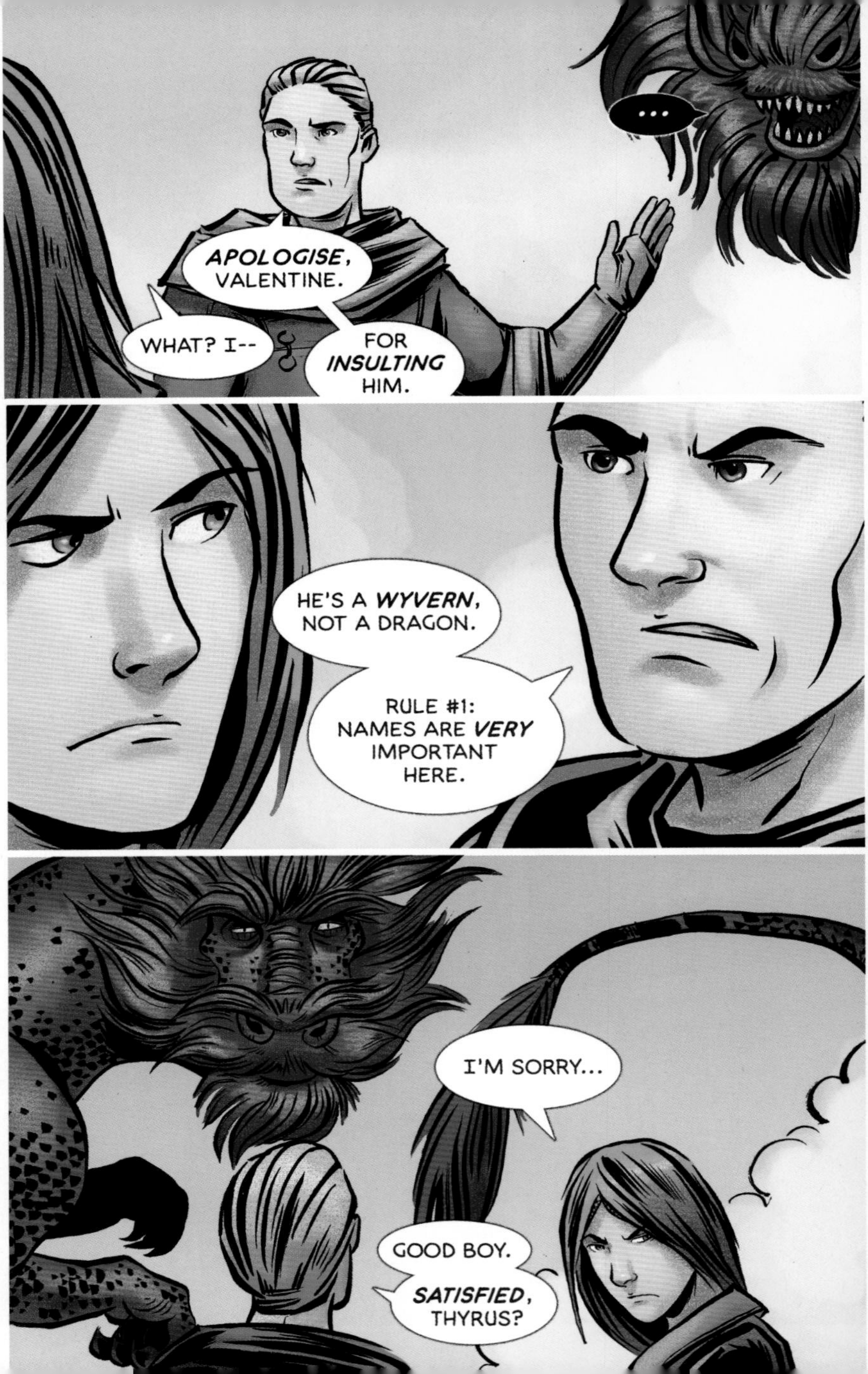
...
APOLOGISE, VALENTINE.
WHAT? I--
FOR INSULTING HIM.
HE'S A WYVERN, NOT A DRAGON.
RULE #1: NAMES ARE VERY IMPORTANT HERE.
I'M SORRY...
GOOD BOY.
SATISFIED, THYRUS?

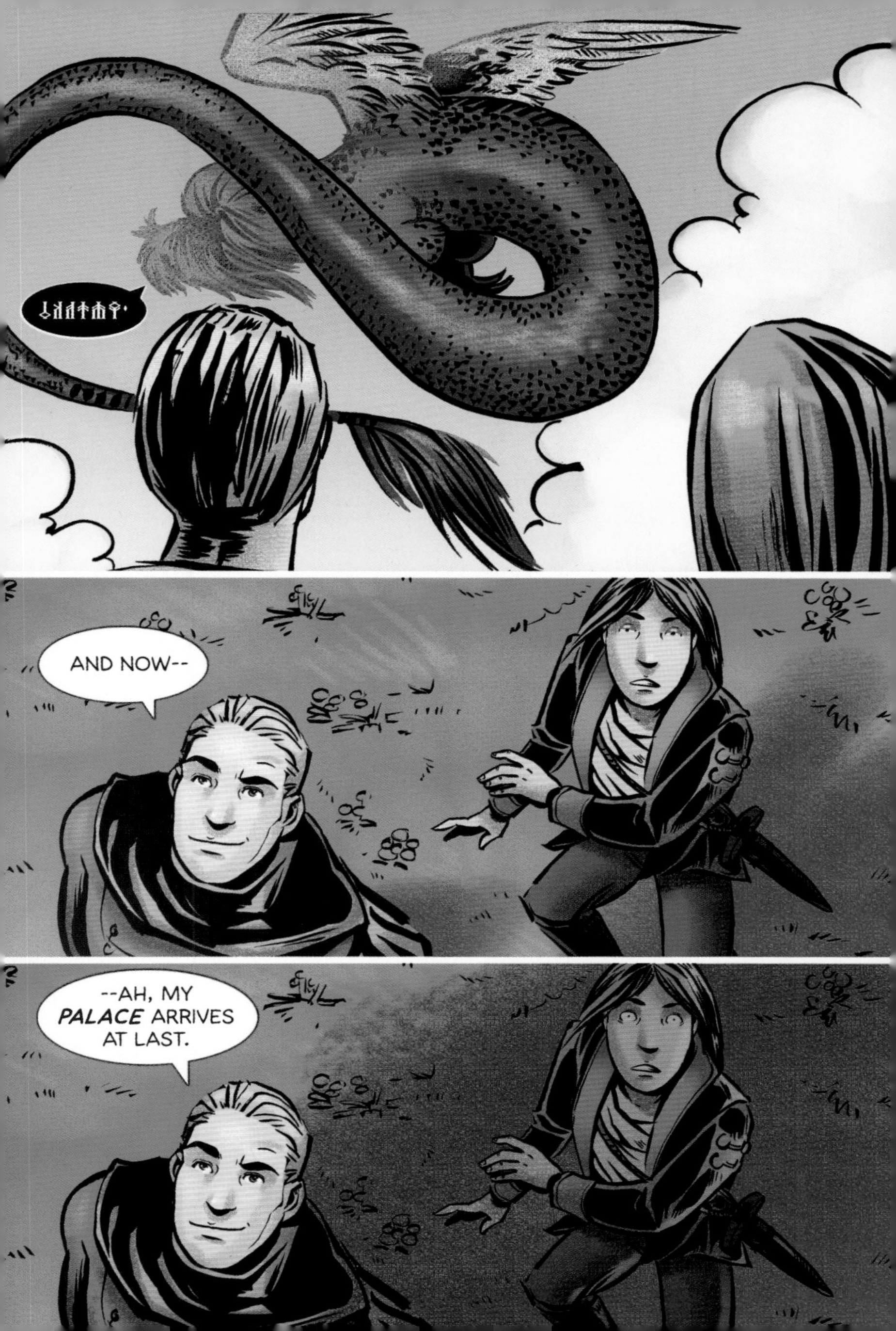
AND NOW--
--AH, MY *PALACE* ARRIVES AT LAST.

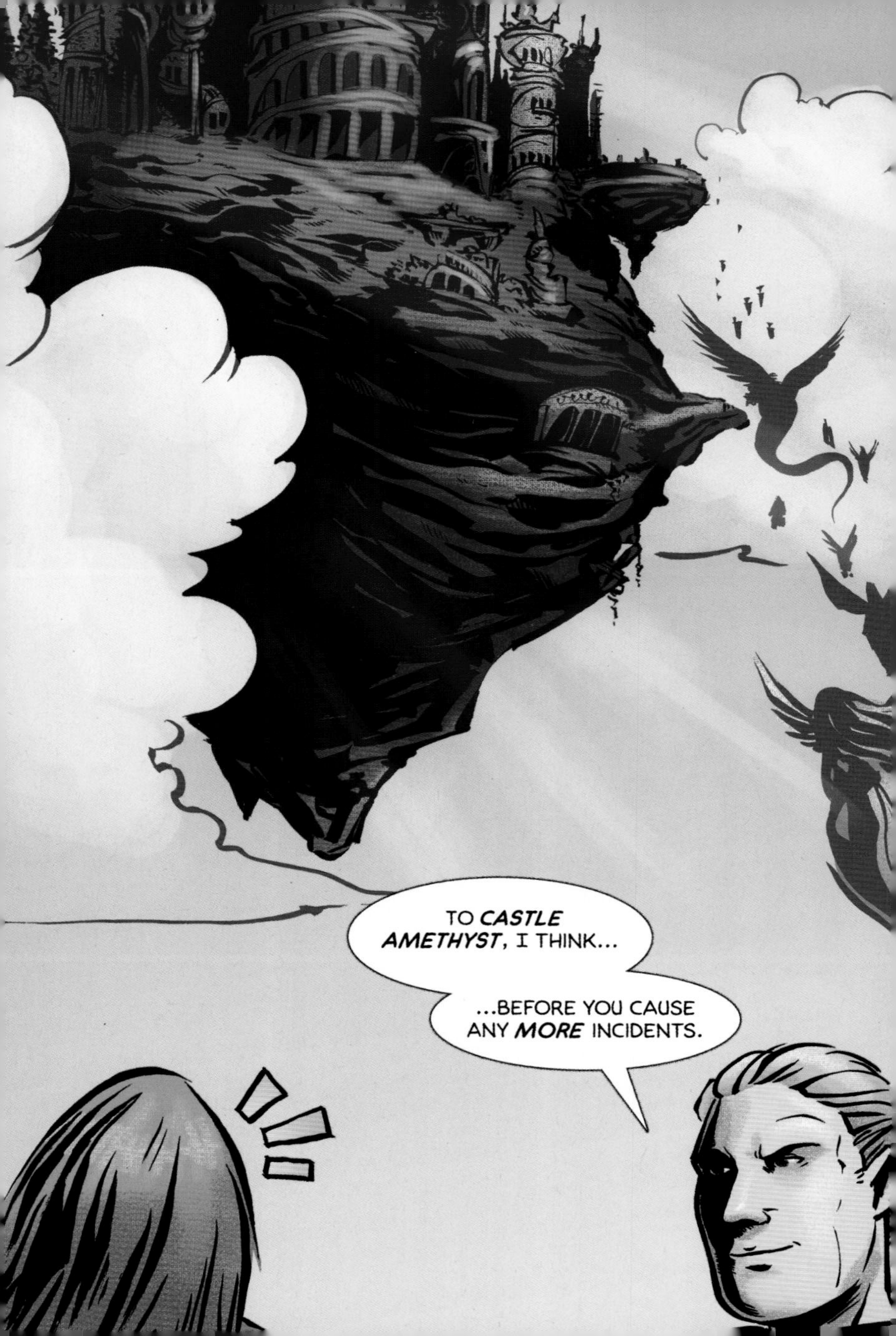
TO CASTLE AMETHYST, I THINK...
...BEFORE YOU CAUSE ANY MORE INCIDENTS.

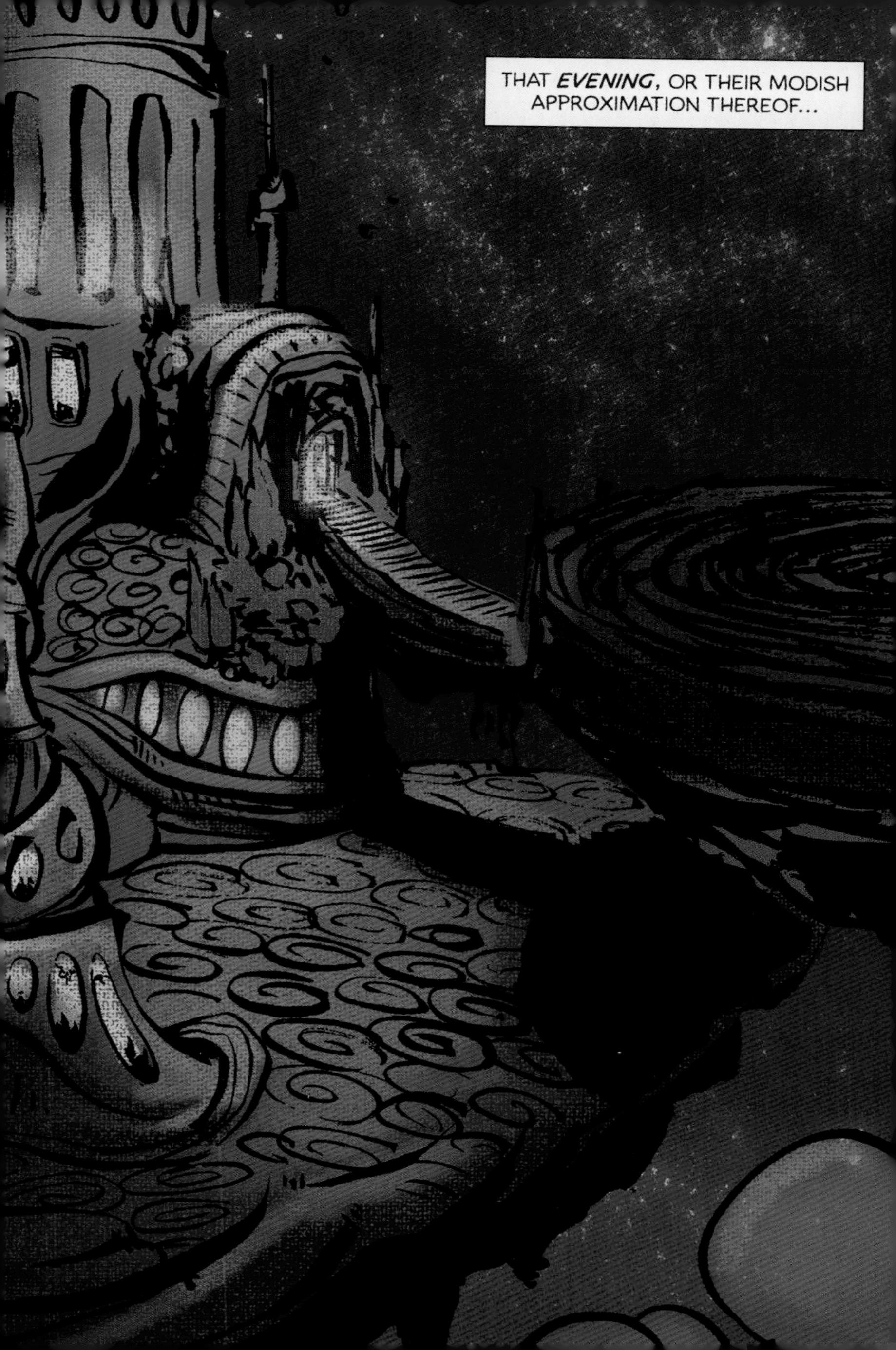
THAT *EVENING*, OR THEIR MODISH APPROXIMATION THEREOF...

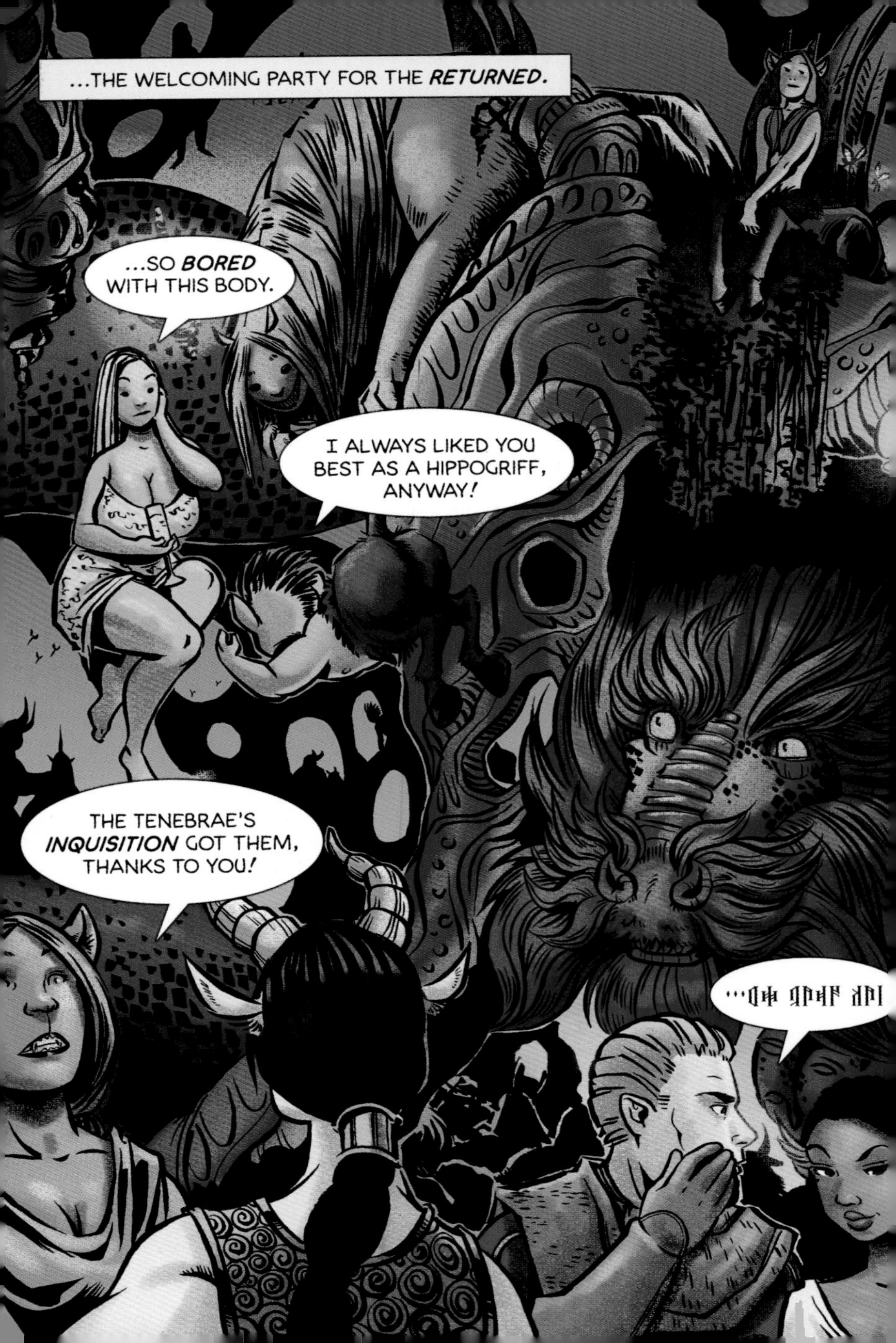
...THE WELCOMING PARTY FOR THE RETURNED.
...SO BORED WITH THIS BODY.
I ALWAYS LIKED YOU BEST AS A HIPPOGRIFF, ANYWAY!
THE TENEBRAE'S INQUISITION GOT THEM, THANKS TO YOU!

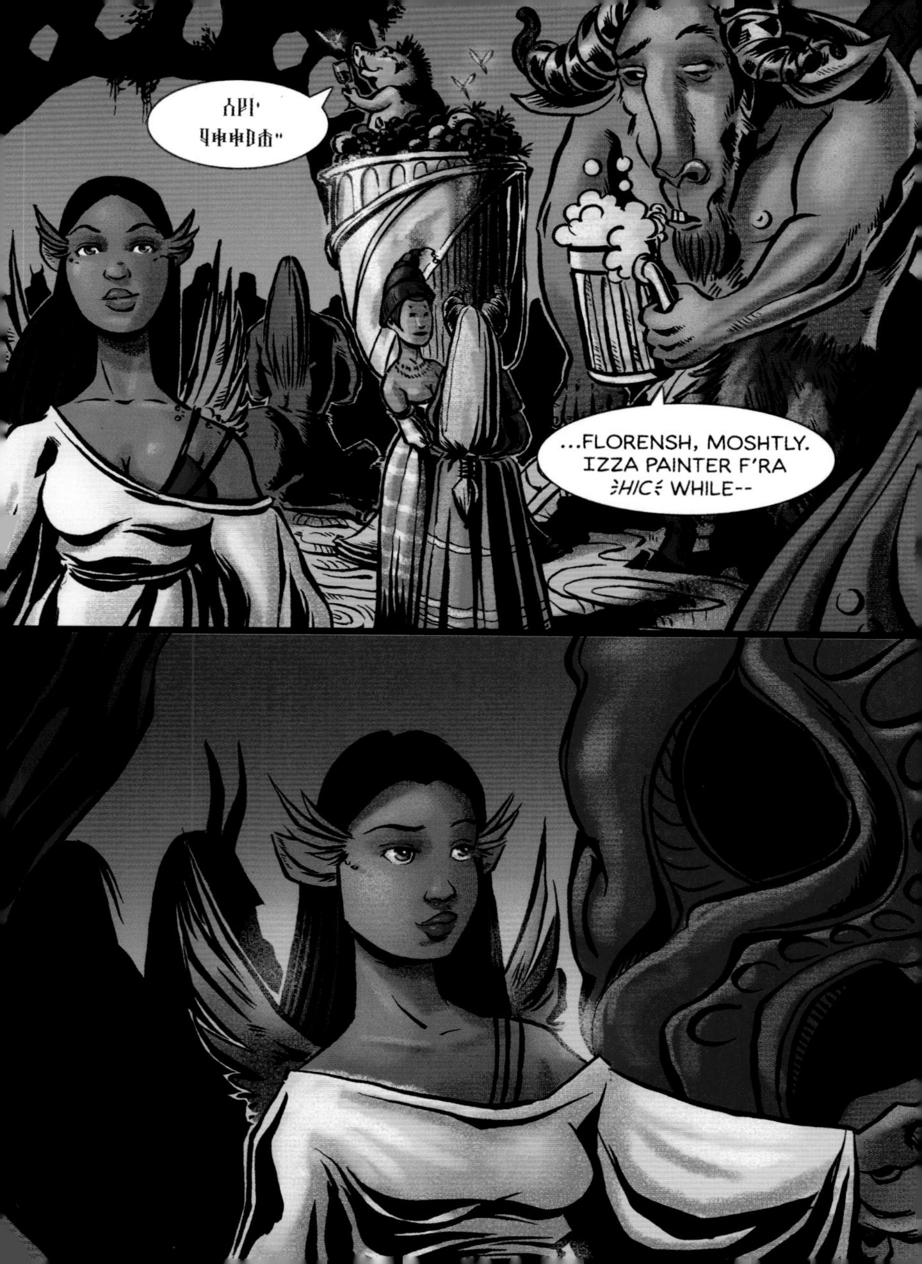
...FLORENSH, MOSHTLY. IZZA PAINTER F'RA HIC WHILE--

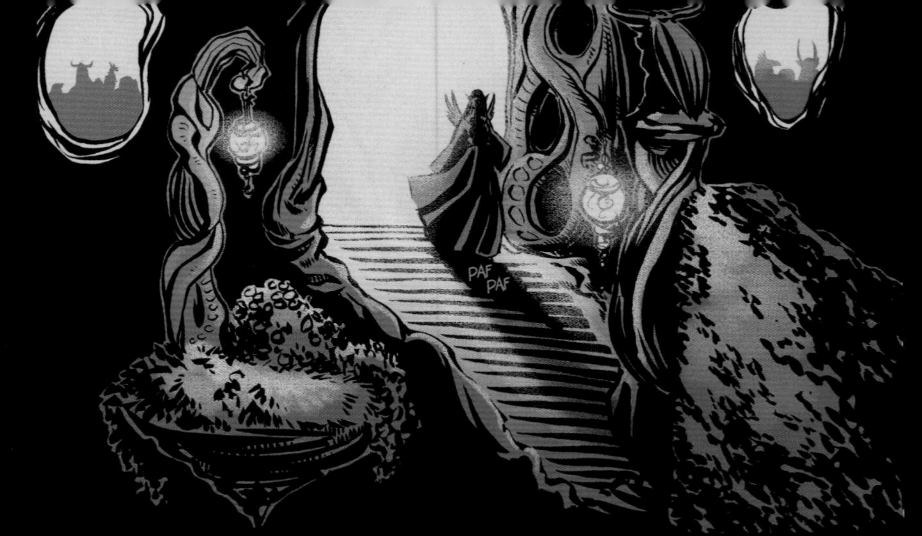
PAF
PAF

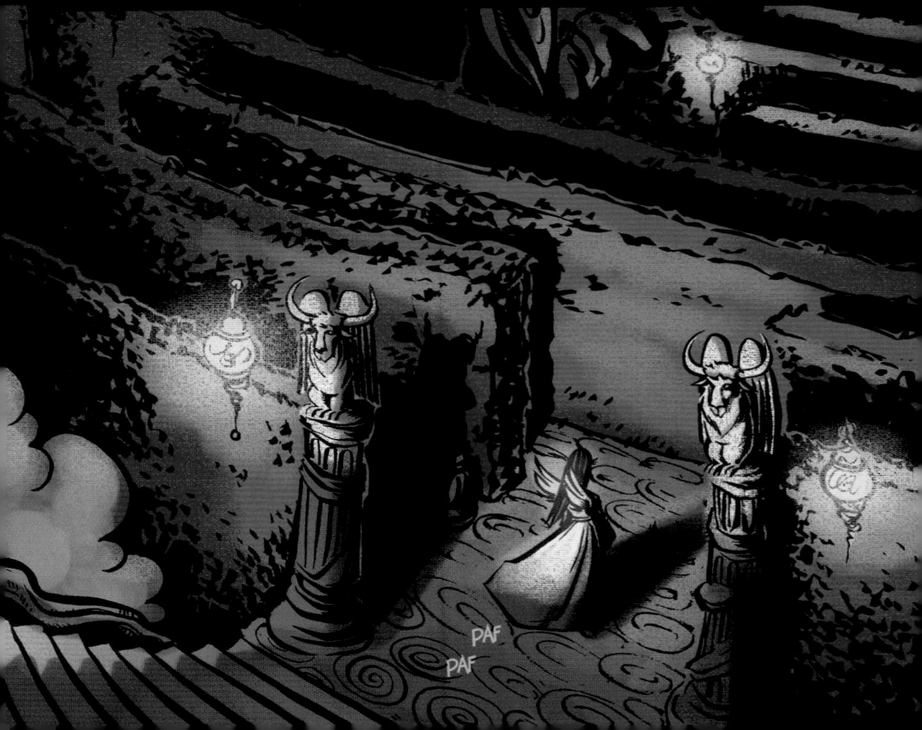
PAF
PAF

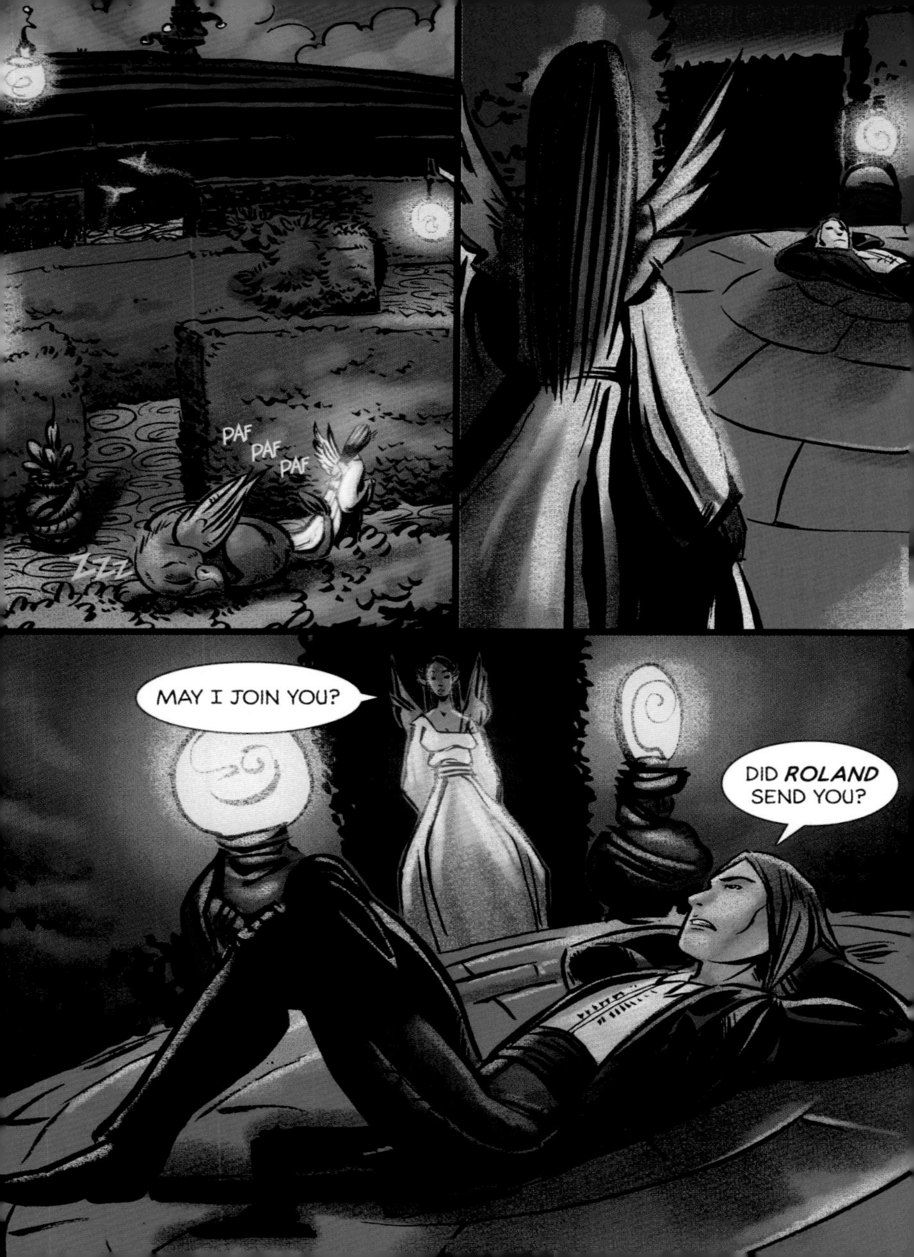
PAF
PAF
PAF
ZZZ
MAY I JOIN YOU?
DID *ROLAND* SEND YOU?

I CAME BECAUSE I WANTED TO *THANK* YOU.
I WAS READY TO *KILL* MYSELF. SO *MANY* OF US ALREADY HAD...
I WAS STUCK IN THAT *BIGOTED*, HORRIBLE WORLD OF YOURS FOR HUNDREDS OF YEARS...
...UNTIL I BEGAN TO *DOUBT* THE DAWN COUNTRY HAD EVER EXISTED.

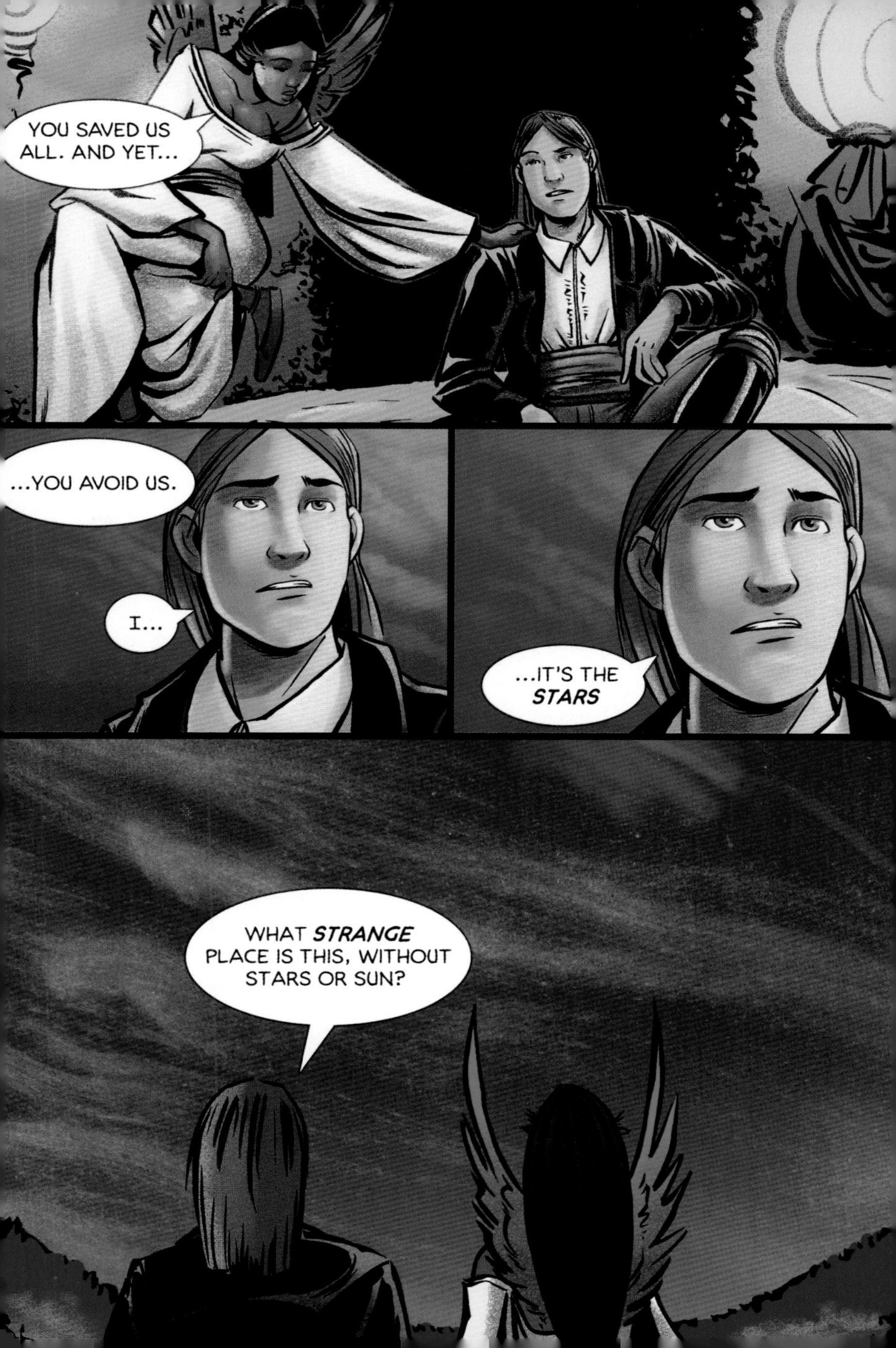
YOU SAVED US ALL. AND YET...
...YOU AVOID US.
I...
...IT'S THE *STARS*
WHAT *STRANGE* PLACE IS THIS, WITHOUT STARS OR SUN?

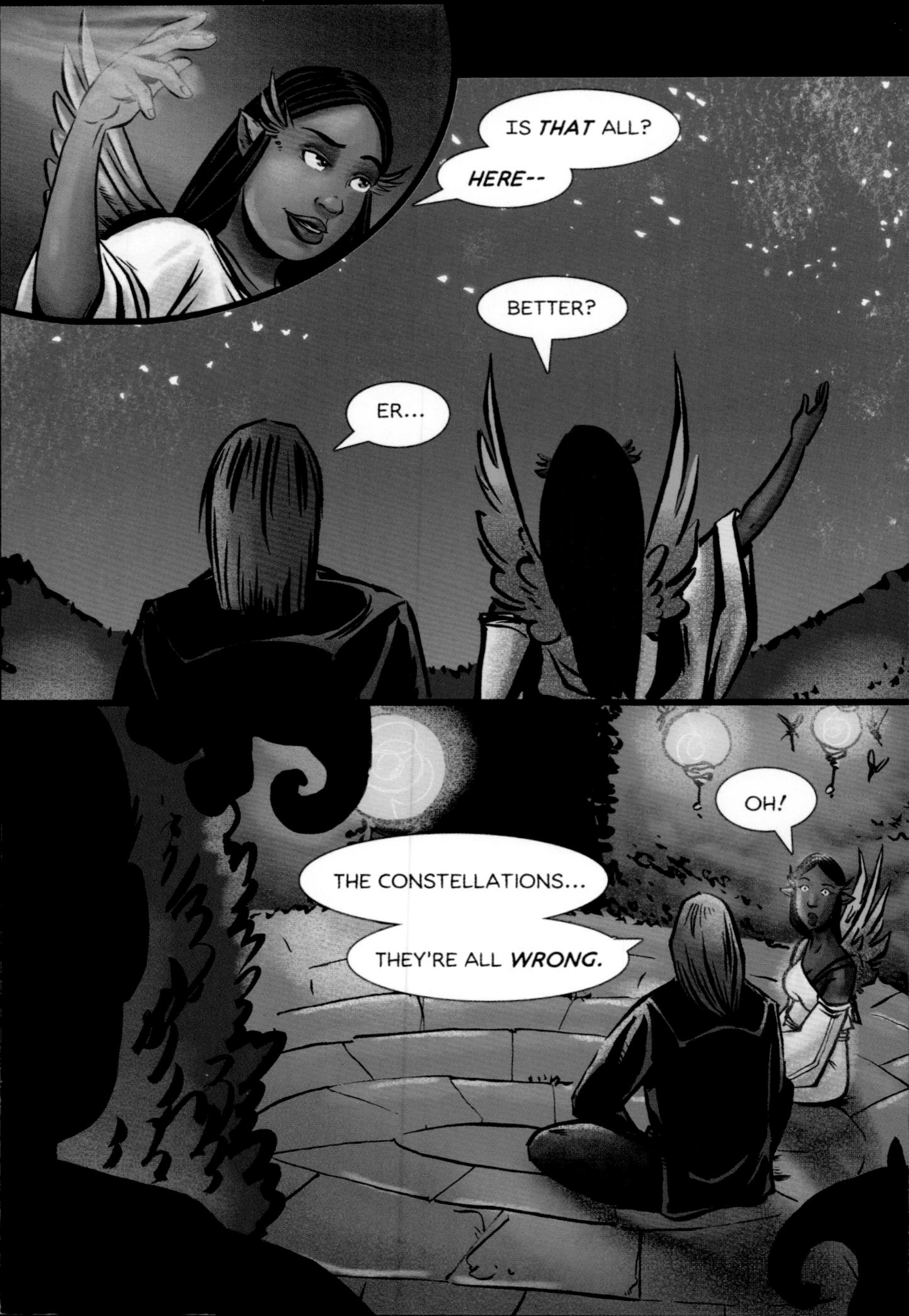
IS *THAT* ALL?
HERE--
BETTER?
ER...
OH!
THE CONSTELLATIONS...
THEY'RE ALL *WRONG.*

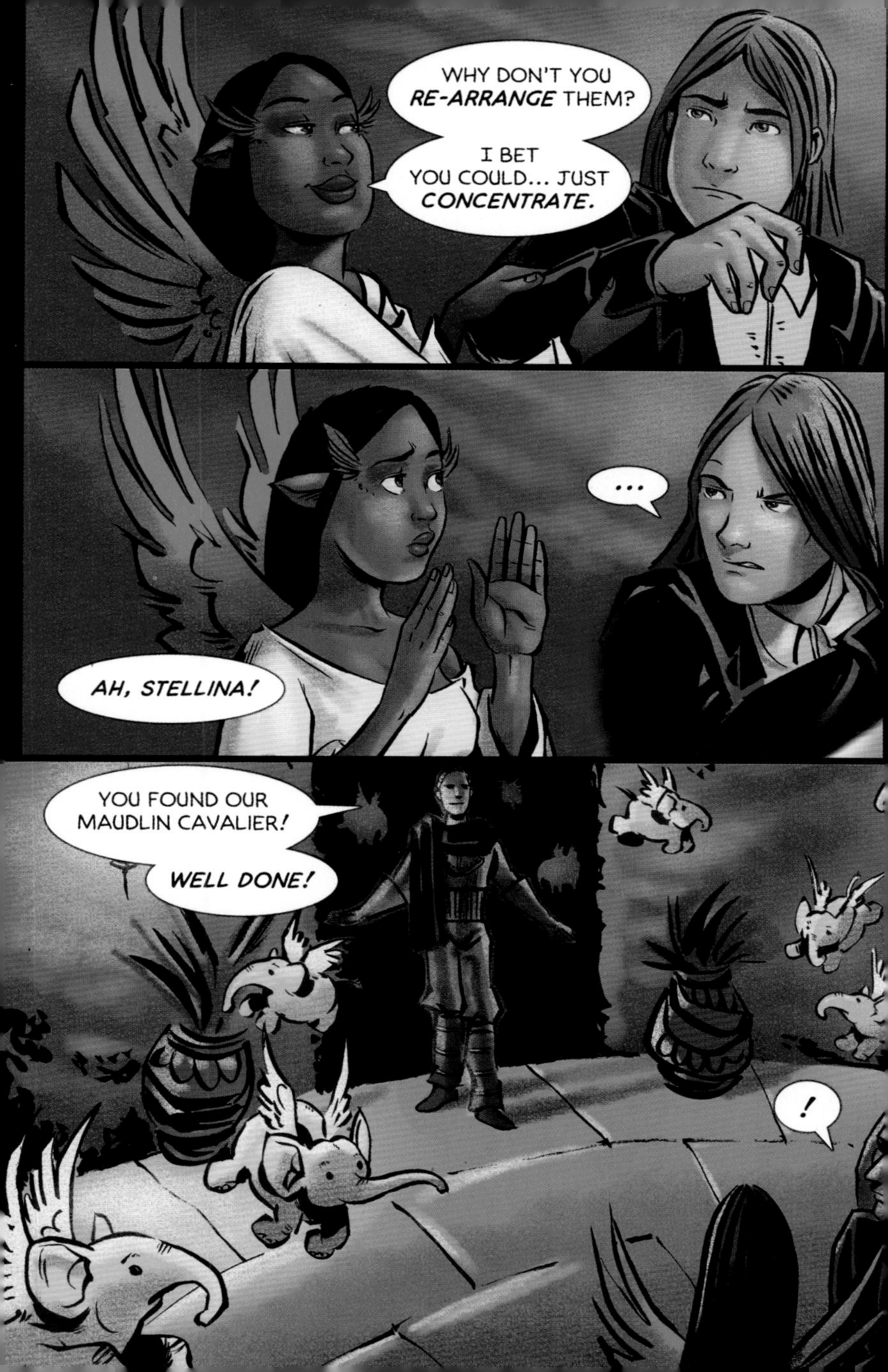
WHY DON'T YOU *RE-ARRANGE* THEM?
I BET YOU COULD... JUST *CONCENTRATE.*
...
AH, STELLINA!
YOU FOUND OUR MAUDLIN CAVALIER!
WELL DONE!
!

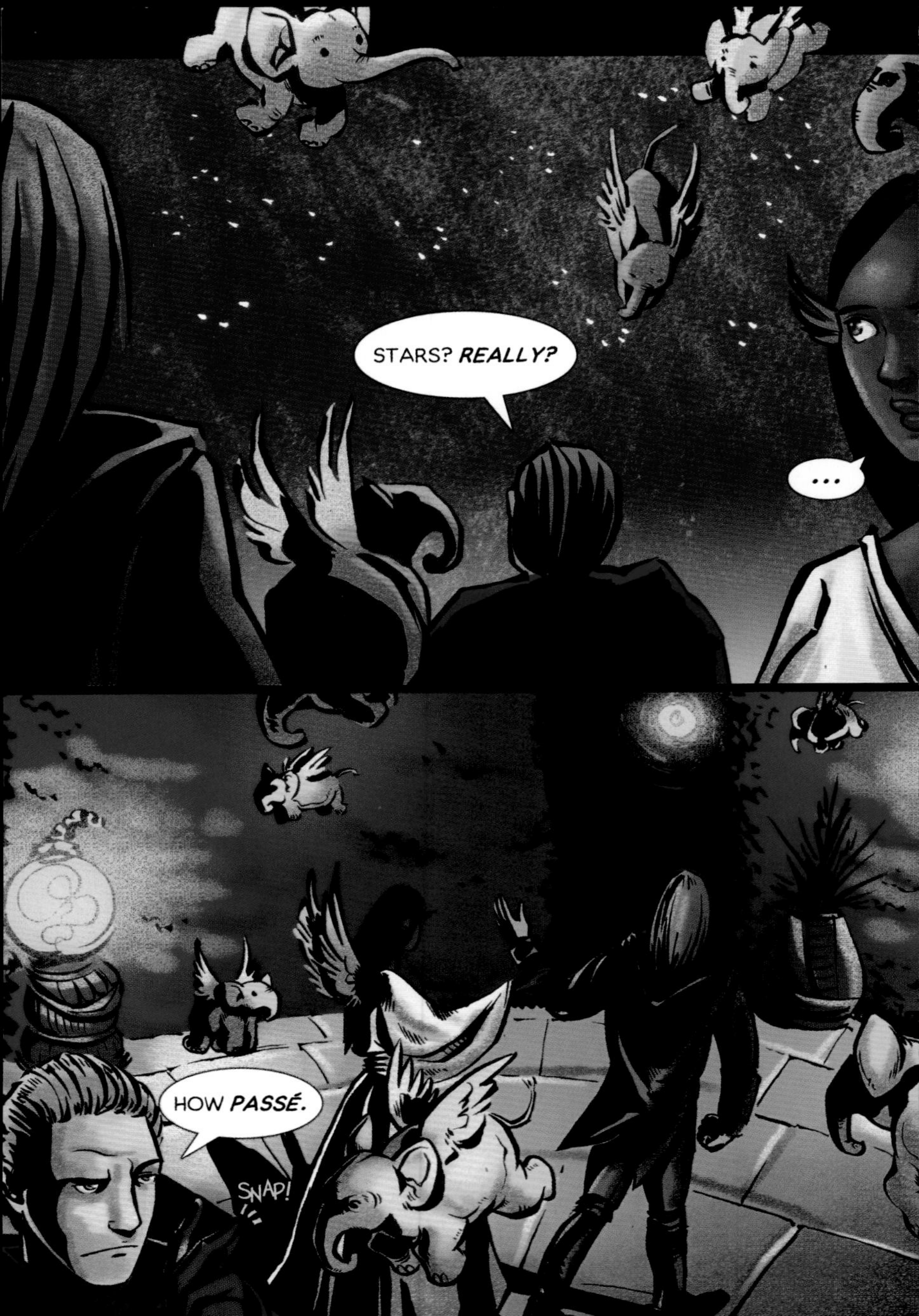
STARS? REALLY?
...
HOW PASSÉ.
SNAP!

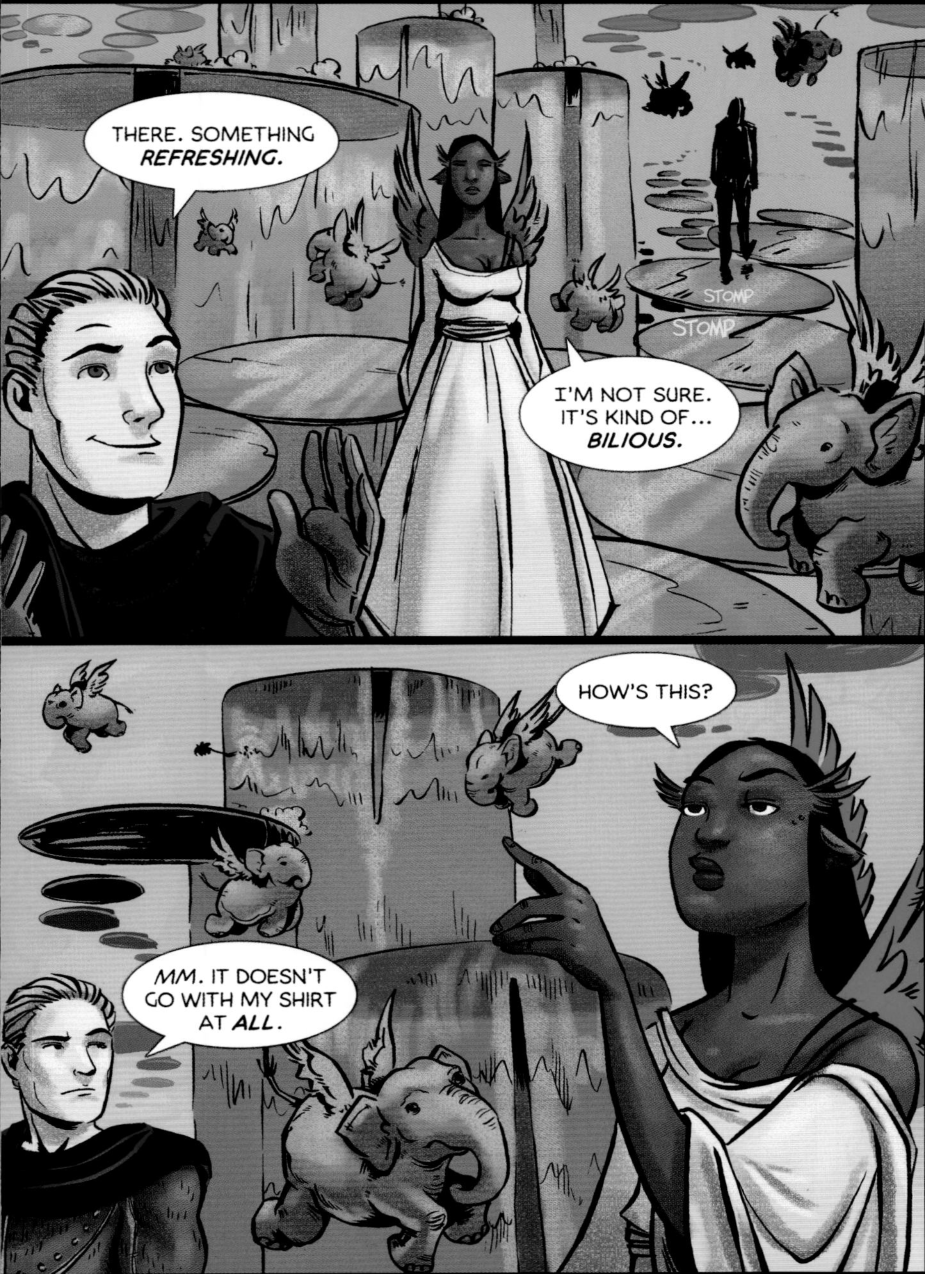
THERE. SOMETHING *REFRESHING.*
STOMP
STOMP
I'M NOT SURE. IT'S KIND OF... *BILIOUS.*
HOW'S THIS?
MM. IT DOESN'T GO WITH MY SHIRT AT *ALL*.

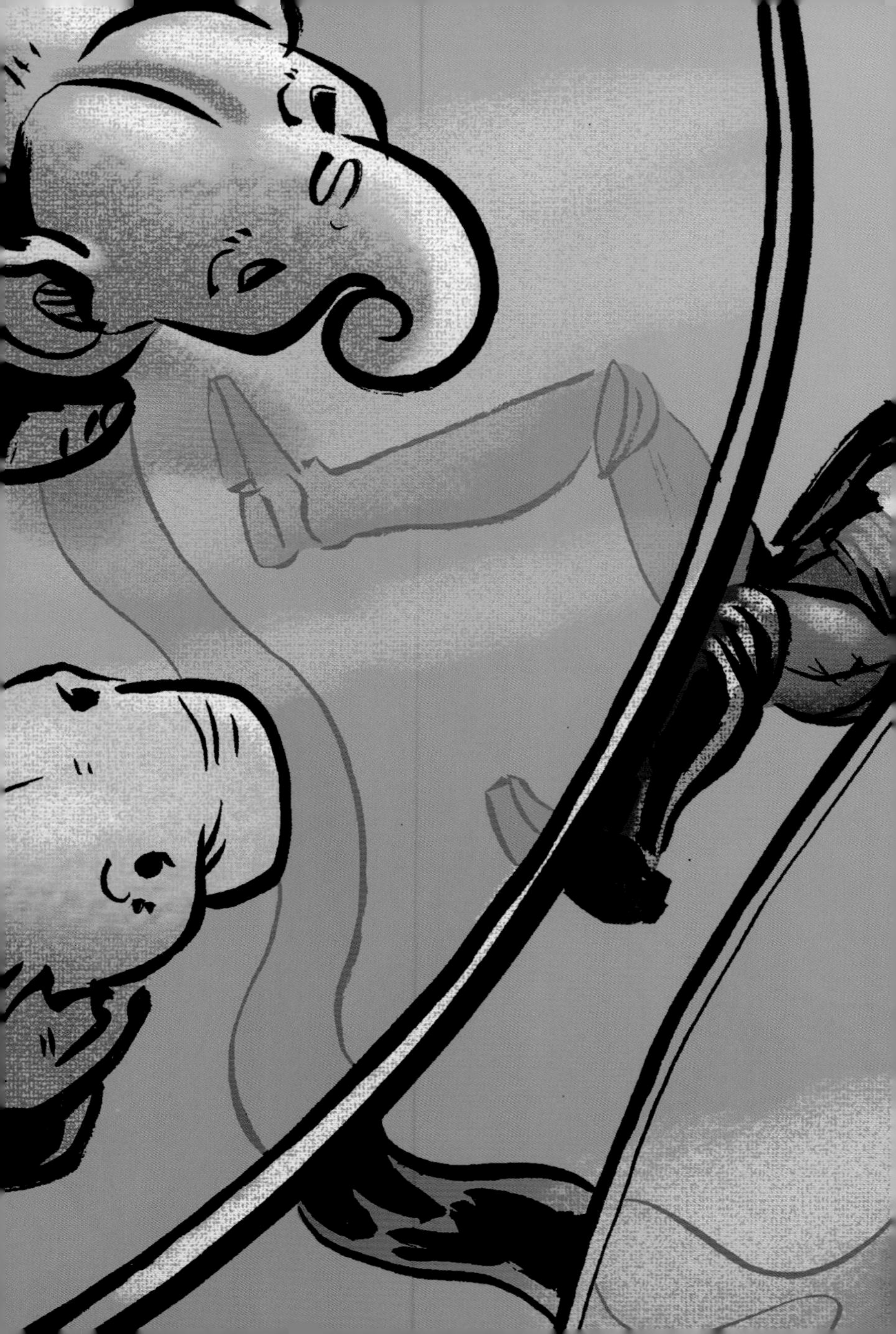

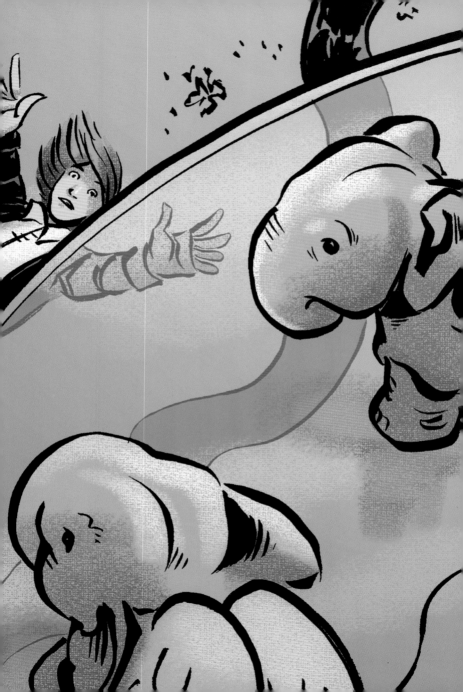

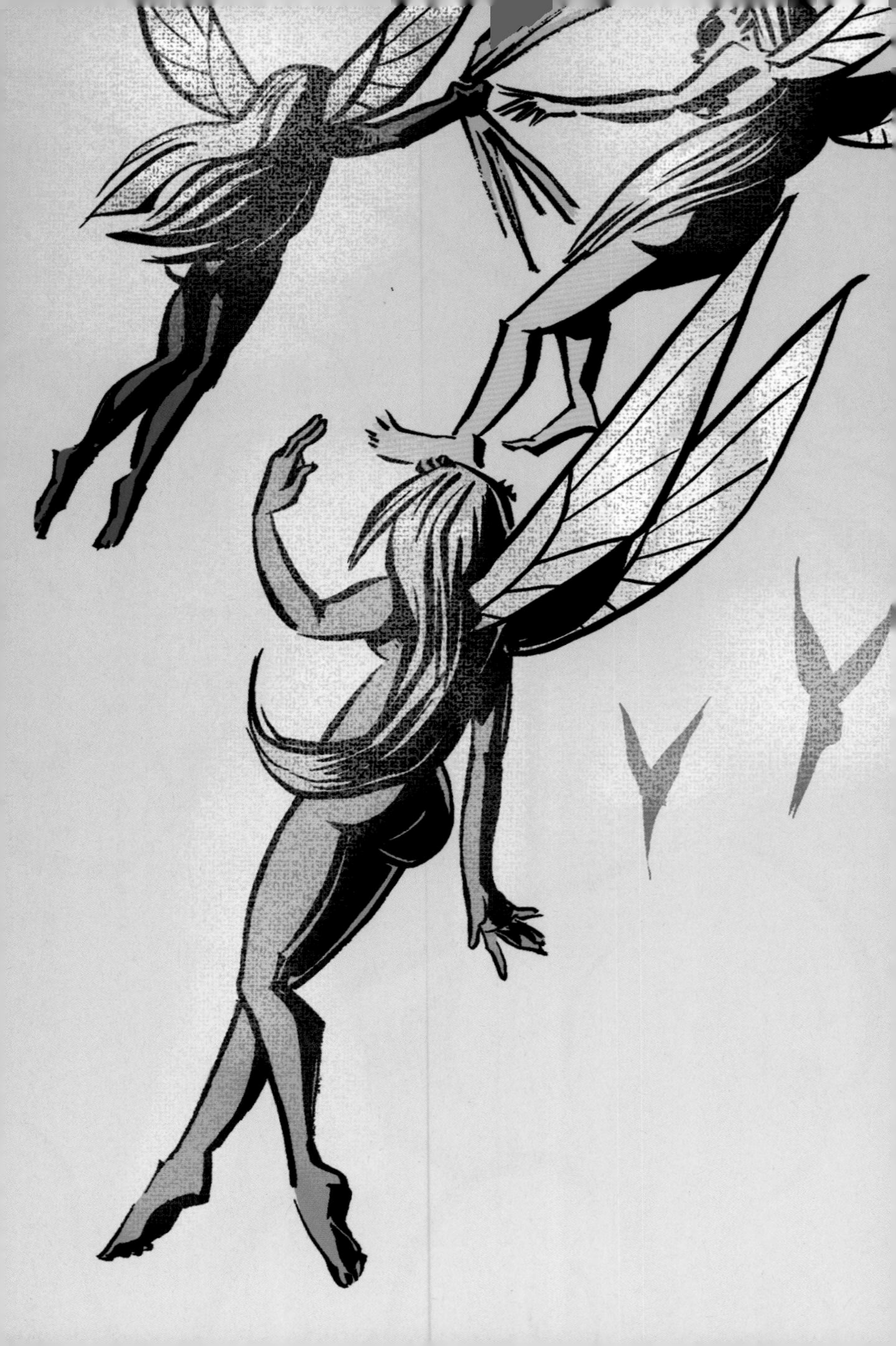

08

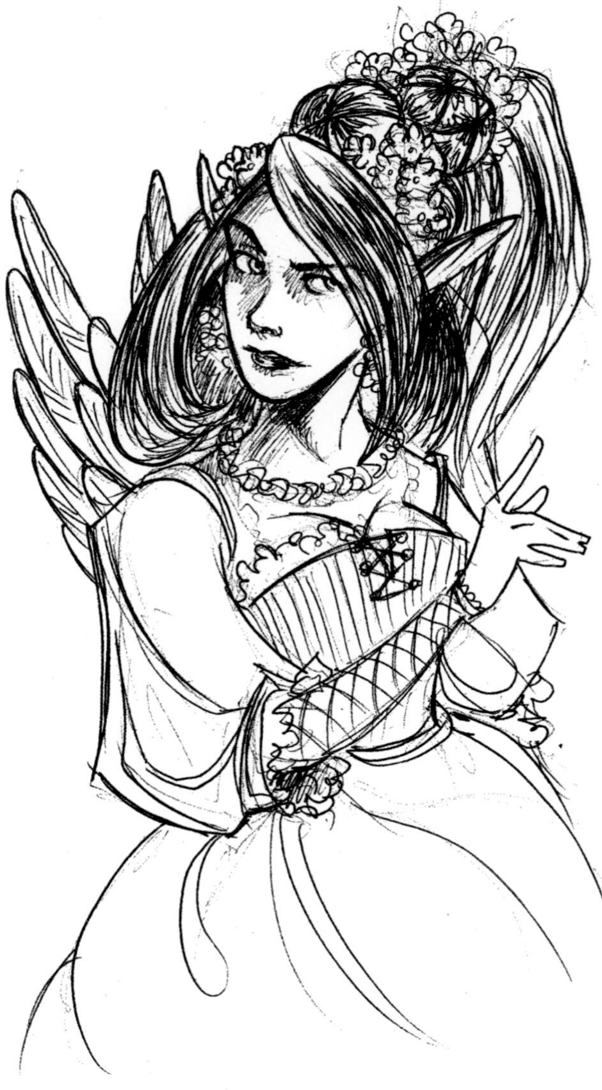

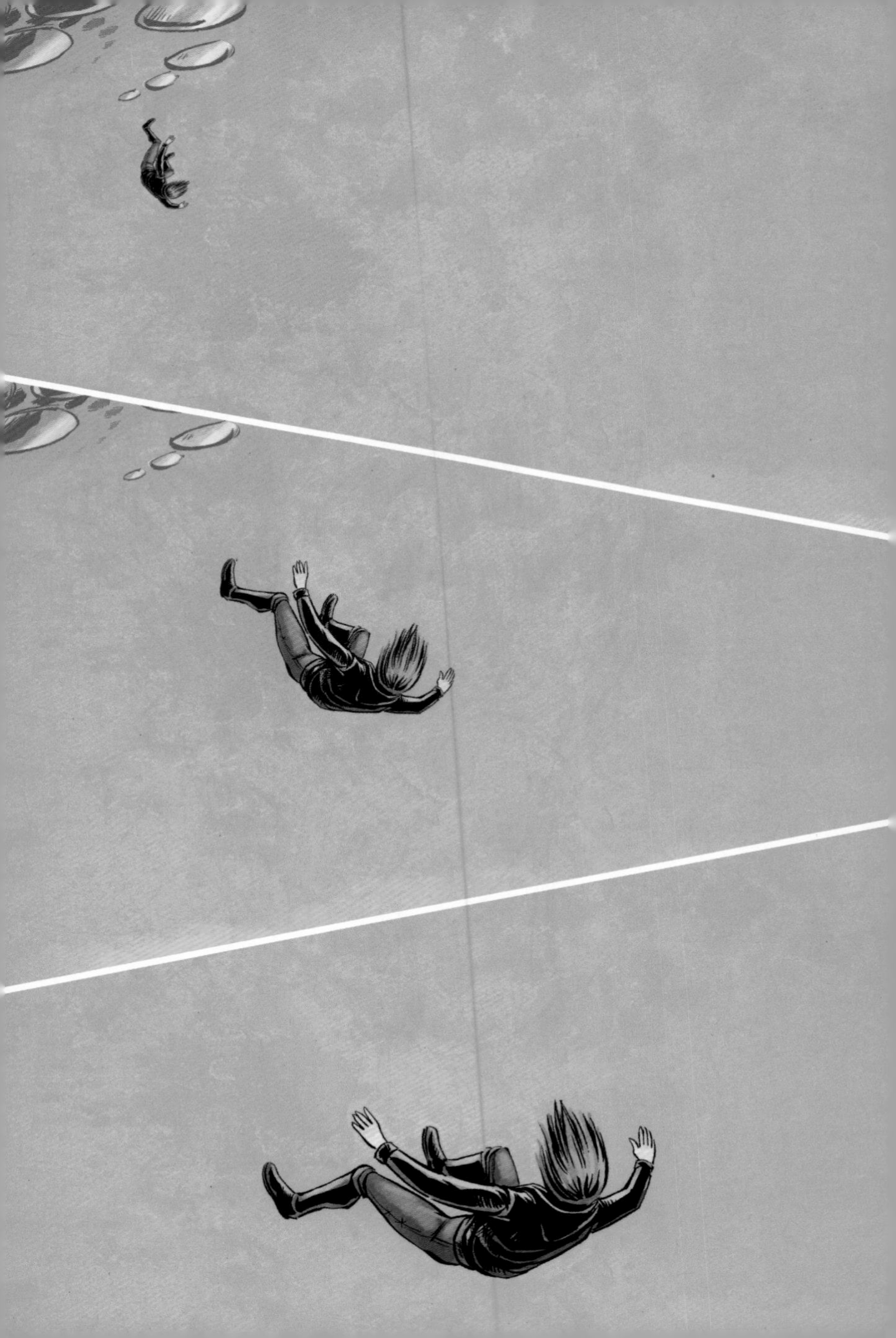

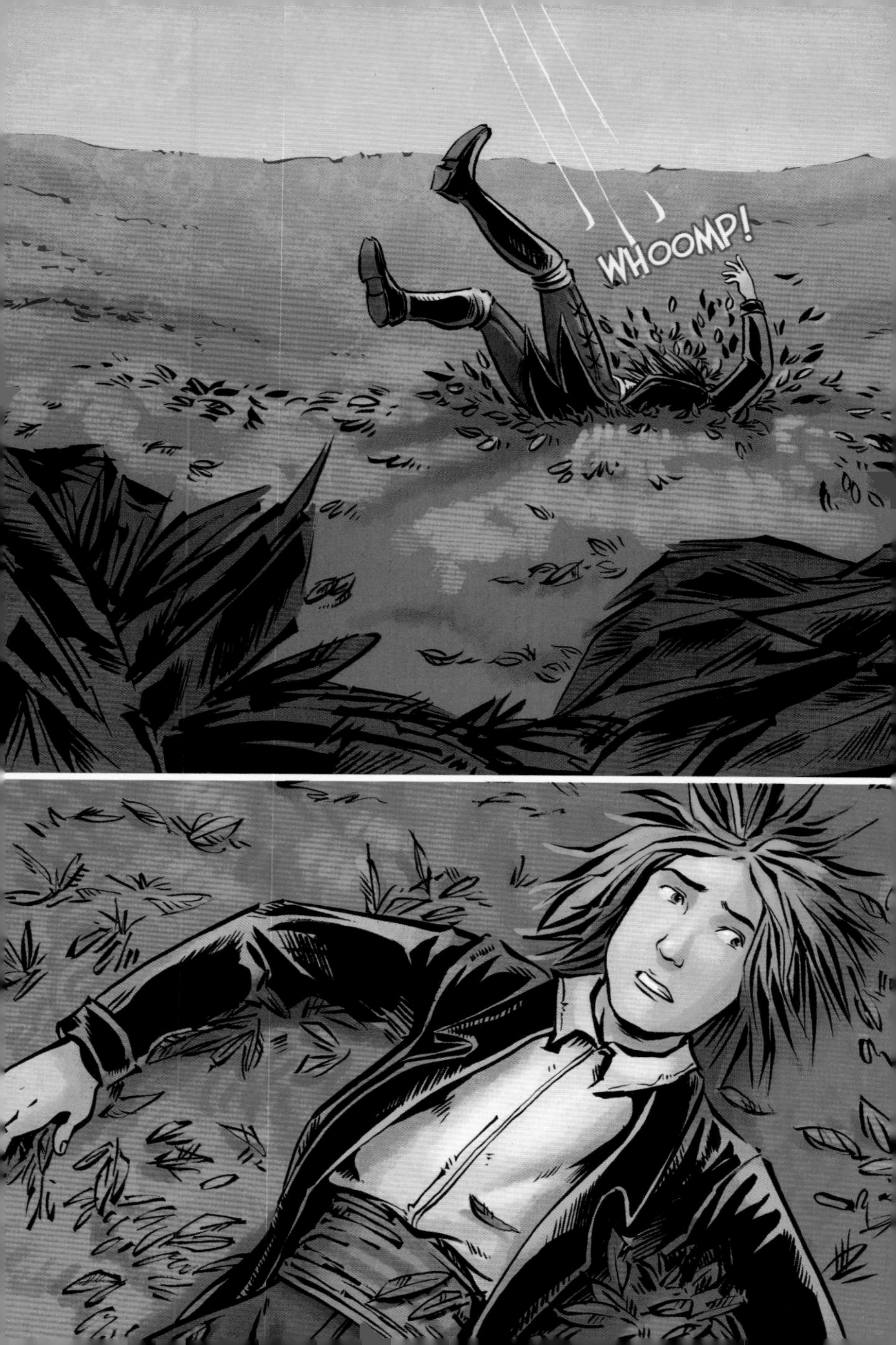
WHOOMP!

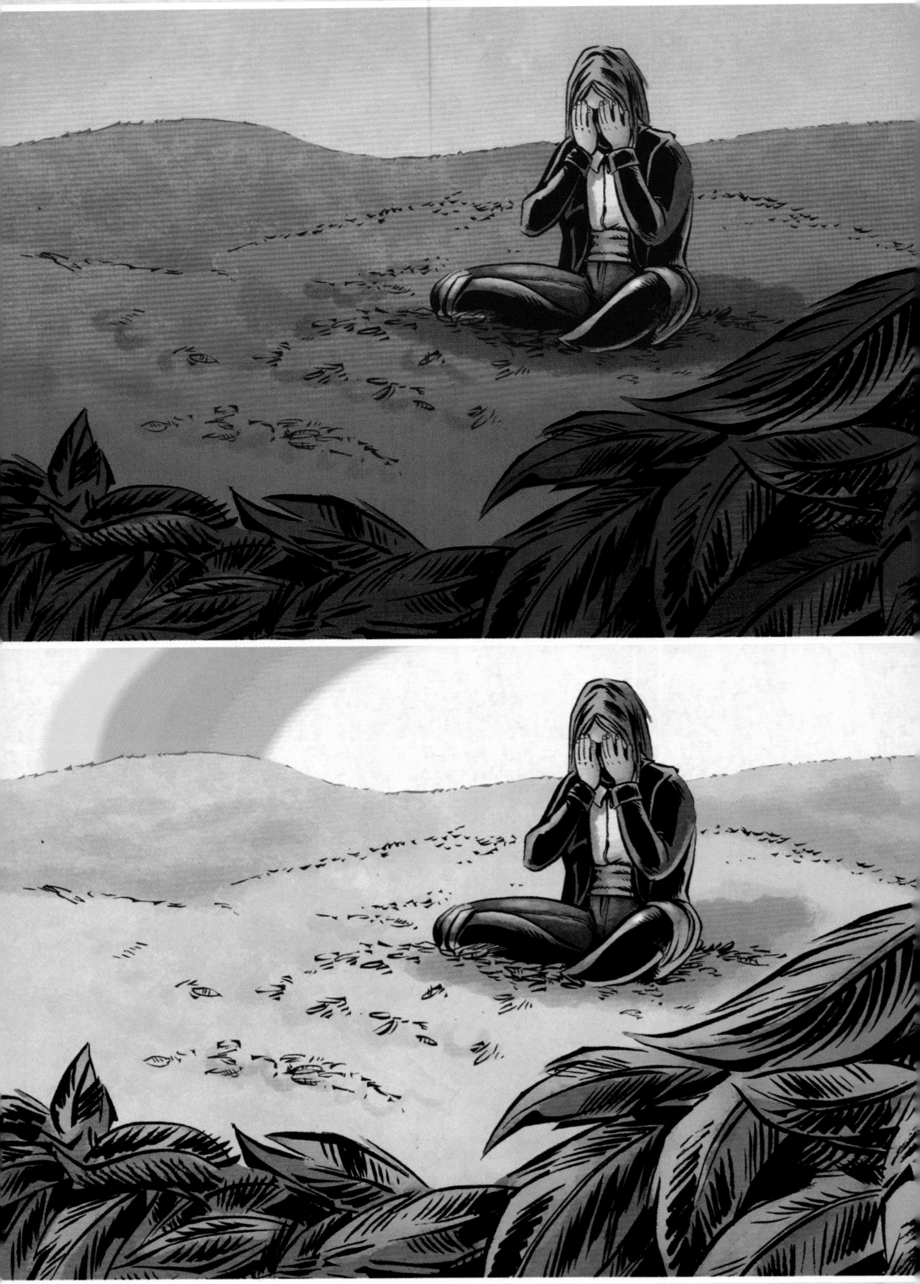

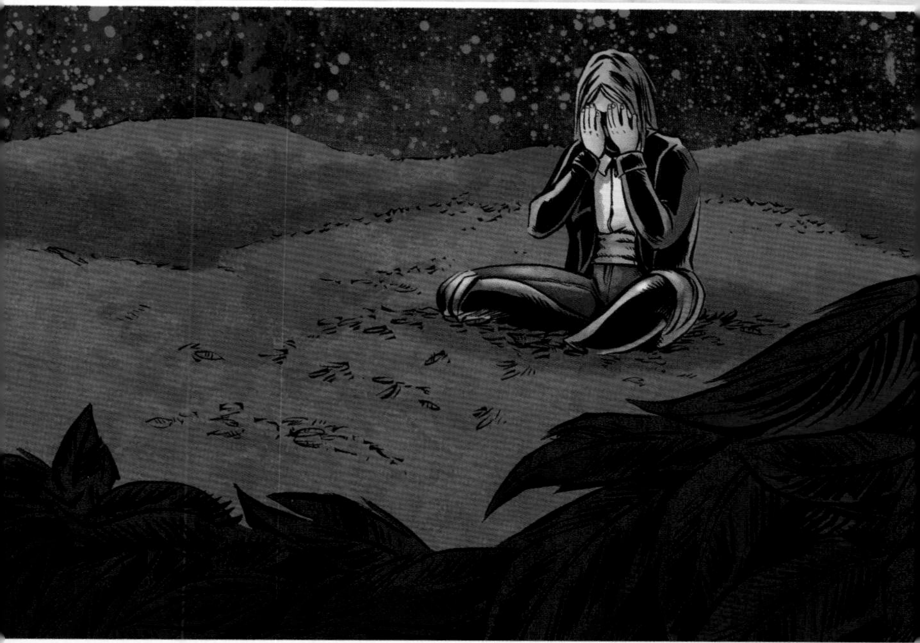

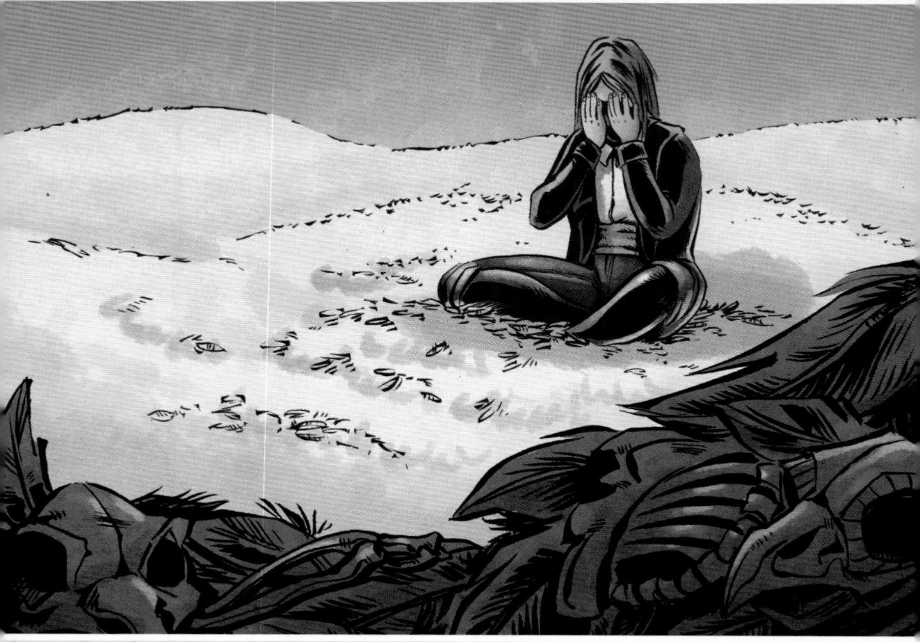

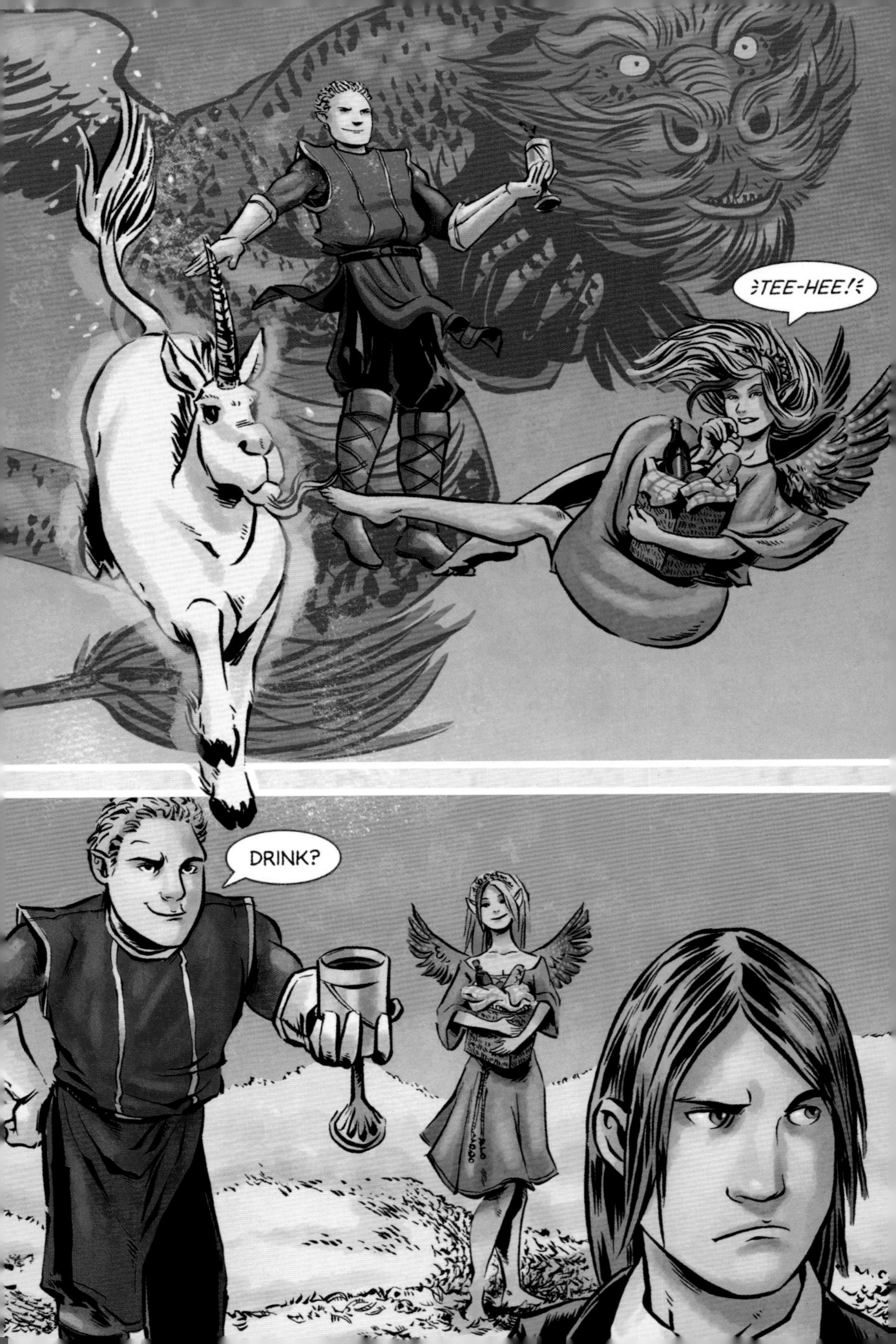
TEE-HEE!
DRINK?

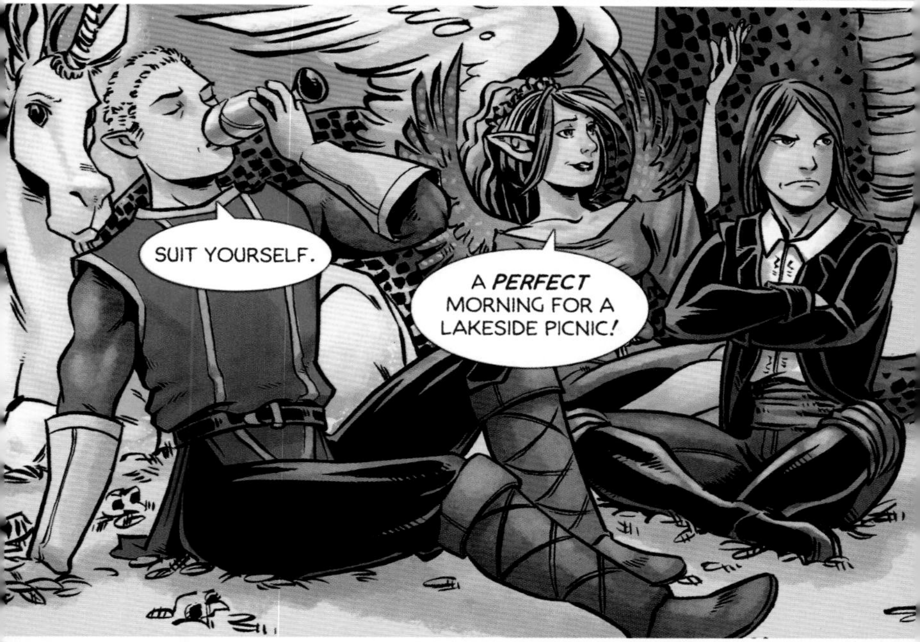
SUIT YOURSELF.
A PERFECT MORNING FOR A LAKESIDE PICNIC!

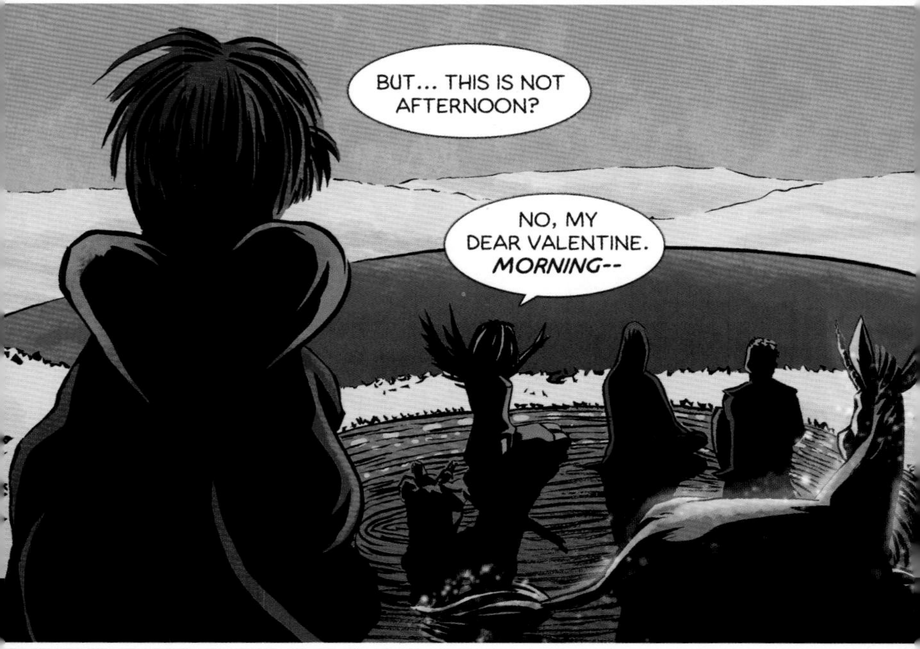
BUT... THIS IS NOT AFTERNOON?
NO, MY DEAR VALENTINE. MORNING--

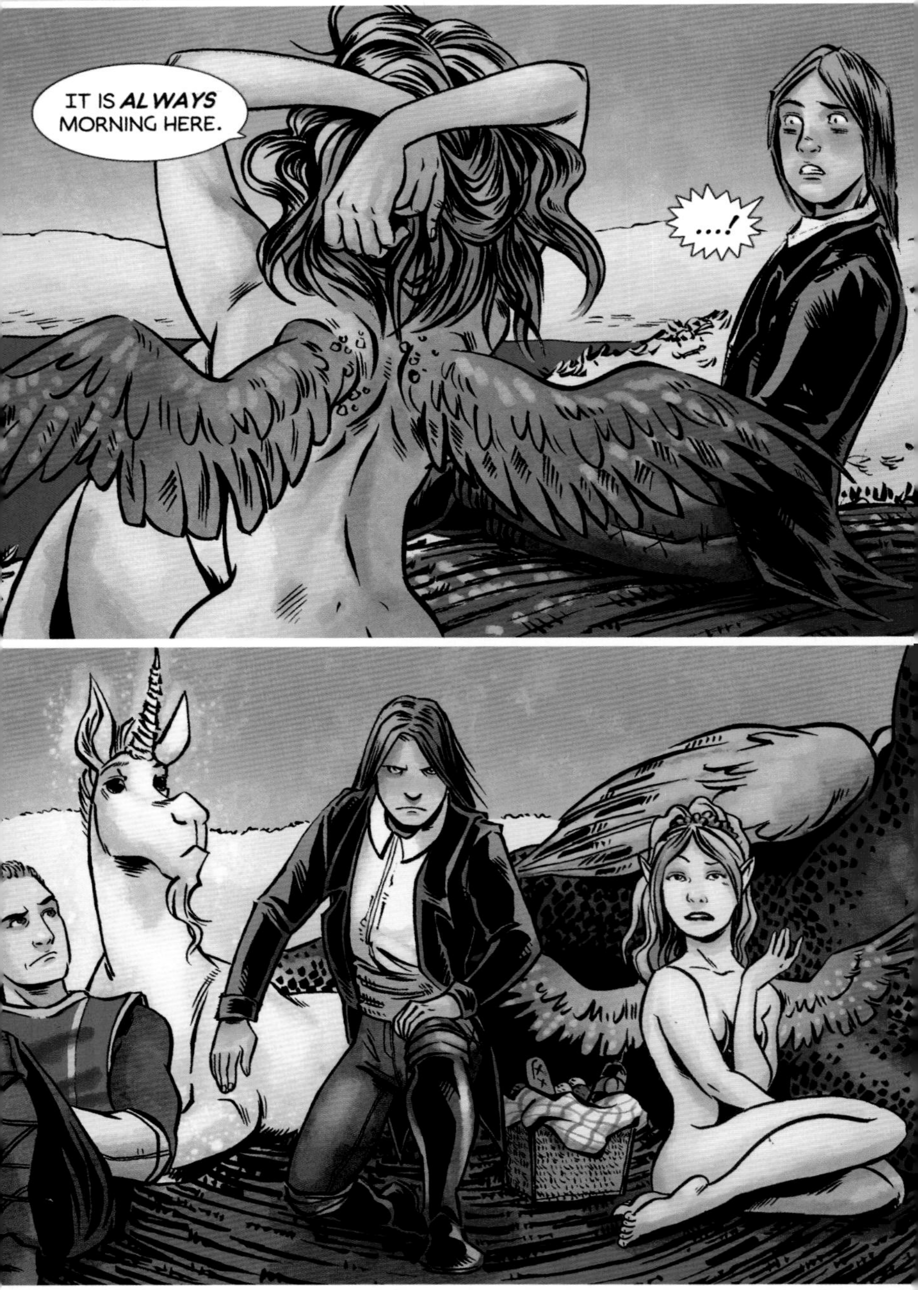
IT IS *ALWAYS* MORNING HERE.
...!

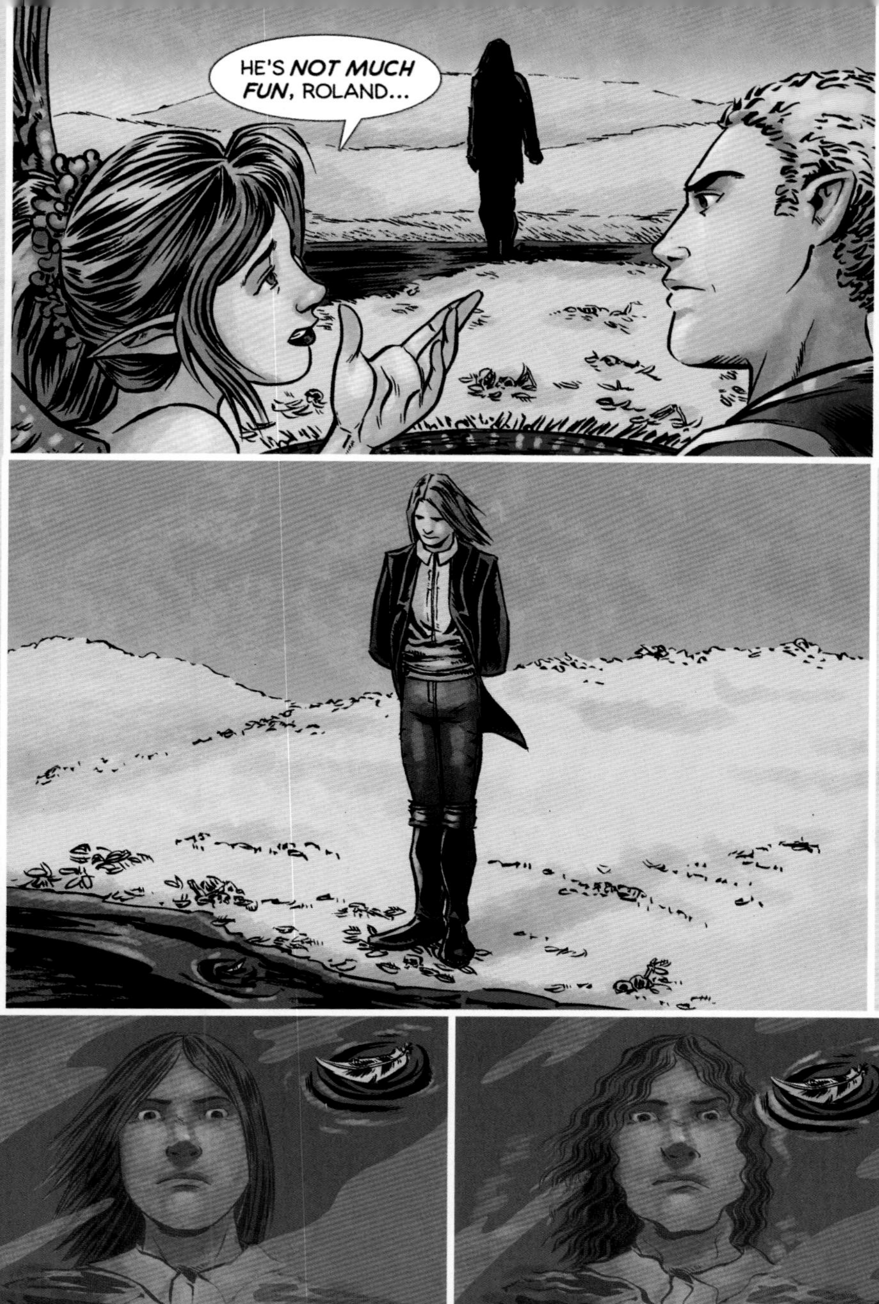
HE'S ***NOT MUCH FUN***, ROLAND...

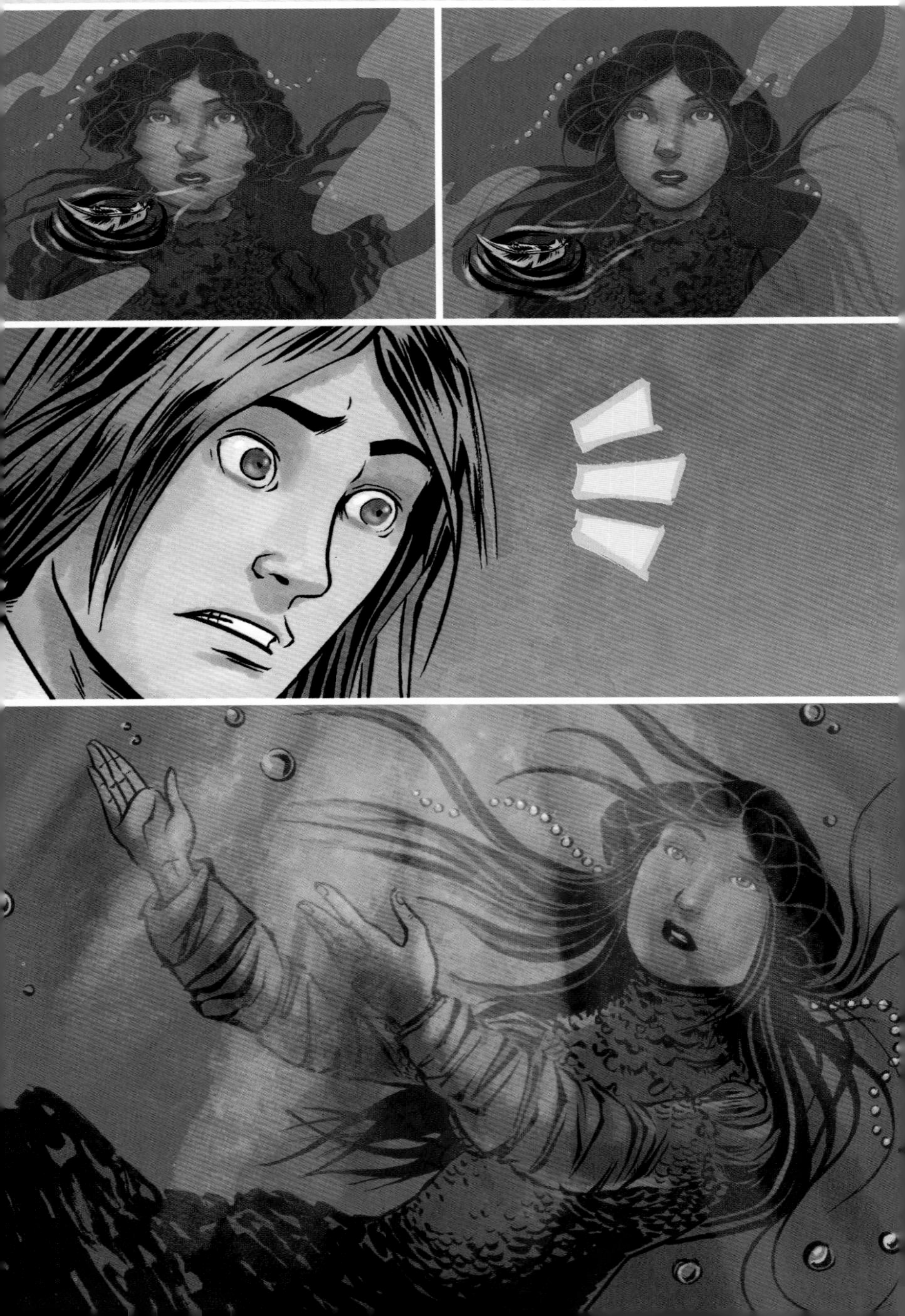

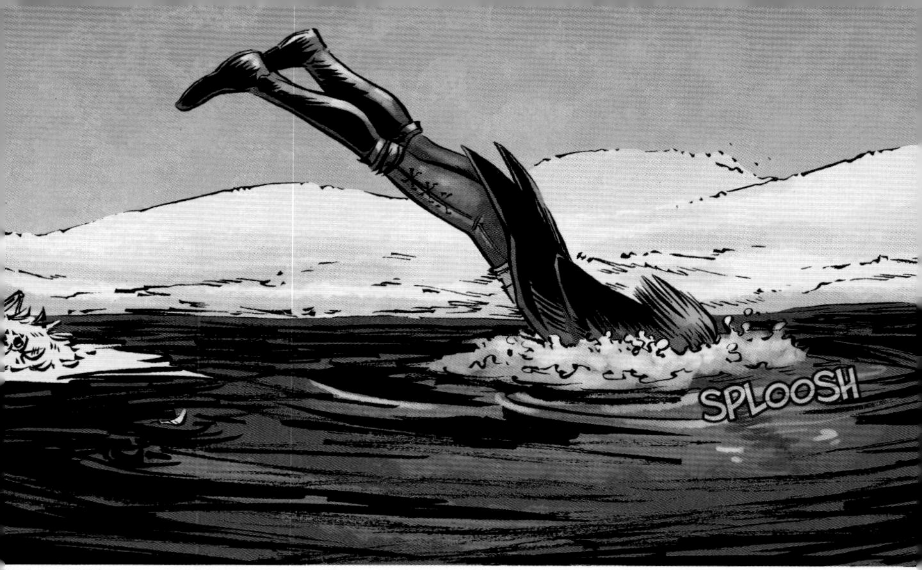
SPLOOSH

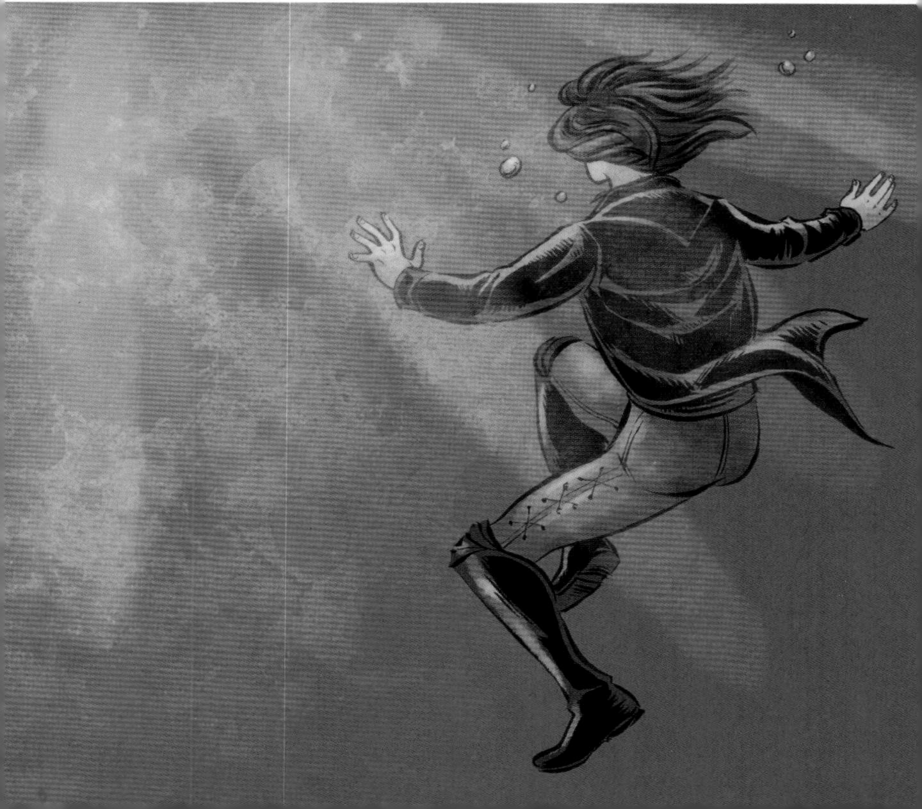

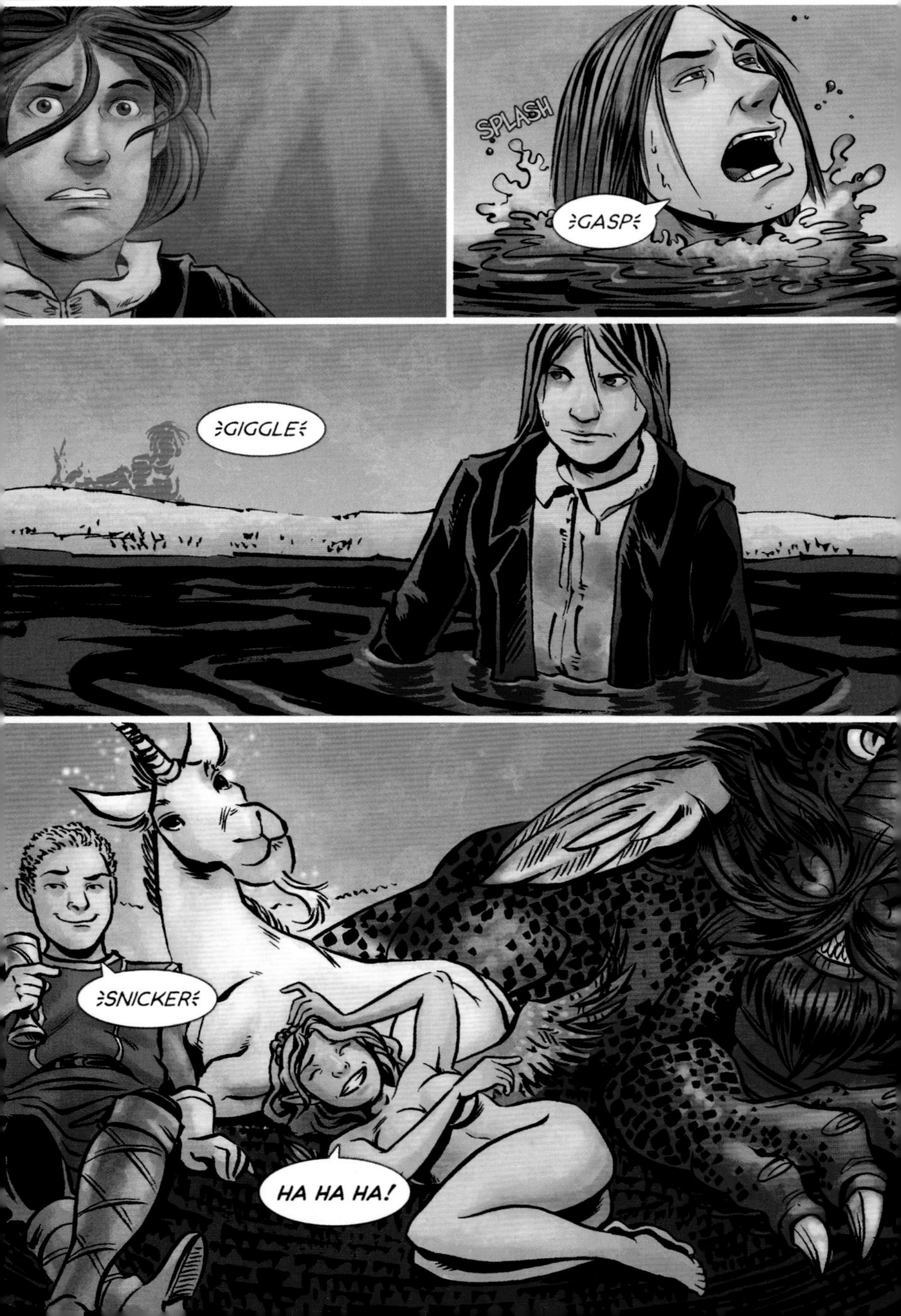
SPLASH
GASP
GIGGLE
SNICKER
HA HA HA!

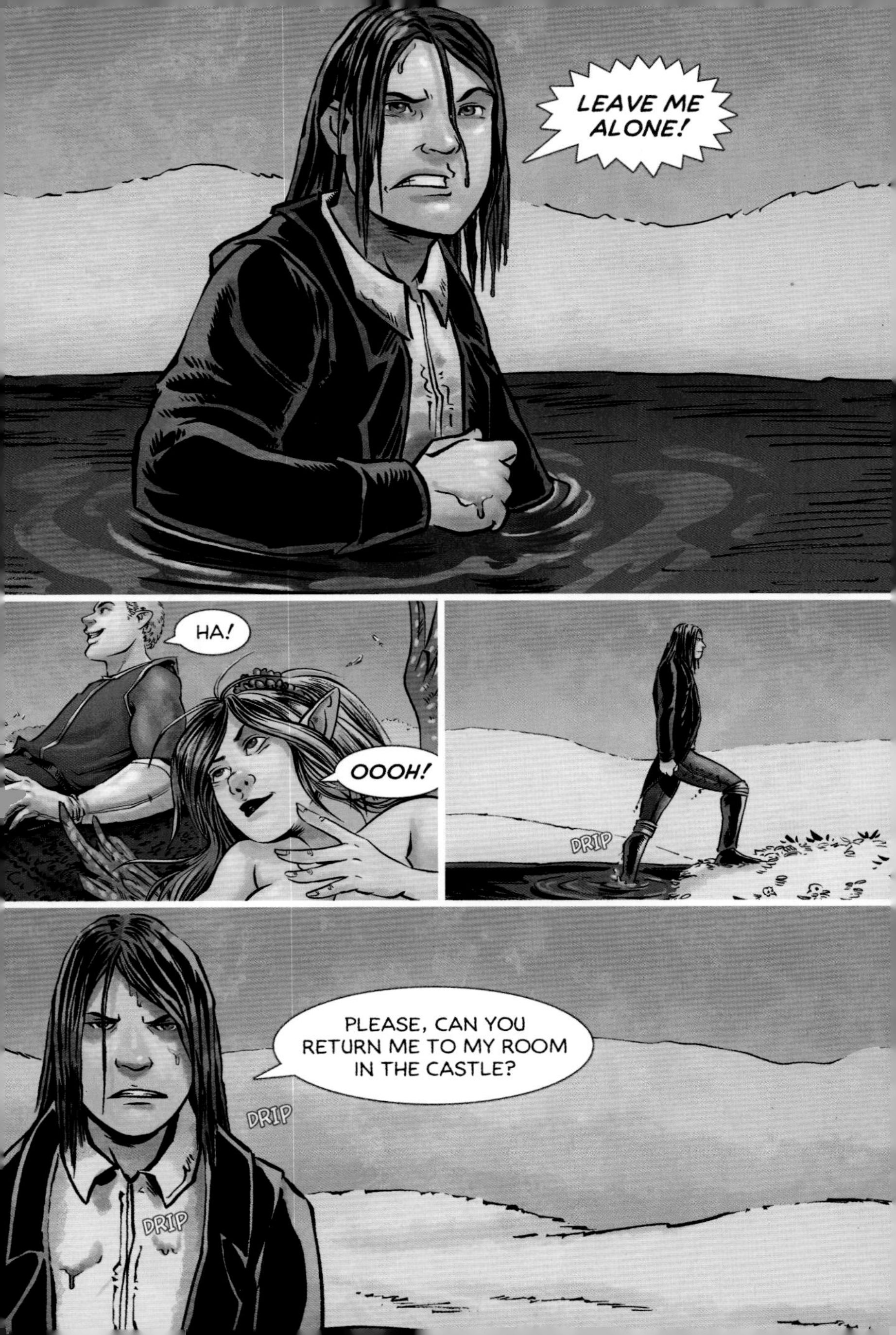
LEAVE ME ALONE!
HA!
OOOH!
DRIP
PLEASE, CAN YOU RETURN ME TO MY ROOM IN THE CASTLE?
DRIP
DRIP

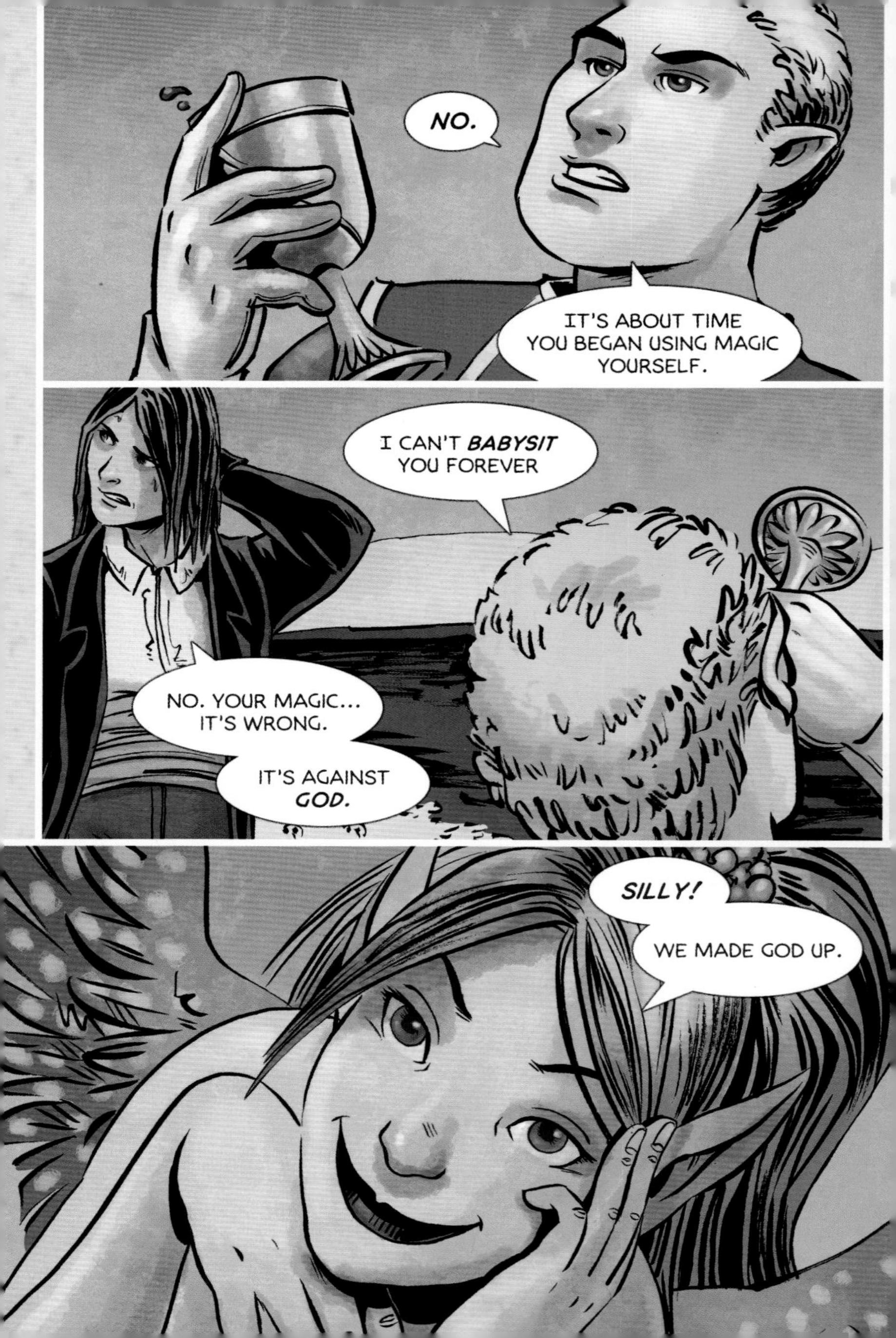
NO.
IT'S ABOUT TIME YOU BEGAN USING MAGIC YOURSELF.
I CAN'T BABYSIT YOU FOREVER
NO. YOUR MAGIC... IT'S WRONG.
IT'S AGAINST GOD.
SILLY!
WE MADE GOD UP.

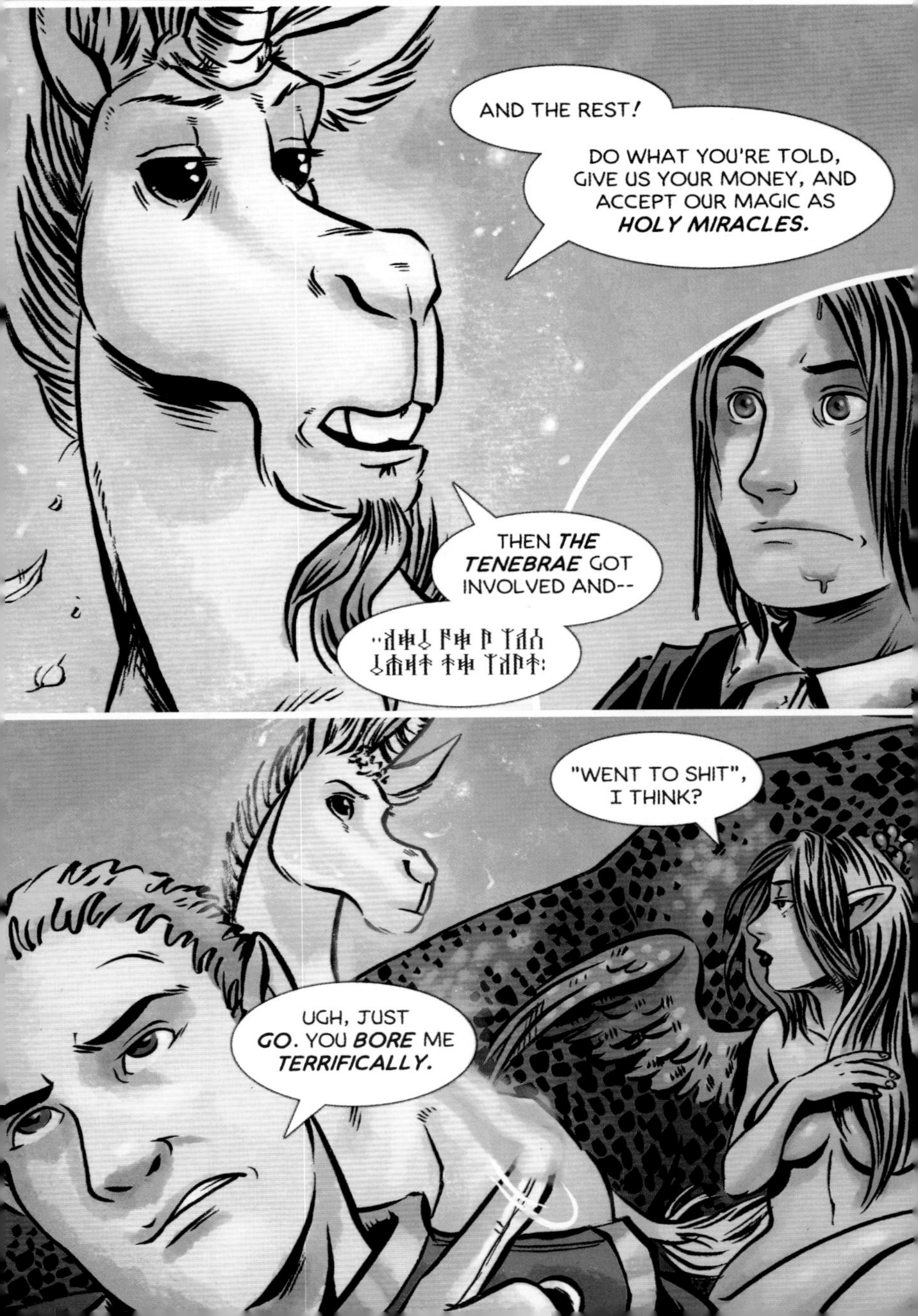
AND THE REST!
DO WHAT YOU'RE TOLD, GIVE US YOUR MONEY, AND ACCEPT OUR MAGIC AS *HOLY MIRACLES.*
THEN *THE TENEBRAE* GOT INVOLVED AND--
"WENT TO SHIT", I THINK?
UGH, JUST *GO*. YOU *BORE* ME *TERRIFICALLY.*

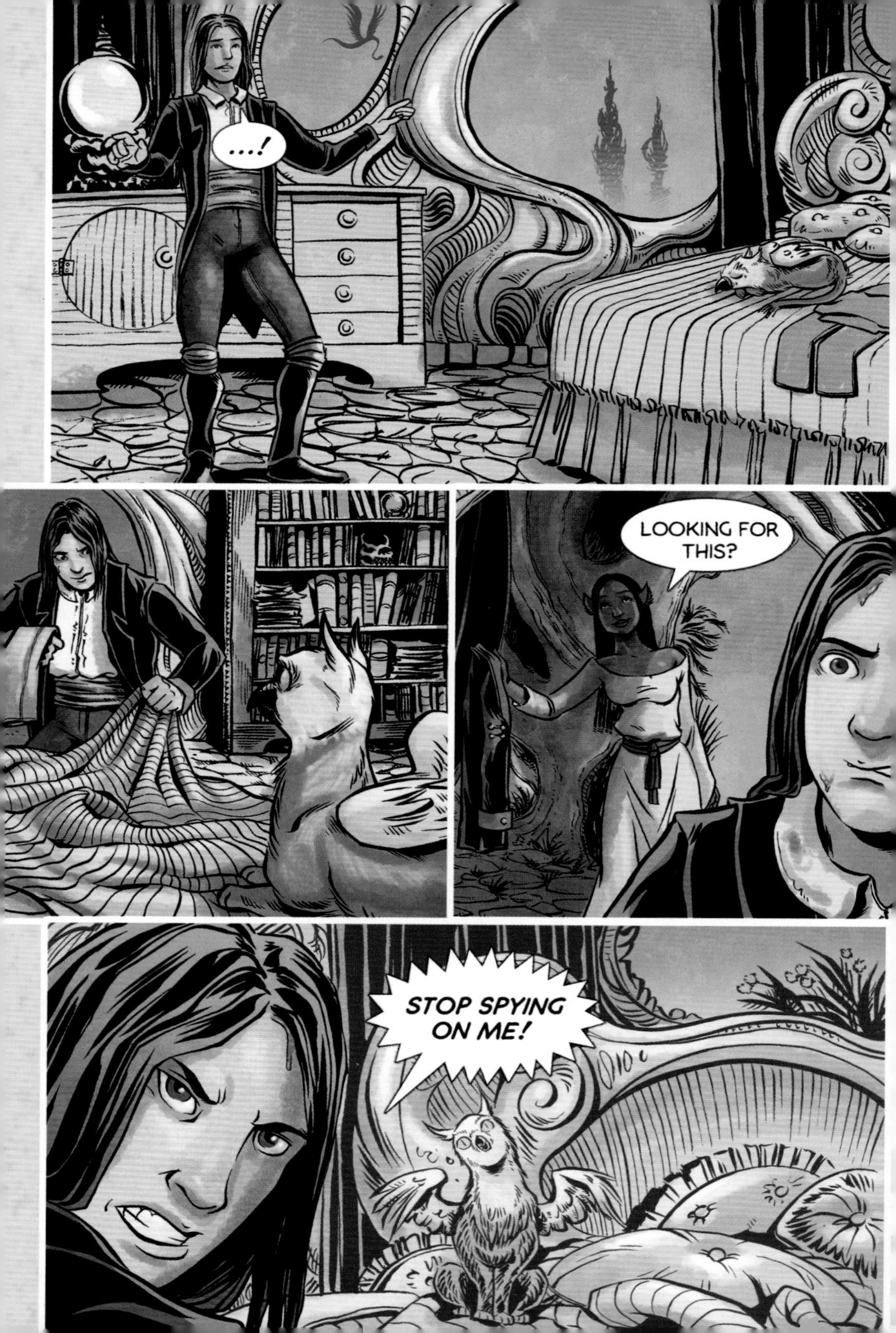
...!
LOOKING FOR THIS?
STOP SPYING ON ME!

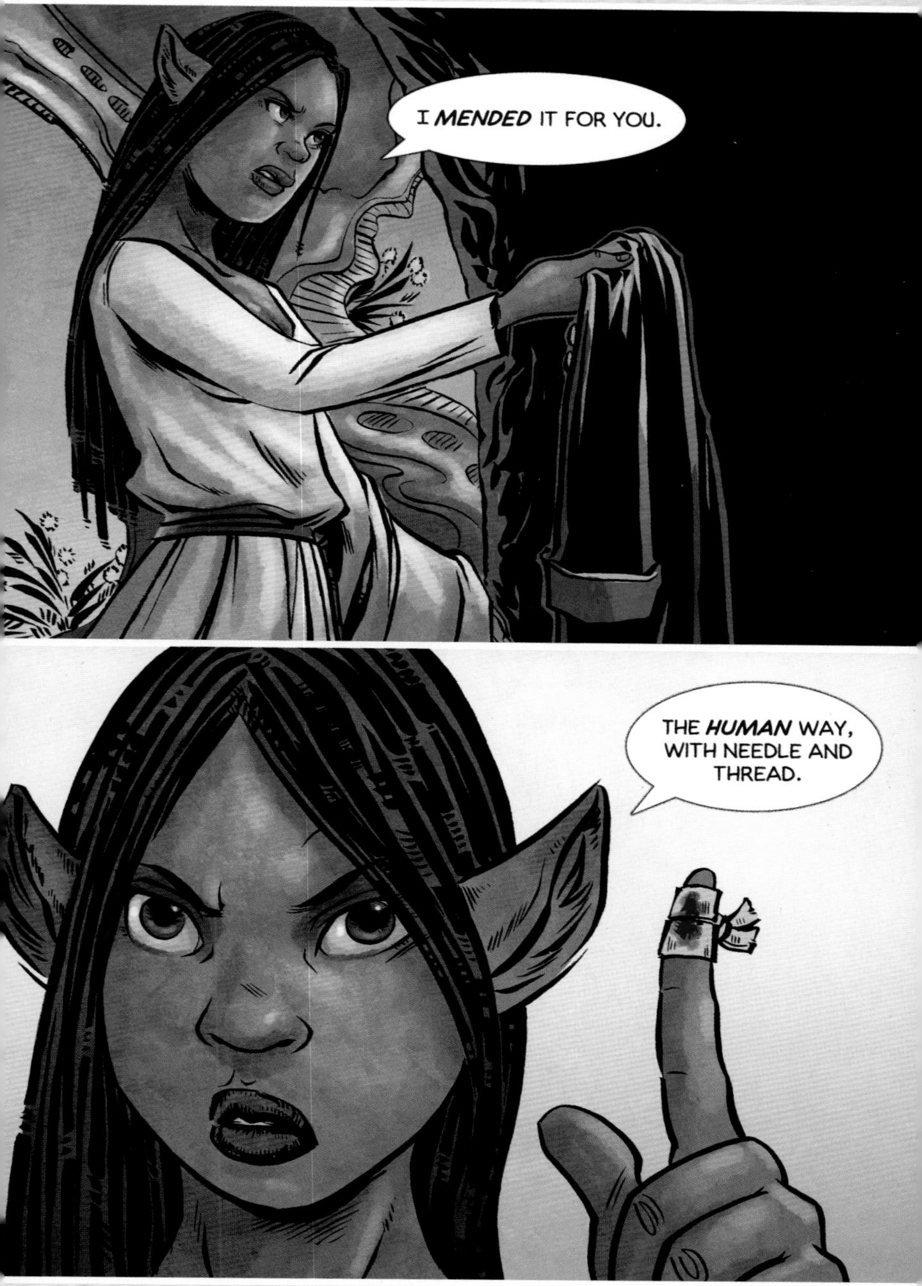
I *MENDED* IT FOR YOU.
THE *HUMAN* WAY, WITH NEEDLE AND THREAD.

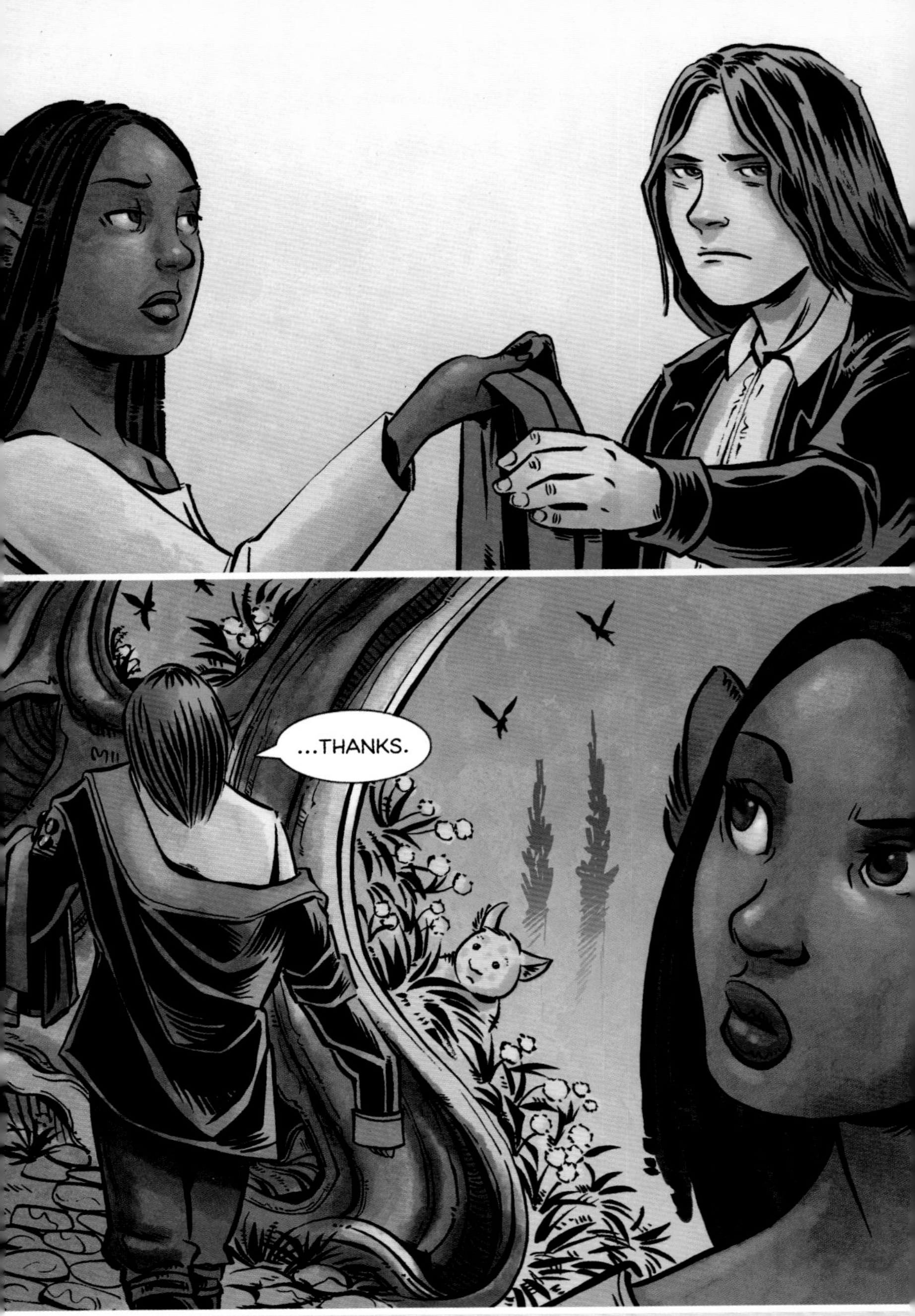
...THANKS.

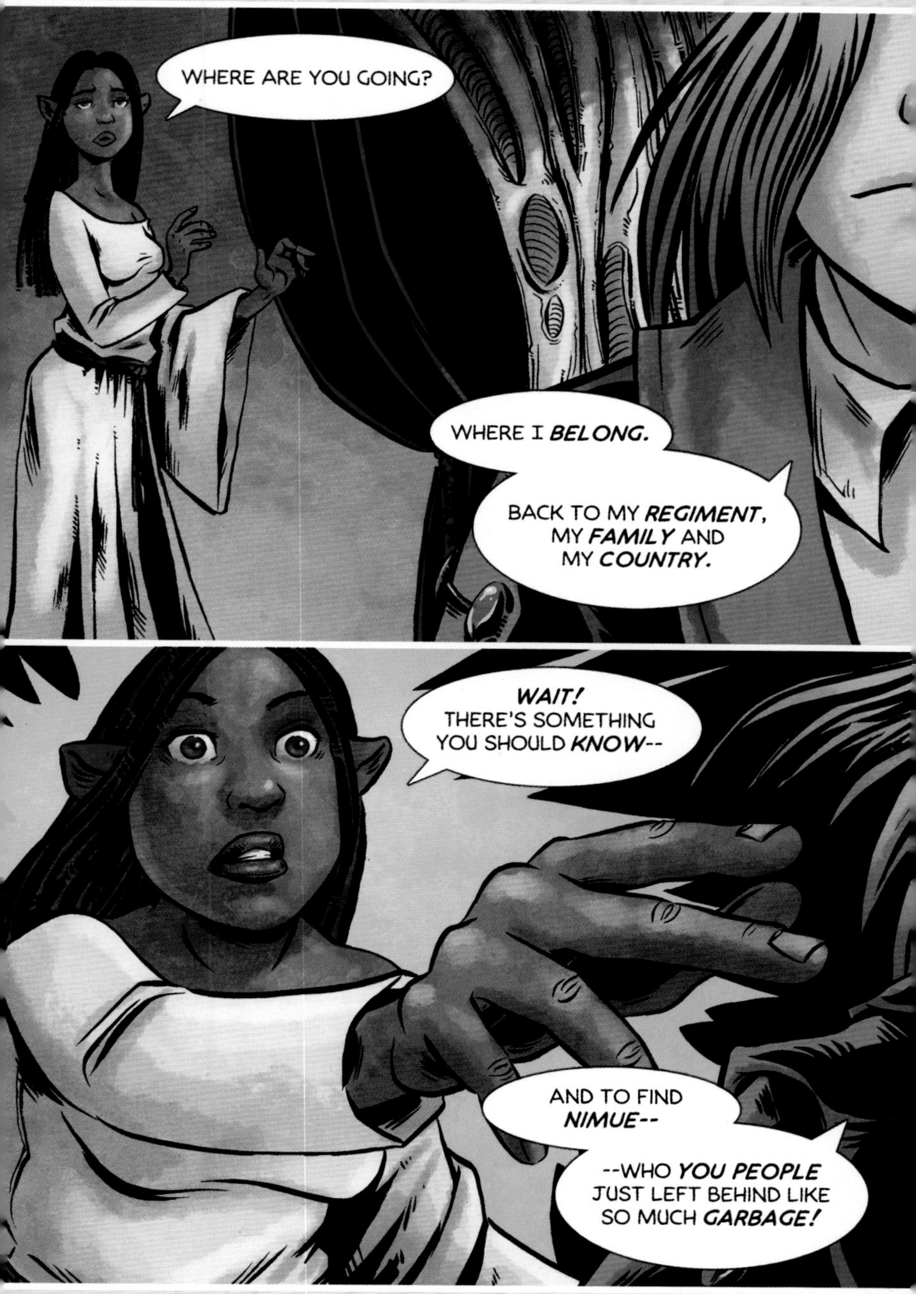
WHERE ARE YOU GOING?
WHERE I BELONG.
BACK TO MY REGIMENT, MY FAMILY AND MY COUNTRY.
WAIT! THERE'S SOMETHING YOU SHOULD KNOW--
AND TO FIND NIMUE--
--WHO YOU PEOPLE JUST LEFT BEHIND LIKE SO MUCH GARBAGE!

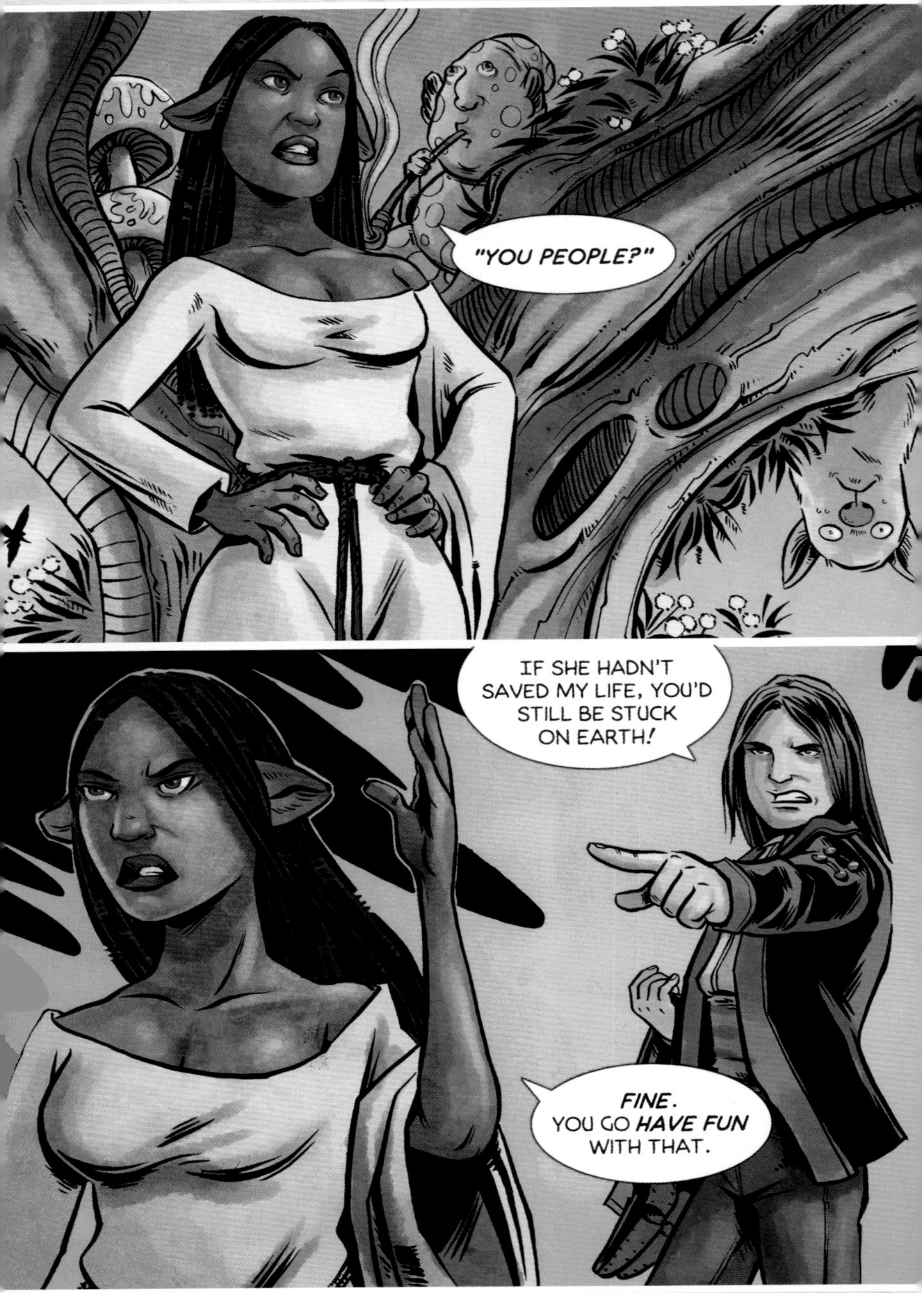
"YOU PEOPLE?"
IF SHE HADN'T SAVED MY LIFE, YOU'D STILL BE STUCK ON EARTH!
FINE. YOU GO HAVE FUN WITH THAT.

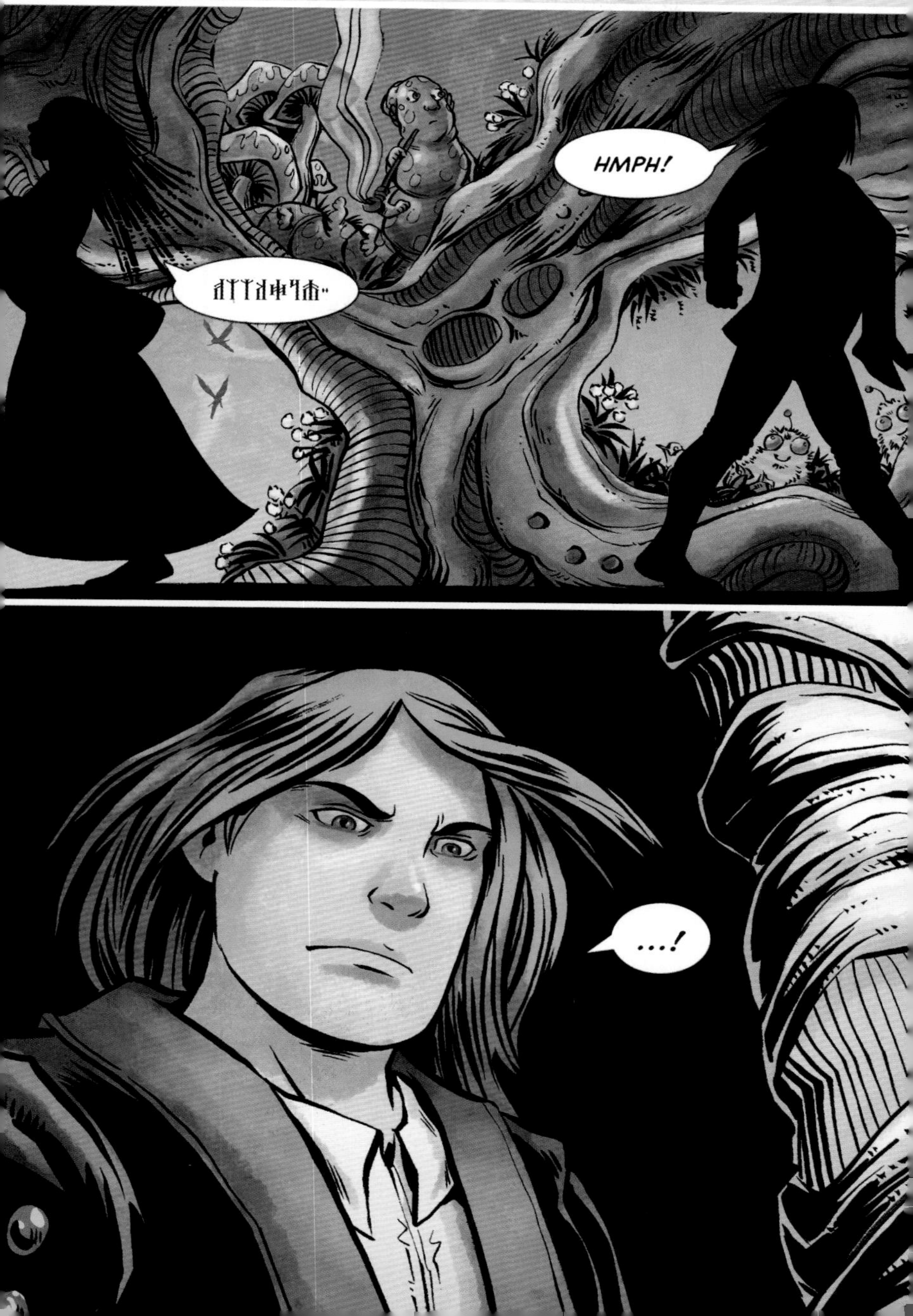
HMPH!
...!

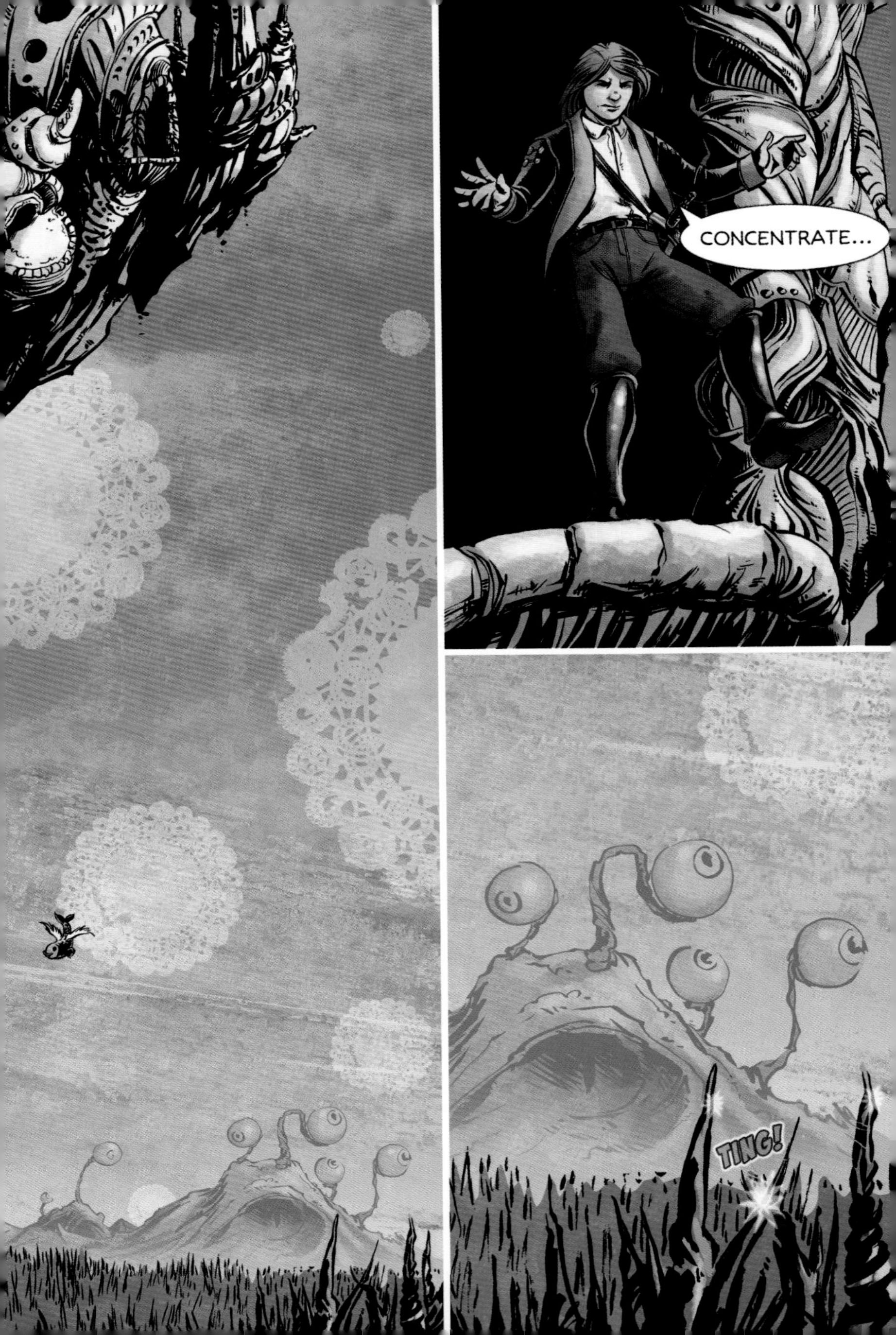
CONCENTRATE...
TING!

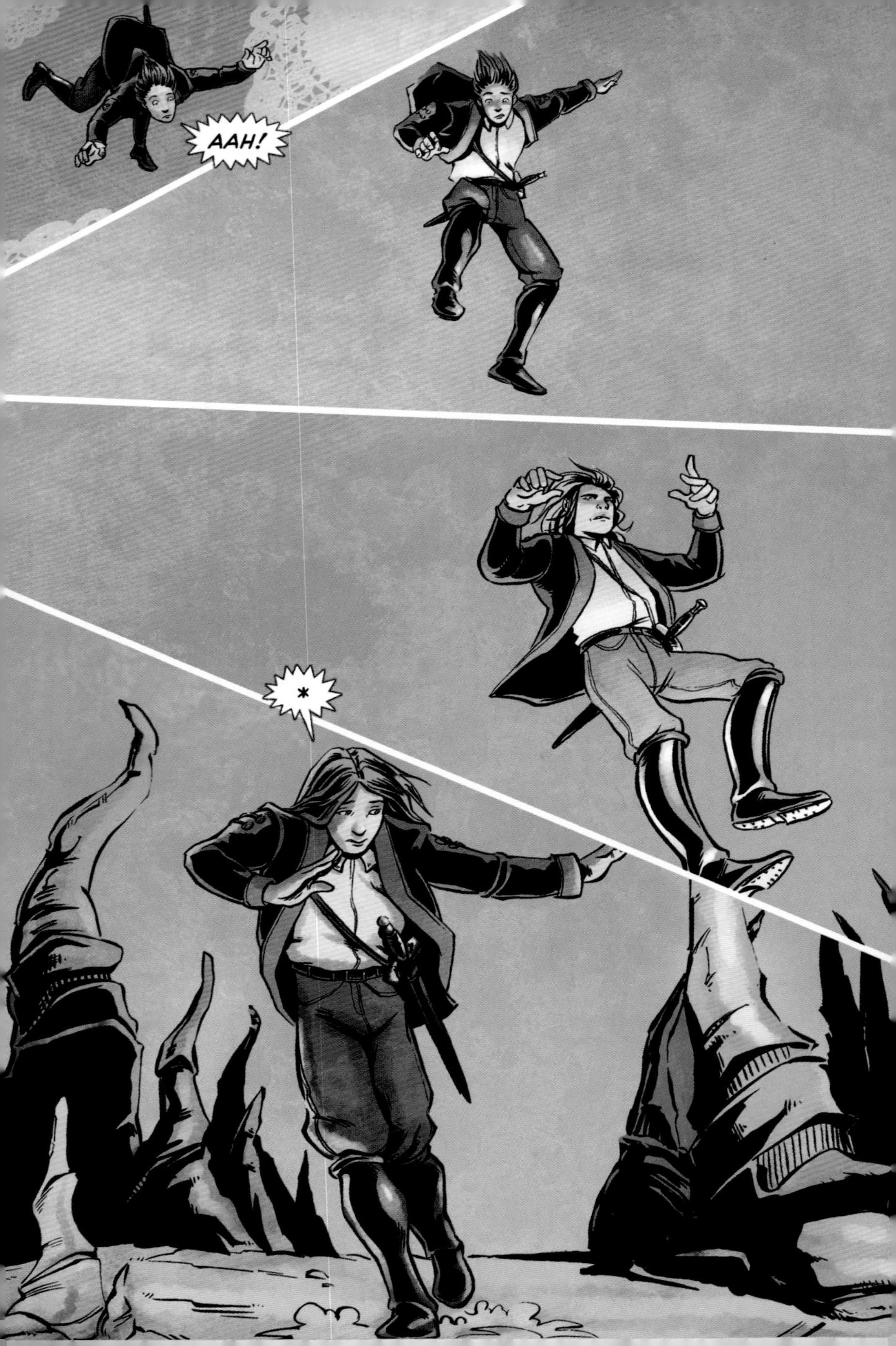

AAH!
*

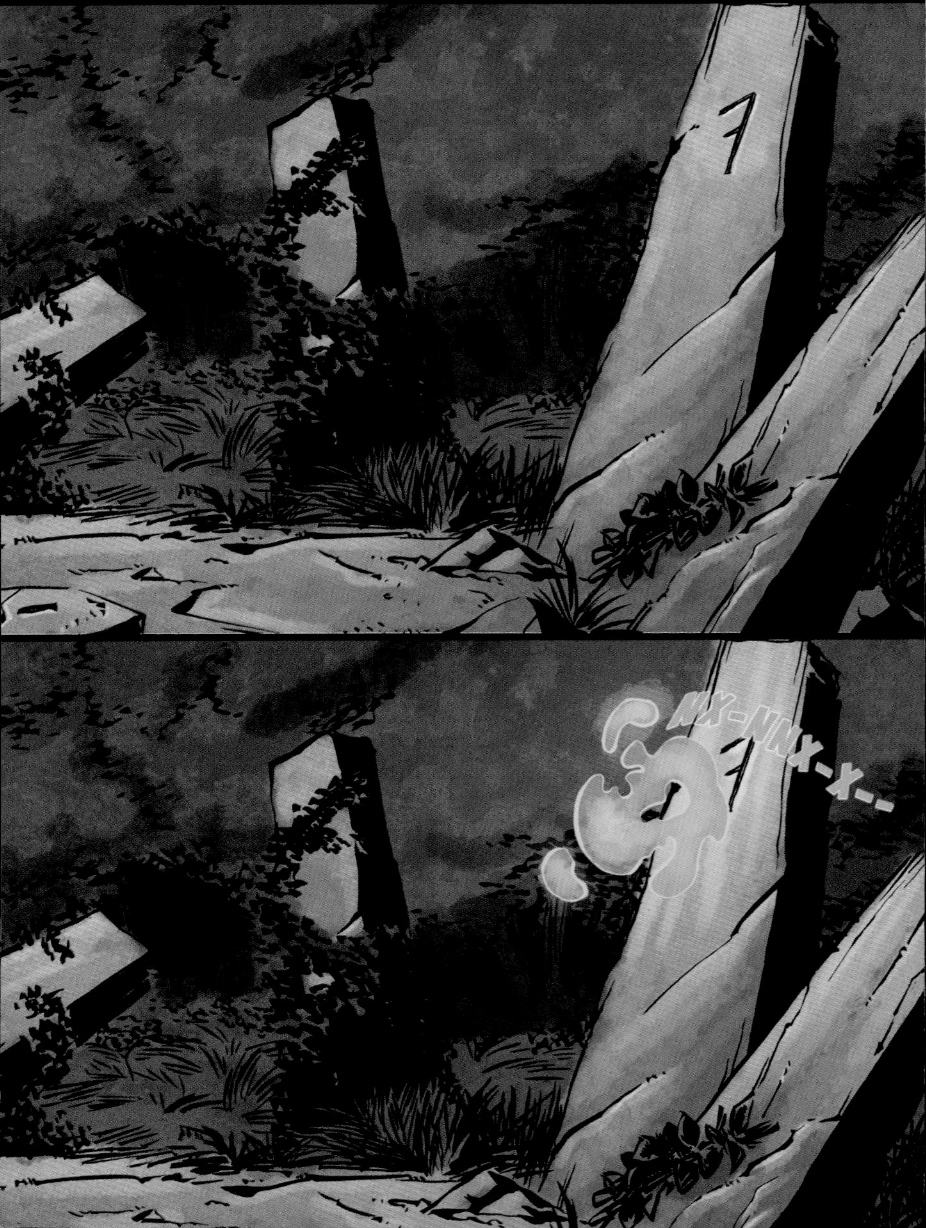
NX-NNX-X--

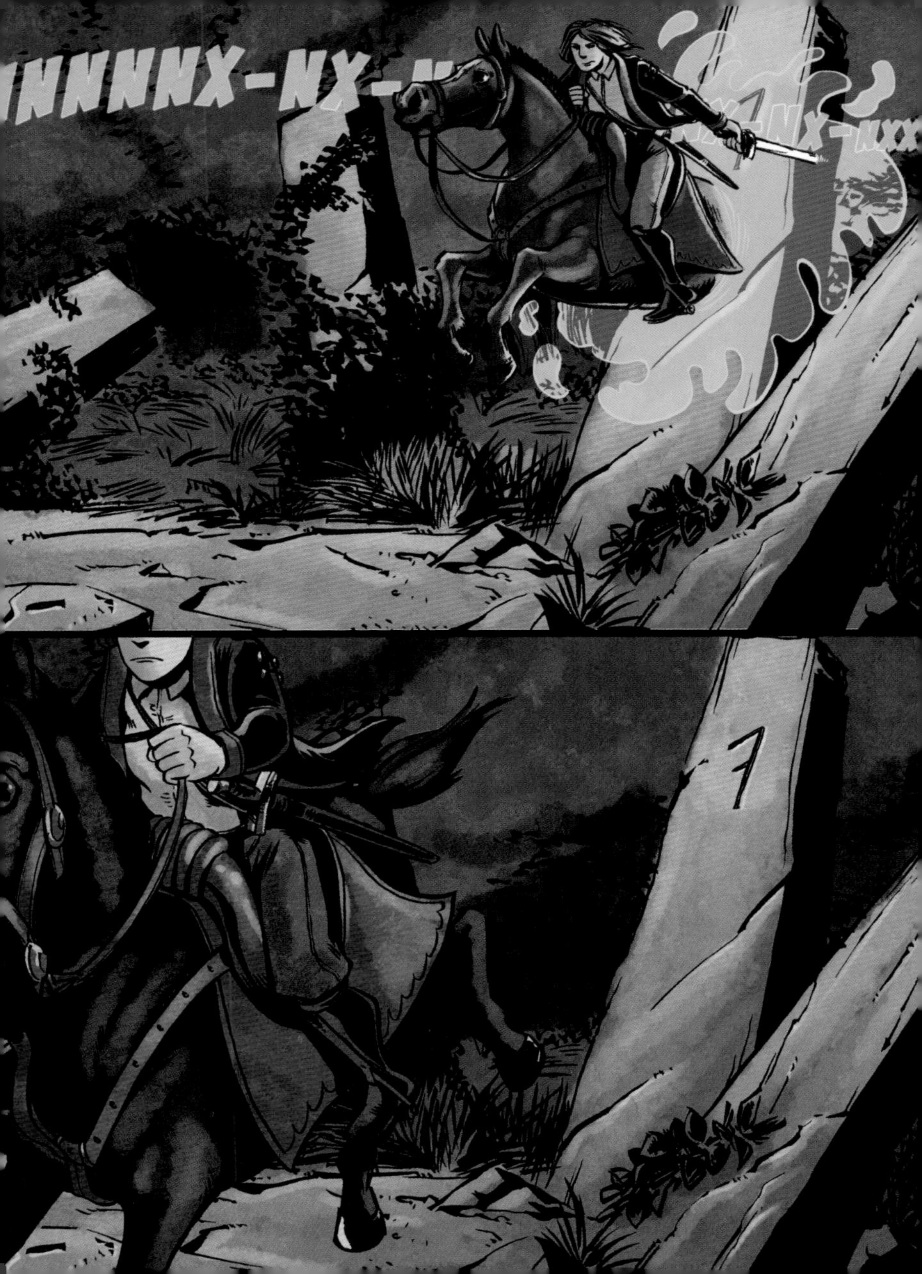
NNNNNX-NX-N
NX-NX-NXX

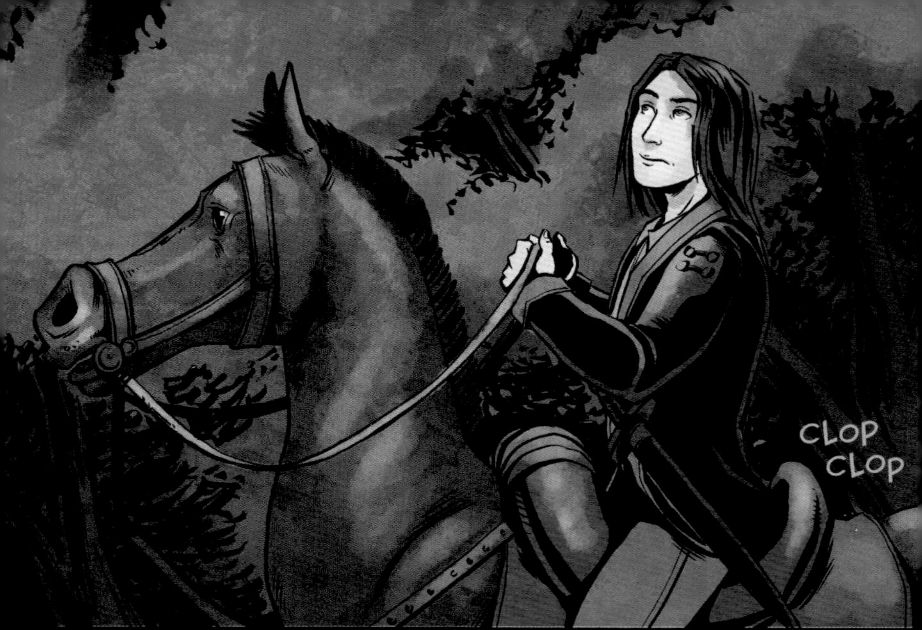
CLOP
CLOP

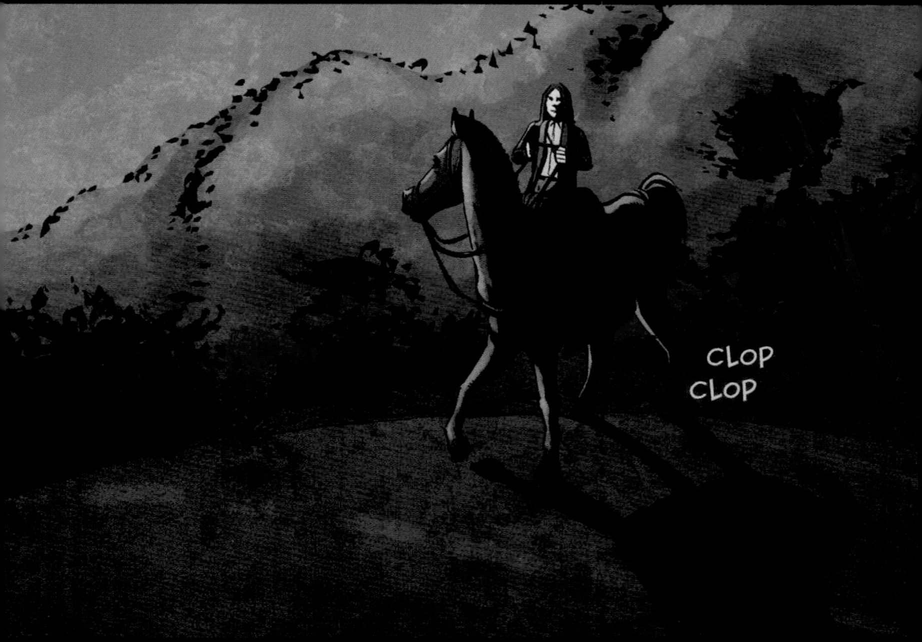
CLOP
CLOP

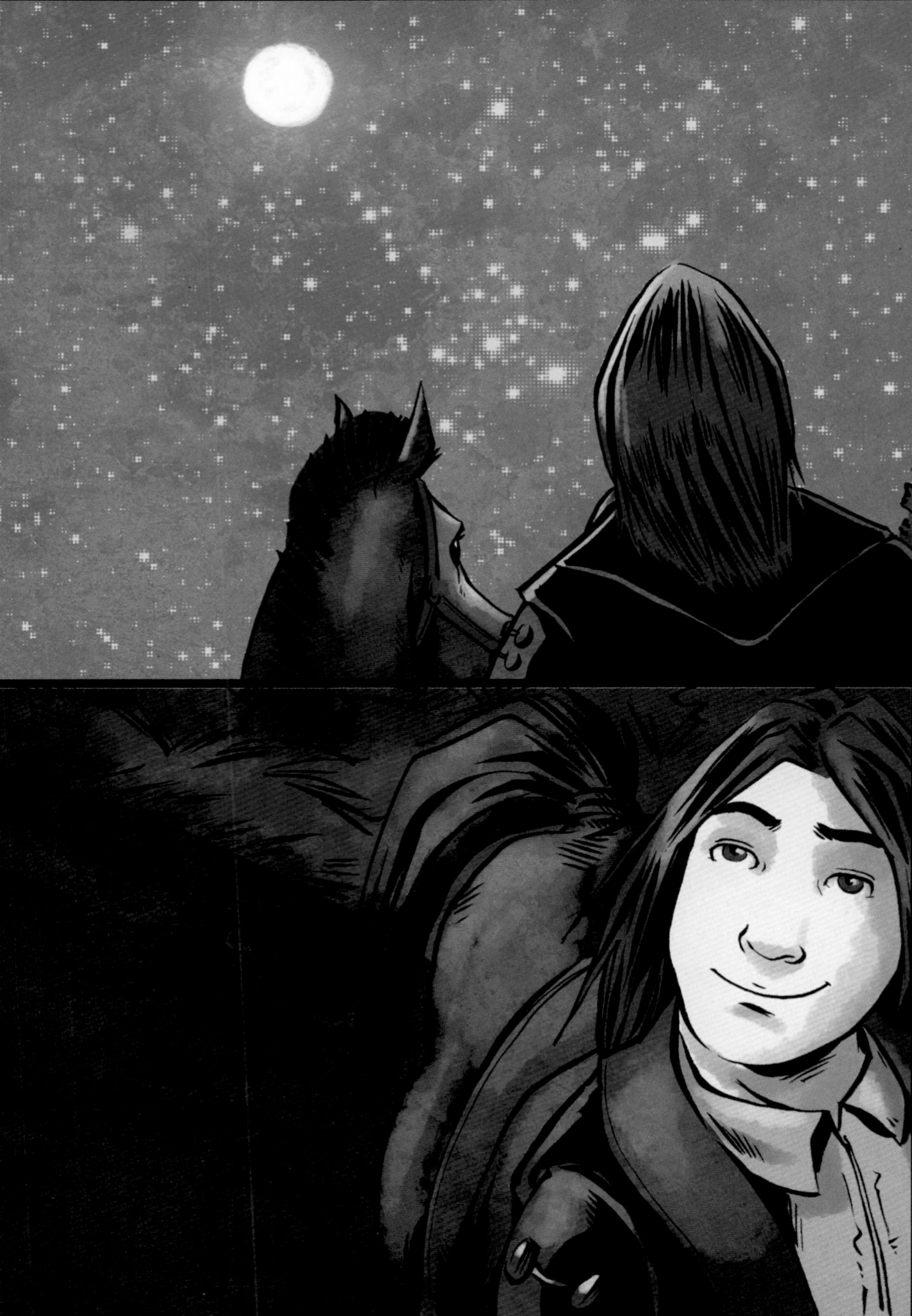

SCREEEEEEEEEEEEEEEEEEEEEEEE

EEEEEEEEEEEEEEEEEE

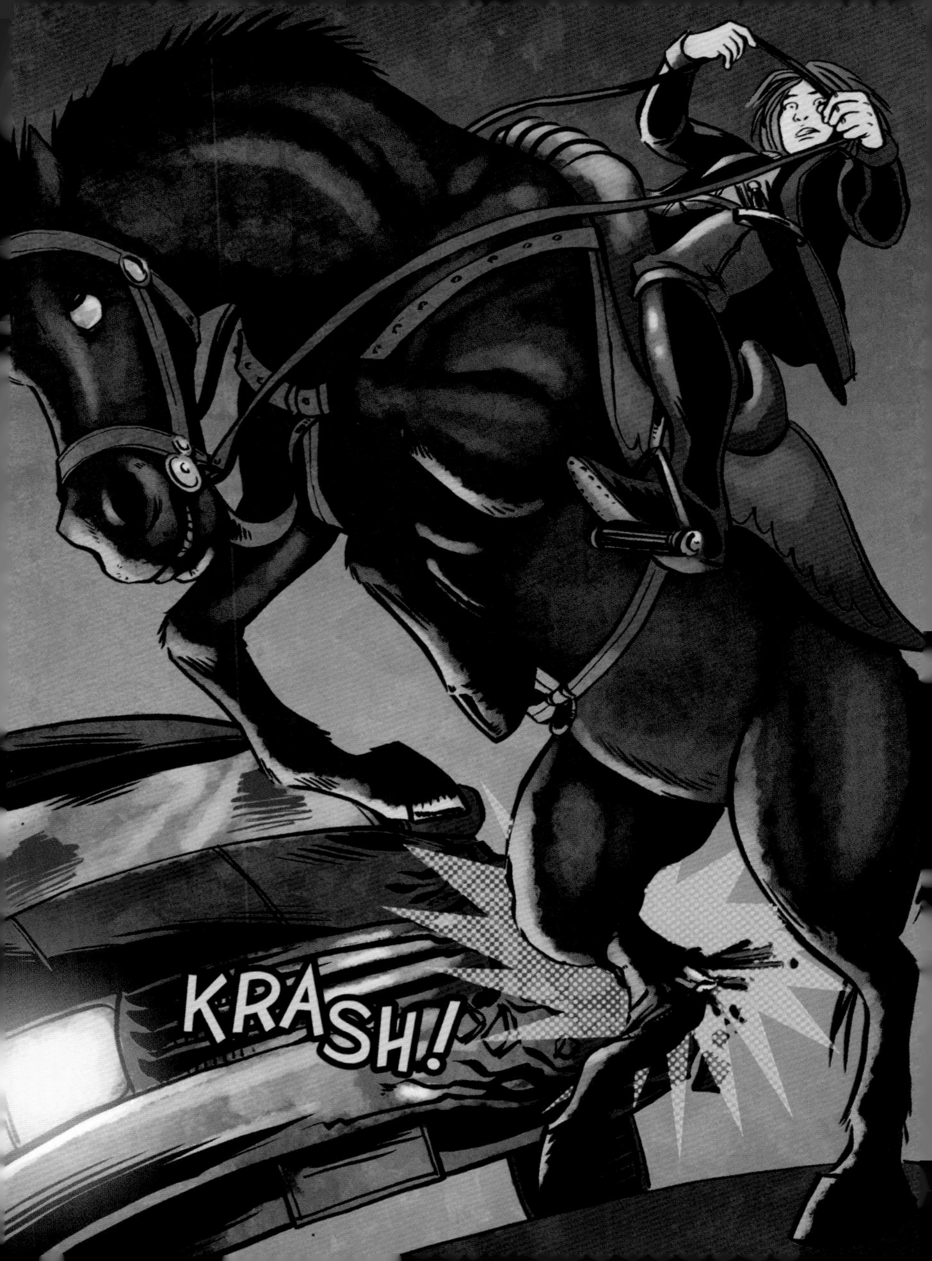
KRASH!!

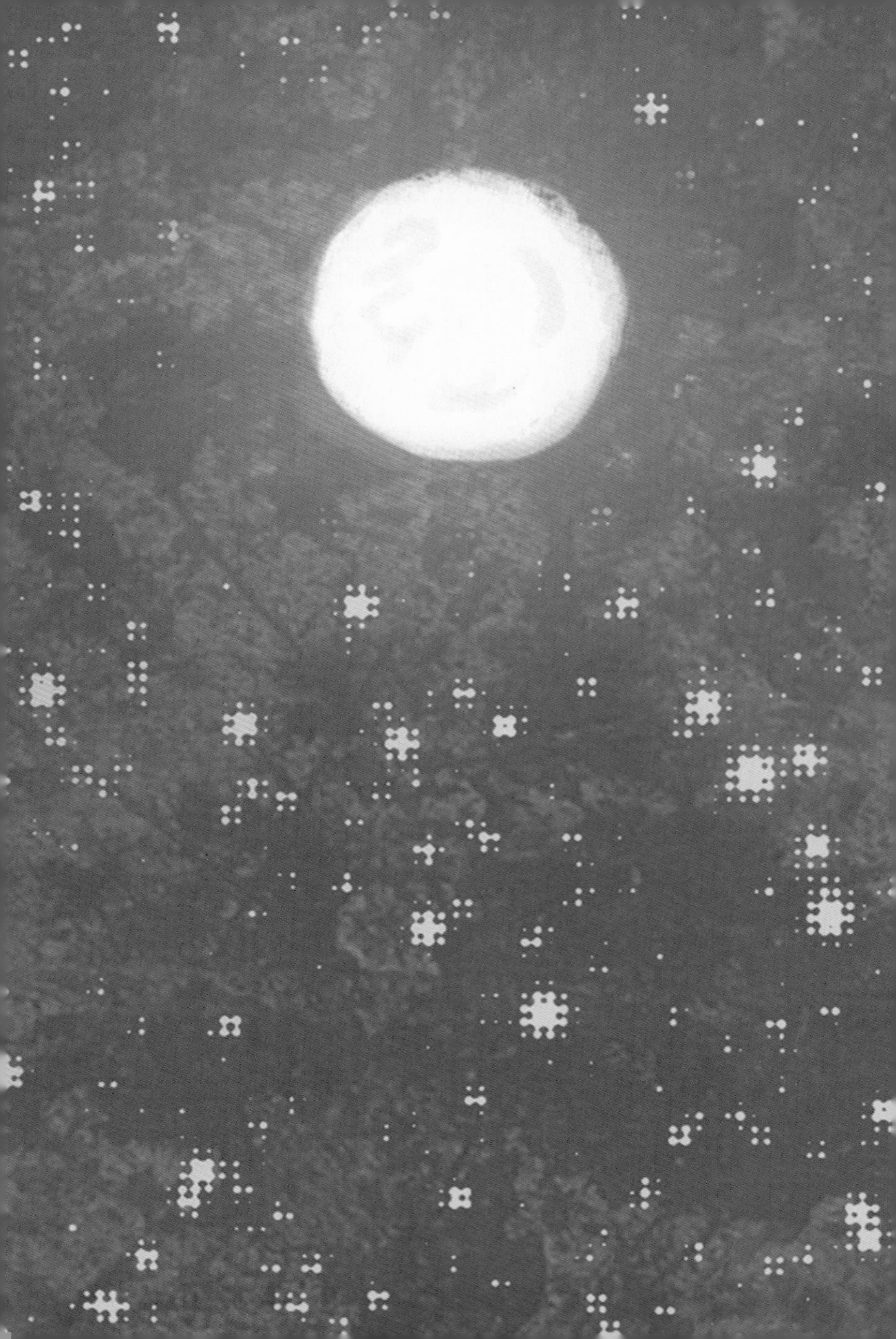

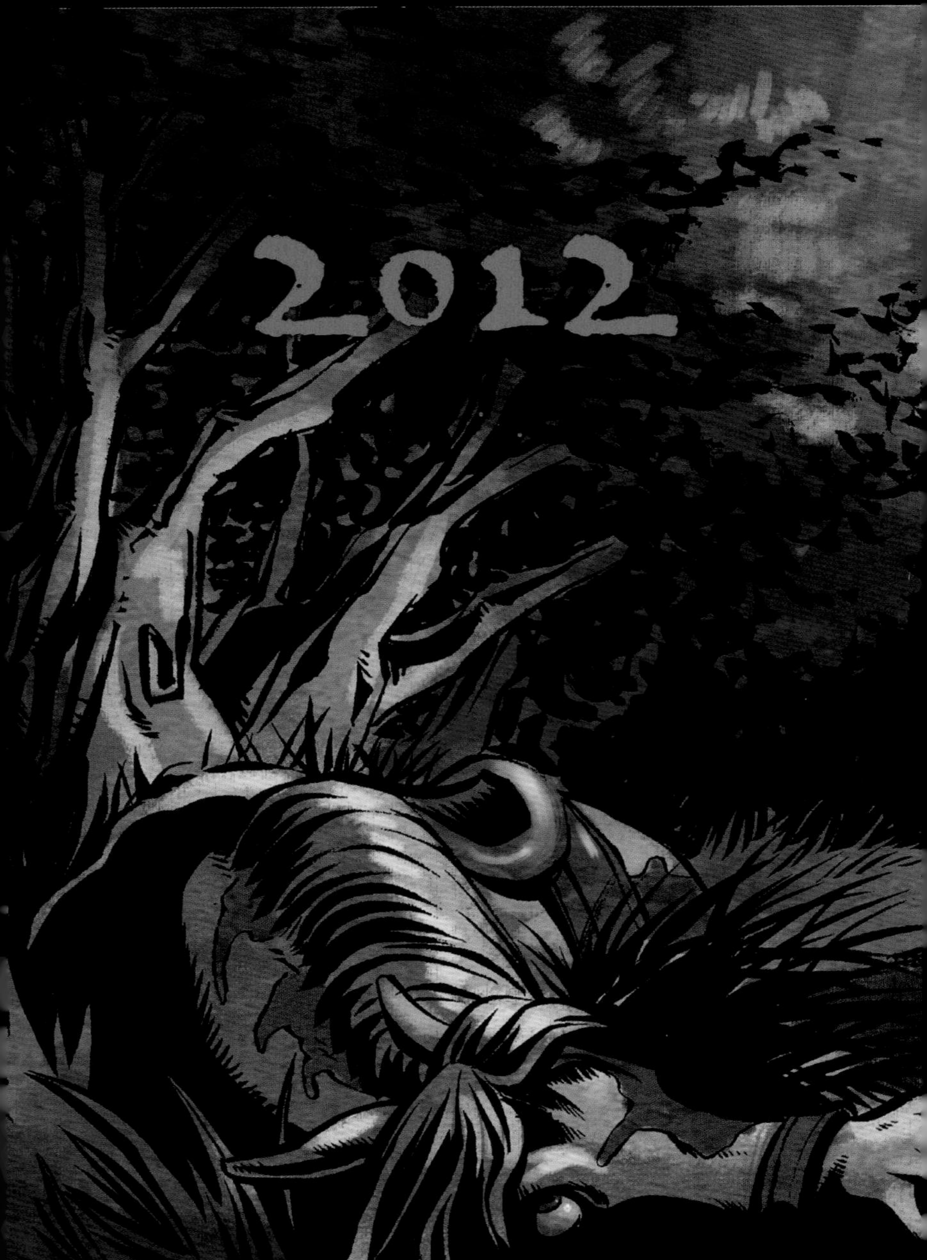
2012

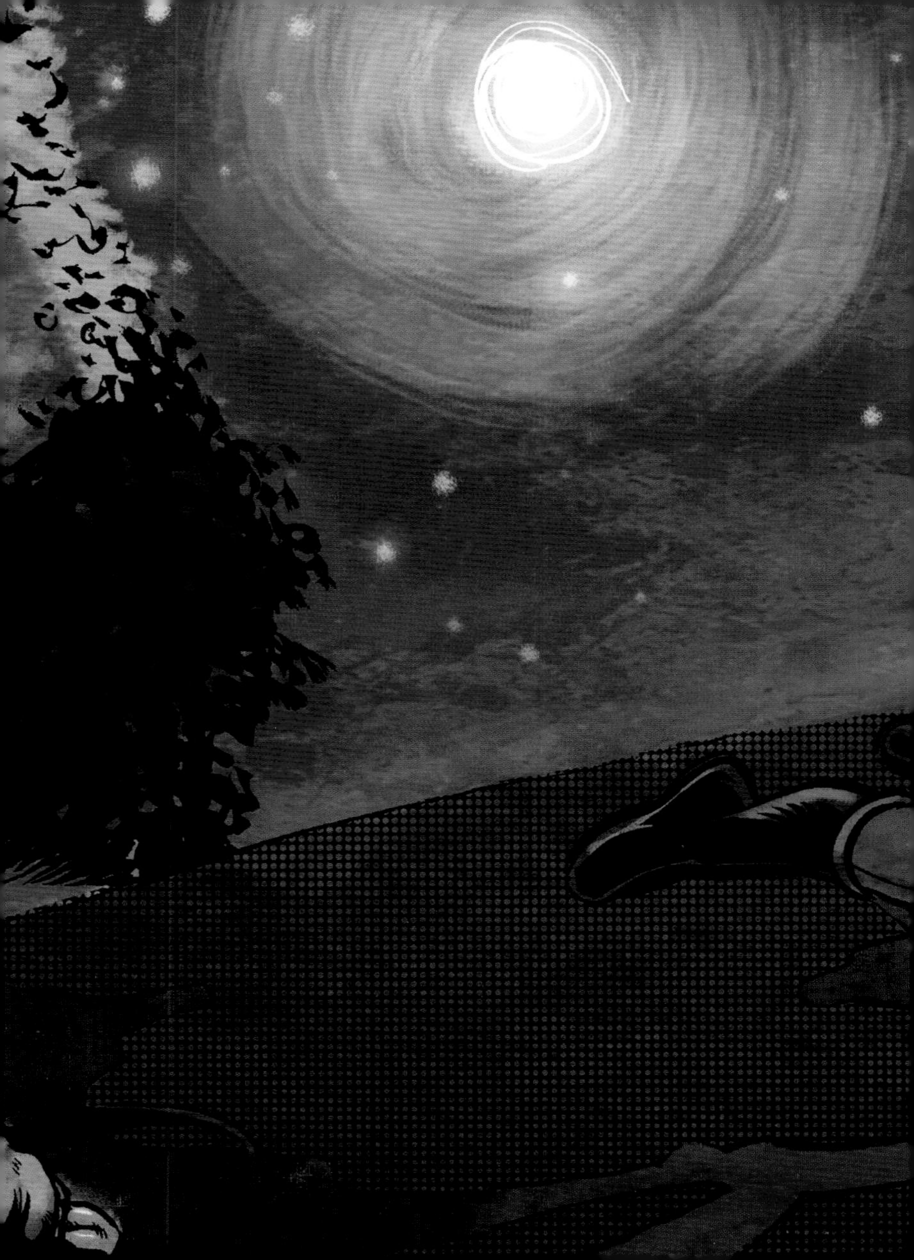

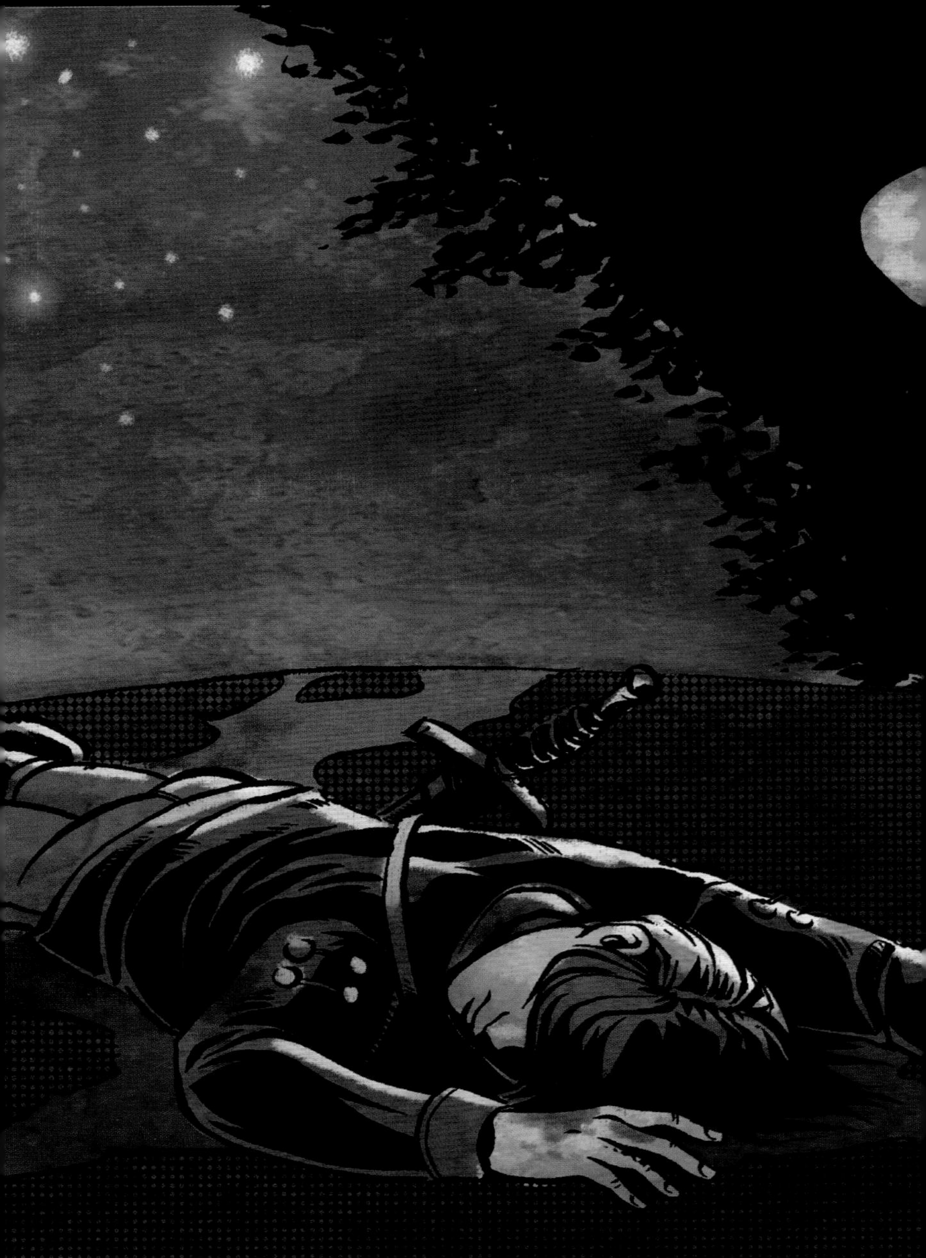

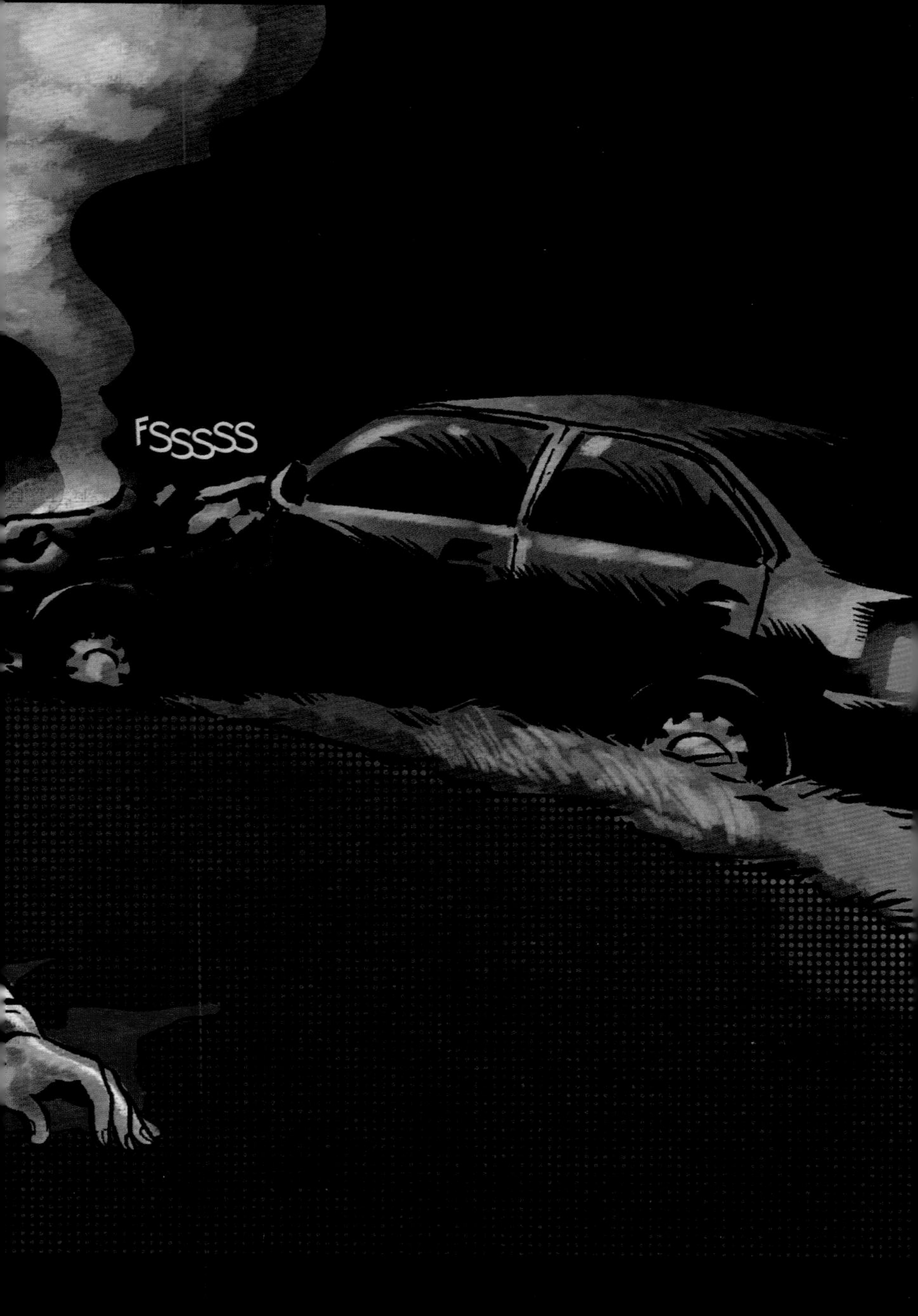
FSSSSS

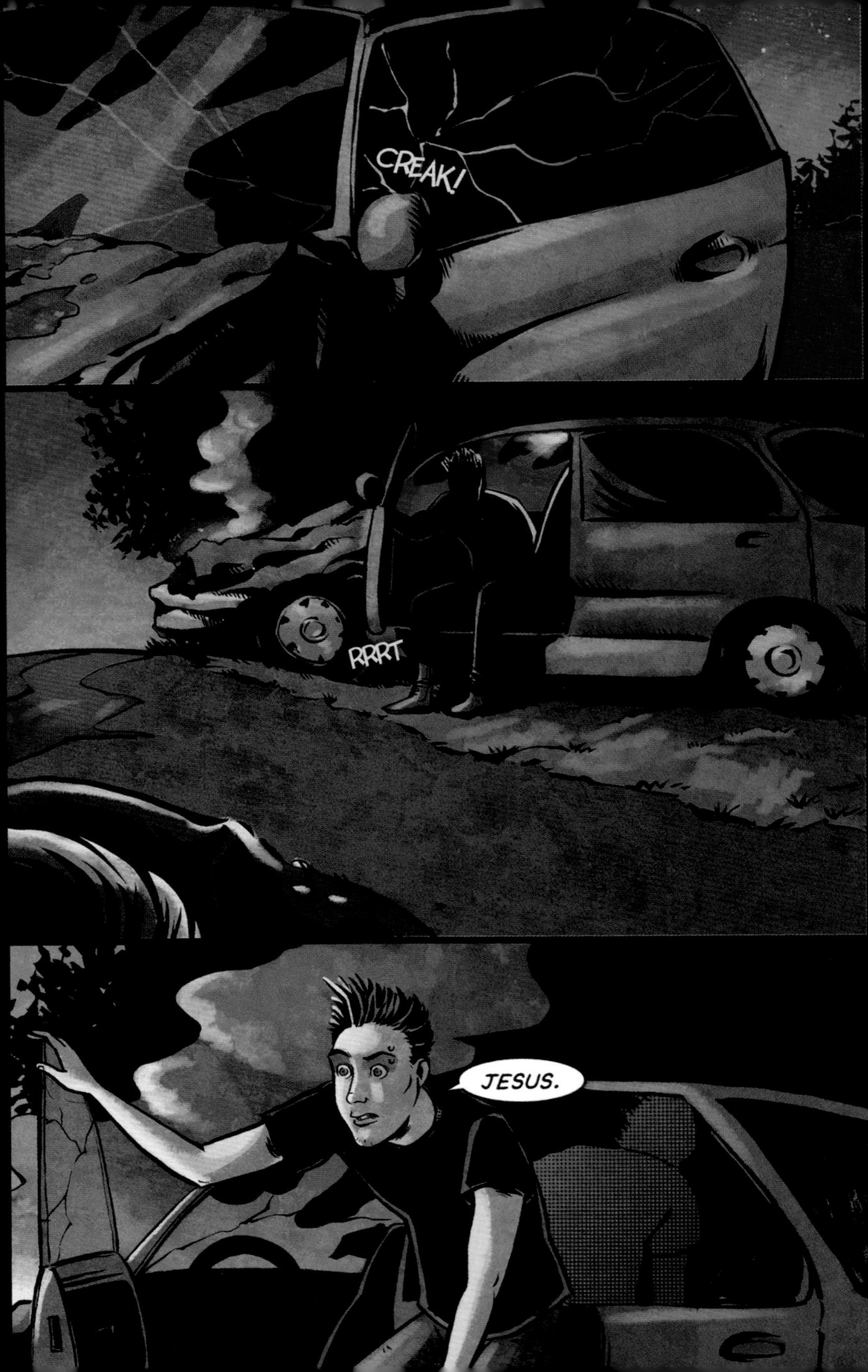
CREAK!
RRRT
JESUS.

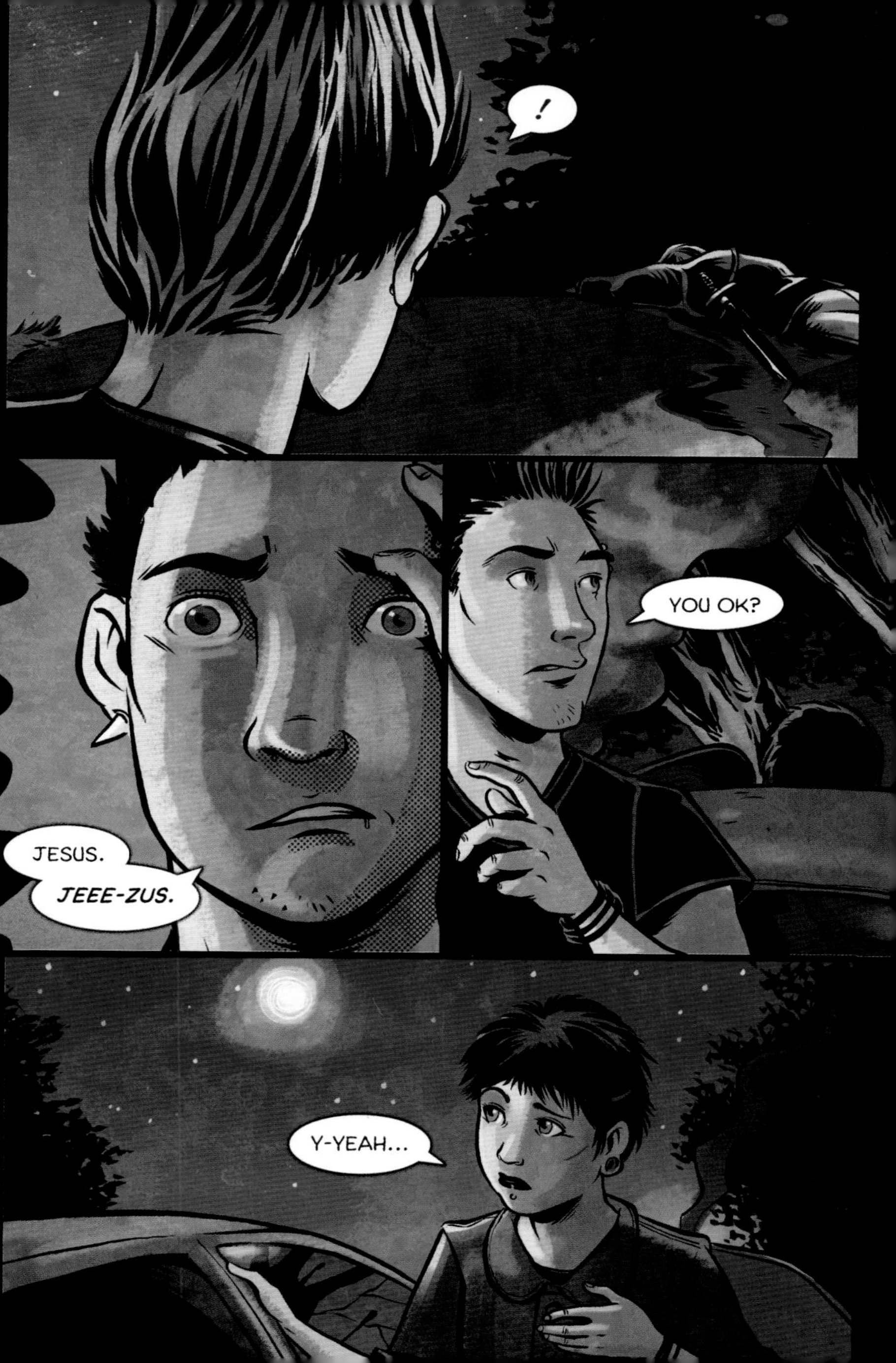
!
JESUS.
JEEE-ZUS.
YOU OK?
Y-YEAH...

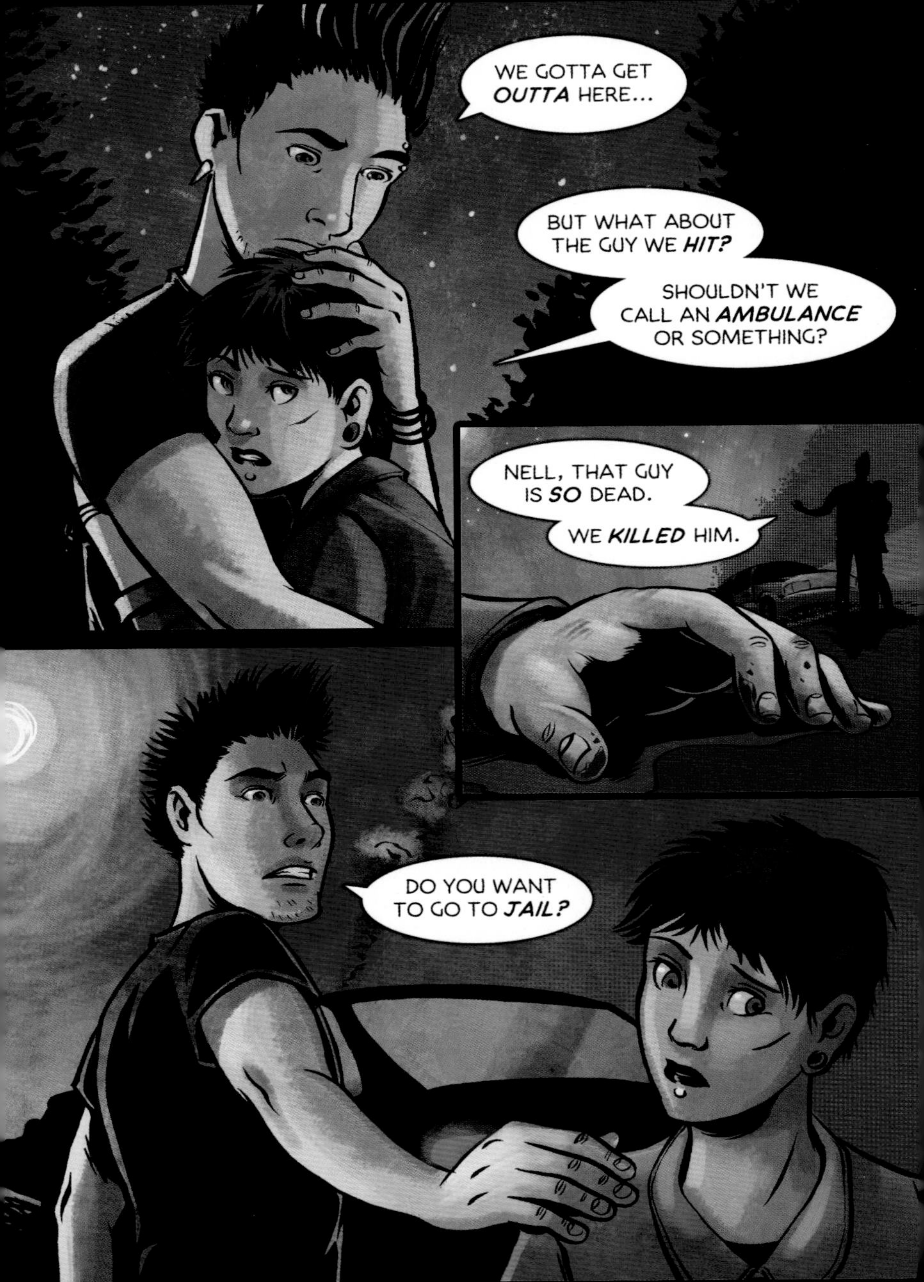
WE GOTTA GET *OUTTA* HERE...
BUT WHAT ABOUT THE GUY WE *HIT?*
SHOULDN'T WE CALL AN *AMBULANCE* OR SOMETHING?
NELL, THAT GUY IS *SO* DEAD.
WE *KILLED* HIM.
DO YOU WANT TO GO TO *JAIL?*

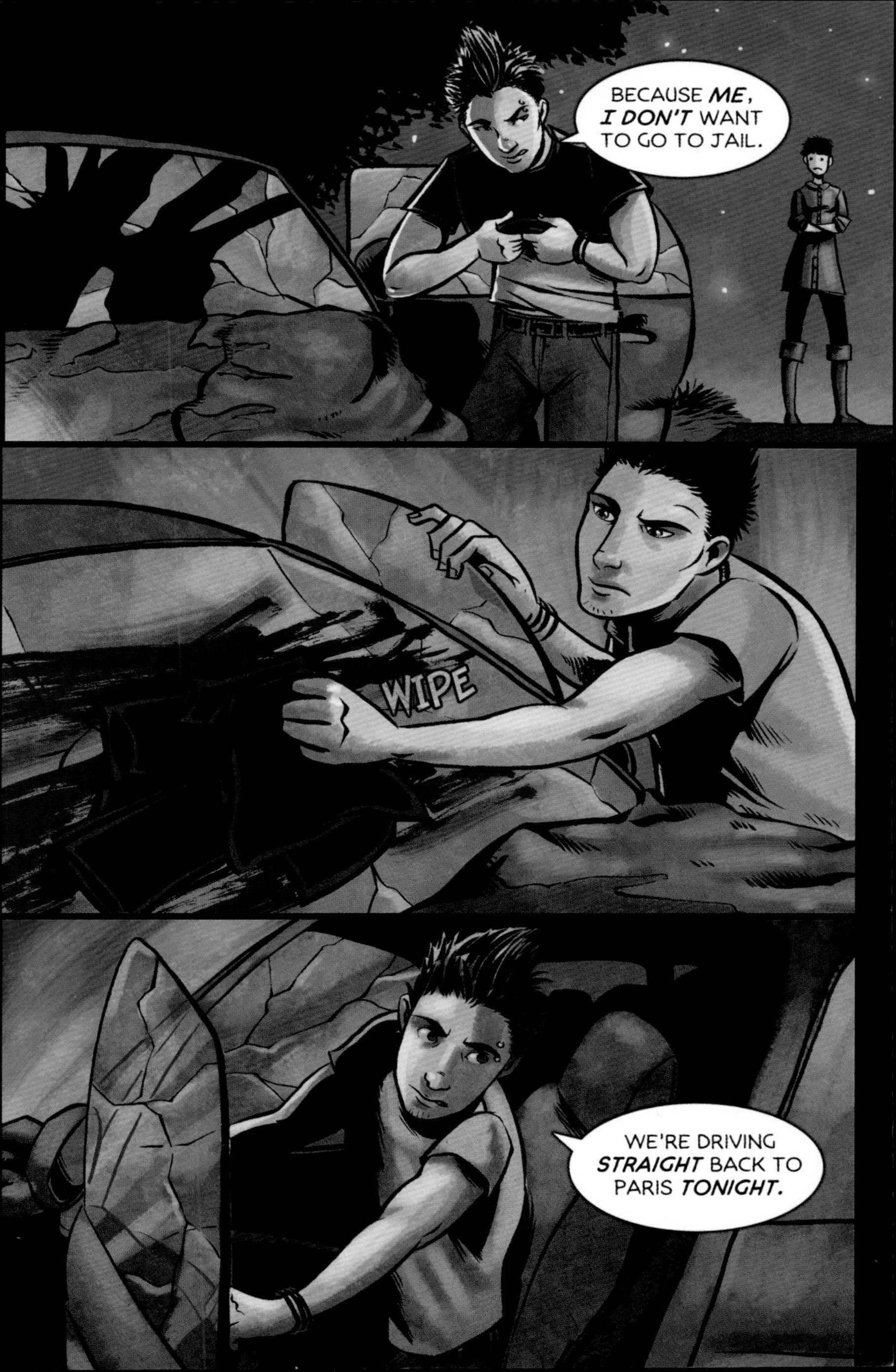
BECAUSE *ME*, *I DON'T* WANT TO GO TO JAIL.
WIPE
WE'RE DRIVING *STRAIGHT* BACK TO PARIS *TONIGHT.*

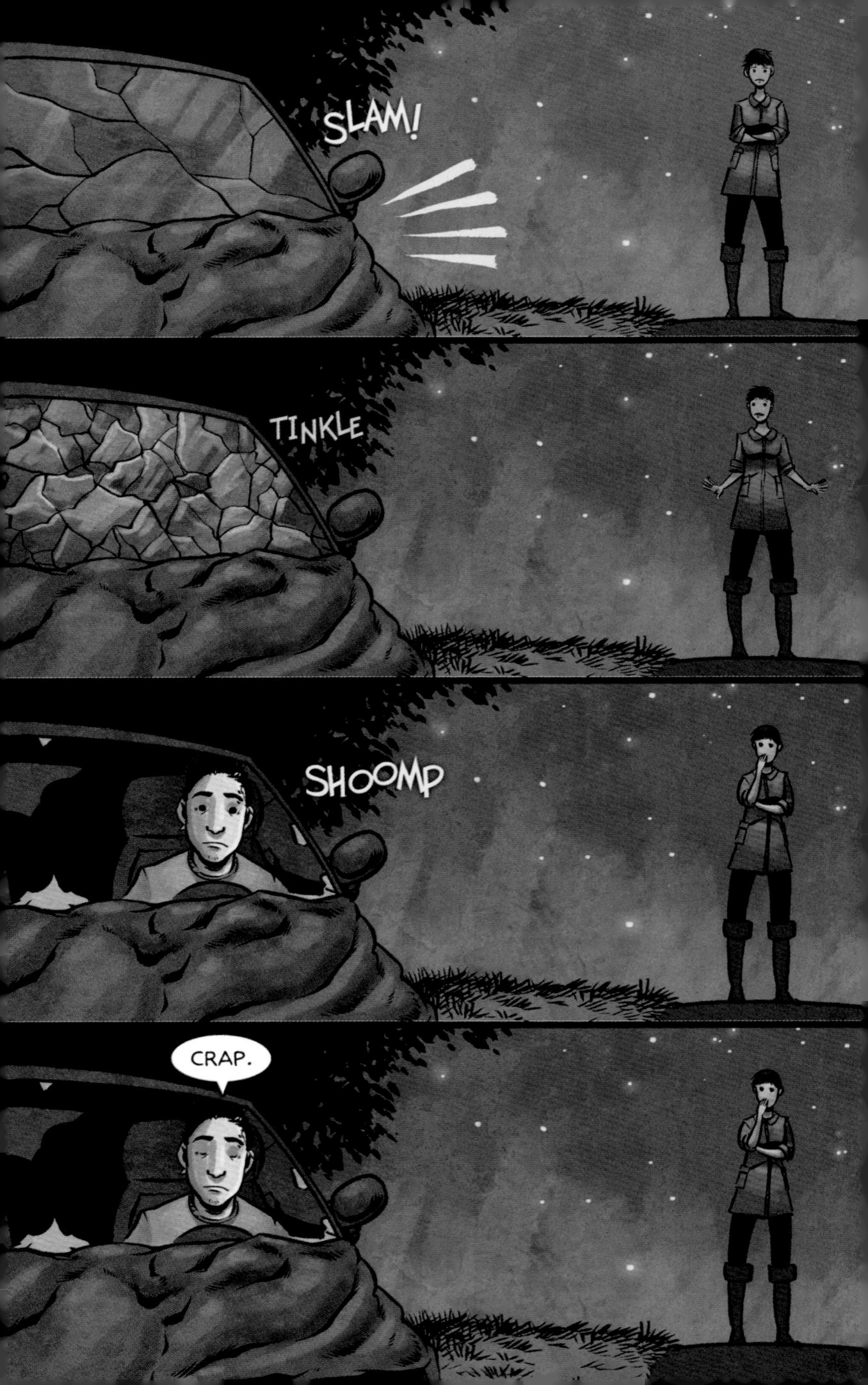
SLAM!
TINKLE
SHOOMP
CRAP.

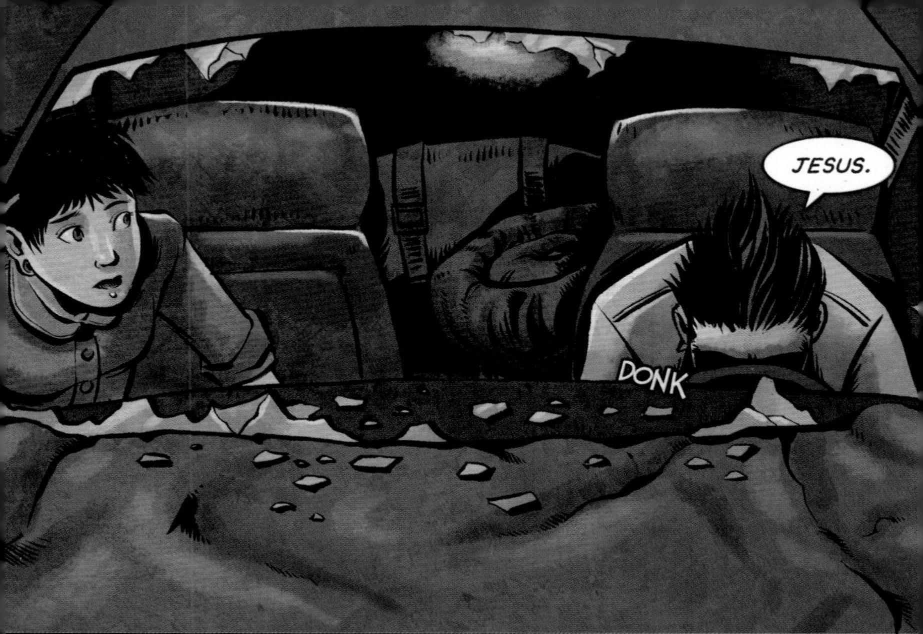
JESUS.
DONK

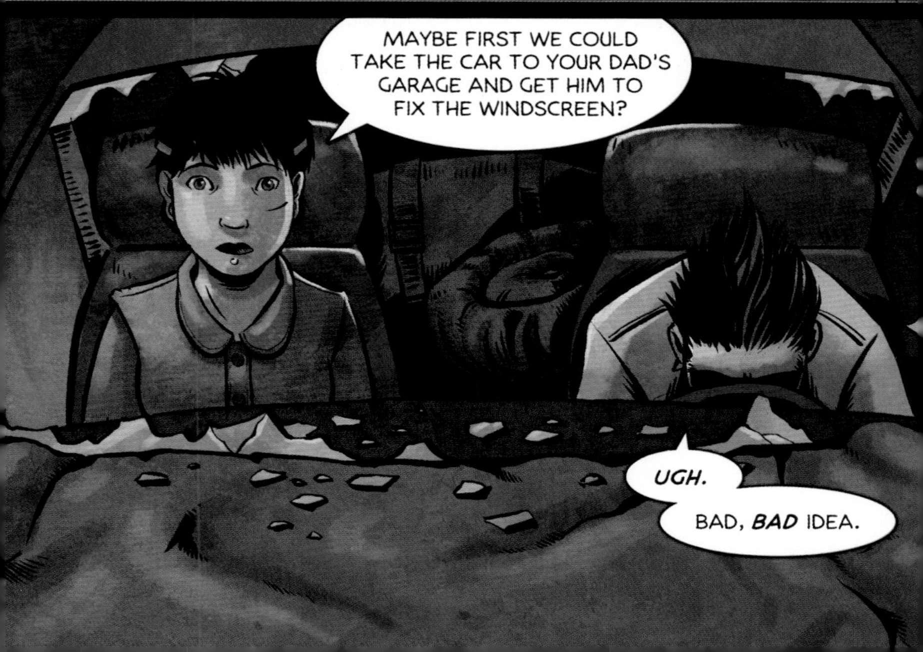
MAYBE FIRST WE COULD TAKE THE CAR TO YOUR DAD'S GARAGE AND GET HIM TO FIX THE WINDSCREEN?
UGH.
BAD, *BAD* IDEA.

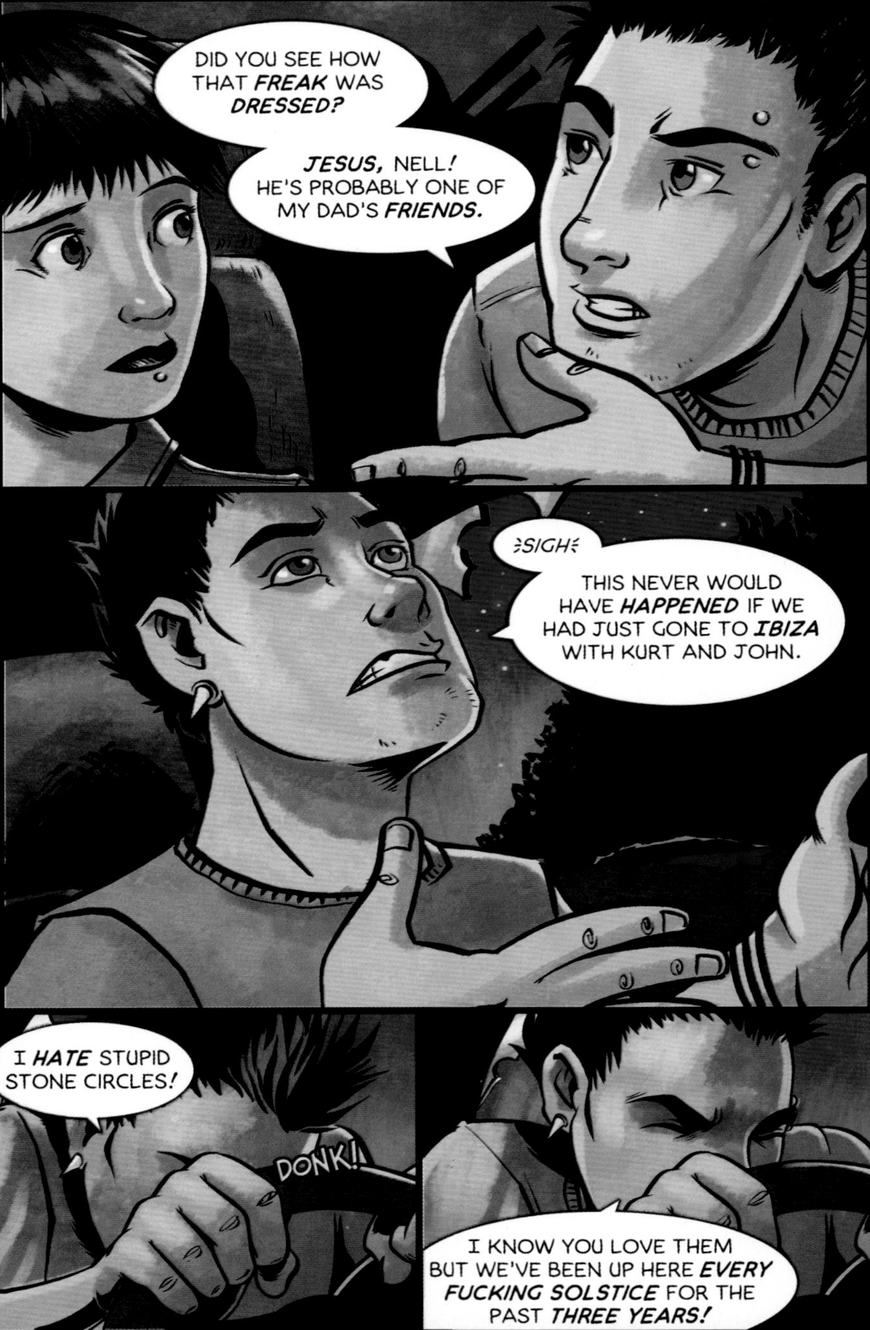
DID YOU SEE HOW THAT *FREAK* WAS *DRESSED?*
JESUS, NELL! HE'S PROBABLY ONE OF MY DAD'S *FRIENDS.*
SIGH
THIS NEVER WOULD HAVE *HAPPENED* IF WE HAD JUST GONE TO *IBIZA* WITH KURT AND JOHN.
I *HATE* STUPID STONE CIRCLES!
DONK!
I KNOW YOU LOVE THEM BUT WE'VE BEEN UP HERE *EVERY FUCKING SOLSTICE* FOR THE PAST *THREE YEARS!*

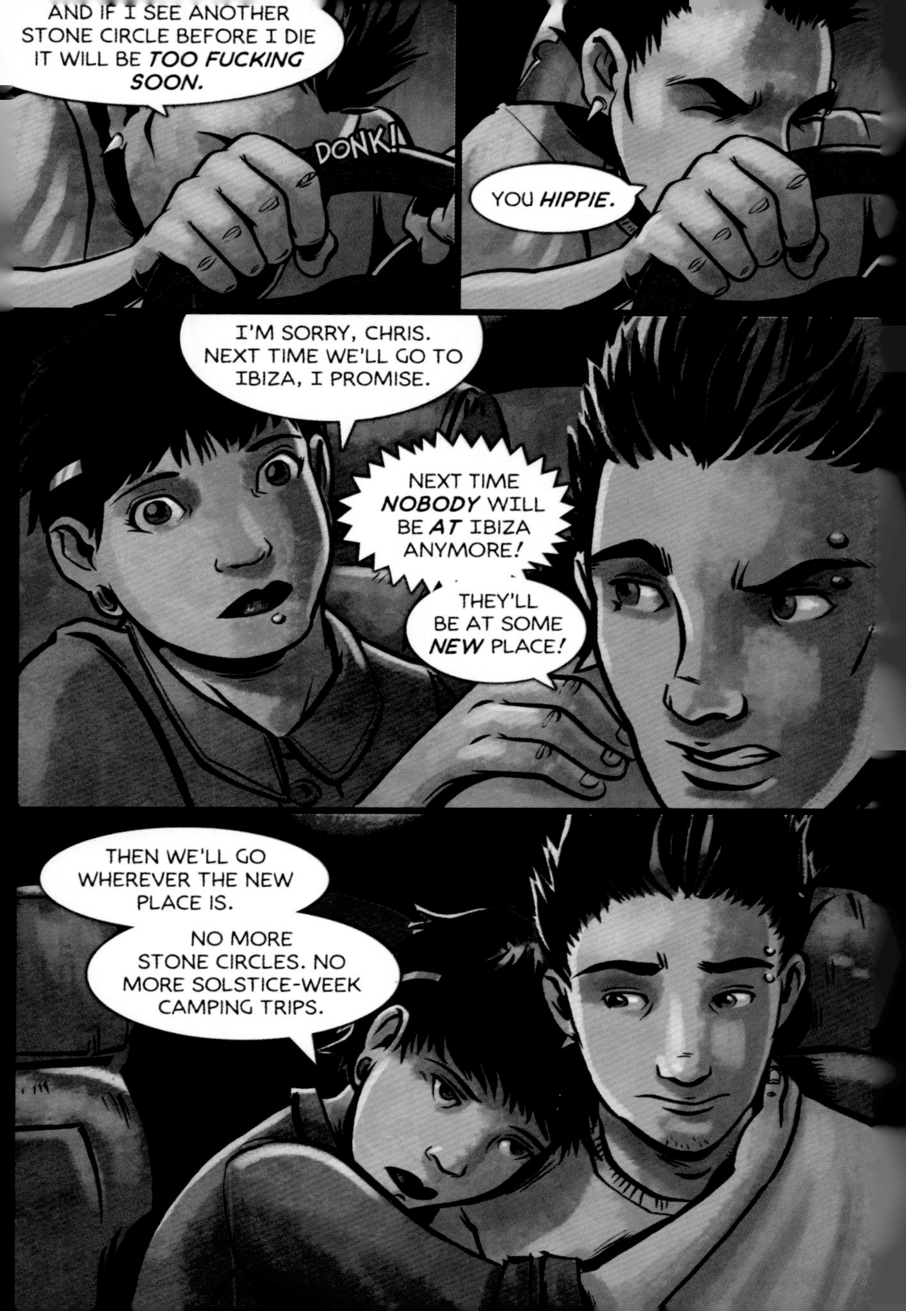
AND IF I SEE ANOTHER STONE CIRCLE BEFORE I DIE IT WILL BE TOO FUCKING SOON.
DONK!!
YOU HIPPIE.
I'M SORRY, CHRIS. NEXT TIME WE'LL GO TO IBIZA, I PROMISE.
NEXT TIME NOBODY WILL BE AT IBIZA ANYMORE!
THEY'LL BE AT SOME NEW PLACE!
THEN WE'LL GO WHEREVER THE NEW PLACE IS.
NO MORE STONE CIRCLES. NO MORE SOLSTICE-WEEK CAMPING TRIPS.

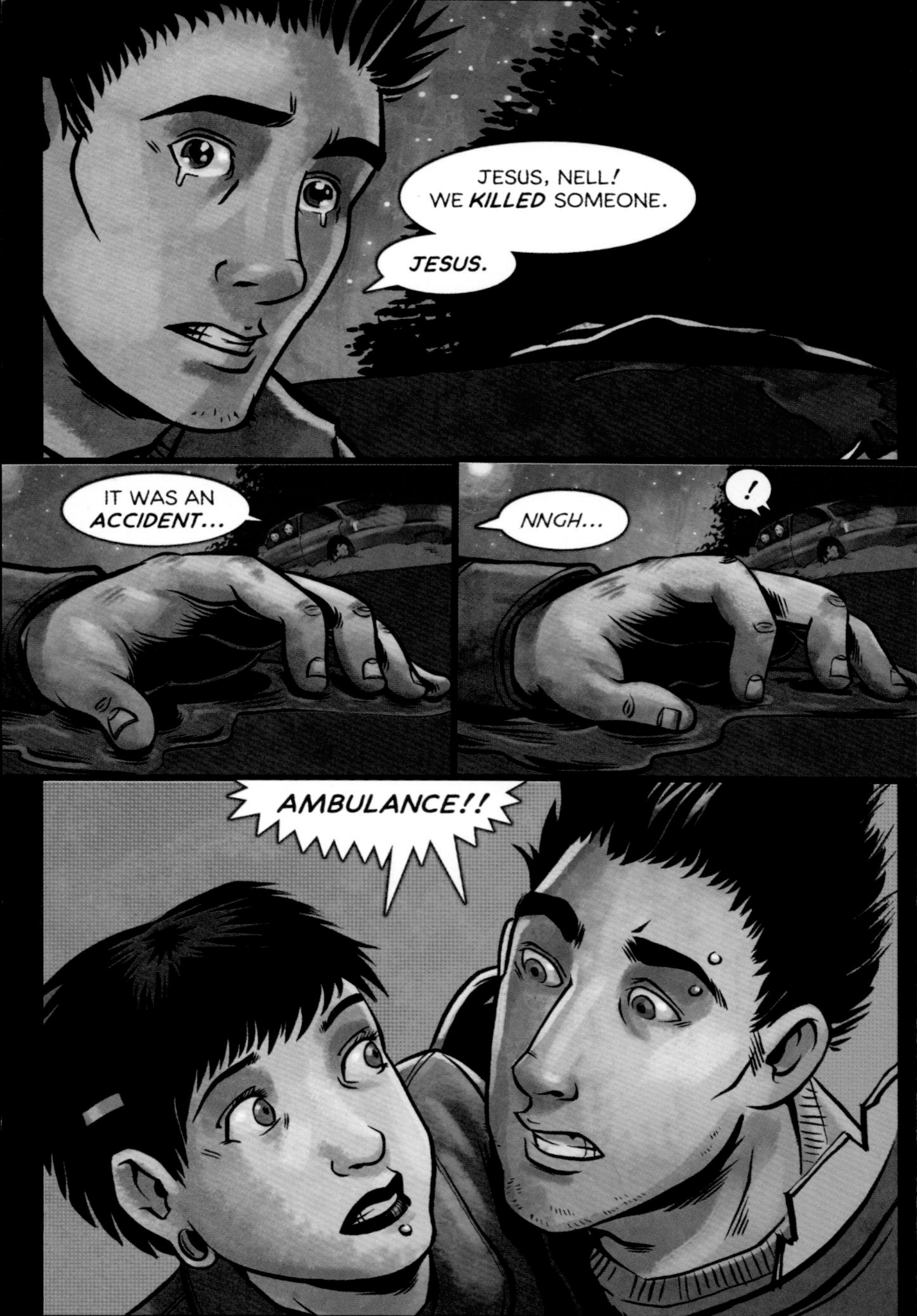
JESUS, NELL! WE KILLED SOMEONE.
JESUS.
IT WAS AN ACCIDENT...
NNGH...
!
AMBULANCE!!

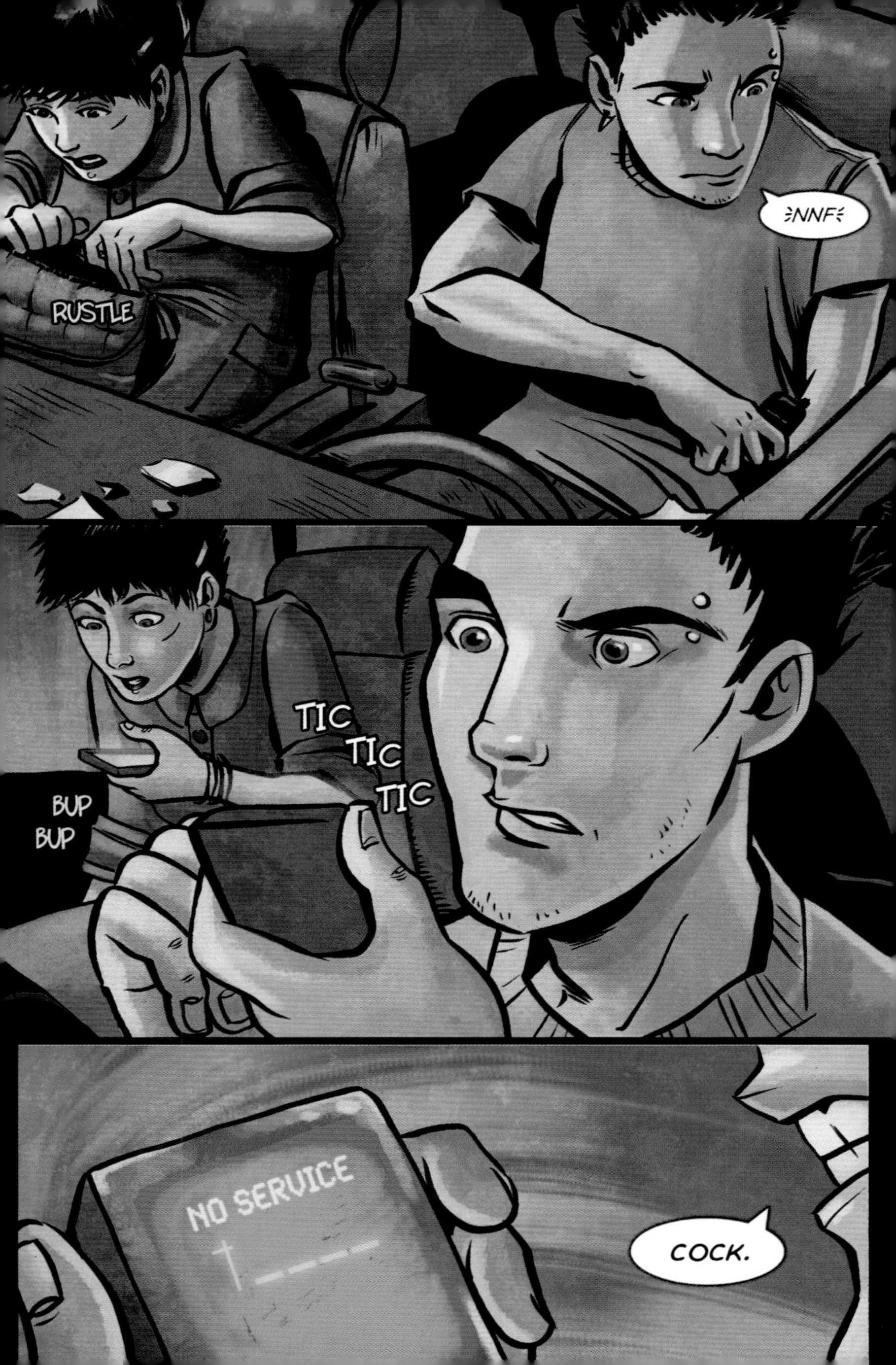
NNF
RUSTLE
TIC
TIC
TIC
BUP
BUP
NO SERVICE
COCK.

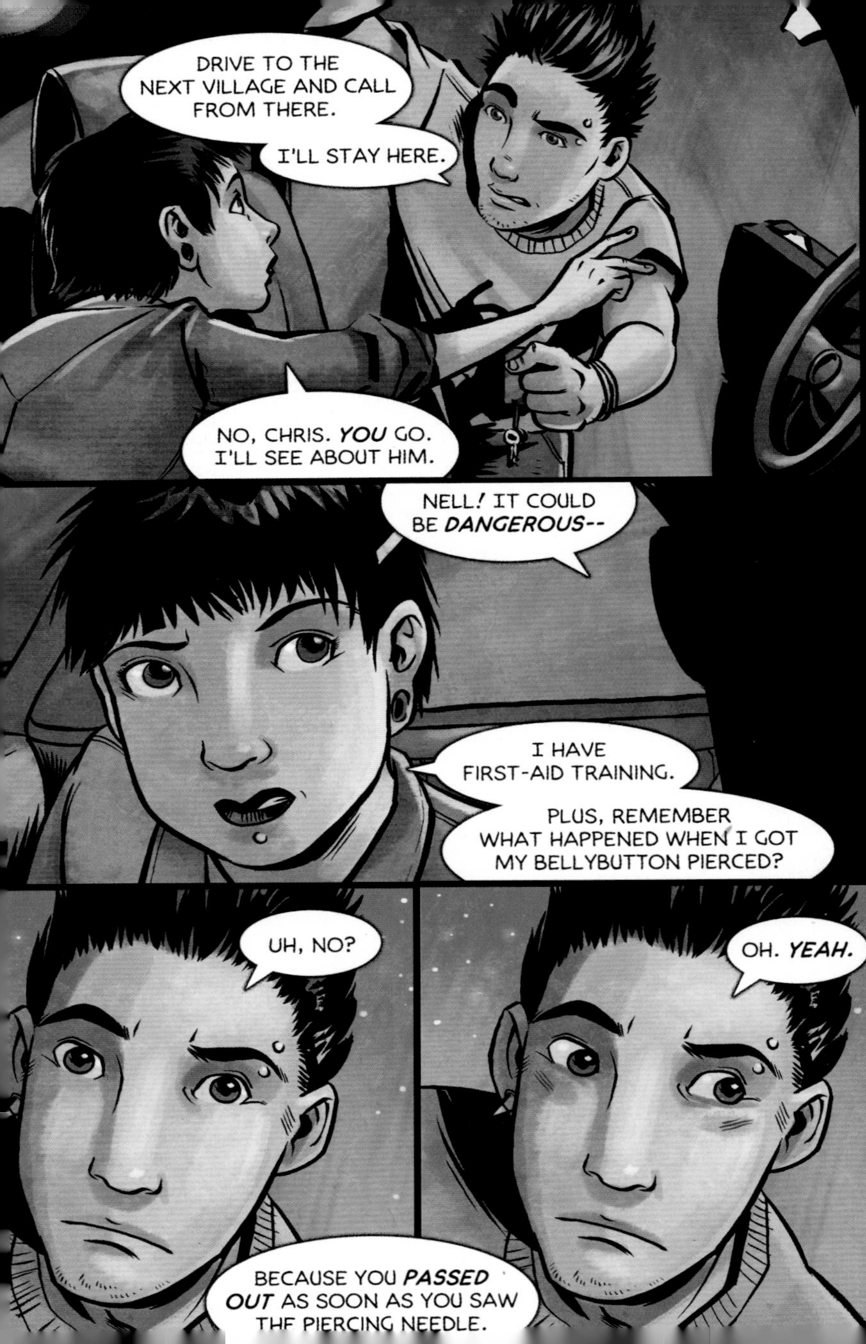
DRIVE TO THE NEXT VILLAGE AND CALL FROM THERE.
I'LL STAY HERE.
NO, CHRIS. *YOU* GO. I'LL SEE ABOUT HIM.
NELL! IT COULD BE ***DANGEROUS***--
I HAVE FIRST-AID TRAINING.
PLUS, REMEMBER WHAT HAPPENED WHEN I GOT MY BELLYBUTTON PIERCED?
UH, NO?
OH. ***YEAH.***
BECAUSE YOU ***PASSED OUT*** AS SOON AS YOU SAW THE PIERCING NEEDLE.

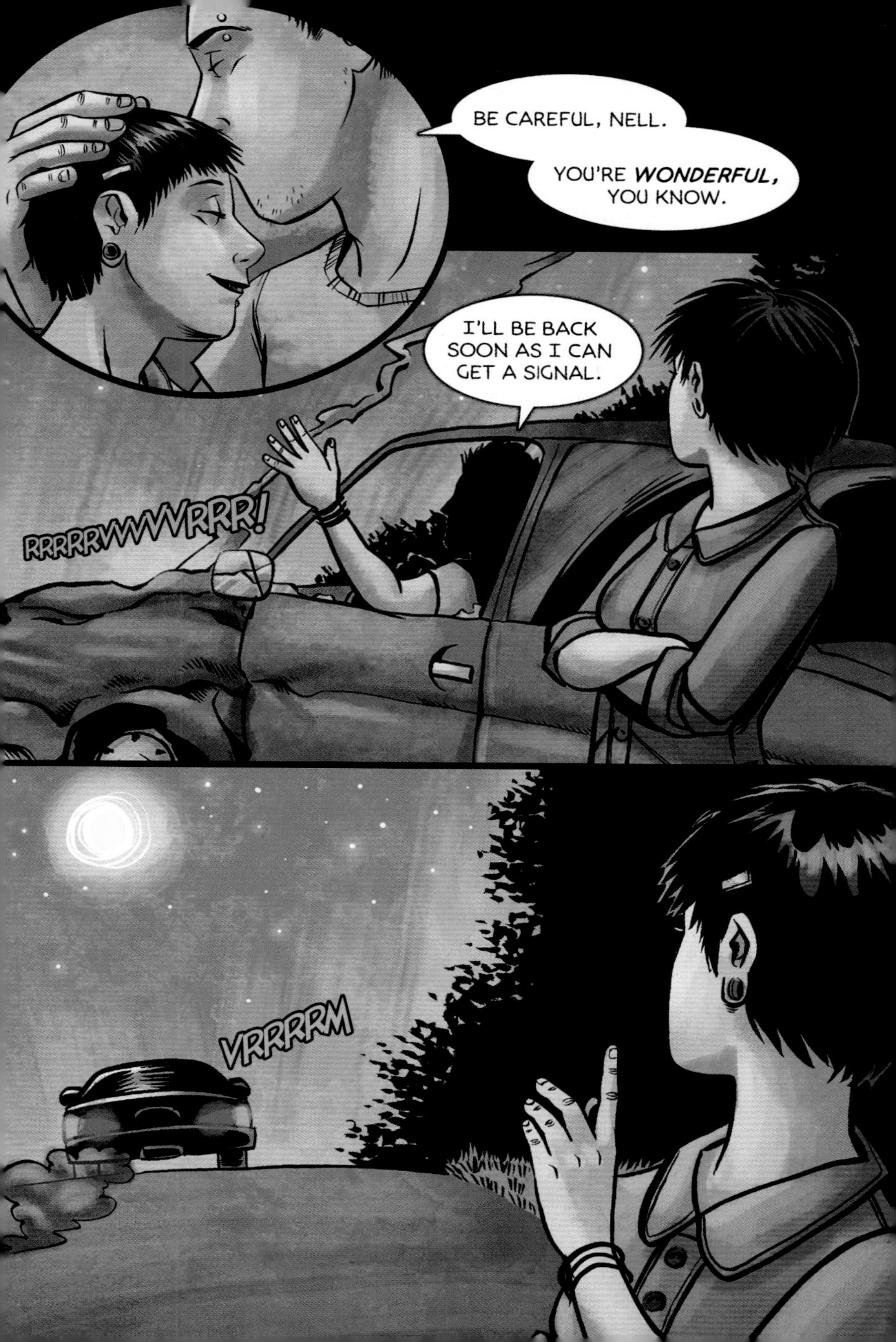
BE CAREFUL, NELL.
YOU'RE **WONDERFUL,** YOU KNOW.
I'LL BE BACK SOON AS I CAN GET A SIGNAL.
RRRRRVVVVVRRR!
VRRRRM

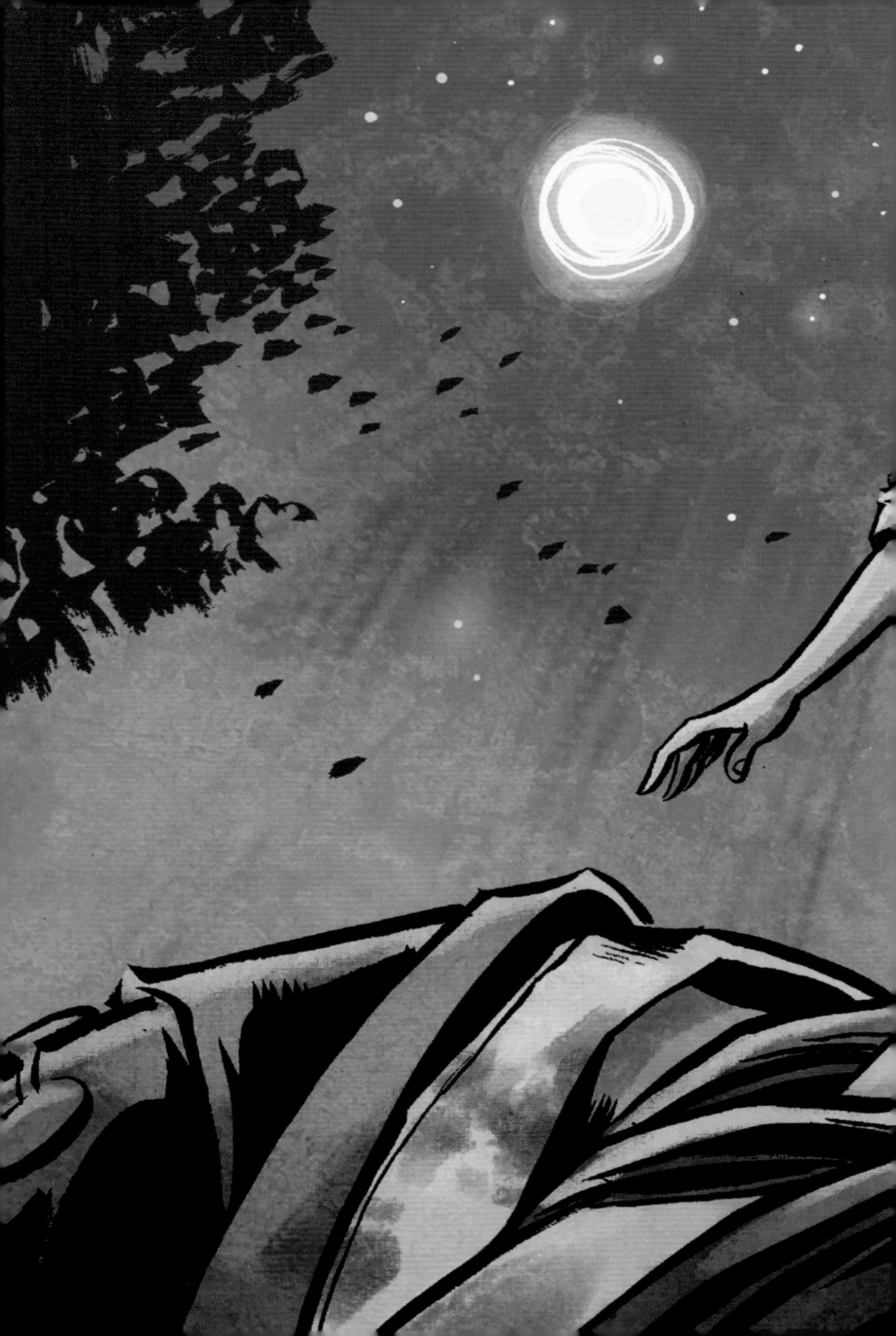

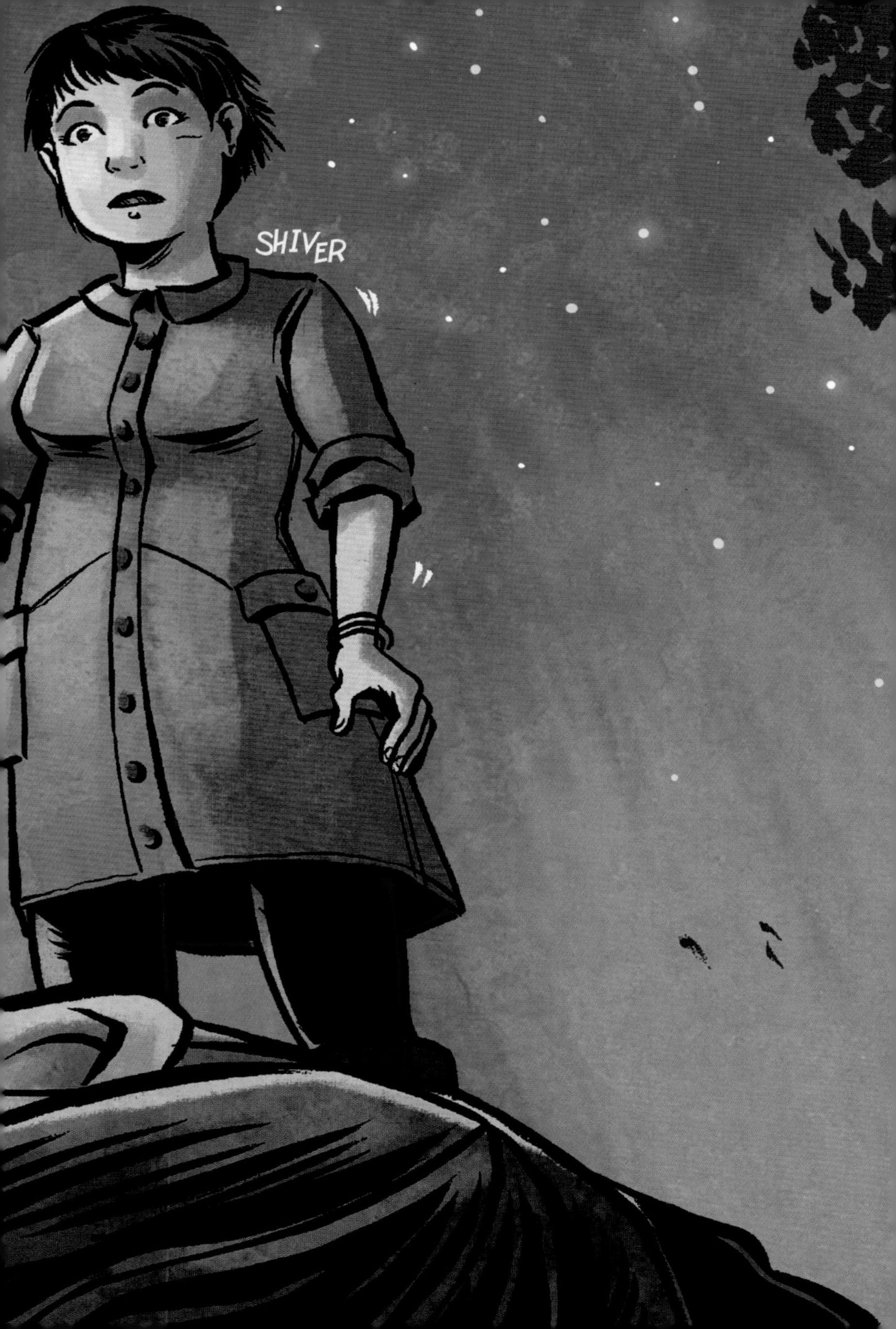
SHIVER

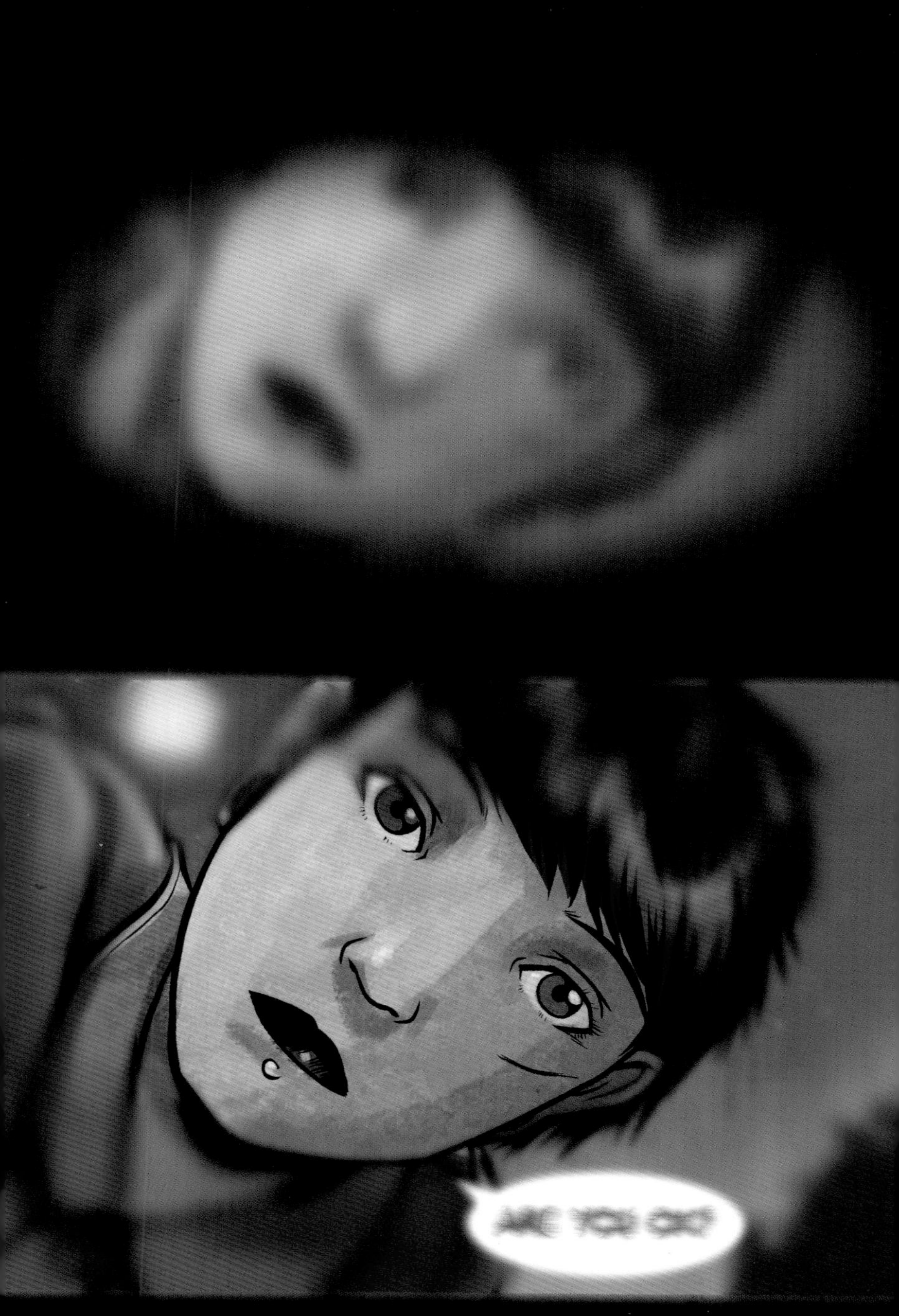
ARE YOU OK?

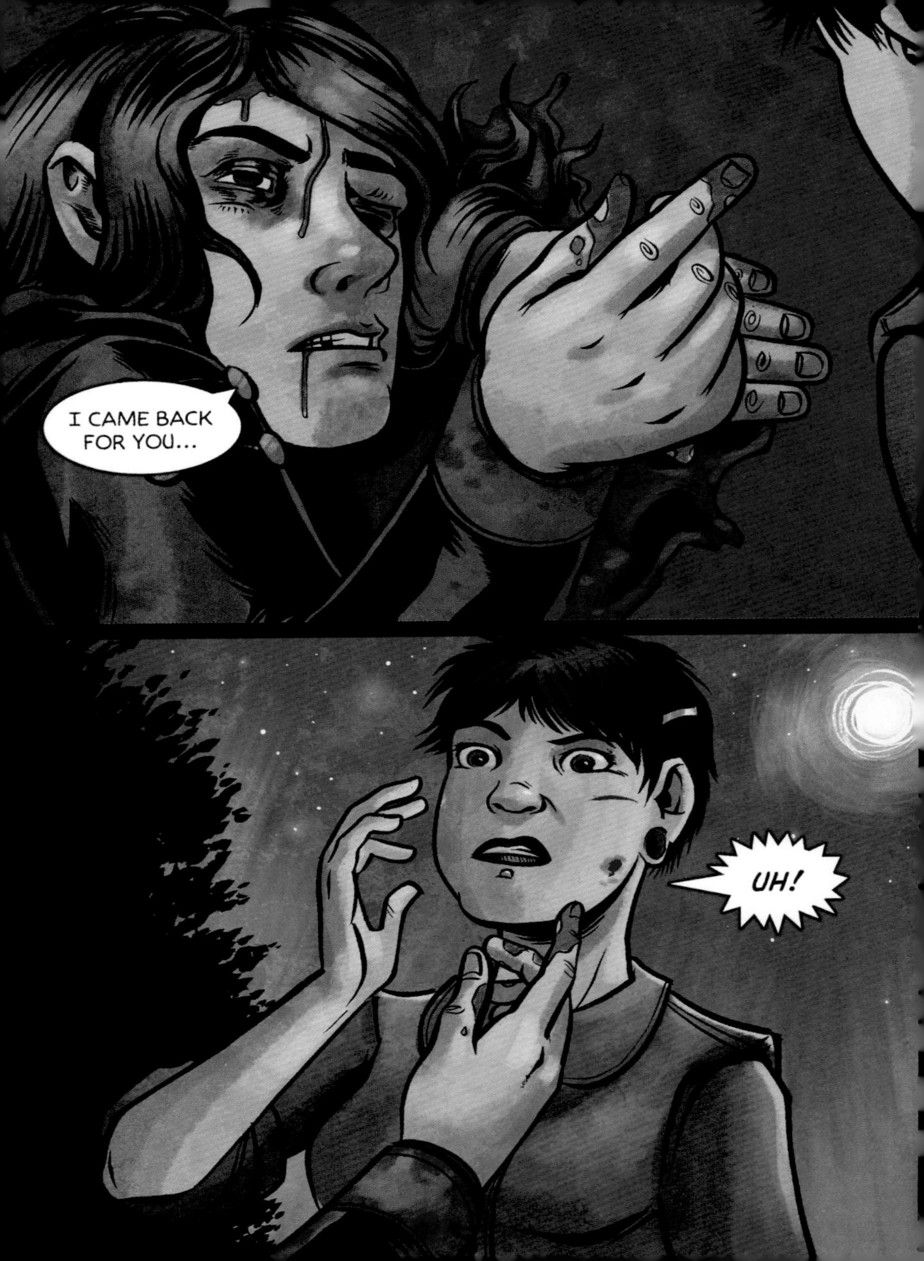
I CAME BACK FOR YOU...
UH!

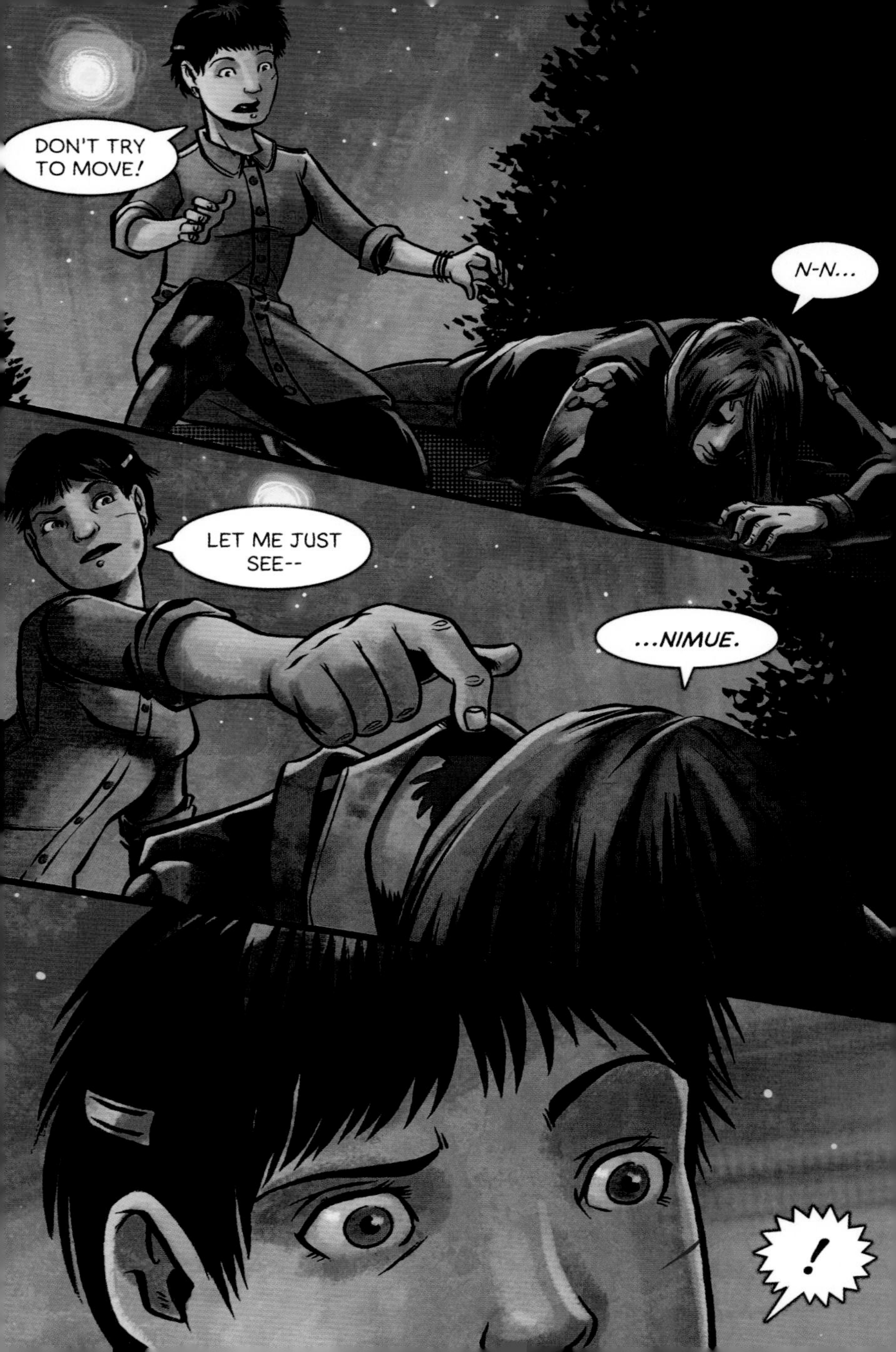
DON'T TRY TO MOVE!
N-N...
LET ME JUST SEE--
...NIMUE.
!

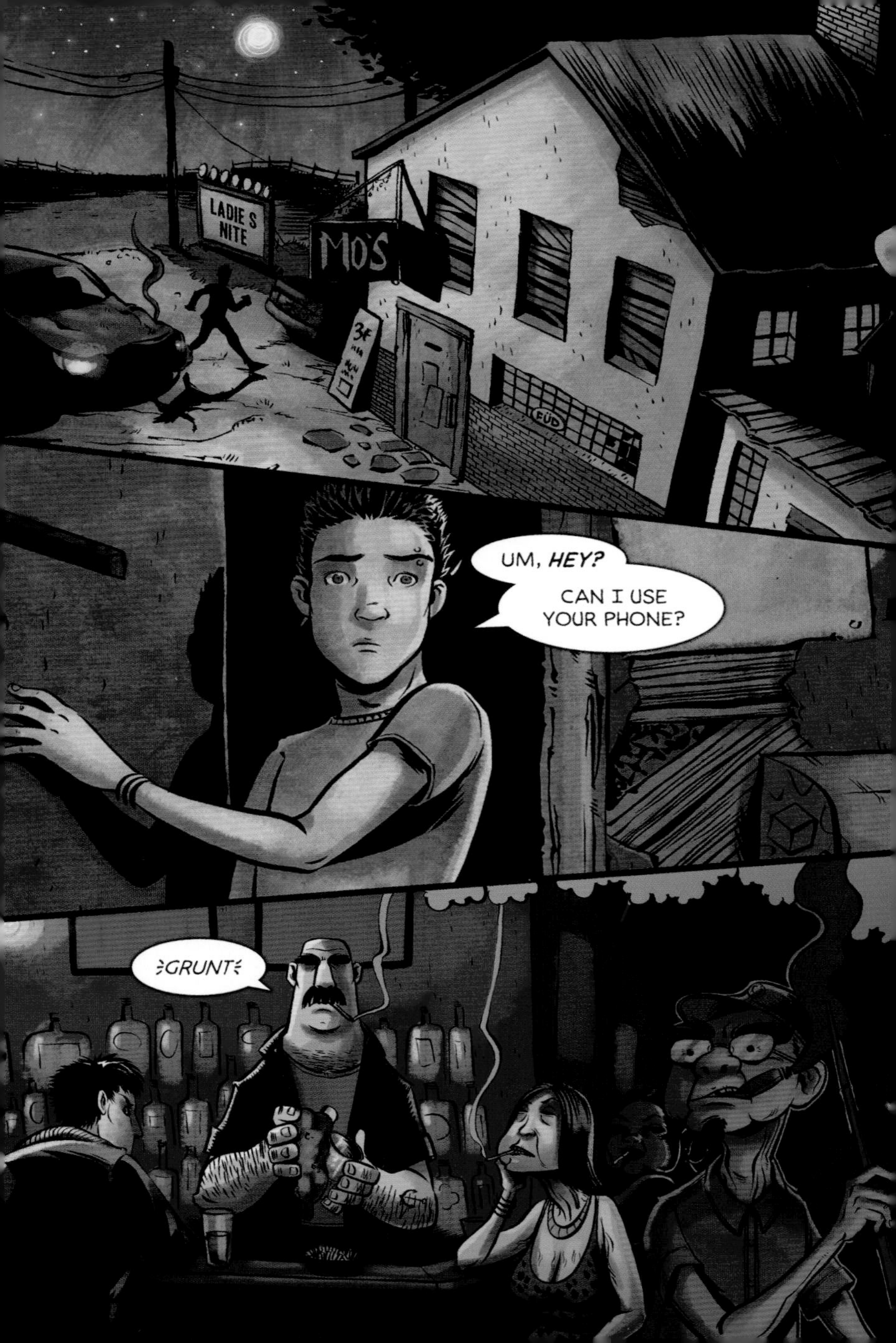
LADIE S NITE
MO'S
FÜD
UM, HEY?
CAN I USE YOUR PHONE?
GRUNT

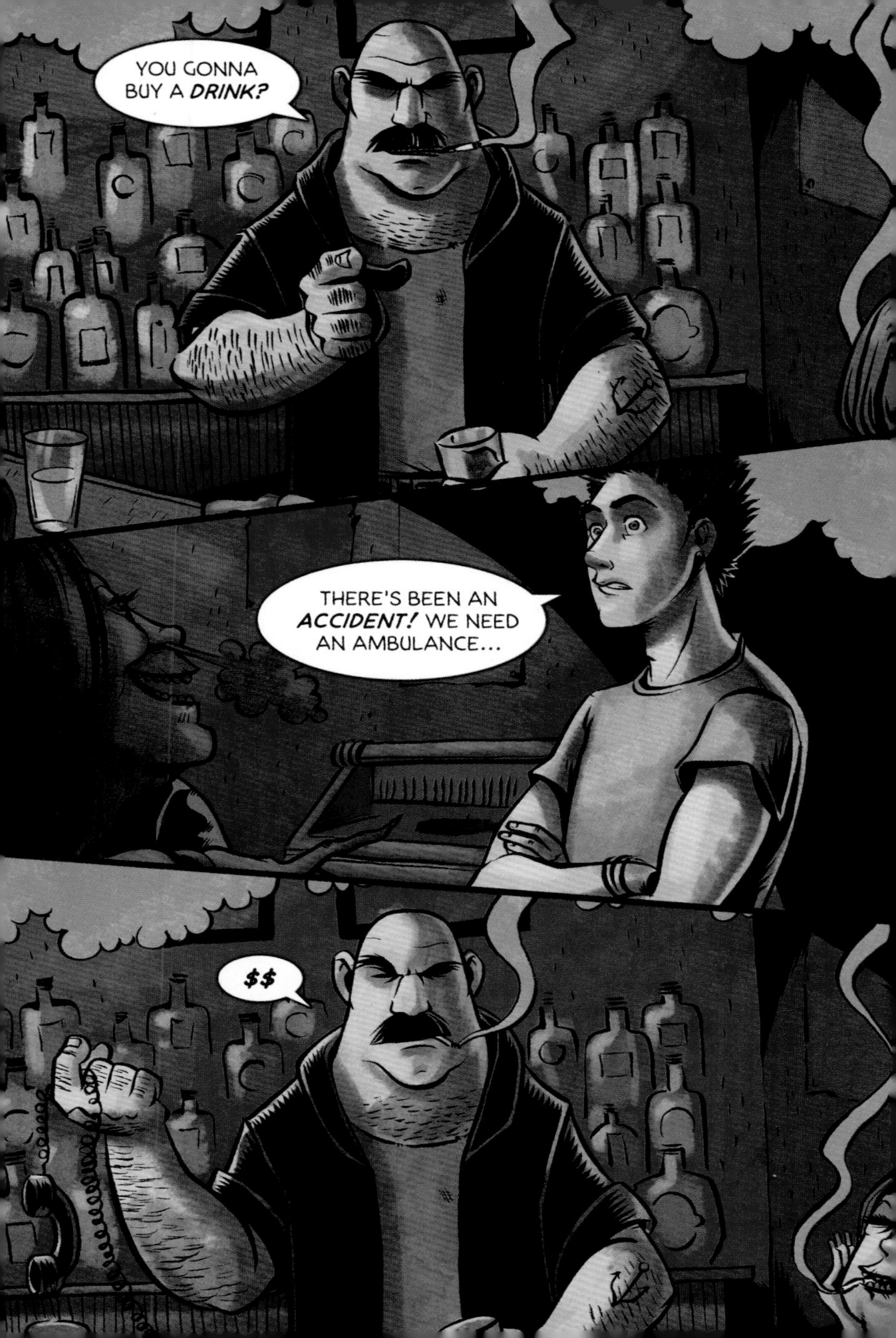
YOU GONNA BUY A *DRINK?*
THERE'S BEEN AN *ACCIDENT!* WE NEED AN AMBULANCE...
$$

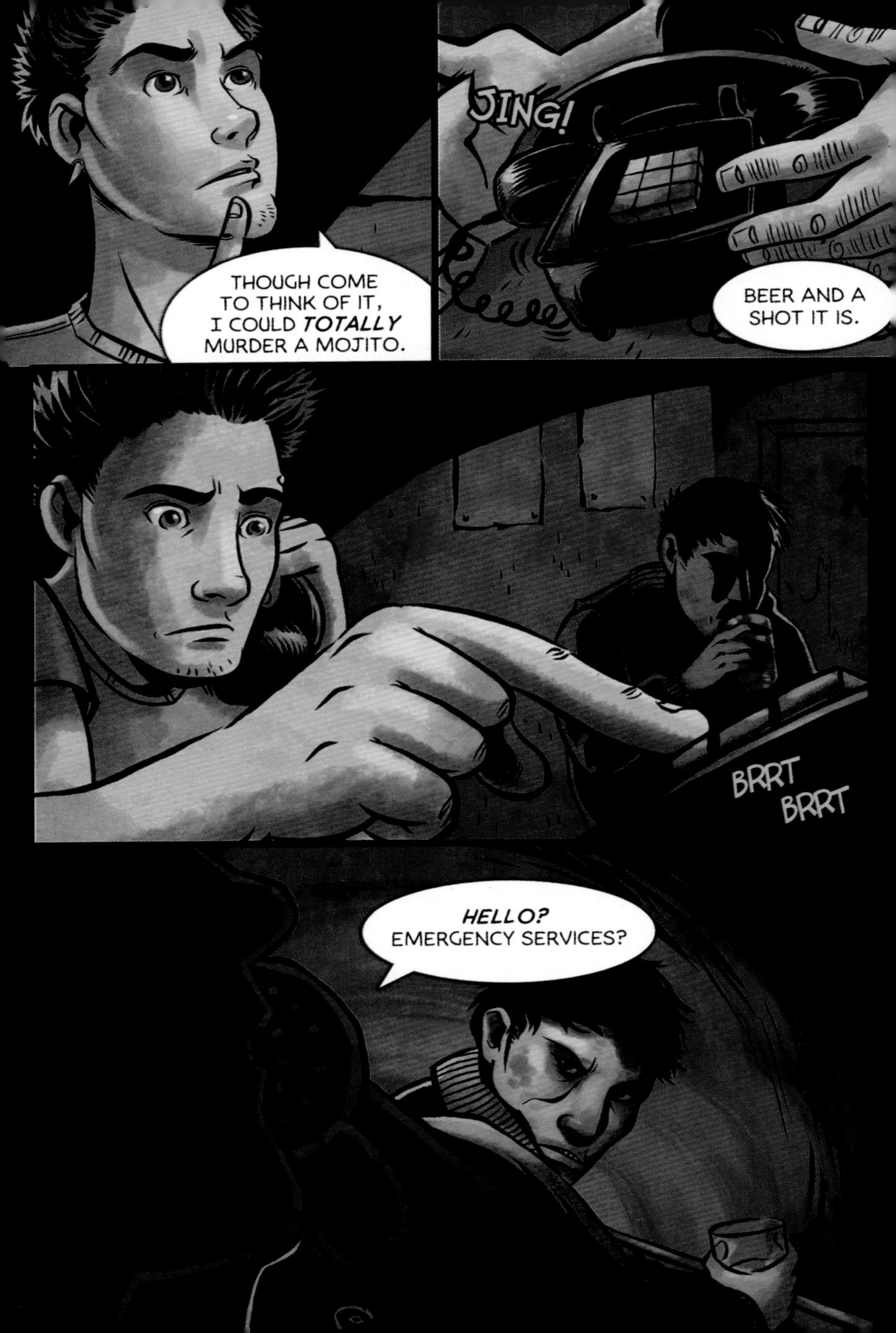
THOUGH COME TO THINK OF IT, I COULD *TOTALLY* MURDER A MOJITO.
JING!
BEER AND A SHOT IT IS.
BRRT BRRT
HELLO? EMERGENCY SERVICES?

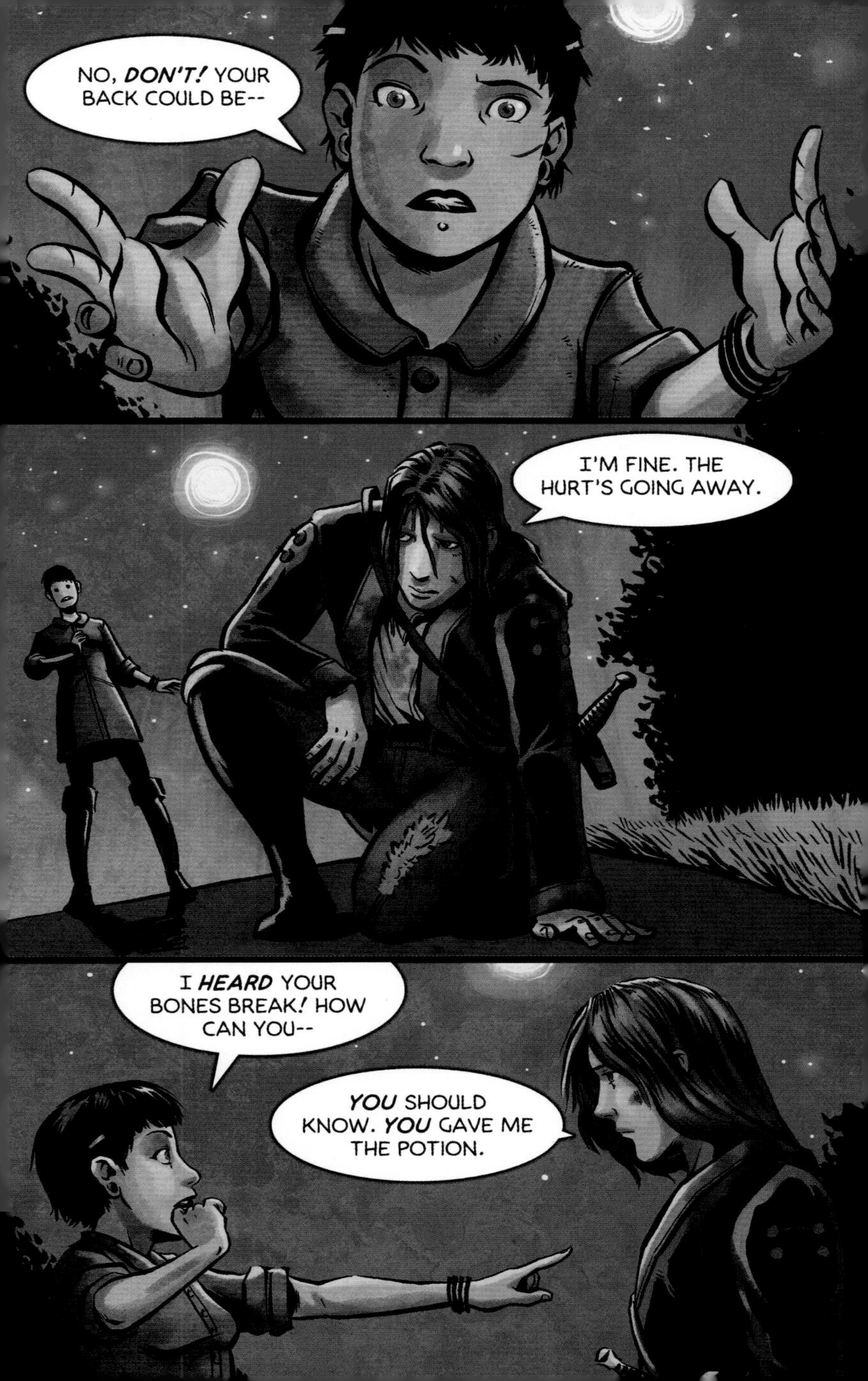
NO, DON'T! YOUR BACK COULD BE--
I'M FINE. THE HURT'S GOING AWAY.
I HEARD YOUR BONES BREAK! HOW CAN YOU--
YOU SHOULD KNOW. YOU GAVE ME THE POTION.

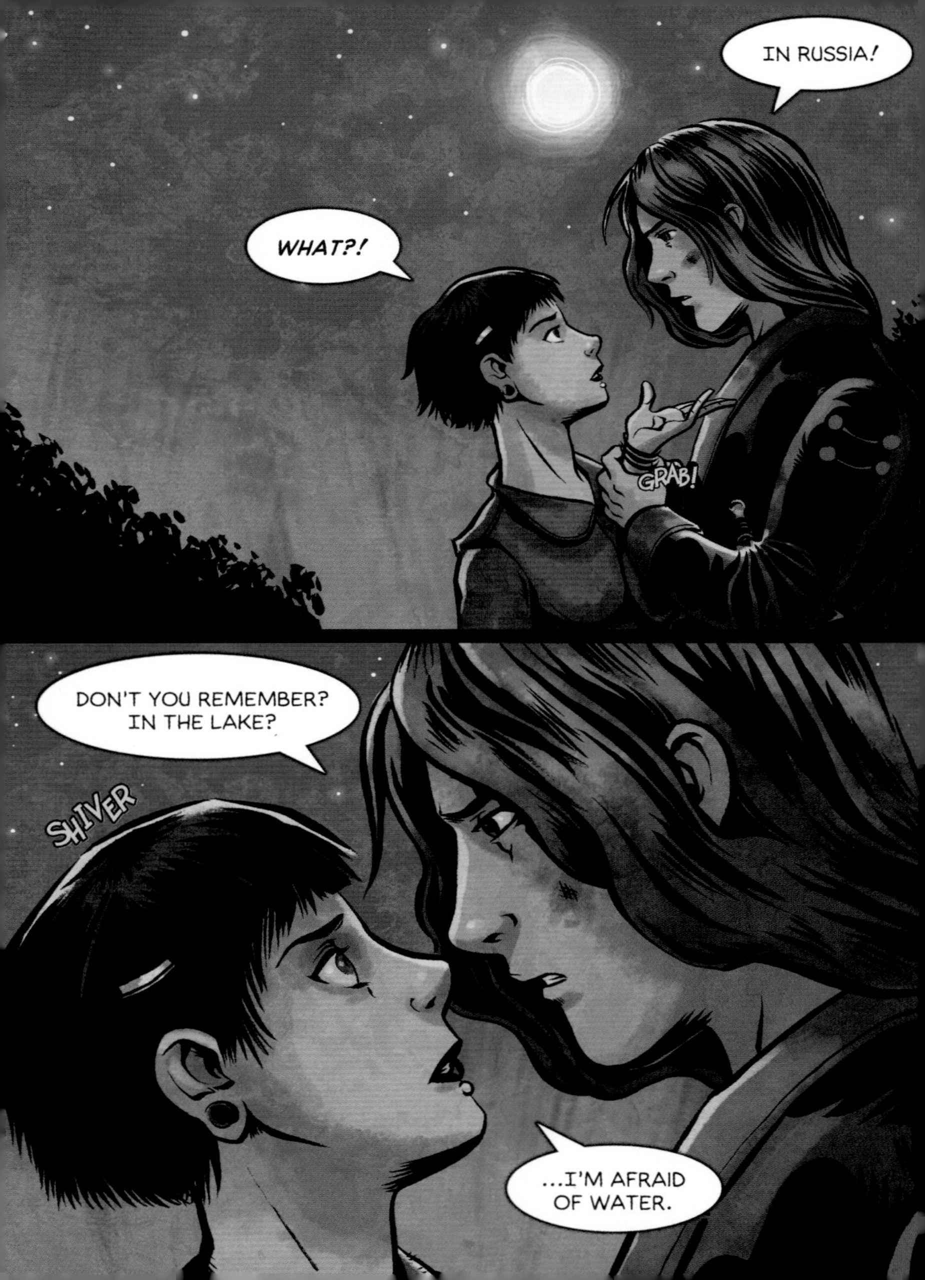
IN RUSSIA!
WHAT?!
GRAB!
DON'T YOU REMEMBER? IN THE LAKE?
SHIVER
...I'M AFRAID OF WATER.

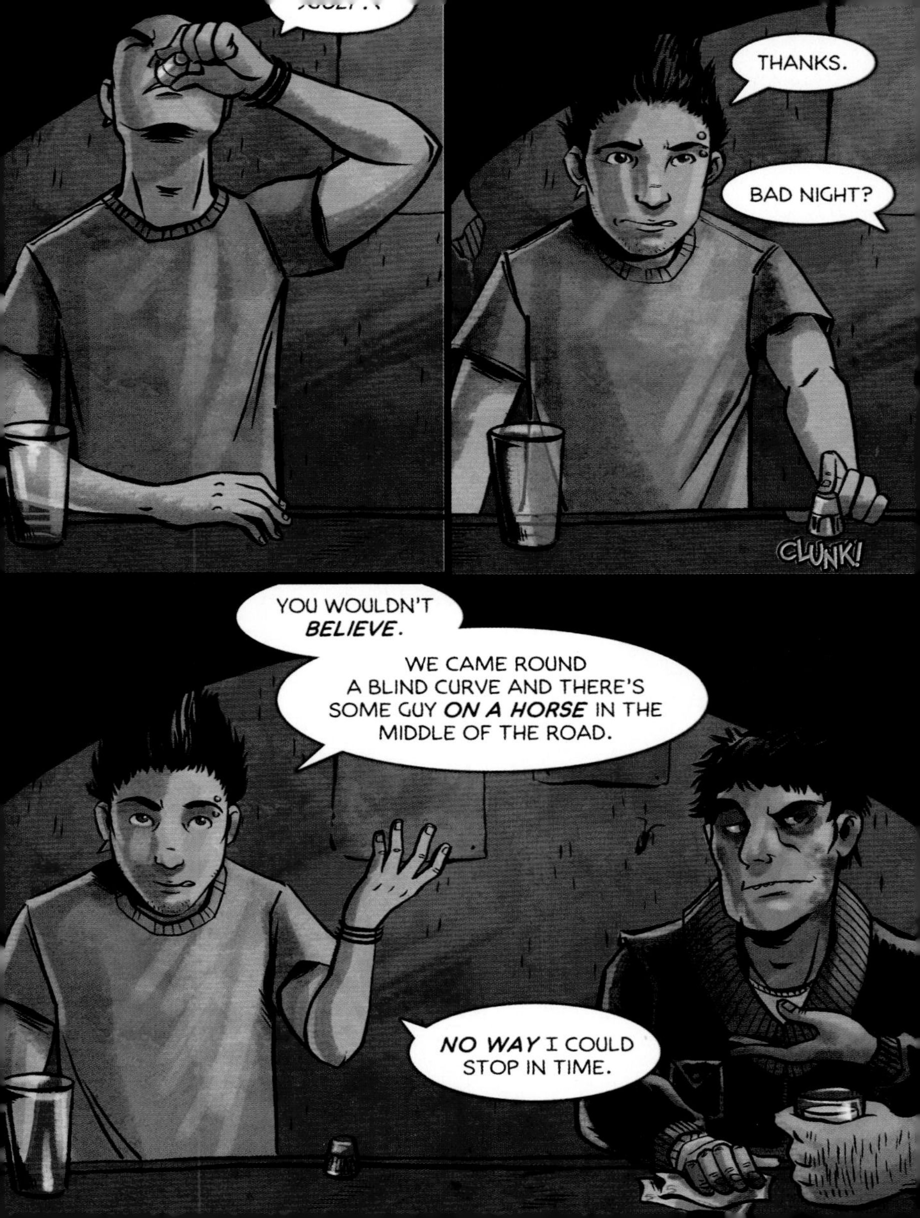
THANKS.
BAD NIGHT?
CLUNK!
YOU WOULDN'T *BELIEVE*.
WE CAME ROUND A BLIND CURVE AND THERE'S SOME GUY *ON A HORSE* IN THE MIDDLE OF THE ROAD.
NO WAY I COULD STOP IN TIME.

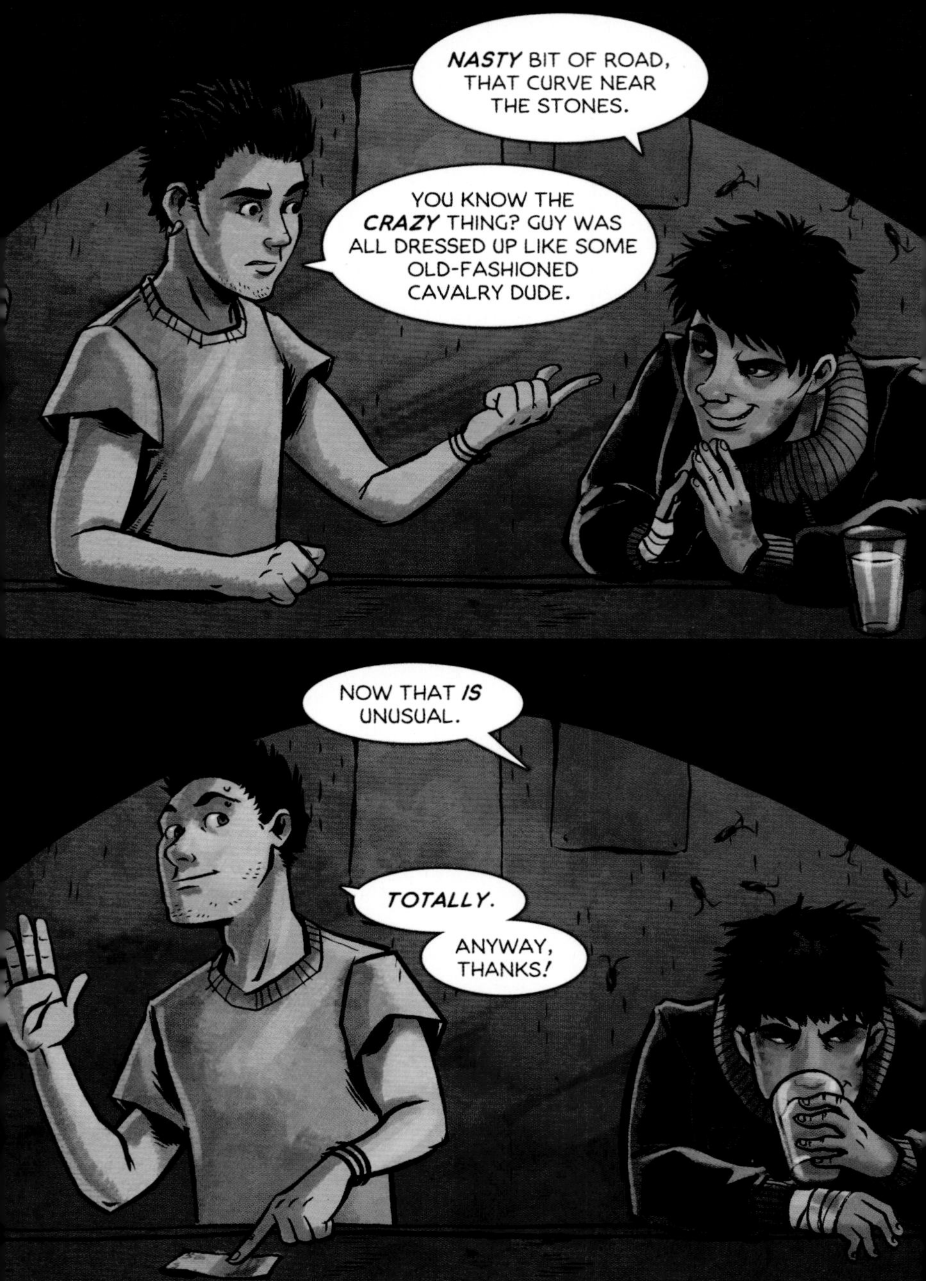
NASTY BIT OF ROAD, THAT CURVE NEAR THE STONES.
YOU KNOW THE CRAZY THING? GUY WAS ALL DRESSED UP LIKE SOME OLD-FASHIONED CAVALRY DUDE.
NOW THAT IS UNUSUAL.
TOTALLY.
ANYWAY, THANKS!

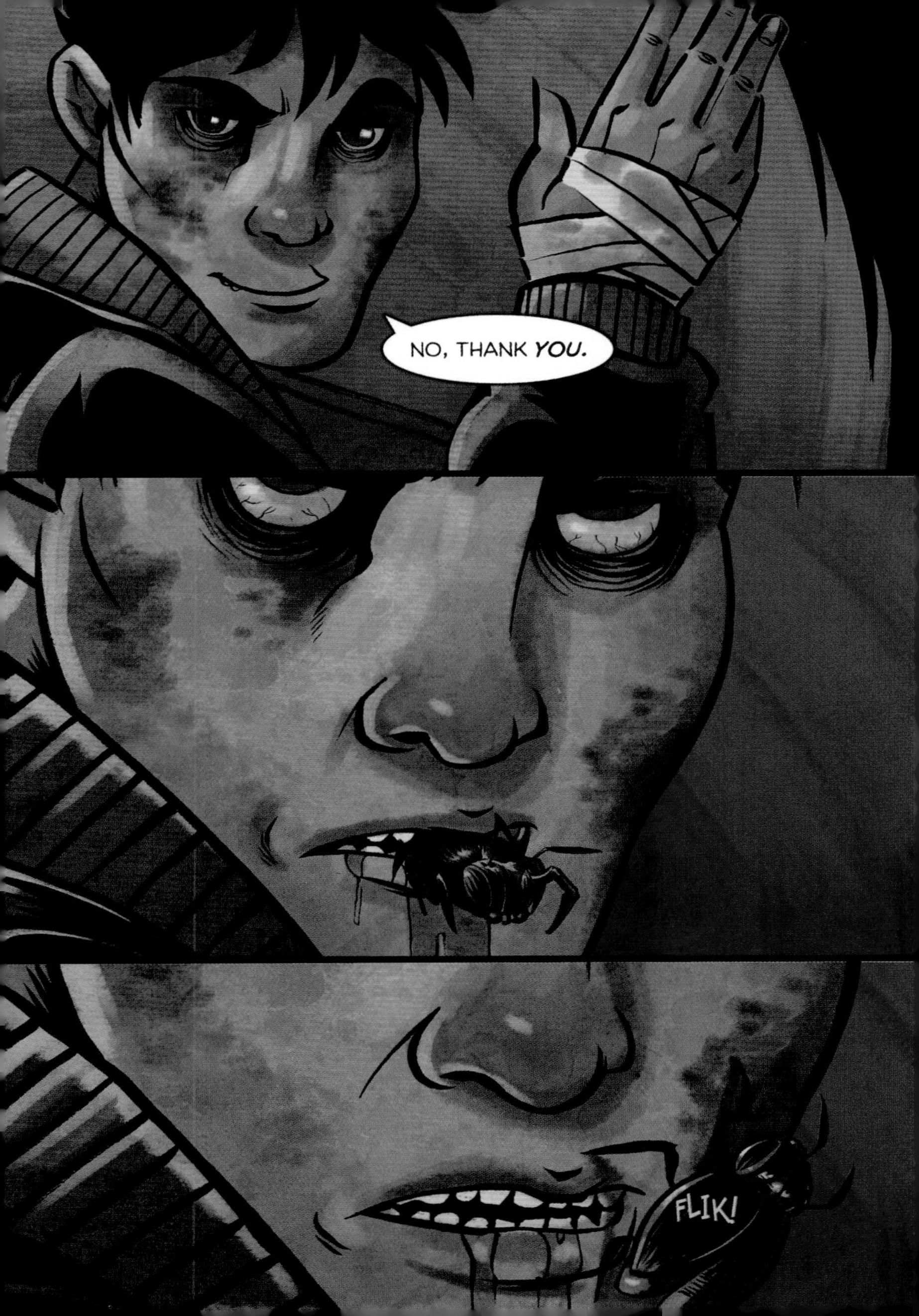
NO, THANK YOU.
FLIK!

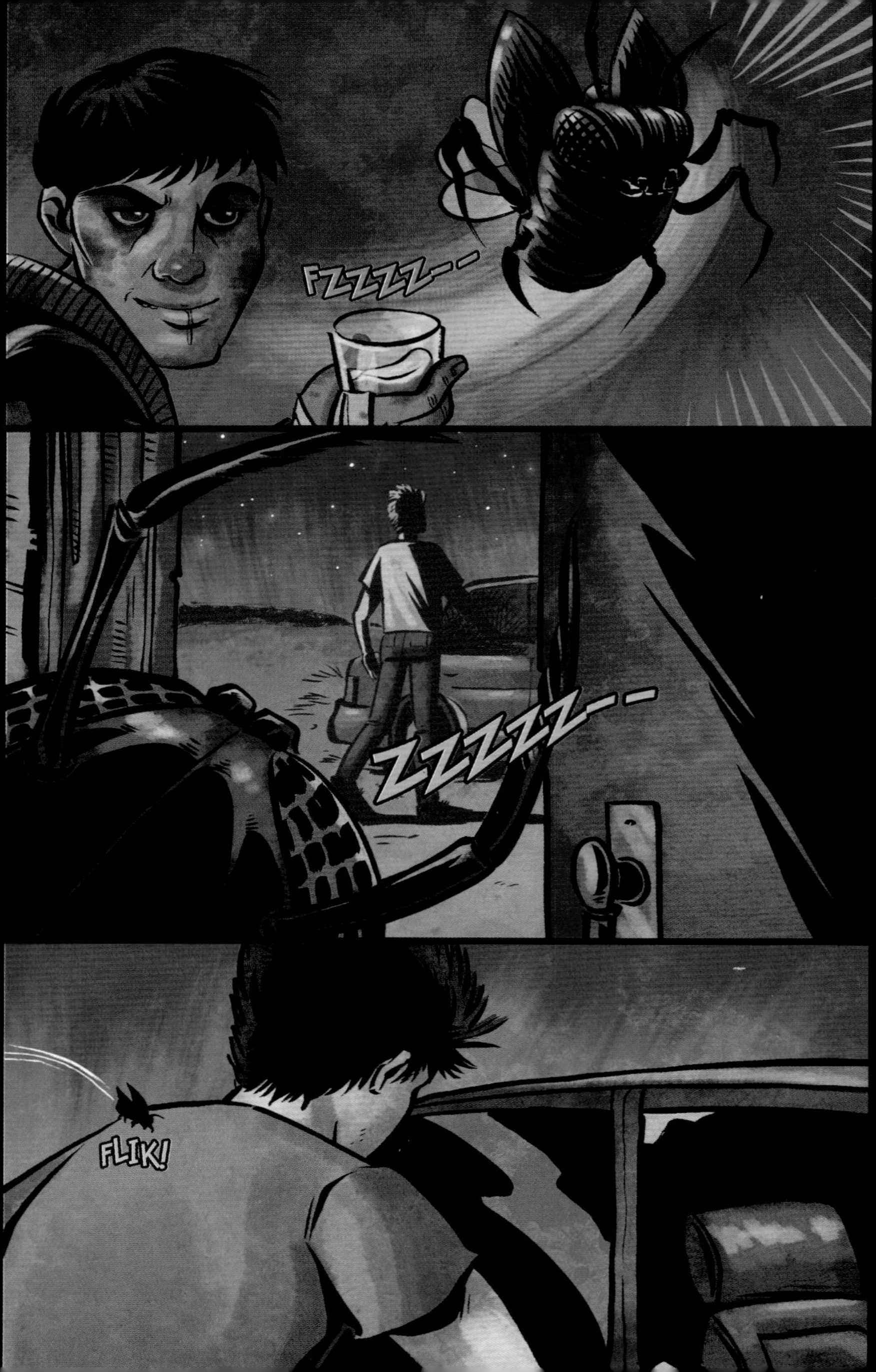
FZZZZ---
ZZZZZ---
FLIK!

10

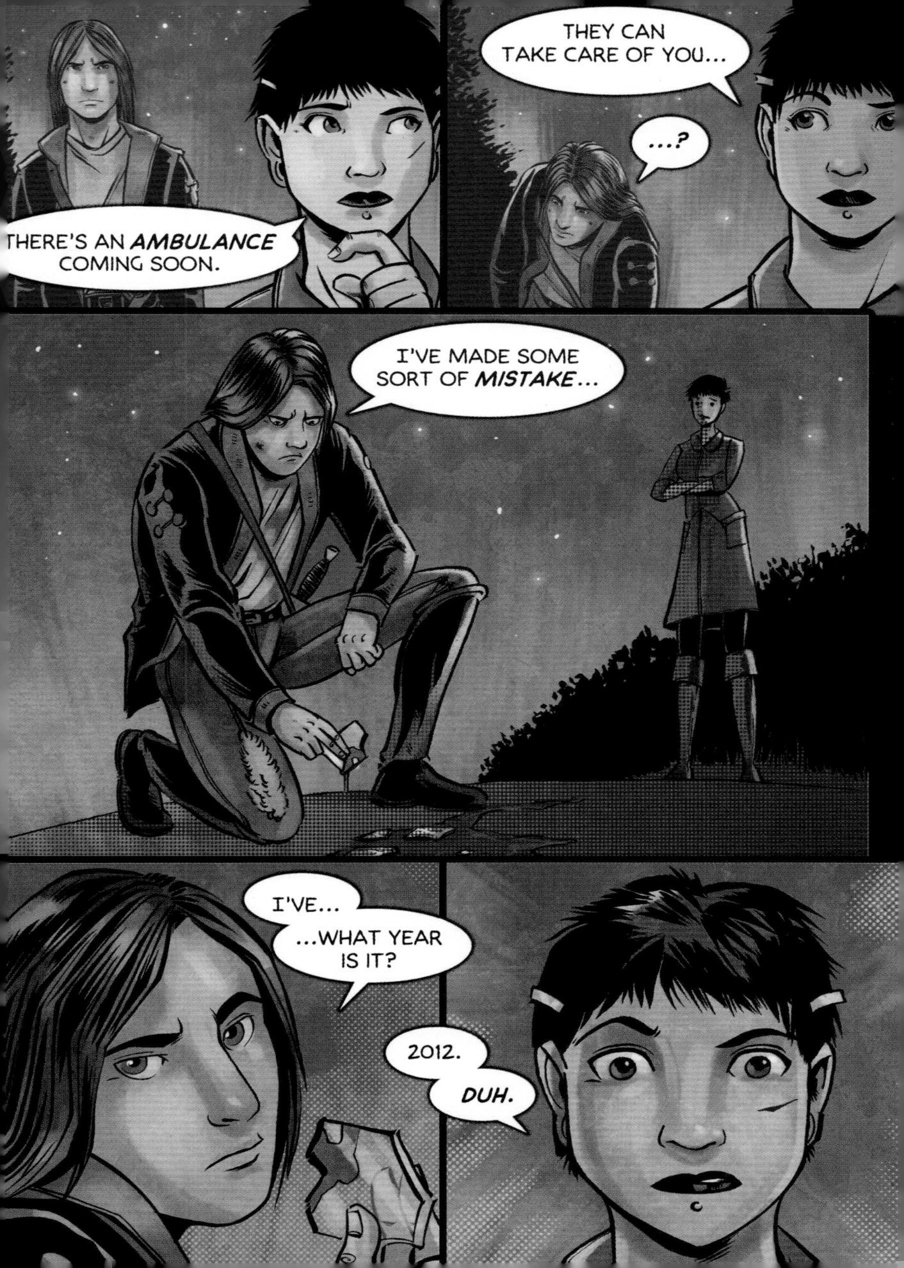
THERE'S AN *AMBULANCE* COMING SOON.
THEY CAN TAKE CARE OF YOU...
...?
I'VE MADE SOME SORT OF *MISTAKE*...
I'VE...
...WHAT YEAR IS IT?
2012.
DUH.

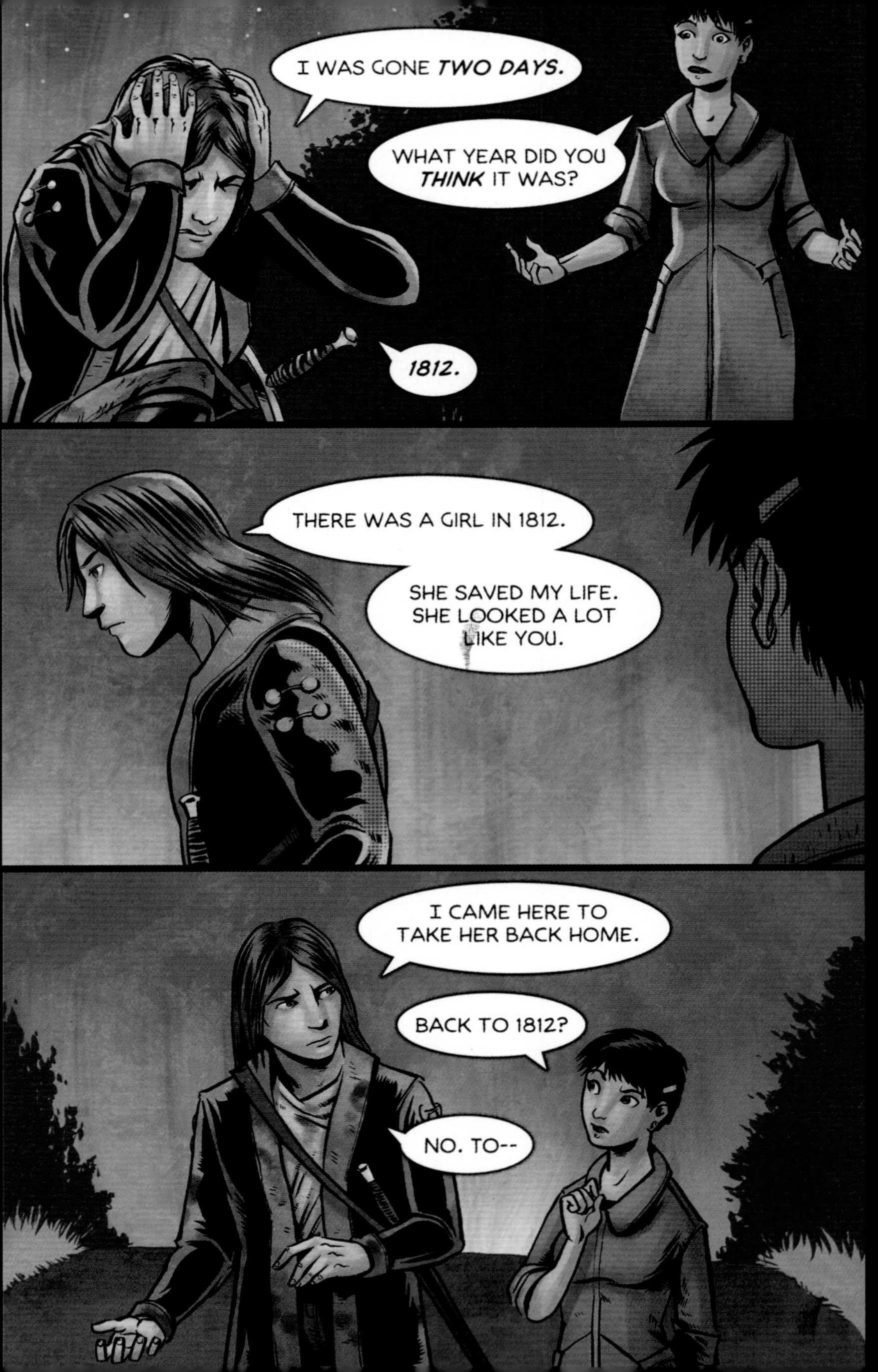

I WAS GONE *TWO DAYS.*
WHAT YEAR DID YOU *THINK* IT WAS?
1812.
THERE WAS A GIRL IN 1812.
SHE SAVED MY LIFE. SHE LOOKED A LOT LIKE YOU.
I CAME HERE TO TAKE HER BACK HOME.
BACK TO 1812?
NO. TO--

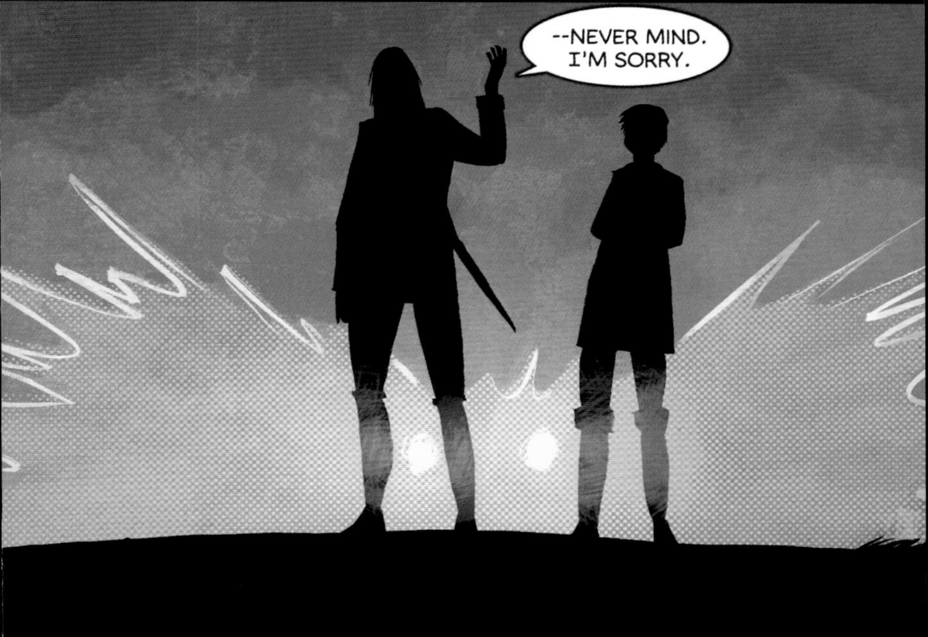
--NEVER MIND.
I'M SORRY.

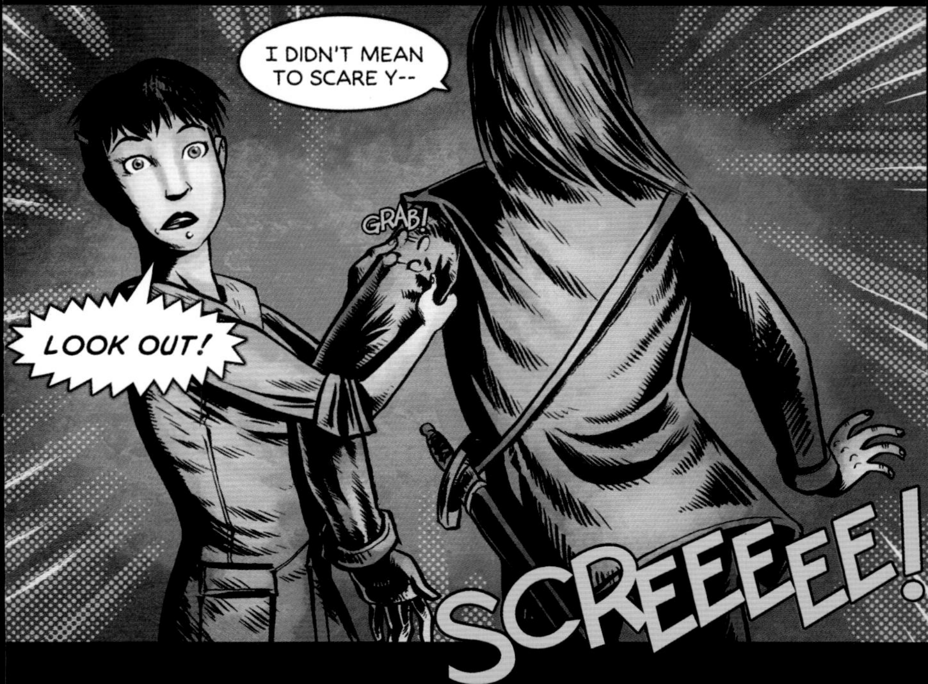
I DIDN'T MEAN TO SCARE Y--
GRAB!
LOOK OUT!
SCREEEEEE!

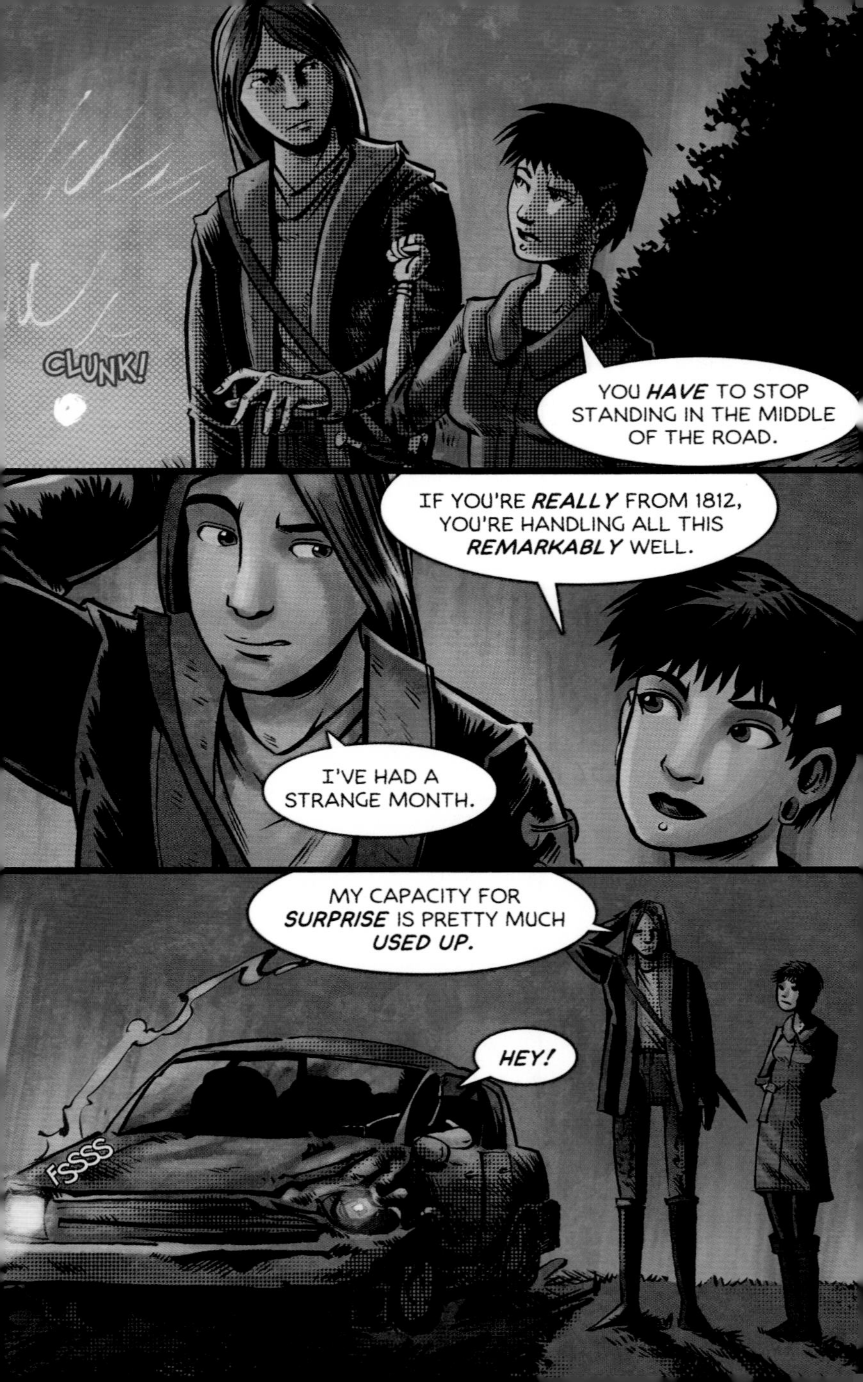
CLUNK!
YOU *HAVE* TO STOP STANDING IN THE MIDDLE OF THE ROAD.
IF YOU'RE *REALLY* FROM 1812, YOU'RE HANDLING ALL THIS *REMARKABLY* WELL.
I'VE HAD A STRANGE MONTH.
MY CAPACITY FOR *SURPRISE* IS PRETTY MUCH *USED UP.*
HEY!
FSSSS

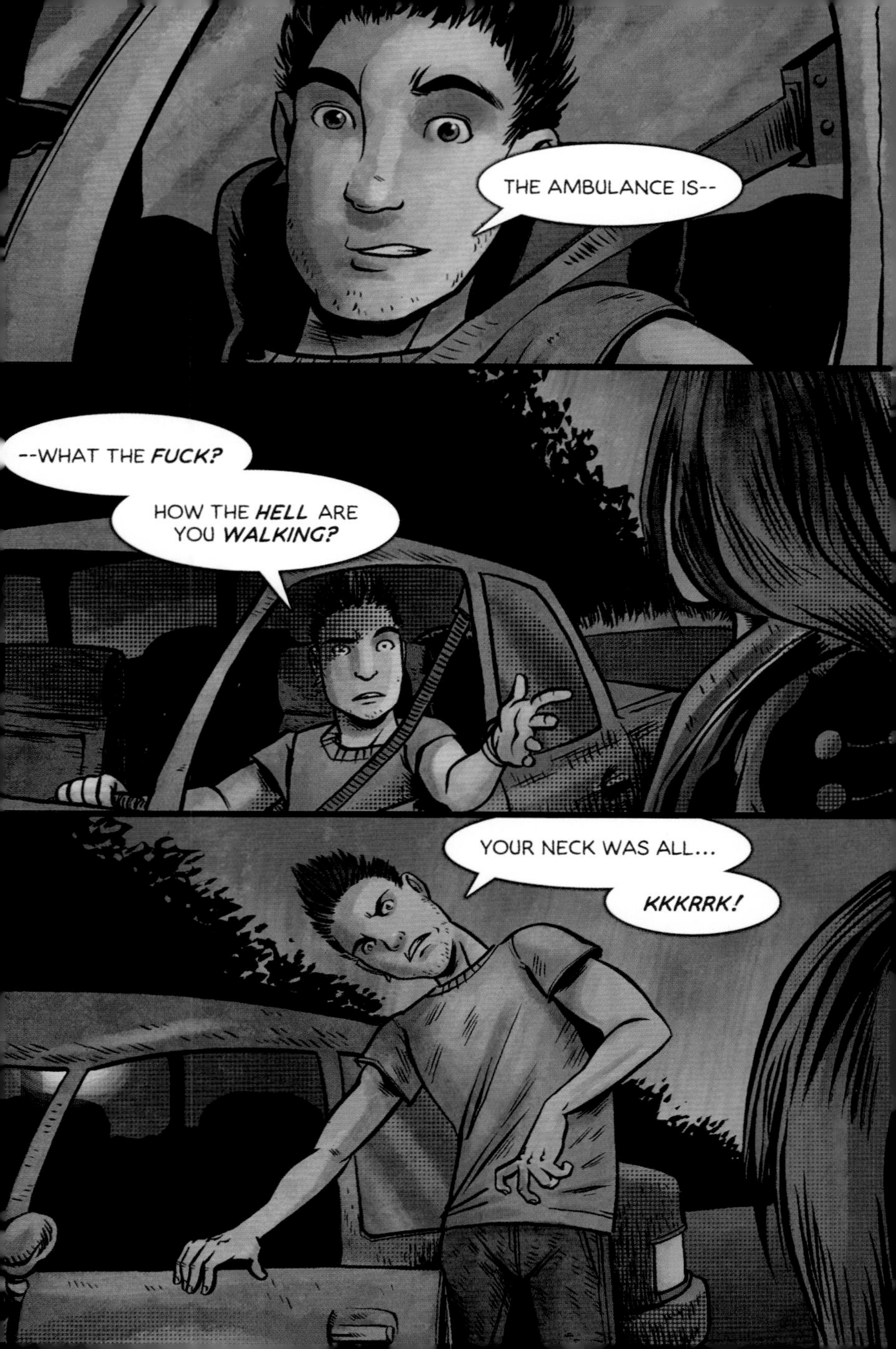
THE AMBULANCE IS--
--WHAT THE *FUCK?*
HOW THE *HELL* ARE YOU *WALKING?*
YOUR NECK WAS ALL...
KKKRRK!

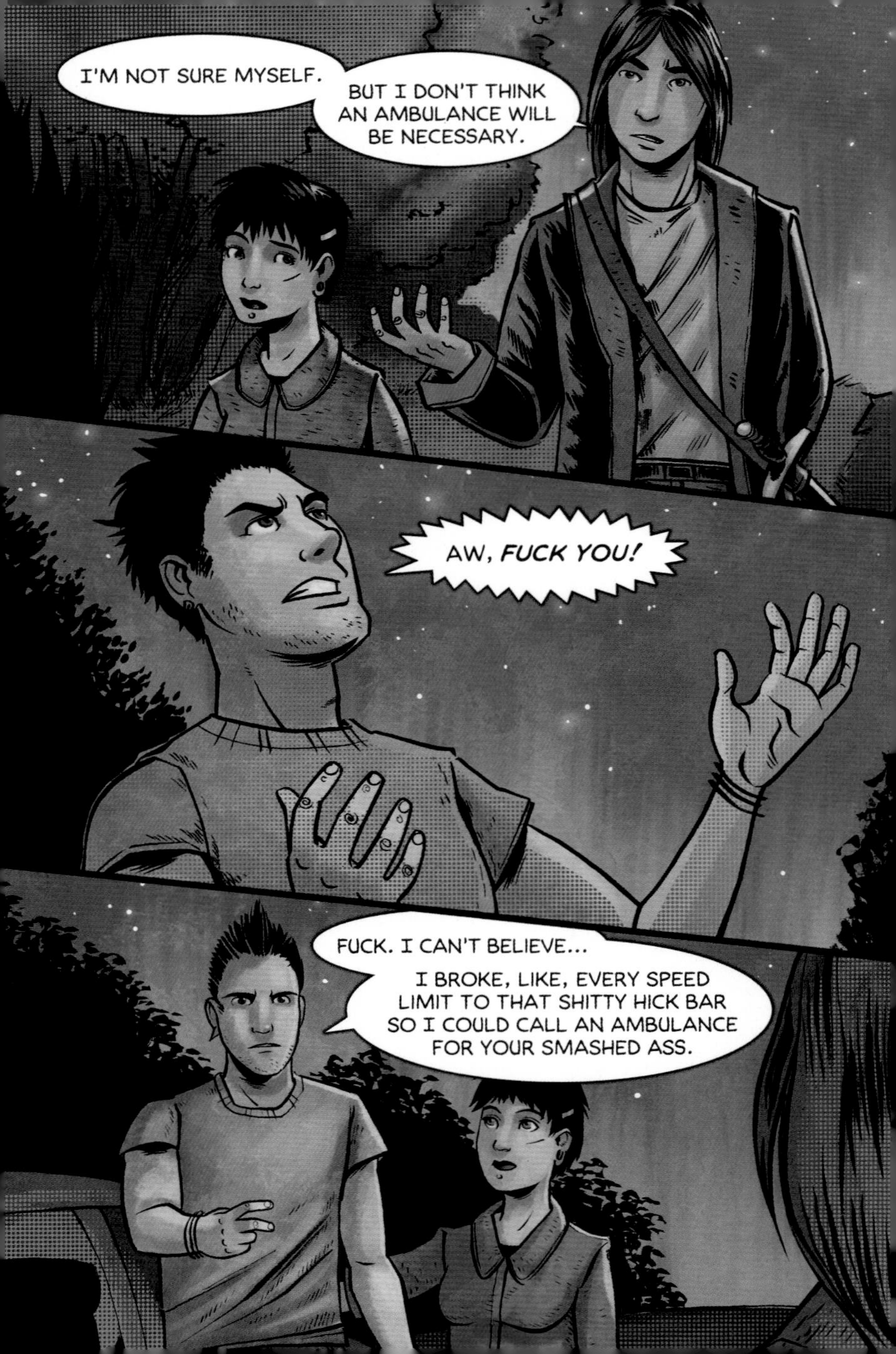
I'M NOT SURE MYSELF.
BUT I DON'T THINK AN AMBULANCE WILL BE NECESSARY.
AW, *FUCK YOU!*
FUCK. I CAN'T BELIEVE...
I BROKE, LIKE, EVERY SPEED LIMIT TO THAT SHITTY HICK BAR SO I COULD CALL AN AMBULANCE FOR YOUR SMASHED ASS.

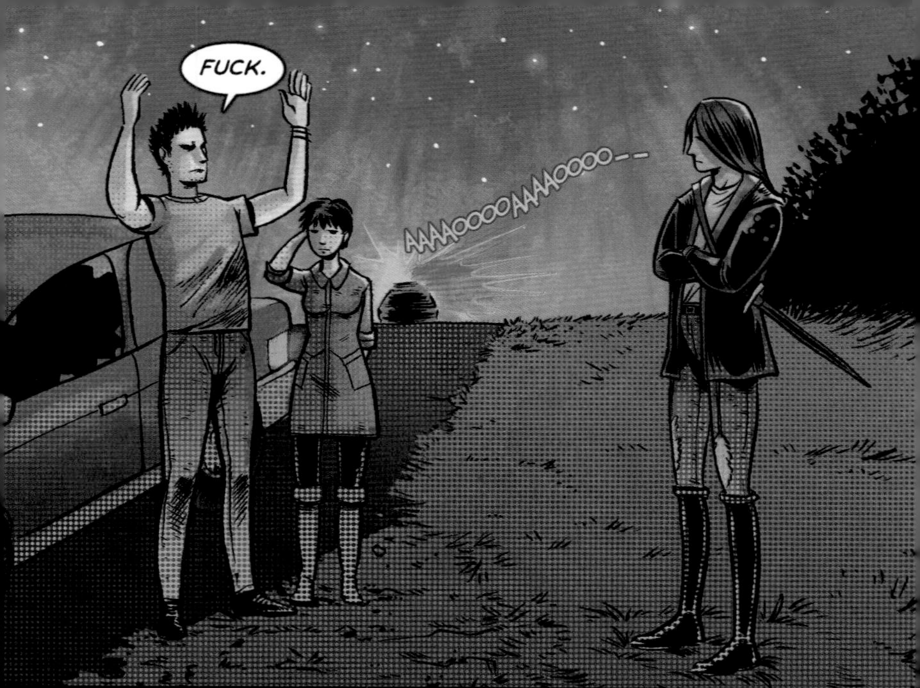
FUCK.
AAAAOOOOAAAAOOOO--
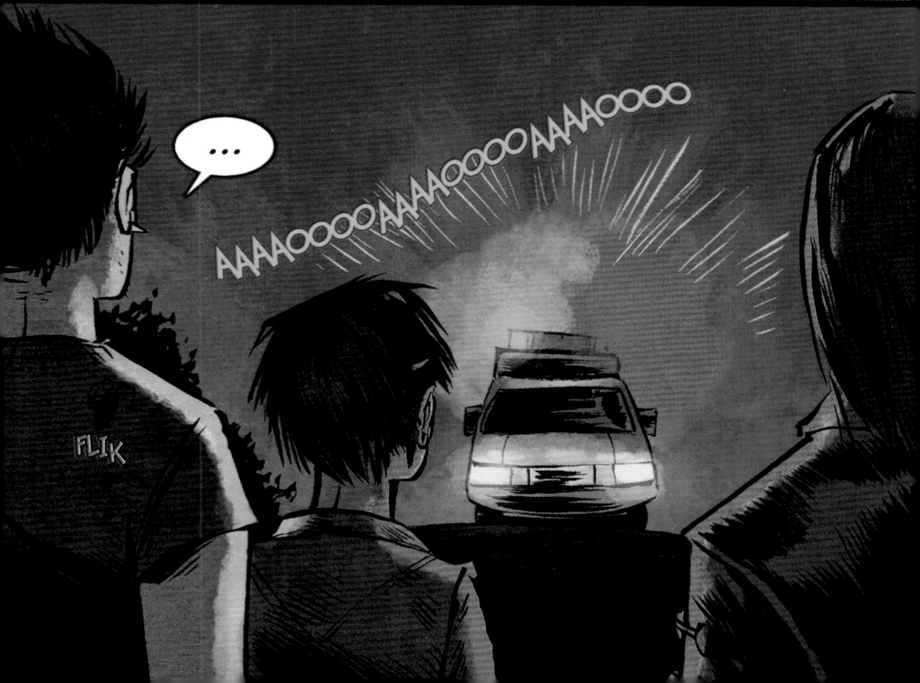
...
AAAAOOOOAAAAOOOOAAAAOOOO
FLIK

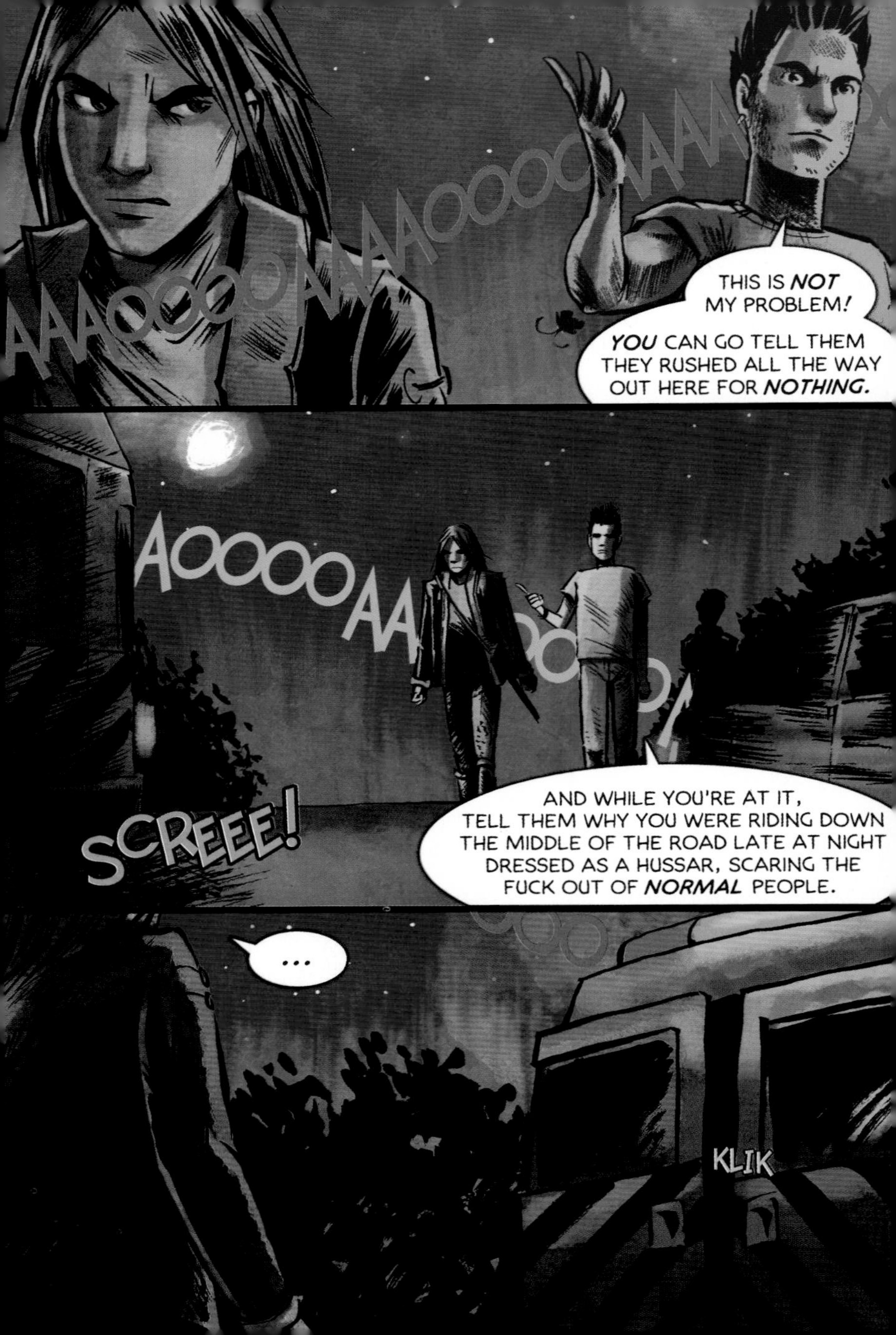
AAAOOOOAAAAOOOOAAAAAOO
THIS IS NOT MY PROBLEM!
YOU CAN GO TELL THEM THEY RUSHED ALL THE WAY OUT HERE FOR NOTHING.
AOOOOAAOOOA
SCREEE!
AND WHILE YOU'RE AT IT, TELL THEM WHY YOU WERE RIDING DOWN THE MIDDLE OF THE ROAD LATE AT NIGHT DRESSED AS A HUSSAR, SCARING THE FUCK OUT OF NORMAL PEOPLE.
...
KLIK

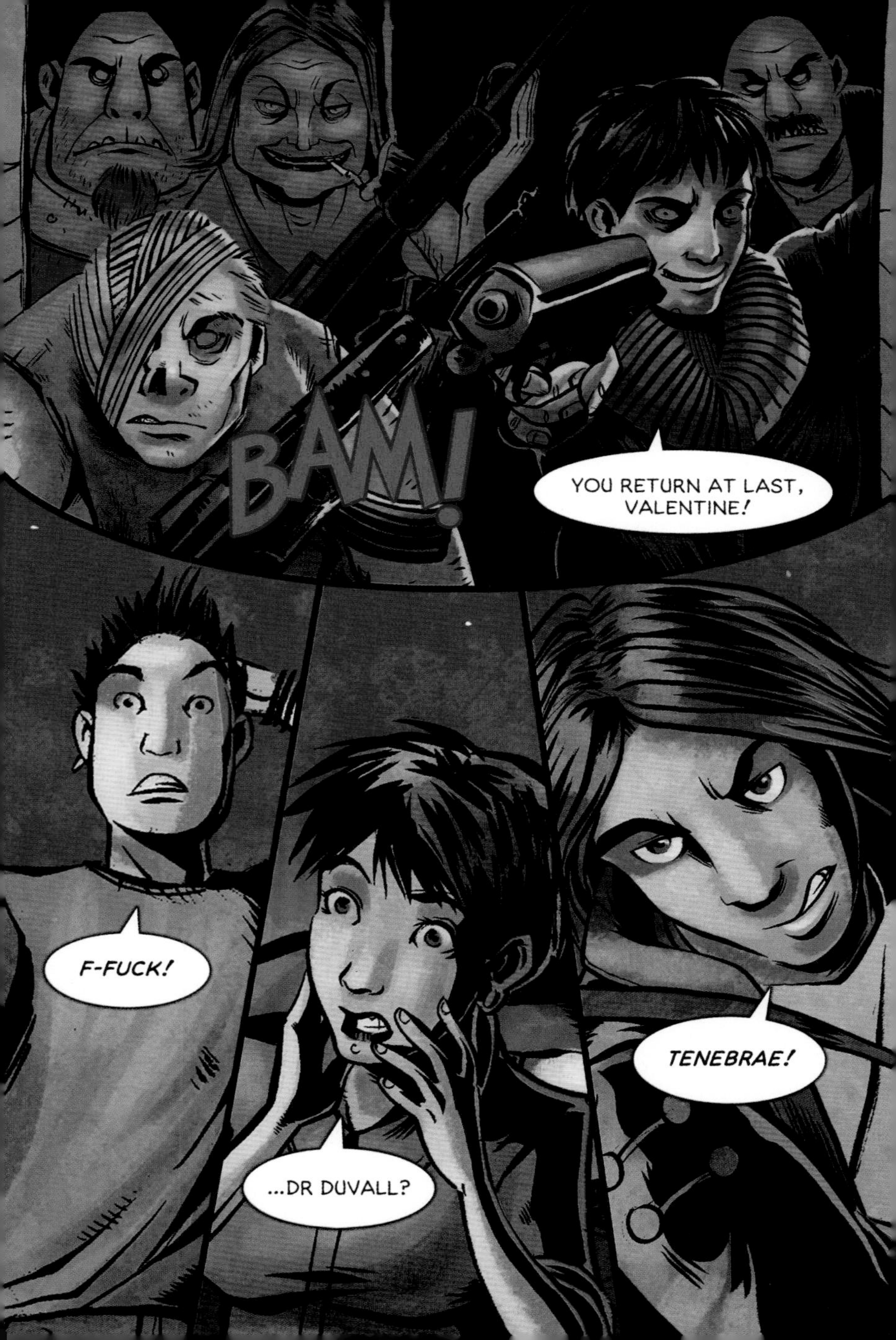
BAM!
YOU RETURN AT LAST, VALENTINE!
F-FUCK!
...DR DUVALL?
TENEBRAE!

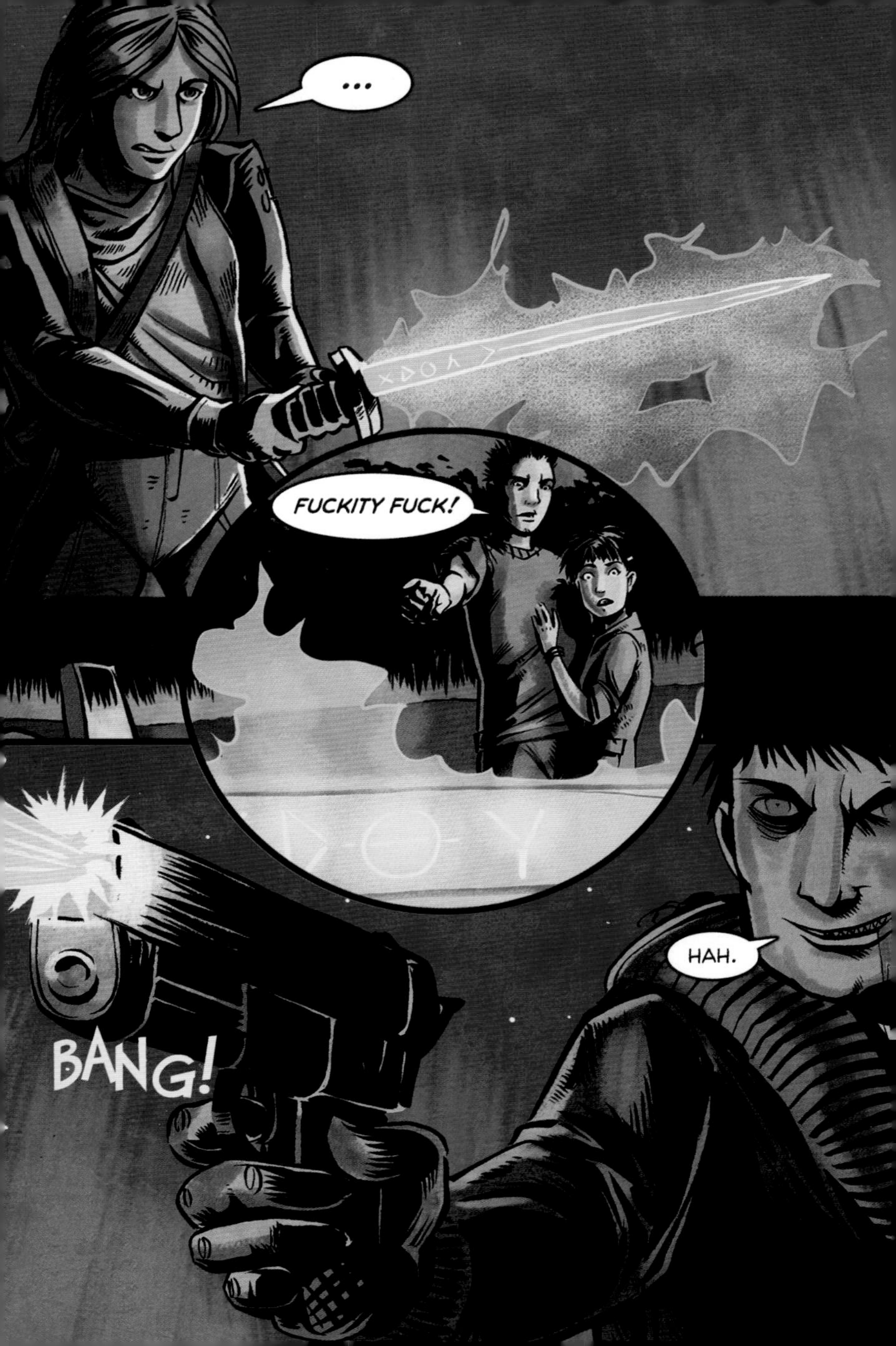
...
FUCKITY FUCK!
HAH.
BANG!

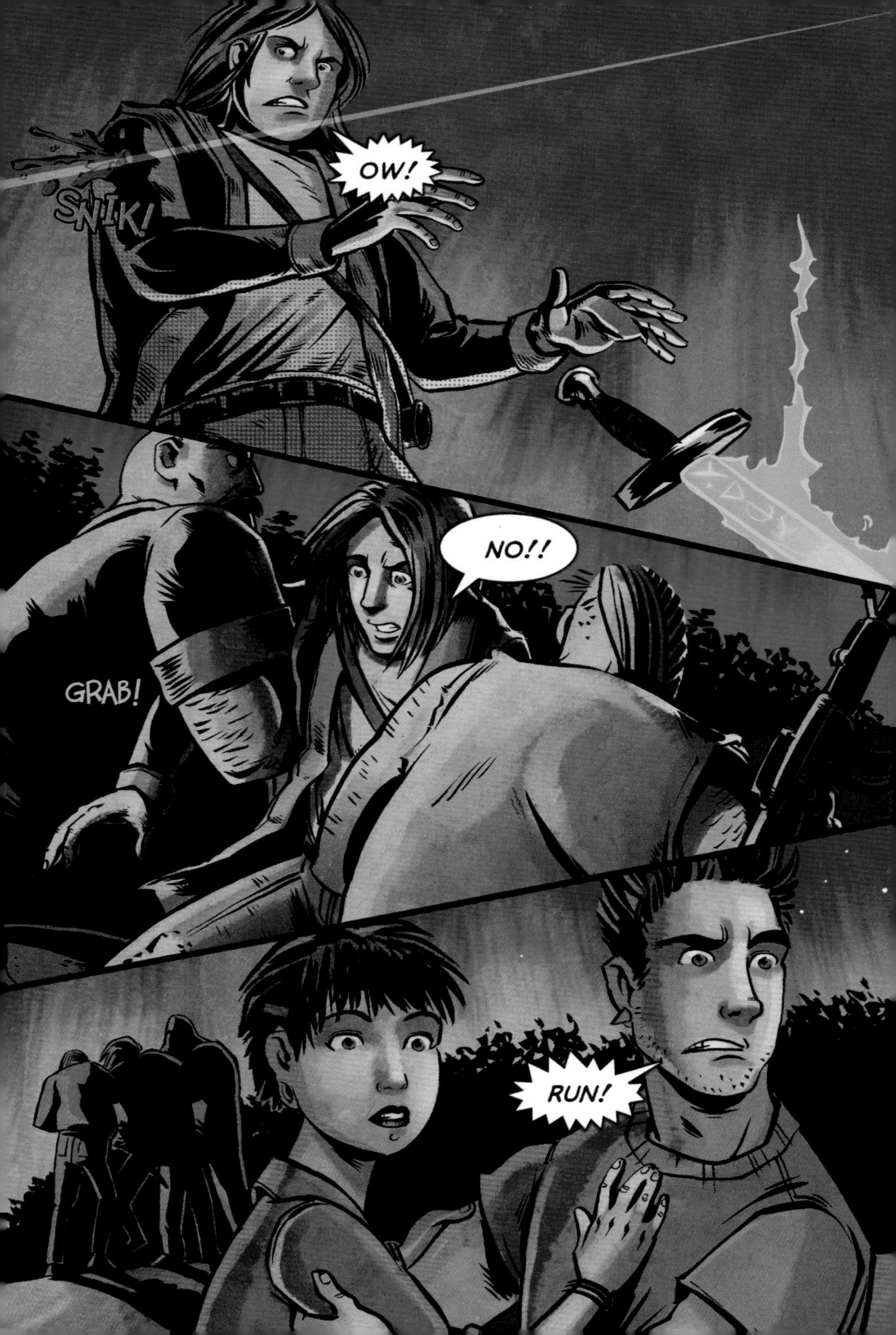
SNIK!
OW!
NO!!
GRAB!
RUN!

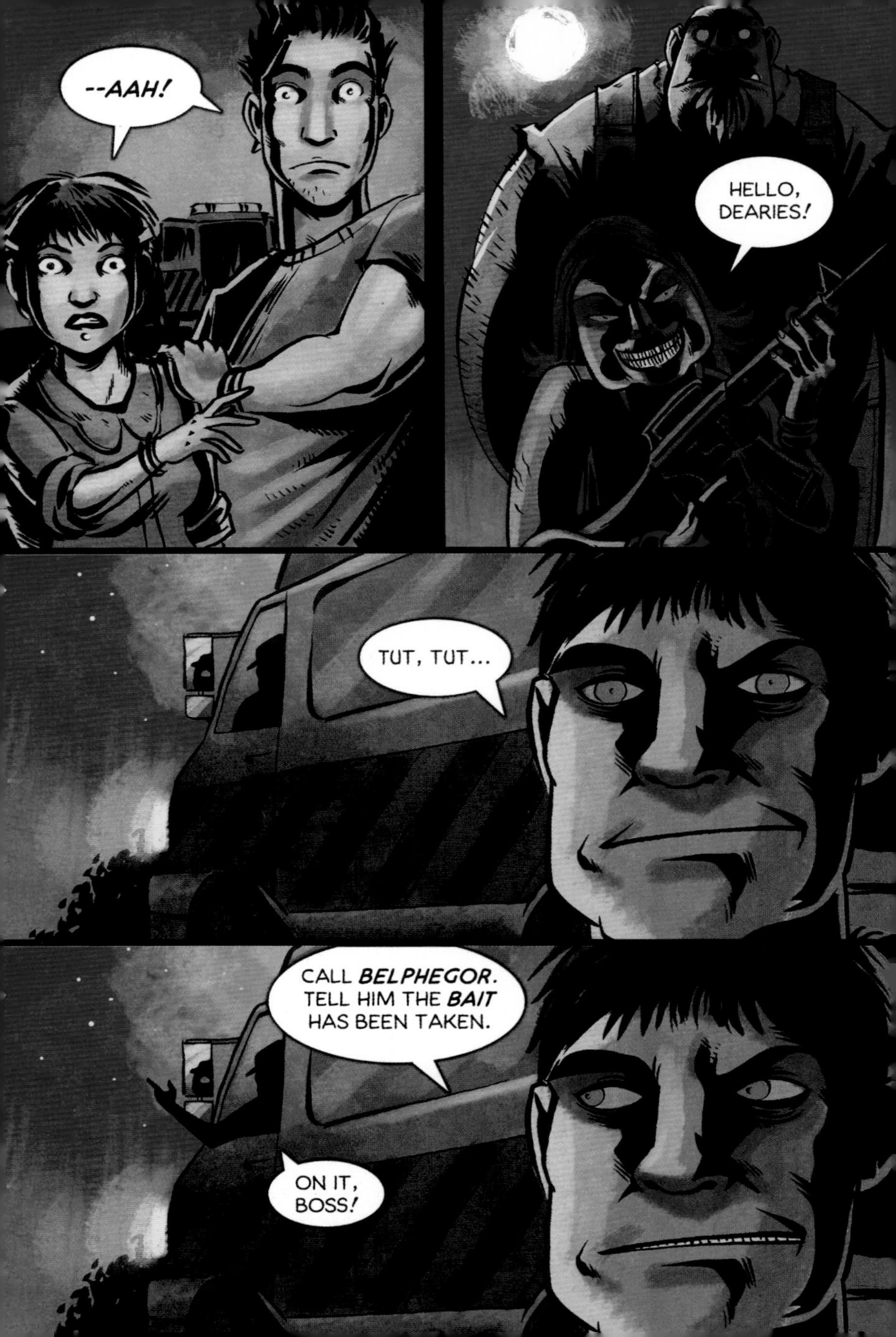
--AAH!
HELLO, DEARIES!
TUT, TUT...
CALL BELPHEGOR. TELL HIM THE BAIT HAS BEEN TAKEN.
ON IT, BOSS!

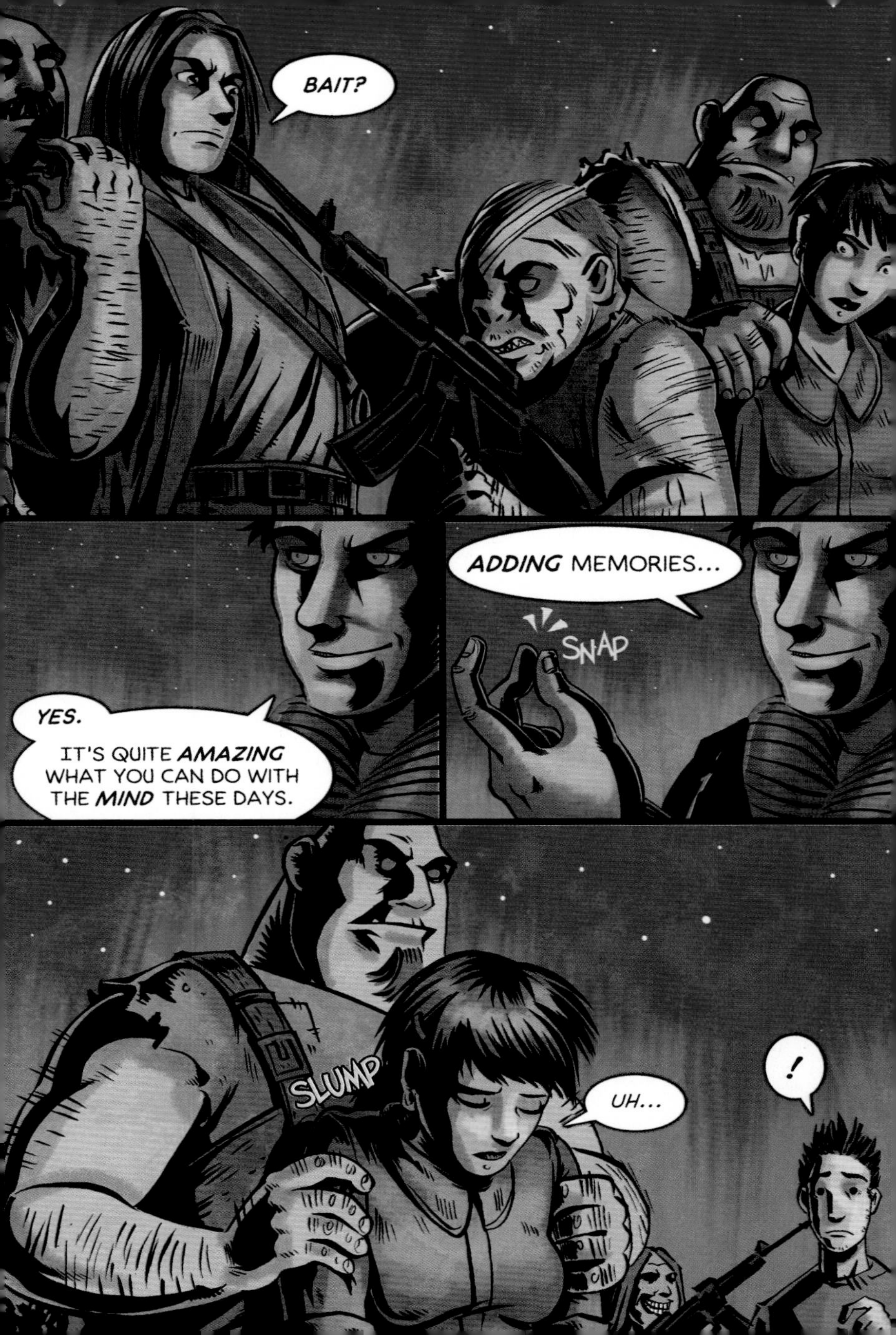
BAIT?
YES.
IT'S QUITE AMAZING WHAT YOU CAN DO WITH THE MIND THESE DAYS.
ADDING MEMORIES...
SNAP
SLUMP
UH...
!

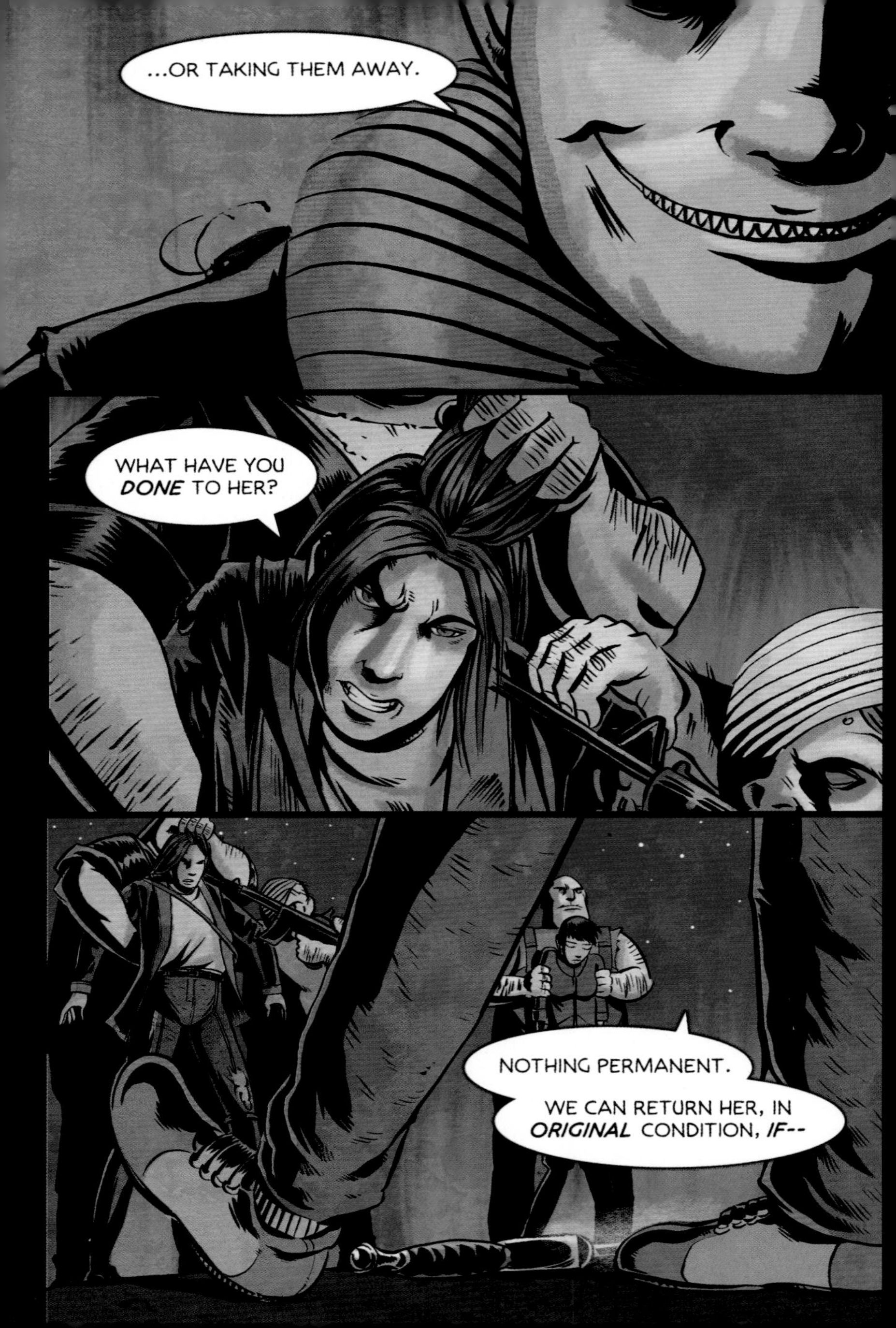
...OR TAKING THEM AWAY.
WHAT HAVE YOU *DONE* TO HER?
NOTHING PERMANENT.
WE CAN RETURN HER, IN *ORIGINAL* CONDITION, *IF--*

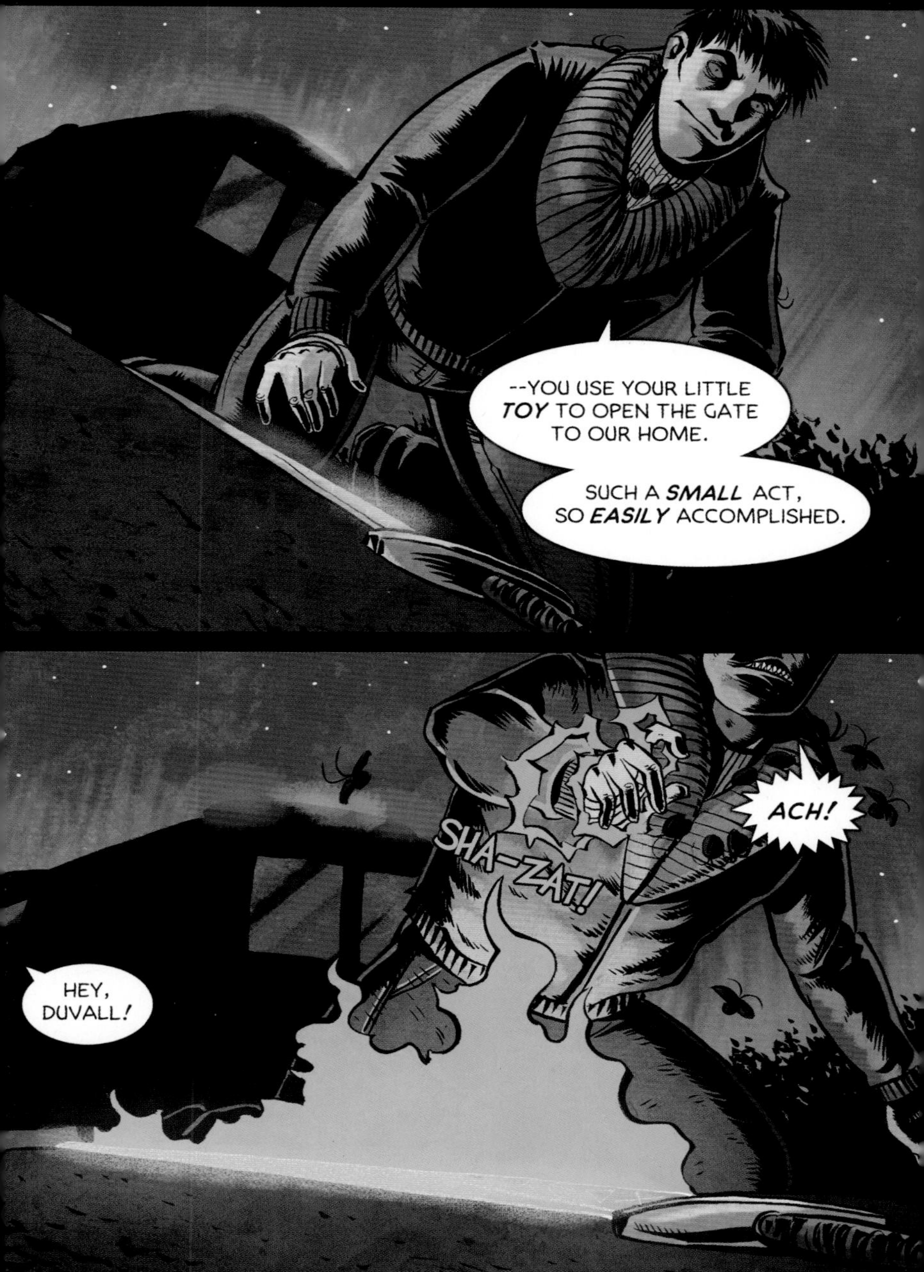
--YOU USE YOUR LITTLE *TOY* TO OPEN THE GATE TO OUR HOME.
SUCH A ***SMALL*** ACT, SO ***EASILY*** ACCOMPLISHED.
SHA-ZAT!
ACH!
HEY, DUVALL!

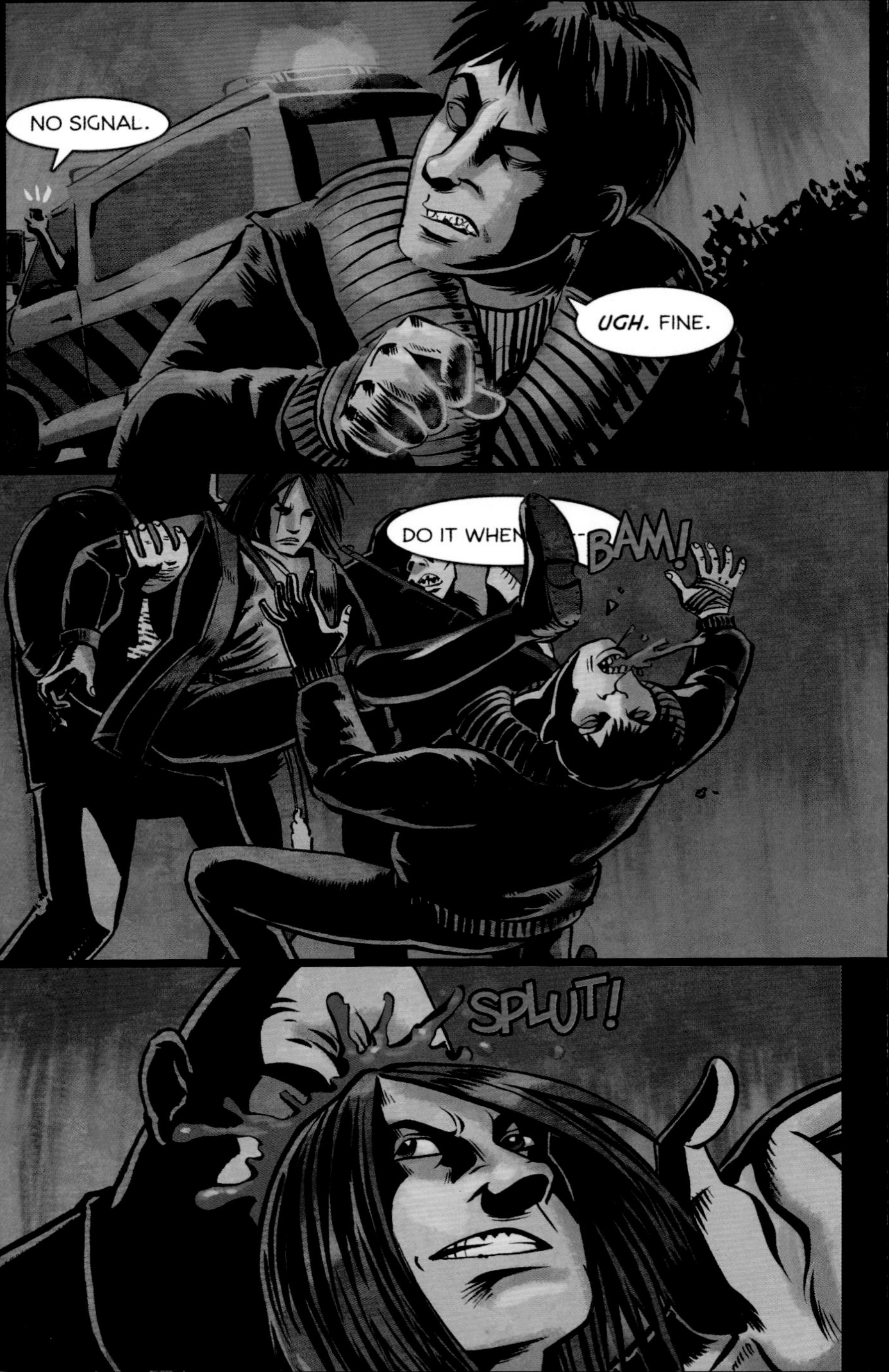
NO SIGNAL.
UGH. FINE.
DO IT WHEN--
BAM!
SPLUT!

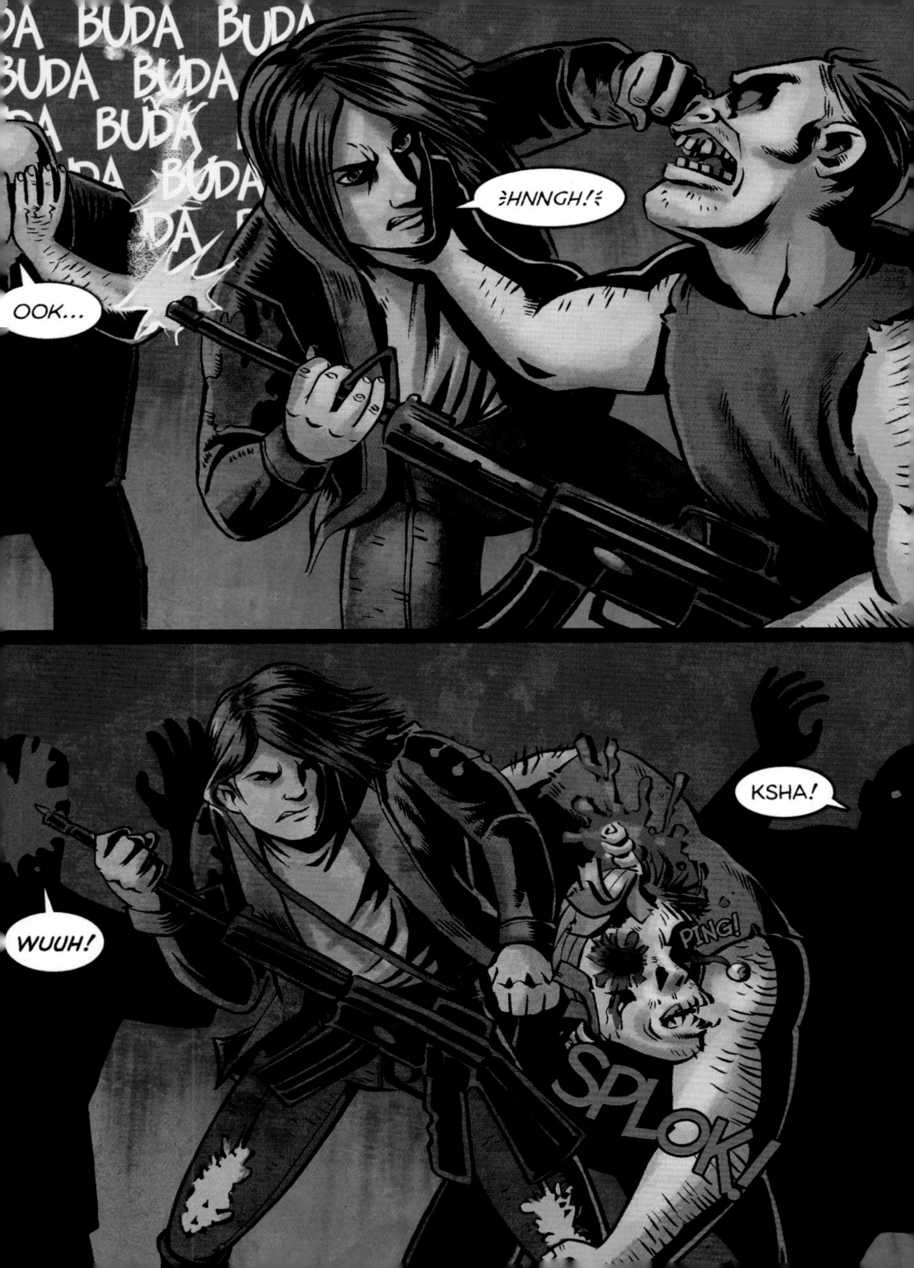
BUDA BUDA
BUDA BUDA
BUDA
BUDA
HNNGH!
OOK...
KSHA!
WUUH!
PING!
SPLOK!

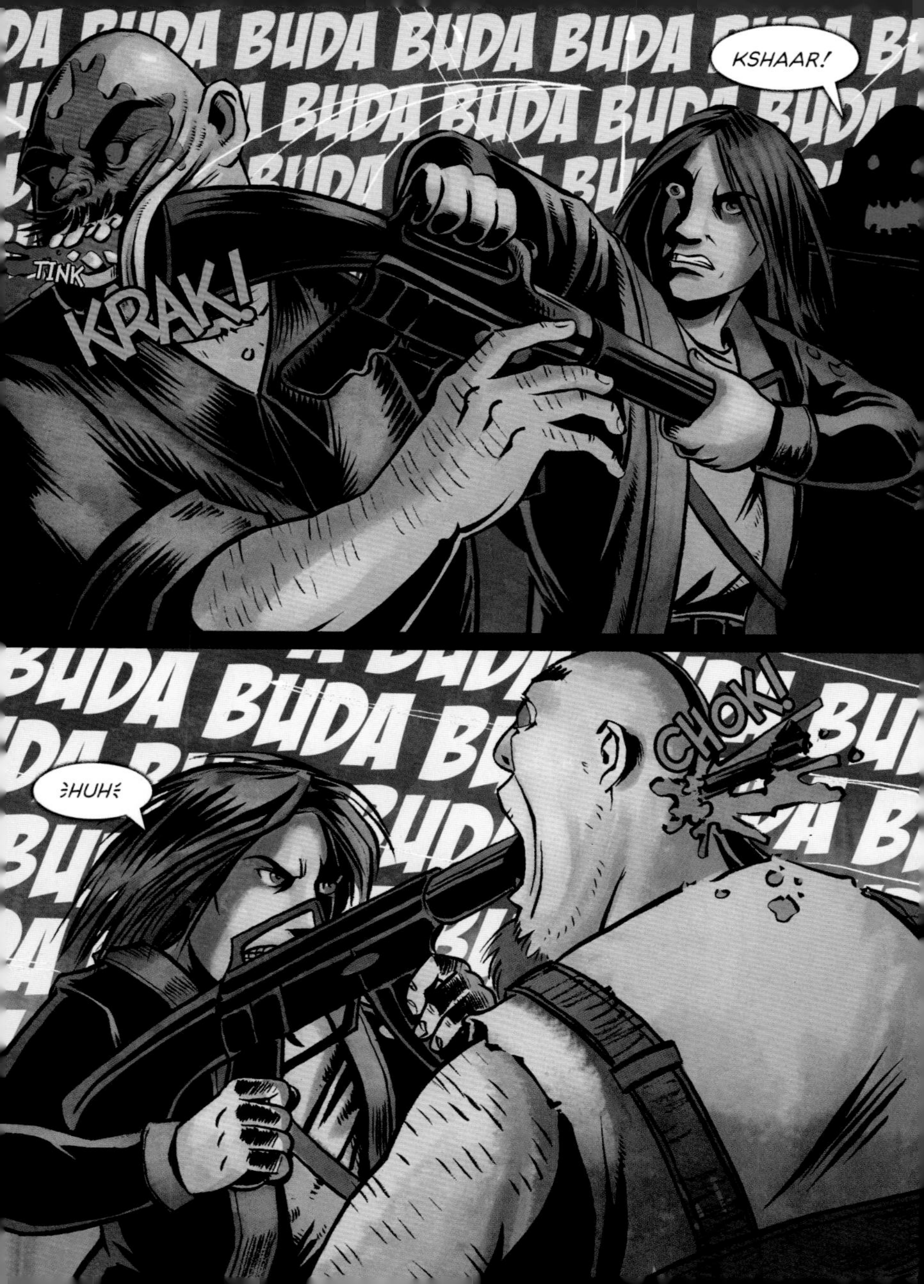
BUDA BUDA BUDA
BUDA BUDA
KSHAAR!
TINK
KRAK!
BUDA BUDA
HUH
CHOK!

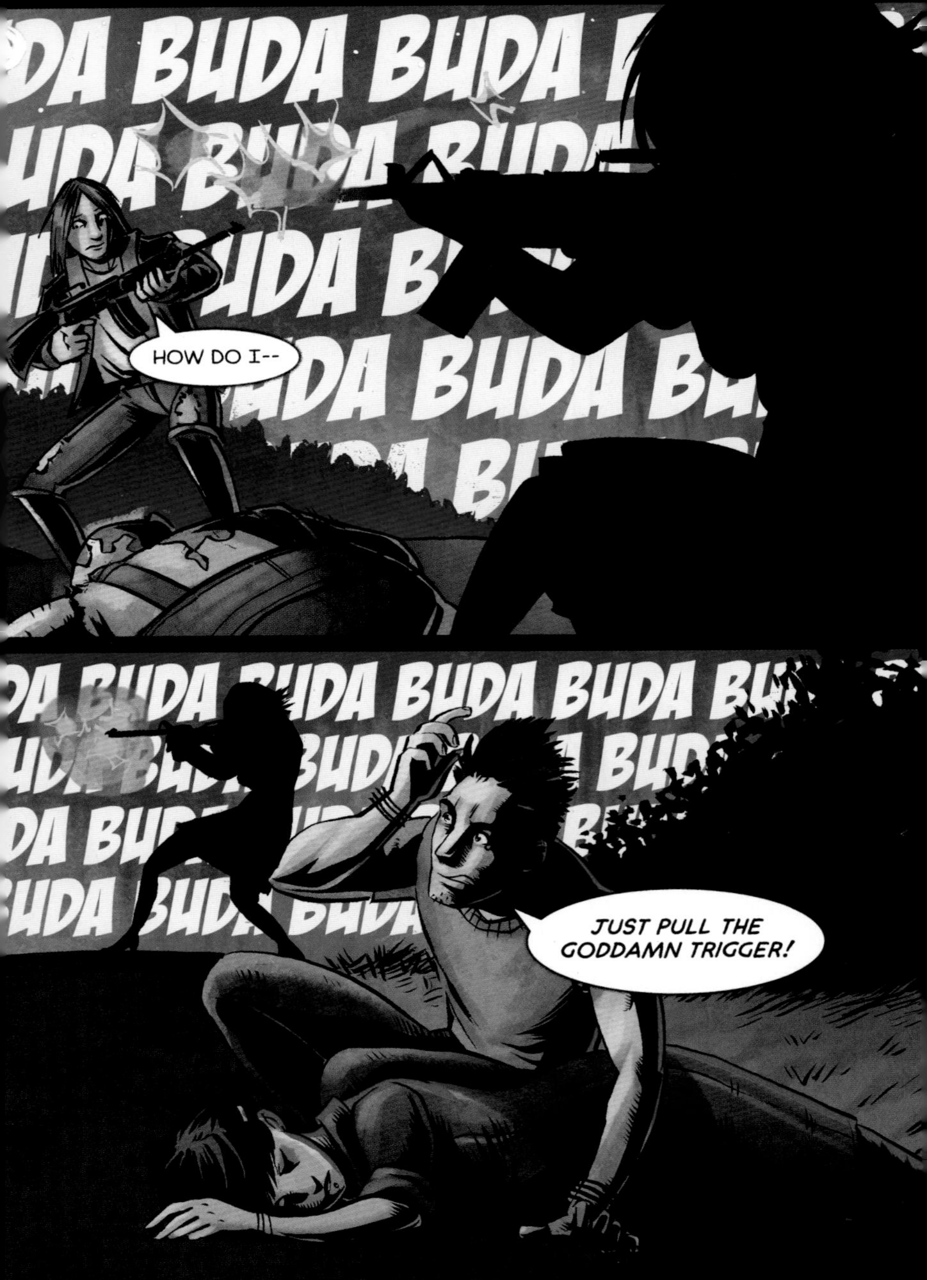
BUDA BUDA BUDA
HOW DO I--
BUDA BUDA BUDA
JUST PULL THE GODDAMN TRIGGER!

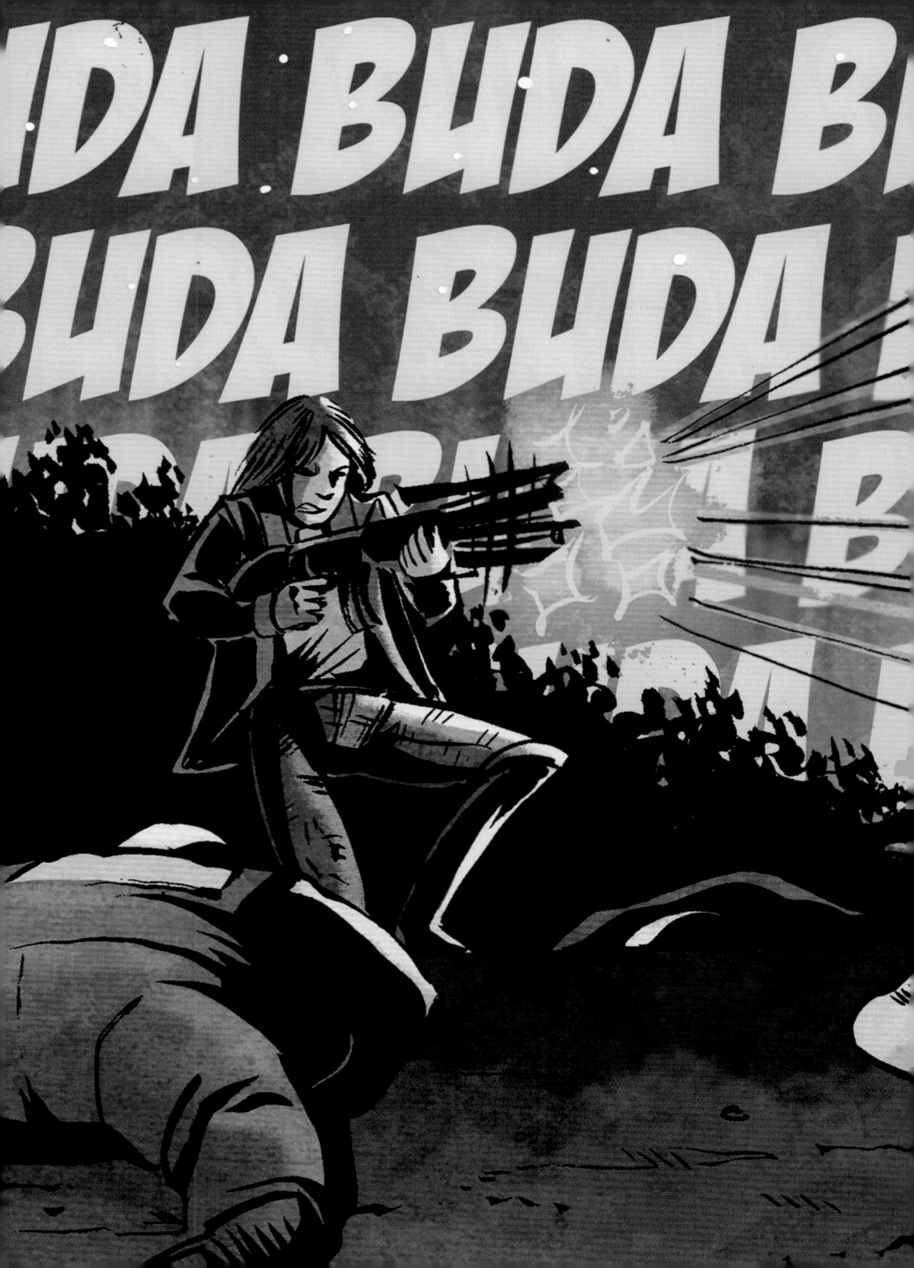
BUDA
BUDA BUDA

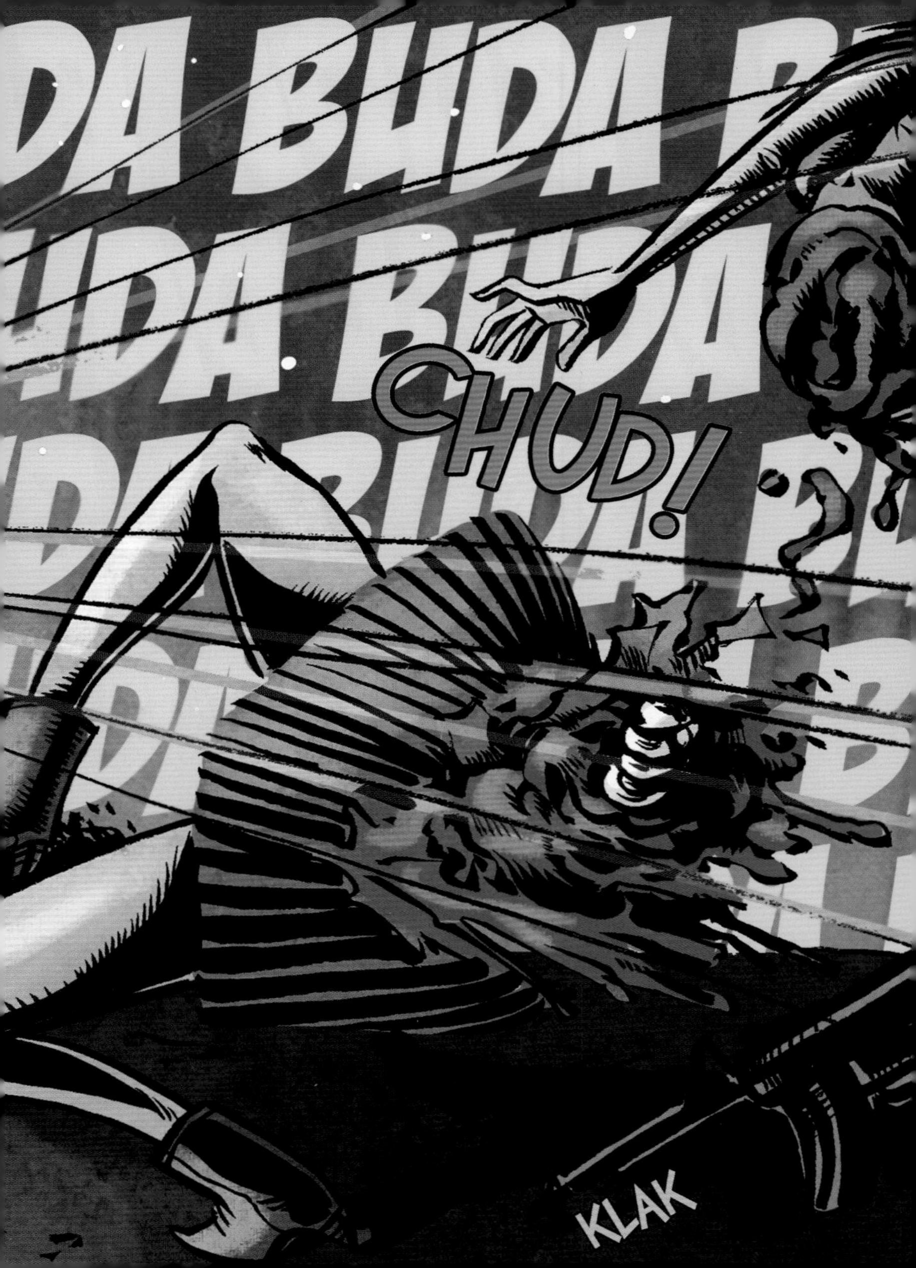
DA BUDA
CHUD!
KLAK

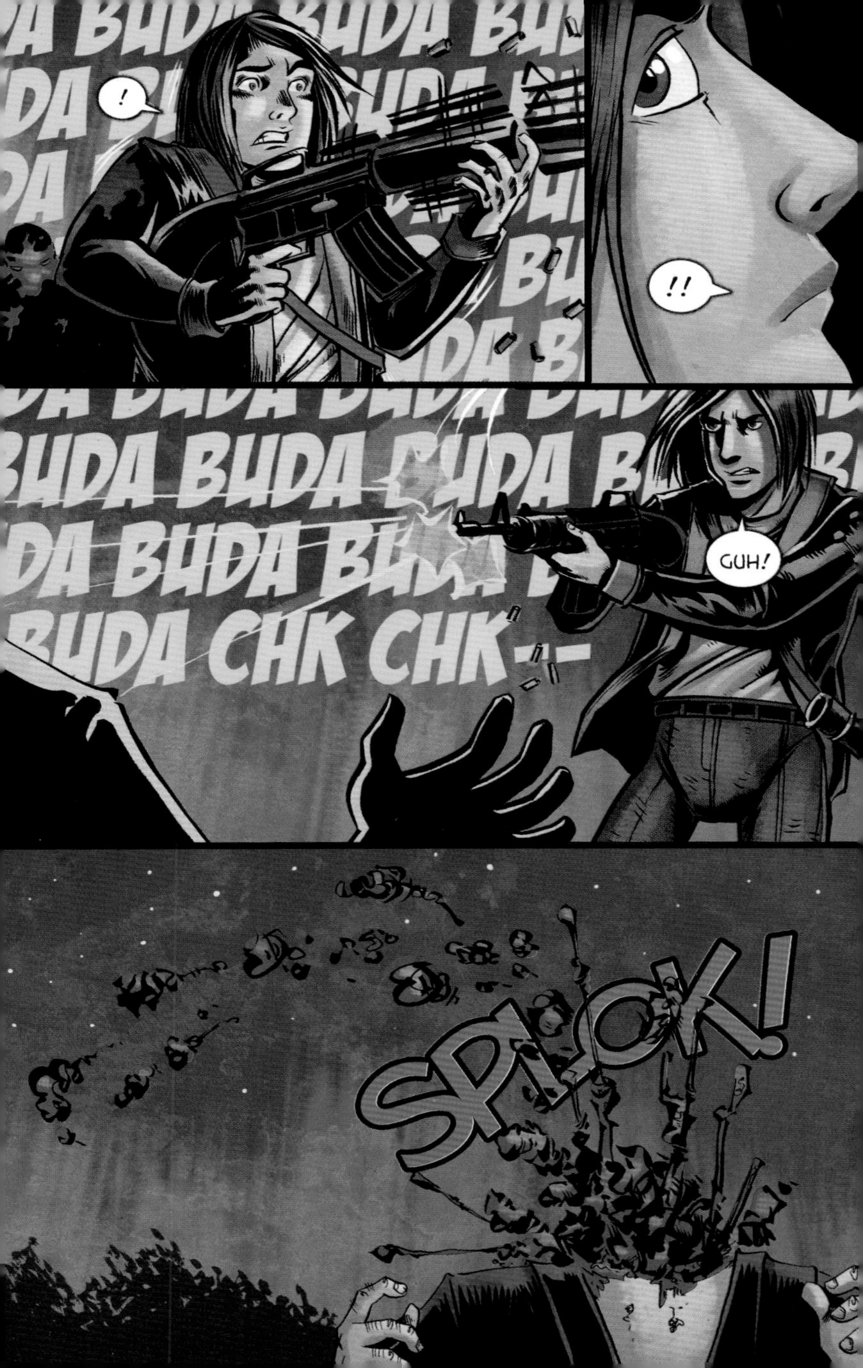
BUDA BUDA
!
!!
BUDA BUDA
BUDA BUDA
BUDA CHK CHK
GUH!
SPLOK!

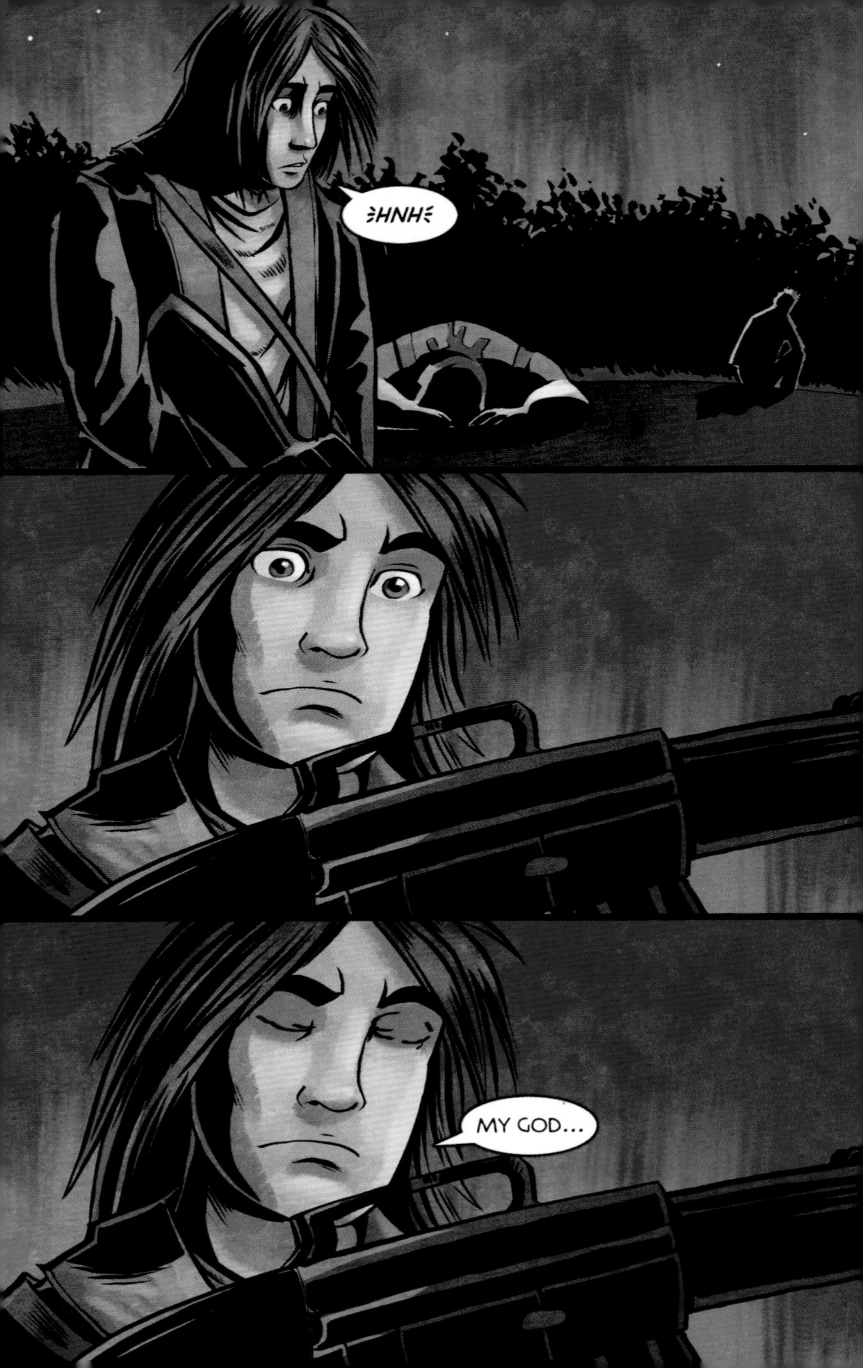
HNH
MY GOD...

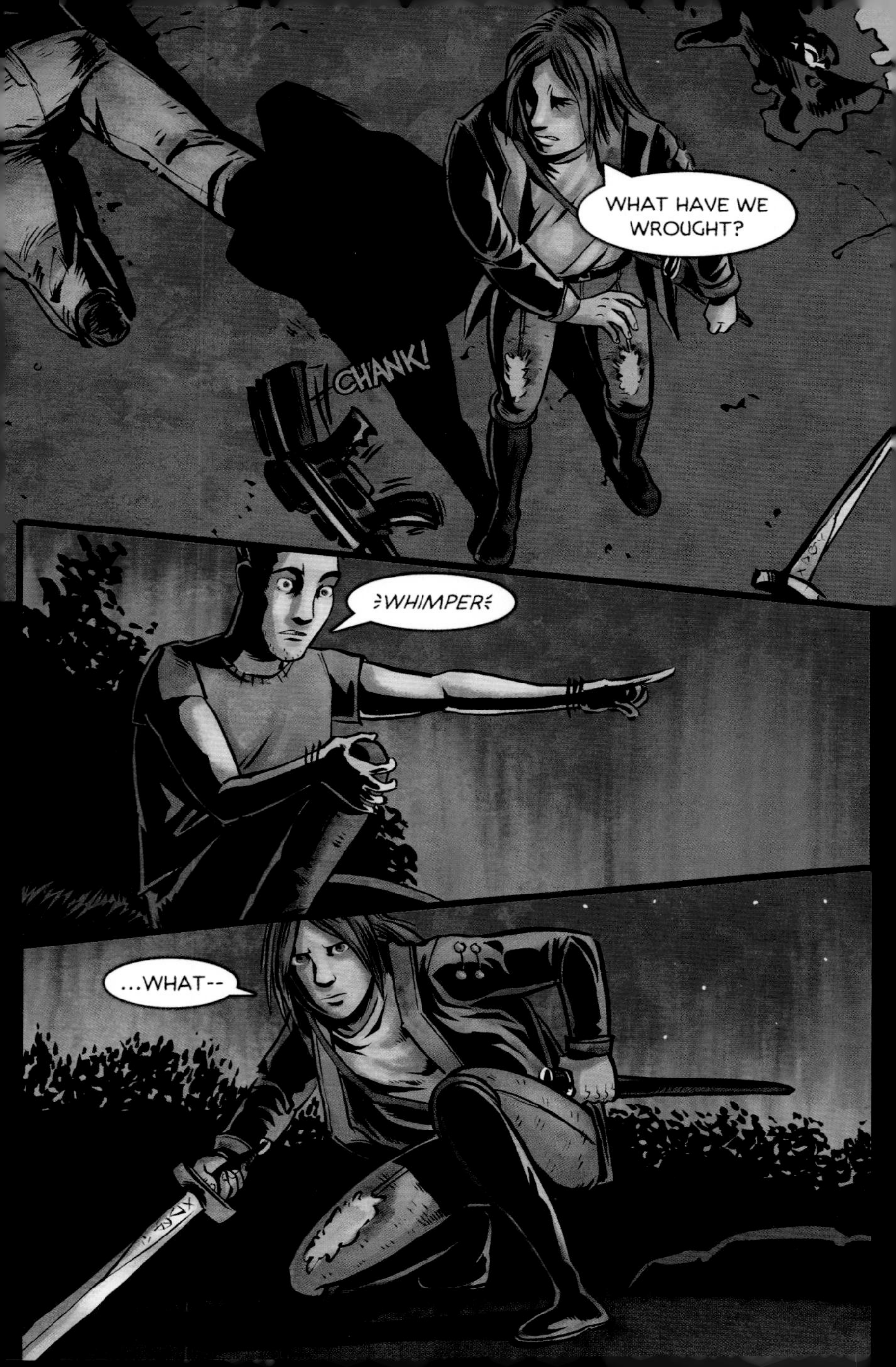
WHAT HAVE WE WROUGHT?
CHANK!
WHIMPER
...WHAT--

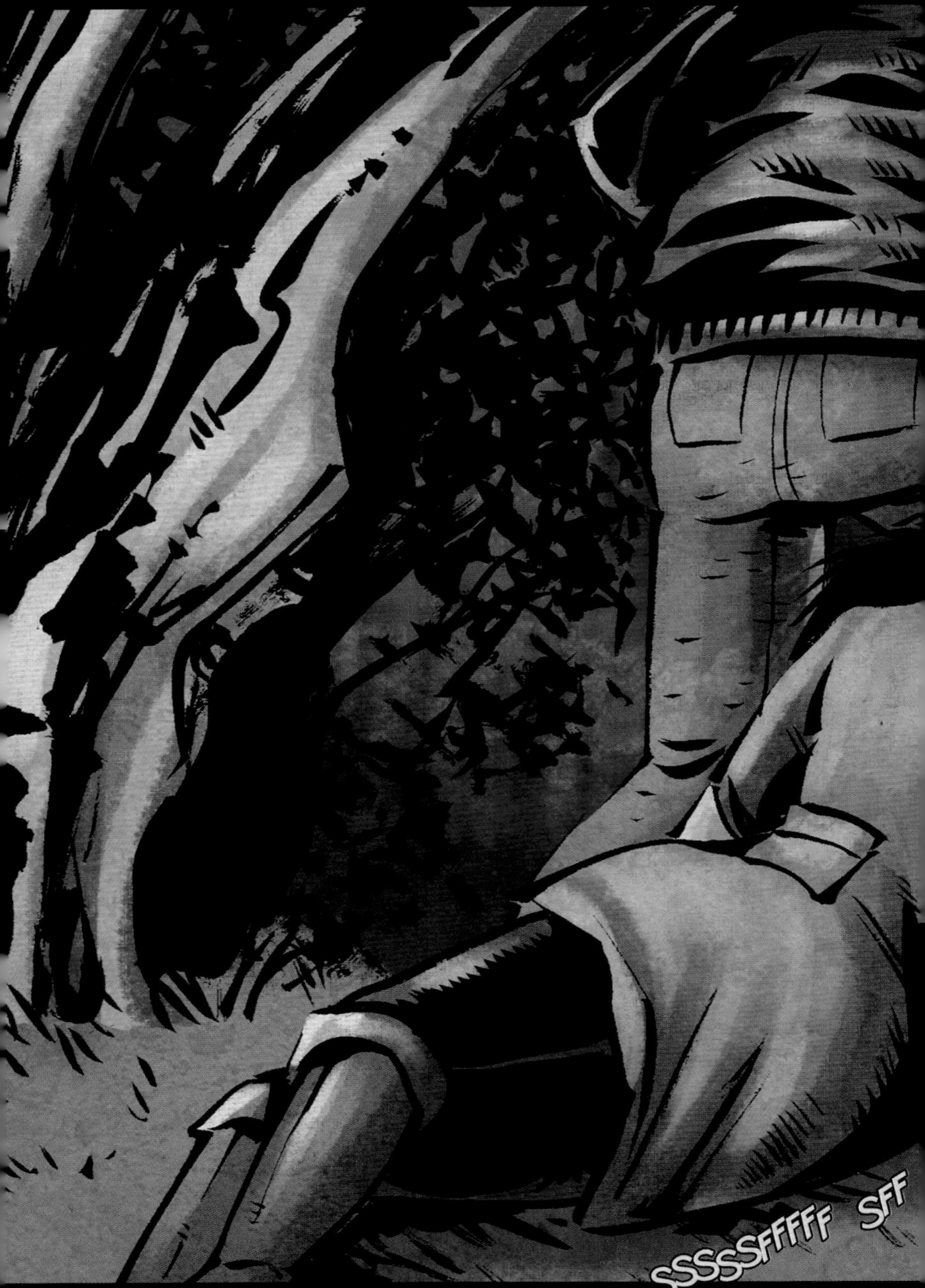
SSSSSFFFFF SFF

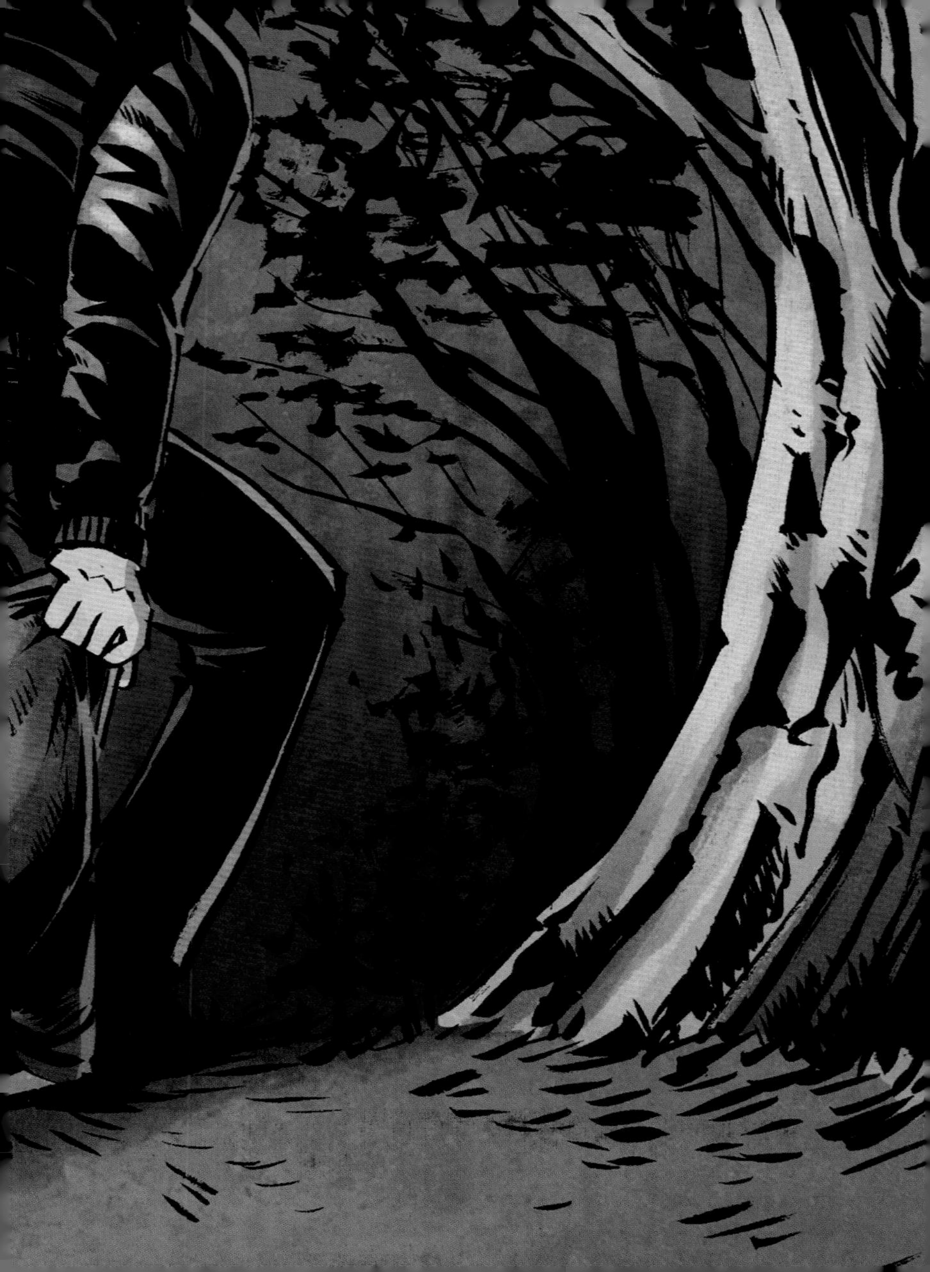

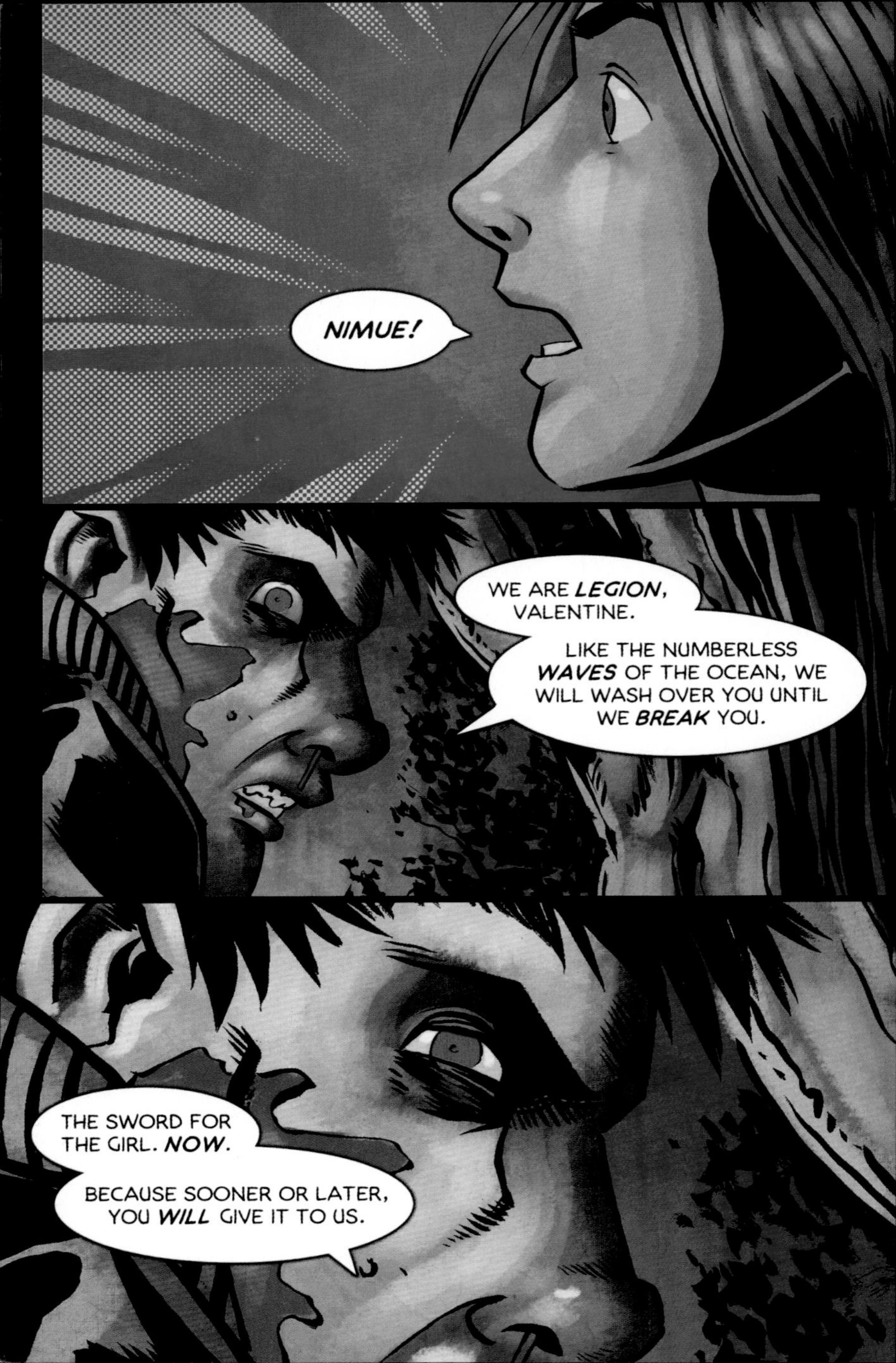
NIMUE!
WE ARE LEGION, VALENTINE.
LIKE THE NUMBERLESS WAVES OF THE OCEAN, WE WILL WASH OVER YOU UNTIL WE BREAK YOU.
THE SWORD FOR THE GIRL. NOW.
BECAUSE SOONER OR LATER, YOU WILL GIVE IT TO US.

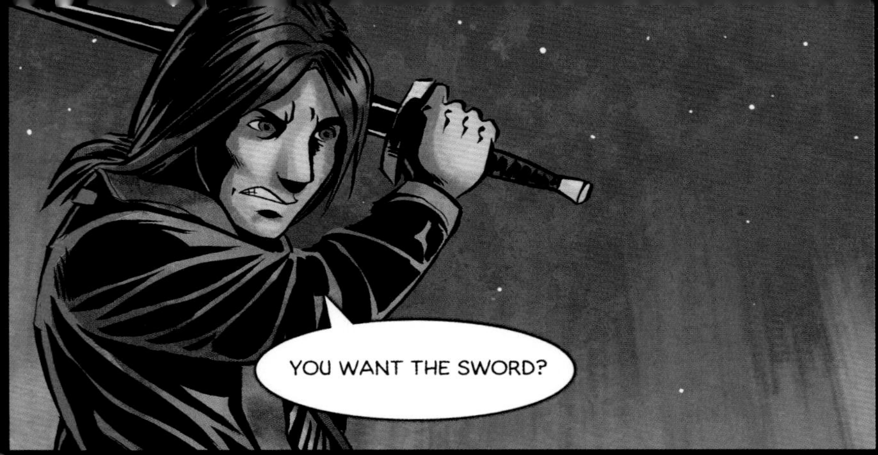
YOU WANT THE SWORD?

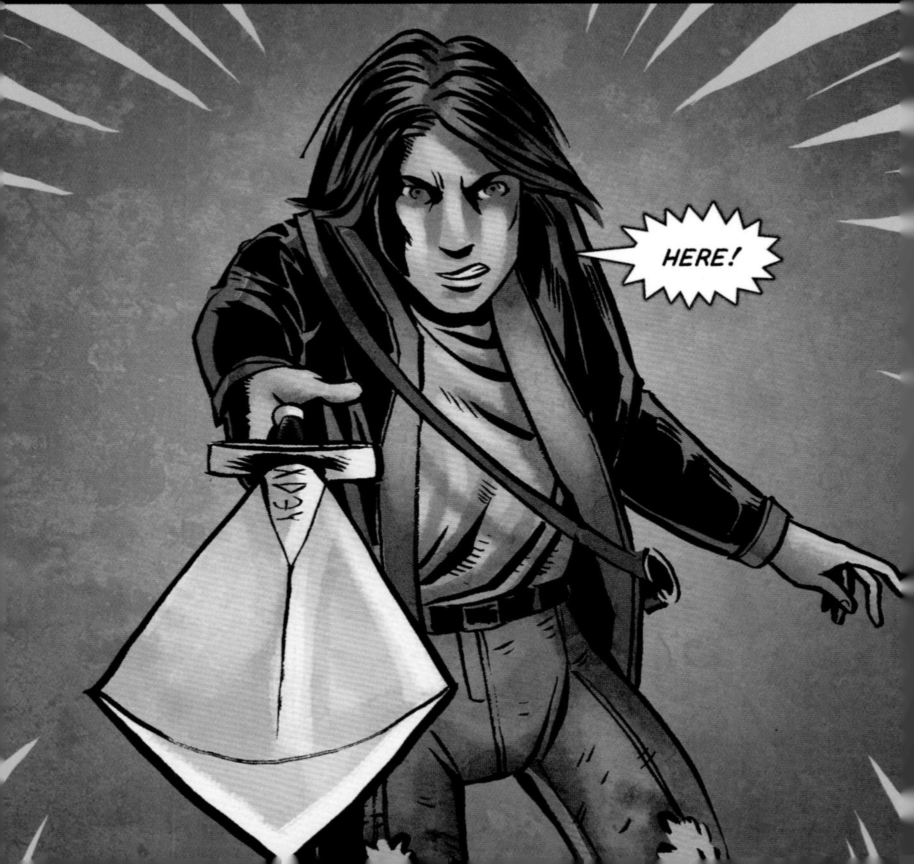
HERE!

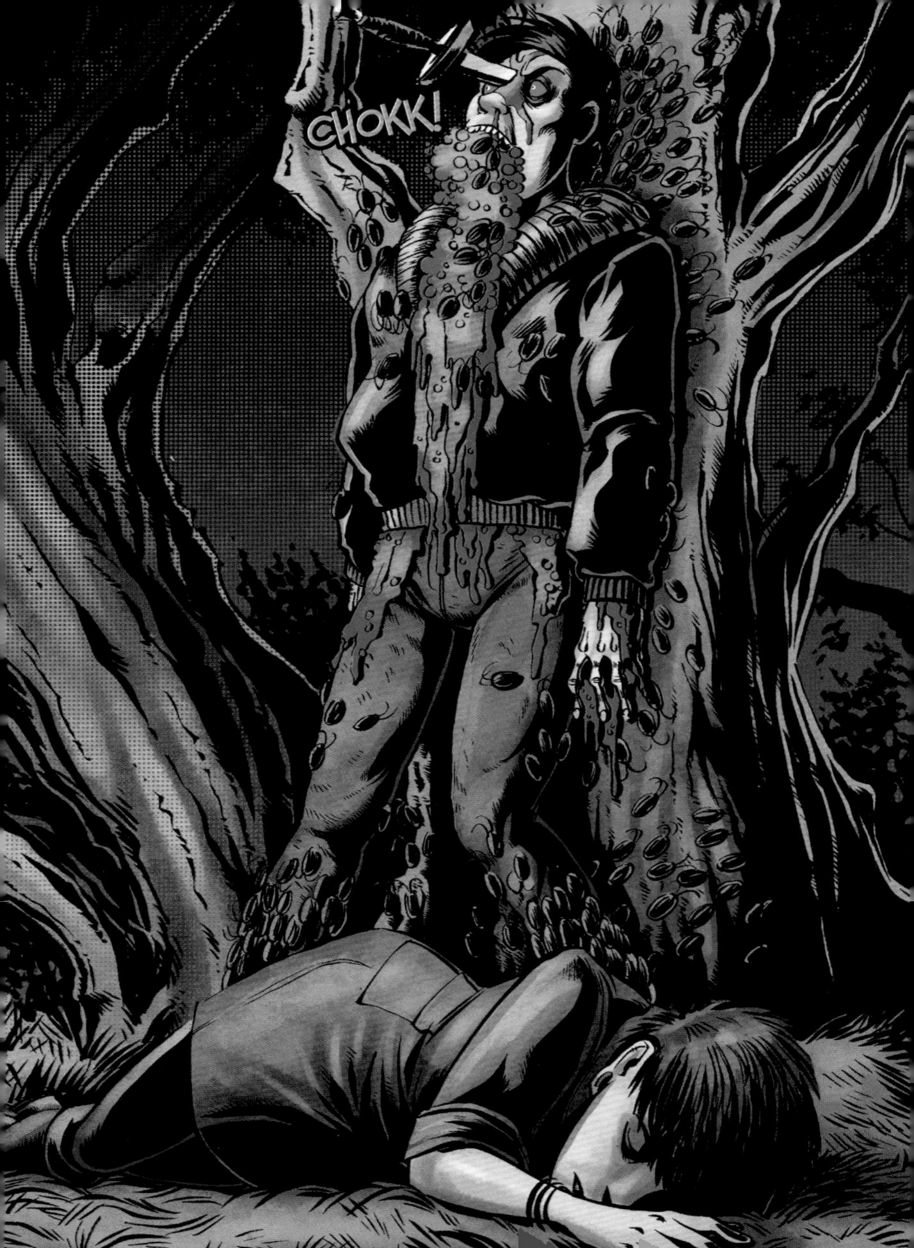
CHOKK!

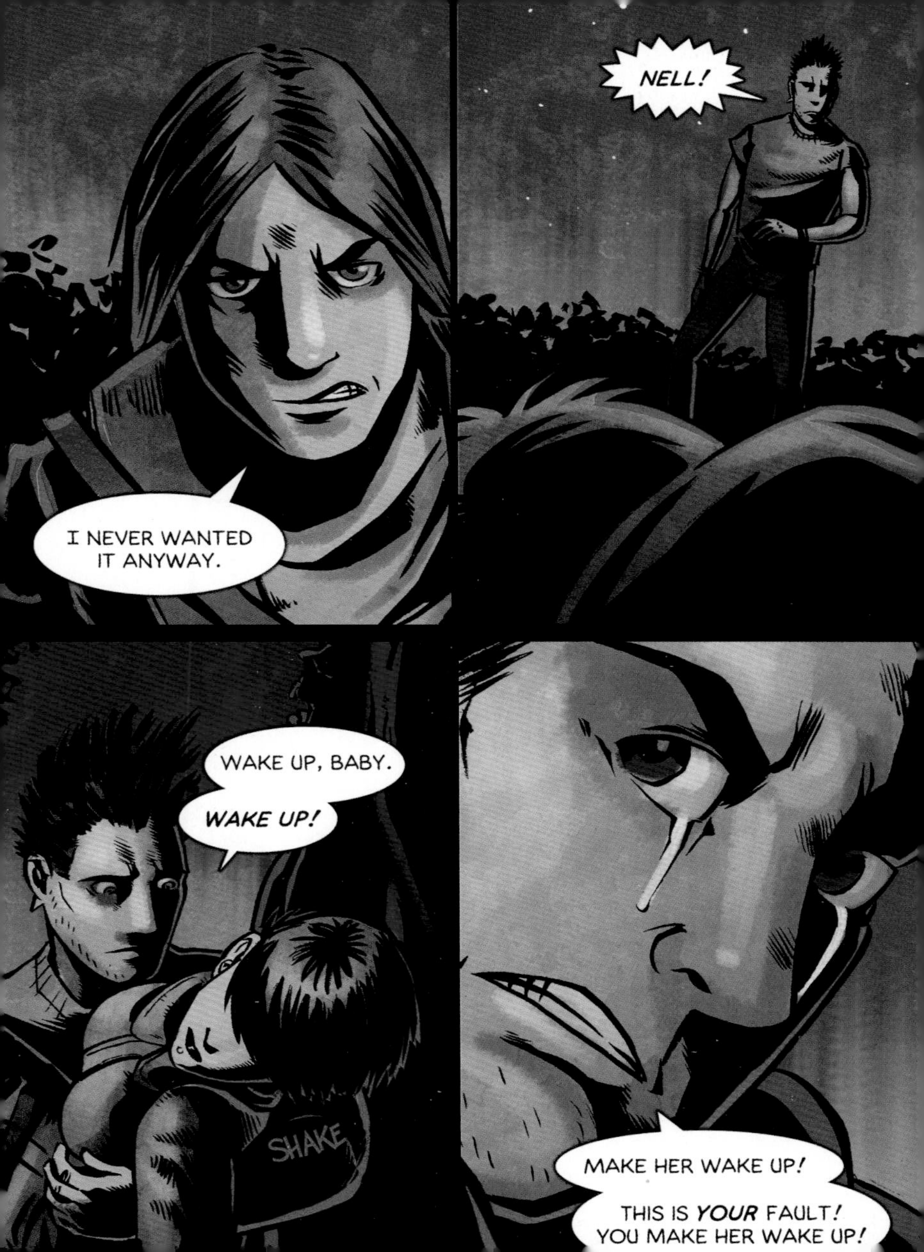
I NEVER WANTED IT ANYWAY.
NELL!
WAKE UP, BABY.
WAKE UP!
SHAKE
MAKE HER WAKE UP!
THIS IS YOUR FAULT! YOU MAKE HER WAKE UP!

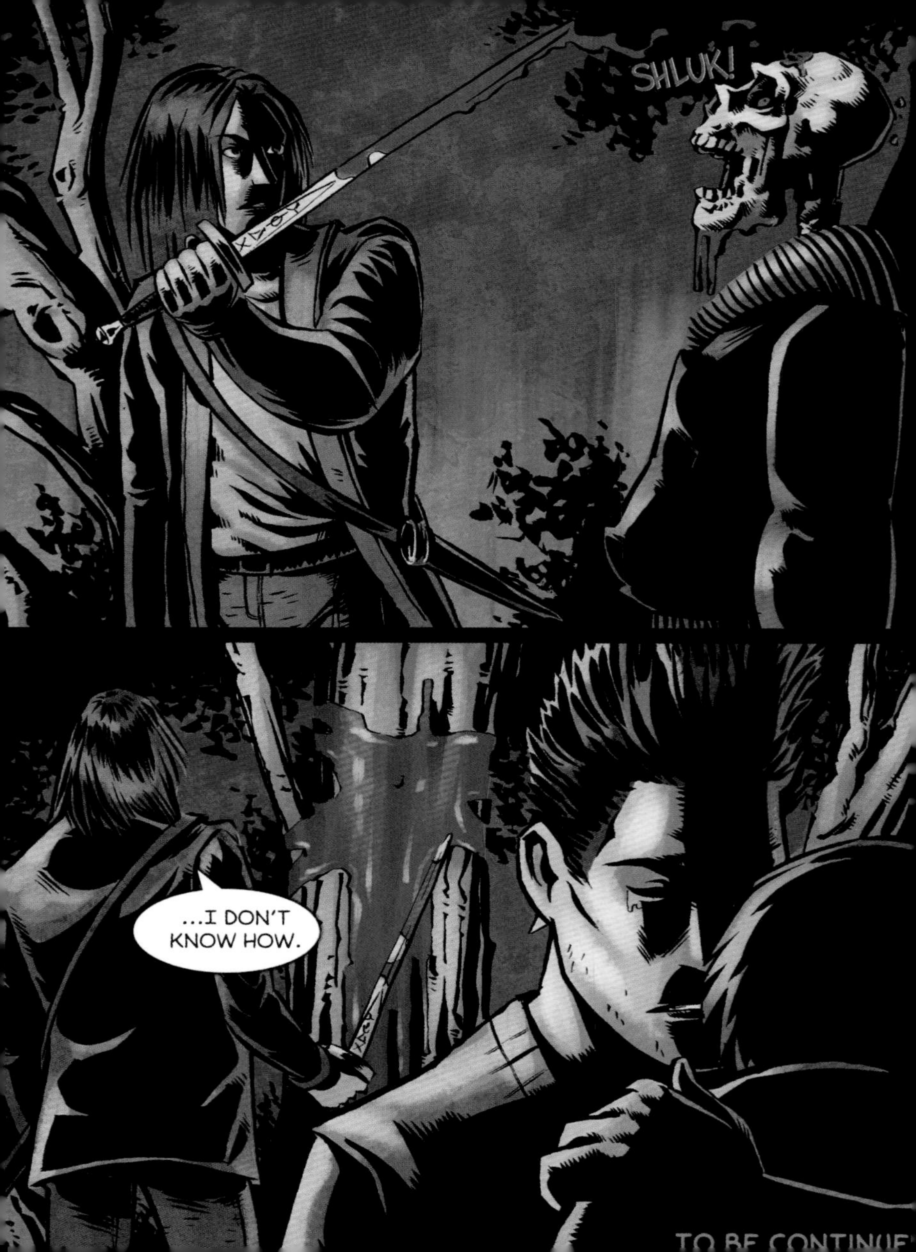
SHLUK!
...I DON'T KNOW HOW.
TO BE CONTINUE

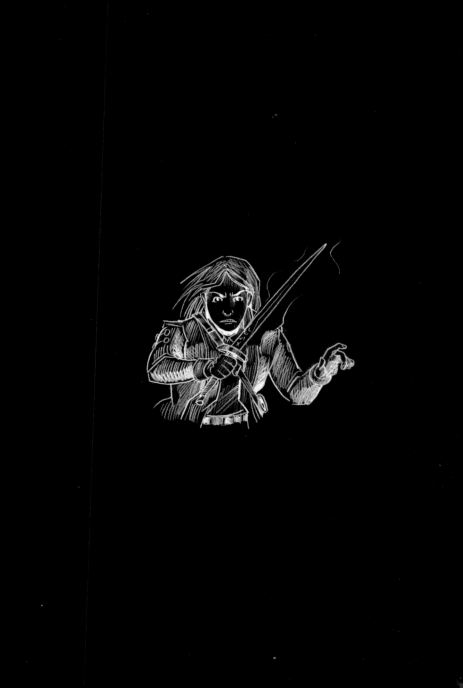

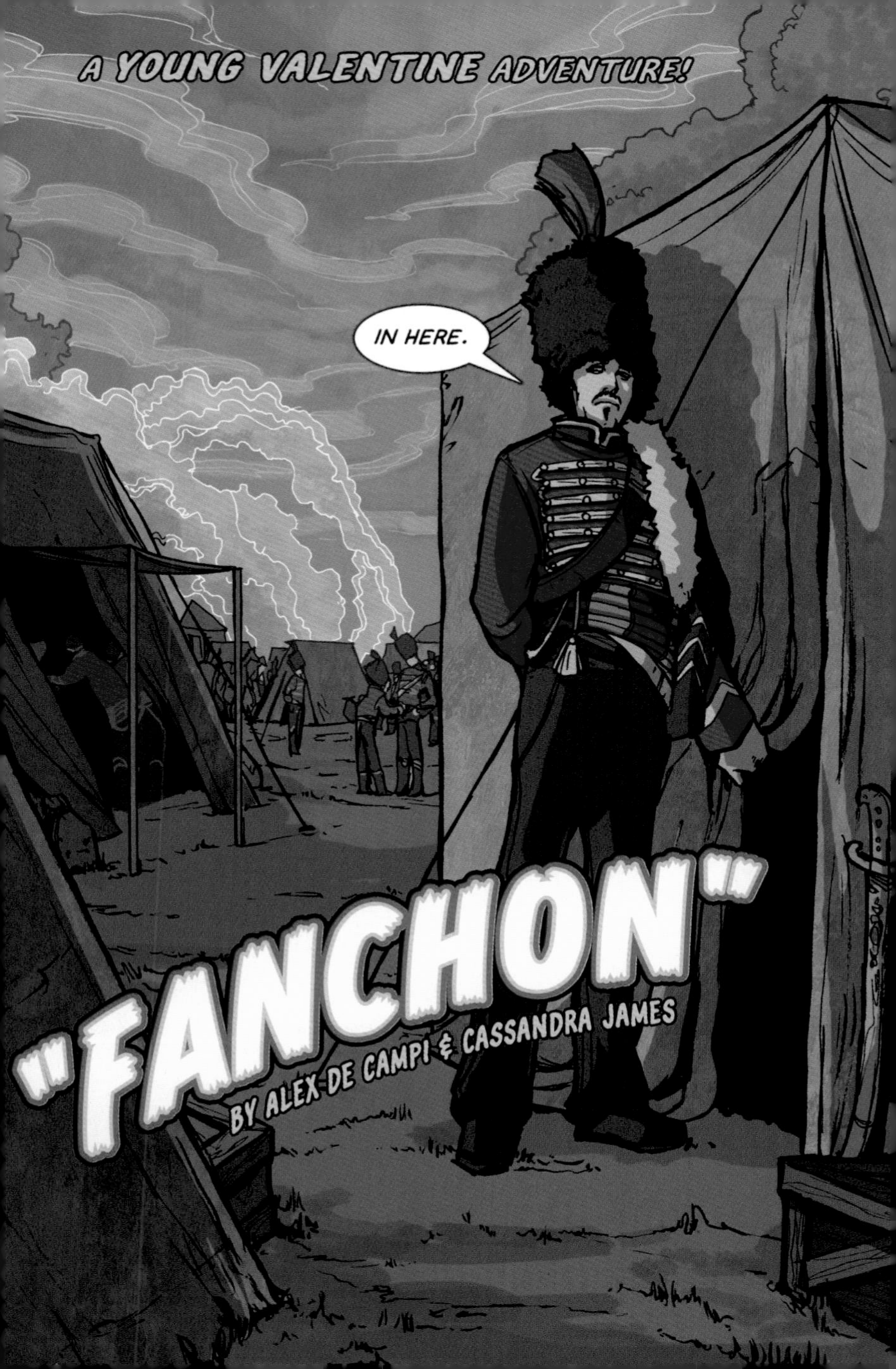
A YOUNG VALENTINE ADVENTURE!
IN HERE.
"FANCHON"
BY ALEX DE CAMPI & CASSANDRA JAMES

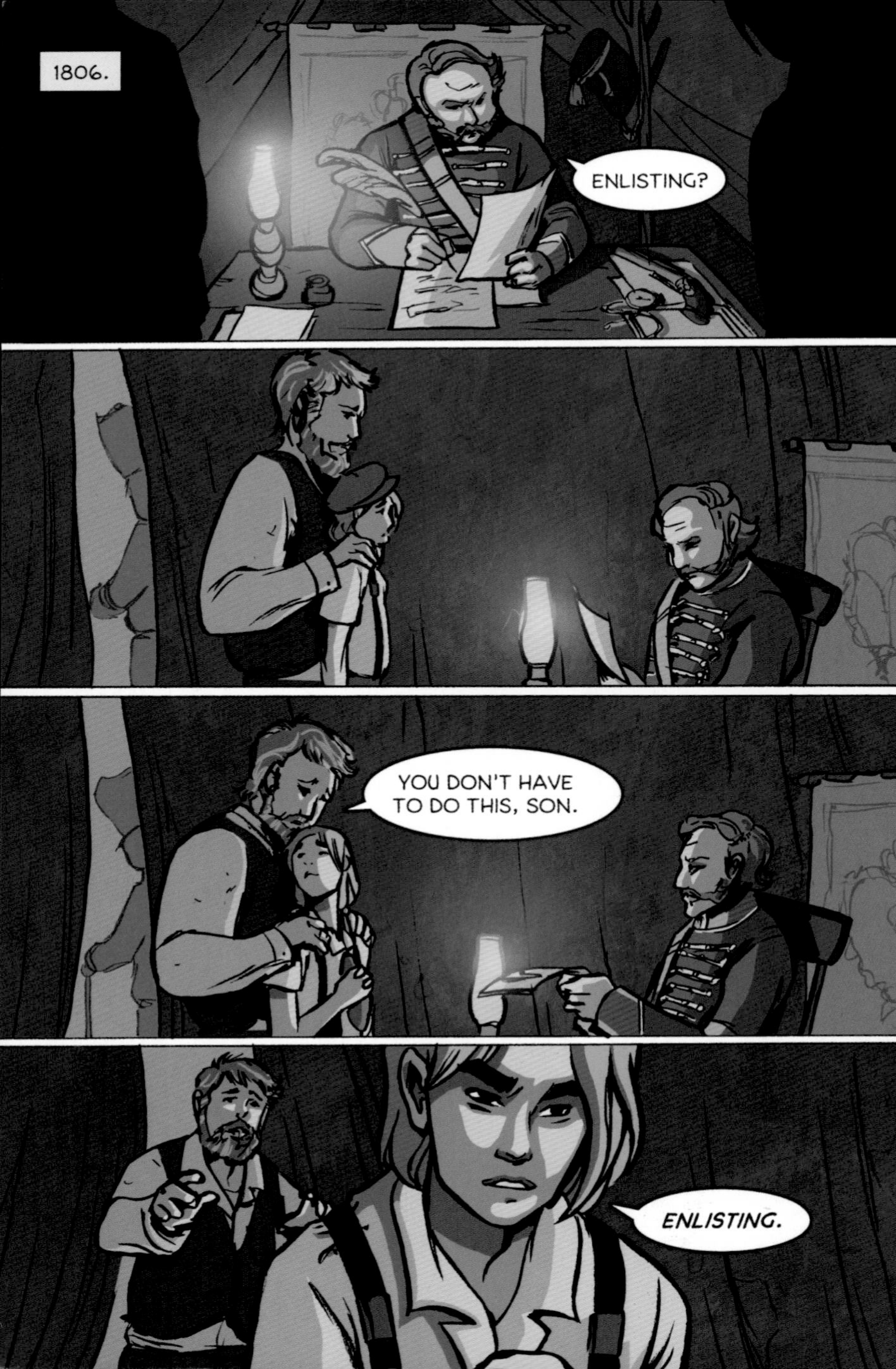
1806.
ENLISTING?
YOU DON'T HAVE TO DO THIS, SON.
ENLISTING.

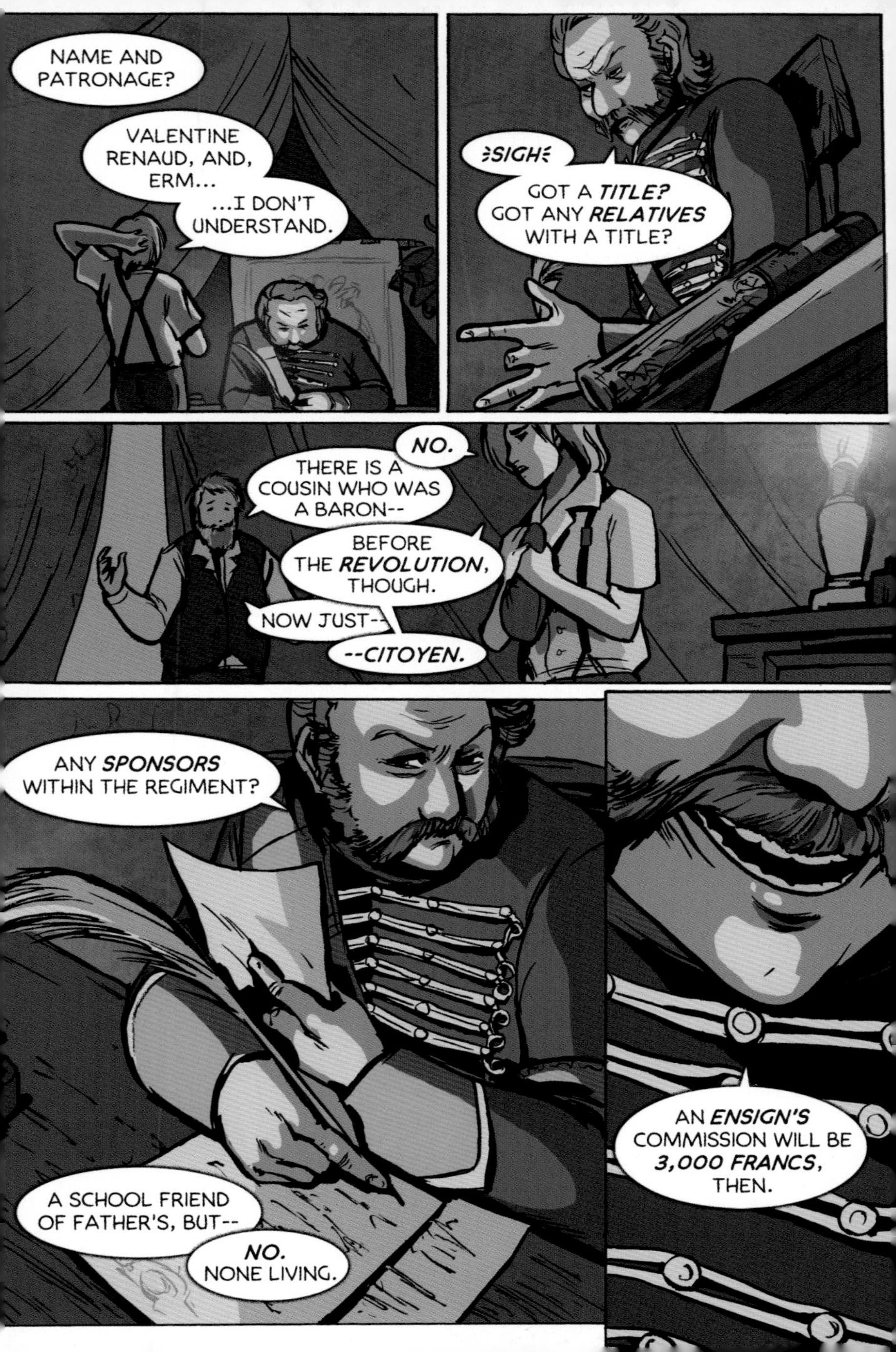

NAME AND PATRONAGE?
VALENTINE RENAUD, AND, ERM...
...I DON'T UNDERSTAND.
SIGH
GOT A *TITLE?* GOT ANY *RELATIVES* WITH A TITLE?
NO.
THERE IS A COUSIN WHO WAS A BARON--
BEFORE THE *REVOLUTION*, THOUGH.
NOW JUST--
--CITOYEN.
ANY *SPONSORS* WITHIN THE REGIMENT?
A SCHOOL FRIEND OF FATHER'S, BUT--
NO. NONE LIVING.
AN *ENSIGN'S* COMMISSION WILL BE *3,000 FRANCS*, THEN.

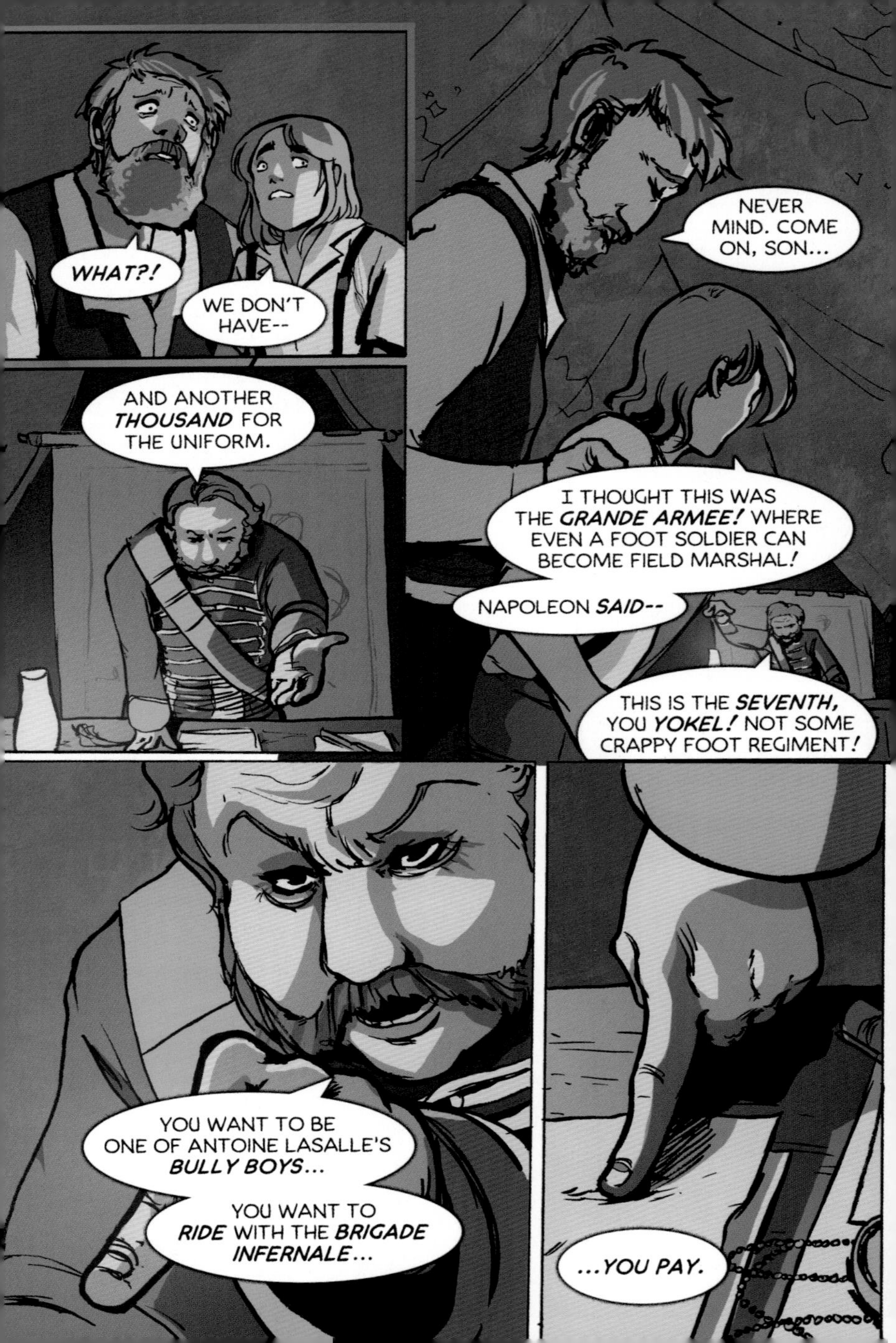
WHAT?!
WE DON'T HAVE--
NEVER MIND. COME ON, SON...
AND ANOTHER *THOUSAND* FOR THE UNIFORM.
I THOUGHT THIS WAS THE *GRANDE ARMEE!* WHERE EVEN A FOOT SOLDIER CAN BECOME FIELD MARSHAL!
NAPOLEON *SAID--*
THIS IS THE *SEVENTH,* YOU *YOKEL!* NOT SOME CRAPPY FOOT REGIMENT!
YOU WANT TO BE ONE OF ANTOINE LASALLE'S *BULLY BOYS...*
YOU WANT TO *RIDE* WITH THE *BRIGADE INFERNALE...*
...YOU PAY.

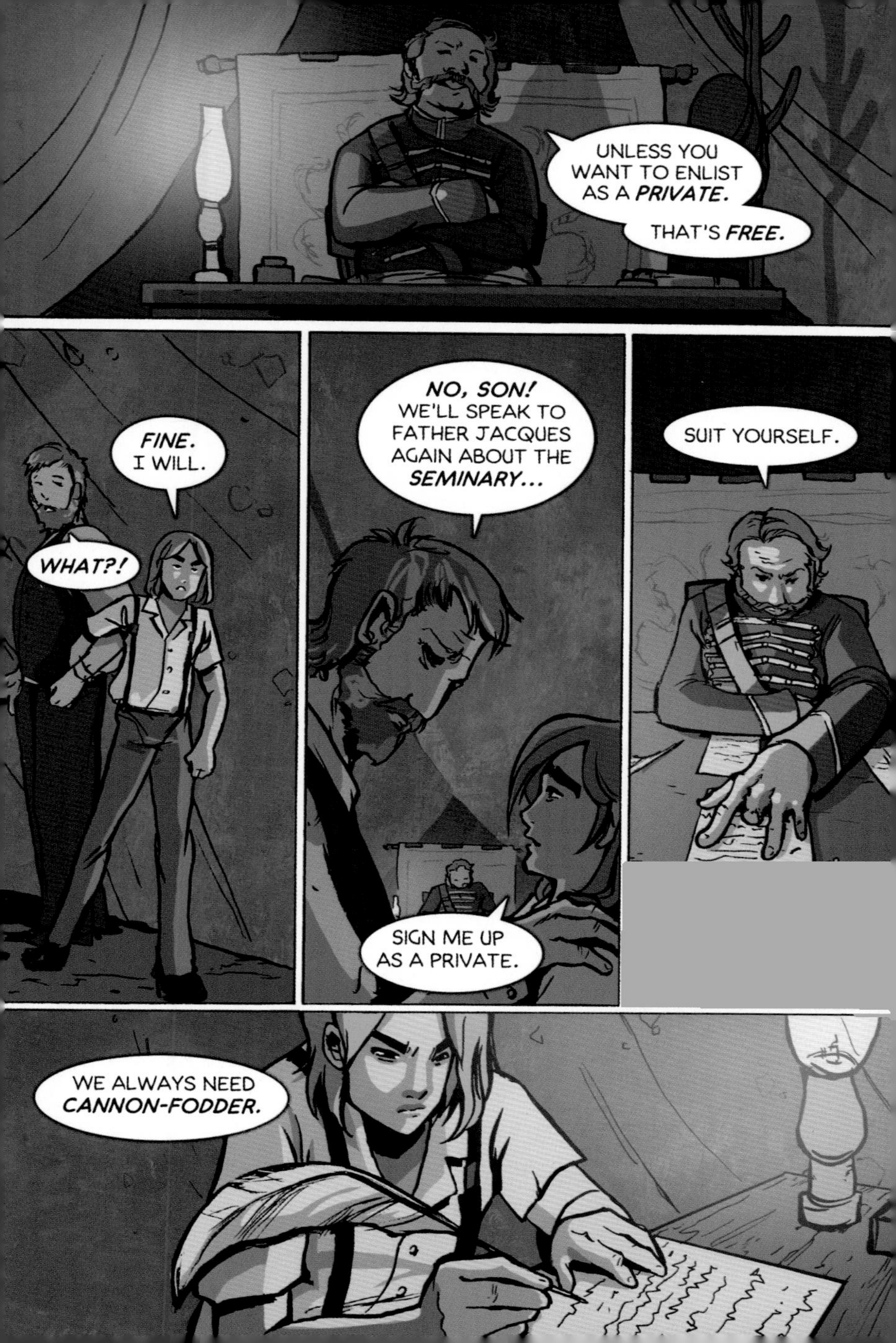
UNLESS YOU WANT TO ENLIST AS A PRIVATE.
THAT'S FREE.
FINE. I WILL.
WHAT?!
NO, SON! WE'LL SPEAK TO FATHER JACQUES AGAIN ABOUT THE SEMINARY...
SIGN ME UP AS A PRIVATE.
SUIT YOURSELF.
WE ALWAYS NEED CANNON-FODDER.

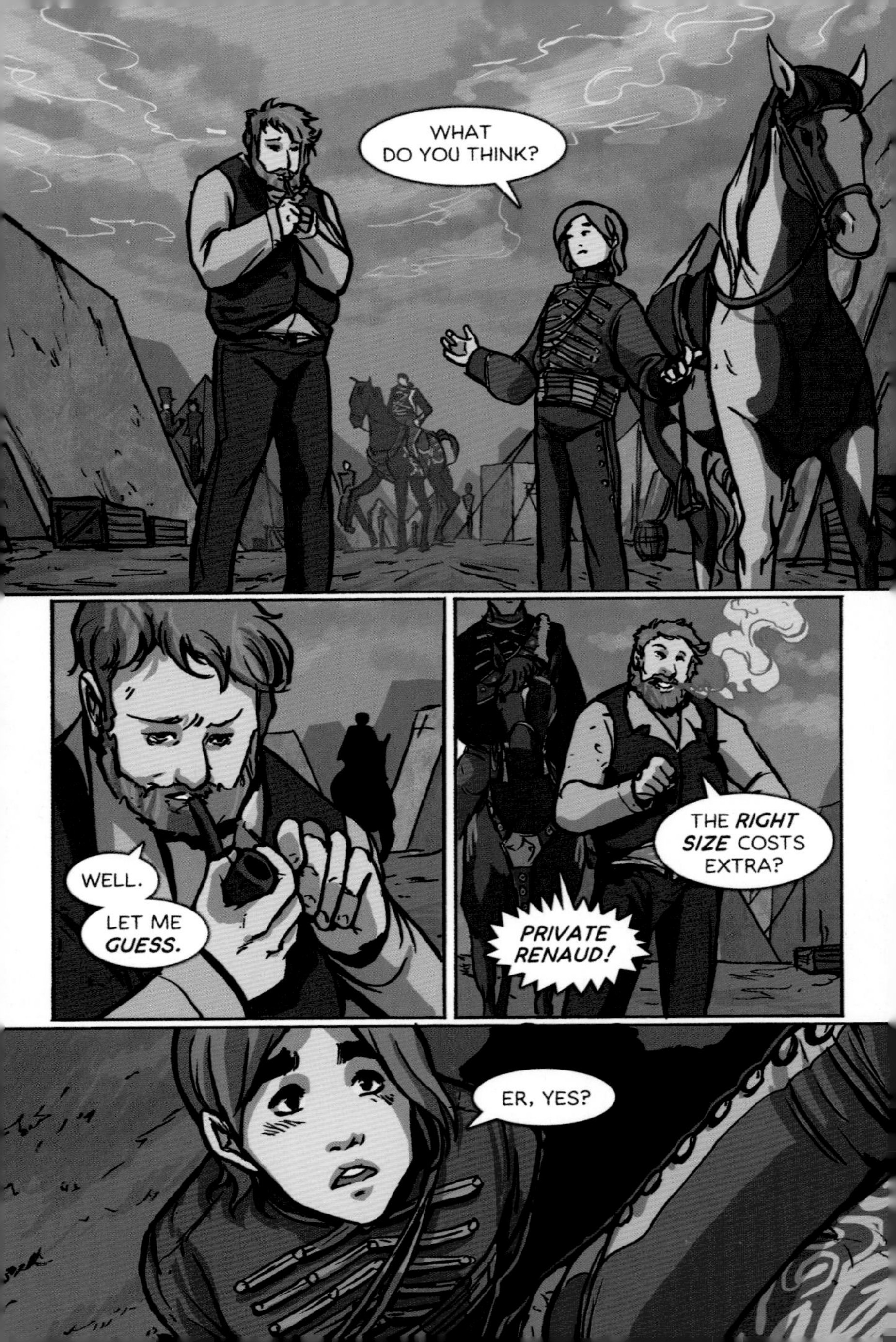
WHAT DO YOU THINK?
WELL.
LET ME *GUESS.*
THE *RIGHT SIZE* COSTS EXTRA?
PRIVATE RENAUD!
ER, YES?

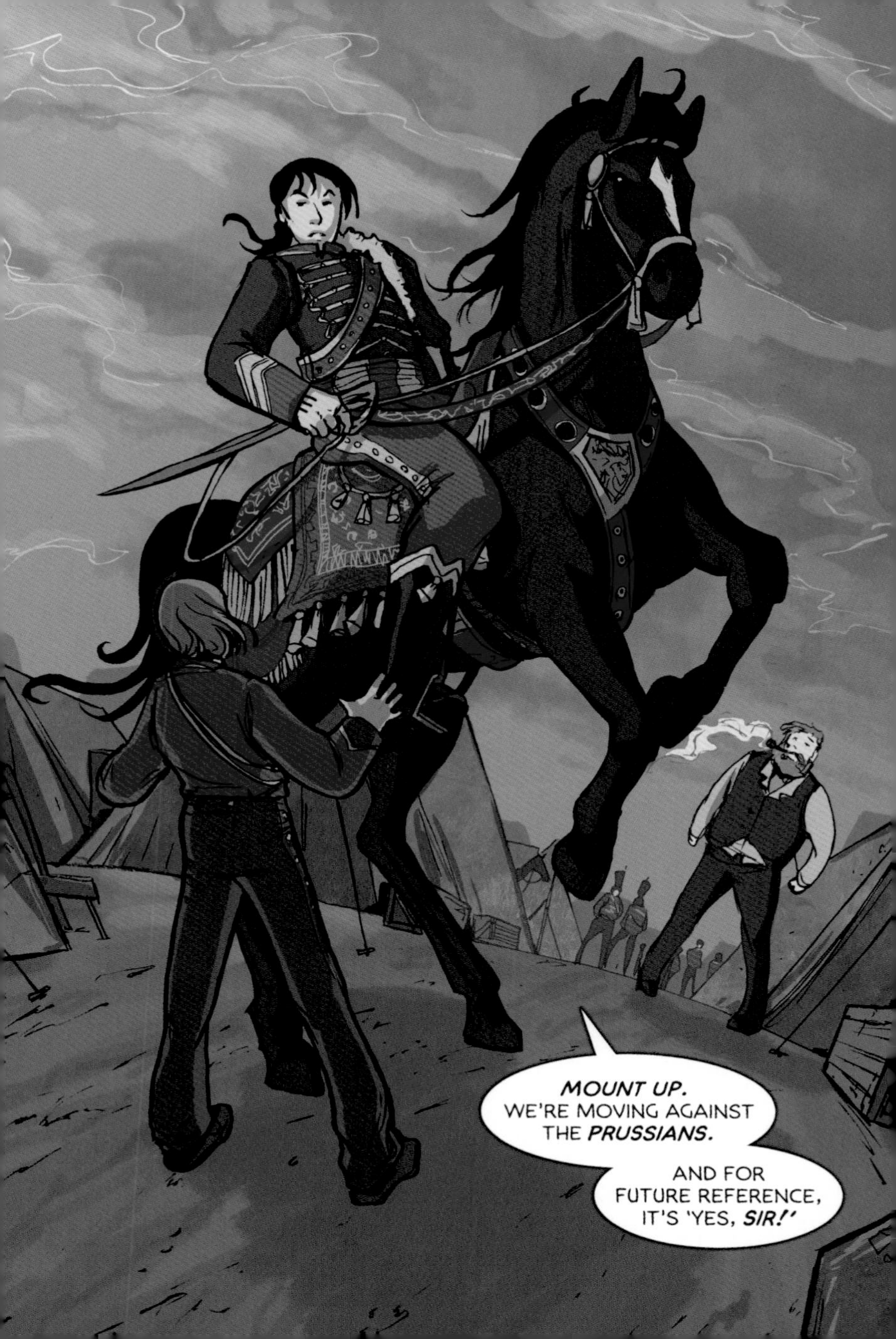
MOUNT UP. WE'RE MOVING AGAINST THE PRUSSIANS.
AND FOR FUTURE REFERENCE, IT'S 'YES, SIR!'

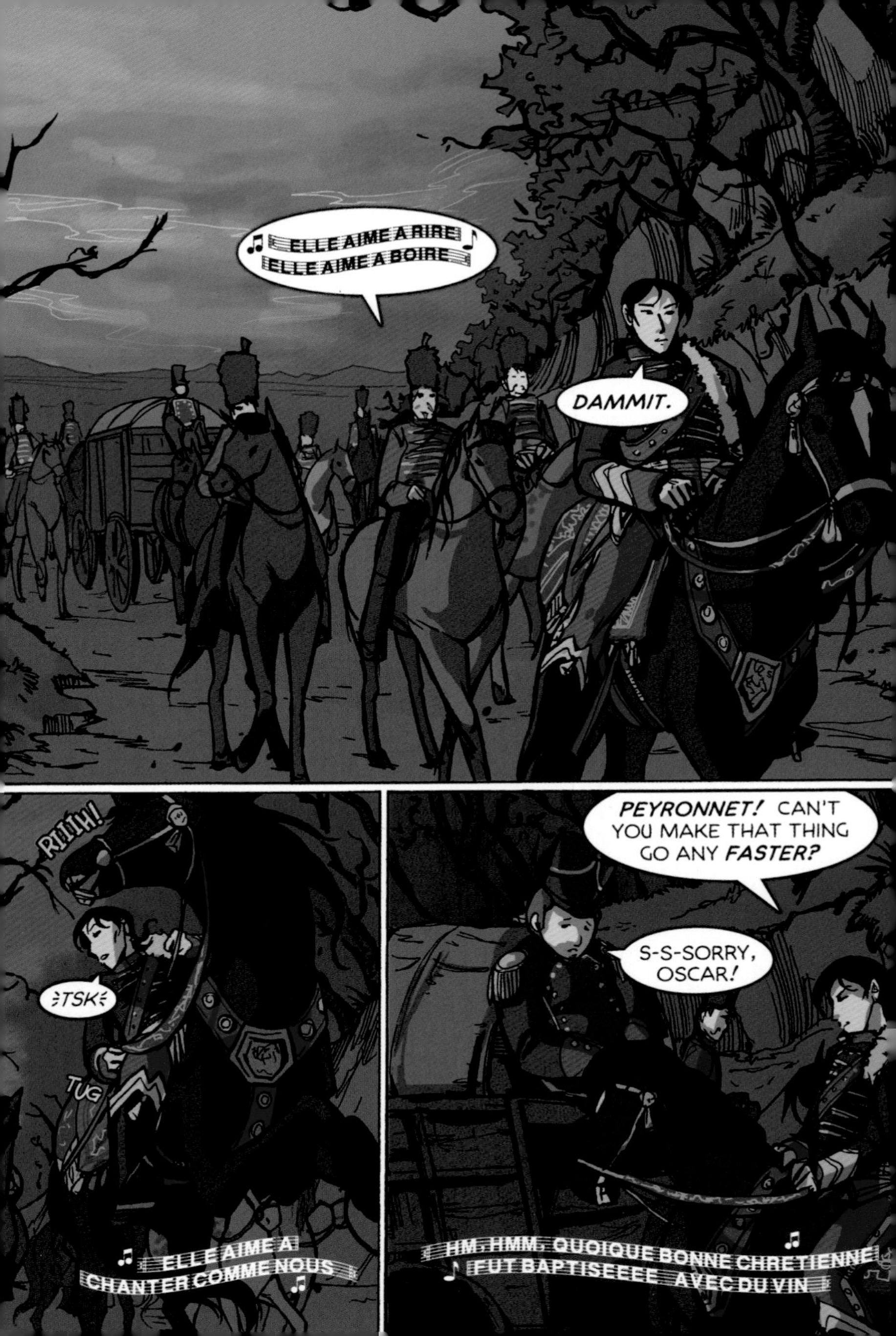
ELLE AIME A RIRE
ELLE AIME A BOIRE
DAMMIT.
RIIIH!
TSK
TUG
ELLE AIME A CHANTER COMME NOUS
PEYRONNET! CAN'T YOU MAKE THAT THING GO ANY FASTER?
S-S-SORRY, OSCAR!
HM, HMM, QUOIQUE BONNE CHRETIENNE
FUT BAPTISEEEE AVEC DU VIN

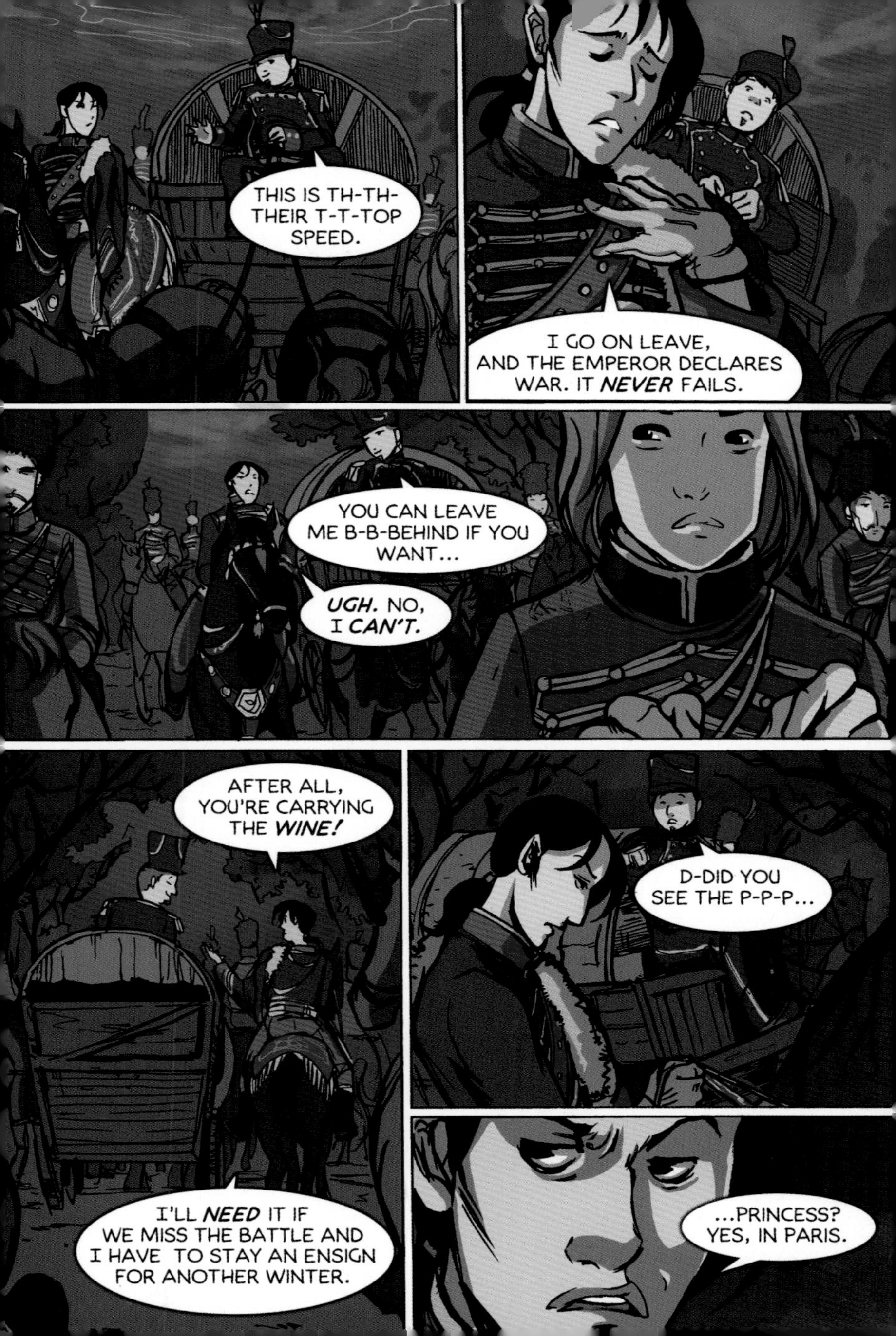
THIS IS TH-TH-THEIR T-T-TOP SPEED.
I GO ON LEAVE, AND THE EMPEROR DECLARES WAR. IT NEVER FAILS.
YOU CAN LEAVE ME B-B-BEHIND IF YOU WANT...
UGH. NO, I CAN'T.
AFTER ALL, YOU'RE CARRYING THE WINE!
I'LL NEED IT IF WE MISS THE BATTLE AND I HAVE TO STAY AN ENSIGN FOR ANOTHER WINTER.
D-DID YOU SEE THE P-P-P...
...PRINCESS? YES, IN PARIS.

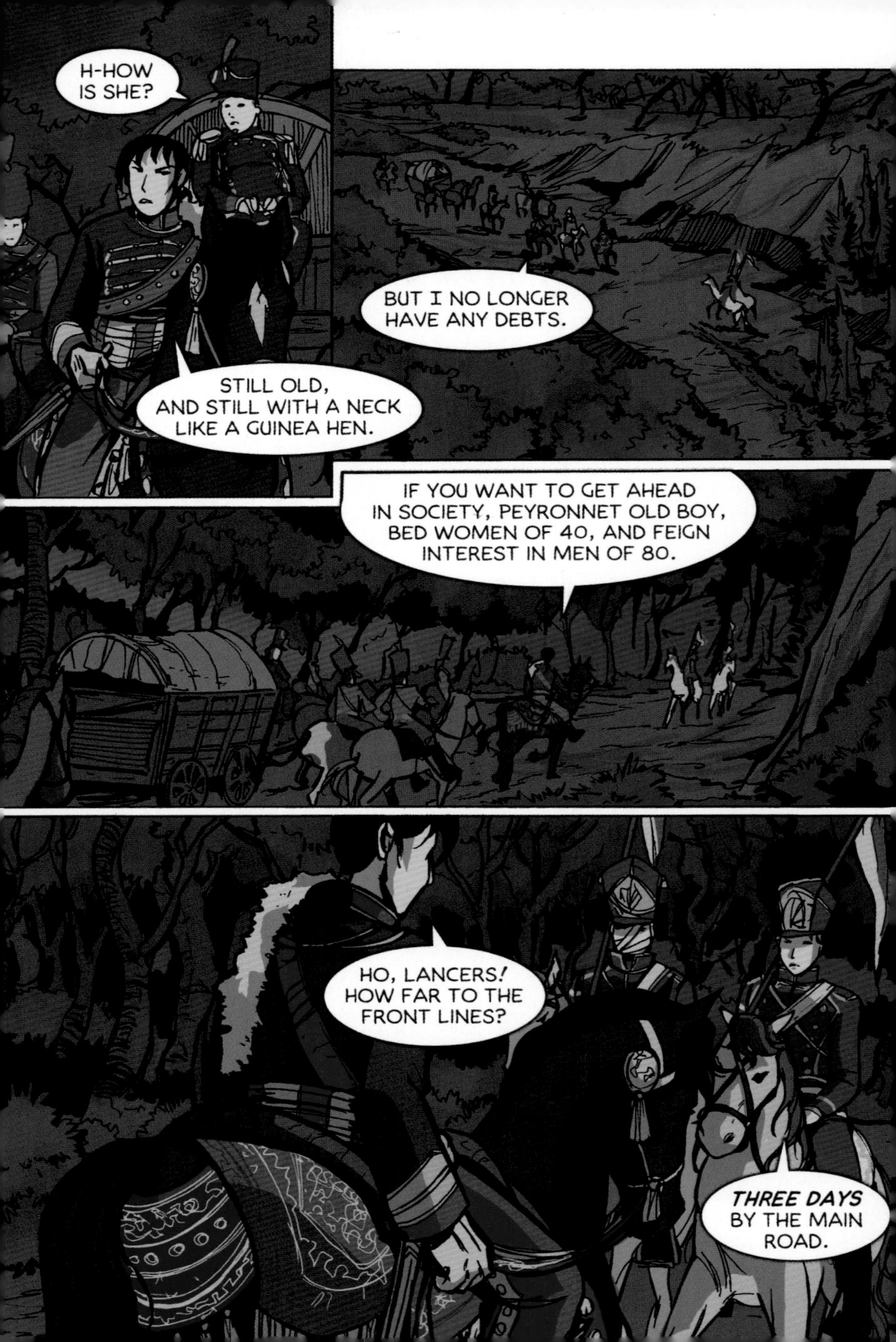
H-HOW IS SHE?
STILL OLD, AND STILL WITH A NECK LIKE A GUINEA HEN.
BUT I NO LONGER HAVE ANY DEBTS.
IF YOU WANT TO GET AHEAD IN SOCIETY, PEYRONNET OLD BOY, BED WOMEN OF 40, AND FEIGN INTEREST IN MEN OF 80.
HO, LANCERS! HOW FAR TO THE FRONT LINES?
THREE DAYS BY THE MAIN ROAD.

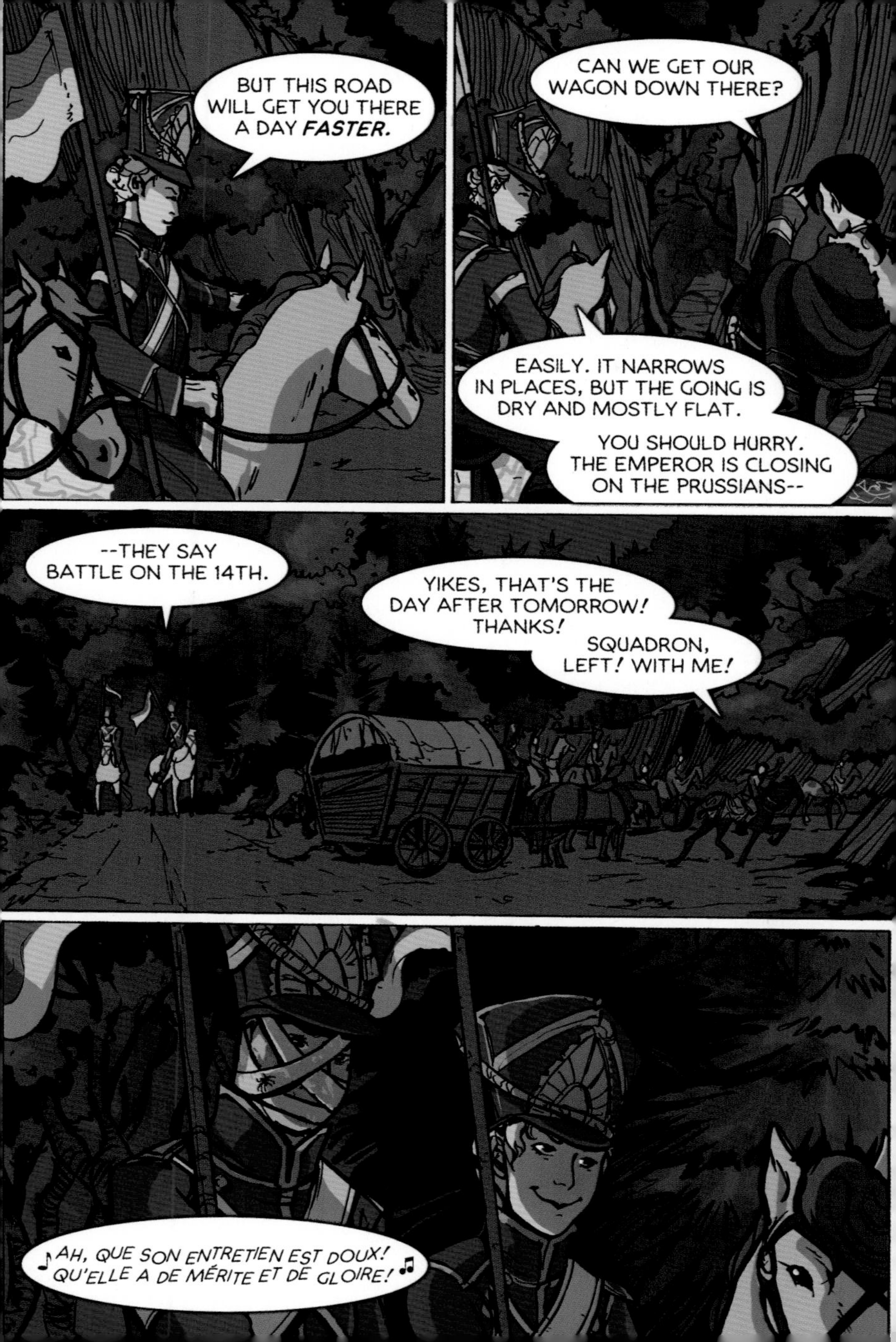
BUT THIS ROAD WILL GET YOU THERE A DAY *FASTER.*
CAN WE GET OUR WAGON DOWN THERE?
EASILY. IT NARROWS IN PLACES, BUT THE GOING IS DRY AND MOSTLY FLAT.
YOU SHOULD HURRY. THE EMPEROR IS CLOSING ON THE PRUSSIANS--
--THEY SAY BATTLE ON THE 14TH.
YIKES, THAT'S THE DAY AFTER TOMORROW! THANKS!
SQUADRON, LEFT! WITH ME!
♪ AH, QUE SON ENTRETIEN EST DOUX! QU'ELLE A DE MÉRITE ET DE GLOIRE! ♫

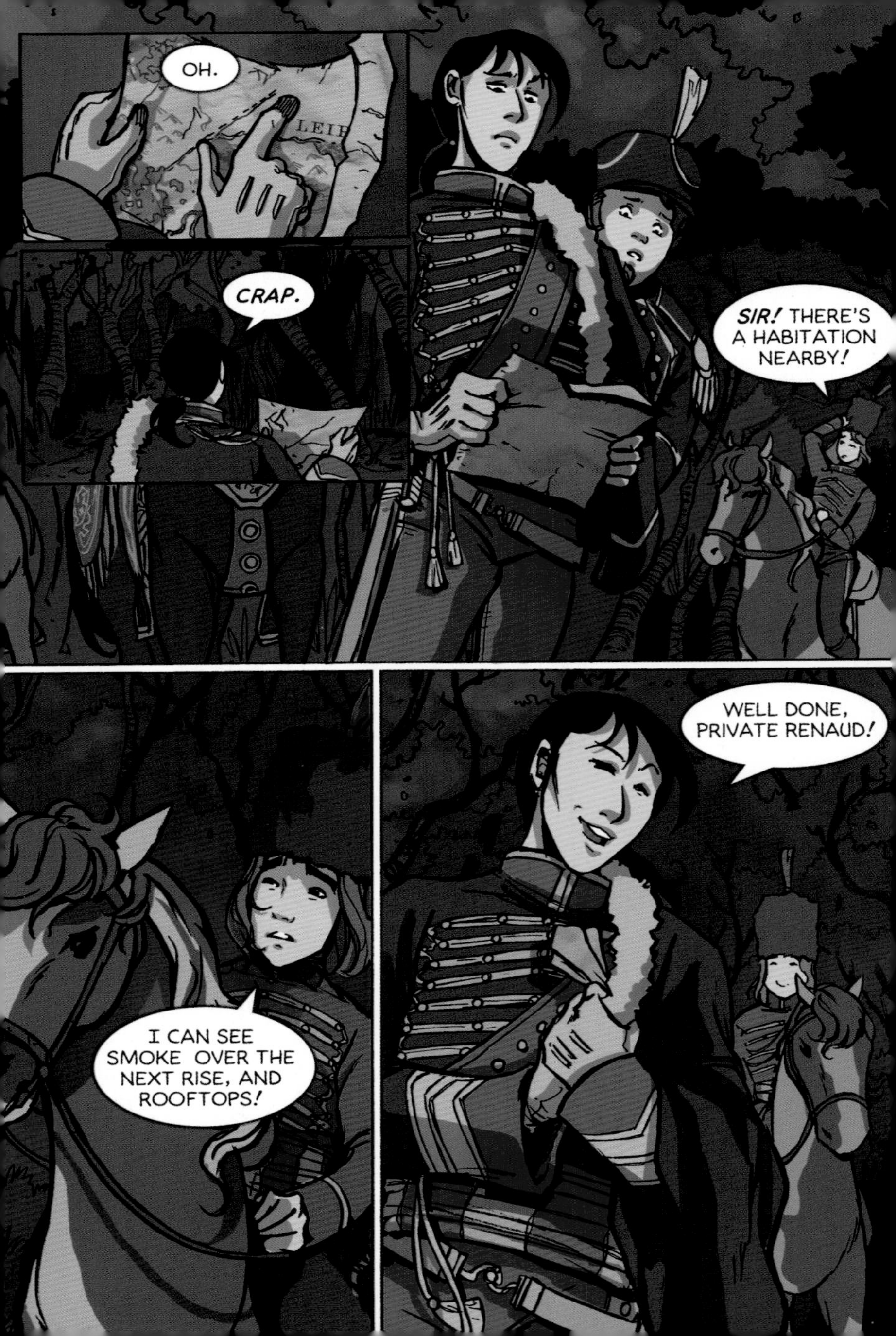
OH.
CRAP.
SIR! THERE'S A HABITATION NEARBY!
I CAN SEE SMOKE OVER THE NEXT RISE, AND ROOFTOPS!
WELL DONE, PRIVATE RENAUD!

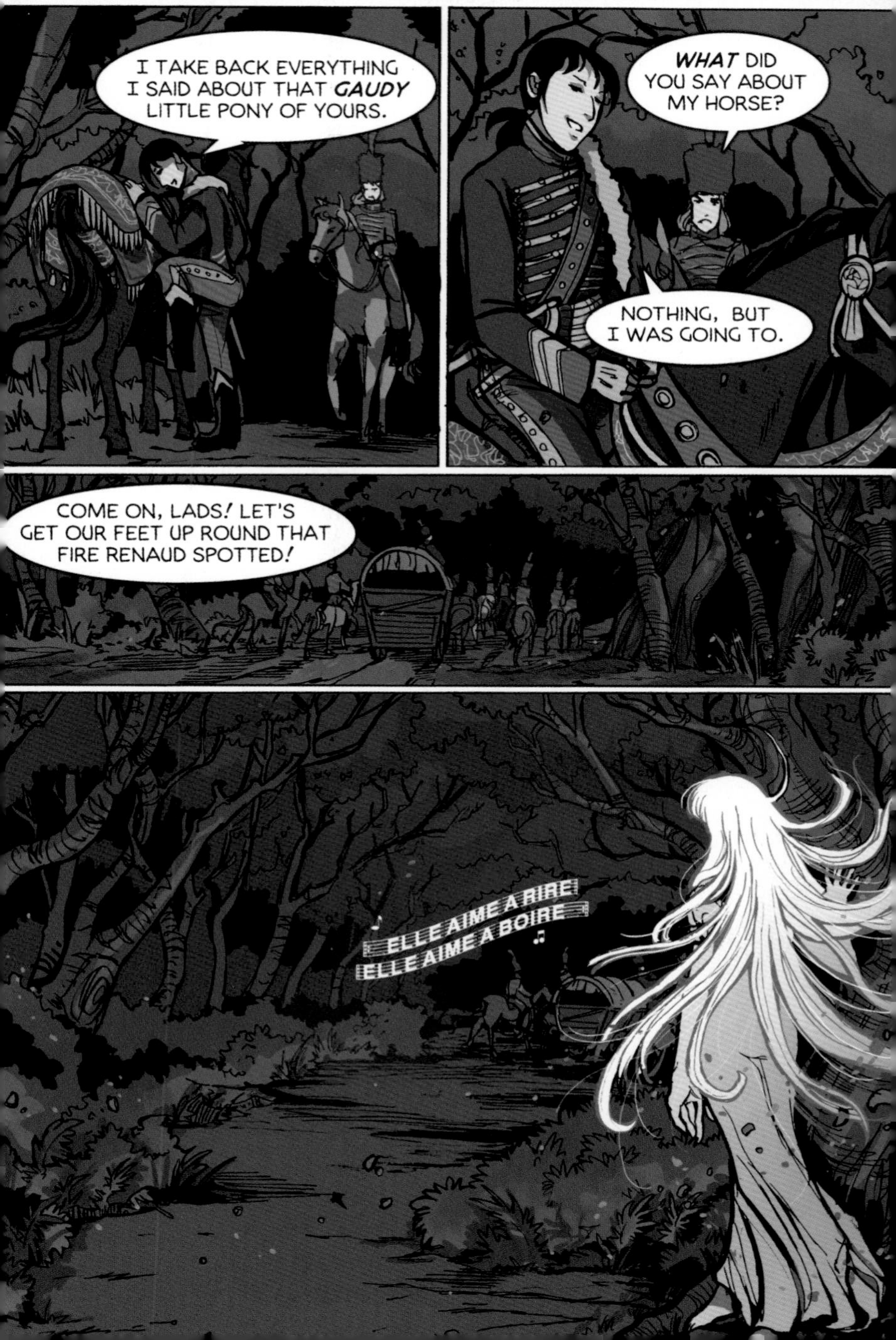
I TAKE BACK EVERYTHING I SAID ABOUT THAT *GAUDY* LITTLE PONY OF YOURS.
WHAT DID YOU SAY ABOUT MY HORSE?
NOTHING, BUT I WAS GOING TO.
COME ON, LADS! LET'S GET OUR FEET UP ROUND THAT FIRE RENAUD SPOTTED!
ELLE AIME A RIRE
ELLE AIME A BOIRE

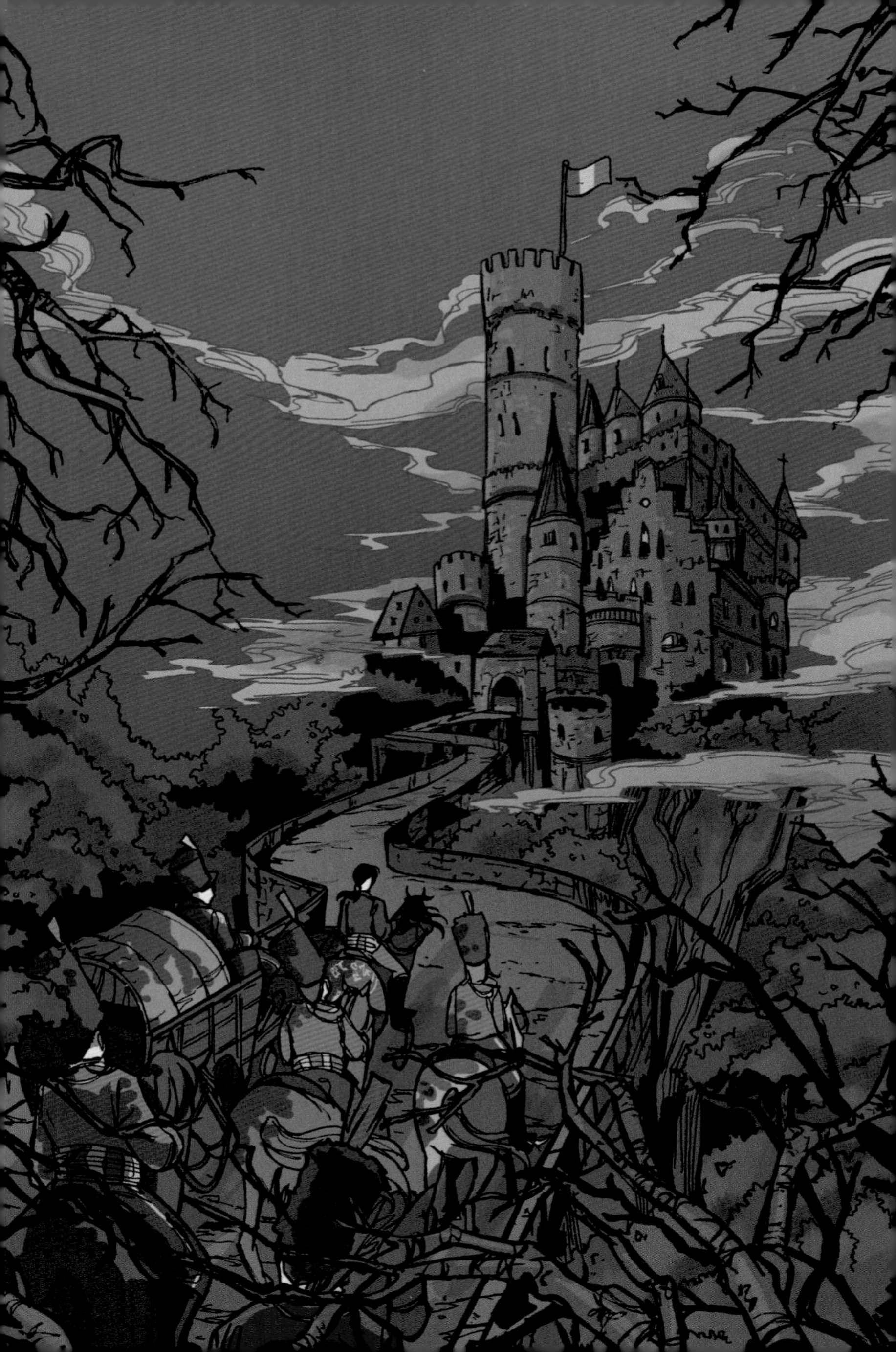

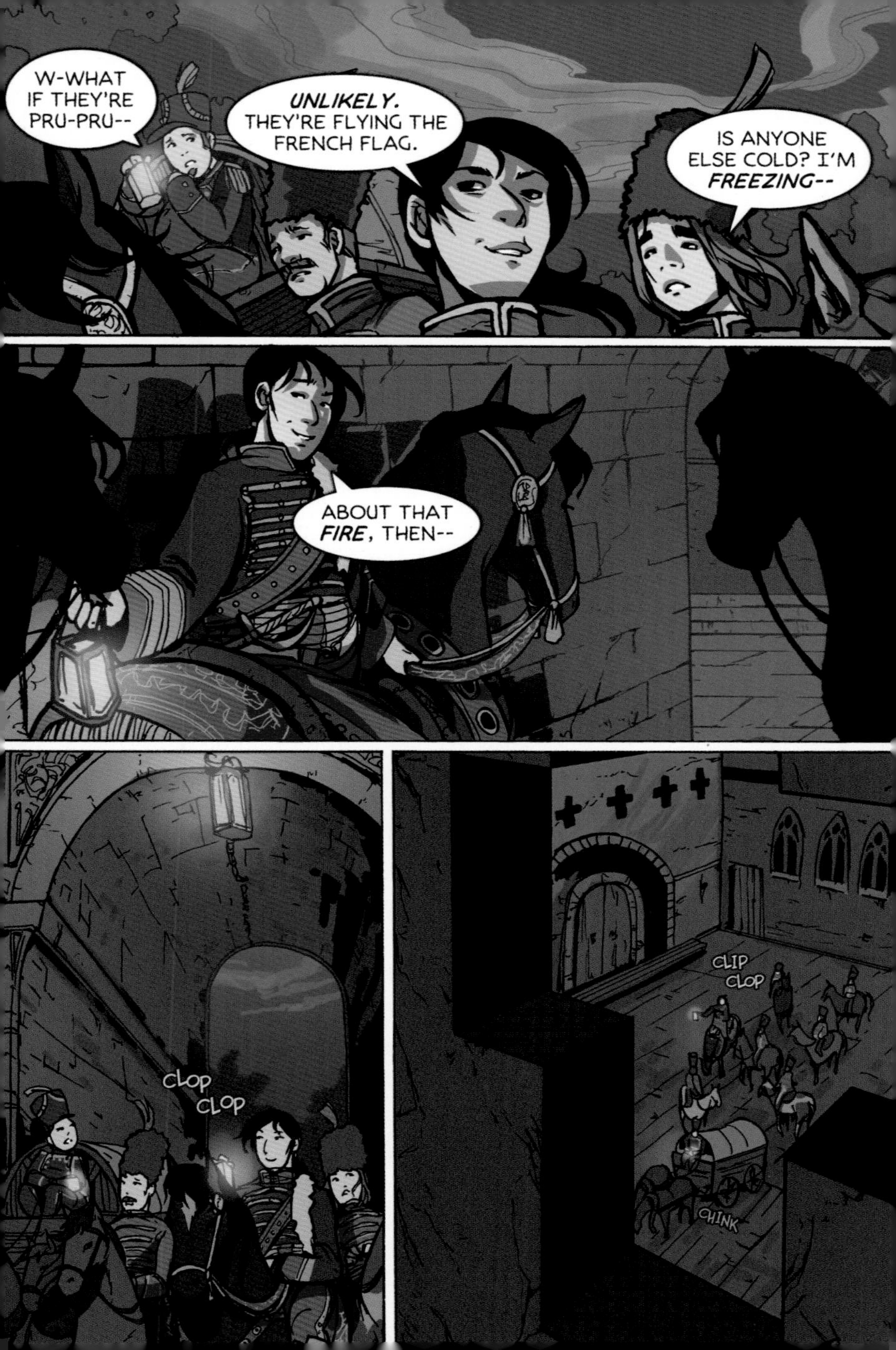
W-WHAT IF THEY'RE PRU-PRU--
UNLIKELY. THEY'RE FLYING THE FRENCH FLAG.
IS ANYONE ELSE COLD? I'M *FREEZING--*
ABOUT THAT *FIRE*, THEN--
CLOP CLOP
CLIP CLOP
CHINK

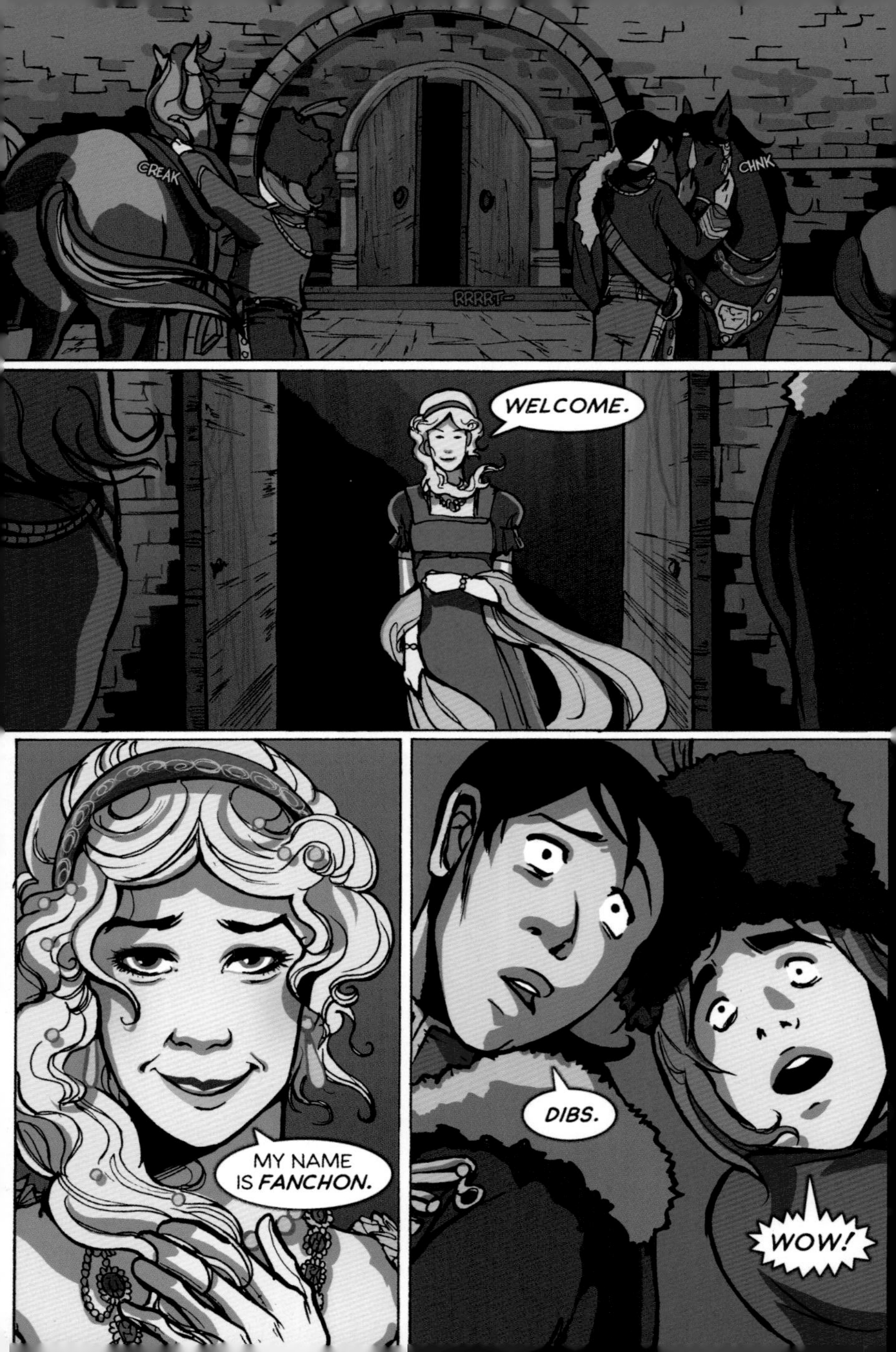
CREAK
CHNK
RRRRT-
WELCOME.
MY NAME IS *FANCHON*.
DIBS.
WOW!

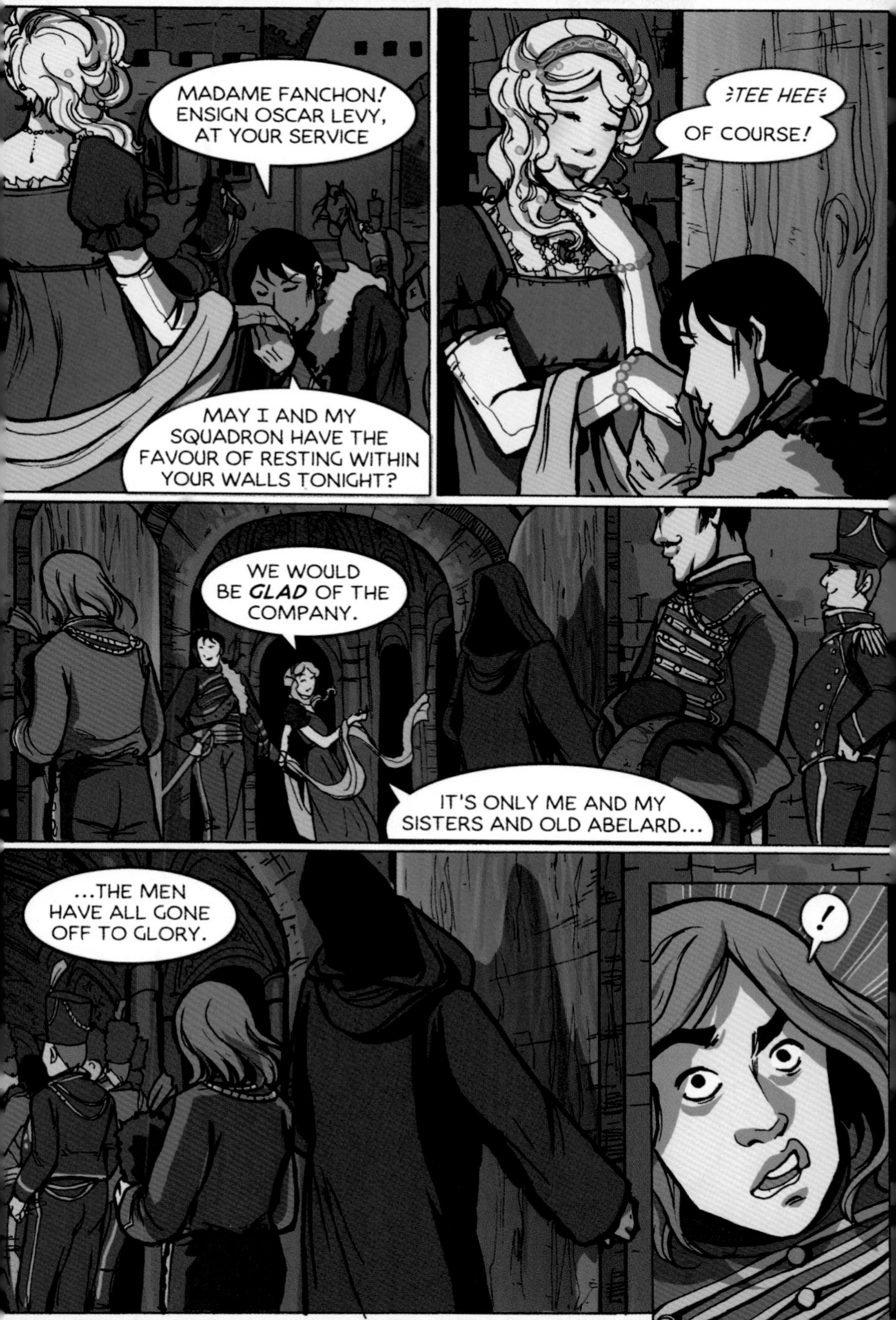
MADAME FANCHON! ENSIGN OSCAR LEVY, AT YOUR SERVICE
MAY I AND MY SQUADRON HAVE THE FAVOUR OF RESTING WITHIN YOUR WALLS TONIGHT?
TEE HEE
OF COURSE!
WE WOULD BE GLAD OF THE COMPANY.
IT'S ONLY ME AND MY SISTERS AND OLD ABELARD...
...THE MEN HAVE ALL GONE OFF TO GLORY.
!

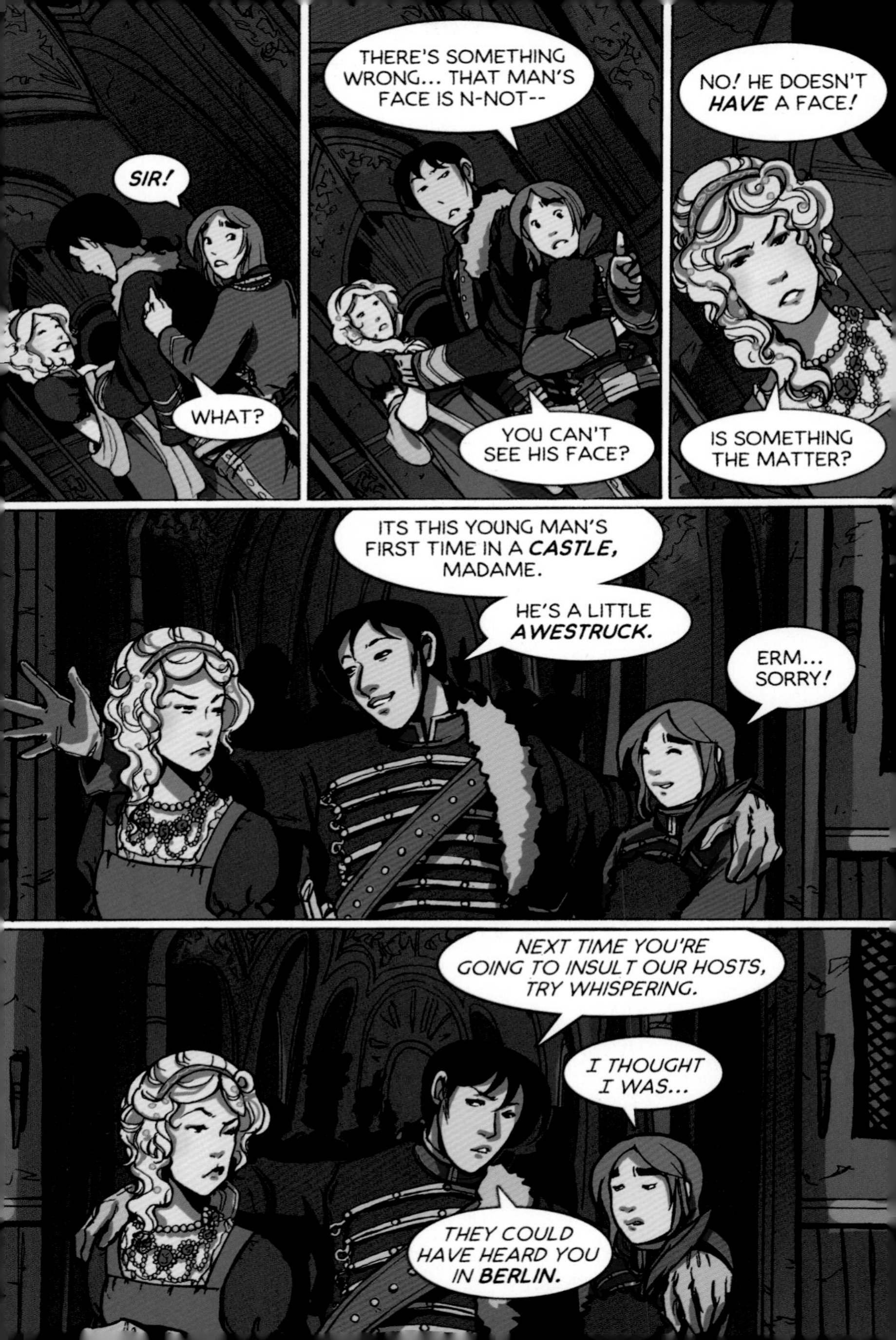
SIR!
WHAT?
THERE'S SOMETHING WRONG... THAT MAN'S FACE IS N-NOT--
YOU CAN'T SEE HIS FACE?
NO! HE DOESN'T *HAVE* A FACE!
IS SOMETHING THE MATTER?
ITS THIS YOUNG MAN'S FIRST TIME IN A *CASTLE,* MADAME.
HE'S A LITTLE *AWESTRUCK.*
ERM... SORRY!
NEXT TIME YOU'RE GOING TO INSULT OUR HOSTS, TRY WHISPERING.
I THOUGHT I WAS...
THEY COULD HAVE HEARD YOU IN ***BERLIN.***

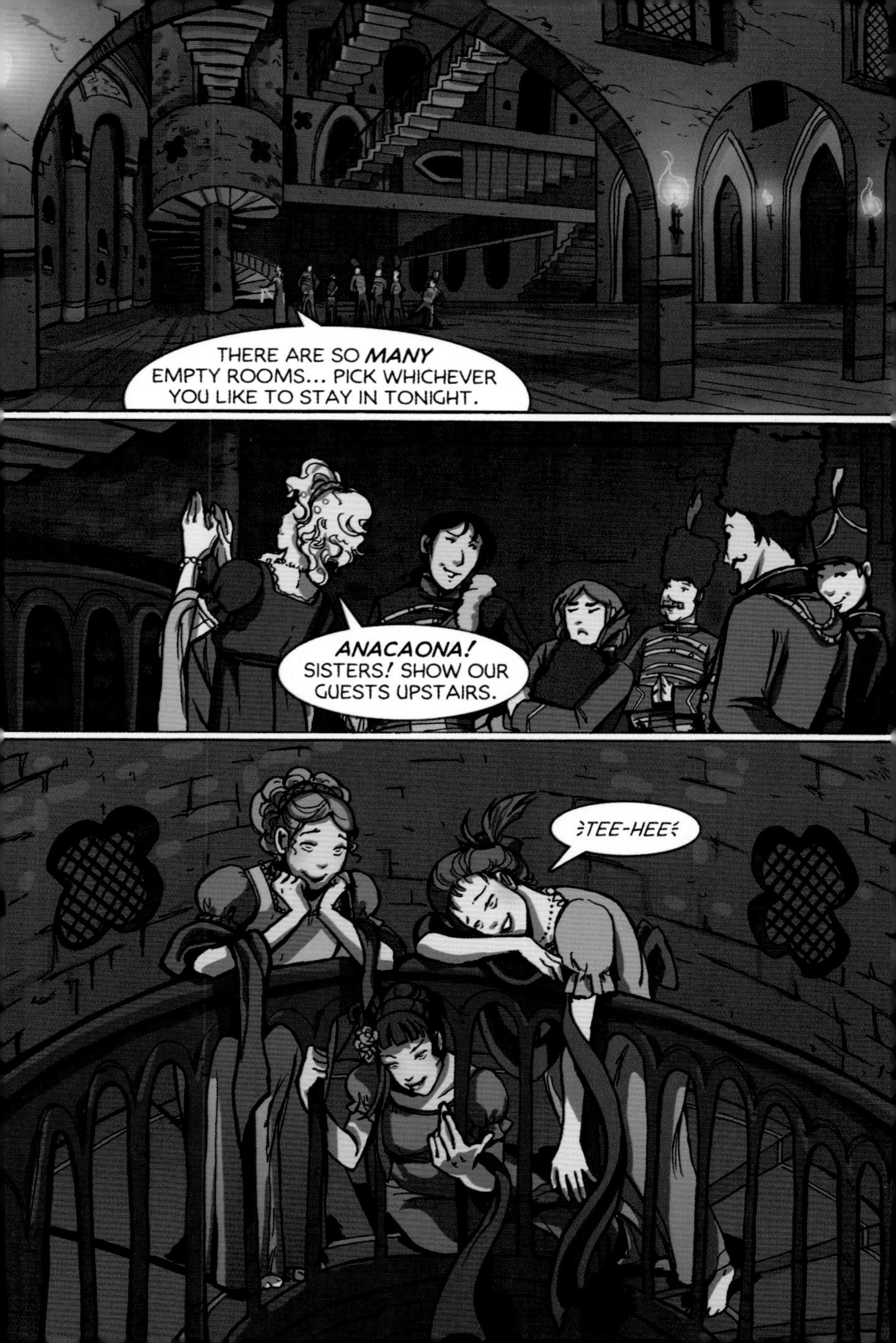
THERE ARE SO MANY EMPTY ROOMS... PICK WHICHEVER YOU LIKE TO STAY IN TONIGHT.
ANACAONA! SISTERS! SHOW OUR GUESTS UPSTAIRS.
TEE-HEE

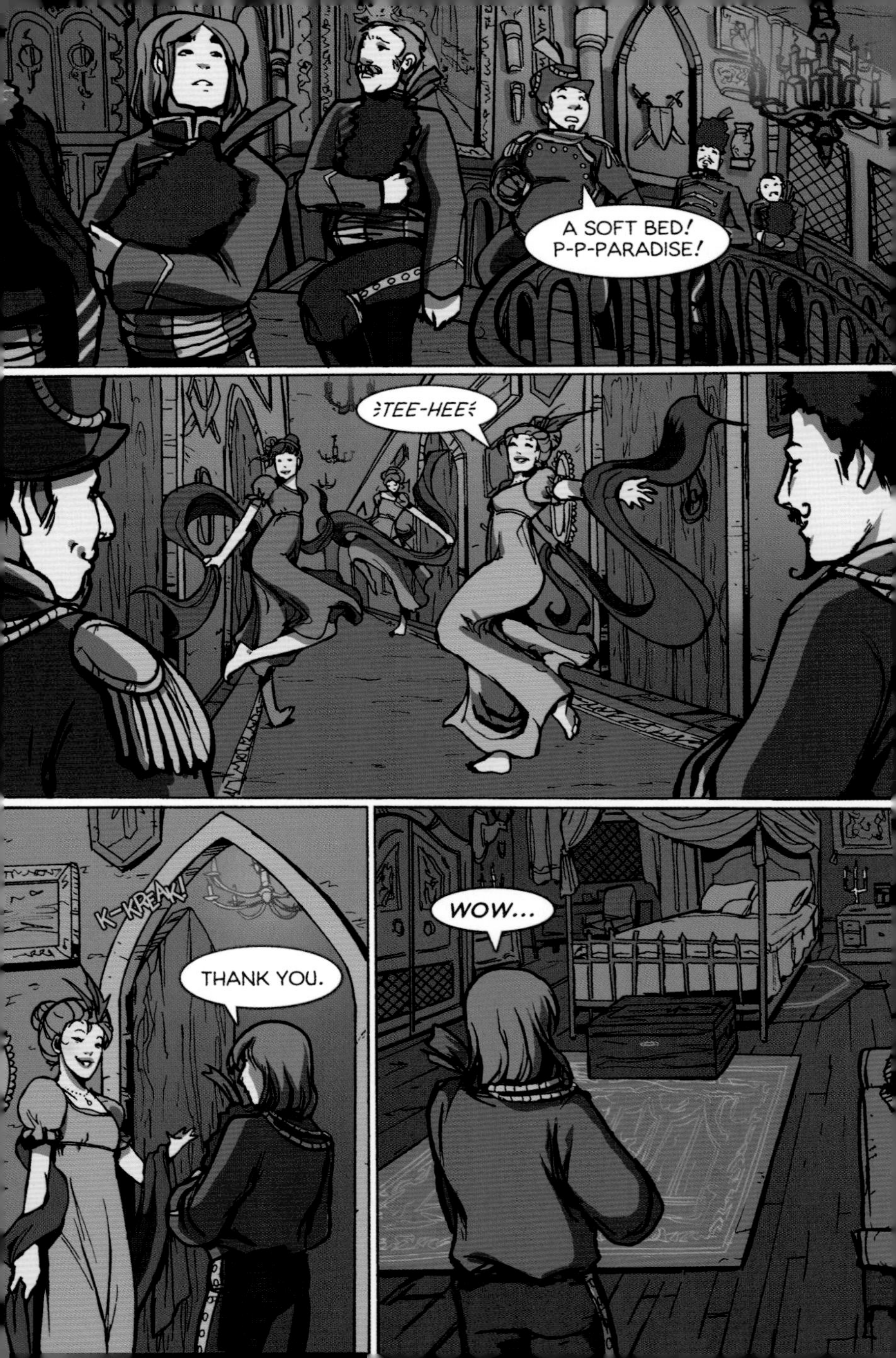
A SOFT BED! P-P-PARADISE!
TEE-HEE
K-KREAK!
THANK YOU.
WOW...

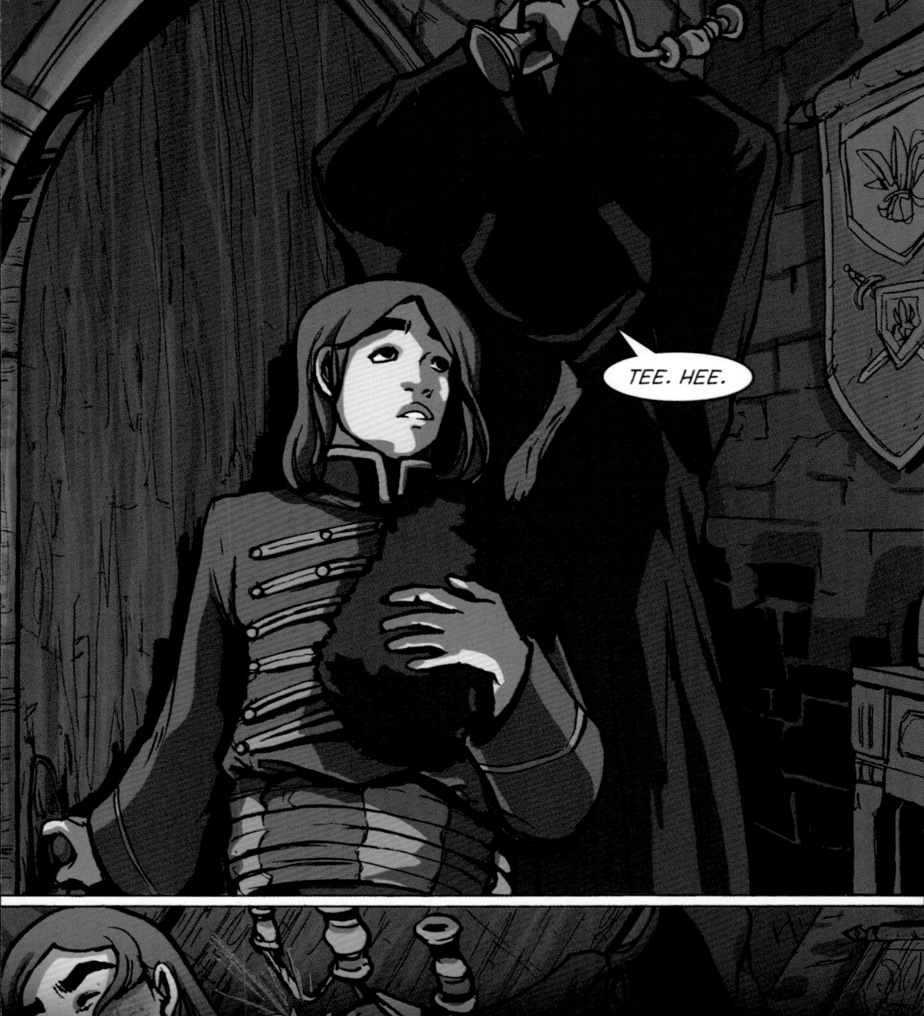
TEE. HEE.
KRAK!

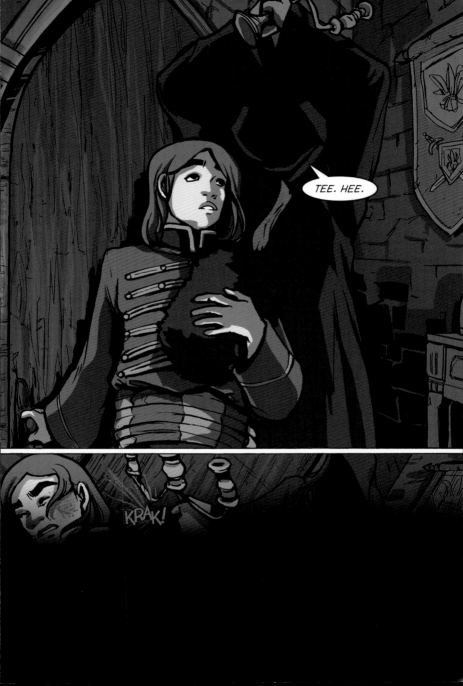

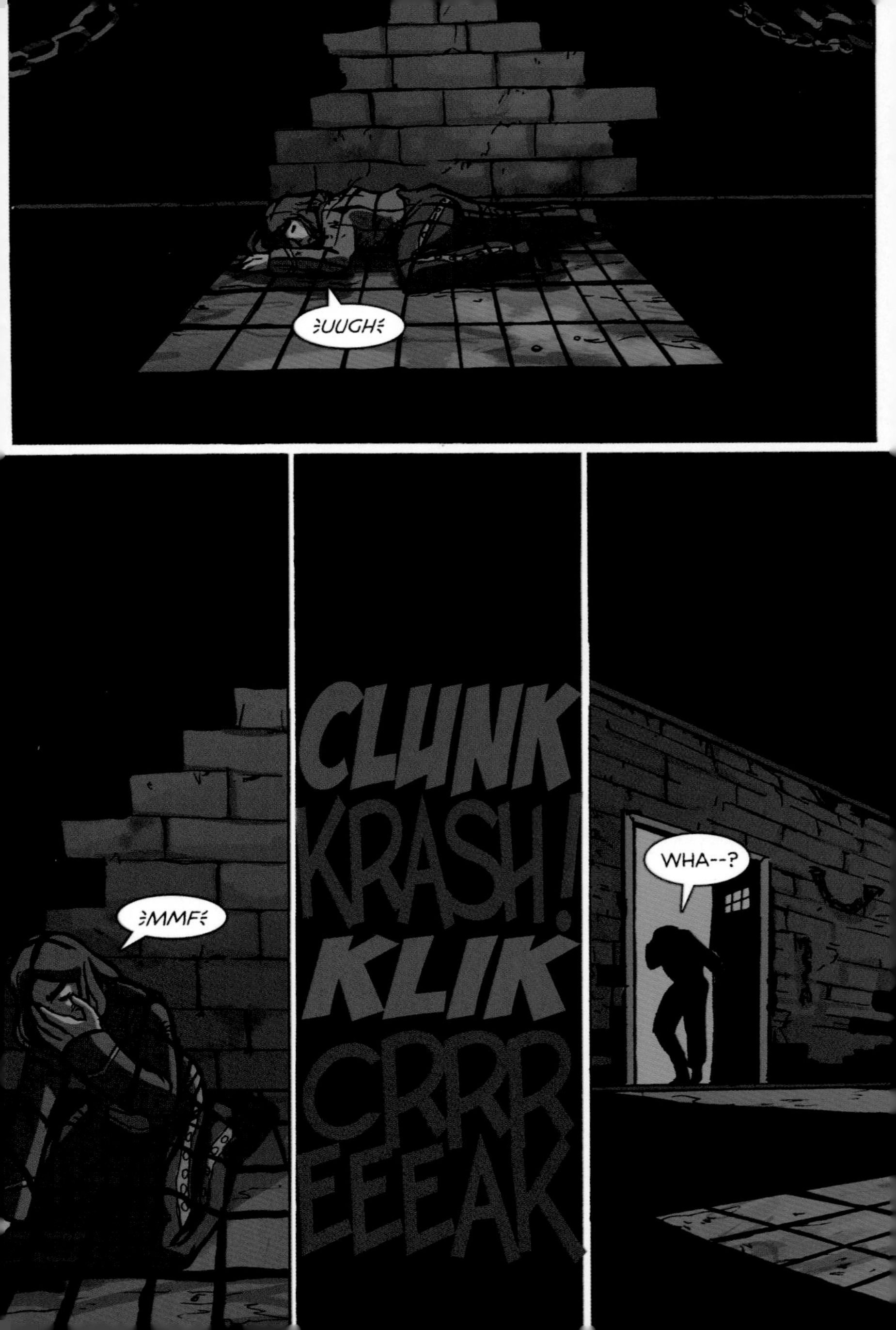
UUGH
MMF
CLUNK
KRASH!
KLIK
CRRR
EEEAK
WHA--?

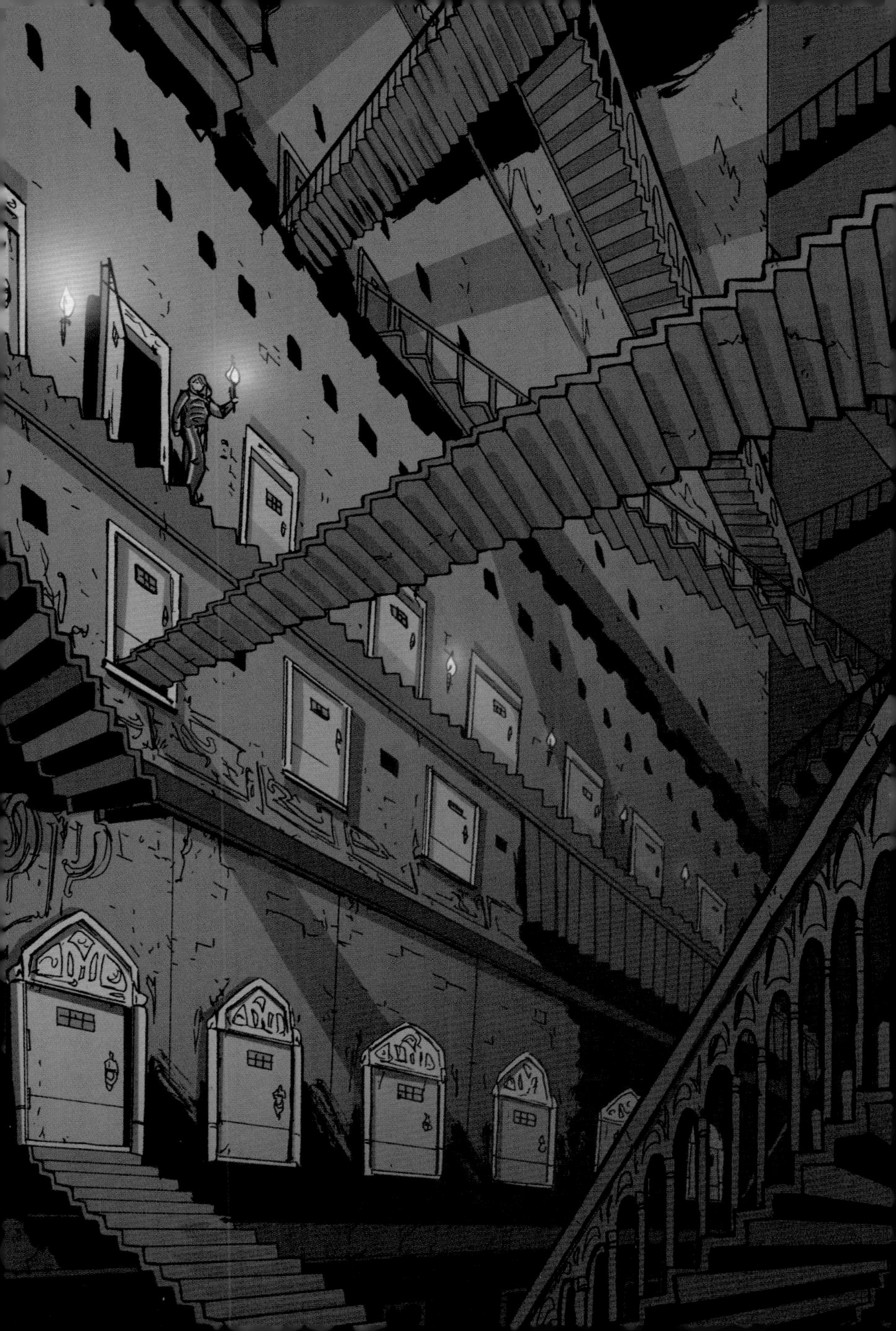

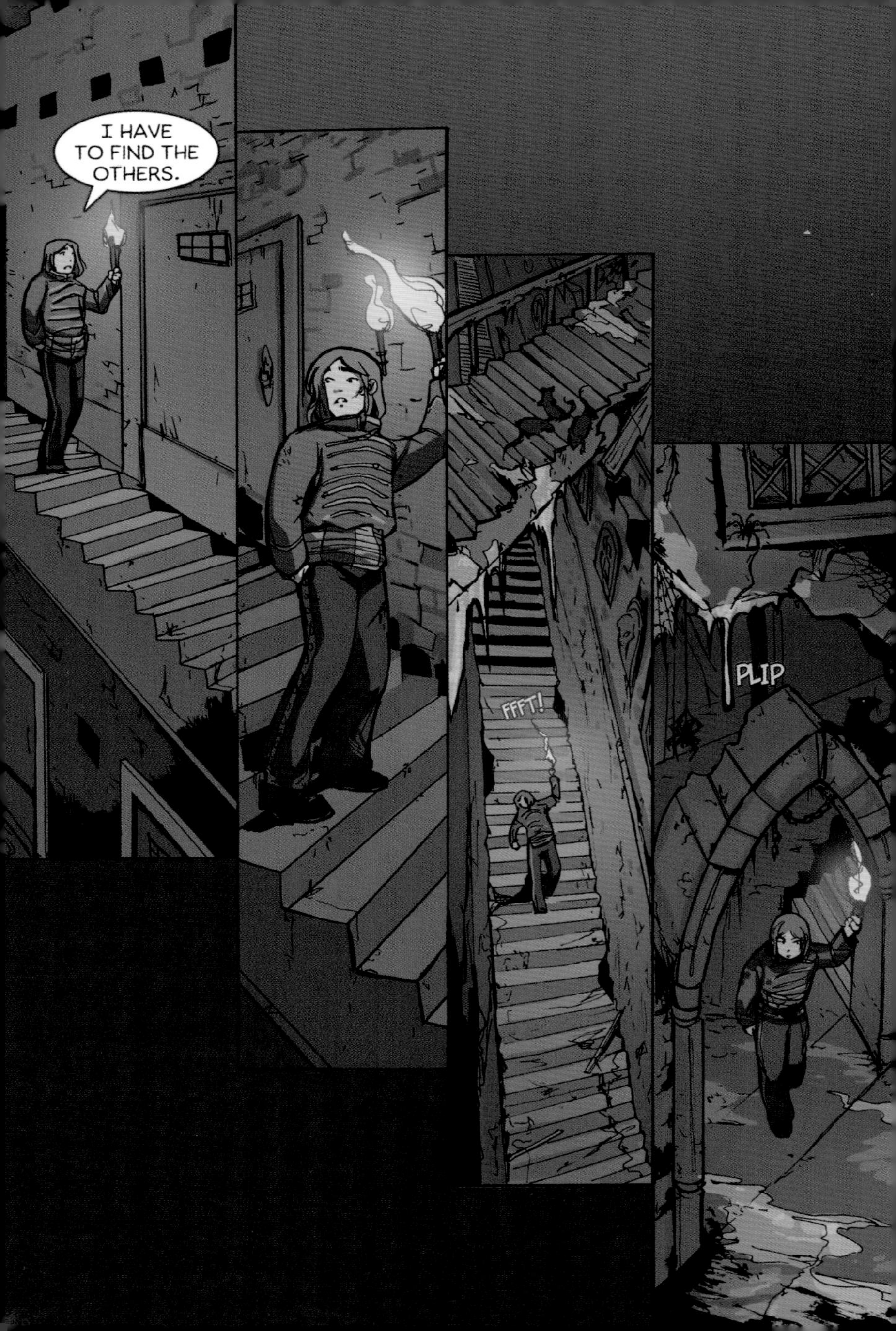
I HAVE TO FIND THE OTHERS.
FFFT!
PLIP

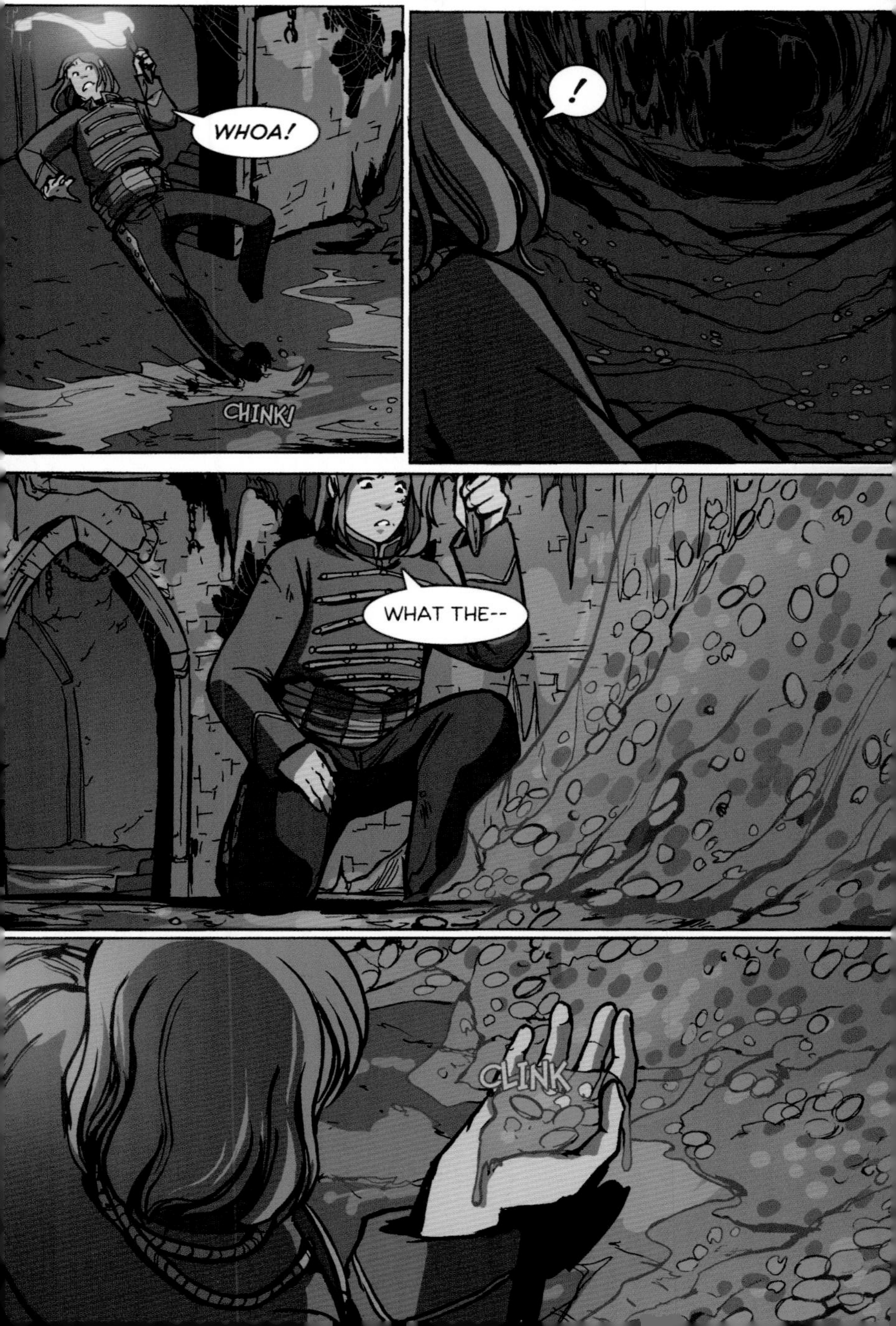
WHOA!
CHINK!
!
WHAT THE--
CLINK

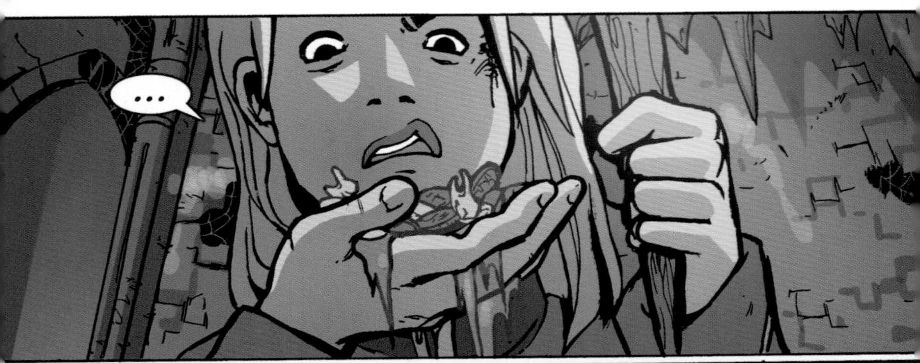
...
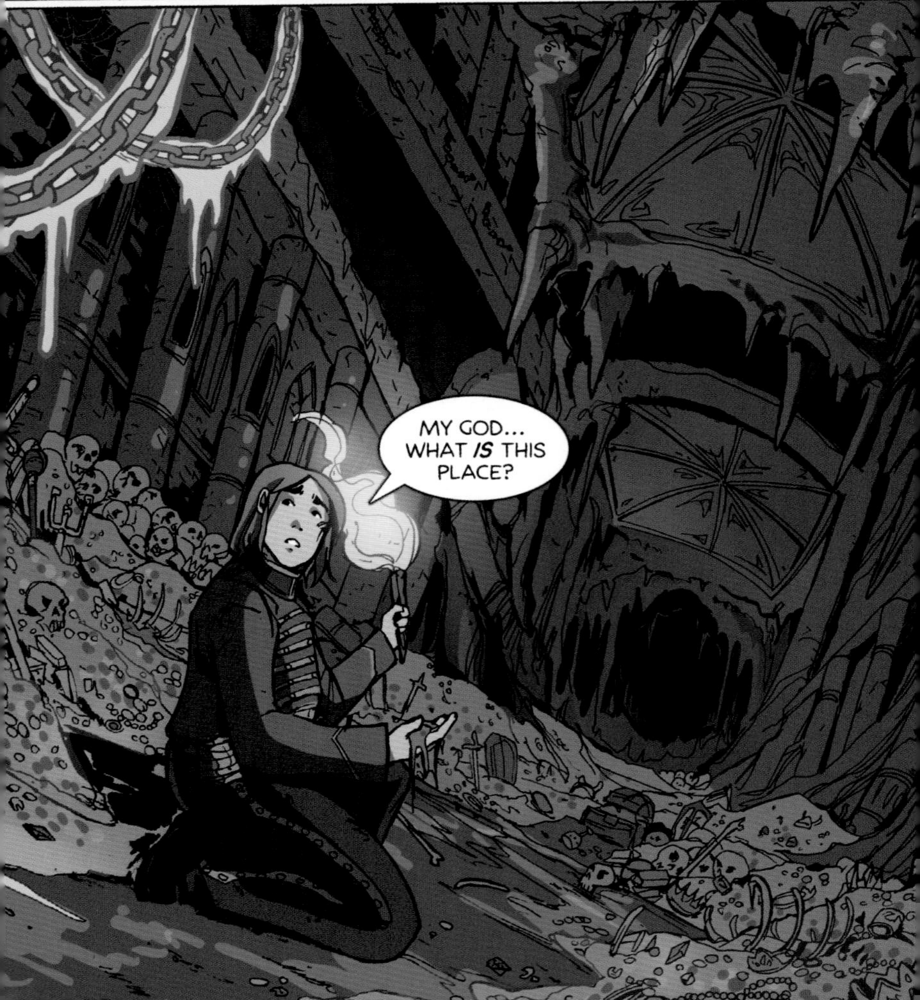
MY GOD... WHAT *IS* THIS PLACE?

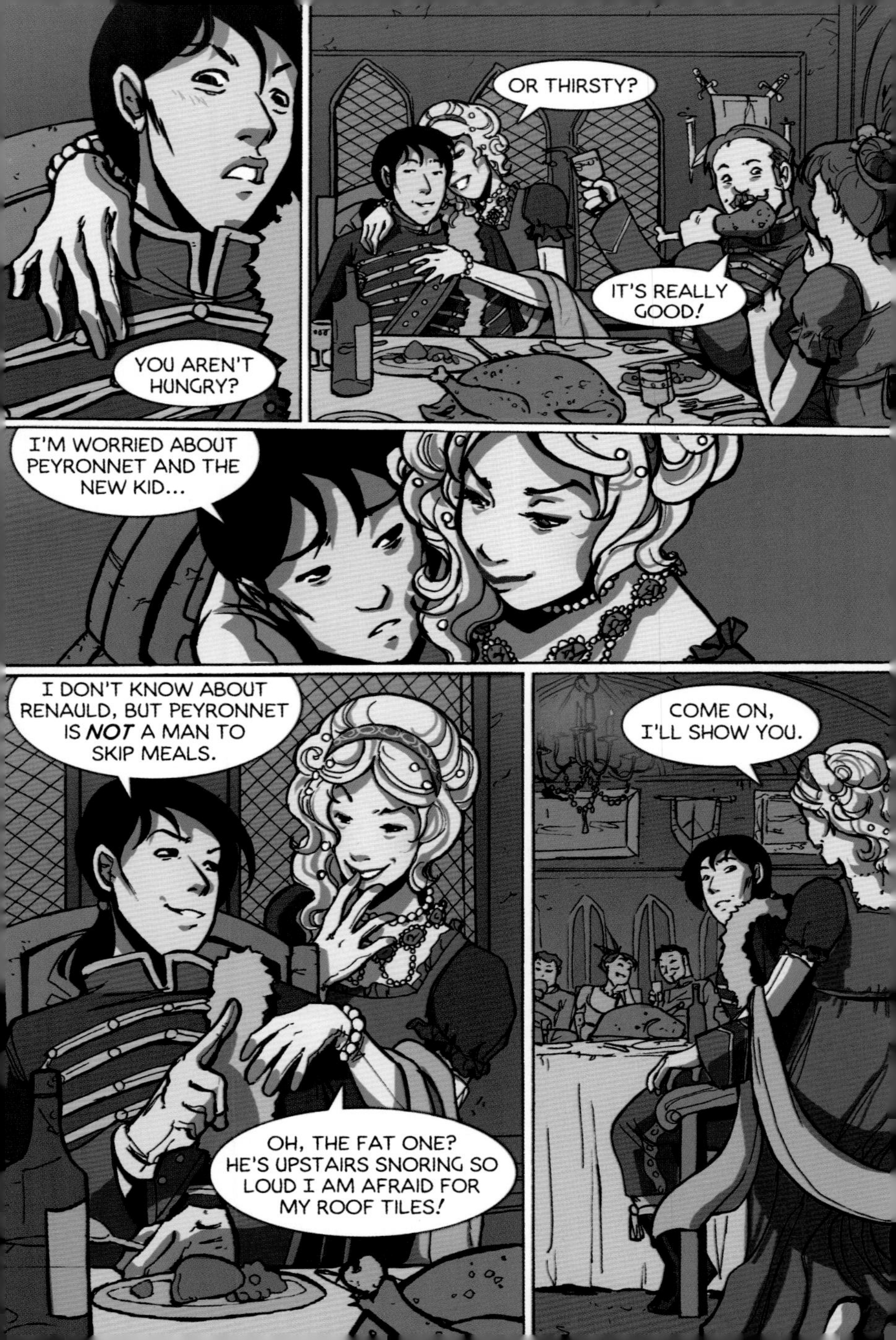
YOU AREN'T HUNGRY?
OR THIRSTY?
IT'S REALLY GOOD!
I'M WORRIED ABOUT PEYRONNET AND THE NEW KID...
I DON'T KNOW ABOUT RENAULD, BUT PEYRONNET IS NOT A MAN TO SKIP MEALS.
OH, THE FAT ONE? HE'S UPSTAIRS SNORING SO LOUD I AM AFRAID FOR MY ROOF TILES!
COME ON, I'LL SHOW YOU.

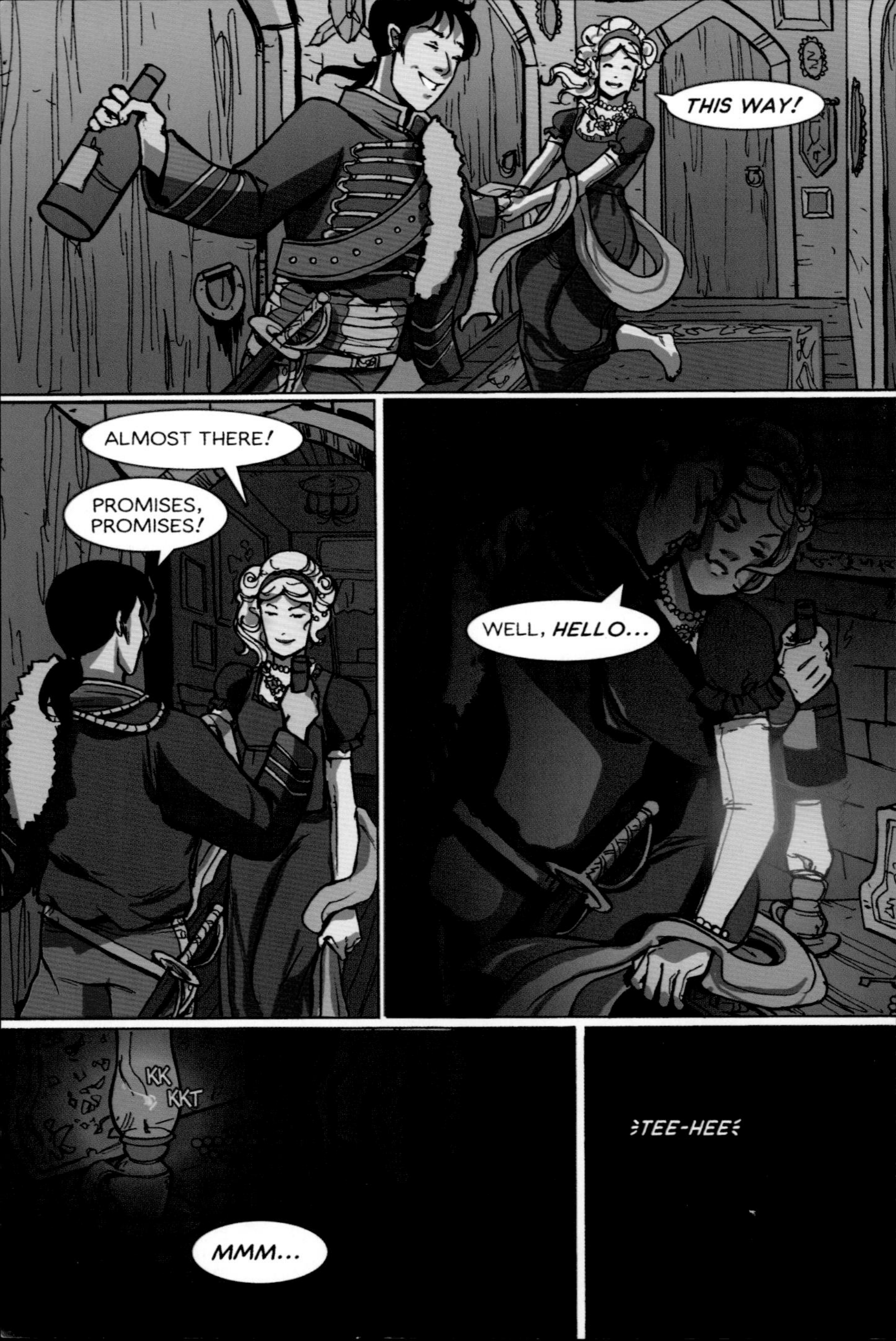
THIS WAY!
ALMOST THERE!
PROMISES, PROMISES!
WELL, HELLO...
KK KKT
MMM...
TEE-HEE

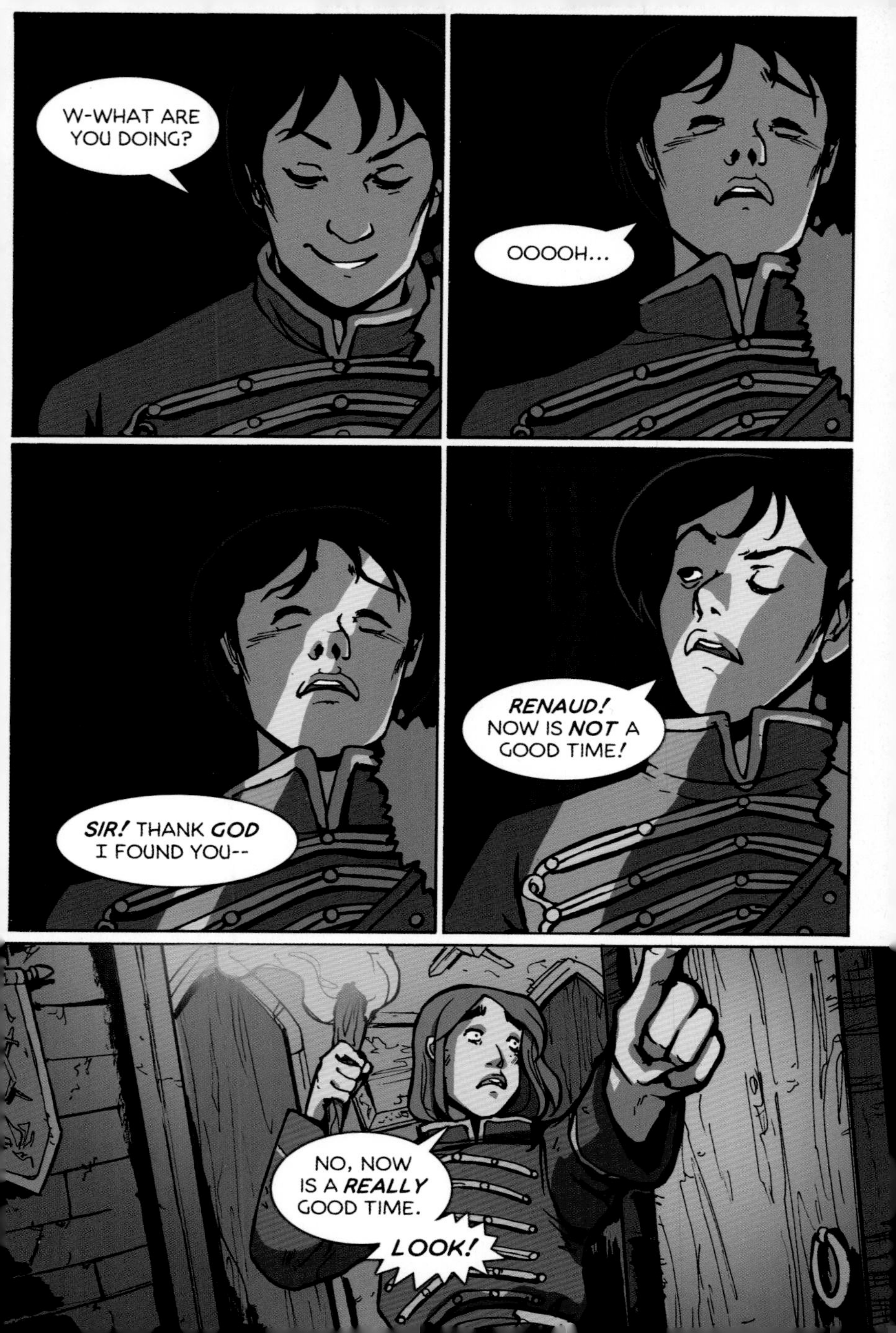
W-WHAT ARE YOU DOING?
OOOOH...
SIR! THANK GOD I FOUND YOU--
RENAUD! NOW IS NOT A GOOD TIME!
NO, NOW IS A REALLY GOOD TIME.
LOOK!

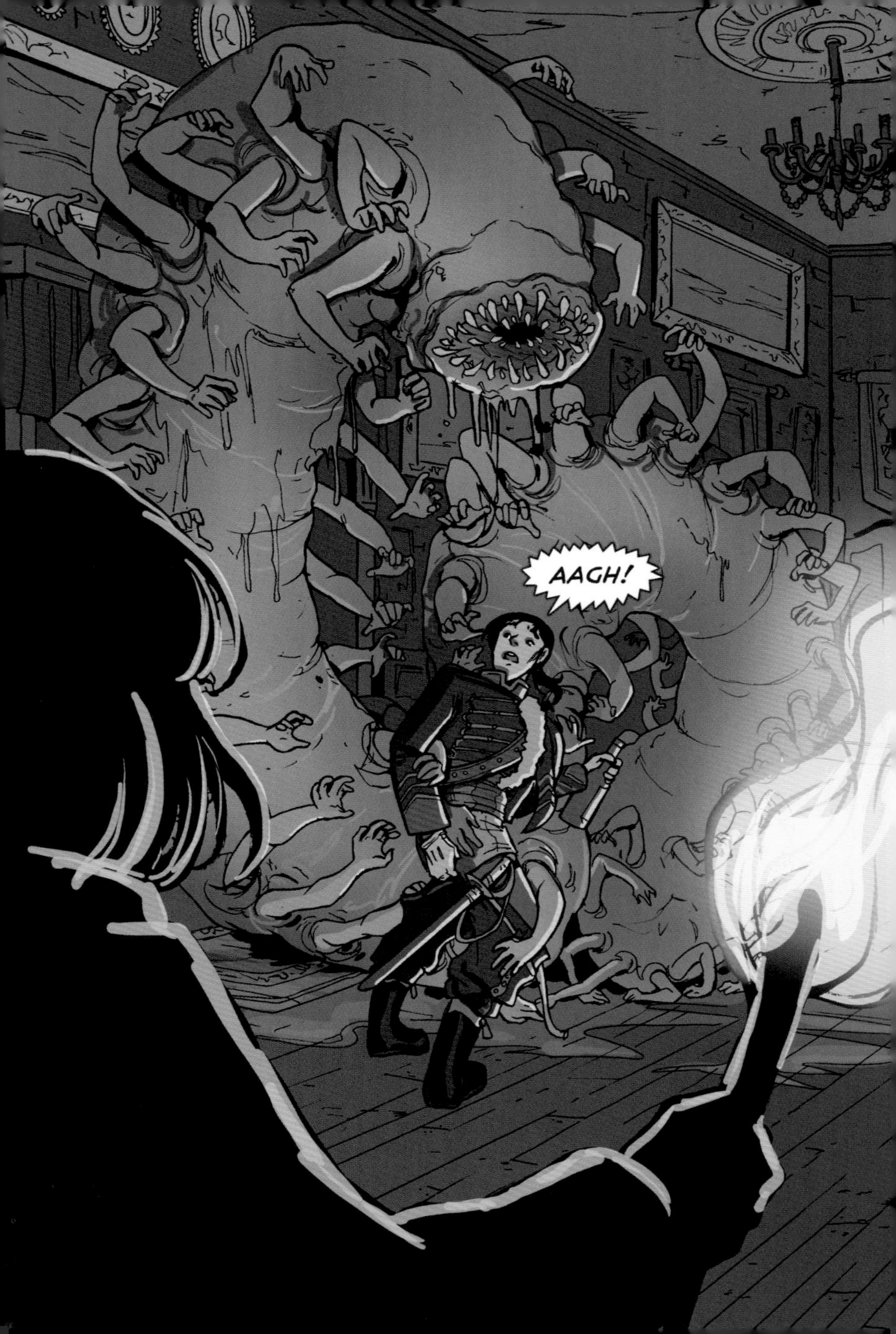
AAGH!

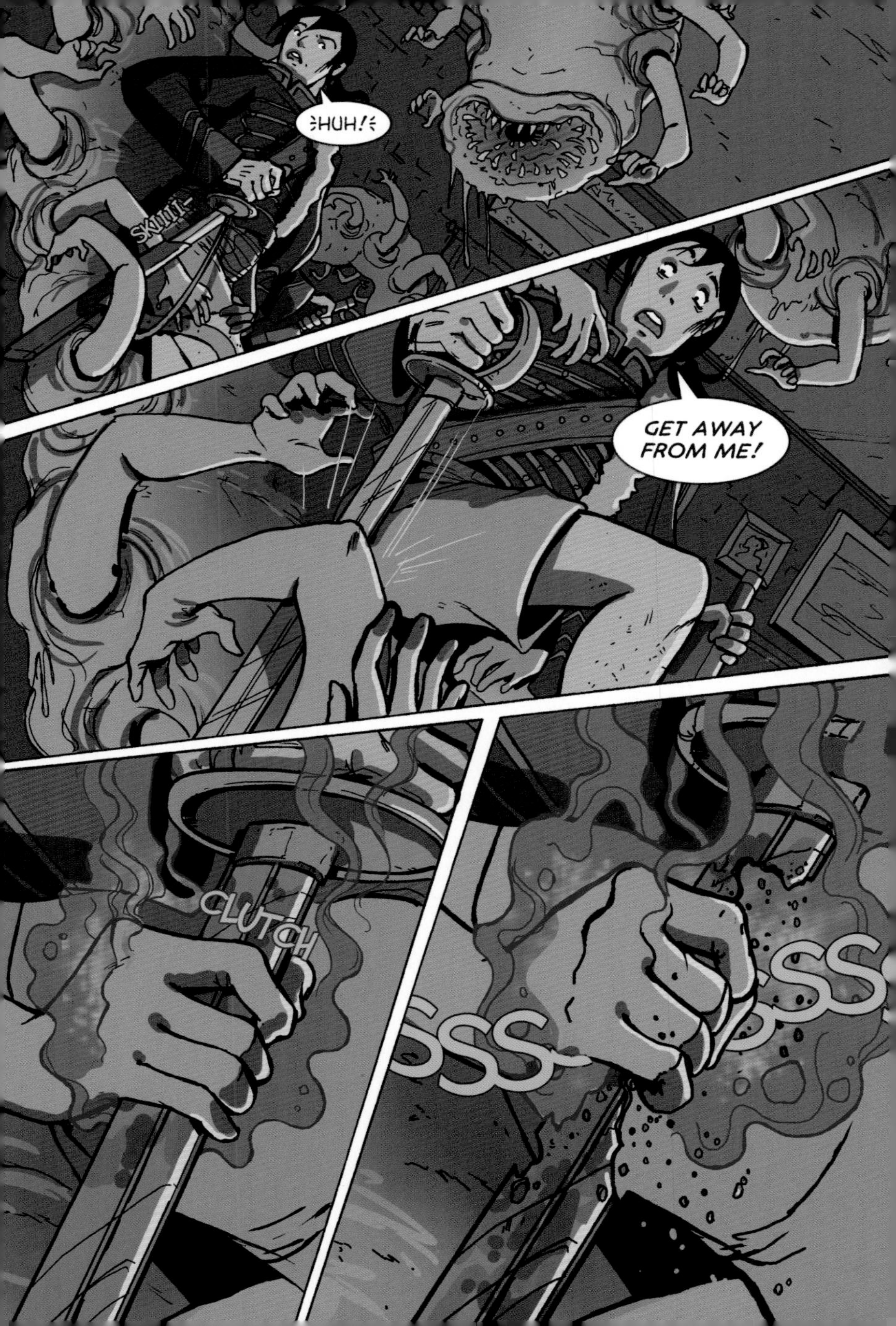

HUH!
SKIIII-
GET AWAY FROM ME!
CLUTCH
SSS
SSS

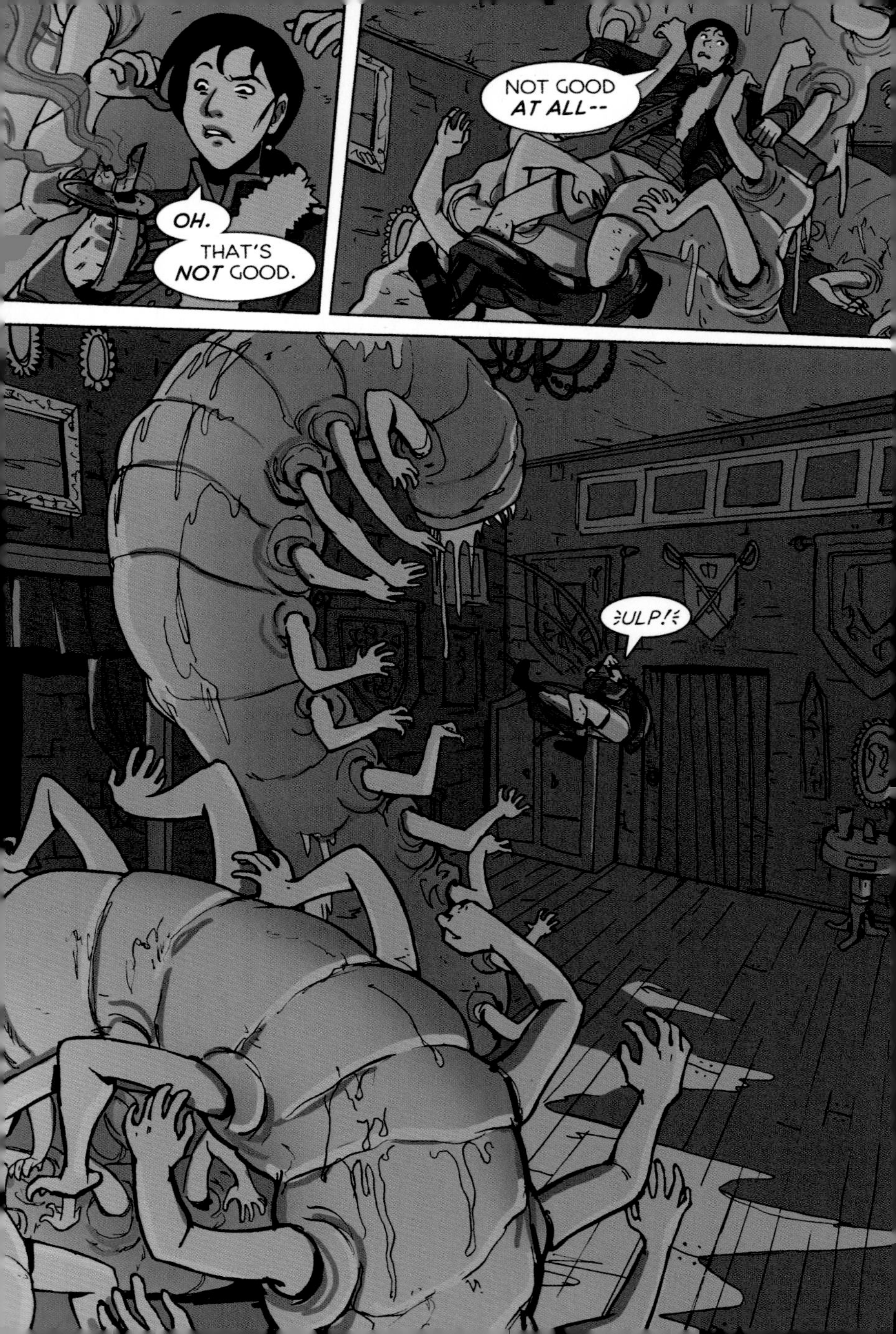
OH.
THAT'S NOT GOOD.
NOT GOOD AT ALL--
ULP!

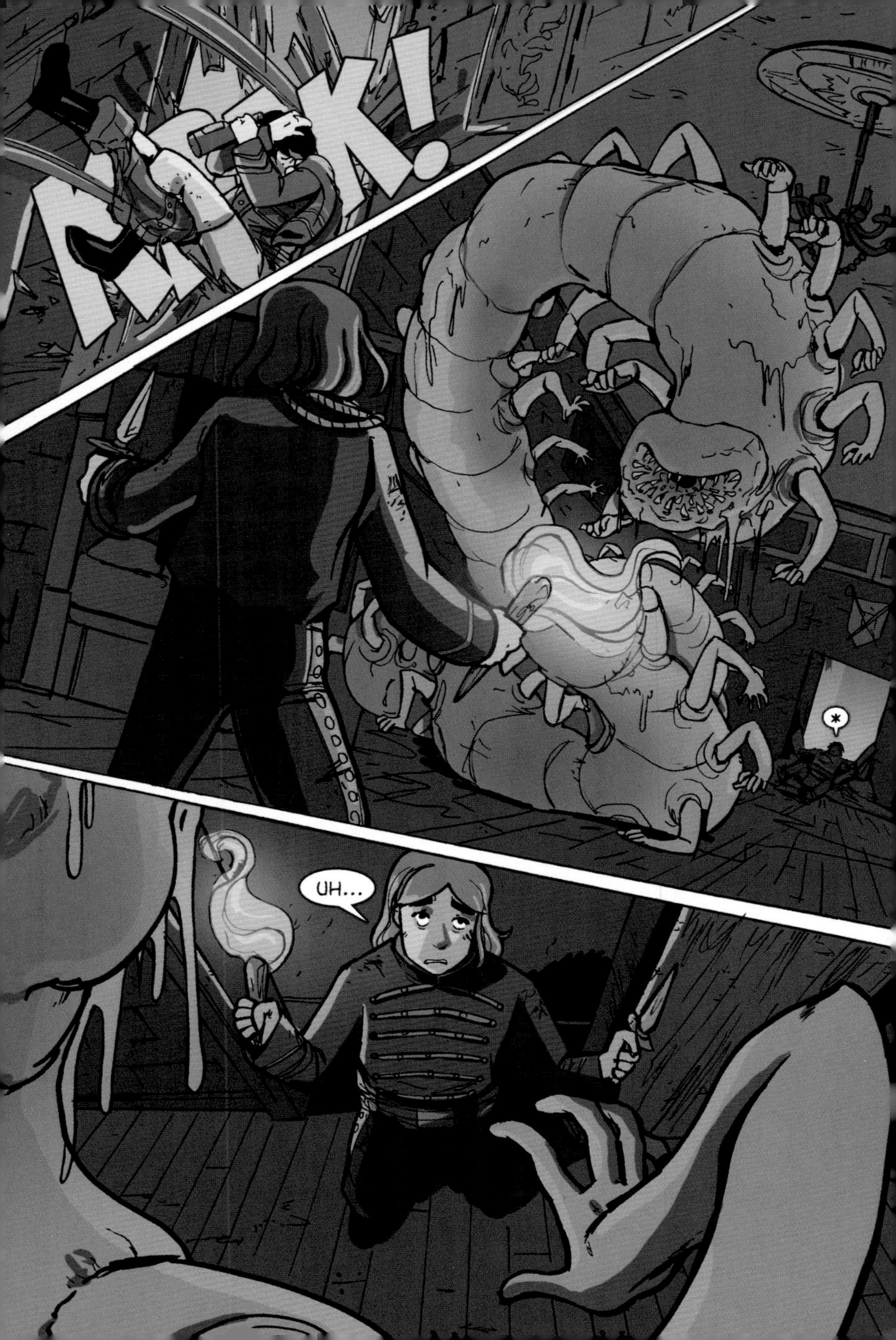

*
UH...

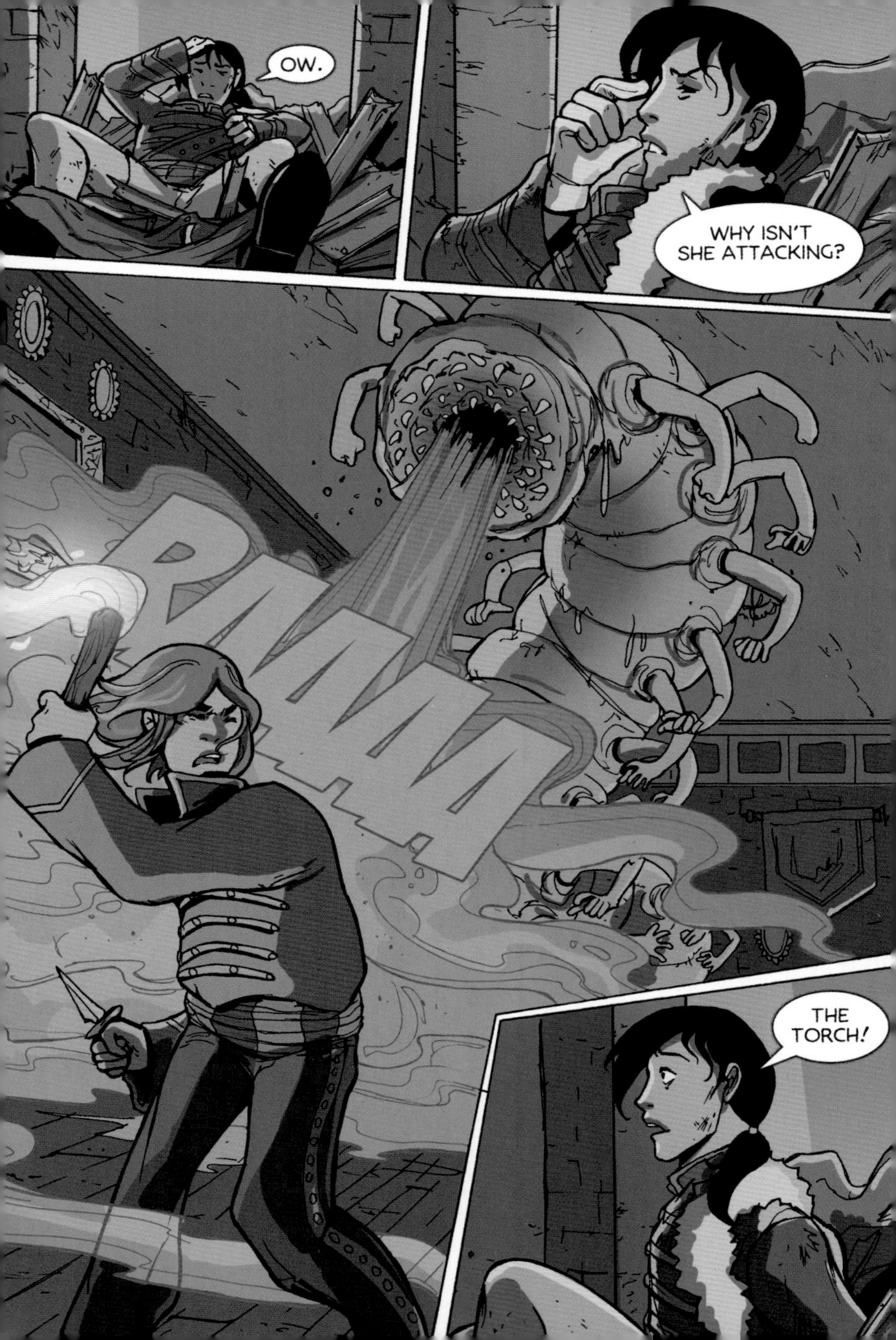
OW.
WHY ISN'T SHE ATTACKING?
BAAAAA
THE TORCH!

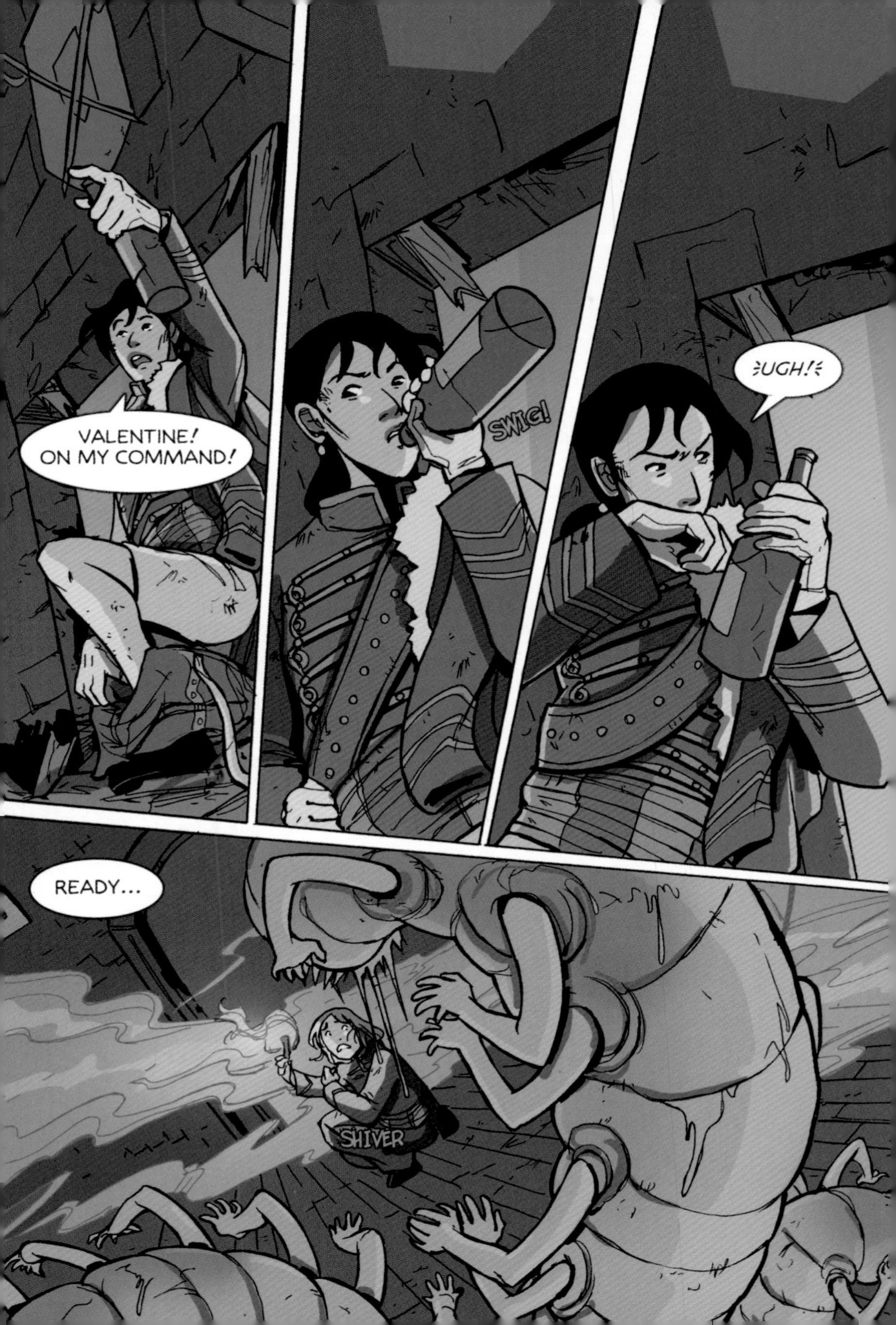

VALENTINE! ON MY COMMAND!
SWIG!
UGH!
READY...
SHIVER

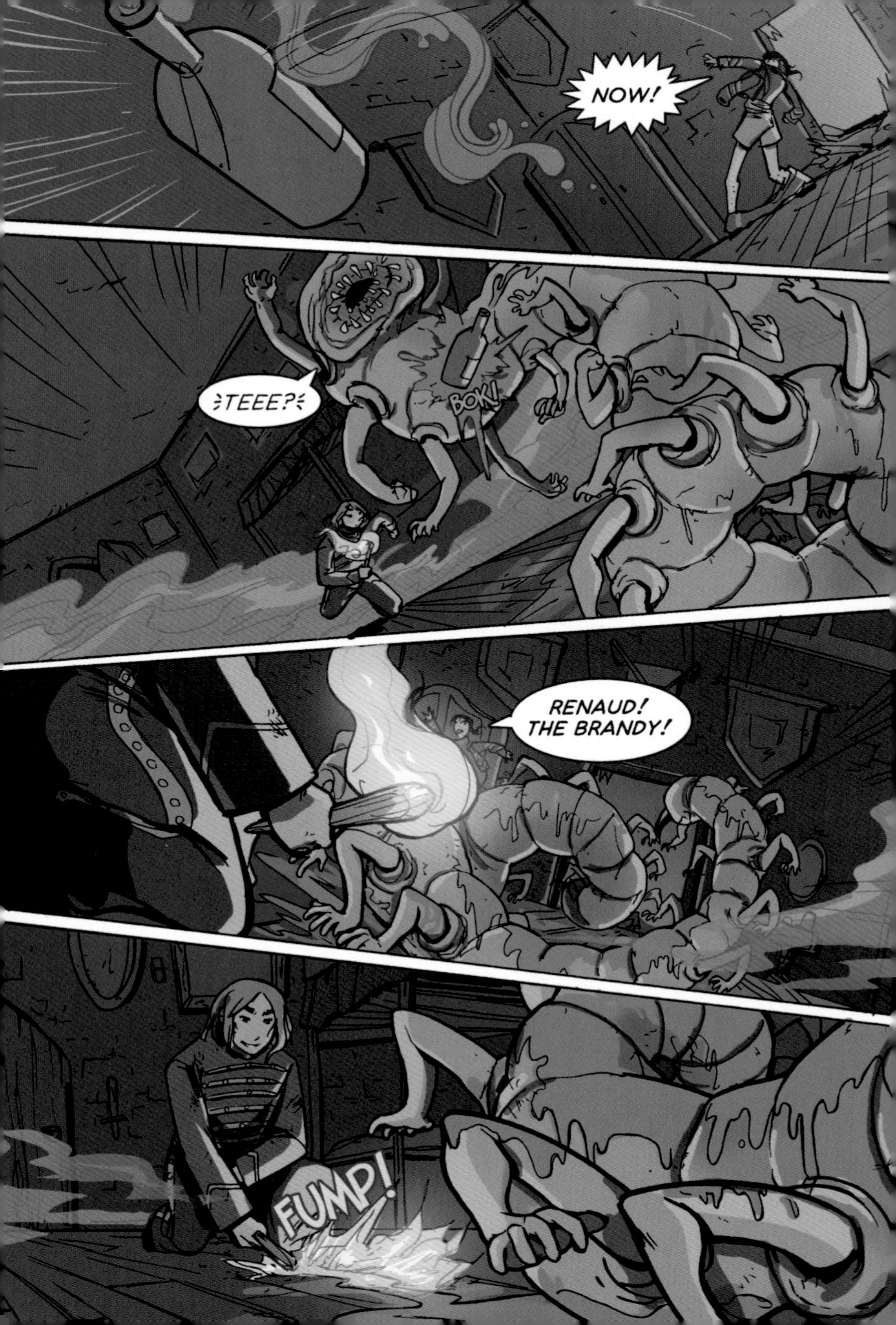
NOW!
TEEE?
BOK!
RENAUD! THE BRANDY!
FUMP!

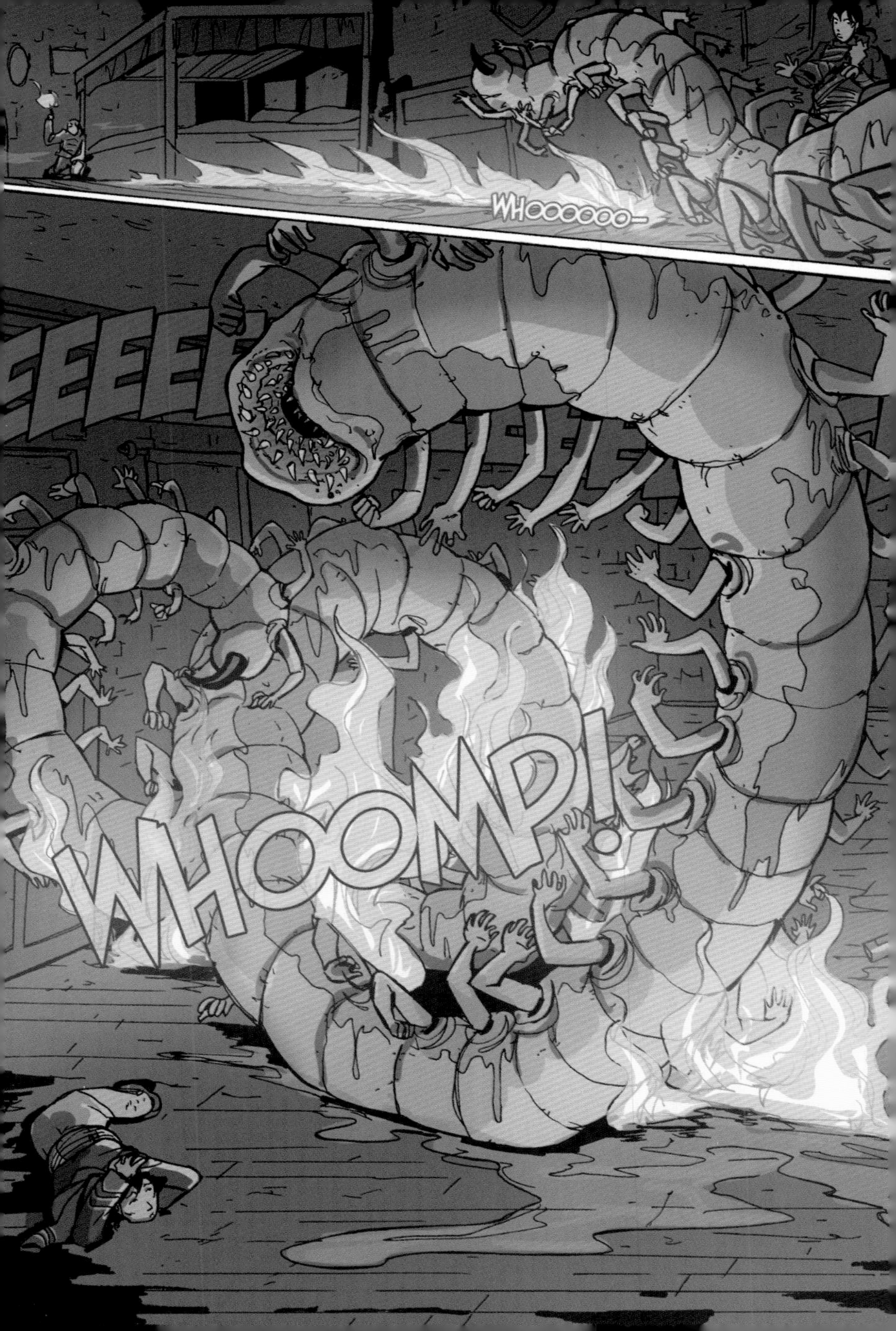
WHOOOOOOO—
EEEEE
WHOOMP!

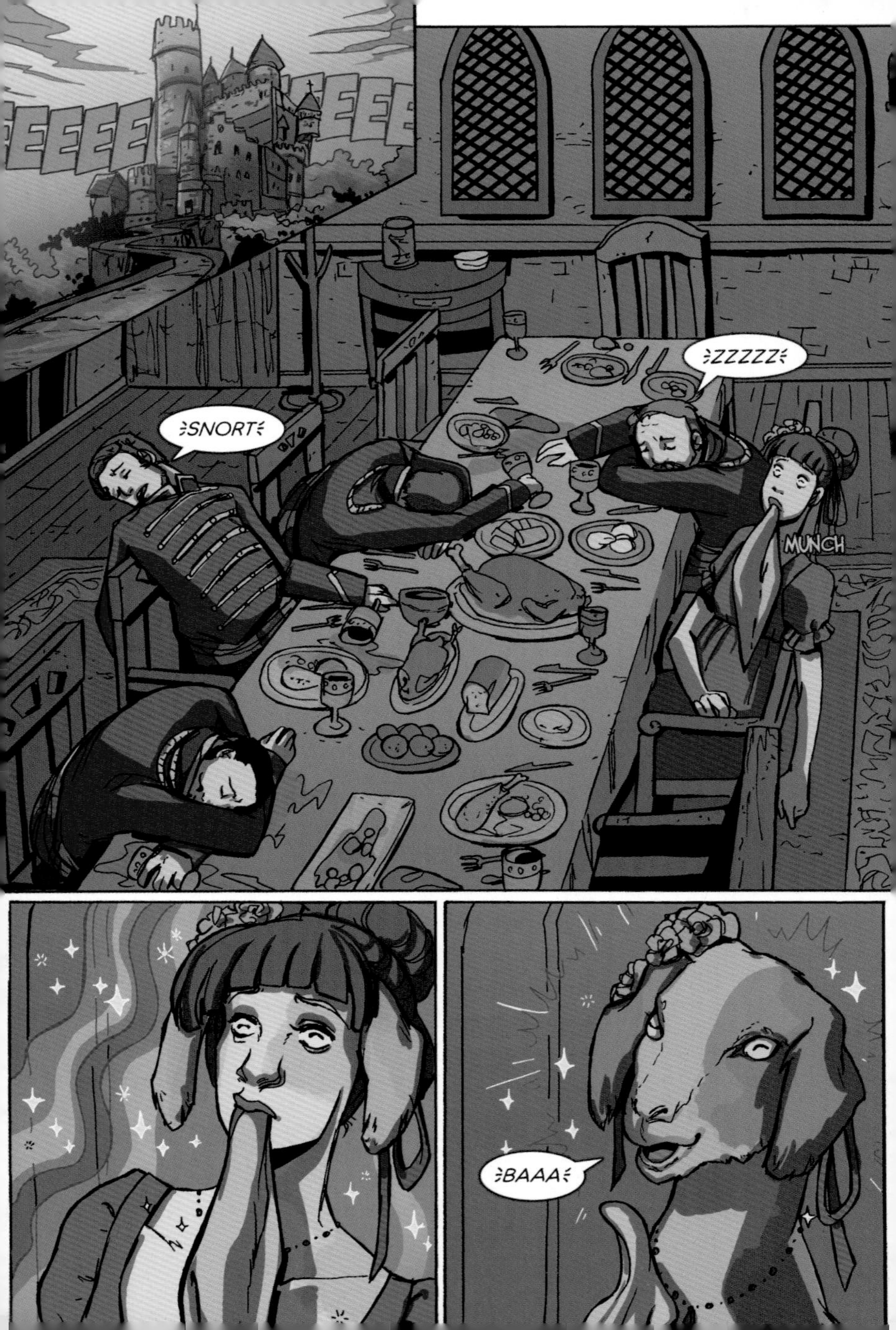
EEEEE
EEEE
SNORT
ZZZZZ
MUNCH
BAAA

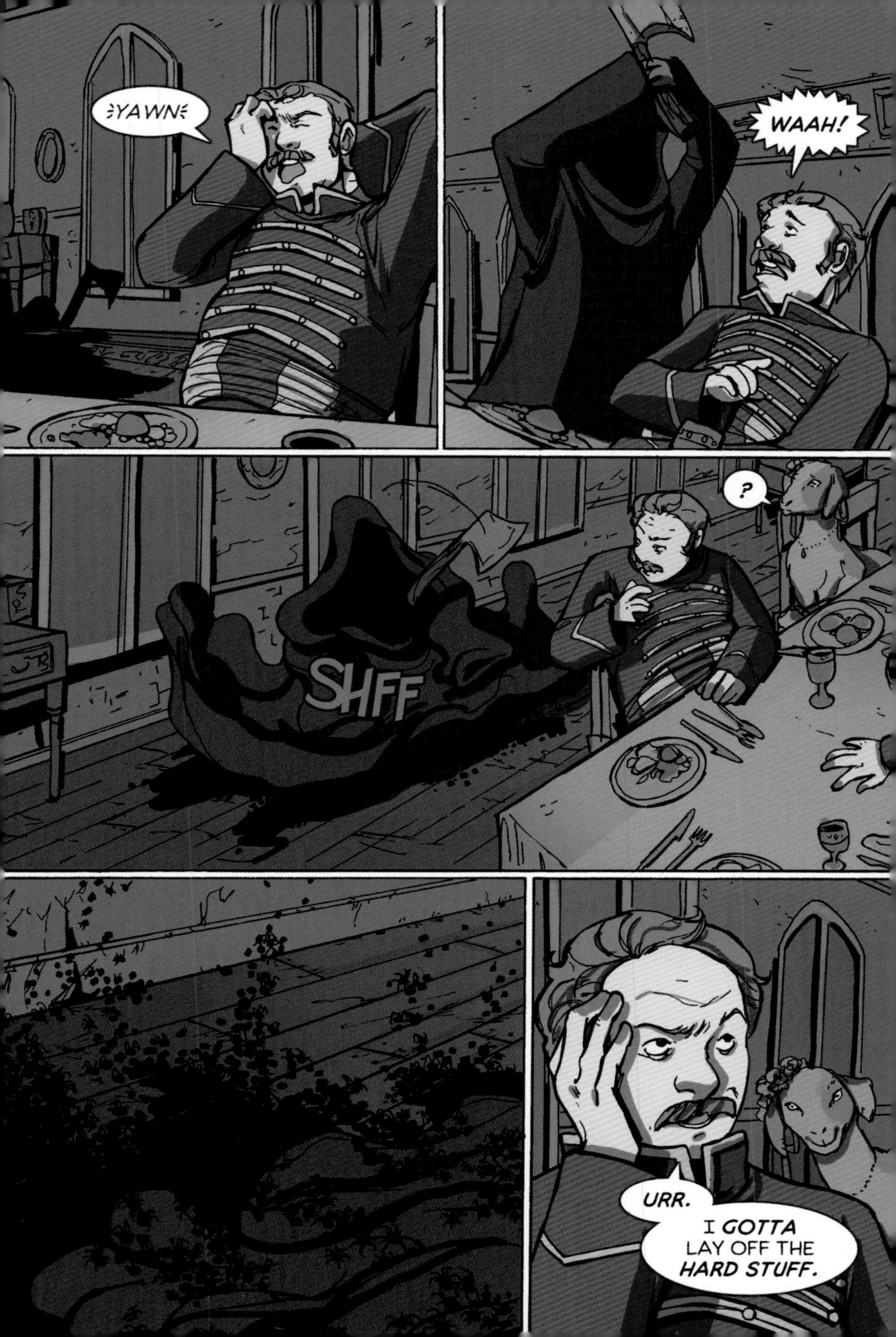
YAWN
WAAH!
SHFF
?
URR.
I GOTTA LAY OFF THE HARD STUFF.

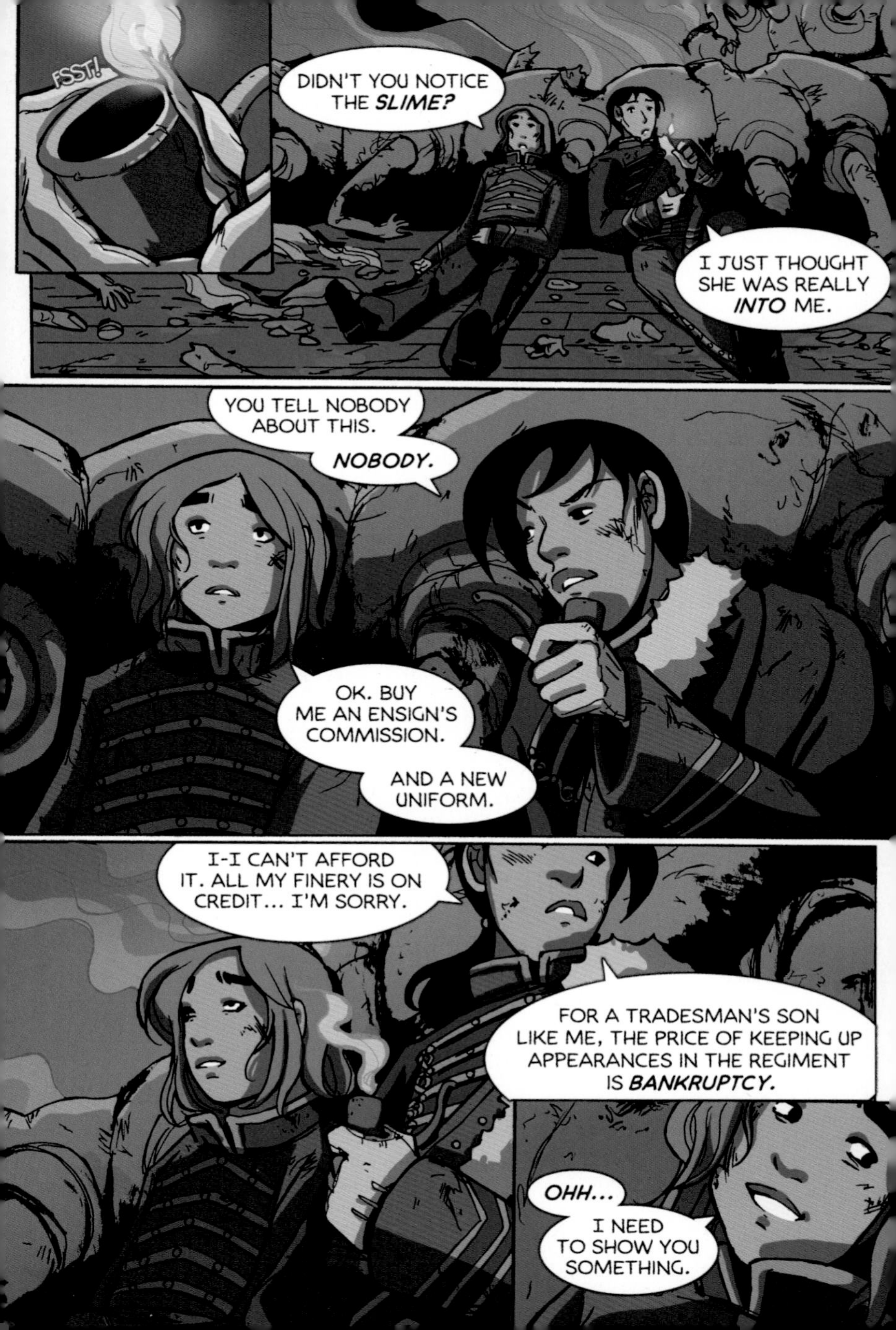
FSST!
DIDN'T YOU NOTICE THE SLIME?
I JUST THOUGHT SHE WAS REALLY INTO ME.
YOU TELL NOBODY ABOUT THIS.
NOBODY.
OK. BUY ME AN ENSIGN'S COMMISSION.
AND A NEW UNIFORM.
I-I CAN'T AFFORD IT. ALL MY FINERY IS ON CREDIT... I'M SORRY.
FOR A TRADESMAN'S SON LIKE ME, THE PRICE OF KEEPING UP APPEARANCES IN THE REGIMENT IS BANKRUPTCY.
OHH...
I NEED TO SHOW YOU SOMETHING.

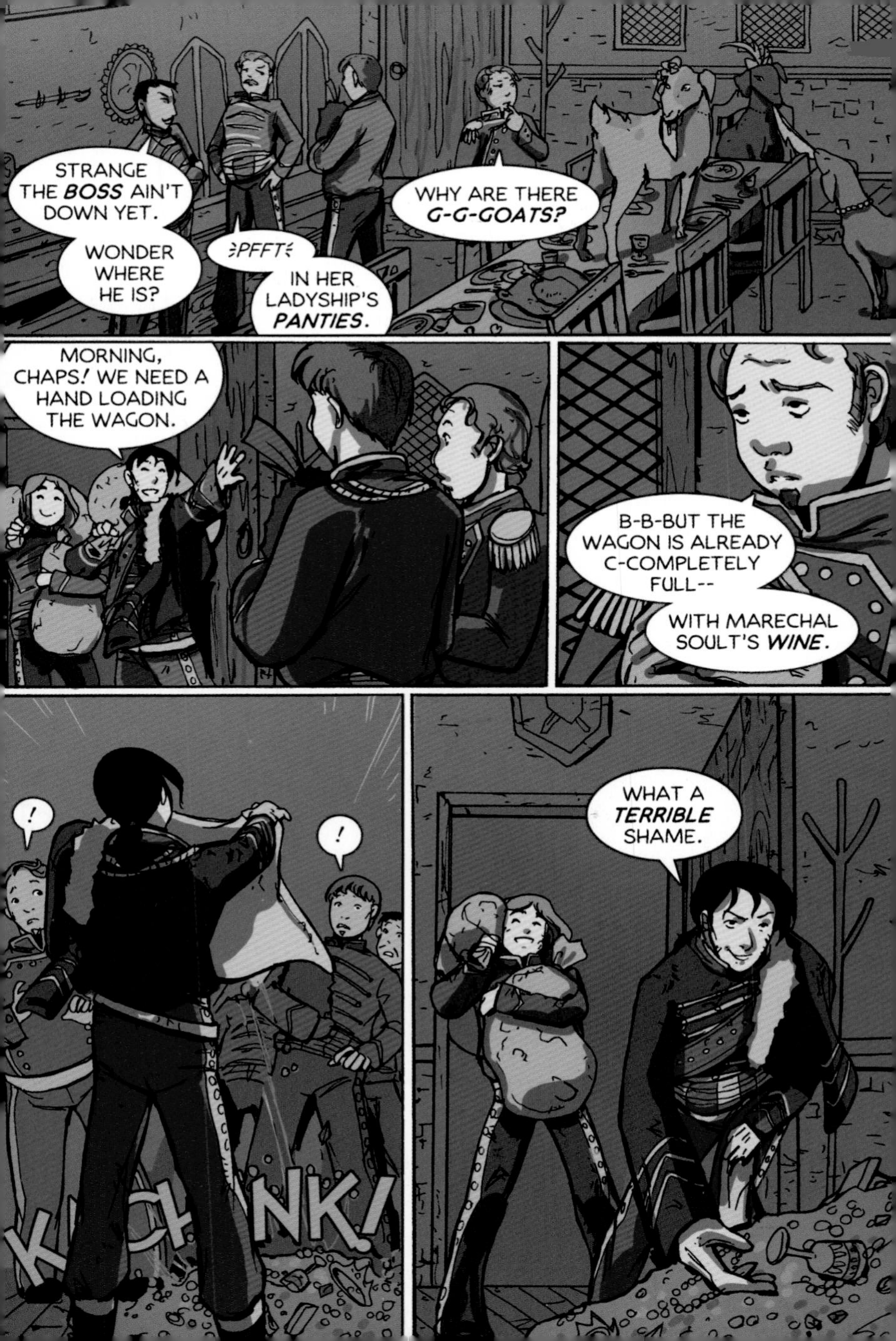
STRANGE THE BOSS AIN'T DOWN YET.
WONDER WHERE HE IS?
PFFT
IN HER LADYSHIP'S PANTIES.
WHY ARE THERE G-G-GOATS?
MORNING, CHAPS! WE NEED A HAND LOADING THE WAGON.
B-B-BUT THE WAGON IS ALREADY C-COMPLETELY FULL--
WITH MARECHAL SOULT'S WINE.
!
!
KLCHUNK!
WHAT A TERRIBLE SHAME.

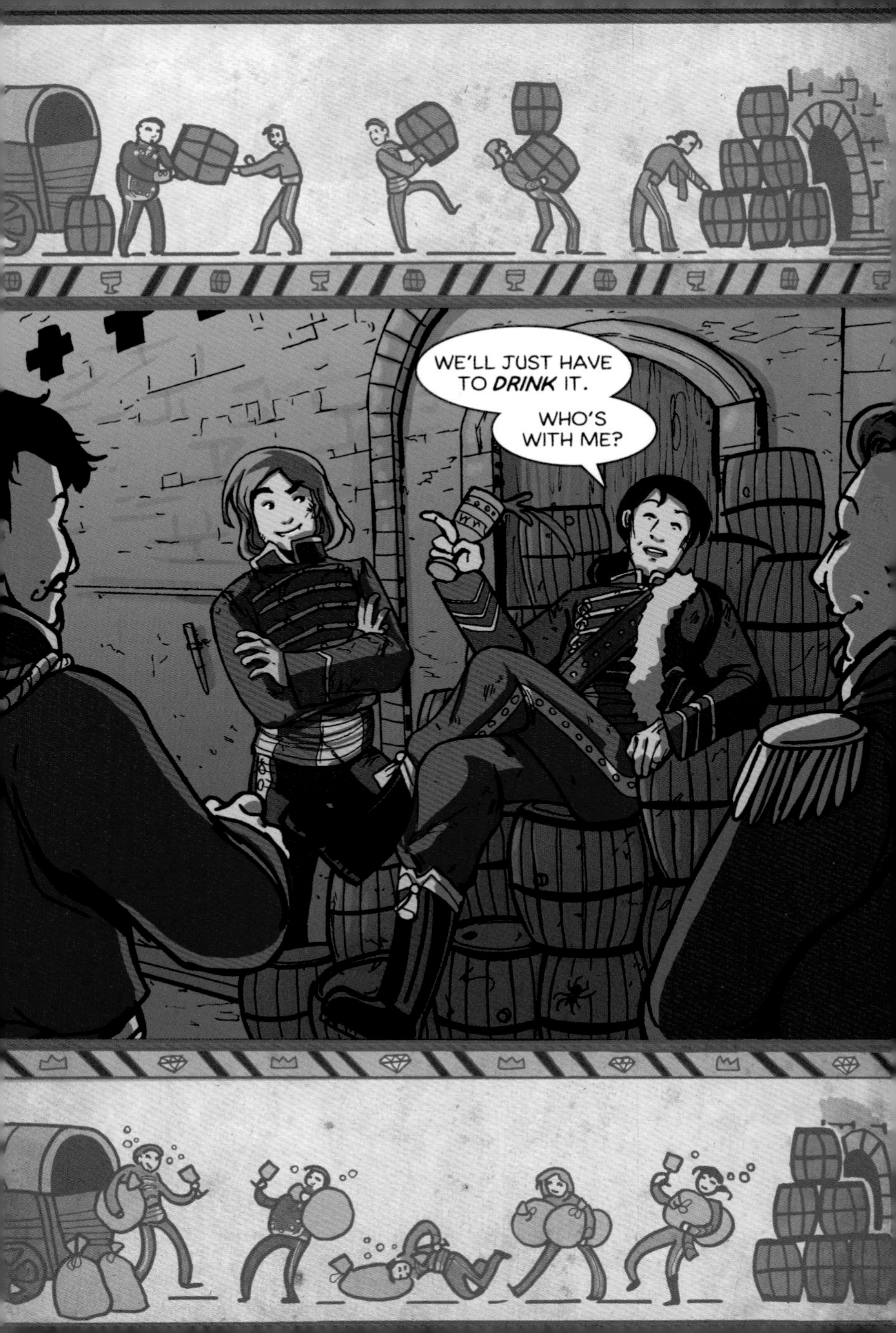
WE'LL JUST HAVE TO DRINK IT.
WHO'S WITH ME?

fin.

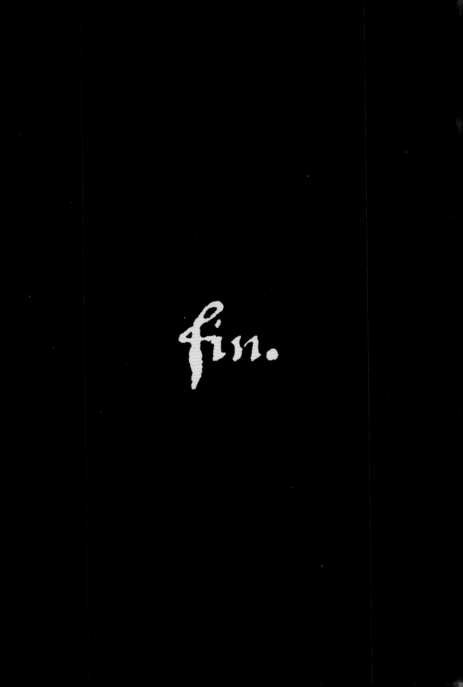

TIM DURNING is an illustrator from Philadelphia, PA. He's lucky enough to have drawn pictures for UPS, The New York Times, and Fantasy Flight Games and his other comic book credits include colors for Shrek, Cut the Rope, and Once Upon a Time Machine. He's got two cats, loves talking craft beer and homebrewing in his tiny South Philadelphia kitchen.

Originating from the pine barrens of central Jersey, CHRISTINE LARSEN is a Harvey Award nominated illustrator fueled by 5 Hour Energy drinks and violent exploitation films. She has done comics for DC Online, Ape Entertainment, Dark Horse and Comixology. Christine is also a part time instructor at the University of the Arts in Philadelphia. Christine resides with her two cats, her fiancé and a sawed off shotgun in a heavily fortified North Philadelphia row home where she awaits the zombie apocalypse.

CASSANDRA JAMES is a comic artist from Tasmania, Australia. Her work has been included in various Gathering comic book anthologies and most recently, the successfully funded Kickstarter project, Womanthology. Cassandra lives with her loving husband, Rowan, and her spoilt cat, Princess Peach.

ALEX DE CAMPI is kept awake at night by the stories in her head. She makes stop-motion films in her garage, walks her dogs in the woods, and hangs out with her daughter at the playground.

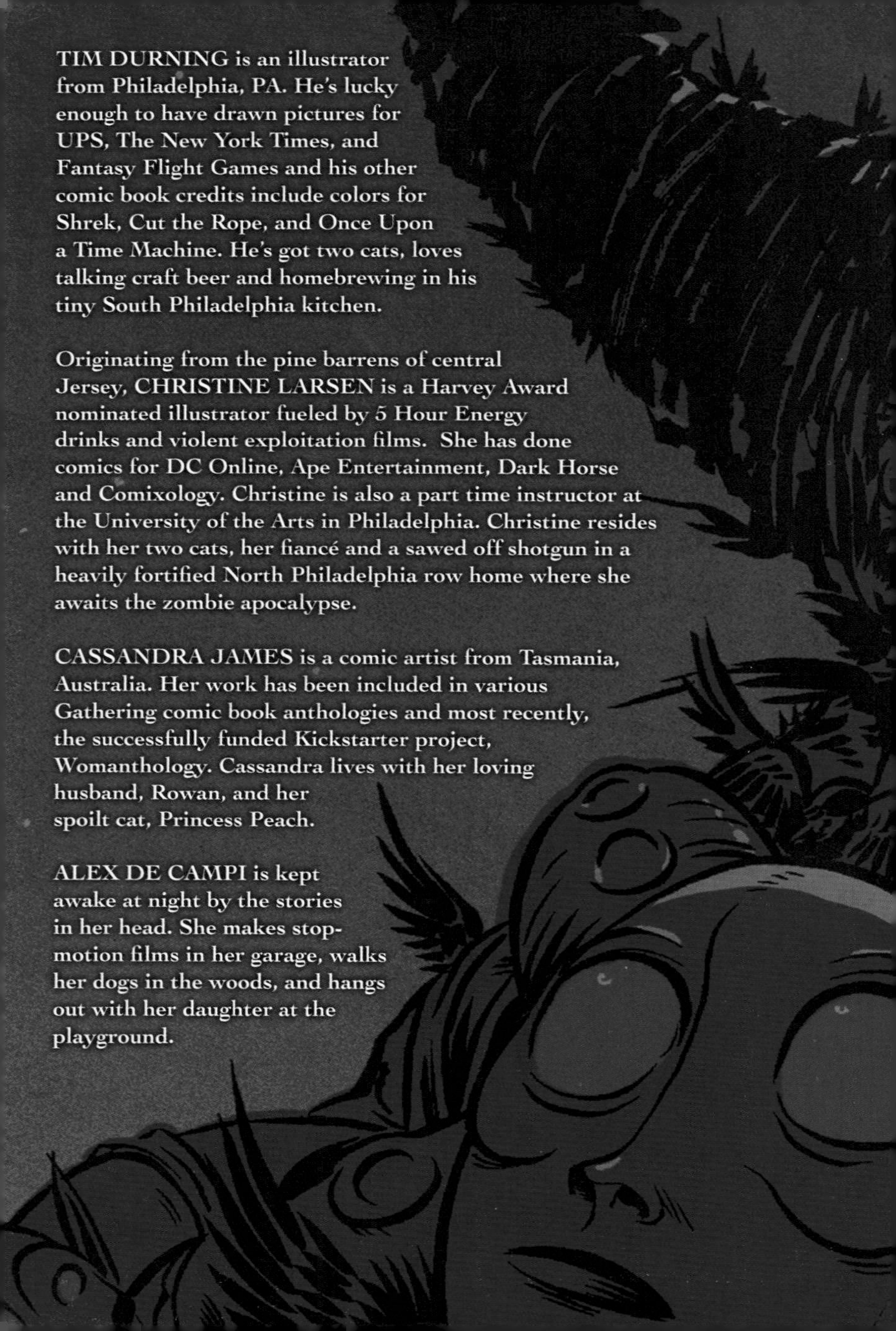